COMMERCIAL LEASES

AUSTRALIA
LBC Information Services
Sydney

CANADA AND USA
Carswell
Toronto

NEW ZEALAND
Brooker's
Auckland

SINGAPORE AND MALAYSIA
Thompson Information (S.E. Asia)
Singapore

COMMERCIAL LEASES

STEPHEN TROMANS, M.A.

Solicitor

Second Edition

LONDON, DUBLIN, HONG KONG
SWEET & MAXWELL
1996

First edition 1987

Published in 1996 by
Sweet & Maxwell Ltd, of
100 Avenue Road, Swiss Cottage
London NW3 3PF
Computerset by
Interactive Sciences Ltd,
Gloucester
Printed and bound in the United Kingdom by
Butler and Tanner Ltd,
Frome and London

**A catalogue record for this
book is available from
the British Library.**

ISBN 0–421–523506

P REFACE TO SECOND EDITION

The first edition of this book was a solo effort, produced in an academic context, but nevertheless with the aim of providing as practical a guide as possible for lawyers faced with the intricacies and pitfalls of commercial leases. This second edition is very much a joint effort, produced within the context of an international law firm, but with exactly the same objective.

All things considered, the text of the first edition appears to have stood the test of time remarkably well, in terms of structure, emphasis and relevance, and as a result this second edition follows an identical format. However, the fecundity of legal imagination, which was apparent in this area at the time of the first edition, has continued to feed the never-ending stream of cases which have had to be incorporated into the text. In addition, new developments both in the area of landlord and tenant law, and property law generally, have necessitated three new chapters in this edition dealing with the Landlord and Tenant (Covenants) Act 1995, VAT and environmental considerations.

THE LANDLORD AND TENANT (COVENANTS) ACT 1995

It is appropriate to comment briefly here on the effect of the Landlord and Tenant (Covenants) Act 1995, particularly for those lawyers who were not practising in this area of the law on January 1, 1996, the day when the Act came into force. For landlord and tenant lawyers that was a momentous day, as the Act effected the greatest change to landlord and tenant law since 1954. The circumstances in which the Act reached the statute book were unusual, and are going to cause problems for property owners, occupiers and their professional advisers for years to come.

The Government had committed itself to abolishing the rule of law whereby the original tenant remained liable under the obligations in a lease even after assignment, but this was fiercely opposed by the landlords' lobby, and the Government had put the idea on one side for the time being. A private member's bill was promoted by Peter Thurnham M.P., with the same aim, but this was defeated in August 1994. However the landlords' and tenants' organisations subsequently agreed a compromise in November 1994 whereby, in exchange for accepting the abolition of the original tenant liability rule, landlords would be given greater control over the identity of assignees. A provision to accomplish this (now section 22 of the Act) was grafted onto the original private member's bill; additionally the Law Commission took the opportunity to suggest the incorporation of a code regulating the manner in which leasehold covenants should operate, and these provisions too were incorporated into the bill.

The entire operation took place within a period of six weeks, which was, it is generally accepted, insufficient time for consideration by the profession of so many changes: the resulting statute is unsatisfactory in many respects, not least the uncertain extent of the very broadly drafted anti-avoidance provisions. It seems very unfortunate that so many ambiguities could be found in a modern Act even before it had come into force. Litigation over the operation of the Act on certain provisions commonly found in leases seems inevitable sooner rather than later, and it is equally certain that the court will then be asked to consider the purpose of the Act, and the comments of ministers during the Act's brief progression through Parliament, in accordance with the House of Lords case of *Pepper v. Hart*.[1]

Practitioners, however, are having to operate the new provisions without the benefit of the court's deliberations on the intricacies of the Act, and I have endeavoured to explain them as lucidly as possible[2]; readers must recall, however, that at the time of going to press the new provisions have been operating for less than six months, and the market has not yet bedded down. For this reason I am particularly indebted to my friend Charles Harpum, the Law Commissioner with responsibility for this area of the law, who was heavily involved in the bill's progress, and who has given me his helpful insights into what was intended by the draftsman of the Act: these views have been incorporated so far as practicable into Chapter 2.

THE WRITING TEAM

As mentioned above, the second edition has been a team effort. I have been exceptionally fortunate that members of the Property Department at Simmons & Simmons have taken responsibility for the updating of the various chapters, and in some cases the provision of entirely new material; colleagues from other areas of the firm assisted in addition where necessary. Those who have contributed in this way are listed below, but particular thanks are due to Peter Williams and Claire Burnett-Scott, who acted as general editors and co-ordinators.

The writing, updating and reviewing team comprised: Margarethe Batteson, Penny Bryce, Stephen Coleclough, Lisa Cristie, Robert Cummins, Stephen Elvidge, Richard Fidler, Duncan Field, Mary Fleming, Jonathan Goodliffe, Grace Gethin, Carol Hewson, Nick Jones, Fiona Larcombe, Jane Mortimer Tracy, Justin Nimmo, Steven Pearce, David Pinner, John Rakowicz, Emily Roche, Michael Roskell, Roy Russell, Carol Shaw, John Sirs, John Storey,

---

[1] [1993] 1 All E.R. 42.
[2] A useful consideration of the reforms enacted by the 1995 Act can be found in "Privity of Contract and Leases—Reform at Last" by Martin Davey, MLR 59:1 January 1996.

David Thompson, Mike Willmott and Simon Yates.

Gratitude should also be expressed to Charles Harpum, as mentioned above; to Anthony Tanney of Falcon Chambers, for his considerable feat of reading and commenting on the entire text at proof stage; and also to Richard Asher of Jones Lang Wootton, for his involvement from a surveyor's point of view at a time when a Chapter on valuation issues was being considered.

Responsibility as to the accuracy of the text remains, as always, that of the author, whose hope is that those who have used, with benefit, the first edition will find the second edition similarly helpful, and that new readers will also come to know the work. The law is stated generally as at May 31, 1996, although minor amendments have been incorporated at proof stage dealing with developments after that date.*

Stephen Tromans
Simmons & Simmons
21 Wilson Street
London EC2M 2TX

July 31, 1996

---

* Regrettably it has not been possible to include any mention of the changes to arbitration law and practice expected to be effected by the Arbitration Act 1996, which was passed on June 17, 1996. While this is not expected to be brought into effect until 1997, it will apply to any arbitration agreement in a lease, whenever the lease was granted.

P REFACE TO FIRST EDITION

My aim in writing this book has been to provide a concise guide to the law of commercial leases for solicitors practising in that field. I have attempted to focus on those practical problems most likely to occur, and for which all too often there is no easy or ready answer.

Drafting is of course a vitally important part of the work of the practitioner in this area, and I hope that the book will provide guidance as to potential pitfalls in the drafting or negotiation of commercial leases. However, I have also attempted to deal with the continuing operation of leases in matters such as rent review, alterations and repairs, and the renewal of leases under Part II of the Landlord and Tenant Act 1954. I have also tried to cover in some detail the law and practice of leasehold conveyancing; this is a subject which is often absent from works on the law of landlord and tenant, and is sometimes only sketchily treated in books on conveyancing.

Those practising in the field of commercial leases will be aware of the extent to which knowledge of property law needs to be supplemented by an awareness of related areas of law, such as planning law, tax law, rating law, insurance law, insolvency law and the law of tort. I have attempted to be mindful of this and to engage in lateral legal thinking where appropriate.

The book contains no precedents. Inclusion of comprehensive precedents would have made it a very bulky tome, and I felt that an arbitrary selection of precedents would have been irritating rather than instructive. In any event, most solicitors have more than adequate access to precedents in this area, and space is probably better devoted to explanation of the law behind the precedents. Space also forbids any detailed treatment of some general aspects of the law of landlord and tenant, such as capacity, distress and forfeiture, which are already very adequately covered by the standard textbooks on landlord and tenant and real property.

A recurring theme throughout the book is the importance of market forces in shaping the rights and obligations of the parties to a lease. This is no new phenomenon — as long ago as 1553 Edward VI was moved to temper such forces by including in the Book of Private Prayer of that date the following Prayer for Landlords:

> We heartily pray thee to send thy holy spirit into the hearts of them that possess the grounds, pastures, and dwelling places of the earth, that they, remembering themselves to be thy tenants, may not rack and stretch out the rents of their houses and lands, nor yet take unreasonable fines and incomes, after the manner of covetous worldlings . . . but so behave themselves in

letting out their tenements, lands, and pastures, that after
this life they may be received into everlasting dwelling
places.

No doubt many a tenant's solicitor, struggling against a non-
negotiable 80 page institutional lease, might echo those
sentiments.

This Preface would be incomplete without an expression of
my deep thanks to the many people who have assisted me by
reading various portions of this book in draft and who have
offered most helpful and constructive advice and suggestions.
Academic colleagues who have helped in this way are Dr
Malcolm Clarke, Mr Charles Harpum, Dr Len Sealy and Mr
John Spencer (all of the Faculty of Law, Cambridge
University), Dr Lakshman Guruswamy of the University of
Durham, Mr Delyth Williams of the Department of
Surveying, Liverpool Polytechnic, and Mr Andy Waite of the
University of Southampton. A number of solicitors in practice
also gave up their valuable time to help in this way, and for
this I am most grateful to Mr Lewis Isaacs and Mr Alan Brett
of Messrs Wild, Hewitson and Shaw, Cambridge, to Mr Greg
Moss and Mr Robert Sweet of Messrs Routh Stacey, London,
and to Mr Richard Woof of Messrs. Debenham & Co.,
London. I am doubly indebted to Mr Isaacs, for as well as
reading part of the manuscript, it was he who first introduced
me to the practicalities of commercial leases during my
articles. Two practising surveyors also gave me the benefit of
their experience and insight in connection with the chapter on
Rent Review — Mr Derek Dazeley of Messrs Douglas L.
January & Partners of Cambridge, and Mr Hugh Stallard of
Messrs Collier & Madge. The efforts of all of them have
greatly enriched the book, but of course they are in no way
responsible for its shortcomings.

I am also most thankful to the editorial staff at Sweet &
Maxwell for their efficiency and encouragement, and to Mr
Roger Bonehill for preparing the index.

Finally, I wish to express my gratitude to my wife, Caroline,
and our children, Amy and Hannah, for their patience and
forbearance while this book was being researched and written.
The period during which it was written coincided with my
wife's pregnancy with our third child, so that we wondered
which of us would be the first to see the fruits of our labours.
In the event my wife won by a comfortable margin—Lucy
arrived a week before the page proofs. As a token of my
gratitude, this book is dedicated to Caroline, Amy, Hannah
and Lucy.

I have attempted to state the law as at April 1, 1987, but it
has been possible to include references to some material
available after that date. Unfortunately it has not been
possible to incorporate into the text references to the new
Town and Country Planning (Use Classes) Order 1987 No.
764 (see p. 108) or to Law Commission Working Paper No.
102 on Compensation for Tenants' Improvements (see
p. 117). Nor has it been possible to deal adequately with two
important Court of Appeal decisions, which were not fully
reported at the page proof stage: these are *Dennis & Robinson*

Ltd v. Kiossis Establishment on rent review clauses (see p. 48) and *Charles Follett Ltd v. Cabtell Investment Co. Ltd* on section 24A interim rent (see p. 178).

Stephen Tromans
Selwyn College,
Cambridge,
June 4, 1987

C ONTENTS

Preface to Second Edition   v
Preface to First Edition   ix
Table of Cases   xxiii
Table of Statutes   lxv
Table of Statutory Instruments and Circulars   lxxiii

CHAPTER 1   INTRODUCTION

General   1
Need for clear drafting   2
Length of leases   4
Standard forms   4
Importance of lease provisions   5
Commercial Property Leases Code of
     Practice   5

**CHAPTER 2   THE RULES OF PRIVITY OF
                      CONTRACT**

Introduction   6
Which rules apply?   6
Anti-avoidance provisions   7
The liability of the tenant   8
Release of the tenant   10
Authorised guarantee agreements
     (AGAs)   10
The liability of a guarantor   11
The liability of the landlord   13
Effect of release of landlords and
     tenants   14
Rights of indemnity between successive
     tenants   15
Assignments of part   16
New safeguards for former tenants   16

CHAPTER 3   THE PARTIES

Introduction   20
The Landlord—Generally   20
Definition of landlord   20
Landlord a single individual   22
Landlord a number of individuals   22
Landlord a company   22
The Tenant—Definition of tenant   23
Tenant an individual   23
Joint tenants   25
Partnerships   26
Companies   27
The Surety—Reason for surety   28
Guarantee or indemnity   28
Advising the sureties   30

Suretyship provisions from the point
of view of the landlord 30
Suretyship provisions from the point
of view of the surety 35
Suretyship provisions from the point
of view of the tenant 37

CHAPTER 4 THE DEMISED PREMISES AND
ANCILLARY RIGHTS

Defining the premises 39
Description and plan 39
Description of part of building 40
More than one parcel of land 42
Fixtures 42
Appurtenant rights 42
Access 43
Service media 44
Parking 44
Use of sanitary and other facilities 45
Signs and advertisements 45
Access to adjoining property 46
Negating implied grants 47
Exceptions and reservations by landlord 47
Rights of access 48
Rights to use service media 48
Rights of entry 48
Right to develop adjoining and
neighbouring premises 49

CHAPTER 5 THE TERM

Introduction 51
Length of term 51
The commencement date 53

CHAPTER 6 RENT AND RENT REVIEW

Rent—Reservation of rent and covenant
to pay 56
Rent-free periods 56
Payment of rent 57
Other payments reserved as rent 57
Rent deposits 57
Interest 58
Rent Review—Generally 58
Preliminary considerations 59
Activating the review provisions 61
Notice to review 62
Default notices 66
Determining the new rent 69
Arbitrator or expert? 69
Appointing the third party 71
Arbitration procedure 72
Procedure on valuation 74

Evidence and comparables 75
Costs 77
Challenging the arbitrator's decision 77
Challenging the expert's decision 80
Evidencing the review 81
Payment of reviewed rent and interest 81
Basis on which new rent to be assessed 82
Basis of valuation 83
When are the premises to be valued? 85
What is to be valued? 85
Rent review provisions in hypothetical
    lease 87
User clause in hypothetical lease 89
The length of term to be assumed 91
Letting with vacant possession 92
Rent-free periods as inducements 94
Letting as a whole 95
Planning permission and development
    potential 96
Matters to be assumed 97
Disregard of tenant's occupation and
    goodwill 99
Disregard of improvements 100
Model forms of clause 103
Indexed rents 105
Turnover rents 105
Geared rents 106

CHAPTER 7   RATES AND STATUTORY
                 REQUIREMENTS

Introduction 108
Uniform business rates 108
Water charges 110
Statutes requiring capital expenditure 110
Apportionment of costs 113
Statutory improvements and rent review 114

CHAPTER 8   SERVICES AND SERVICE CHARGES

Introduction 115
Obligation on landlord to provide
    services 116
The expenditure covered by the service
    charge 118
Apportionment of the cost 120
Certification of expenditure and
    apportionment 122
Method of payment 124
Replacement and reserve funds 125

CHAPTER 9   REPAIRS, REDECORATIONS AND
                 DILAPIDATIONS

Introduction 127
Repairs—The allocation of liability 128

The tenant's covenant to repair 130
The timing of the obligation 130
The spatial extent of the obligation 131
The defects covered by the covenant 134
Design and construction defects 136
Whether work is "repair" 136
Exclusion of liability for inherent defects 138
Other similar obligations 139
Desirability of a survey 140
Tenant's rights against third parties 140
Subrogation 142
Collateral warranties 143
Other possible solutions 143
The standard of repair required 144
Insured risks 145
Covenant to repair on notice 145
The landlord's covenant to repair 145
Redecoration—Specification of work 148
Timing of work 148
Redecoration after repairs 149
Miscellaneous provisions relating to
condition 149
Dilapidations and Remedies—Breach of
tenant's repairing obligations 150
Measure of damages 153
Injunction 154
Breach of landlord's repairing
obligations 154

CHAPTER 10 PROVISIONS AS TO USE

Introduction 157
Nuisance and annoyance 157
Restrictions affecting the reversion 158
Planning 158
Uses requiring specific licences 159
Preventing the premises falling vacant 159
Sunday trading 160
Restriction to specified use 160
Consent to change of use 163
Effect of user provisions on alienability 164
Protecting the tenant's use of the
premises 164
Attacking user restrictions 166

CHAPTER 11 IMPROVEMENTS, ALTERATIONS AND FIXTURES

Improvements and alterations—Generally 167
Express covenants against alterations 167
The extent of the demise 169
The law of waste 169
Consent to alterations and improvements 170
Conditions of consent 172
Compensation for improvements 173

Improvements and rent review   174
Other implications of improvements   175
Fixtures—Generally   175
Fixture or chattel   175
Landlord's or tenant's fixture   176
Removal of tenant's fixtures   177
Fixtures and rent review   178
Compensation for fixtures   178
Capital allowances   178

CHAPTER 12 ALIENATION

Introduction   180
Construction generally   180
Covenant against assignment   180
Covenant against underletting   181
Covenant against parting with
        possession   181
Covenant against sharing possession   182
Alienation of whole or part   182
Absolute and qualified covenants   183
No fine to be payable for consent   183
Effect of unreasonable refusal of consent 184
Timing of reasons for refusal   186
Incorporating conditions for assignment
        into the lease   186
Criteria for judging reasonableness
        of refusal   187
Common reasons for refusal of consent   189
Offer-to-surrender clauses   194

**CHAPTER 13 INSURANCE, REINSTATEMENT AND
                SUSPENSION OF RENT**

Introduction   196
Insurance—Matters to be covered   196
What is to be insured   196
Who is to insure   197
With which insurer   199
Subrogation   200
Insurance in joint names   200
Against what risks   201
The sum insured   202
Invalidation of the insurance policy   203
Reinstatement—Generally   205
Time of reinstatement   205
Shortfall in insurance monies   206
Standard of reinstatement   206
Where reinstatement is impossible   207
Where the landlord does not wish to
        reinstate   208
Suspension of rent—Proviso for
        suspension of rent   208
Length of period of suspension   209

CHAPTER 14 PROVISIONS AS TO FORFEITURE

Generally   210
Conditions   210
Forfeiture clauses   210
Exercising the right of forfeiture   212
Waiver   213
Statutory requirements and relief against
    forfeiture   215
Underlessees and mortgagees   217
Law Commission recommendations   218

CHAPTER 15 MISCELLANEOUS PROVISIONS

Introduction   220
Covenants—Protection of easements   220
Refuse and effluent   220
Overloading of floors and wiring   221
Planning and other compensation   222
Statutory notices and planning
    applications   222
Regulations of landlord   222
Indemnity to landlord   223
Provisos—Arbitration   223
Service of notices   223
Costs   224

CHAPTER 16 SECURITY OF TENURE

Introduction   225
Quiet enjoyment—Purpose of covenant
    for quiet enjoyment   225
Nature of the covenant   225
Implications for leasehold conveyancing   227
Break clauses—Purpose of break clauses   227
Requirements as to exercise   228
Effect of exercise   229
Power to break on condition   229
Interaction of tenant's break notice with
    section 26 of the 1954 Act   230
Options to renew—Introduction   231
Drafting   231
Protecting the option   232
Exercising the option   232
Security of tenure under the Landlord
    and Tenant Act 1954—
    Introduction   234
Scope of the Act   235
Occupation of the premises   235
Occupation for the purposes of a
    business   237
Occupation by the tenant   237
Mixed use   238
Unauthorised uses   239
Occupations excluded from the Act   239
Licences and tenancies-at-will   240
Excluding the Act by agreement   242
The operation of the Act   244

Common rules and concepts under
    the Act 245
Landlord's section 25 notice 250
Tenant's response to section 25 notice 252
Tenant's section 26 request 252
Landlord's response to section 26
    request 253
Renewal of tenancy by agreement 253
Tenant's application for a new tenancy 254
Interim rent 254
Obtaining information under section 40 255
Opposing the grant of a new tenancy 256
Ground (a): disrepair caused by tenant 256
Ground (b): delay in paying rent 257
Ground (c): other substantial breaches 257
Ground (d): alternative accommodation 258
Ground (e): property to be let as a
    whole 258
Ground (f): demolition and
    reconstruction 259
Ground (g): landlord intends to occupy 263
Landlord's opposition successful 266
Grant of new tenancy 266
The property to be compromised in
    the tenancy 267
The duration of the new tenancy 267
The terms of the new tenancy other
    than the rent 269
Rent under the new tenancy 270
Costs of the proceedings 272
After the order for a new tenancy 272
Statutory compensation 272

CHAPTER 17 INTERPRETATION AND RECTIFICATION OF LEASES

Introduction 275
Interpretation—General principles 275
Extrinsic evidence 277
Other rules of construction 279
Rectification—Generally 280
Requirements for rectification 281
The common intention 281
Execution of a document which fails to
    record the intention accurately 282
Mistake of both parties or known to one 283
Discretionary remedy 284

CHAPTER 18 LEASEHOLD CONVEYANCING

Introduction 285
Grant of lease—Preliminary matters 285
Creating a binding contract 286
Allocation of costs 288
Searches and preliminary enquiries 289
Procedure for negotiating 292

Agreement for lease   293
Investigating the landlord's title   294
Pre-completion searches   296
Completion   297
Post-completion matters   299
Assignment of a lease—Generally   300
Printed conditions of sale   301
Title   301
Terms of the lease   302
Compliance with the terms of the lease   303
Obtaining landlord's consent   305
The assignment: implied covenants   308
Form of deed of assignment   310
Post-completion matters   311
Grant of underlease—Generally   311
Investigation of title   312
Landlord's consent to underletting   313
Assignment of underlease   314
Title   314
Surrender—Reasons for surrender   315
Form of surrender   316
Effect of surrender   316
Surrender subject to underleases   318
Surrender of registered lease   318
Possession before completion—
    Generally   319
Allowing the tenant into occupation
    prior to grant of lease   319
Occupation pending assignment of
    lease   324
Occupation pending grant of underlease   325

CHAPTER 19 VALUE ADDED TAX

Introduction   327
General Principles—Basis of charge   327
Input tax and output tax   328
VAT invoices   329
Penalties and interest   329
Supplies   330
Time of supply   331
Value of supply   331
Types of supply   332
The election to waive the exemption
    (option to tax)   333
VAT considerations during the term of a
    lease—Service charges   334
Insurance rents   335
Improvements carried out pursuant to
    section 3 of the Landlord and
    Tenant Act 1927   335
Tenants paying landlord's solicitors and other
    professional costs   336
Other miscellaneous circumstances   337

VAT considerations arising on the grant
    of a lease, and on the sale and
    purchase of a lease—Generally   338
Points to be ascertained by the
    purchaser   338
The purchaser's VAT position   339
The purchase price   340
Stamp duty on VAT   341
Land Registry fees   341

CHAPTER 20 ENVIRONMENTAL CONSIDERATIONS

Introduction   342
Liability relating to current use—
    Applicable legislation   342
Potential liability upon the landlord 343
Compliance with notices   345
Common law nuisance   345
Protecting the landlord   346
Protecting the tenant   347
Liability relating to past uses—Nature of
    liability   347
Allocation of risk between landlord and
    tenant   349
General covenants   349
Protecting the tenant   350
Protecting the landlord   352
Migration of contamination from other
    land   353

Index   355

TABLE OF CASES

A.B.B. Power v. Customs and Excise Commissioners (1992) 5 VATTR 491,
   Manchester Tribunal 19–04
A.B.C. Coupler and Engineering Co., *Re* (No. 3) [1970] 1 W.L.R. 702; [1970]
   1 All E.R. 650 18–27
Abbey National Building Society v. Maybeech [1985] Ch. 190; [1984] 3
   W.L.R. 793; [1984] 3 All E.R. 262; (1984) 271 E.G. 995 14–06
Abrahams v. Macfisheries Ltd [1925] 2 K.B. 18 12–07
Accuba v. Allied Shoe Repairs [1975] 1 W.L.R. 1559; [1975] 3 All E.R. 782;
   (1975) 30 P. & C.R. 403 6–10
Ackland v. Lutley (1839) 9 A & E 879 5–03
Adelphi (Estates) v. Christien (1984) 269 E.G. 221, C.A. 8–04
Adler v. Upper Grosvenor Street Investment [1957] 1 W.L.R. 227; [1957] 1 All
   E.R. 229 1–02
Agip SpA v. Navigazione Alta Italia SpA; Nai Genova and Nai Superba, The
   [1984] 1 Lloyd's Rep. 353, C.A. 18–06
Ahern (P.F.) v. Hunt [1988] 21 E.G. 69, C.A. 16–40
Air India v. Balabel [1993] 30 E.G. 90 .... 12–10, 12–14
Aircool Installations v. British Telecommunications, April 26, 1995
   (unreported) 11–16
Aireps v. City of Bradford Metropolitan Council [1985] 2 EGLR 143; (1985)
   276 E.G. 1067, C.A. 16–16
Al Saloom v. James (Shirley) Travel Services (1981) 42 P. & C.R. 181,
   C.A. 6–10
Alan Estates v. W.G. Stores [1982] Ch. 511; [1981] 3 W.L.R. 892; [1981] 3 All
   E.R. 481; (1981) 260 E.G. 173, C.A. 18–10
Aldin v. Latimer Clark, Muirhead & Co. [1894] 2 Ch. 437 10–11
Aldridge v. Fearne (1886) 17 Q.B.D. 212 7–04
—— v. Wright [1929] 2 K.B. 117 4–14
Aldwych Club v. Copthall Property Co. (1962) 185 E.G. 219 16–46
Alghussein Establishment v. Eton College [1988] 1 W.L.R. 587 .... 18–07, 18–17
Ali v. Booth (1969) 199 E.G. 641 14–06
—— v. Knight (1984) 272 E.G. 1165 16–31
Allied London Investments v. Hambro Life Assurance (1985) 50 P. & C.R.
   207; [1985] EGLR 45; (1985) 274 E.G. 81 .... 2–04, 6–06
Allnatt London Properties v. Newton [1984] 1 All E.R. 423; (1983) 45 P. &
   C.R. 94; (1983) 265 E.G. 601, C.A. 12–15
Allum v. Dickinson (1882) 9 Q.B.D. 632 7–04
Altmann v. Boatman (1963) 186 E.G. 109, C.A. 4–07
Amalgamated Estates v. Joystretch Manufacturing (1980) 257 E.G. 489,
   C.A. 6–11
Amalgamated Investment & Property Co. (in liquidation) v. Texas Commerce
   International Bank [1982] Q.B. 84; [1981] 3 W.L.R. 565; [1981] 3 All
   E.R. 577 17–03
Amarjee v. Barrowfen Properties [1993] 2 EGLR 133; [1993] 30 E.G. 98 ... 16–47
Amax International v. Custodian Holdings [1986] 2 EGLR 111; (1986) 279
   E.G. 279 .... 6–27, 17–04
Amherst v. Walker (James) Goldsmith and Silversmith (1980) 254 E.G. 123,
   C.A. 6–10
—— v. —— (No. 2) [1983] Ch. 305; [1983] 3 W.L.R. 334; [1983] 2 All E.R.
   1067; (1984) 47 P. & C.R. 85; (1982) 267 E.G. 163, C.A. 6–10

Amika Motors v. Colebrook Holdings (1981) 259 E.G. 243, C.A. 16–45
Amoco Australia Pty. v. Rocco Bros. Motor Engineering Co. Pty. [1975] A.C.
    561; [1975] 2 W.L.R. 779; [1975] 1 All E.R. 968, P.C. 10–12
Anglia Building Society v. Sheffield City Council (1982) 266 E.G. 311,
    C.A. 10–09, 12–14
Angus Restaurants Ltd v. Day, August 19, 1982 (unreported) 12–14
Antaios Compania Naviera S.A. v. Salen Rederierna A.B. [1985] A.C. 191;
    [1984] 3 W.L.R. 592; [1984] 3 All E.R. 229, H.L. 17–02
Antoniades v. Villiers [1990] 1 A.C. 417 16–22
Appleby Developments Ltd v. Hollway (1962) 183 E.G. 861 10–08
Arc v. Scofield [1990] 38 E.G. 113 16–11
Arding v. Economic Printing and Publishing Company Ltd (1898) 79 L.T.
    622 7–04
Argy Trading Development Co. v. Lapid Developments [1977] 1 W.L.R. 444;
    [1977] 3 All E.R. 785 13–04
Arnold v. National Westminster Bank [1991] 2 A.C. 93; [1991] 2 W.L.R. 1177;
    [1991] 3 All E.R. 41; [1991] 2 EGLR 109, H.L. 6–19, 17–02
—— v. —— (No. 2) [1994] EGCS 44, C.A. 6–19
Art and Sound v. West London Litho; Same v. Tampo Supplies (1991) 64 P. &
    C.R. 28; [1992] 1 EGLR 138; [1992] 14 E.G. 110 6–10
Artoc Bank & Trust v. Prudential Assurance Co. [1984] 1 W.L.R. 1181; [1984]
    3 All E.R. 538; (1984) 271 E.G. 454 16–32
Asco Developments v. Gordon (1978) 248 E.G. 683 9–27
Ashburn Anstalt v. Arnold (W.J.) & Co. [1988] 2 All E.R. 147; (1987) 284 E.G.
    1375; (1988) 55 P. & C.R. 137, C.A. 6–02
—— v. —— (No. 2) [1988] 2 W.L.R. 706; [1988] 23 E.G. 128, C.A. 16–22,
                                                                          18–07
Ashby v. Wilson [1900] 1 Ch. 66 10–11
Ashton v. Sobelman [1987] 1 W.L.R. 177; [1987] 1 All E.R. 755; (1987) 231
    E.G. 303; [1987] 1 EGLR 33 14–04
Aslan v. Clintons (a firm) (1984) 134 L.J. 584 1–05
Aspen Trader, The [1981] 1 Lloyd's Rep. 273 6–11
Aspinall Finance v. Viscount Chelsea [1989] 9 E.G. 77 16–16
Associated British Ports v. Bailey (C.H.) [1990] 2 A.C. 703; [1990] 2 W.L.R.
    812; [1990] 1 All E.R. 929; [1990] 16 E.G. 65 9–24
Associated Dairies v. Pierce (1983) 265 E.G. 127, C.A.; (1982) 43 P. & C.R.
    208, D.C. 3–13, 3–15
Associated Deliveries v. Harrison (1984) 50 P. & C.R. 91; (1984) 272 E.G.
    321, C.A. 14–04
Atkin v. Rose [1923] 1 Ch. 522 10–08
Att.-Gen.'s Reference (No. 1 of 1994) *The Independent*, January 31, 1995 20–03
Austin Company of UK Ltd LON/91/1990X (7981) 19–04
Australian Mutual Provident Society v. Overseas Telecommunications Com-
    mission (Australia) Ltd [1972] N.S.W.L.R. 806 6–30
Austruther-Gough-Calthorpe v. McOscar [1924] 1 K.B. 716 9–16
Avagil Investments v. Corner, October 3, 1975 (unreported) C.A. 8–03
Averbrian v. Willmalight [1994] C.L.Y. 2799 .... 5–02, 18–21
Avon County Council v. Alliance Property Co. (1981) 258 E.G. 1181 6–30

B.L. Holdings Ltd v. Market Investments Ltd (1978) 249 E.G. 849 9–24
Bacon v. Chesney (1816) 1 Stark 192 3–15
Badcock v. Hunt (1888) 22 Q.B.D. 145 7–03
Bader Properties v. Linley Property Investments (1968) 19 P. & C.R. 620;
    (1968) 205 E.G. 655 .... 9–24, 18–17

Bagettes v. G.P. Estates [1956] Ch. 290; [1956] 2 W.L.R. 773; [1956] 1 All
    E.R. 729, C.A.; [1955] 3 W.L.R. 602; [1955] 3 All E.R. 451 16–16
Baglarbasi v. Deedmethod [1991] 2 EGLR 71; [1991] 29 E.G. 137 16–26
Bailey (C.H.) v. Memorial Enterprises [1974] 1 W.L.R. 728; [1974] 1 All E.R.
    1003; (1973) 27 P. & C.R. 188, C.A. 6–01
Bairstow Eves (Securities) v. Ripley (1992) 65 P. & C.R. 220; [1992] 32 E.G.
    52 .... 9–21, 14–07, 16–13
Baker v. Merckel, Anson (Third Party) [1960] 1 Q.B. 657; [1960] 2 W.L.R.
    492; [1960] 1 All E.R. 668, C.A. 18–26
Balabel v. Mehmet [1990] 26 E.G. 176, C.A. 18–17, 18–31
Balfour v. Kensington Gardens Mansions (1932) 49 T.L.R. 29 12–14
Band v. Kirklington and Piccadilly Estates [1947] L.Y.R. 884 16–13
Bandar Property Holdings v. Darwen (J.S.) (Successors) [1968] 2 All E.R. 305;
    (1968) 19 P. & C.R. 785 13–05
Bandy v. Cartwright (1853) 8 Exch. 913 16–03
Bank of India v. Trans Continental Commodity Merchants [1983] 2 Lloyd's
    Rep. 298 3–16
Baptist v. Masters of the Bench and Trustees of the Honourable Society of
    Grays Inn [1993] 42 E.G. 287 .... 6–24, 16–47
Barbecue (Leicester Square) v. Berkeley Laboratories (London) (1964) 190
    E.G. 1055 4–11
Barclays Bank v. Ascott [1961] 1 W.L.R. 717; [1961] 1 All E.R. 782 16–26
—— v. Daejan Investments (Grove Hall) Ltd [1995] 18 E.G. 117 10–09,
                                                                                                    11–05, 12–09
—— v. O'Brien [1994] 1 A.C. 180; [1993] 3 W.L.R. 786; [1993] 4 All E.R.
    417, H.L. 3–14
Baring Securities v. D.G. Durham Group plc [1993] EGCS 192 18–17
Barnes v. City of London Real Property Company [1918] 2 Ch. 18 8–02
Barrett Estate Services v. David Grieg (Retail) [1991] 2 EGLR 123; [1991] 36
    E.G. 155 6–11
Barth v. Pritchard [1990] 20 E.G. 65 16–40
Barton v. Fitzgerald (1812) 15 East 530 17–02
—— v. Reed [1932] 1 Ch. 362 10–08
Barton (W.J.) v. Long Acre Securities [1982] 1 W.L.R. 398; [1982] 1 All E.R.
    465; (1982) 263 E.G. 877, C.A. 6–15
Basildon Development Corp. v. Mactro [1986] 1 EGLR 137; (1985) 278 E.G.
    406, C.A. 10–08
Basingstoke and Deane Borough Council v. Host Group [1988] 1 W.L.R. 348;
    [1988] 1 All E.R. 824; (1987) 284 E.G. 1587; (1988) 56 P. & C.R. 31,
    C.A.; (1986) 279 E.G. 505 6–26
Bass Holdings v. Morton Music [1988] Ch. 493; [1987] 3 W.L.R. 543; [1987]
    2 All E.R. 1001; (1987) 54 P. & C.R. 135; [1987] 1 EGLR 214; (1986)
    280 E.G. 1435; [1986] 2 EGLR 50 .... 16–13, 18–13
Bassett v. Whitely (1983) 45 P. & C.R. 87, C.A. 16–13
Baxendale (Robert) v. Davstone (Holdings); Carobene v. Collier Menswear
    [1982] 1 W.L.R. 1385; [1982] 3 All E.R. 496; (1983) 45 P. & C.R. 127;
    (1982) 264 E.G. 713, C.A. 16–31
Baynton v. Morgan (1888) 22 Q.B.D. 74 2–04
Beacon Carpets v. Kirby [1985] Q.B. 755; [1984] 3 W.L.R. 489; [1984] 2 All
    E.R. 726; (1984) 48 P & C.R. 445 13–15
Beale v. Kyte [1907] 1 Ch. 564 17–10
Beard (formerly Coleman) v. Williams [1986] 1 EGLR 148, (1986) 278 E.G.
    1087, C.A. 16–37
Beaumont Property Trust v. Tai (1983) 265 E.G. 872 .... 6–08, 17–04
Becker v. Partridge [1966] 2 Q.B. 155; [1966] 2 W.L.R. 803; [1966] 2 All E.R.
    266, C.A. 18–24

Beer v. Bowden [1981] 1 W.L.R. 522; [1981] 1 All E.R. 1071; (1976) 41
P. & C.R. 317, C.A. 6–02, 17–02
Beesly v. Hallwood Estates [1961] Ch. 105; [1961] 2 W.L.R. 36; [1961] 1 All
E.R. 90 .... 16–12, 18–10
Balfour v. Weston (1786) 1 T.R. 310 13–17
Bell v. Franks (Alfred) & Bartlett Co. [1980] 1 W.L.R. 340; [1980] 1 All E.R.
356; (1979) 39 P. & C.R. 591; (1979) 253 E.G. 903, C.A. 4–09, 16–20
Bellinger v. Southern London Stationers (1979) 252 E.G. 699 6–11
Belvedere Motors v. King (1981) 260 E.G. 813 6–15
Bentray Investments v. Venner Time Switches [1985] 1 EGLR 39; (1985) 274
E.G. 43 18–10
Berton v. Alliance Economic Investment Co [1922] 1 K.B. 759 .... 10–08, 20–03
Best v. Glenville [1960] 1 W.L.R. 1198; [1960] 3 All E.R. 478; (1960) 12
P. & C.R. 48 18–05
Beswick v. Beswick [1966] 3 W.L.R. 396; [1966] 3 All E.R. 1, C.A. 3–03
Bethway v. Moss Ltd MAN/86/331 (2667) unreported 19–19
Betty's Cafés v. Phillips Furnishing Stores [1956] 3 W.L.R. 1134; [1957] 1 All
E.R. 1, C.A. 16–34, 16–40, 16–45
Bewlay (Tobacconists) v. British Bata Shoe Co. [1959] 1 W.L.R. 45; [1958] 3
All E.R. 652, C.A. 16–40
Beyfus v. Lodge [1925] 1 Ch. 350 18–16
Bhojwani v. Kingsley Investment Trust [1992] 39 E.G. 138 14–06
Bickel v. Courtenay Investments (Nominees) [1984] 1 W.L.R. 795; [1984] 1
All E.R. 657; (1984) 48 P. & C.R. 1 18–17
Bickmore v. Dimmer [1903] 1 Ch. 158 11–02
Biddor Building Co. Ltd v. Tricia Guild Associates Ltd, January 25, 1985,
(unreported), Q.B.D. 9–08, 13–15
Bier v. Danser (1951) 157 E.G. 552 10–08
Bigos v. J.R.S.S.T. Charitable Trust (Trustees of) (1965) 193 E.G. 1035 16–20
Billson v. Residential Apartments [1992] 1 A.C. 494; [1992] 2 W.L.R. 15;
[1992] 1 All E.R. 141; (1991) 63 P. & C.R. 122; [1992] 1 EGLR 43,
H.L. 14–06
Birch (A. & W.) v. P.B. (Sloane) Ltd and Cadogan Settled Estates Co. (1956)
167 E.G. 283 16–40
Birmingham, Dudley & District Banking Co. v. Ross (1888) 38 Ch.D 295 ... 4–18
Bishop v. Consolidated London Properties Ltd (1933) 102 LJKB 257 .. 9–10, 9–19
Bissett v. Marwin Securities (1987) 281 E.G. 75; [1987] 1 EGLR 115 6–38
Blackburn v. Hussain [1988] 22 E.G. 78; [1988] EGLR 77, C.A. 16–40
Blake (Victor) (Menswear) v. Westminster City Council (1978) 38 P. & C.R.
448; (1978) 249 E.G. 543 16–32
Blore v. Giulini [1903] 1 K.B. 356 2–09
Blumenthal v Gallery Five Ltd (1971) 220 E.G. 31 6–38
Blundell v. Obsdale (1958) 171 E.G. 491 9–05
Bocardo S.A. v. S. & M. Hotels [1980] 1 W.L.R. 17; [1979] 3 All E.R. 737;
(1979) 39 P. & C.R. 287; (1979) 252 E.G. 59, C.A. 12–12, 12–15
Bodfield Ltd v. Caldew Colour Mates Ltd [1985] 1 EGLR 110 6–08
Boldmark v. Cohen [1986] 1 EGLR 47; (1985) 277 E.G. 745, C.A. 8–03, 8–06
Bolton (H.L.) (Engineering) Co. v. Graham (T.J.) & Sons [1957] 1 Q.B. 159;
[1956] 3 W.L.R. 804; [1956] 3 All E.R. 624 16–40
Banner v. Tottenham and Edmonton Permanent Investment Building Society
[1899] 1 Q.B. 161 18–22
Boots the Chemist v. Pinkland, Thorn EMI v. Same [1992] 28 E.G. 118;
[1992] 2 EGLR 98 16–45
—— v. Street (1983) 268 E.G. 817 .... 17–07, 17–09, 17–10
Boswell v. Crucible Steel Co. [1925] 1 K.B. 119 .... 9–05, 11–12
Bourne & Tant v. Salmon & Gluckstein Ltd [1907] 1 Ch. 616 7–03

Bovis Group Pension Fund v. G.C. Flooring & Furnishing (1984) 269 E.G.
1252, C.A. 6–33, 10–02
Bowes Earl of Strathmore v. Vane, *Re* (1888) 37 Ch. D. 128 3–08
Bowes-Lyon v. Green [1963] A.C. 420; [1961] 3 W.L.R. 1044; [1961] 3 All
E.R. 843, H.L. 16–24
Boyer (William) & Sons v. Adams (1975) 32 P. & C.R. 89 16–16
Bracey v. Read [1963] Ch. 88; [1962] 3 W.L.R. 1194; [1962] 3 All E.R.
472 16–16
Bracknell Development Corp. v. Greenlees Lennards (1981) 260 E.G.
500 .... 16–11, 17–03
Braddon Towers Ltd v. International Stores [1987] 1 EGLR 206 10–06
Bradley v. Chorley Borough Council [1985] 2 EGLR 49; (1985) 275 E.G. 801,
C.A. 9–22
Bradley (C.) & Sons v. Telefusion (1981) 259 E.G. 337 6–10
Bradshaw v. Pawley [1980] 1 W.L.R. 10; [1979] 3 All E.R. 273; (1979) 40
P. & C.R. 496; (1979) 253 E.G. 693 .... 5–03, 6–01
Braid v. W.L. Highway & Sons (1964) 191 E.G. 433 18–22
Bramhall Tudor Cinema Properties v. Brennan's Cinemas (1955) 166 E.G.
528 6–39
Branhills v. Town Tailors (1956) 168 E.G. 642 16–40
Brent L.B.C. v. Ladbroke Rentals [1981] R.A. 153; (1980) 258 E.G. 857,
C.A. 7–02
Bretherton v. Paton [1986] 1 EGLR 172 (1986) 278 E.G. 615, C.A. 16–22,
18–31
Brett v. Brett Essex Golf Club, The (1986) 52 P. & C.R. 330; [1986] 1 EGLR
154, (1986) 278 E.G. 1476 C.A. 6–36
Brew Bros. Ltd v. Snax (Ross) [1970] 1 Q.B. 612; [1969] 3 W.L.R. 657; [1970]
1 All E.R. 587; (1969) 207 E.G. 341 .... 9–06, 9–08, 9–09, 20–05
Brewers' Company v. Viewplan [1989] 2 EGLR 133; [1989] 45 E.G.
153 .... 10–08, 17–02
Bridgers v. Stanford [1991] 2 EGLR 265; (1991) 63 P. & C.R. 18 16–26
Brigg v. Thornton [1904] 1 Ch. 386 10–11
Brilliant v. Michaels [1945] 1 All E.R. 121 5–03
Brimican Investments Ltd v. Blue Circle Heating [1995] EGCS 18 ..... 6–08, 17–07
British Airways v. Heathrow Airport [1992] 1 EGLR 141; [1992] 19 E.G.
157 .... 6–08, 6–24, 6–26
British Anzani (Felixstowe) v. International Marine Management (U.K.)
[1980] Q.B. 637; [1979] 3 W.L.R. 451; [1979] 2 All E.R. 1063; (1978) 39
P. & C.R. 189; (1978) 250 E.G. 1183 9–27
British Bakeries (Midlands) v. Testler & Co. [1986] 1 EGLR 64; (1985) 277
E.G. 1245 12–14
British Gas v. Dollar Land Holdings [1992] 1 EGLR 135; [1992] 12 E.G.
141 6–28
British Gas Corporation v. Universities Superannuation Scheme [1986] 1
W.L.R. 398; [1986] 1 All E.R. 978; (1986) 52 P. & C.R. 111; [1986] 1
EGLR 120; (1986) 277 E.G. 980 6–27
British Home Stores v. Ranbrook Properties [1988] 16 E.G. 80 6–27
B.P. Pension Trust v. Behrendt (1986) 52 P. & C.R. 117; [1985] 2 EGLR 97;
(1985) 276 E.G. 199, C.A. 14–06
British Rail Pension Trustee Co. v. Cardshops [1987] 1 EGLR 127; (1986) 282
E.G. 331 6–11
British Railways Board v. Elgar House (1969) 209 E.G. 1313 6–40
British Red Ash Collieries Ltd, *Re* [1920] 1 Ch. 326 11–13
British Telecom v. Sun Life Assurance Society [1995] 3 W.L.R. 622 9–19
Broadgate Square plc v. Lehman Brothers Ltd [1995] 1 E.G. 111 6–23,
6–27, 6–30, 6–31, 17–02

Bromley Park Gardens Estates v. Moss [1982] 1 W.L.R. 1019; [1982] 2 All
E.R. 890; (1982) 44 P. & C.R. 266; (1983) 266 E.G. 1189, C.A. 12–13
Bromsgrove District Council v. Carthy (1975) 30 P. & C.R. 34, D.C. 20–03
Brown v. Gould [1972] Ch. 53; [1971] 3 W.L.R. 344; [1971] 2 All E.R. 1505;
(1971) 22 P. & C.R. 871 16–11
Brown & Root Technology Ltd v. Sun Alliance and London Assurance Co. Ltd
[1995] 3 W.L.R. 558 16–06
Browne v. Flower [1911] 1 Ch. 219 10–11
Buckle v. Fredericks (1890) 44 Ch. D. 244 10–08
Budd-Scott v. Daniell [1902] 2 K.B. 351 16–03
Buffalo Enterprises v. Golden Wonder [1991] 1 EGLR 171; [1991] 24 E.G.
171 .... 6–23, 6–27
Bullock v. Dommitt (1796) 6 T.R. 650 9–17
Bulstrode v. Lambert [1953] 1 W.L.R. 1064; [1953] 2 All E.R. 728 4–07
Burchell v. Clark (1876) 2 C.P.D. 88 17–08
Burfort Financial Investments v. Chotard (1976) 239 E.G. 891 14–06
Burgess v. Hunsden Properties Ltd (1962) 182 E.G. 373 17–02
Burnett (Marjorie) v. Barclay (1980) 125 S.J. 199; (1980) 258 E.G. 642 16–11
Busby v. Co-operative Insurance Society [1994] 6 E.G. 141 16–50
Butler v. Mountview Estates [1951] 2 K.B. 563; [1951] 1 All E.R. 693 18–18
Butler Estates Co. v. Bean [1942] 1 K.B. 1 18–18

CBS United Kingdom v. London Scottish Properties [1985] 2 EGLR 125;
(1985) 275 E.G. 718 16–45
C.I.B.C. Mortgages v. Pitt [1994] 1 A.C. 200; [1993] 3 W.L.R. 802; [1993] 4
All E.R. 433, H.L. 3–14
CIN Properties v. Barclays Bank [1986] 1 EGLR 59; (1985) 277 E.G. 973,
C.A. 8–05
—— v. Gill (1992) 67 P. & C.R. 288; [1993] 38 E.G. 152 12–11
C & A Pensions Trustees v. British Vita Investments (1984) 272 E.G. 63 6–28
Cabell v. Vaughan (1669) 1 Wms. Saund. 288 3–09
Cadogan v. McCarthy & Stone Developments Ltd [1996] EGCS 94 16–40
Cadogan (Earl) v. Guinness [1936] Ch. 515 5–03
Caerns Motor Services v. Texaco [1995] 1 All E.R. 247 3–03
Cafeteria (Keighley) Ltd v. Harrison (1956) 168 E.G. 668 16–17
Cairnplace v. CBL (Property Investments) Co. [1984] 1 W.L.R. 696; [1984] 1
All E.R. 315; (1984) 47 P. & C.R. 531; (1984) 269 E.G. 542 ...... 3–15, 16–46
Calabar Properties v. Seagull Autos [1969] 1 Ch. 451; [1968] 2 W.L.R. 361;
[1968] 1 All E.R. 1 14–04
—— v. Stitcher [1984] 1 W.L.R. 287; [1984] 3 All E.R. 759; (1983) 268 E.G.
697, C.A. 9–27
Calabar (Woolwich) v. Tesco Stores (1977) 245 E.G. 479, C.A. 10–08, 17–02
Calderbank v. Calderbank [1976] Fam. 93; [1975] 3 W.L.R. 586; [1975] 3 All
E.R. 333 6–18
Cam Gears v. Cunningham [1981] 1 W.L.R. 1011; [1981] 2 All E.R. 560;
(1982) 43 P. & C.R. 144; (1981) 258 E.G. 749, C.A. 16–41
Cambro Contractors Ltd v. John Kennelly Sales, *The Times*, April 14, 1994,
C.A. 17–07
Camden L.B.C. v. Bromley Park Gardens Estate [1985] 2 EGLR 179; (1985)
276 E.G. 928 7–02
Camden Theatre Ltd v. London Scottish Properties Ltd, 1984 (un-
reported) 13–14
Campden Hill Towers v. Gardner [1977] Q.B. 823; [1977] 2 W.L.R. 159;
[1977] 1 All E.R. 739; (1976) 242 E.G. 375, C.A. 9–05

Canada Square Corporation Ltd v. Versafood Services Ltd [1980] 101 DLR
    (3d) 743 5–03
Canas Property Co. Ltd v. K.L. Television Services Ltd [1970] 2 Q.B. 433;
    [1970] 2 W.L.R. 1133; [1970] 2 All E.R. 795; (1970) 21 P. & C.R. 601,
    C.A. 14–04
Cannock v. Jones (1849) 3 Ex. 233 9–16
Cannon v. Villars (1878) 8 Ch.D. 415 4–07
Cantor Art Services v. Kenneth Bieber Photography [1969] 1 W.L.R. 1226;
    [1969] 3 All E.R. 843; (1969) 20 P. & C.R. 766, C.A. 18–32
Capital & Counties Freehold Equity Trust v. B.L. (1987) 283 E.G. 563 8–03,
                                                                                                                        8–06
Caplan (I. & H.) v. Caplan (No. 2) [1963] 1 W.L.R. 1247; [1961] 3 All E.R.
    1174 16–16
Capocci v. Goble (1987) 284 E.G. 230, C.A. 16–40
Cardigan Properties v. Consolidated Property Investments [1991] 7 E.G.
    132 .... 14–05, 14–06
Cardiothoracic Institute v. Shrewdcrest [1986] 1 W.L.R. 368; [1986] 3 All E.R.
    633; [1986] 2 EGLR 57; (1986) 279 E.G. 69 .... 16–23, 18–03, 18–31
Cardshops v. Davies [1971] 1 W.L.R. 591; [1971] 2 All E.R. 721; (1971) 22
    P. & C.R. 499, C.A. 16–46
—— v. Lewis (John) Properties [1983] Q.B. 161; [1982] 3 W.L.R. 803; [1982]
    3 All E.R. 746; (1983) 45 P. & C.R. 197; (1982) 263 E.G. 791, C.A. ... 16–50
Carlisle Cafe Co. v. Muse Brothers & Co. (1897) 67 L.J. Ch. 53 4–03
Carter v. White (1883) 25 Ch. D. 666 3–16
Caselton (A.) & Co. v. Jack (1950) 155 E.G. 478, C.A. 9–19
Celsteel v. Alton House Holdings (No. 2) [1987] 1 W.L.R. 291 (1987) 281
    E.G. 1446; [1987] 1 EGLR 48 16–03
Central Estates Ltd v. Secretary of State for the Environment [1995] NPC 106,
    C.A. 6–10
Central Estates (Belgravia) v. Woolgar (No. 2) [1972] 1 W.L.R. 1048; [1972]
    3 All E.R. 610 14–05
Central and Metropolitan Estates v. Compusave (1982) 266 E.G. 900 17–07,
                                                                                                                        17–10
Centrovincial Estates v. Bulk Storage (1983) 46 P. & C.R. 393; (1983) 268
    E.G. 59 2–04
Cerex Jewels v. Peachey Property Corporation [1986] 2 EGLR 65 (1986) 279
    E.G. 971, C.A. 16–40
Chapman v. Freeman [1978] 1 W.L.R. 1298; [1978] 3 All E.R. 878; (1978)
    247 E.G. 295; (1978) 36 P. & C.R. 323, C.A 16–18
—— v. Mason (1910) 103 L.T. 390 13–10
Charalambous v. Ktori [1972] 1 W.L.R. 951; [1972] 3 All E.R. 701; (1972) 24
    P. & C.R. 253 18–07
Charles Hunt Ltd v. Palmer [1931] Ch. 287 18–15
Charles Follett v. Cabtell Investment Co. Ltd; See Follett (Charles) v. Cabtell
    Investment Co. Ltd.
Chartered Trust v. Maylands Green Estate Co. (1984) 270 E.G. 845 6–11
Chatterton v. Terrell [1923] A.C. 578 12–07
Chelsea Building Society v. R. & A. Millett (Shops) Ltd [1994] 9 E.G.
    182 6–10
Chelsea Cloisters (In Liquidation), Re (1980) 41 P. & C.R. 98, C.A. 8–07
Chelsfield MH Investments Ltd v. British Gas plc [1995] NPC 169 10–08
Cheryl Investments v. Saldanha; Royal Life Saving Society v. Page [1978] 1
    W.L.R. 1329; [1979] 1 All E.R. 5; (1978) 37 P. & C.R. 349; (1978) 248
    E.G. 591, C.A. 16–19
Chester v. Buckingham Travel [1981] 1 W.L.R. 96; [1981] 1 All E.R. 386;
    (1981) 42 P. & C.R. 221 18–07

Chez Garard v. Greene (1983) 268 E.G. 575, C.A. 16–40
Child v. Edwards [1909] 2 K.B. 753 6–01
Chilton Court (Baker Street) Residents v. Wallabrook Property Co. [1989] 43
    E.G. 173, C.A. 16–06
Chipperfield v. Shell (U.K.). *See* Warwick & Warwick (Philately) v. Shell
    (U.K.).
Chiswell v. Griffon Land & Estates [1975] 1 W.L.R. 1181; [1975] 2 All E.R.
    665; (1975) 30 P. & C.R. 211, C.A. 16–25
Chrisdell v. Johnson and Tickner (1987) 54 P. & C.R. 257; (1987) 283 E.G.
    1553, C.A. 14–05
Church v. Brown (1808) 15 Ves. 258 18–07
Church Commissioners for England v. Nodjoumi (1986) 51 P. & C.R. 155,
    D.C. 14–05
City Hotels Group Ltd v. Total Property Investments Ltd [1985] 1 EGLR
    253 12–14
City of London Corporation v. Fell; Herbert Duncan Ltd v. Cluttons (A Firm)
    [1994] A.C. 458; [1993] 3 W.L.R. 1164; [1993] 4 All E.R. 968; [1993] 49
    E.G. 113, H.L. 2–04, 5–01
City Offices v. Bryanston Insurance Co. [1993] 11 E.G. 129 6–31
City Offices (Regent Street) v. Europa Acceptance Group [1990] 5 E.G. 71,
    C.A. 4–03, 9–05
City of Westminster Properties v. Mudd [1959] Ch. 129 17–03
Clark v. Chief Land Registrar; Chancery v. Ketteringham [1994] Ch. 370;
    [1994] 3 W.L.R. 593; [1994] 4 All E.R. 96, C.A. 18–07
Clarke v. Findon Developments (1984) 270 E.G. 426 6–34
Clayhope Properties v. Evans and Jennings [1986] 1 W.L.R. 1223; [1986] 2 All
    E.R. 795; (1986) 52 P. & C.R. 149; [1986] 2 EGLR 34; (1986) 279 E.G.
    855 9–27
Clayton v. Sale Urban District Council [1926] 1 K.B. 415 20–08
Clerical General and Medical Life Assurance Society v. Fanfare Properties Ltd,
    June 2, 1981 (unreported), Ch. D. 11–06
Cleveland Shoe Co. Ltd v. Murrays Book Sales (Kings Cross) (1973) 229 E.G.
    1465, C.A. 13–17
Clore v. Theatrical Properties [1936] 3 All E.R. 483 16–22
Cluttenham v. Anglian Water Authority, *The Times*, August 14, 1986,
    C.A. 9–19
Clydebank District Council v. Monaville [1982] S.L.T. (Sh. Ct.) 46 20–08
Coastplace v. Hartley [1987] Q.B. 984; [1987] 2 W.L.R. 1289; (1987) 54 P. &
    C.R. 272; (1987) 282 E.G. 64 3–03
Coates v. Diment [1951] 1 All E.R. 890 .... 16–08, 17–04
Coatsworth v. Johnson (1886) 55 L.J.Q.B. 220 18–07
Cockburn v. Smith [1924] 2 K.B. 119 4–03
Colchester Estates (Cardiff) v. Carlton Industries [1986] Ch. 80; [1984] 3
    W.L.R. 693; [1984] 2 All E.R. 601; (1984) 271 E.G. 778 9–24
Coldunell v. Gallon [1986] Q.B. 1184; [1986] 2 W.L.R. 466; [1986] 1 All E.R.
    429 3–14
Collins v. Flynn [1963] 2 All E.R. 1068 .... ·9–08
Colquhoun v. Brooks (1888) 21 Q.B.D. 52 17–04
Commercial General Administration v. Thomsett (1979) 250 E.G. 547,
    C.A. 10–08
Commercial Union Life Assurance Company v. Woolworths [1994] EGCS
    191 6–26
Commission for the New Towns v. Cooper (Great Britain) (Formerly Coopind
    U.K.) [1995] 2 W.L.R. 677 .... 17–09, 18–03, 18–06
—— v. Levy (R.) & Co. [1990] 28 E.G. 119 6–10

Commissioners of Inland Revenue v. Southend-on-Sea Estates Co. Ltd [1915] A.C. 428 16–08
Commissioners of Works v. Hull [1922] 1 K.B. 205 12–02
Computer Machinery Co. v. Drescher [1983] 1 W.L.R. 1379; [1983] 3 All E.R. 153 16–48
Concorde Graphics v. Andromeda Investments S.A. (1982) 265 E.G. 386 ... 8–05, 8–07
Connaught Restaurants v. Indoor Leisure [1994] 1 W.L.R. 501 9–27
Conns Water Properties Ltd v. Wilson (1986) 16 *Chartered Surveyor Weekly*, September 25, 928; Northern Ireland High Court of Justice 10–11, 17–03
Conservative and Unionist Central Office v. Burrell [1982] 1 W.L.R. 522; [1982] 2 All E.R. 1 8–07
Conway v. Arthur [1988] 40 E.G. 120, C.A. 16–32
Cook v. Mott (1961) 178 E.G. 637, C.A. 16–40
—— v. Shoesmith [1951] 1 K.B. 752 12–07
Co-operative Insurance Society Ltd v. Argyll Stores (Holdings) Ltd [1996] 3 W.L.R. 27; [1996] 9 E.G. 128, H.L. 10–06
—— v. Centremoor (1983) 268 E.G. 1027, C.A. 6–40, 17–05, 17–07, 17–08
Co-operative Wholesale Society Ltd v. National Westminster Bank plc [1995] 1 E.G. 111 .... 6–23, 6–31, 17–02
Coopers & Lybrand v. William Schwarz Construction Co. (1980) 116 D.L.R. (3d) 450 12–14
Cordon Bleu Freezer Food Centres v. Marbleace [1987] 2 EGLR 143; (1987) 284 E.G. 786 6–10
Cornillie v. Saha [1996] EGCS 21 14–05
Cornwall Coast Country Club v. Cardgrange [1987] 1 EGLR 146; (1987) 282 E.G. 1664 .... 6–15, 6–24, 6–33
Cornish (Formerly Humes) v. Midland Bank [1985] 3 All E.R. 513, C.A. ... 3–14
Coronation Street Industrial Properties v. Ingall Industries [1989] 1 W.L.R. 304; [1989] 1 All E.R. 979; [1989] 24 E.G. 125; (1990) 59 P. & C.R. 8 3–15
Corporation of Bristol v. Westcott (1879) 12 Ch. D. 461 3–10
Corson v. Rhuddlan Borough Council (1990) 59 P. & C.R. 185; [1990] 1 EGLR 255, C.A. 16–11
Cosh v. Fraser (1964) 189 E.G. 421, C.A. 12–14
Cosh's Contract, *Re* [1897] 1 Ch. 9 12–09
Cosser v. Collinge (1832) 3 My. & K. 283 18–22
Costa v. Georghiou, 1984 (unreported), C.A. 6–08
Costain Property Developments v. Finlay & Co. [1989] 1 EGLR 237, D.C. 10–06
County Personnel (Employment Agency) v. Pulver (Alan R.) & Co. [1987] 1 W.L.R. 916; [1987] 1 All E.R. 289; [1986] 2 EGLR 246 .... 1–05, 18–06
Coward v. Gregory (1886) L.R. 2 C.P. 153 14–05
Craddock v. Fieldman (1960) 175 E.G. 1149 .... 16–08, 16–27
Crago v. Julian [1992] 1 W.L.R. 372; [1992] 1 All E.R. 744; [1992] 1 EGLR 84; [1992] 17 E.G. 108 18–19
Crawford v. Newton (1886) 36 W.R. 54 9–20
Crawley Borough Council v. Ure [1995] 3 W.L.R. 95 3–10
Crédit Suisse v. Beegas Nominees Ltd [1994] 11 E.G. 151; [1993] EGCS 157 .... 9–19, 17–04
Creech v. Mayorcas (1966) 198 E.G. 1091 18–32
Creedon v. Collins (1964) 191 E.G. 123, C.A. 4–09
Creery v. Summersell and Flowerdew & Co. [1949] Ch. 751; [1949] L.J.R. 1166 12–12
Cressey v. Jacobs, October 14, 1977 (unreported) 3–16
Cristina v. Seear [1985] 2 EGLR 128; (1985) 275 E.G. 898, C.A. 16–17

Crowhurst Park, *Re* [1974] 1 W.L.R. 583; [1974] 1 All E.R. 991; (1973) 28
P. & C.R. 14 16–26
Crusoe d. Blencowe v. Bugby (1771) 3 Wils. K.B. 234 3–08
Cryer v. Scott Brothers (Sunbury) (1986) 55 P. & C.R. 183, C.A. 10–09,
11–05, 11–06
Culworth Estates v. Society of Licensed Victuallers [1991] 2 EGLR 54; [1991]
39 E.G. 132; (1991) 62 P. & C.R. 211, C.A. 9–25
Cumshaw Ltd v. Bowen (1987) 281 E.G. 68; [1987] 1 EGLR 30 6–38
Cunliffe v. Goodman [1950] 2 K.B. 237; [1950] 1 All E.R. 720, C.A. 16–40
Currie v. Misa (1875) L.R. 10 Ex. 153 18–18
Cutler v. Simons (1816) 2 Mer. 104 18–31
Cutts v. Head [1984] Ch. 290; [1984] 2 W.L.R. 349; [1984] 1 All E.R.
597 6–18
Cynon Valley Borough Council v. Secretary of State for Wales and Oi Mee Lam
(1987) 53 P. & C.R. 68; [1986] 2 EGLR 191; (1986) 280 E.G. 195 10–02

DAF Motoring Centre (Gosport) v. Hatfield & Wheeler (1982) 263 E.G. 976,
C.A. 16–40
D. & F. Estates v. Church Commissioners [1989] A.C. 177; [1988] 2 EGLR
213 .... 9–12, 9–19
Daejan Investments v. Cornwall Coast Country Club (1984) 49 P. & C.R. 157;
[1985] 1 EGLR 77; (1985) 273 E.G. 1122 .... 6–24, 6–33
Daiches v. Bluelake Investments (1985) 51 P. & C.R. 51; [1985] 2 EGLR 67;
(1985) 275 E.G. 462 9–27
Daleo v. Iretti (1972) 224 E.G. 61 16–41
Dallman v. King (1837) Bing. N.C. 105 11–06
Dalton v. Pickard [1926] 2 K.B. 545n 18–27
Dann v. Spurrier (1803) 3 Bos. & P. 399 16–06
Darlington v. Hamilton (1854) Kay. 550 18–21
Darlington Borough Council v. Waring & Gillow (Holdings) [1988] 45 E.G.
102, D.C. 6–10
—— v. Wiltshier Northern [1995] 3 All E.R. 895; [1995] 1 W.L.R. 68 9–12
David Allen Neon Displays Ltd v. Spanton (1958) 171 E.G. 679 16–40
Davies v. Yadegar (1990) 22 H.L.R. 232; [1990] 9 E.G. 67 .... 4–03, 11–03
Davies' Agreement, *Re*, Davies v. Fagarazzi (1970) 21 P. & C.R. 328 18–17
Davis and Carey, *Re* (1888) 40 Ch. D. 601 18–15
Davstone Estate's Leases, *Re*, Manprop v. O'Dell [1969] 2 Ch. 378; [1969] 2
W.L.R. 1287; [1969] 2 All E.R. 849; (1969) 20 P. & C.R. 395 8–05
Davy Ltd v. Guy Salmon (Service) Ltd, *Chartered Surveyor Weekly*, July 23,
1992 20–06
De Falbe, *Re* [1901] 1 Ch. 523 11–13
De Lasalle v. Guildford [1901] 2 K.B. 215 17–03
De Meza v. Ve-Ri-Best Manufacturing Co. (1952) 160 E.G. 364, C.A. 4–07,
8–02
Dean v. Prince [1954] Ch. 409; [1954] 2 W.L.R. 538; [1954] 1 All E.R.
749 5–08
—— v. Walker [1996] NPC 78 4–12
Dean and Chapter of Canterbury Cathedral v. Whitbread [1995] 24 E.G.
148 16–22
Dean and Chapter of Chichester Cathedral v. Lennards (1977) 35 P. & C.R.
309; (1977) 244 E.G. 807, C.A. 6–10
Deanplan v. Mahmoud [1993] Ch. 151; [1992] 3 W.L.R. 467; [1992] 3 All
E.R. 945; (1992) 64 P. & C.R. 409; [1992] 1 EGLR 79; [1992] 16 E.G.
100 2–04

Debtor, A, *Re* [1995] 1 W.L.R. 1127 14–05
Decca Navigator Co. v. Greater London Council [1974] 1 W.L.R. 748; [1974]
    1 All E.R. 1178; (1973) 28 P. & C.R. 107, C.A. 16–40, 16–48
Dellneed v. Chin (1987) 53 P. & C.R. 172; (1987) 281 E.G. 531 ..... 16–17, 16–22
Delronne v. Clohessy-Mart [1975] C.L.Y. 1850 9–10
Demetriou v. Robert Andrews (Estate Agencies) (1990) 63 P. & C.R. 536;
    [1991] 25 E.G. 113, C.A. 16–16
Denley's Trust Deed, *Re*, Holman v. Martyn (H.H.) & Co. [1969] 1 Ch. 373;
    [1968] 3 W.L.R. 457; [1968] 3 All E.R. 65 8–07
Dennett v. Atherton (1872) L.R. 7 Q.B. 316 .... 10–11, 18–05
Dennis and Robinson v. Kiossos Establishment (1987) 54 P. & C.R. 282;
    (1987) 282 E.G. 857; [1987] 1 EGLR 133, C.A. 6–08, 6–24, 6–29
Department of the Environment v. Allied Freehold Property Trust [1992] 45
    E.G. 156 16–32
—— v. Royal Insurance (1987) 54 P. & C.R. 26; (1987) 282 E.G. 208; [1987]
    1 EGLR 83 16–50
—— v. Thomas Bates [1991] 1 A.C. 499; [1990] 3 W.L.R. 457; [1990] 2 All
    E.R. 943; [1990] 46 E.G. 115, H.L. 9–12
Dickinson v. St. Aubyn [1944] 1 K.B. 454 .... 9–04, 16–07
Dikstein v. Kanersky (1947) V.L.R. 216 4–07
Direct Spanish Telegraph Co. Ltd v. Shepherd (1884) 13 Q.B.D. 202 7–03
Distributors and Warehousing, *Re* [1986] 1 EGLR 90; (1985) 278 E.G. 1363
    .... 3–03, 3–16
Dixey (C.W.) & Sons Ltd v. Parsons (1964) 192 E.G. 197 18–22
Dodds v. Walker [1981] 1 W.L.R. 1027; [1981] 2 All E.R. 609; (1981) 42
    P. & C.R. 131, H.L. 16–25
Dodson Bull Carpet Co. v. City of London Corporation; Same v. Same [1975]
    1 W.L.R. 781; [1975] 2 All E.R. 497; (1974) 29 P. & C.R. 311 16–20
Doe d. Goodbehere v. Bevan (1815) 3 M. & S. 353 3–08
Doe d. Henniker v. Watt (1828) 8 B. & C. 308 14–02
Doe d. Ambler v. Woodbridge (1829) 9 B. & C. 376 14–05
Domer v. Gulf Oil (Great Britain) (1975) 119 S.J. 392 16–34
Dong Bang Minerva (U.K.) v. Davina [1995] 5 E.G. 162 .... 12–10, 18–17
Double Shield Window Co. Ltd MAN/84/227 (1771) unreported 19–19
Douglas-Scott v. Scorgie [1984] 1 W.L.R. 716; [1984] 1 All E.R. 1086; (1984)
    48 P. & C.R. 109; (1984) 269 E.G. 1164 9–05
Dowse v. Davis (1961) 179 E.G. 335 11–05
Drake Investments v. Lewisham London Borough Council (1984) 269
    E.G. 133 7–02
Drebbond v. Horsham District Council (1978) 37 P. & C.R. 237; (1978) 246
    E.G. 1013, D.C. 6–10
Dresden Estates v. Collinson (1988) 55 P. & C.R. 47; (1987) 281 E.G. 1321;
    [1987] 1 EGLR 45, C.A. 16–22
Drieselman v. Winstanley (1909) 53 S.J. 631 7–03
Drive Yourself Hire Co. (London) v. Strutt [1954] 1 Q.B. 250; [1953] 3
    W.L.R. 1111; [1953] 2 All E.R. 1475, C.A. 18–24
Drummond v. S. & U. Stores (1980) 258 E.G. 1293 9–25
D'Silva v. Lister House Development [1971] Ch. 17; [1970] 2 W.L.R. 563;
    [1970] 1 All E.R. 858; (1970) 21 P. & C.R. 230 16–20
Duke of Devonshire v. Brookshaw (1899) 81 L.T. 83 10–02
Duke of Westminster v. Guild [1985] Q.B. 688; [1984] 3 W.L.R. 630; [1984]
    3 All E.R. 144; (1984) 48 P. & C.R. 42; (1983) 267 E.G. 763, C.A. 4–07,
                                                8–02, 9–02, 9–19
Dukeminster (Ebbgate House One) v. Somerfield Properties Co. Ltd [1996]
    EGCS 56 17–04

Dun & Bradstreet Software Services (England) Ltd v. Provident Mutual Life
    Assurance Society [1996] NPC 57 16–06
Dunning (A.J.) & Sons (Shopfitters) v. Sykes & Son (Poole) [1987] Ch. 287;
    [1987] 2 W.L.R. 167; [1987] 1 All E.R. 700; (1987) 53 P. & C.R.
    385 4–02
Dunns Motors Ltd v. Cashman (J.P.) & Sons Ltd, January 11, 1982 (unre-
    ported), C.A. 16–23
Dunster v. Hollis [1918] 2 K.B. 795 4–07
Durham City Estates v. Felicetti [1990] 3 E.G. 71, C.A. 6–10, 17–01
Duvan Estates Ltd v. Rossette Sunshine Savouries Ltd (1981) 261 E.G.
    364 .... 6–17, 6–28

Earl of Lonsdale v. Att.-Gen [1982] 1 W.L.R. 887; [1982] 3 All E.R. 579;
    (1983) 45 P. & C.R. 1 17–02
Earl of Stradbroke v. Mitchell. *See* Rouse v. Mitchell.
East Coast Amusement Co. v. British Transport Board [1965] A.C. 58; [1963]
    2 W.L.R. 1426 6–36
Eastwood v. Ashton [1915] A.C. 900 4–02
Edicron v. Whitely (William) [1984] 1 W.L.R. 59; [1984] 1 All E.R. 219;
    (1983) 47 P. & C.R. 625; (1983) 268 E.G. 1035, C.A. 16–50
Edler v. Auerbach [1950] 1 K.B. 359; (1949) 65 T.L.R. 645; [1949] 2 All E.R.
    692; 1 P. & C.R. 10 18–05
Edlingham v. M.F.I. Furniture Centres (1981) 259 E.G. 421 6–11
Edmonton Corporation v. Knowles (W.M.) & Son (1962) 60 L.G.R. 124 8–02
Edwardes v. Barrington (1901) 85 L.T. 650 12–04
Edwards v. Thompson [1990] 29 E.G. 41; (1990) 60 P. & C.R. 222 16–40
Edwards (J.H.) & Sons v. Central London Commercial Estates; Eastern Bazaar
    v. Central London Commercial Estates (1984) 271 E.G. 697, C.A. 16–45
Edwin Woodhouse Trustee Co. Ltd v. Sheffield Brick Co. plc (1983) 270 E.G.
    548 6–10
Egerton v. Jones [1939] 2 K.B. 702 14–07
Eichner v. Midland Bank Executor and Trustee Co. [1970] 1 W.L.R. 1120;
    [1970] 2 All E.R. 597; (1970) 21 P. & C.R. 503, C.A. 16–37
Electricity Supply Nominees v. F.M. Insurance Co. [1986] 1 EGLR 143;
    (1986) 278 E.G. 523 6–27
—— v. I.A.F. Group [1993] 1 W.L.R. 1059; [1993] 3 All E.R. 372; [1993] 37
    E.G. 155; (1992) 67 P. & C.R. 28 .... 8–02, 9–27
—— v. London Clubs [1988] 34 E.G. 71 6–15
Elfer v. Beynon-Lewis (1972) 222 E.G. 1955 18–17
Elite Investments v. T.I. Bainbridge Silencers (No. 2) (1987) 283 E.G. 747;
    [1986] 2 EGLR 43 .... 9–06, 9–08, 9–09
Ellis v. Lawrence (1969) 210 E.G. 215 18–17
Elmcroft Developments v. Tankersley-Sawyer; Same v. IAB; Same v. Rogers
    (1984) 270 E.G. 140, C.A. 9–08
Enfield L.B.C. v. Arajah [1995] EGCS 164 18–02
Englefield Holdings and Sinclair's Contract, *Re*, Rosslyn and Lorimer Estates
    v. Englefield Holdings [1962] 1 W.L.R. 1119; [1962] 3 All E.R. 503 18–16
English Exporters (London) v. Eldonwall; Same v. Same [1973] Ch. 415;
    [1973] 2 W.L.R. 435; [1973] 1 All E.R. 726; (1972) 25 P. & C.R.
    379 .... 6–17, 16–32
Enlayde Ltd v. Roberts [1917] 1 Ch. 109 17–02
Equity and Law Life Assurance Society v. Bodfield (1987) 54 P. & C.R. 290;
    (1987) 281 E.G. 1448; [1987] 1 EGLR 124, C.A. 6–27
—— v. Coltness Group (1983) 267 E.G. 949 .... 17–09, 17–10

Errington v. Birt (1911) 105 L.T. 373 10–02
Escalus Properties Ltd v. Robinson [1995] 4 All E.R. 852; [1995] 3 W.L.R.
    524; [1995] 31 E.G. 71, C.A. 8–07, 14–07
Espresso Coffee Machine Co. v. Guardian Assurance Co. (1959) 173 E.G. 353
    [1959] 1 W.L.R. 250; [1959] 1 All E.R. 458 .... 16–40, 16–41
Esselte A.B. v. Pearl Assurance plc [1995] 37 E.G. 173 16–24
Essexcrest v. Evenlex [1994] 1 W.L.R. 992 16–23
Esso Petroleum v. Fumegrange [1994] 46 E.G. 199 16–22
—— v. Harper's Garage (Stourport) [1968] A.C. 269; [1967] 2 W.L.R. 871;
    [1967] 1 All E.R. 699 10–12
Essoldo (Bingo) Underlease, *Re*, Essoldo v. Elcresta (1971) 23 P. & C.R.
    1 6–09
Estates Gazette v. Benjamin Restaurants [1995] 1 All E.R. 129 2–04
Estates Projects v. Greenwich London Borough (1979) 251 E.G. 851 6–36
Euripides v. Gascoyne Holdings Ltd [1995] EGCS 119 6–19
Europark (Midlands) v. Town Centre Securities [1985] 1 EGLR 88; (1985)
    274 E.G. 289 16–41
Euston Centre Properties v. Wilson (H. & J.) (1982) 262 E.G. 1079 6–35
Evans v. Clayhope Properties [1988] 1 W.L.R. 358; [1988] 1 All E.R. 444;
    [1988] 3 E.G. 95, C.A. 9–27
Evans Construction Co. v. Charrington & Co. and Bass Holdings [1983] Q.B.
    810; [1983] 2 W.L.R. 117; [1983] 1 All E.R. 310; (1982) 264 E.G.
    347 16–31
Evans (D.R.) & Co. v. Chandler (1969) 211 E.G. 1381 10–02
Evans (F.R.) (Leeds) v. English Electric Co. (1977) 36 P. & C.R. 185; (1977)
    245 E.G. 657 .... 6–24, 6–30, 6–32
Exchange Theatre v. Iron Trades Mutual Insurance Co. [1984] 1 Lloyd's Rep.
    149, C.A. 13–10
Exclusive Properties v. Cribgate [1986] 2 EGLR 123; (1986) 280 E.G.
    529 6–33
Exeter Golf and Country Club v. Customs and Excise Commissioners [1981]
    S.T.C. 211; [1979] VAT T.R. 70 19–15
Expert Clothing Service & Sales v. Hillgate House [1986] Ch. 340; [1985] 3
    W.L.R. 359; [1985] 2 All E.R. 998; (1985) 50 P. & C.R. 317; [1985] 2
    EGLR 85; (1985) 275 E.G. 1011, 1129 .... 14–05, 14–06
Eyre v. Hall [1986] 2 EGLR 95; (1986) 280 E.G. 193, C.A. 3–08

F. & G. Sykes Ltd v. Finefare Ltd; *See* Sykes (F. & G.) (Wessex) v. Fine
    Fare.
F.W. Woolworth & Co. Ltd v. Lambert; *See* Woolworth (F.W.) & Co. Ltd v.
    Lambert.
F.W. Woolworth plc v. Charlwood Alliance Properties Ltd; *See* Woolworth
    (F.W.) plc v. Charlwood Alliance Properties Ltd.
Factory Holdings Group v. Leboff International (1986) 282 E.G. 1005; [1987]
    1 EGLR 135 6–10
Fairmount Investments v. Secretary of State for the Environment [1976] 2 All
    E.R. 865; *sub nom.* Fairmount Investments and Southwark London
    Borough Council v. Secretary of State for the Environment [1976] 1
    W.L.R. 1255, H.L. 6–15
Falcon Pipes v. Stanhope Gate Property Co. (1967) 204 E.G. 1243 16–26
Falgor Commercial S.A. v. Alsabahia [1986] 1 EGLR 41; (1985) 277 E.G.
    185, C.A. 12–14
Family Management v. Gray (1979) 253 E.G. 369, C.A. 6–34, 9–25
Farimani v. Gates (1984) 271 E.G. 887 .... 9–24, 13–12, 14–05

Farlow v. Stevenson [1900] 1 Ch. 128 7–04
Farnham v. Royal Insurance Co. [1976] 2 Lloyd's Rep. 437 13–10
Farrows Bank Ltd, *Re* [1921] 2 Ch. 164 3–10
Faruqi v. English Real Estates [1979] 1 W.L.R. 963; (1978) 38 P. & C.R. 318;
    (1978) 251 E.G. 1285 18–14
Fawke v. Viscount Chelsea [1980] Q.B. 441; [1979] 3 W.L.R. 508; [1979] 3 All
    E.R. 568; (1979) 38 P. & C.R. 504; (1979) 250 E.G. 855, C.A. .. 6–34, 16–32
Felsman v. Mansell (1962) 184 E.G. 331 18–15
Felthouse v. Bindley (1863) 11 C.B. (N.S.) 869 6–11
Fencing Supplies v. Customs and Excise Commissioners [1993] VATTR
    302 19–10
Field v. Curnick (1926) 95 L.J.K.B. 756 9–05
Filering Ltd v. Taylor Commercial [1996] EGCS 95 18–26
Finchbourne v. Rodrigues [1976] 3 All E.R. 581, C.A. 8–05
Fine Fare v. Kenmore Investments [1989] 1 EGLR 143; [1989] 21 E.G.
    81 6–19
First Leisure Training v. Dorita Properties [1991] 1 EGLR 133; [1991] 23
    E.G. 116 .... 6–24, 6–35
First National Finance Corp. v. Goodman [1983] BCLC 203; [1983]
    Com.L.R. 184, C.A. 3–15
Fischer v. Toumazos [1991] 2 EGLR 204; [1991] 48 E.G. 123, C.A. 18–17,
                                                                                                    18–32
—— v. Taylor's Furnishing Stores Ltd [1956] 2 Q.B. 78; [1956] 3 W.L.R. 985;
    [1956] 2 All E.R. 78, C.A. 16–41
Fitz v. Iles [1893] 1 Ch. 77 10–11
Flexman v. Corbett [1930] 1 Ch. 672 .... 18–07, 18–15
Flight v. Barton (1832) 3 My. & K. 282 18–22
Foley v. Addenbroke (1844) 13 M. & W. 174 11–03
Follett (Charles) v. Cabtell Investment Co. (1988) 55 P. & C.R. 36; (1987) 283
    E.G. 195; [1986] 2 EGLR 76, C.A. 16–32, 16–45
Forbuoys v. Newport Borough Council [1994] 24 E.G. 156 6–08
Fordgate (Bingley) Ltd v. National Westminster Bank plc [1994] 39 E.G.
    135 .... 6–11, 6–12, 6–13
Forte & Co. v. General Accident Life Assurance (1987) 54 P. & C.R. 9; [1986]
    2 EGLR 115; (1986) 279 E.G. 1227 .... 6–28, 6–30, 6–36
Foulger v. Arding [1902] 1 K.B. 700 7–04
Foundling Hospital v. Crane [1911] 2 K.B. 367 18–10
Fowler v. Fowler (1979) 10 Fam. Law 119; (1859) 4 De G. & J. 250 17–07
Fox v. Jolly [1916] 1 A.C. 1 14–06
—— v. Swann (1655) Sty. 482 3–08
—— v. Wellfair (P.G.) (1982) 263 E.G. 589 6–13
Fox Chemical Engineering Works Ltd v. Martin (1957) 169 E.G. 297 10–08
France v. Shaftward Investments, June 25, 1981, (unreported) C.A. 16–41
Francis v. Cowcliffe (1977) 33 P. & C.R. 368; (1976) 239 E.G. 977,
    D.C. 9–27
Fraser Pipestock v. Gloucester City Council [1995] 36 E.G. 141 .... 6–40, 17–02
Frederick Berry Ltd v. Royal Bank of Scotland [1949] 1 K.B. 619 4–11
Freehold & Leasehold Shop Properties v. Friends Provident Life Office (1984)
    271 E.G. 451, C.A. 6–40, 17–02
French v. Commercial Union Assurance Co. [1993] 24 E.G. 115 16–32
Frend v. Buckley (1870) L.R. 5 Q.B. 213 18–14
Friends Provident Life Office v. British Railways Board [1996] 1 All E.R. 336;
    [1995] 48 E.G. 106 .... 2–04, 2–05, 2–12,
                                                                                    3–15, 18–26
Frish v. Barclays Bank [1955] 2 Q.B. 541; [1955] 3 W.L.R. 439; [1955] 3 All
    E.R. 185 16–41

Frobisher (Second Investments) v. Kiloran Trust Co. [1980] 1 W.L.R. 425; [1980] 1 All E.R. 488; (1979) 40 P. & C.R. 442; (1979) 253 E.G. 1231 8–07
Fryer v. Ewart [1902] A.C. 187 3–11
Fuller v. Judy Properties (1991) 64 P. & C.R. 176; [1992] 1 EGLR 75; [1992] 14 E.G. 106, C.A. 18–09
Fuller's Theatre and Vaudeville Company Ltd v. Rofe [1923] A.C. 435 P.C. 12–14

G.P. & P. v. Bulcraig & Davis [1988] 12 E.G. 103, C.A. 18–05
G.S. Fashions v. B. & Q. [1995] 9 E.G. 324 14–04
GUS Property Management Ltd v. Texas Homecare Ltd [1993] 27 E.G. 130 2–04
Ganton House Investments v. Corbin [1988] 43 E.G. 76 18–17
—— v. Crossman Investments, May 19, June 14, 1993, Colchester Cty. Ct. 16–47
Garrard v. Frankel (1862) 30 Beav. 445 17–10
Garston v. Scottish Widows Fund and Life Assurance Society [1996] 1 W.L.R. 834; [1996] 23 E.G. 131 16–09
General Accident Fire and Life Assurance Corp. v. Electronic Data Processing Co. (1987) 53 P. & C.R. 189; (1987) 281 E.G. 65; [1987] 1 EGLR 113 .... 6–23, 6–26, 6–27
Gentle v. Faulkner [1900] 2 Q.B. 267 12–03
Gian Singh & Co. v. Nahar; See Singh (Gian) & Co. v. Nahar.
Gilmour Caterers v. St. Bartholemew's Hospital Governors [1956] 1 Q.B. 387; [1956] 2 W.L.R. 419; [1956] 1 All E.R. 314 16–40
Glass v. Kencakes Ltd [1966] 1 Q.B. 611 14–06
Glegg, Ex p. (1881) 19 Ch. D. 7 18–27
Gleneagles Hotel v. Customs and Excise Commissioners (No. LON/85/473) [1986] VATTR 196; [1987] 2 C.M.L.R. 269, V.A.T. Tribunal 19–13
Gleniffer Finance Corp. v. Bamar Wood & Products (1978) 37 P. & C.R. 208; [1978] 2 Lloyd's Rep. 49 13–09
Glessing v. Green [1975] 1 W.L.R. 863; [1975] 2 All E.R. 696; (1975) 29 P. & C.R. 461, C.A. 18–10
Globe Equities Ltd, MAN/93/1449 (13105), unreported 19–12
Glofield Properties v. Morley [1988] 2 E.G. 62 6–11
—— v. —— (No. 2) [1988] 33 E.G. 59 6–25
Godbold v. Martin (The Newsagents) (1983) 268 E.G. 1202 .... 6–36, 11–07
Gold v. Brighton Corporation [1956] 1 W.L.R. 1291; [1956] 3 All E.R. 442, C.A. 16–46
Goldberg v. Edwards [1950] Ch. 247, C.A. 4–12
Goldman v. Abbott [1989] 48 E.G. 151, C.A. 12–10, 18–17
Goldsmiths' Co. v. West Metropolitan Rail Co. [1904] 1 K.B. 1 16–25
Goldstein v. Sanders [1915] 1 Ch. 549 12–14
Gooch v. Clutterbuck [1899] 2 Q.B. 148 18–18
Gooderham & Worts v. Canadian Broadcasting Corporation [1947] A.C. 66 9–10
Good's Lease, Re [1954] 1 W.L.R. 309; [1954] 1 All E.R. 275 12–04
Gordon v. Selico Co. [1986] 1 EGLR 71; (1986) 278 E.G. 53, C.A. 18–05
Gosling v. Woolf [1893] 1 Q.B. 39 18–24
Goulston Discount Co. v. Clark [1967] 2 Q.B. 493; [1966] 3 W.L.R. 1280; [1967] 1 All E.R. 61 3–13
Graham v. Philcox [1984] Q.B. 747; [1984] 3 W.L.R. 150; [1984] 2 All E.R. 643; (1984) 48 P. & C.R. 354 .... 4–07, 4–13

Granada T.V. Network Ltd v. Great Universal Stores Ltd (1963) 187 E.G. 391 12–14

Granada Theatres v. Freehold Investment (Leytonstone) [1959] Ch. 592; [1959] 1 W.L.R. 570; [1959] 2 All E.R. 176 9–05

Grand Junction Co. v. Bates [1954] 2 Q.B. 160; [1954] 3 W.L.R. 45; [1954] 2 All E.R. 385 12–04

Graysim Holdings Ltd v. P & O Holdings Ltd [1995] 3 W.L.R. 854; [1995] 4 All E.R. 831; [1996] 3 E.G. 124, H.L. 16–16

Graystone Property Investments v. Margulies (1984) 47 P. & C.R. 472; (1984) 296 E.G. 538, C.A. 4–03

GREA Real Property Investments v. Williams (1979) 250 E.G. 651 6–36

Great Northern Railway Co. v. Harrison (1852) 12 C.B. 576 1–02

Greater London Council v. Connolly [1970] 2 Q.B. 100; [1970] 2 W.L.R. 658; [1970] 1 All E.R. 870, C.A. 17–02

—— v. Minchin, February 25, 1981, unreported 16–22

Greater London Properties' Lease, Re; Taylor Bros. (Grocers) v. Covent Garden Properties Co. [1959] 1 W.L.R. 503; [1959] 1 All E.R. 728 ...... 12–08, 12–14, 13–05

Green's Case (1582) Cro. Eliz. 3 14–05

Greenhaven Securities v. Compton [1985] 2 EGLR 117; (1985) 275 E.G. 628 6–11

Greenwich London Borough v. Discreet Selling Estates [1990] 48 E.G. 113; (1990) 61 P. & C.R. 405, C.A. 14–05

Gregson v. Lord Cyril [1963] 1 W.L.R. 41; [1962] 3 All E.R. 907, C.A. 16–40

Groveside Properties v. Westminster Medical School (1984) 47 P. & C.R. 507; (1983) 267 E.G. 593, C.A. 16–16, 16–18

Gruhn v. Balgray Investments (1963) 185 E.G. 455; (1963) 107 S.J. 112, C.A. 17–04

Guardian Assurance Co. v. Gants Hill Holdings (1983) 267 E.G. 678 10–09

Guild & Co. v. Conrad [1894] 2 Q.B. 885 3–13

Gurton v. Parrott [1991] 1 EGLR 98; [1991] 18 E.G. 161 16–18

Guys' n' Dolls v. Sade Brothers Catering (1984) 269 E.G. 129, C.A. 17–03

Hadley v. Baxendale (1854) 9 Exch. 341 9–27

Haedicke and Lipski's Contract, Re [1901] 2 Ch. 666 18–15

Hafton Properties v. Camp; Camp v. Silchester Court (Croydon) Management Co. [1994] 3 E.G. 129 8–02

Hagee (London) v. Co-operative Insurance Society (1991) 63 P. & C.R. 362; [1992] 1 EGLR 57; [1992] 7 E.G. 122 11–02

—— v. Erikson (A.B.) and Larson [1976] Q.B. 209; [1975] 3 W.L.R. 272; [1975] 3 All E.R. 234; (1975) 29 P. & C.R. 512, C.A. 16–22, 16–23

Haines v. Florensa [1990] 1 EGLR 73; [1990] 9 E.G. 70 .... 4–03, 11–03

Hair v. Prudential Assurance Co. [1983] 2 Lloyd's Rep. 667 13–10

Hambros Bank Executor & Trustee Co. v. Superdrug Stores [1985] 1 EGLR 99; (1985) 274 E.G. 590 6–36

Hamilton v. Martell Securities [1984] Ch. 226; [1984] 2 W.L.R. 699; [1984] 1 All E.R. 665; (1984) 48 P. & C.R. 69 9–24

Hamish Cathie Travel England v. Insight International Tours [1986] 1 EGLR 244 6–36

Hammersmith and Fulham L.B.C. v. Monk; Barnet L.B.C. v. Smith [1992] 1 A.C. 478; [1990] 3 W.L.R. 1144; [1992] 1 All E.R. 1; (1991) 63 P. & C.R. 373; [1992] 1 EGLR 65; [1992] 9 E.G. 135 3–10

Hampshire v. Wickens (1878) 7 Ch.D. 55 18–07

Hampson (t/a Abbey Self Storage) v. Newcastle-upon-Tyne City Council
[1996] EGCS 4 7–02
Hampstead & Suburban Properties v. Diomedous [1969] 1 Ch. 248; [1968] 3
W.L.R. 990; [1968] 3 All E.R. 545; (1969) 19 P. & C.R. 880 10–02
Hancock & Willis v. G.M.S. Syndicate (1983) 265 E.G. 473, C.A. 16–16
Handel v. St. Stephen's Close [1994] 5 E.G. 159 4–07
Hankey v. Clavering [1942] K.B. 326 16–06
Harben Style Ltd v. Rhodes Trust [1995] 17 E.G. 125 6–08
Hare v. Groves (1796) 3 Anst. 687 13–17
Harewood Hotels v. Harris [1958] 1 W.L.R. 108; [1958] 1 All E.R. 104 6–34
Hargreaves Transport v. Lynch [1969] 1 W.L.R. 215; [1969] 1 All E.R. 455;
(1969) 20 P. & C.R. 143, C.A. 18–05
Harman v. Ainslie [1904] 1 K.B. 698 14–03
Harmsworth Pension Funds Trustees v. Charringtons Industrial Holdings
(1985) 49 P. & C.R. 297; [1985] 1 EGLR 97; (1985) 274 E.G. 588 6–34
Harris v. Black (1983) 46 P. & C.R. 366, C.A. 3–10
Harris v. Boots Cash Chemists (Southern) [1904] 2 Ch. 376 18–18
Harry Lay Ltd v. Fox (1963) 186 E.G. 15 12–03
Hart v. Emelkirk; Howroyd v. Emelkirk [1983] 1 W.L.R. 1289; [1983] 3 All
E.R. 15; (1983) 267 E.G. 946 9–27
—— v. Windsor (1843) 12 M. & W. 68 9–02
Hart Dyke (Sir W.), Ex p., Morrish, Re (1882) 22 Ch.D. 410 18–27
Haskell v. Marlow [1928] 2 K.B. 95 9–06
Hastie and Jenkenson v. McMahon [1990] 1 W.L.R. 1575; [1991] 1 All E.R.
255 16–25
Hastings Corporation v. Letton [1908] 1 K.B. 378 3–13
Havenridge v. Boston Dyers [1994] 49 E.G. 111 13–05
Haviland v. Long (Dunn Trust, Third Parties) [1952] 2 Q.B. 80; [1952] 1
T.L.R. 576; [1952] 1 All E.R. 463 9–25
Hayns v. Secretary of State for the Environment (1977) 36 P. & C.R. 317,
(1978) 245 E.G. 53 4–07
Heard v. Stuart (1907) 24 T.L.R. 104 .... 4–11, 11–02
Heath v. Drown [1973] A.C. 498; [1972] 2 W.L.R. 1306; [1972] 2 All E.R.
561; (1971) 23 P. & C.R. 351, H.L. 16–40
Heinnemann v. Cooper (1987) 284 E.G. 1237, C.A. 18–12
Hemingway Securities Ltd v. Dunraven [1995] 9 E.G. 322 .... 12.02
Henderson Group v. Superabbey [1988] 39 E.G. 87, D.C. 6.12
Henry Smith's Charity Trustees v. AWADA Trading & Promotion Services Ltd
(1984) 269 E.G. 729 .... 6–11, 17–03
—— v. Hemmings (1982) 265 E.G. 383 18–07
Henry Southeran v. Norwich Union Life Insurance Society [1992] 2 EGLR 9;
[1992] 31 E.G. 70 6–15
Herbert Duncan Ltd v. Cluttons (A Firm); See City of London Corporation v.
Fell; Herbert Duncan Ltd v. Cluttons (A Firm).
Herongrove v. Wates City of London Properties [1988] 24 E.G. 108 16–26
Hesketh Estates Ltd v. Cohen (1948) 151 E.G. 465 11–05
Heywood v. Mahalitu (1883) 25 Ch.D. 357 18–14
Hibernian Property Co. v. Liverpool Corporation [1973] 1 W.L.R. 751; [1973]
2 All E.R. 1117; (1973) 25 P. & C.R. 477 9–25
Higgins and Percival, Re (1888) 57 L.J.Ch. 807 18–16
Highett and Bird's Contract, Re [1903] 1 Ch. 287 18–16
Hill v. Barclay (1811) 18 Ves. 56 9–26
—— v. East & West India Dock Company (1884) 9 App. Cas. 448 3–15
—— v. Griffin (1987) 282 E.G. 85; [1987] 1 EGLR 81, C.A. 14–07
—— v. Harris [1965] 2 Q.B. 601; [1965] 2 W.L.R. 1331; [1965] 2 All E.R.
358 .... 6–33, 18–05, 18–22

Hill Samuel Life Assurance v. Preston Borough Council [1990] 36 E.G. 111 .... 6–30, 6–32

Hill Street Investments Ltd v. Bellshore Property Investments Ltd [1996] NPC 20 14–06

Hill (William) (Southern) v. Cabras (1987) 54 P. & C.R. 42; (1987) 281 E.G. 309; [1987] 1 EGLR 37, C.A. 4–18

Hillgate House v. Expert Clothing Services & Sales (1987) 282 E.G. 715; [1987] 1 EGLR 65 16–03

Hilliard Property Co. Ltd v. Nicholas Clarke Investments Ltd (1984) 269 E.G. 1257 9–08

Hillil Property and Investment Co. v. Naraine Pharmacy (1979) 39 P. & C.R. 67; (1979) 252 E.G. 1013, C.A. 16–18

Hills (Patents) v. University College Hospital Board of Governors [1956] 1 Q.B. 90; [1955] 3 W.L.R. 523; [1955] 3 All E.R. 365 16–18

Hilton v. Smith (James) & Sons (Norwood) (1979) 257 E.G. 1063, C.A. 4–02, 10–02, 10–11

Hindcastle v. Barbara Attenborough Associates Ltd [1996] 1 All E.R. 737; [1994] 4 All E.R. 129, H.L. 2–04, 3–08, 3–15

Historic Houses Hotels Ltd v. Cadogan Estates [1995] 11 E.G. 140 6–36

Hizzett v. Hargreaves, April 28, 1986, C.A.T. No. 419 .... 6–02, 18–08

Hodgson v. Armstrong [1967] 2 Q.B. 299; [1967] 2 W.L.R. 311; [1967] 1 All E.R. 307 16–25

Hogarth Health Club v. Westbourne Investments [1990] 2 E.G. 69; (1990) 59 P. & C.R. 212 11–07

Hogg Bullimore & Co. v. Co-operative Insurance Society (1984) 49 P. & C.R. 105 16–25

Hoggett v. Hoggett (1979) 39 P. & C.R. 121, C.A. 18–26

Holden v. White [1982] Q.B. 679; [1982] 2 W.L.R. 1030; [1982] 2 All E.R. 328, C.A. 4–07

Holicater v. Grandred [1993] 23 E.G. 129; [1993] 1 EGLR 135, C.A. 1–02, 6–10

Holiday Fellowship v. Hereford [1959] 1 W.L.R. 211; [1959] 1 All E.R. 433 9–05

Holme v. Brunskill (1878) 3 Q.B.D. 495 3–15

Hooper v. Sherman [1994] NPC 153 18–03

Hope Bros Ltd v. Cowan [1913] 2 Ch. 312 4–03

Hopcutt v. Carver (1969) 209 E.G. 1069, C.A. 16–36

Horner v. Franklin [1905] 1 K.B. 479 7–05

Hornidge v. Wilson (1840) 11 Ad. & El. 645 3–08

Horowitz v. Ferrand [1956] C.L.Y. 4843 16–36

Horsey Estate Ltd v. Steiger [1899] 2 Q.B. 79 3–11

Horsfall v. Testar (1817) 7 Taunt. 385 9–18

Houlder Bros & Co. v. Gibbs [1925] Ch. 198, 575 12–13

Howard de Walden Settled Estates v. The Pasta Place Ltd [1995] 22 E.G. 143 3–15

Howell v. Kightley (1856) 21 Beav. 331 18–16

Hua Chiao Commercial Bank v. Chiaphua Industries (formerly known as Chiap Hua Clocks & Watches) [1987] A.C. 99; [1987] 2 W.L.R. 179; [1985] 1 All E.R. 1110; (1987) 54 P. & C.R. 52 6–05

Huber (J.J.) (Investments) v. Private DIY Co., The [1995] EGCS 112 .... 17–07, 17–09, 17–10, 18–06

Hudson (A.) v. Legal & General Life of Australia [1986] 280 E.G. 1434; [1986] 2 EGLR 130, P.C. 6–20

Hunt v. Bishop (1853) 3 Ex. 675 9–16

—— v. Decca Navigator Co. (1972) 222 E.G. 625 16–41

Hunts Refuse Disposals v. Norfolk Environmental Waste Services Ltd [1996]
NPC 88 16–22
Hurstfell v. Leicester Square Property Co. [1988] 37 E.G. 109, C.A. 16–36
Hussain v. Brown, *The Times*, December 15, 1995, C.A. 13–10
Hyams v. Titan Properties (1972) 24 P. & C.R. 359; (1972) 224 E.G. 2017,
C.A. 8–03, 16–46
Hyman v. Rose [1912] A.C. 623 11–04
Hynes v. Twinsectra [1995] 35 E.G. 136 14–04

IBM United Kingdom v. Rockware Glass [1980] F.S.R. 335 .... 18–05, 18–17
Iceland Frozen Foods v. Starlight Investments [1992] 1 EGLR 126; [1992] 2
E.G. 117, C.A. 6–30
Ideal Film Renting Co. v. Nielson [1921] 1 Ch. 575 12–10
Imprint (Print and Design) v. Inkblot Studios (1985) 129 S.J. 133 16–25
Imray v. Oakshette [1897] 2 Q.B. 218 18–24
Industrial Properties (Barton Hill) v. Associated Electrical Industries [1977]
Q.B. 580; [1977] 2 W.L.R. 726; [1977] 2 All E.R. 293; (1977) 242 E.G.
955 3–06
International Drilling Fluids v. Louisville Investments (Uxbridge) [1986] Ch.
513; [1986] 1 W.L.R. 581; [1986] 1 All E.R. 321; [1986] 1 EGLR 39;
(1985) 277 E.G. 62 .... 12–13, 12–14
Iperion Investments Corp. v. Broadwalk House Residents [1992] 2 EGLR
235 .... 14–05, 14–06
Ipswich Borough Council v. Fisons [1990] Ch. 709; [1990] 2 W.L.R. 108;
[1990] 1 All E.R. 730; [1990] 4 E.G. 127 6–19
Irvine v. Moran (1991) 24 H.L.R. 1; [1991] 1 EGLR 261 9–05
Isaac v. Hotel de Paris [1960] 1 W.L.R. 239 16–22
Isow's Restaurants v. Greenhaven (Piccadilly) Properties Ltd (1969) 213 E.G.
505 12–14
Italica Holdings S.A. v. Bayadea [1985] 1 EGLR 70; (1985) 273 E.G. 888 .. 16–25
Ivory Gate v. Capital City Leisure [1993] EGCS 76 6–36
Izon v. Garton (1839) 5 Bing (N.C.) 501 13–15

J.F. Crossman LON/89/398 (5417) unreported 19–04
J.T. Developments v. Quinn (1990) 62 P. & C.R. 33; [1991] 2 EGLR 257,
C.A. 16–31
J.T. Sydenham & Co. v. Enichers Elastomers [1989] 1 EGLR 257 6–20
Jackson v. Bishop (1979) 48 P. & C.R. 57, C.A. 4–02
—— v. Mumford (1904) 52 W.R. 342 9–07
—— v. Simons [1923] 1 Ch. 373 12–05
Jacob Isbicki & Co. v. Goulding & Bird [1989] 1 EGLR 236 8–03
James v. British Crafts Centre (1988) 55 P. & C.R. 56; (1987) 282 E.G. 1251;
[1987] 1 EGLR 139, C.A. 6–28
—— v. Heim Gallery (London) (1980) 41 P. & C.R. 269; (1980) 256 E.G.
819, C.A. 6–10
Janes (Gowns) v. Harlow Development Corporation (1979) 253 E.G.
799 .... 6–17, 16–32, 16–47
Jaskel v. Sophie Nursery Products [1993] EGCS 42, C.A. 6–05
Javad v. Aqil [1991] 1 W.L.R. 1007; [1991] 1 All E.R. 243; [1990] 41 E.G.
61 .... 16–22, 18–31
Jebco Properties v. Mastforce [1992] NPC 42 18–17
Jeffries v. O'Neill (1983) 46 P. & C.R. 376; (1984) 269 E.G. 131 6–26

Jenkins v. Price [1907] 2 Ch. 229 12–09
Jervis v. Harris [1996] 1 All E.R. 303; [1996] 2 W.L.R. 220, C.A. 9–24
Job v. Barrister (1856) 2 K. & J. 374 16–13
Jocelyne v. Nissen [1970] 2 Q.B. 86 17–07
Joel v. Montgomery & Taylor [1967] Ch. 272; [1967] 2 W.L.R. 21; [1966] 3 All
    E.R. 763 18–31
John Lewis Properties v. Viscount Chelsea (1993) 67 P. & C.R. 120; [1993] 34
    E.G. 116 .... 14–05, 17–03
Johnsey Estates v. Lewis & Manley (Engineering) (1987) 284 E.G. 1240 18–18
—— v. Webb [1990] 19 E.G. 84 .... 3–15, 3–16
Johnsey Estates (1990) Ltd v. Newport Marketworld [1996] EGCS 87 18–10
Johnstone v. Holdway [1963] 1 Q.B. 601; [1963] 2 W.L.R. 147; [1963] 1 All
    E.R. 432, C.A. 17–04
Jones v. Jenkins (1985) 277 E.G. 644; [1986] 1 EGLR 113, C.A. 16–41
—— v. Lavington [1903] 1 K.B. 253 16–03
—— v. Sherwood Computer Services [1992] 1 W.L.R. 277; [1992] 2 All E.R.
    170 6–20
—— v. Watts (1890) 43 Ch.D. 574 18–08
Joseph v. London County Council (1914) 111 L.T. 276 11–02
Junction Estates v. Cope (1974) 27 P. & C.R. 482 3–15
Junior Books v. Veitchi Co., The [1983] A.C. 520; [1982] 3 W.L.R. 477;
    [1982] 3 All E.R. 201 9–12

K/S Norjal A/S v. Hyundai Heavy Industries Co. [1992] Q.B. 863; [1991] 3
    W.L.R. 1025; [1991] 3 All E.R. 211, C.A. 6–14
Kammin's Ballrooms Co. v. Zenith Investments (Torquay) [1971] A.C. 850;
    [1970] 3 W.L.R. 287; [1970] 2 All E.R. 871; (1971) 22 P. & C.R. 74,
    H.L. 16–25
Kaye v. Shop Investments (1966) 198 E.G. 1091 12–14
Keats v. Graham [1960] 1 W.L.R. 30; [1959] 3 All E.R. 919 9–25
Keith Bayley Rogers & Co. (A Firm) v. Cubes (1975) 31 P. & C.R. 412 16–26
Kelly v. Battershell [1949] 2 All E.R. 830 10–11
—— v. Rogers [1892] Q.B. 910 16–03
Kelsen v. Imperial Tobacco Co. (of Great Britain and Ireland) [1957] 2 Q.B.
    334; [1957] 2 W.L.R. 1007; [1957] 2 All E.R. 343 .... 4–03, 14–18
Kemp v. Bird (1877) 5 Ch.D. 974 10–11
—— v. Neptune Concrete [1988] 48 E.G. 71 .... 17–07, 17–09
Kened Ltd v. Connie Investments Ltd [1995] EGCS 87 12–10
Kent Coast Property Investments v. Ward [1990] 45 E.G. 107, C.A. 16–19
Kent County Council v. Beaney [1993] Env.L.R. 225 20–03
Kewal Investments v. Arthur Maiden [1990] 15 E.G. 58 16–16
Kiddle v. City Business Properties [1942] 1 K.B. 269 9–19
Kilgour v. Gaddes [1904] 1 K.B. 457 15–02
Killick v. Second Covent Garden Property Co. [1973] 1 W.L.R. 658; [1973] 2
    All E.R. 337; (1973) 25 P. & C.R. 332, C.A. 12–14, 17–03, 17–04
King, Re, Robinson v. Gray [1963] Ch. 459; [1963] 2 W.L.R. 629; [1963] 1 All
    E.R. 781 .... 13–15, 18–16
King v. Cave-Brown-Cave [1960] 2 Q.B. 222; [1960] 3 W.L.R. 204; [1960] 2
    All E.R. 751 7–03
Kings (Estate Agents) v. Anderson [1992] 1 EGLR 121; [1992] 5 E.G.
    166 6–10
King's Motors (Oxford) v. Lax [1970] 1 W.L.R. 426; [1969] 3 All E.R. 665   16–11
Kings Reach Investments v. Reed Publishing Holdings (1984) (Unreported),
    C.A. 4–03
Kings North Trust v. Bell [1986] 1 W.L.R. 119; [1986] 1 All E.R. 423 3–14

Kitney v. Greater London Properties (1984) 272 E.G. 786 .... 16–12, 16–13
—— v. MEPC [1977] 1 W.L.R. 981; [1978] 1 All E.R. 595; (1977) 243 E.G.
   131 16–12
Knight v. Williams [1901] 1 Ch. 256 18–27
Koumoudouros & Marathon Realty Co. Re (1978) 89 D.L.R. (3d) 551
   Ont.H.C.J. 14–06
Kramer (Michael) & Co. v. Airways Pension Fund Trustees (1976) 246 E.G.
   911, C.A. 16–32
Kumar v. Dunning [1989] Q.B. 193, C.A. 3–15

La Salle Recreations v. Canadian Camdex Investments (1969) 4 D.L.R. (3d)
   549 11–11
Labone v. Litherland Urban District Council; Liverpool Co-operative Society
   & Gourley Bros (Third Parties) [1956] 1 W.L.R. 522; [1956] 2 All E.R.
   215 10–08
Lace v. Chantler [1944] K.B. 368; [1944] 1 All E.R. 305 5–01
Ladyman v. Wirral Estates [1968] 2 All E.R. 197; (1969) 19 P. & C.R.
   781 5–03
Laing Investments Co. v. Dunn (G.A.) & Co. (1982) 263 E.G. 879 6–14
Lam Kee Ying Sdn. Bhd. v. Lam Shes Tong (Trading as Lian Joo Co.) [1975]
   A.C. 247; [1974] 3 W.L.R. 784; [1974] 3 All E.R. 137, P.C. 12–05
Lamas v. Peak [1947] 2 All E.R. 574 20–03
Lambert v. Keymood Ltd [1996] NPC 58 13–06
—— v. Woolworth & Co. [1938] Ch. 883; [1938] 2 All E.R. 664, C.A. 11–05
Lambourne v. McLellan [1903] 2 Ch. 268 .... 11–13, 17–03, 17–04
Land and Premises at Liss, Hants, Re [1971] Ch. 986; [1971] 3 W.L.R. 77;
   [1971] 3 All E.R. 380; (1971) 22 P. & C.R. 861 16–23
Land Reclamation Co. v. Basildon District Council; Re Pitsea Access Road,
   Basildon [1979] 1 W.L.R. 767; [1979] 2 All E.R. 993; (1979) 250 E.G.
   549 16–16
Land Securities v. Westminster City Council [1993] 1 W.L.R. 286; [1993] 4 All
   E.R. 124; (1992) 65 P. & C.R. 387; [1992] 44 E.G. 153 6–17
—— v —— (No. 2) [1995] 1 EGLR 245 6–19
Langford v. Selmes (1857) 3 K. & J. 220 12–03
Langton v. Henson (1905) 92 L.T. 805 3–10
Laura Investments v. Havering (No. 2) [1993] 8 E.G. 120 .... 6–30, 6–36, 6–40
Laurence v. Lexcourt Holdings [1978] 1 W.L.R. 1128; [1978] 2 All E.R.
   810 18–05
Law Land Co. v. Consumers' Association (1980) 255 E.G. 617, C.A. 6–28
Lawrence v. Carter (1956) 17 E.G. 222; [1956] J.P.L. 432 16–38
Lawrence (Frederick) v. Freeman Hardy & Willis [1959] Ch. 731; [1959] 3
   W.L.R. 275; [1959] 3 All E.R. 77 .... 16–41, 16–45
Lawrie v. Lees (1881) 14 Ch. D. 249; (1981) 7 App.Cas. 19 18–16
Lawson Mardon Group Pension Scheme, LON/92/492 (10231),
   (unreported) 19–10
Lear v. Blizzard [1983] 3 All E.R. 662; (1983) 268 E.G. 1115 .. 6–24, 6–27, 16–11
Learmonth Property Investment Co. v. Amos Hinton & Sons [1985] 1 EGLR
   13; (1984) 274 E.G. 725 6–19
Leathwoods v. Total Oil (G.B.) (1986) 51 P. & C.R. 20; [1985] 2 EGLR 237;
   (1984) 270 E.G. 1083 .... 16–40, 16–41
Lee v. Railway Executive [1949] 2 All E.R. 581 17–04
Lee-Parker v. Izzet [1971] 1 W.L.R. 1688; [1971] 3 All E.R. 1099 9–27
—— v. —— (No. 2) [1972] 1 W.L.R. 775; [1972] 2 All E.R. 800; (1972) 23
   P. & C.R. 301 18–31

Lee-Verhulst (Investments) v. Harwood Trust [1973] 1 Q.B. 204; [1972] 3
  W.L.R. 772; [1972] 3 All E.R. 619; (1972) 24 P. & C.R. 346, C.A. 16–16
Legal and General Assurance (Pension Management) v. Cheshire County
  Council (1984) 269 E.G. 40, C.A. 6–10
Leggott v. Barrett (1880) 15 Ch. D. 306 18–10
Lehmann v. McArthur (1868) L.R. 3 Ch.App. 496 18–17
Leppard v. Excess Insurance Co. [1979] 1 W.L.R. 512; [1979] 2 All E.R. 668;
  (1979) 250 E.G. 751, C.A. 13–09
Leschellas v. Woolf [1908] 1 Ch. 641 16–27
Levene v. Clapham Super Market Ltd (1958) 171 E.G. 719 10–11
Levermore v. Jobey [1956] 1 W.L.R. 697; [1956] 2 All E.R. 362 .... 1–01, 17–03
Levy, *ex p.* Walton *Re*, (1881) 17 Ch. D. 746 17–02
Levy (A) & Son v. Martin Brent Developments [1987] 2 EGLR 93; [1987] 28
  E.G. 646 16–40
Lewington v. Trustees for the Protection of Ancient Buildings (1983) 45 P. &
  C.R. 336; (1983) 266 E.G. 997, C.A. 16–27
Lewis v. Baker [1905] 1 Ch. 46 .... 5–02, 18–21
—— v. M.T.C. (Cars) [1975] 1 W.L.R. 457; [1975] 1 All E.R. 874; (1975) 29
  P. & C.R. 495, C.A. 16–26
—— v. Weldcrest [1978] 1 W.L.R. 1107; [1978] 3 All E.R. 1226; (1978) 37
  P. & C.R. 331; (1978) 247 E.G. 211, C.A. 16–15
Lewis (A.) & Co. (Westminster) v. Bell Property Trust [1940] Ch.
  345 10–08
Lewis Vintners t/a Smokey Joe v. Speight (V.O.) (LVC/497/1983) (1984) 272
  E.G. 1177; (1984) 25 R.V.R. 85, Lands Tribunal 11–09
Lex Services v. Johns (1990) 59 P. & C.R. 427; [1990] 10 E.G. 67 16–25
—— v. Oriel House B.V. [1991] 39 E.G. 139; [1991] 2 EGLR 126 6–17
Lilley & Skinner Ltd v. Crump (1929) 73 S.J. 366 2–11
Linden v. Department of Health and Social Security [1986] 1 W.L.R. 164;
  [1986] 1 All E.R. 691; (1985) 51 P. & C.R. 317; (1985) 277 E.G.
  543 16–16
Linden Gardens Trust v. Lenesta Sludge Disposals; St. Martins Property Corp.
  v. Sir Robert McAlpine & Sons [1995] F.S.R. 686; [1994] 1 A.C. 85;
  [1993] 3 W.L.R. 408; [1993] 3 All E.R. 417, H.L. 9–12
Lipinski's Will Trusts, *Re* [1976] Ch. 235; [1976] 3 W.L.R. 522; [1977] 1 All
  E.R. 33 8–07
Lipmans Wallpaper v. Mason and Hodghton [1969] 1 Ch. 20, [1968] 2 W.L.R.
  881; [1968] 1 All E.R. 1123; (1969) 19 P. & C.R. 224 18–17
Lister v. Lane and Nesham [1893] 2 Q.B. 212 .... 9–06, 9–08
Lister Locks v. T.E.I. Pensions Trust (1982) 264 E.G. 827 .... 6–27, 17–03
Little v. Courage, *The Times*, January 6, 1995, C.A. 16–13
Liverpool City Council v. Irwin [1977] A.C. 239; (1976) 238 E.G. 879 4–07,
                                                                      8–02, 9–02, 9–19
Liverpool Properties v. Oldbridge Investments [1985] 2 EGLR 111; (1985)
  276 E.G. 1352, C.A. 14–04
Livestock Underwriting Agency v. Corbett & Newson (1955) 165 E.G.
  469 16–40
Lloyd v. Stanbury [1971] 1 W.L.R. 535; [1971] 2 All E.R. 267; (1971) 22 P. &
  C.R. 432 18–31
Lloyds Bank v. City of London Corp. [1983] Ch. 192; [1982] 3 W.L.R. 1138;
  [1983] 1 All E.R. 92; (1983) 45 P. & C.R. 287; (1982) 264 E.G. 1001,
  C.A. 16–50
—— v. Lake [1961] 1 W.L.R. 884; [1961] 2 All E.R. 30 9–25
Lloyd's Bank and Lillington's Contract, *Re* [1912] 1 Ch. 601 18–21
Lobb (Alec) (Garages) v. Total Oil Great Britain [1985] 1 W.L.R. 173; [1985]
  1 All E.R. 303; [1985] 1 EGLR 33 10–12

Lockharts v. Bernard Rosen & Co. [1922] 1 Ch. 433 18–16
London & County (A. & D.) v. Wilfred Sportsman; Greenwoods (Hosiers & Outfitters) Third Party [1971] Ch. 764; [1970] 3 W.L.R. 418 14–04
London & Leeds Estates v. Paribas (1993) 66 P. & C.R. 218; [1993] 30 E.G. 89 6–30
London & Manchester Assurance Co. v. Dunn & Co. (G.A.) (1983) 265 E.G. 39, 131, C.A. 6–10, 6–25
London and Provincial Millinery Stores v. Barclays Bank [1962] 1 W.L.R. 510; [1962] 2 All E.R. 163 16–45
London Borough of Tower Hamlets v. London Docklands Development Corporation, April 13, 1992 (unreported) Knightsbridge Crown Ct. 20–03
London County Council v. Hutter [1925] Ch. 626 .... 4–11, 11–02
London Hilton Jewellers v. Hilton International Hotels [1990] 1 EGLR 112; [1990] 20 E.G. 69, C.A. 16–41
London Merchant Securities v. Islington L.B.C. [1988] A.C. 303; [1987] 3 W.L.R. 173; [1987] 2 All E.R. 961; (1987) 283 E.G. 954 7–02
London Regional Transport v. Wimpey Group Services (1987) 53 P. & C.R. 356; [1986] 2 EGLR 41; (1986) 280 E.G. 898 .... 6–23, 17–07, 17–08
London Scottish Properties Ltd v. Council for Professions Supplementary to Medicine, November 8, 1977, (unreported), C.A. 6–28
Long Acre Securities v. Electro Acoustic Industries [1990] 1 EGLR 91; [1990] 6 E.G. 103; (1989) 61 P. & C.R. 177, C.A. 16–24
Long (Nevill) & Co. (Boards) v. Firmenich and Co. (1984) 47 P. & C.R. 59; (1983) 268 E.G. 572, C.A. 16–16
Longman v. Viscount Chelsea (1989) 58 P. & C.R. 1989; [1989] 2 EGLR 242, C.A. 18–10, 18–17
Lonrho v. Shell Petroleum Co. (No. 2) [1982] A.C. 173, [1980] 1 W.L.R. 627, H.L. 6–15
Lord Bernstein of Leigh v. Skyviews and General Ltd [1978] Q.B. 479 4–03
Lord Hodson v. Cashmore (1973) 226 E.G. 1203 .... 3–10, 16–17
Lord Newborough v. Jones [1975] Ch. 90 16–25
Lord Windsor v. Burry (1582) 1 Dyer. 456 3–08
Lotteryking Ltd v. AMEC Properties Ltd [1995] 28 E.G. 100 18–03
Lovely and Orchard Services v. Daejan Investments (1977) 246 E.G. 651 16–47
Lowther v. Clifford [1927] 1 K.B. 130 7–04
Lubbock Fine & Co. v. Customs & Excise Commissioners (Case C–63/92) [1994] Q.B. 571; [1994] 3 W.L.R. 261; [1994] 3 All E.R. 705; [1994] 2 C.M.L.R. 633, E.C.J. 19–06
Lucas Industries v. Welsh Development Agency [1986] Ch. 500; [1986] 3 W.L.R. 80; [1986] 2 All E.R. 858; (1987) 53 P. & C.R. 198; [1986] 1 EGLR 147; (1986) 278 E.G. 878 6–19
Lurcott v. Wakely and Wheeler [1911] 1 K.B. 905 9–06
Luxmore v. Robson (1818) 1 B. & Ald. 584 9–04
Lynnthorpe Enterprises v. Sidney Smith (Chelsea) [1990] 40 E.G. 130, C.A. 6–26, 6–28
Lyons v. Central Commercial Properties, London [1958] 1 W.L.R. 869; [1958] 2 All E.R. 767 16–35
Lyons (J.) & Co. v. Knowles [1943] 1 K.B. 366 2–04
Lyons (John) Charity v. Haysport Properties [1995] EGCS 171 13–05

MEPC v. Scottish Amicable Life Assurance Society; Eckley (Neville Richard) (Third Party) (1993) 67 P. & C.R. 314 3–08
M.F.I. Properties v. BICC Group Pension Trust [1986] 1 All E.R. 974; [1986] 1 EGLR 115 .... 6–27, 17–02

MMC Investments Ltd v. Bossevain, October 7, 1993, C.A. (unreported)   2–04
M. & P. Enterprises (London) v. Norfolk Square Hotels [1994] 14 E.G.
    128   16–26
McCausland v. Duncan Lawrie [1996] EGCS 103, C.A.   18–03
McGreal v. Wake (1984) 128 S.J. 116; (1984) 269 E.G. 1254 .... 9–19, 9–22
McZiraith v. Grady [1968] 1 Q.B. 468; [1967] 3 W.L.R. 1331   4–07
MacKusick v. Carmichael [1917] 2 K.B. 581   12–04
McLaughlin v. Walsall Arcade (1956) 167 E.G. 356   16–47
McMullen v. Great Southern Cemetery and Crematorium Co., The (1958)
    172 E.G. 855, C.A.   16–26
Maison Kaye Fashions v. Horton's Estate (1967) 202 E.G. 23   16–36
Mammouth Greetings Cards v. Agra [1990] 29 E.G. 45   6–11
Mancetter Developments v. Garmanson & Givertz [1986] Q.B. 1212; [1986]
    2 W.L.R. 871; [1986] 1 EGLR 240 .... 11–04, 11–13
Manchester Bonded Warehouse Co. v. Carr (1880) 5 C.P.D. 507   9–06
Manchester City Council v. National Car Parks (1982) 262 E.G. 1297,
    C.A.   16–21
Manchester Garages v. Petrofina (U.K.) (1974) 233 E.G. 509, C.A.   16–40
Manfield & Sons v. Botchin [1970] 2 Q.B. 612; [1970] 3 W.L.R. 120   16–22
Mannai Investment Co. v. Eagle Star Life Assurance Co. [1995] 1 W.L.R.
    1508 .... 6–10, 16–06
Manor House Drive v. Shahbazian (1965) 109 S.J. 666; 195 E.G. 283   8–05
Maraday v. Sturt Properties [1988] 46 E.G. 99   6–10
Mark v. Arnold [1902] 1 K.B. 761   7–05
Marks v. Warren [1979] 1 All E.R. 29; (1978) 37 P. & C.R. 275; (1978) 248
    E.G. 503 .... 12–02, 12–04
Marsden v. Edward Heyes Ltd [1927] 2 K.B. 1   11–04
Maskell v. Ivory [1970] 1 Ch. 502; [1970] 2 W.L.R. 844; (1970) 21 P. & C.R.
    360   18–31
Massey v. Midland Bank [1995] 1 All E.R. 929   3–14
Matcham's Park (Holdings) v. Dommett (1984) E.G. 549, C.A.   16–21
Mather v. Barclays Bank [1987] 2 EGLR 254, D.C.   9–25
Matlodge v. Miller (1973) 227 E.G. 2247   4–17
Matthew v. Curling [1922] 2 A.C. 180 .... 9–04, 9–17
Maughan, Re (1885) 14 Q.B.D. 956   18–07
Max Factor v. Wesleyan Assurance Society [1996] EGCS 82 .... 12–15, 16–06
Meadfield Properties v. Secretary of State for the Environment [1994] EGCS
    144   5–03
Meadows v. Clerical, Medical and General Life Assurance Society [1981] Ch.
    70; [1980] 2 W.L.R. 639; [1980] 1 All E.R. 454; (1979) 40 P. & C.R. 238;
    (1979) 255 E.G. 883   14–04
Mecca Leisure v. Renown Investments (Holdings) [1985] 49 P. & C.R.
    12; (1984) 271 E.G. 989, C.A.   6–11
Meggeson v. Groves [1917] 1 Ch. 158   5–03
Mehmet v. Dawson (1984) 270 E.G. 139, C.A.   16–27
Melluish (Inspector of Taxes) v. BMI (No. 3); Same v. BMI (No. 6); Same v.
    BMI (No. 9); Same v. Fitzroy Finance; Same v. Barclays Mercantile
    Business Finances [1994] 3 W.L.R. 1032   11–16
Melville v. Grapelodge Developments (1978) 39 P. & C.R. 179   9–27
Melzak v. Lilienfield [1926] 1 Ch. 480   18–22
Memvale Securities Application, Re, LP/37/1973 [1975] J.P.L. 160, Lands
    Tribunal   10–12
Mercury Communications v. Director General of Telecommunications [1995]
    1 W.L.R. 48   6–20
Method Developments v. Jones [1971] 1 W.L.R. 168; [1971] 1 All E.R. 1027;
    (1971) 22 P. & C.R. 141, C.A. 16–40, 16–41

Metrolands Investments v. Dewhurst (J.H.) [1986] 3 All E.R. 659; (1986) 52
    P. & C.R. 232; [1986] 1 EGLR 125, C.A. 6–10
Metropolitan Properties Co. (F.G.C.) v. Cordery (1979) 39 P. & C.R. 10
    (1979) 251 E.G. 561, C.A. 14–05
Meyer v. Riddick [1990] 18 E.G. 97 16–41
Micrografix v. Woking 8 Ltd [1995] 37 E.G. 179 16–06
Middlegate Properties v. Bilbao, Caroline Construction Co. Third Party
    (1972) 24 P. & C.R. 329 18–18
—— v. Gidlow-Jackson (1977) 34 P. & C.R. 4, C.A. 9–24
—— v. Messimeris [1973] 1 W.L.R. 168; [1973] 1 All E.R. 645; (1973) 25
    P. & C.R. 76, C.A. 9–24
Midland Bank v. Chart Enterprises [1990] 44 E.G. 68 12–10
—— v. Shephard [1988] 3 All E.R. 17, C.A. 3–14
Mile End Old Town (Vestry) v. Whitby (1898) 78 L.T. 80 7–04
Miller v. Emcer Products [1956] Ch. 304; [1956] 1 All E.R. 237 7–09
Miller (James) & Partners v. Whitworth Street Estates (Manchester) [1970]
    A.C. 583; [1970] 2 W.L.R. 728; [1970] 1 All E.R. 796, H.L. 17–03
Millett (R. & A.) (Shops) v. Leon Allan International Fashions [1989] 18 E.G.
    107 .... 17–02, 18–33
Millshaw Property Co. Ltd v. Preston Borough Council [1995] EGCS
    186 17–02
Milmo v. Carreras [1946] K.B. 306 .... 5–02, 18–21
Milner v. Staffordshire Congregational Union (Incorporated) [1956] Ch. 275;
    [1956] 2 W.L.R. 556; [1956] 1 All E.R. 494 18–17
Milverton Group v. Warner World (1994) 68 P. & C.R. D9 2–04
Mint v. Good [1951] 1 K.B. 517; [1950] 2 All E.R. 1159 20–05
Mira v. Aylmer Square Investments (1990) 22 H.L.R. 182; [1990] 22 E.G.
    61 16–03
Miramar Maritime Corp. v. Holborn Trading; Miramar, The [1984] A.C. 676;
    [1984] 3 W.L.R. 10; [1984] 2 All E.R. 326; [1984] 2 Lloyd's Rep. 129,
    H.L. 17–02
Mirza v. Nicola [1980] 30 E.G. 92, C.A. 16–41
Moat v. Martin [1950] K.B. 175; [1949] 2 All E.R. 646 .... 12–08, 12–14
Molton Builders v. City of Westminster London Borough Council (1975) 119
    S.J. 627; 30 P. & C.R. 182, C.A. 10–11
Molyneaux v. Hawtrey [1903] 2 K.B. 487 18–15
Montross Associated Investments SA v. Moussaieff (1991) 63 P. & C.R.
    31; [1992] 2 E.G. 160, D.C. 10–08
Moody v. Steggles (1879) 12 Ch. D. 261 4–11
Moonraker's Guest House [1992] STC 544, Q.B. 19–19
Moore Stephens & Co. v. Local Authorities' Mutual Investment Trust [1992]
    1 EGLR 33 6–19
Moran v. Lloyd's [1983] Q.B. 542; [1983] 2 W.L.R. 672; [1983] 2 All E.R.
    200; [1983] 1 Lloyd's Rep. 472, C.A. 6–19
Morar v. Chauhan [1985] 1 W.L.R. 1263; [1985] 3 All E.R. 493; (1985) 51
    P. & C.R. 59; (1985) 276 E.G. 300; [1985] 2 EGLR 137, C.A. 16–41
Morgan v. Fear [1907] A.C. 425 15–02
Morris v. Patel (1987) 281 E.G. 419, [1987] 1 EGLR 75, C.A. 16–26
Morris-Thomas v. Petticoat Lane Rentals (1987) 53 P. & C.R. 238, C.A. 9–02
Morrison Holdings v. Manders Property (Wolverhampton) [1976] 1 W.L.R.
    533; [1976] 2 All E.R. 205; (1975) 32 P. & C.R. 218, C.A. 16–16
Morrow v. Nadeem [1986] 1 W.L.R. 1381; [1987] 1 All E.R. 237; (1987) 53
    P. & C.R. 203; [1986] 2 EGLR 73; (1986) 279 E.G. 1083, C.A. 16–26,
    16–27
Moschi, Re B. (Ex p. R. Moschi) v. Lep Air Services [1973] A.C. 331; [1972]
    2 W.L.R. 1175 3–13

Moss v. Mobil Oil Co. [1988] 6 E.G. 109, C.A. 4–04, 16–26
Moss Empires v. Olympian (Liverpool) [1939] A.C. 544 9–25
Moule v. Garrett (1872) L.R. 7 Ex. 101 2–10
Mowats v. Hudson Bros. (1911) 105 L.T. 400 11–12
Mucklow (A. & J.) (Birmingham) v. Metro-Cammell Weymann [1994] EGCS
    64 .... 16–06, 16–13
Mularczyk v. Azralnove Investments [1985] 2 EGLR 141; (1985) 276 E.G.
    1065, C.A. 16–40
Mullaney v. Maybourne Grange (Croydon) Management Co. [1986] 1 EGLR
    70; (1988) 277 E.G. 1350 .... 8–03, 9–08
Multon v. Cordell [1986] 1 EGLR 44; (1985) 277 E.G. 189 16–13
Mumford Hotels v. Wheler [1964] Ch. 117; [1963] 3 W.L.R. 735; [1963] 3 All
    E.R. 250 13–11
Munro v. Lord Burghclere [1918] 1 K.B. 291 7–05
Murphy v. Brentwood District Council [1991] 1 A.C. 398; [1990] 3 W.L.R.
    414; [1990] 2 All E.R. 908, H.L. 9–12
—— v. Sawyer-Hoare [1993] 27 E.G. 127 3–15
My Kinda Town v. Castlebrook Properties [1986] 1 EGLR 120; (1986) 277
    E.G. 1144 6–19

N.E. Railway v. Lord Hastings [1900] A.C. 260 17–02
National Car Parks v. Paternoster Consortium [1990] 15 E.G. 53 16–45
National Carriers v. Panalpina (Northern) [1981] A.C. 675; [1981] 2 W.L.R.
    45 13–15
National Electric Theatres Ltd v. Hudgen [1939] 1 Ch. 553 11–07
National Employers' Mutual General Insurance Association v. Haydon [1980]
    2 Lloyd's Rep. 149, C.A. 13–04
National Jazz Centre, Re, [1988] 38 E.G. 142 14–05
National Rivers Authority v. Welsh Development Agency (1994) 158 J.P. 506;
    [1993] EGCS 160 20–03
National Schizophrenia Fellowship v. Ribble Estates S.A. [1994] 3 E.G.
    132 10–02
National Westminster Bank v. BSC Footwear (1981) 42 P. & C.R. 90; (1980)
    257 E.G. 227, C.A. 16–11
—— v. Riley [1986] BCLC 268, [1986] F.L.R. 213, C.A. 3–15
—— v. Young (Arthur) McCelland Moores & Co. [1985] 1 W.L.R. 1123;
    (1985) 272 E.G. 717, C.A. 6–27
Naylor v. Uttoxeter Urban District Council (1974) 231 E.G. 619 6–39
Network Housing Association v. Westminster City Council, *The Times*, Novem-
    ber 8, 1994, D.C. 20–04
Never-Stop Railway (Wembley) Ltd v. British Empire Exhibition (1924)
    Incorporated [1926] 1 Ch. 877 11–06
Neville Russell [1987] VATTR 14 (2484) 19–10, 19–13
New England Properties v. Portsmouth New Shops; Sterling Surveys v. New
    England Properties; New England Properties v. Ex-Electronics (U.K.)
    (1993) 67 P. & C.R. 141; [1993] 23 E.G. 130 9–19
New Pinehurst Residents Association (Cambridge) v. Silow [1988] 1 EGLR
    227 8–05
New Zealand Government Property Corp. v. H.M. & S. [1982]
    Q.B. 1145; (1982) 263 E.G. 765 .... 6–30, 6–36,
                                    16–47, 11–12, 11–13, 11–14, 18–27
Newby v. Sharpe (1877) 8 Ch. D. 39 10–11
Newey & Eyre v. Curtis (J.) & Son (1984) 271 E.G. 891 16–47
Newman v. Jones, March 22, 1982 (unreported) 4–08

—— v. Real Estate Debenture Corporation Ltd [1940] 1 All E.R. 131 10–11
Nicholls v. Kinsey [1994] 2 W.L.R. 622; [1994] 16 E.G. 145 16–23
Nikko Hotels (U.K.) v. MEPC [1991] 2 EGLR 103 .... 6–19, 8–05
99 Bishopsgate v. Prudential Assurance (1985) 273 E.G. 984, C.A. 6–30, 6–32
No. 1, Albemarle St W1, *Re* [1959] Ch. 531; [1959] 2 W.L.R. 171; [1959] 1
   All E.R. 250 16–44
North Eastern Co-operative Society v. Newcastle Upon Tyne City Council
   (1987) 282 E.G. 1409 6–13
North Hertfordshire District Council v. Hitchin Industrial Estate [1992] 37
   E.G. 133; [1992] EGCS 71 6–10
Northcote Laundry v. Donnelly (Frederick) [1968] 1 W.L.R. 562 16–41
Northways Flats Management Co. (Camden) v. Wimpey Pension Trustees
   [1992] EGLR 42, C.A. 8–05
Norwich Union Life Insurance Society, LON/90/1809 X (7205) un-
   reported 19–16
—— v. British Railways Board (1987) 283 E.G. 846 .... 6–26, 6–34, 9–06
—— v. Low Profile Fashions (1991) 64 P. & C.R. 187; [1992] 1 EGLR 86;
   [1992] 21 E.G. 104, C.A. 2–04, 12–14
—— v. P. & O. Property Holdings. *See* P. & O. Property Holdings v. Norwich
   Union Life Insurance Society.
—— v. Sketchley [1986] 2 EGLR 126 .... 6–10, 6–11
—— v. Trustee Savings Banks Central Board [1986] 1 EGLR 136; (1985) 278
   E.G. 162 6–29
—— v. Waller (Tony) (1984) 128 S.J. 300; (1984) 270 E.G. 42 6–10
Nozari-Zadeh v. Pearl Assurance (1987) 283 E.G. 457, C.A. 16–17
Nuflats & Properties v. Sheckman (1959) 174 E.G. 39 .... 16–18, 17–16
Nunes v. Davies Laing & Dick (1985) 51 P. & C.R. 310; (1985) 277 E.G.
   416 6–11
Nurit Bar v. Pathwood Investments (1987) 54 P. & C.R. 178; (1987) 282 E.G.
   1538 16–31
Nursey v. Currie (P.) (Dartford) [1959] 1 W.L.R. 273; [1959] 1 All E.R.
   497 16–41

O'Brien v. Robinson [1973] A.C. 912; [1973] 2 W.L.R. 393; [1973] 1 All E.R.
   583; (1973) 25 P. & C.R. 239, H.L. 9–19
O'Callaghan v. Elliott [1966] 1 Q.B. 601; [1965] 3 W.L.R. 746; [1965] 3 All
   E.R. 111, C.A. 16–21
Ocean Accident & Guarantee Corporation v. Next plc; Commercial Union
   Assurance Company plc v. Next plc [1995] EGCS 187 .... 6–26, 11–14
Old Grovebury Manor Farm v. Seymour (W.) Plant Sales and Hire (No. 2)
   [1979] 1 W.L.R. 263, [1979] 3 All E.R. 504, (1979) 252 E.G. 1103,
   C.A. 12–02
Olympia & York Canary Wharf v. Oil Property Investments [1994] 2 EGLR 48;
   [1994] 29 E.G. 121, C.A. 12–14, 16–06
O'May v. City of London Real Property Co. Ltd [1983] 2 A.C. 726; [1982] 2
   W.L.R. 407; [1982] 1 All E.R. 660; (1982) 43 P. & C.R. 351; (1982) 261
   E.G. 1185, H.L. 8–01, 9–02, 16–46
Onyx (U.K.) Ltd v. Beard [1996] EGCS 55 5–01
Optilon v. Commission for the New Towns [1993] 35 E.G. 125 .... 9–19, 18–10
Orakpo v. Manson Investments [1978] A.C. 95; [1977] 3 W.L.R. 229; (1977)
   36 P. & C.R. 1, H.L. 9–13
Orchid Lodge U.K. v. Extel Computing [1991] 32 E.G. 57; [1991] 2 EGLR
   116, C.A. 6–26, 6–28, 6–30
Oreinstein v. Donn, May 5, 1983, (unreported) C.A. 16–45

Oriani v. Dorita Properties (1987) 282 E.G. 1001; [1987] 1 EGLR 88, C.A. 16–47

Orlik (G.) (Meat Products) v. Hastings & Thanet Building Society (1974) 29 P. & C.R. 126; (1975) 234 E.G. 281 16–44

Our Boy's Clothing Company Ltd v. Holborn Viaduct Land Co. Ltd (1896) 12 T.L.R. 344 10–02

Overcom Properties v. Stockleigh Hall Residents Management [1989] 14 E.G. 78; (1989) 58 P. & C.R. 1 14–18

Owen v. Gadd [1956] 2 Q.B. 99; [1956] 2 W.L.R. 945; [1956] 2 All E.R. 28, C.A. 4–18

Owen Owen Estate v. Livett [1956] Ch. 1; [1955] 3 W.L.R. 1; [1955] 2 All E.R. 513 11–07

Owers, *Re* [1941] Ch. 17 3–08

Oxfordshire County Council v. Chancellor Masters and Scholars of Oxford University, *The Times*, December 10, 1980, D.C. 7–04

P. & A. Swift Investments v. Combined English Stores Group [1988] 2 All E.R. 885 .... 3–03, 3–15

P. & O. Property Holdings v. Norwich Union Life Insurance Society; *sub nom.* Norwich Union Life Insurance Society v. P. & O. Property Holdings (1994) 68 P. & C.R. 261, H.L. 6–20

Packaging Centre v. Poland Street Estate (1961) 178 E.G. 189 12–14

Pakwood Transport v. 15 Beauchamp Place (1977) 36 P. & C.R. 112; (1977) 245 E.G. 309, C.A. 14–06

Palacath v. Flanagan [1985] 2 All E.R. 161; [1985] 1 EGLR 86; (1985) 274 E.G. 143 6–13

Palmer v. Goren (1856) 25 L.J. Ch. 841 18–16

—— v. Pronk, Davis & Rusby Ltd (1954) 164 E.G. 608 9–25

Panavia Air Cargo v. Southend-on-Sea Borough Council [1988] 22 E.G. 82; (1988) 56 P. & C.R. 365, C.A. 6–10

Panther Shop Investments v. Keith Pople (1987) 282 E.G. 594 6–36

Panton St, (No. 5) Haymarket, *Re* (1959) 175 E.G. 49 16–46

Papillon v. Brunton (1860) 5 H. & N. 518 16–25

Parker v. Camden L.B.C.; Newman v. Camden L.B.C. [1986] Ch. 162; [1985] 3 W.L.R. 47; [1985] 2 All E.R. 141, C.A. 9–27

—— v. Jones [1910] 2 K.B. 32 18–28

—— v. Taswell (1858) 2 De G. & J. 559 18–07

Parkinson v. Barclays Bank [1951] 1 K.B. 368; [1950] 2 All E.R. 936, C.A. 16–08

Parkside Clubs (Nottingham) Ltd v. Armgrade Ltd [1995] 48 E.G. 104, C.A. 6–33

Parkside Knightsbridge v. The German Food Centre [1987] NPC 10 6–17

Parry v. Harbert (1539) 1 Dyer 456 3–08

—— v. Robinson-Wyllie (1987) 54 P. & C.R. 187; (1987) 283 E.G. 559 6–22

Patel v. Earlspring Properties [1991] 46 E.G. 153; [1991] 2 EGLR 131, C.A. 6–10, 6–11

Patel (Bhanubhai) v. Peel Investments (South) [1992] 30 E.G. 88 6–11

Payne v. Burridge (1844) 12 M. & W. 727 7–04

Pearce v. Maryon-Wilson [1935] 1 Ch. 188 10–11

Pearl Assurance v. Shaw [1985] 1 EGLR 92 .... 6–28, 11–06

Pearson v. Alyo [1990] 25 E.G. 90; (1989) 60 P. & C.R. 56 16–26

Peel Developments (South) v. Siemens [1992] 47 E.G. 103 16–06

Pegler v. Graven [1952] 2 Q.B. 693; [1952] 1 All E.R. 685, C.A. 16–17

—— v. White (1864) 33 Beav. 403 18–16

Pembroke St. Georges v. Cromwell Developments [1991] 2 EGLR 129; [1991] 40 E.G. 115 6–10

Peninsular Maritime v. Padseal (1981) 259 E.G. 860, C.A. 9–27, 14–04

Pennell v. Payne [1995] 2 W.L.R. 261; [1995] 6 E.G. 152 16–07

Penniall v. Harborne (1848) 11 Q.B. 368 13–06

Perry v. Chotzner (1893) 9 T.L.R. 488 9–20

Philipson-Stow v. Square (Trevor) (1980) 257 E.G. 1262 16–26

Philpots (Woking) v. Surrey Conveyancers [1986] 1 EGLR 97, C.A. ... 6–08, 17–02

Phipps-faire v. Malbern Construction (1987) 282 E.G. 460; [1987] 1 EGLR 129 6–11

Phipos v. Callegari (1910) 54 S.J. 635 18–28

Photo Centre v. Grantham Court Properties (Mayfair) (1964) 191 E.G. 505 16–42

Pimms v. Tallow Chandlers Co. [1964] 2 Q.B. 547; [1964] 2 W.L.R. 1129; [1964] 2 All E.R. 145, C.A. 12–13

Pinemain v. Tuck (unreported) 3–15

——— v. Welbeck International (1984) 272 E.G. 1116, D.C. 3–03, 3–15

Pioneer Shipping v. B.T.P. Tioxide; Nema, The [1982] A.C. 724; [1981] 3 W.L.R. 292; [1981] 2 All E.R. 1030; [1981] 2 Lloyd's Rep. 239, H.L. 6–19, 17–02

Piper v. Muggleton [1956] 2 Q.B. 569; [1956] 2 W.L.R. 1093; [1956] 2 All E.R. 249, C.A. 16–25

Pips (Leisure) Productions v. Walton (1982) 43 P. & C.R. 415 18–17

Pitcher v. Tovey (1692) 4 Mod. 71 3–08

Pittalis v. Sherefettin [1986] Q.B. 868; [1986] 2 W.L.R. 1003; [1986] 2 All E.R. 227; [1986] 1 EGLR 130; (1986) 278 E.G. 153, C.A. 6–11

Pivot Properties Ltd v. Secretary of State for the Environment (1980) 41 P. & C.R. 248 6–29

Pleasurama v. Sun Alliance and London Insurance [1979] 1 Lloyd's Rep. 389 13–09

Pleasurama Properties v. Leisure Investments (West End) [1986] 1 EGLR 145; (1986) 278 E.G. 732, C.A. 6–36, 11–06, 11–09

Plesser (A.) & Co. v. Davis (1983) 267 E.G. 1039 3–15

Plinth Property Investments v. Mott, Hay & Anderson (1978) 38 P. & C.R. 361; (1978) 249 E.G. 1167, C.A. 6–28

Plumrose v. Real & Leasehold Estates Investment Society [1970] 1 W.L.R. 52; [1969] 3 All E.R. 1441; (1970) 21 P. & C.R. 52 16–11

Polak v. Everett (1876) 1 Q.B.D. 669 3–15

Pole Properties v. Feinberg (1981) 43 P. & C.R. 121, C.A. 8–04

Polyviou v. Seely [1980] 1 W.L.R. 55; [1973] 3 All E.R. 853; (1979) 39 P. & C.R. 164; (1979) 252 E.G. 375, C.A. 16–25

Ponderosa International Development Inc. v. Pengap Securities (Bristol) [1986] 1 EGLR 66; (1986) 277 E.G. 1252 12–14

Ponsford v. H.M.S. Aerosols [1979] A.C. 63; [1978] 3 W.L.R. 241; [1978] 2 All E.R. 837; (1978) 38 P. & C.R. 270; (1978) 247 E.G. 1171, CA. 6–17, 6–24, 6–26, 6–36

Pontsarn Investments v. Kansallis-Osake-Pankki [1992] 1 EGLR 148; [1992] 22 E.G. 103 6–30

Poole's Case (1703) 1 Salk. 368 11–12

Port v. Griffith [1938] 1 All E.R. 295 10–11

Porter v. Shephard (1796) 6 Term. Rep. 665 2–09

Portavon Cinema Co. Ltd v. Price [1939] 4 All E.R. 601 13–04

Posner v. Scott-Lewis [1987] Ch. 25; [1986] 3 W.L.R. 531; [1986] 3 All E.R. 513; [1986] 1 EGLR 56 8–02

Post Office v. Aquarius Properties [1987] 1 All E.R. 1055; (1987) 54 P. & C.R. 61; [1987] 1 EGLR 40, C.A. 4–07, 9–04

Post Office Counters v. Harlow District Council (1991) 63 P. & C.R. 46;
 [1991] 2 EGLR 121; [1991] 36 E.G. 151 6–26
Postel Properties and Daichi Lire (London) v. Greenwell [1992] 47 E.G.
 106 6–20
Potts (Norman E.) (Birmingham) v. Rootes (1957) 170 E.G. 39 16–31
Power Securities (Manchester) v. Prudential Assurance Co. (1986) 281 E.G.
 1327; [1987] 1 EGLR 121 6–40
Premier Confectionery (London) Co. v. London Commercial Sale Rooms
 [1933] Ch. 904 12–14
Prenn & Simmonds [1971] 1 W.L.R. 1381; [1971] 3 All E.R. 237, H.L. 17–03
Preston v. Lindlands (1976) 239 E.G. 653 6–03
Price v. Bouch (1987) 53 P. & C.R. 257; [1986] 2 EGLR 179; (1986) 279 E.G.
 1226 10–09
—— v. Esso Petroleum Co. (1980) 255 E.G. 243 16–40
—— v. Jenkins (1877) 5 Ch. D. 619 18–18
—— v. West London Investment Building Society [1964] 1 W.L.R. 616; [1964]
 2 All E.R. 318, C.A. 16–25
—— v. Worwood (1859) 4 H. & N. 512 14–05
Propert v. Parker (1832) 3 My. & K. 280 18–07
Property & Bloodstock v. Emerton; Bush v. Property & Bloodstock [1968] Ch.
 94; [1967] 3 W.L.R. 973; [1967] 3 All E.R. 321, C.A. 18–17
Prothero v. Bell (1906) 22 T.L.R. 370 10–08
Proudfoot v. Hart (1890) 25 Q.B.D. 42 .... 9–04, 9–06, 9–16, 9–20
Proudreed v. Microgen Holdings [1996] 12 E.G. 127, C.A. 14–04,
 18–26
Prudential Assurance Co. v. Gray (1987) 283 E.G. 648 6–25
—— v. London Residuary Body [1992] 2 A.C. 386; [1992] 3 W.L.R. 279;
 [1992] 3 All E.R. 504; (1992) 64 P. & C.R. 193; [1992] 36 E.G. 129,
 H.L. 5–01
—— v. Grand Metropolitan Estates [1993] 32 E.G. 74 6–35
—— v. 99 Bishopsgate [1992] 1 EGLR 119; [1992] 3 E.G. 120 .... 6–23, 6–27
—— v. Salisbury's Handbags (1992) 65 P. & C.R. 129; [1992] 1 EGLR 153;
 [1992] 23 E.G. 117 .... 6–26, 6–29
Provident Mutual Life Assurance Association v. Greater London Employers'
 Association [1996] 23 E.G. 129 16–24
Prudential Nominees v. Greenham Trading [1995] 1 E.G. 111 6–30,
 6–31, 6–37
Prudential Property Services v. Capital Land Holdings (1992) 66 P. & C.R.
 398; [1993] 15 E.G. 147 6–11
Pugh v. Smiths Industries; Welch (F.A.) Holdings v. Smiths Industries; Smiths
 Industries v. Pugh (1982) 264 E.G. 823 .... 6–27, 17–07
Pulleng v. Curran (1980) 44 P. & C.R. 58 16–19

Queensway Marketing v. Associated Restaurants [1988] 32 E.G. 41, C.A. 16–03
Quennell v. Salaman (1955) 165 E.G. 285 8–02
Quick v. Taff-Ely Borough Council [1986] Q.B. 809; [1985] 3 W.L.R. 981;
 [1985] 3 All E.R. 321; [1985] 2 EGLR 50; (1985) 276 E.G. 452,
 C.A. 7–07, 9–08

R. v. CPC (U.K.) [1994] NPC 112 20–07
—— v. Gravesend County Court, ex p. Patchett [1993] 26 E.G. 125; [1993]
 C.O.D. 12 16–32

—— v. London Borough of Southwark, noted in [1986] Environmental Data
Services Report No. 132 at 17 10–02
—— v. Paulson [1921] 1 A.C. 271 14–05
—— v. Thurrock Borough Council, ex p. Tesco Stores, Same v. Same, ex p.
J. Sainsbury; Same v. Same, ex p. Safeway Stores [1993] EGCS 176;
[1993] P.L.R. 114 10–08
RPH v. Mirror Group (Holdings) Ltd; sub nom. Mirror Group Holdings, Re
(Holdings) (1992) 65 P. & C.R. 252; [1993] 13 E.G. 113 2–10
Railstore Ltd v. Playdale [1988] 35 E.G. 87 6–33
Rance v. Elvin (1985) 49 P. & C.R. 9, C.A. 4–10, 8–03
Rapid Results College v. Angell [1986] 1 EGLR 53; (1986) 277 E.G. 856,
C.A. 8–03, 9–05
Ratners (Jewellers) v. Lemnoll (1980) 255 E.G. 987 16–32
Ravenseft Properties' Application, Re; See Ravenseft Properties v. Director-
General of Fair Trading 7–02, 10–12
Ravenseft Properties v. Davstone (Holdings) [1980] Q.B. 12; [1979] 2 W.L.R.
898; [1979] 1 All E.R. 929; (1978) 249 E.G. 51; (1978) 37 P. & C.R.
502 9–08
—— v. Director General of Fair Trading [1977] 1 All E.R. 47; sub nom.
Ravenseft Properties' Application, Re [1978] Q.B. 52; [1977] 2
W.L.R. 432 .... 7–02, 10–12
Rawashden v. Lane [1988] 40 E.G. 109 16–42
Rayburn v. Wolf (1985) 2 EGLR 235; (1985) 50 P. & C.R. 463 12–13
Rayner v. Preston (1881) 18 Ch. D. 1 13–11
Reardon Smith Line v. Yngvar Hansen-Tangen [1976] 1 W.L.R. 989 17–03
Reckitt v. Cody [1920] 2 Ch. 452 18–18
Record v. Bell [1991] 1 W.L.R. 853; [1991] 4 All E.R. 471; (1990) 62 P. &
C.R. 192 18–03
Redfern v. Reeves (1978) 37 P. & C.R. 364; [1978] 247 E.G. 991, C.A. 16–40
Redleaf Investments Ltd v. Talbot [1995] BCC 1091 .... 2–05, 14–04
Reed Personnel Services Ltd v. American Express [1996] NPC 7 16–07
Reeve v. Berridge (1888) 20 Q.B.D. 523 18–15
Regent Jewellers (London) Ltd v. C.H. (Bournemouth) Ltd (1968) 207 E.G.
629 6–17
Regional Properties v. City of London Real Property (1980) 257 E.G.
64 .... 4–17, 9–25
Regis Property Co. v. Dudley [1959] A.C. 370; [1958] 3 W.L.R. 647; [1958]
3 All E.R. 491 9–06
—— v. Redman [1956] 2 Q.B. 612; [1956] 3 W.L.R. 95; [1956] 2 All E.R.
335 4–09
Relvok Properties v. Dixon (1972) 25 P. & C.R. 1, C.A. 14–04
Rendall v. Andreae (1892) 61 L.J.Q.B. 630 3–08
Rene Claro (Haute Coiffure) v. Hallé Concerts Society [1969] 1 W.L.R. 909;
[1969] 2 All E.R. 842; (1969) 20 P. & C.R. 378 16–26
Reohorn v. Barry Corporation [1956] 1 W.L.R. 845; [1956] 2 All E.R.
742 16–40
Reston v. Hudson [1990] 37 E.G. 86 8–03
Reynard v. Arnold (1875) L.R. 10 Ch. 386 13–04
Reynolds v. Pheonix Assurance Co. [1978] 2 Lloyd's Rep. 22; (1978) 247 E.G.
995 13–09
Rhyl Urban District Council v. Rhyl Amusements [1959] 1 W.L.R. 465; [1959]
1 All E.R. 257 18–26
Ricehurst v. Pimenta [1993] 1 W.L.R. 519; [1993] 2 All E.R. 559 6–11
Richard West and Partners (Inverness) v. Dick; See West (Richard) and
Partners v. Dick 18–05
Richards (C.) & Son Ltd v. Karenita Ltd (1972) 221 E.G. 25 6–10

Richmond v. Satin [1926] 2 K.B. 530 18–27
Ridgeon's Bulk v. Customs and Excise Commissioner [1994] S.T.C. 427,
    Q.B.D. 19–15
Ridley v. Taylor [1965] 1 W.L.R. 611; [1965] 2 All E.R. 51; 16 P. & C.R.
    113   6–36
Riggs, ex p. Lovell, Re [1901] 2 K.B. 16   3–08
Rignall Developments v. Halil [1988] Ch. 190; [1987] 3 W.L.R. 394; [1987] 3
    All E.R. 170; (1987) 54 P. & C.R. 245; (1987) 282 E.G. 1414; [1987] 1
    EGLR 193 18–05
Riley (E.J.) Investments v. Eurostile Holdings [1985] 1 W.L.R. 1139; (1985)
    129 S.J. 523; [1985] 3 All E.R. 181; [1985] 2 EGLR 124; (1985) 51 P. &
    C.R. 36; (1985) 135 New L.J. 887; (1985) 82 L.S.Gaz. 2500, C.A. 16–25
Rimmer v. Liverpool City Council [1985] Q.B. 1; [1984] 2 W.L.R. 426; [1984]
    1 All E.R. 930; (1984) 47 P. & C.R. 516; (1984) 269 E.G. 319   9–19
Ritz Hotel (London) Ltd v. Ritz Casinos [1989] 46 E.G. 95 .... 6–15, 6–29
Riverlate Properties v. Paul [1975] Ch. 133; [1974] 3 W.L.R. 564; [1974] 2 All
    E.R. 656; (1974) 28 P. & C.R. 220 17–10
Robert Baxendale v. Davstone (Holdings); see Baxendale (Robert) v. Davstone
    (Holdings); Carobene v. Collier Menswear.
Roberts (A.) & Co. v. Leicestershire County Council [1961] Ch. 555; [1961]
    2 W.L.R. 1000; [1961] 2 All E.R. 545 17–09
Robinson v. Kilvert (1884) 41 Ch. D. 88 10–11
Roffey v. Bent (1867) L.R. 3 Eq. 759 10–08
Rom Tyre & Accessories Co. Ltd v. Crawford Street Properties Ltd (1966) 197
    E.G. 565 16–48
Romulus Trading v. Comet Properties [1996] NPC 52 10–11
—— v. Henry Smith's Charity Trustees [1990] 32 E.G. 41; (1989) 60
    P. & C.R. 62 16–40
Ross Auto Wash v. Herbert (1978) 250 E.G. 971 16–17
Rossi v. Hestdrive Ltd [1985] 1 EGLR 50 .... 10–08, 12–14
Rother v. Colchester Corporation [1969] 1 W.L.R. 720; [1969] 2 All E.R.
    600 .... 10–08, 10–11
Rothschild v. Moser [1986] NPC 46 .... 4–03, 4–17
Rous v. Mitchell, sub nom. Earl of Stradbroke v. Mitchell [1991] 1 W.L.R. 469;
    [1991] 1 All E.R. 676; (1990) 61 P. & C.R. 314; [1991] 1 EGLR 1; [1991]
    3 E.G. 128; (1990) 140 New L.J. 1386, C.A. 16–26
Rowlands (Mark) v. Berni Inns [1985] Q.B. 211; [1985] 3 W.L.R. 964; (1985)
    276 E.G. 191, C.A. 13–06
Rowley v. Adams (1839) 4 Myl. & Cr. 534   3–08
Royal Bank of Scotland plc v. Jennings [1995] 35 E.G. 140   6–08
Royal Borough of Kingston-upon-Thames v. Marlow [1995] NPC 160 7–02,
                                                                                                                14–04
Royal Exchange Assurance v. Bryant Samuel Properties [1985] 1 EGLR 84;
    (1985) 272 E.G. 132   6–24
Royal Life Insurance v. Philips [1990] 43 E.G. 70; (1990) 61 P. & C.R.
    182   6–11
Royal Life Saving Society v. Page; see Cheryl Investments v. Saldanha 16–19
Royton Industries Ltd v. Lawrence [1994] 20 E.G. 151   6–01
Rubery v. Stevens (1832) 4 B. & Ad. 241   3–08
Rugby School Governors v. Tannahill [1935] 1 K.B. 87 14–06
Rush & Tompkins v. Greater London Council [1989] A.C. 1280, H.L.   6–15
Rushmoor Borough Council v. Goacher (1986) 52 P. & C.R. 255; [1985] 2
    EGLR 140; (1985) 276 E.G. 304   6–33
Russ and Brown's Contract, Re [1934] 1 Ch. 34 18–24
Russell v. Beecham [1924] 1 K.B. 525 .... 12–02, 12–07
Rutter v. Michael John Ltd (1960) 201 E.G. 299 18–17

S.E.D.A.C. Investments v. Tanner [1982] 1 W.L.R. 1342; (1982) 264 E.G. 615 .... 9–24, 9–26
S. Turner (Cabinet Works) Ltd v. Young (1955) 165 E.G. 632 13–12
St Anne's Well Brewery Co. v. Roberts [1929] 140 L.T. 1 20–05
St Edmundsbury and Ipswich Diocesan Board of Finance v. Clark (No. 2) [1975] 1 W.L.R. 468; [1975] 1 All E.R. 772; (1974) 29 P. & C.R. 336 17–04
St Martin's Theatre; Re, Bright Enterprises v. Willoughby De Broue [1959] 1 W.L.R. 872; [1959] 3 All E.R. 298 16–34
St Marylebone Property Co. v. Tesco Stores [1988] 27 E.G. 72 10–08
Sacher Investments Pty v. Forma Stereo Consultants Pty [1976] 1 N.S.W.L.R. 5 3–03
Salisbury v. Gilmore [1942] 2 K.B. 38 9–25
Salomon v. Akiens [1992] 1 P. & C.R. 364; [1993] 14 E.G. 97, C.A. 16–25, 16–31
Sampson v. Floyd [1989] 33 E.G. 41, C.A. 16–03
Sampson v. Hodson-Pressinger [1981] 3 All E.R. 710; (1982) 261 E.G. 891 20–05
Samuel Properties (Developments) v. Hayek [1972] 1 W.L.R. 1296; 116 S.J. 764; [1972] 3 All E.R. 473; (1972) 24 P. & C.R. 223, C.A. 6–10
Sanders v. Pope (1806) 13 Ves. Jun. 283 14–06
Sanderson v. Berwick-on-Tweed Corporation (1884) 13 Q.B.D. 547 10–11
Sandill v. Franklin (1875) L.R. 10 C.P. 377 5–03
Sandhu v. Ladbroke Hotels Ltd [1995] 39 E.G. 152 .... 6–34, 9–16
Sansom and Narbeth's Contract, Re [1910] 1 Ch. 741 4–02
Savva v. Houssein [1996] NPC 64 14–06
Scala House and District Property Co. Ltd v. Forbes [1974] 1 Q.B. 575; [1973] 3 W.L.R. 14; [1973] 3 All E.R. 308; (1973) 26 P. & C.R. 164 .. 14–05, 14–06
Scarfe v. Adams [1981] 1 All E.R. 843 4–02
Scheggia v. Gradwell [1963] 1 W.L.R. 1049 18–17
Scholl Manufacturing Co. v. Clifton (Slim Line) [1967] 1 Ch. 41; [1966] 3 W.L.R. 575; [1966] 3 All E.R. 16 .... 16–14, 16–26
Schuler (L.) AG v. Wickman Machine Tools Sales [1974] A.C. 235; [1973] 2 W.L.R. 683; 117 S.J. 340; [1973] 2 All E.R. 39; [1973] 2 Lloyd's Rep. 53, H.L. 17–02, 17–03
Scott & Alverez's Contract, Re [1895] 1 Ch. 596 18–14
Scottish Amicable Life Assurance Society v. Middleton Potts & Co.; Co-operative Wholesale Society Ltd v. National Westminster Bank plc; Prudential Nominees v. Greenham Trading and Broadgate Square plc v. Lehman Brothers Ltd [1995] 1 E.G. 111 .... 6–23, 6–31
Scottish & Newcastle Breweries v. Secretary of State for the Environment (1992) 64 P. & C.R. 290; [1992] 2 P.L.R. 147 .... 6–26, 6–36
—— v. Sir Richard Sutton's Settled Estates [1985] 2 EGLR 130; (1985) 276 E.G. 77 6–30
Secretary of State for the Environment v. Euston Centre Investments [1994] 3 W.L.R. 1081, C.A. 6–19
—— v. Reed International [1994] 6 E.G. 137 .... 6–13, 6–35
Sector Properties v. Meah (1974) 229 E.G. 1097 16–25
Securicor v. Postel Properties [1985] 1 EGLR 102; (1985) 274 E.G. 730 6–27
Seers v. Hind (1791) 1 Ves. Jun. 294 3–08
Sefton v. Tophams Ltd (No. 2) [1967] A.C. 50; [1966] 2 W.L.R. 814 10–08
Segama N.V. v. Penny Le Roy (1984) 269 E.G. 322 6–17
Selous Street Properties v. Oronel Fabrics (1984) 270 E.G. 643 .... 2–04, 3–15
Serjeant v. Nash, Field & Co. [1903] 2 K.B. 304 12–04
Sevenarts v. Busvine [1968] 1 W.L.R. 1929; [1969] 1 All E.R. 392; (1968) 20 P. & C.R. 79 16–41

Shankie-Williams v. Heavey [1986] 2 EGLR 139; (1986) 279 E.G. 316,
C.A. 9–11
Shannon, The v. Venner [1965] 1 Ch. 682; [1965] 2 W.L.R. 718; [1965] 1 All
E.R. 590 17–03
Sharma v. Knight [1986] 1 W.L.R. 757 16–31
Sharman and Meade's Contract, Re [1936] Ch. 755 4–02
Shave v. Rosner [1954] 2 Q.B. 113; [1954] 2 W.L.R. 1057; [1954] 2 All E.R.
280 20–03
Shaw v. Kay (1847) 1 Exch. 412 5–03
—— v. Robberds (1837) 6 Ad. & El. 75 13–10
—— v. Stenton (1858) 2 H. & N. 858 10–11
Shaw's Application (1995) 68 P. & C.R. 591 3–03
Sheerness Steel Co. v. Medway Ports Authority [1992] 1 EGLR 133; [1992] 12
E.G. 138, C.A. 6–26, 6–28, 6–36
Shelley v. United Artists Corp. [1990] 16 E.G. 73; (1989) 60 P. & C.R. 241,
C.A. 16–25
Shell-Mex & B.P. v. Manchester Garages [1971] 1 W.L.R. 612; [1971] 1 All
E.R. 841 16–22
Shield Properties & Investments v. Anglo-Overseas Transport Co. (No. 2)
(1987) 53 P. & C.R. 215; [1986] 2 EGLR 112; [1985] 1 EGLR 7; (1986)
279 E.G. 1088 6–22
Shiloh Spinners v. Harding [1973] A.C. 691; [1973] 2 W.L.R. 28; [1973] 1 All
E.R. 90; (1973) 25 P. & C.R. 48 14–06
Shires v. Brock (1977) 247 E.G. 127 18–17
Shirlcar Properties v. Heinetz (1983) 268 E.G. 362, C.A. 6–11
Shirreff v. Hastings (1877) 6 Ch. D. 610 3–08
Shuwa Ashdown House Corporation v. Grayrigg Properties [1992] 2 EGLR
127; [1992] 46 E.G. 108 6–10
Sidnell v. Wilson [1966] 2 Q.B. 67; [1966] 2 W.L.R. 560; [1966] 1 All E.R.
681 9–24
Sidney Bolsom Investment Trust v. Karmios (E.) & Co. (London) [1956] 1
Q.B. 529 16–28
Simmonds v. Egyed [1985] C.L.Y. 1908 16–19
Simons v. Associated Furnishers Ltd [1930] All E.R. 427 16–07
Singh Gian & Co. v. Nahar [1965] 1 W.L.R. 412; [1965] 1 All E.R. 768,
P.C. 3–10
Skillion v. Keltec Industrial Research [1992] 1 EGLR 123; [1992] 5 E.G.
162 17–04
Slater v. Hoskins [1982] 2 N.Z.L.R. 541 16–03
Smedley v. Chumley & Hawkes (1982) 44 P. & C.R. 50; (1982) 261 E.G.
775 .... 9–05, 9–08, 17–02
Smiley v. Townsend [1950] 2 K.B. 311; [1950] 1 All E.R. 530; (1950) 155
E.G. 110 9–25
Smith v. Bradford City M.B.C. (1982) 44 P. & C.R. 171 9–02
—— v. Butler [1900] 1 Q.B. 694 18–17
—— v. City Petroleum [1940] 1 All E.R. 260 .... 11–12, 11–13
—— v. Draper (1990) 60 P. & C.R. 252 16–26
—— v. East Anglian Entertainment Activities Ltd [1985] 1 EGLR 206 16–22
—— v. Metropolitan City Properties Ltd [1986] 1 EGLR 52; (1985) 277 E.G.
753 14–06
—— v. Mills (1899) 16 T.L.R. 59 9–05
—— v. Mulvihill, C.A., May 10, 1985 (unreported) 9–25
Smith (A.J.A.) Transport v. British Railways Board (1980) 257 E.G.
1257 .... 16–27, 16–42
Smith's Lease, Re, Smith v. Richards [1951] 1 All E.R. 346 12–12

Solomons v. Gertzentein (R.) [1954] 2 Q.B. 243; [1954] 3 W.L.R. 317; [1954] 2 All E.R. 625 15–08

South Shropshire District Council v. Amos [1986] 1 W.L.R. 1271; (1986) 130 S.J. 803; [1987] 1 All E.R. 340; [1986] 2 EGLR 194; (1986) 280 E.G. 635 .... 6–12, 6–15

South Tottenham Land Securities v. R. & A. Millett (Shops) [1984] 1 W.L.R. 710; (1984) 128 S.J. 365; [1984] 1 All E.R. 614; (1984) 48 P. & C.R. 159; (1984) 269 E.G. 630 .... 6–19, 6–22

Southport Old Links v. Naylor [1985] 1 EGLR 66; (1985) 273 E.G. 767 .... 16–08, 16–25

Sovmots Investments v. Secretary of State for the Environment; Brompton Securities v. Same [1979] A.C. 144; [1977] 2 W.L.R. 951; [1977] 2 All E.R. 385; (1977) 35 P. & C.R. 350; (1977) 75 L.G.R. 510; [1977] J.P.L. 443; *sub non.* Sovmots Investments and Brompton Securities v. Secretary of State for the Environment (1977) 243 E.G. 995, H.L. 4–07

Spall v. Owen (1981) 44 P. & C.R. 36 4–02

Spark's Lease, *Re* [1905] 1 Ch. 456 12–14

Spectrum Investment Co. v. Holmes [1981] 1 W.L.R. 221; [1981] 1 All E.R. 6; (1980) 41 P. & C.R. 133 18–29

Spencer v. Marriott (1823) 1 B. & C. 457 16–03

Spike and Rocco Group, *Re* [1979] 107 D.L.R. (3d) 62 10–11

Spon Engineering Co. Ltd v. Kossman Manufacturing Co. Ltd (1965) 195 E.G. 645 4–07

Spook Erection v. British Railways Board [1988] 21 E.G. 73, C.A. 16–40

Sport International Bussum BV v. Inter-Footwear [1984] 1 W.L.R. 776; [1984] 2 All E.R. 321 18–07

Stacey v. Hill [1901] 1 K.B. 660 3–15

Stadium Finance Co. v. Helm (1965) 109 S.J. 471 3–13

Staines Warehousing Co. v. Montagu Executor & Trustee Co. (1987) 54 P. & C.R. 302; (1987) 283 E.G. 458, C.A. 6–10

Stait v. Fenner [1912] 2 Ch. 504 2–09

Standard Chartered Bank v. Walker [1982] 1 W.L.R. 1410; [1982] 3 All E.R. 938; (1982) 264 E.G. 345 3–15

Standard Life Assurance Co. v. Oxoid; Oxoid v. Standard Life Assurance (1987) 283 E.G. 1219; [1986] 1 EGLR 123; (1985) 277 E.G. 1248 6–23

Stanhope Pension Trust v. Registrar of Companies [1994] BCC 84 2–10

Stanley v. Kenneth Properties Ltd (1957) 170 E.G. 133 10–11

Starrokate v. Burry (1983) 265 E.G. 871 .... 9–23, 9–24

Stening v. Abrahams [1931] 1 Ch. 470 12–05

Stent v. Monmouth District Council (1987) 54 P. & C.R. 193; (1987) 282 E.G. 705; [1987] 1 EGLR 59 9–07

Stephens v. Junior Army and Navy Stores Ltd [1914] 2 Ch. 516 14–05

Stephenson v. Orca Properties [1989] 44 E.G. 81 .... 6–10, 16–25

Sterling Land Office Developments Ltd v. Lloyds Bank (1984) 271 E.G. 894 6–28

Stevenage Development Corporation v. Baby Carriages & Toys (Stevenage) Ltd (1968) 207 E.G. 531 10–08

Stevens & Cutting v. Anderson [1990] 11 E.G. 70 16–31

Stevenson and Rush (Holdings) v. Langdon (1978) 38 P. & C.R. 208; (1978) 249 E.G. 743, C.A. 16–48

Stewart v. Chapman [1951] 2 K.B. 792; [1951] 2 All E.R. 613 16–25

Stidolph v. American School in London Educational Trusts (1969) 211 E.G. 925; (1969) 20 P. & C.R. 802, C.A. 16–26

Stile Hall Properties v. Gooch [1980] 1 W.L.R. 62; [1979] 3 All E.R. 848; (1979) 39 P. & C.R. 173 .... 16–25, 16–26

Stokes v. Mixconcrete (Holdings) (1978) 38 P. & C.R. 488, C.A. 18–05

Strand Securities v. Caswell [1965] Ch. 958; [1965] 2 W.L.R. 958; [1965] 1 All
  E.R. 820 18–11
Strandley Investments v. Barpress (1987) 282 E.G. 1124; [1987] 1 EGLR 69,
  C.A. 4–03
Stratton (R.J.) v. Wallis Tomlin & Co. [1986] 1 EGLR 104; (1985) 277 E.G.
  409, C.A. 16–24
Stream Properties v. Davis [1972] 1 W.L.R. 645; [1972] 2 All E.R. 746; (1971)
  23 P. & C.R. 294 16–32
Street v. Mountford [1985] A.C. 809; [1985] 2 W.L.R. 877; (1985) 277 E.G.
  1355 .... 12–04, 16–22, 18–31
Stuart v. Diplock (1889) 43 Ch. D. 343 .... 10–08, 10–11
Sturge v. Hackett [1962] 1 W.L.R. 1257; [1962] 3 All E.R. 166 4–03
Sturcke v. Edwards (S.W.) Ltd (1971) 23 P. & C.R. 185 9–17
Stylo Shoes v. Prices Tailors [1960] Ch. 396; [1960] 2 W.L.R. 8; [1959] 3 All
  E.R. 901 16–25
Sudbrook Trading Estate v. Eggleton [1983] 1 A.C. 444; [1982] 3 W.L.R. 315;
  [1982] 3 All E.R.; (1982) 44 P. & C.R. 153; (1983) 265 E.G. 215 16–11,
                                                                                                          17–02
Sun Alliance & London Assurance Co. v. British Railways Board [1989] 2
  EGLR 237 .... 8–03, 9–23
—— v. Hayman [1975] 1 W.L.R. 177; [1975] 1 All E.R. 248; (1974) 29 P. &
  C.R. 422 16–25
Supasnaps Ltd v. Bailey [1995] EGCS 89 6–10
Sutton v. Temple (1843) M. & W. 52 20–07
Swain v. Ayres (1888) 21 Q.B.D. 289 18–07
Swallow Securities v. Brand (1983) 45 P. & C.R. 328; (1981) 260 E.G. 63 .. 9–24
Sweet & Maxwell v. Universal News Services [1964] 2 Q.B. 699; [1964] 3
  W.L.R. 356 17–02
Sykes v. Midland Bank Executor and Trustee Co. [1971] 1 Q.B. 113; [1970]
  3 W.L.R. 273; [1970] 2 All E.R. 471, C.A. 18–06
Sykes (F. & G.) (Wessex) v. Fine Fare [1967] 1 Lloyd's Rep. 53, C.A. 17–02

T.S.B. Bank plc v. Botham [1995] EGCS 3 11–11
—— v. Camfield [1995] 1 W.L.R. 430; [1995] 1 All E.R. 951 3–14
Tandon v. Trustees of Spurgeon's Homes [1982] A.C. 755; [1982] 2 W.L.R.
  735; [1982] 1 All E.R. 1086; (1982) 44 P. & C.R. 307; (1982) 263 E.G.
  349, H.L. 16–19
Tarjomari v. Panther Securities (1983) 46 P. & C.R. 32 16–24
Taunton and West of England Perpetual Benefit Building Society and Roberts'
  Contract, Re [1912] 2 Ch. 381 18–16
Taylor v. British Legal Life Assurance Co. Ltd [1925] 1 Ch. 395 4–08
—— v. Pendleton Overseers (1887) 19 Q.B.D. 288 16–16
—— v. Webb [1937] 2 K.B. 283 16–03
Taylor Fashions v. Liverpool Victoria Friendly Society; [1981] Q.B. 133;
  [1981] 2 W.L.R. 576; [1981] 1 All E.R. 897; (1979) 251 E.G. 159 16–12
Taylor Woodrow Property Co. v. Lonrho Textiles (1986) 52 P. & C.R. 28;
  [1985] 2 EGLR 120; (1985) 275 E.G. 632 6–11
Taylor Woodrow Property Management v. National Rivers Authority [1994]
  Env. L.R. D20; The Times, July 14, 1994; (1995) 158 J.P. 1101, D.C. ... 20–03
Tea Trade Properties v. C.I.N. Properties [1990] 22 E.G. 67 .... 6–28, 6–33
Teasdale v. Walker [1958] 1 W.L.R. 1076; [1958] 3 All E.R. 307 16–17
Techno v. Allied Dunbar [1993] 22 E.G. 109 6–19
Teesside Indoor Bowls v. Stockton-on-Tees Borough Council [1990] 46
  E.G. 116, C.A. 16–41

Telegraph Properties (Securities) v. Courtaulds (1981) 257 E.G. 1153 6–10
Temple & Crook v. Capital & Countries Property [1990] 38 E.G.
    118 .... 6–13, 6–19
Tennant Radiant Heat v. Warrington Development Corp. [1988] 11 E.G.
    71 .... 9–02, 9–19
Terrell v. Mabie Todd & Co. (1953) 70 R.P.C. 97, C.A. 18–17
Tesco Holdings v. Jackson [1990] 10 E.G. 71 6–19
Tetley v. Chitty [1986] 1 All E.R. 663 10–02
Texaco Antilles v. Kernochan (Dorothy) [1973] A.C. 609; [1973] 2 W.L.R.
    381; [1973] 2 All E.R. 118 .... 10–08, 17–02
Thames Manufacturing Co. v. Perrotts (Nichol & Peyton) (1984) 49 P. & C.R.
    1; (1984) 271 E.G. 284 2–04
Theodorou v. Bloom [1964] 1 W.L.R. 1152; [1964] 3 All E.R. 399 18–17
Thomas v. Hammond-Lawrence [1986] 1 W.L.R. 456; [1986] 2 All E.R. 214;
    [1986] 1 EGLR 141; (1986) 278 E.G. 414 16–32
Thomas Bates & Son Ltd v. Wyndham's (Lingerie) Ltd [1981] 1 W.L.R. 505;
    [1981] 1 W.L.R. 505; [1981] 1 All E.R. 1077; (1980) 257 E.G. 381;
    (1980) 41 P. & C.R. 345, C.A. 17–02, 17–07
Thompson v. Lapworth (1868) L.R. 3 C.P. 149 7–04
Thorn E.M.I. Pension Trust v. Quinton Hazell (1984) 269 E.G. 414 6–10
Thornton (J.W.) v. Blacks Leisure Group (1987) 53 P. & C.R. 223; [1986] 2
    EGLR 61; (1986) 279 E.G. 588, C.A. 16–41
Tideway Investments and Property Holdings v. Wellwood [1952] Ch. 791;
    [1952] 2 All E.R. 514 11–03
Tidswell v. Whitworth (1867) L.R. 2 C.P. 326 7–04
Tod-Heatly v. Benham (1888) 40 Ch. D. 80 10–02
Tollbench v. Plymouth City Council (1988) 56 P. & C.R. 194; [1988] 23 E.G.
    132 10–09
Tootal Clothing v. Guinea Properties Management (1992) 64 P. & C.R. 452;
    [1992] 41 E.G. 117 18–03
Top Shop Estates v. Danino (C.) [1985] 1 EGLR 9; (1985) 273 E.G.
    197 6–19
Tophams v. Sefton (Earl of) [1967] A.C. 50; [1966] 2 W.L.R. 814; [1966] 1 All
    E.R. 1039 20–03
Torminster Properties v. Green [1983] 1 W.L.R. 676; [1983] 2 All E.R. 457;
    (1983) 45 P. & C.R. 391; (1983) 267 E.G. 256; [1982] 1 W.L.R.
    751; C.A. 3–16, 18–27
Torrens v. Walker [1906] 2 Ch. 166 9–06
Tote Bookmakers v. Development & Property Holdings Co. [1985] Ch. 261;
    [1985] 2 W.L.R. 603; [1985] 2 All E.R. 555; (1984) 49 P. & C.R. 232;
    [1985] 1 EGLR 94; (1984) 247 E.G. 585 6–11
Tottenham Hotspur Football and Athletic Co. v. Princegrove Publishers [1974]
    1 W.L.R. 113; [1974] 1 All E.R. 17; (1973) 27 P. & C.R. 101 16–23
Touche Ross & Co. v. Secretary of State for the Environment (1983) 46 P. &
    C.R. 187; (1983) 265 E.G. 982, C.A. 6–10
Town Centre Securities Ltd v. Wm. Morrison Supermarkets (1982) 263 E.G.
    435 6–17
Town Investments v. Department of the Environment [1978] A.C. 359; [1977]
    2 W.L.R. 450; [1977] 1 All E.R. 813; (1977) 34 P. & C.R. 48, H.L. 16–18
Town Investments Underlease, Re [1954] Ch. 301; [1954] 2 W.L.R. 355;
    [1954] 1 All E.R. 585 12–14
Toyota (G.B.) v. Legal and General Assurance (Pensions) Management [1989]
    42 E.G. 104; (1990) 59 P. & C.R. 435, C.A. 5–03, 6–29, 17–02
Trailfinders v. Razuki [1988] 30 E.G. 59 .... 4–16, 17–04
Trane (U.K.) v. Provident Mutual Life Assurance [1995] 3 E.G.
    122 .... 5–03, 16–07, 16–13

Trans-Britannia Properties v. Derby Properties [1986] 1 EGLR 151; (1986) 278 E.G. 1254, C.A. 16–16
Trave Schiffahrtsgesellschaft GmbH & Co. K.G. v. Ninemia Maritime Corp. [1986] Q.B. 802; [1986] 2 W.L.R. 773; [1986] 2 All E.R. 244 6–15
Tropis Shipping v. Ibex Property Corporation [1967] E.G.D. 433 16–26
Trustees of National Deposit Friendly Society v. Beatties of London [1985] 2 EGLR 59; (1985) 275 E.G. 54 16–11
Tucker v. Granada Motorway Services [1979] 1 W.L.R. 683; [1979] 2 All E.R. 801 6–39
Tudor v. Hamid [1988] 1 EGLR 251 18–32
Tulapam Properties v. De Almeida (1981) 260 E.G. 919 .... 12–06, 17–02
Turner v. Stevenage Borough Council [1996] 14 E.G. 94 .... 6–15, 6–19
Turner v. Wandsworth L.B.C. [1994] 25 E.G. 148 16–40
Turner & Bell (trading as Avro Luxury Coaches) v. Searles (Stanford-le-Hope) (1977) 33 P. & C.R. 208; (1977) 244 E.G. 1023, C.A. 16–37
Turone v. de Walden (Howard) Estates (1983) 267 E.G. 440 16–45
29 Equities v. Bank Leumi (U.K.) [1986] 1 W.L.R. 1490; [1987] 1 All E.R. 108; (1987) 54 P. & C.R. 114; [1986] 2 EGLR 251 .... 12–10, 18–17
Tydeman's Lease, Re, Cross v. Tydeman (1961) 177 E.G. 259 12–14

UBH (Mechanical Services) v. Standard Life Assurance Co. The Times, November 13, 1986 .... 8–02, 9–26, 18–17
U.D.S. Tailoring v. B.H. Holdings (1982) 261 E.G. 49 6–28
Unit Four Cinemas v. Tosara Investment [1993] 44 E.G. 121 .... 6–13, 6–19
United London Co-operatives v. Sun Alliance & London Assurance Co. (1986) 282 E.G. 91 6–14
United Scientific Holdings v. Burnley Borough Council; Cheapside Land Development Co. v. Messels Service Co. [1978] A.C. 904; [1977] 2 W.L.R. 806; (1977) 33 P. & C.R. 220; (1977) 243 E.G. 43, H.L. 6–01, 6–10, 16–13
University of Reading v. Johnson-Houghton [1985] 2 EGLR 113; (1985) 276 E.G. 1353 16–22
Upsons v. Robins (E.) [1956] 1 Q.B. 131; [1955] 3 W.L.R. 584; [1955] 3 All E.R. 348 16–45
Urban Small Space v. Burford Investment Co. [1990] 28 E.G. 116 6–15

V.T. Engineering v. Barland (Richard) & Co. (1968) 19 P. & C.R. 890; (1968) 207 E.G. 247 4–07
Valpy v. St Leonard's Wharf Co. (1903) 67 L.T. 402 7–04
Van v. Corpe (1834) 3 My. & K. 269 18–21
Vangeen v. Benjamin (1976) 239 E.G. 647 .... 18–07, 18–31
Varley v. Coppard (1872) L.R. 7 C.P. 505 3–10
Vaux Group v. Lilley [1991] 4 E.G. 136 12–14
Venetian Glass Gallery v. Next Properties [1989] 30 E.G. 92 .... 12–14, 18–10, 18–17
Victoria Laundry (Windsor) v. Newman Industries, Coulson & Co. (Third Parties) [1949] 2 K.B. 528; [1949] 1 All E.R. 997 9–27
Villenex Co. v. Courtney Hotel (1969) 20 P. & C.R. 575 7–04
Vincent v. Premo Enterprises (Voucher Sales) [1969] 2 Q.B. 609; [1969] 2 W.L.R. 1256; [1969] 2 All E.R. 941; (1969) 20 P. & C.R. 591, C.A. 18–10
Violet Yorke Ltd v. Property Holding & Investment Trust Ltd (1967) 205 E.G. 429 16–47

Viscount Tredegar v. Harwood [1929] A.C. 72 .... 12–13, 13–05
Vural v. Security Archives (1990) 60 P. & C.R. 258 .... 13–11, 13–14

W. H. Smith v. Bath City Council CC (unreported) noted (1986) 277 E.G.
    822 16–47
—— v. Daw, March 31, 1987 (unreported), C.A. 9–19
Wadman v. Calcraft (1804) 10 Ves. Jun. 67 14–06
Wainwright v. Leeds City Council (1984) 82 L.G.R. 657; [1984] 270 E.G.
    1289 9–06
Waite v. Jennings [1906] 2 K.B. 11 12–09
Walker Property Investments (Brighton) v. Walker (1947) 177 L.J. 204,
    C.A. 17–03
Walsh v. Lonsdale (1882) 21 Ch. D. 9 .... 18–07, 18–31
Wandsworth L.B.C. v. Attwell and Donald [1996] 1 E.G. 100 15–10
—— v. Singh (1991) 62 P. & C.R. 219; [1991] 2 EGLR 75; [1991] 33 E.G.
    90 .... 16–16, 16–18
Ward v. Day (1863) 4 B. & S. 337 14–05
Warren v. Keen [1954] 1 Q.B. 15; [1953] 3 W.L.R. 702; [1953] 2 All
    E.R. 1118 9–02
—— v. Marketing Exchange for Africa [1988] 2 EGLR 247 12–13
Warrington and Runcorn Development Corp. v. Greggs (1987) 281 E.G.
    1075; [1987] 1 EGLR 9 6–19
Warwick & Warwick (Philately) v. Shell (U.K.); Chipperfield v. Shell (U.K.)
    (1980) 125 S.J. 99; (1980) 257 E.G. 1042, C.A. 16–45
Watney Combe Reid & Co. v. Westminster (City) London Borough Council
    (1970) 214 E.G. 1631 7–05
Webb v. Frank Bevis Ltd [1940] 1 All E.R. 247 11–12
Webb's Lease, Re, Sandom v. Webb [1951] 1 Ch. 808 4–14
Weeds v. Blaney (1977) 247 E.G. 211, C.A. 17–10
Weeton v. Woodcock (1840) 7 M. & W. 14 11–13
Weller v. Akehurst [1981] 3 All E.R. 411; (1981) 42 P. & C.R. 320; (1980) 257
    E.G. 1259 6–10
West (Richard) and Partners (Inverness) v. Dick [1969] 2 Ch. 424; [1969] 2
    W.L.R. 1190; [1969] 1 All E.R. 943 18–05
West Central Investments v. Borovik (1976) 241 E.G. 609 8–05
West County Cleaners (Falmouth) v. Saly [1966] 1 W.L.R. 1485; [1966] 3 All
    E.R. 210; (1966) 119 E.G. 563 16–13
West Horndon Industrial Park v. Phoenix Timber [1995] 20 E.G. 137 17–04
West Layton v. Ford (Executrix of the Estate of Joseph, decd.) [1979] Q.B.
    593; [1979] 3 W.L.R. 14; [1979] 2 All E.R. 657; (1978) 38 P. & C.R.
    304 12–13
West Pennine Water Board v. Migael (Jon) (North West) (1975) 73 L.G.R.
    420, C.A. 7–03
Westacott v. Hahn [1918] 1 K.B. 495 .... 8–02, 9–19, 17–02
Western Assurance Co. v. Harrison (1903) 33 S.C.R. 473 13–10
Western Credit v. Alberry [1964] 1 W.L.R. 945; [1964] 2 All E.R. 938 3–13
Western Electric Ltd v. Welsh Development Agency [1983] 1 Q.B. 796 9–02
Westminster Bank v. Lee [1956] Ch. 7; [1955] 3 W.L.R. 376; [1955] 2 All E.R.
    883 17–10
Westminster City Council v. Croyalgrange [1986] 1 W.L.R. 674; [1986] 2 All
    E.R. 353 20–03
—— v. Duke of Westminster (1992) 24 H.L.R. 572 .... 10–08, 17–02
—— v. Select Management [1985] 1 W.L.R. 576; [1985] 1 All E.R. 897;
    [1985] 1 EGLR 245 7–04

Wetherall v. Smith [1980] 1 W.L.R. 1290; [1980] 2 All E.R. 530; (1980) 40 P. & C.R. 205; (1980) 256 E.G. 163, C.A. 16–19

Wheeldon v. Burrows (1879) 12 Ch. D. 31 .... 4–13, 4–14

Wheeler v. Mercer [1957] A.C. 416; [1956] 3 W.L.R. 841; [1956] 3 All E.R. 631 16–22

Whelton Sinclair (A Firm) v. Hyland [1992] 41 E.G. 112, C.A. 5–03

White v. Bijou Mansions [1937] Ch. 610 18–08

—— v. Harrow (1902) 86 L.T. 4 .... 4–18, 17–02, 17–04

—— v. Hay (1895) 72 L.T. 281 18–23

White and Smith's Contract, *Re* [1896] 1 Ch. 637 18–15

Whiteminster Estates v. Hodges Menswear (1974) 232 E.G. 715 12–14

Wiggington and Milner v. Winster Engineering [1978] 1 W.L.R. 1462; [1978] 3 All E.R. 436; (1977) 36 P. & C.R. 203, C.A. 4–02

Wilchick v. Marks and Silverstone [1934] 2 K.B. 56 20–05

Wilkinson v. Collyer (1884) 13 Q.B.D. 1 7–04

William Hill (Football) Ltd v. Willen Key & Hardware (1964) 108 S.J. 482 18–27

William Hill (Southern) v. Cabras, *see* Hill (William) (Southern) v. Cabras .. 4–11, 4–13, 4–18, 16–06, 16–07

William Sindall v. Cambridgeshire C.C. [1994] 1 W.L.R. 1016; [1994] 3 All E.R. 932 18–05

William Skelton & Son Ltd v. Harrison and Pinder Ltd [1975] Q.B. 361 18–21

Williams v. Gabrial [1906] 1 K.B. 155 16–03

—— v. Spargo [1893] W.N. 100 18–11

Willis v. Association of Universities of the British Commonwealth [1965] 1 Q.B. 140; [1964] 2 W.L.R. 946; [1964] 2 All E.R. 39, C.A. 16–41

Willison v. Cheverell Estates Ltd [1995] 26 E.G. 133 .... 5–01, 16–24

Willmott v. London Road Car Co. [1910] 2 Ch. 525 .... 12–08, 13–05

Wilson v. Hagon (1958) 109 L.J. 204 14–05

—— v. Rosenthal (1906) 22 T.L.R. 233 12–07

—— v. Tavener [1901] 1 Ch. 578 .... 4–11, 16–16

—— v. Whately (1860) 1 J. & H. 436 17–04

Wimbush (A.D.) & Son v. Franmills Properties [1961] 2 W.L.R. 498; [1961] 2 All E.R. 197; (1960) 176 E.G. 119 16–40

Wolff v. Endfield London Borough (1988) 55 P. & C.R. 78; (1987) 281 E.G. 1320; [1987] 1 EGLR 119, C.A. 6–33

Wong v. Beaumont Property Trust [1965] 1 Q.B. 173; [1964] 2 W.L.R. 1329; [1964] 2 All E.R. 119 17–02

Woodhouse (Edwin) Trustee Co. v. Sheffield Brick Co. (1983) 270 E.G. 548 6–09

Woolcott v. Sun Alliance and London Insurance [1978] 1 W.L.R. 493; [1978] 1 All E.R. 1253 13–10

Woolworth (F.W.) v. Charlwood Alliance Properties (1987) 282 E.G. 585; [1987] 1 EGLR 53 .... 10–06, 12–14

Woolworth (F.W.) & Co. v. Lambert [1937] Ch. 37 .... 11–02, 11–05

"Wonderland", Cleethorpes, *Re*; East Coast Amusement Co. v. British Transport Commission; *see* East Coast Amusement Co. v. British Transport Board

Wrenbridge Ltd v. Harries (Southern Properties) Ltd (1981) 260 E.G. 1195 .... 6–09, 6–14

Wright, *Re*, Landau v. The Trustee [1949] Ch. 729; [1949] 2 All E.R. 605 .... 3–07, 3–08

Wright v. Dean [1948] Ch. 686; [1948] 2 All E.R. 415 16–12

—— v. Robert Leonard (Developments) [1994] NPC 49; [1994] EGCS 69, C.A. 18–03

—— v. Simpson (1802) 6 Ves. Jun. 714 3–15

Wright Davies v. Marler (unreported) but noted at [1995] 10 C.L. 122   4–02
Wychavon District Council v. National Rivers Authority [1993] 1 W.L.R. 125;
    [1993] 2 All E.R. 440 20–03
Wycombe Area Health Authority v. Barnett (1982) 264 E.G. 619   9–10

X.L. Fisheries v. Leeds Corporation [1955] 2 Q.B. 636; [1955] W.L.R. 393;
    [1955] 2 All E.R. 875 16–25
Xey S.A. v. Abbey Life Assurance Co. Ltd [1994] EGCS 190   3–15

Yamaha-Kemble Music (U.K.) v. ARC Properties [1990] 1 EGLR 261 16–26
Yianni v. Evans (Edwin) & Sons [1982] Q.B. 438; [1981] 3 W.L.R. 843;
    (1981) 259 E.G. 969   9–11
Yorkbrook Investments v. Batten (1986) 52 P. & C.R. 51; [1985] 2 EGLR 100;
    (1985) 276 E.G. 493, C.A.   8–02
Young v. Ashley Gardens Properties [1903] 2 Ch. 112 18–17
—— v. Dalgety (1987) 281 E.G. 427; [1987] 1 EGLR 116 ..... 6–26, 6–36, 11–11,
                                                  11–12, 11–14
Youngmin v. Health [1974] 1 W.L.R. 135; [1974] 1 All E.R. 461; (1973) 26
    P. & C.R. 570, C.A.   3–08

Zermalt Holdings S.A. v. Nu-Life Upholstery Repairs [1985] 2 EGLR 14;
    (1985) 275 E.G. 1134   6–19
Zubaida v. Hargreaves [1995] 9 E.G. 320   6–11

TABLE OF STATUTES

1774 Fire Prevention (Metropolis) Act (14 Geo. 3, c. 78)
    s. 83 13–11

1852 Common Law Procedure Act (15 & 16 Vict., c. 76)
    s. 210 14–06
    s. 211 14–06
    s. 212 14–06

1870 Apportionment Act (33 & 34 Vict., c. 35)
    ss. 2–4 18–27

1890 Partnership Act (53 & 54 Vict., c. 39)
    s. 9 3–10
    s. 20(1) 3–10

1891 Stamp Act (54 & 55 Vict., c. 39)
    s. 15 18–11
    s. 56 19–20
    s. 72 18–11
    s. 75 18–11
    Sched. 1 .... 5–02, 18–11

1908 Law of Distress Amendment Act 12–14

1914 Bankruptcy Act (4 & 5 Geo. 5, c. 17) 3–08

1922 Law of Property Act (12 & 13 Geo. 5, c. 16) 16–11
    s. 145 16–11
    Sched. 15 16–11

1925 Trustee Act (15 Geo. 5, c. 19)
    s. 26 3–08
    (2) 3–08
    Law of Property Act (15 Geo. 5, c. 20) 12–14
    s. 25 18–08
    (9) 18–08
    s. 34(2) 3–10
    s. 44 .... 18–22, 18–24
    (2) 18–08, 18–14, 18–22, 18–24
    (3) 18–24
    (4) 18–22
    (5) 18–08
    s. 45(2) 18–14, 18–16, 18–22, 18–24

1925 Law of Property Act—cont.
    s. 45(3) 18–24
    s. 49(2) 18–17
    s. 52 18–26
    (1) 18–10
    s. 54(2) 18–10
    s. 56 3–03
    s. 61 17–04
    s. 62 .... 4–08, 4–13, 16–44
    s. 77(1)(c) 2–10, 18–18
    (d) 2–10
    s. 78 3–03
    s. 79 3–03
    s. 81 3–05
    (3) 3–05
    s. 84(1) 10–12
    (12) 10–12
    s. 86(1) 12–04
    s. 87(1) 12–04
    s. 139 18–28
    s. 142 3–03
    s. 144 12–09
    s. 146 .... 9–24, 14–06, 15–11
    (1) 14–06
    (2) 9–24, 14–04, 14–06
    (3) 9–24
    (4) 12–14, 14–03
    (5)(a) 18–07
    (10) 14–03
    (13) 14–06
    s. 147 9–21
    s. 149(3) 5–03
    s. 150 18–28
    s. 196 15–10
    (5) 15–10
    s. 198 18–08
    s. 205(1)(xxi) 18–22
    (xxiv) 18–22
    Sched. 2
    Pt IX 18–18
    Land Registration Act (15 Geo. 5, c. 21) 3–03, 4–12, 5–03, 18–11
    s. 10 18–14
    s. 19(2) 18–11
    s. 22 5–03

1925 Land Registration Act
—cont.
    s. 22(1) 18–20
        (2) 18–11
    s. 24(1)(b) 2–10, 18–18
    s. 50(2) 18–08
    s. 64(1) 18–11
        (c) 18–11
    s. 70(1)(g) 16–12
    s. 77(1) 18–14
    s. 123 .... 5–03, 18–11
        (1) 18–20
    Administration of Estates
        Act (15 & 16 Geo. 5,
        c. 23)
    s. 9(1) 3–04
        (2) 3–04
    s. 34 3–08
    s. 36 3–04
    Sched. 1, Pt I 3–08
1927 Landlord and Tenant Act
        (17 & 18 Geo. 5,
        c. 36) 6–36, 12–15
    s. 1 11–07
        (1) 11–14, 11–15
    s. 2(1)(b) 11–07
    s. 3 .... 11–05, 19–13
        (1) 11–07, 18–31
        (4) 11–05
        (5) 11–07
    s. 9 11–07
    s. 16 11–09
    s. 17(1) 18–31
    s. 18 .... 9–24, 9–25
    s. 19(1) 2–06, 12–04,
        12–09, 12–10, 12–12
        (a) 12–08, 12–12
        (b) 6–40,
            12–08, 12–14
        (1A)–(1E) 12–12
        (1B) 12–12
        (1C) 12–12
        (2) 11–05
        (3) 10–09
    s. 23 2–12
        (2) 16–25
    s. 25(1) 18–31
    s. 27 19–13
    Pt I 11–05, 18–31
1931 Finance Act (21 & 22
        Geo. 5, Ch. 21)
    s. 28(1) 18–11, 18–20
1936 Public Health Act (26
        Geo. 5 & 1 Edw. 8,
        c. 49) 7–04
    s. 27 15–03

1936 Public Health Act—cont.
    s. 290 7–05
1937 Public Health (Drainage
        of Trade Premises)
        Act (1 Edw. 8 & 1
        Geo. 6, c. 40)–
    s. 1(1) 11–05, 15–03
1938 Leasehold Property (Re-
        pairs) Act (1 & 2 Geo.
        6, c. 34)
    s. 1 9–24
        (1) 9–24
        (3) 9–24
        (4) 9–24
        (5) 9–24
        (6) 9–24
    s. 7(1) 9–24
1939 London Building Acts
        (Amendment) Act (2
        & 3 Geo. 6, c. 97) 7–04
    s. 4(1) 4–03
    s. 107 7–05
    Pt VI 4–03
1950 Arbitration Act (14 Geo.
        6, c. 27) 6–13
    s. 1(6) 6–15
    s. 12(1) 6–15
    s. 18 6–18
    s. 19 6–18
    s. 22 6–18
    s. 23 6–19
    s. 27 6–11
1954 Landlord and Tenant Act (2
        & 3 Eliz. 2, c. 56) 2–04,
        3–08, 3–15, 5–02, 16–05,
        16 06, 16 08, 16–42,
        16–43, 18–21, 18–31
    s. 23 .... 16–12, 16–15
        (1) 16–19
        (2) 16–18
        (3) 16–44
        (4) 16–20
    ss. 24–28 6–08
    s. 24 .... 16–24, 16–45,
            16–49
        (1) 12–15, 16–24
        (2) 16–24, 18–26
        (3)(a) 16–24
    s. 24A 6–08, 6–27,
            16–25, 16–32
        (3) 16–32
    s. 25 .... 4–03, 4–06,
            16–08, 16–24, 16–25,
            16–26, 16–27, 16–34,
            16–40, 16–50

1954   Landlord and Tenant
         Act—*cont.*
         s. 25(2) 16–25, 16–26
              (3) 16–26
              (b) 16–26
              (4) 16–26
              (5) 16–26, 16–27
              (6) 16–26
         s. 26 .... 16–09, 16–24,
              16–25, 16–34, 16–50
              (2) 6–28, 16–09,
                                  16–25
              (3) 16–28
              (4) 16–09, 16–28
              (5) 16–25, 16–28
              (6) 16–25, 16–29
         s. 27 16–24
              (1) 16–25
              (2) 16–24, 16–25
         s. 28 .... 16–24, 16–25,
                                  16–30
         s. 29 .... 2–02, 16–24
              (1) 16–31, 16–43
              (2) 16–25, 16–27
              (3) 16–25, 16–31
         s. 30 .... 16–25, 16–26
                           16–29, 16–34
              (1)(a) 16–35
                  (b) 16–36
                  (c) 16–37
                  (d) 16–38
                  (e) 16–39
                  (f) 13–16, 16–40
                  (g) 16–41
              (2) 16–41
              (3) 16–41
         s. 31A 16–40
              (1)(a) 16–40
                  (b) 16–40
              (2) 16–40
         ss. 32–35 16–43
         s. 32(1) 16–44
              (2) 16–44
              (3) 16–44
         s. 33 16–45
         s. 34 6–24,
              6–36, 11–14, 16–32, 16–46
              (1)(a) 6–35
                  (b) 6–35
              (3) 16–47
              (4) 16–47
         s. 35(1) 16–46
              (2) 16–48
         s. 36(1) 16–49
              (2) 16–49

1954   Landlord and Tenant
         Act—*cont.*
         s. 37 ... 13–16, 16–50, 19–06
              (2) 16–50
              (3) 16–50
                  (a) 16–50
                  (b) 16–50
              (4) 16–42
              (5) 16–50
              (7) 16–50
              (8) 16–50
         s. 38(1) 12–15, 16–09,
              16–23, 16–24, 16–48,
                                  18–31
              (2) 16–50
              (3) 16–50
              (4) 16–23
                  (a) 16–23, 16–24
                  (b) 12–15
         s. 40 16–33
              (2) 16–33
              (3) 16–33
         s. 41(1) 16–17
              (2) 16–41
         s. 41A 3–10, 16–27
              (6) 16–46
         s. 42(2) 16–17
         s. 43(1)(a) 16–19, 16–21
                  (b) 16–21
              (2) 16–21
              (3) 16–21, 18–31
         s. 43A 16–27
         s. 44 16–25
              (2) 16–25
              (3) 16–25
         s. 48(1) 11–07
         s. 49 11–07
         s. 57 16–21
         s. 58 16–21
         s. 60 16–21
         s. 60A 16–21
         s. 60B 16–21
         s. 63 16–31
         s. 64 .... 16–45, 16–49
              (1) 16–42
              (2) 16–42
         s. 69(2) 16–43
         Sched. 6 16–25
              para. 6 16–26
         Pt II 1–06, 3–10,
              5–02, 6–08, 6–29, 8–04,
              11–07, 12–07, 12–14,
              12–15, 16–01, 16–14,
              16–23, 18–02, 18–03,
              18–07, 18–12, 18–26,
                                  18–31

1958 Costs of Leases Act (6 & 7
      Eliz. 2, c. 52) 16–46
      s. 1 18–04
    Finance Act (6 & 7 Eliz. 2,
      c. 56)
      s. 34(8) 18–20

1961 Factories Act (10 & 11
      Eliz. 2, c. 34) 7–04
      s. 121 7–04
      s. 122 7–04
      s. 155 7–04
      s. 169 11–05
      s. 170 7–05
      s. 176 7–04
    Public Health Act (10 &
      11 Eliz. 2, c. 64) 7–04
    Housing Act (10 & 11
      Eliz. 2, c. 65)
      s. 32 20–05

1962 Recorded Delivery Serv-
      ice Act (10 & 11 Eliz.
      2, c. 27)
      s. 1(1) 16–25

1963 Finance Act (c. 25)
      s. 55 18–20
    Offices, Shops and Rail-
      way Premises Act (c.
      41) 7–04
      s. 42 7–04
      s. 63 7–04
      s. 73(1) 11–05
      (2) 7–05

1964 Perpetuities and Accumu-
      lations Act (c. 55)
      s. 1 8–07
      (1) 4–08

1967 General Rate Act (c. 9) .. 7–02
    Leasehold Reform Act (c.
      88) 16–19

1969 Law of Property Act (c.
      59) 6–36, 16–14

1971 Fire Precautions Act (c.
      40)
      s. 1 7–04
      s. 6(5) 7–04
      s. 25 7–04
      s. 28(2) 11–05
      (3) 7–05
      (A) 7–05
      Sched. 2 7–04
    Banking and Financial
      Dealings Act (c. 80)
      s. 1(4) 6–01
      Sched. 1 6–01

1972 Defective Premises Act (c.
      35) 15–08

1972 Defective Premises Act
      —cont.
      ss. 1–3 9–19
      s. 4 9–19
      (2) 9–02, 9–19
      (4) 9–02, 9–24
    Land Charges Act (c.
      61) 3–03,
                4–12, 16–24
      s. 2(4) 18–09
      s. 3(7) 18–09
      s. 5(1)(b) 18–09
      s. 6(1)(b) 18–08
      s. 10(4) 18–08
      s. 17(1) 18–08

1974 Health and Safety at Work
      etc. Act (c. 37) 7–04,
              9–23, 15–08
      s. 2(2)(d) 7–04
      s. 4 7–04

1975 Sex Discrimination Act (c.
      65)
      s. 31 12–08

1976 Race Relations Act (c.
      74)
      s. 24 12–08

1977 Rent Act (c. 42) 16–19
      s. 24(3) 16–19
    Criminal Law Act (c. 45)
      s. 6 14–04
    Unfair Contract Terms
      Act (c. 50) 8–02, 9–27
      s. 3 8–02
      Sched. 1
      para. 1(b) 8–02

1978 Civil Liability (Contribu-
      tors) Act (c. 47) 2–10

1979 Arbitration Act (c. 42) 6–13
      s. 1 6–19
      (3) 6–19
      (4) 6–19
      (5) 6–15
      s. 3 6–15

1980 Local Government, Plan-
      ning and Land Act (c.
      65)
      s. 193 16–50
      Sched. 33
      para. 4 16–50

1981 Supreme Court Act (c.
      54)
      s. 35A 6–05
      s. 37(1) 9–27
      s. 38(1) 14–06

1982 Supply of Goods and
       Services Act (c. 29) .. 6–13
       s. 13 8–02
       s. 14 8–02
1984 Telecommunications Act
       (c. 12)
       s. 96 11–05
       County Courts Act (c.
       28)
       s. 18 16–23
       s. 89(1) 6–06
       s. 139(2) 14–06
       Sched. 2
       Pt II
       para. 5 14–06
       Building Act (c. 55)
       s. 1 7–04
       s. 24 7–04
       s. 71 7–04
       s. 72 7–04
       s. 102 7–05
       Sched. 3
       Pt. II
       para. 5 7–04
1985 Companies Act (c. 6)
       s. 36A(2) 18–10
             (4) 18–10
             (5) 18–10
       s. 395 6–05
       s. 725 16–25
       s. 736 16–17
       Administration of Justice
       Act (c. 61)
       s. 55 14–06
       Housing Act (c. 68) 9–02
       s. 8 9–02
       s. 11 9–02
1986 Agricultural Holdings Act
       (c. 5) 16–19
       Land Registration Act
       (c. 26)
       s. 1(1) 18–14
       s. 2(1) 18–11
             (b) 18–20
       Gas Act (c. 44)
       Sched. 5
       para. 19(1)(b) 11–11
       Insolvency Act (c. 45)
       ss. 178–182 3–11
       s. 181(2) 3–15
       s. 252(1) 3–08
       s. 253(1) 3–08
       s. 264(2) 3–08
       s. 273(2) 3–08
       s. 306 3–08
       ss. 315–321 3–08

1986 Insolvency Act—cont.
       s. 315(1) 3–08
             (5) 3–08
       s. 320 3–09
       s. 321(3) 3–09
       Financial Services Act
       (c. 60) 18–03
1987 Fire Safety and Safety at
       Places of Sport Act (c.
       27)
       s. 16 7–04
1988 Income and Corporation
       Taxes Act (c. 1)
       s. 34(2) 11–09
             (3) 11–09
             (5) 11–09
       Local   Government
       Finance Act (c. 9)
       s. 45 7–02
       s. 46A 7–02
       s. 65(1) 7–02
             (2) 7–02
       Sched. 4A 7–02
       Landlord and Tenant Act
       (c. 26) 10–09, 12–10,
                   12–14, 18–17, 18–32
       s. 1 12–12
             (1) 12–10
             (3) 12–10
             (4) 12–10
             (5) 12–10
       s. 3 12–10
       s. 4 .... 12–10, 18–17
1989 Finance Act (c. 26) 6–34
       Electricity Act (c. 29)
       Sched. 6 para. 9 11–11
       Law of Property (Miscel-
       laneous   Provisions)
       Act (c. 34)
       s. 2 ..... 18–02, 18–03, 18–31
       Companies Act (c. 40)
       Sched. 16 18–09
       Local Government and
       Housing Act (c. 42)
       Sched. 5, para. 36 7–02
       Sched. 7 16–50
1990 Capital Allowances Act
       (c. 1)
       s. 22 11–16
       s. 52(1) 11–16
       Town   and   County
       Planning Act (c. 8)
       s. 69 18–05
       s. 188 18–05
       s. 191 18–05
             (2) 18–05

1990	Planning (Hazardous Substances) Act (c. 10)
	s. 4 20–02
	Landlord and Tenant (Licensed Premises) Act (c. 39) 16–21
	Environmental Protection Act (c. 43) .. 20–08, 20–10
	s. 6 20–02
	s. 13 20–04
	s. 14 20–04
	s. 33 20–02
	s. 34 15–03
	s. 42(5) 20–04
	s. 78A(9) 20–08
	s. 78E 20–04, 20–08
	s. 78F 20–08
	(4) 20–08
	(5) 20–08
	s. 79(7) 20–08
	s. 80 20–04
	(2) 20–04, 20–08
	Pt IIA 20–08, 20–12, 20–13
1991	Water Industry Act (c. 56)
	s. 118 20–02
	Water Industry Act (c. 56)
	s. 144 7–03
	(1)(b) 7–03
	s. 179(4) 11–11
	Pt. IV, Ch. III 15–03
	Water Resources Act (c. 57)
	s. 85(6) 20–03
	s. 88(1)(a) 20–02
	s. 161(3) 20–08
	Sched. 10 20–02
1992	Access to Neighbouring Land Act (c. 23)
	s. 1(1) 4–12
	(2) 4–12
	(4) 4–12
	(5) 4–12
	s. 4(1) 4–12
1993	Radioactive Substances Act (c. 12)
	s. 6 20–02
	s. 13 20–02
	s. 14 20–02
	Reinsurance (Acts of Terrorism) Act (c. 18) ...13–08
	Finance Act (c. 34)
	s. 201 18–20

1993	Railways Act (c. 43) 7–04
1994	Finance Act (c. 9)
	s. 111 18–11
	s. 240 18–11
	s. 243 18–26
	Sunday Trading Act (c. 20)
	s. 3 10–07
	Value Added Tax Act (c. 23)
	s. 1(2) 19–02
	s. 2(1) 19–03
	s. 3(1) 19–02
	s. 4(1) 19–02
	(2) 19–09
	s. 5(2)(a) 19–15
	s. 6(4) 19–19
	s. 19(2) 19–08, 19–19
	(3) 19–08
	s. 24(1) 19–03
	s. 25(1) 19–03
	(2) 19–03
	(3) 19–03
	s. 26(2) 19–03
	s. 59 19–05
	s. 60 19–05
	s. 61 19–05
	s. 63 19–05
	s. 64 19–05
	s. 80 19–05
	s. 89(2) 19–19
	Sched. 1, para. 1(1) 19–02
	para. 9 19–02
	Sched. 8, group 5 19–09
	n. 3 19–17
	n. 5 19–17
	Sched. 8, group 6 19–09
	Sched. 9, group 1 19–09
	item 1 19–09
	para. (h) 19–09
	group. 5 19–21
	Sched. 10, para. 2(1) ...19–10
	(2) ...19–17
	para. 3(3) ...19–10
	(5) ...19–10
	(6) ...19–10
	(9) ...19–10
	Law of Property (Miscellaneous Provisions) Act (c. 36) 18–18
	s. 1(1)(b) 18–10
	(2)(b) 18–10
	(3) 18–10
	(b) 18–10
	s. 2(1) 18–03
	(a) 18–18

1994   Law of Property (Miscellaneous Provisions)
Act—*cont.*
s. 2(1)(b) 18–18
     (2) 18–03, 18–18
     (3) 18–03, 18–18
     (5) 18–03
s. 3(1) 18–18
     (3) 18–18
s. 4 .... 18–18, 18–27
     (1) 18–18
     (2) 18–22
s. 6 18–18
     (2) 18–22
s. 8 18–18
s. 14 3–04

1995   Finance Act (c. 4)
s. 26 19–02

Environment Act (c. 25)   20–08
s. 57 20–08

Landlord and Tenant
(Covenants) Act
(c. 30) .. 1–01, 2–01, 3–03,
3–12, 6–05, 6–26, 12–13,
12–14, 16–46, 16–47,
18–12
s. 1(3) 2–02, 18–18
     (5) 2–02
     (6) 2–02, 3–15
     (7) 2–02
s. 3(1) 2–04, 3–03,
3–07
     (2) 2–04
       (a)(i) 3–03
          (ii) 3–03
     (3) 6–05
       (a)(i) 3–03
          (ii) 3–03
     (5) 10–11
     (6)(a) 3–03
       (b) 3–03
s. 5 2–07
     (2) 2–05
     (3) 2–05
s. 6(2)(a) 2–08
s. 7(2) 2–08
     (4) 2–08
s. 8 2–08
     (3) 2–08
s. 11(1) 2–05, 5–02
     (2) 3–08

1995   Landlord and Tenant
(Covenants) Act
—*cont.*
s. 12 8–02
s. 13 2–10
s. 13(1) 2–05
s. 16 .... 2–06, 2–07
     (1) 2–07
     (3) 2–06
     (4) 2–06
     (5) 2–06
     (6) 2–06
     (8) 2–06
s. 17 .... 2–04, 2–06, 2–07,
2–12, 3–16
     (2) 2–12
     (4) 2–12
     (5) 2–12
     (6) 2–12
s. 18 .... 2–04, 2–07, 2–12
     (3) 3–15
     (4) 2–12
s. 19 .... 2–02, 3–16
     (1) 2–12
     (2) 2–12
     (5) 2–12
     (6)(b) 2–12
     (7) 2–12
     (8) 2–12
s. 20(1) 2–12
     (2) 2–12
     (6) 2–12
s. 22 .... 2–06, 12–12
s. 24(1)(a) 2–09
     (2) 2–07, 3–16
     (4) 2–09
s. 25(1) 2–03, 2–07,
2–08, 3–16
     (2) 2–03
     (3) 2–03
s. 30 2–10
     (4) 3–03
Sched. 1, para. 3 16–47
        para. 14 16–46

Civil Evidence Act
(c. 38) 6–17, 9–06

Disability Discrimination
Act (c. 50) 7–04
s. 6 11–05
s. 15 11–05
s. 16 11–05
s. 19(2) 11–05
s. 21 11–05
s. 22 11–05
s. 27 11–05

TABLE OF STATUTORY INSTRUMENTS AND DEPARTMENT OF THE ENVIRONMENT CIRCULARS

Statutory Instruments

1925   Land Registration Rules (S.I. 1925 No. 1093)
r. 113(1) 4–02
r. 200 18–29
r. 205 18–29
r. 287 18–09
r. 289 18–09

1954   Landlord and Tenant (Determination of Rateable Value Procedure) Rules (S.I. 1954 No. 1255) 16–50

1965   Rules of the Supreme Court (S.I. 1965 No. 1776)
Ord. 65, r. 5 16–25
Ord. 97, r. 7 16–42

1972   Town and Country Planning (Use Classes) Order (S.I. 1972 No. 1385) 10–08

1976   Fire Certificates (Special Premises) Regulations (S.I. 1976 No. 2003) 7–04

1981   County Court Rules (S.I. 1981 No. 1687)
Ord. 3, r. 4 16–23
Ord. 43, r. 20 16–23

1983   Landlord and Tenant Act 1954 Part II (Notices) Regulations (S.I. 1983 No. 133)
reg. 2.2 16–26
Form 1 16–26
Form 8 16–28
Form 9 16–33
Form 10 16–33

1985   Supply of Services (Exclusion of Implied Terms) Order (No. 1) (S.I. 1985 No. 1) 6–13
Building (Inner London) Regulations (S.I. 1985 No. 1936) 7–04

1986   Local Government Reorganisation (Miscellaneous Provision) Order (S.I. 1986 No. 452) 7–04
Rules of the Supreme Court (Amendment No. 2) Order (S.I. 1986 No. 1187)
r. 2 14–07
r. 3 14–07
County Court (Amendment No. 2) Rules (S.I. 1986 No. 1189)
r. 2 14–07
Insolvency Rules (S.I. 1986 No. 1925)
Chap. 14 3–08
Chap. 15 3–11

1987 Town and Country Planning (Use Classes) Order (S.I. 1987 No. 764) 10–04, 10–08
Building (Inner London) Regulations (S.I. 1987 No. 798) 7–04

1988   Town and Country Planning (General Development) Order (S.I. 1988 No. 1813) 10–04

1989   Fire Precautions (Factories, Offices, Shops and Railway Premises) Order (S.I. 1989 No. 76) 7–04

1989   Landlord and Tenant Act 1954 Part II (Notices) (Amendment) Regulations (S.I. 1989 No. 1548) 16–26

Non-Domestic Rating (Unoccupied Property) Regulations (S.I. 1989 No. 2261) 7–02

1990   Landlord and Tenant Act 1954 (Appropriate Multiplier) Regulations (S.I. 1990 No. 363) 16–50

1991   Building Regulations (S.I. 1991 No. 2768) 7–04

Environmental Protection (Duty of Care) Regulations (S.I. 1991 No. 2839) 15–03

1994   Foreign Companies (Execution of Documents) Regulations (S.I. 1994 No. 950) 18–10

Waste Management Licensing Regulations (S.I. 1994 No. 1056) 20–02
reg. 20 15–03

Land Registration (Execution of Deeds) Rules (S.I. 1994 No. 1130) 18–10

Construction (Design and Management) Regulations (S.I. 1994 No. 3140) 7–04, 11–06

1995   Value Added Tax (Buildings and Land) Order (S.I. 1995 No. 279) 19–10
art. 4 19–10
(b) 19–10

Value Added Tax (Land) Order (S.I. 1995 No. 282)
art. 3 19–09
art. 4 19–09

1995   Value Added Tax (Special Provisions) Order (S.I. 1995 No. 1268)
art. 5 19–06
(3) 19–18

Value Added Tax Regulations (S.I. 1995 No. 2518)
reg. 13 ...... 19–04, 19–19
(5) 19–05
reg. 14 19–04
reg. 29(2) 19–04
reg. 37(3)(b) 19–03
(c) 19–03
reg. 84(2) 19–07
reg. 85 19–07
reg. 101 19–03
reg. 114(2) 19–03
Pt. XV 19–03

Landlord and Tenant (Covenants) Act 1995 (Notices) Regulations (S.I. 1995 No. 2964)
Form 1 2–12
Form 2 2–12
Form 3 2–08
Form 4 2–08
Form 5 2–08
Form 6 2–08

Land Registration (Overriding Leases) Rules 1995 (S.I. 1995 No. 3154) 2–12

Department of the Environment Circulars

19/91   Environmental Protection Act 1990 Section 34: The Duty of Care 15–03

11/94   The Environmental Protection Act 1990: Part II Waste Management Licensing: the Framework Directive on Waste
Annex 8 15–03

1 INTRODUCTION

1–01 General

In some respects a lease of commercial property granted today would be familiar to a lawyer practising 100 years ago. Many traditional provisions have changed little in substance over the years. On the other hand some very significant changes have occurred, partly as a result of developments in the property world and the economy generally, and partly as a result of changes in drafting style and working practice among the legal profession.

Influences on lease terms   Attitudes to commercial property as an investment have led to changes, particularly the demand for lease terms which remove as much risk and expenditure as possible from the landlord and thus maximise the landlord's return.[1] This has meant for example that provisions for rent review have become both universally accepted and increasingly sophisticated. The more recent effects of economic recession have also made their contribution to law and practice. Landlords increasingly require the provision of sureties, and there has been a resurgence of interest in the ability of the landlord to enforce the provisions of the lease against the original tenant, should an assignee's business fail,[2] or to regain possession of the premises. The exigencies of recession have also lent an increased sharpness to the scrutiny to which existing lease terms are subjected, particularly in the area of rent review. The decline in importance of certain types of commercial property, such as large industrial premises, and the development of new sectors, such as shopping centres and business parks, have created a need to tailor traditional leasehold provisions to the type of property and tenant in question. Finally, the over-supply of new premises resulting from the development boom of the mid 1980s, followed in turn by economic recession and a dearth of willing tenants, led to a shift towards lease terms which weighed heavily in the tenant's favour.

It also seems likely that the legal profession has played a part in these developments, although perhaps more by way of reaction to external pressures than by instigating change.

Influence of reported cases   Important judicial decisions on commercial leases are reported with, it seems, an ever-increasing frequency, although often not in the mainstream law reports but in specialist series such as the *Estates Gazette Law Reports*. It seems clear that such decisions do become known to many (though by no means all) of the solicitors practising in this field. Accordingly, the response to such decisions is often to amend leasehold precedents to counter a potential problem or

---

[1] Often termed a "clear lease": see para. 8–01 below.
[2] The landlord's recourse to the original or any former tenant is however now severely limited by the Landlord and Tenant (Covenants) Act 1995. See Chap. 2 below.

neutralise an unfavourable decision. In other cases, knowledge of the decision may suggest to a solicitor a possible interpretation of an existing lease, until then unseen. This may be disputed by the other party, and possibly lead to further litigation. In this way, a large body of case law may accumulate around a particular type of provision with alarming rapidity.[3]

1–02 Need for clear drafting

Modern drafting style The practice of drafting itself evolves, albeit slowly, and undoubtedly a large proportion of the legal profession does seriously attempt to draft in a modern style, using clear and simple words and an open-textured format. Sadly, however, many commercial leases remain forbidding and impenetrable documents—heavily laced with repetitious and pompous language, and capable of being mediated to the parties only by the priestly offices of a solicitor, or in an extreme case counsel. This is a pity, since a lease should be a practical document,[4] capable of being used by the parties or their property advisers to resolve ordinary difficulties, without always needing recourse to legal advice.[5]

Though each lawyer will have his own preferences as to drafting techniques, the following general guidelines may help in achieving clarity and precision.[6]

Logical format (1) It is sensible to follow (a) a logical, and (b) a familiar[7] format. The lease will read more easily and the relevant provision will be more swiftly located. A table of contents, giving the pages of each provision and placed at the start of the lease, will easily repay the time spent in preparing it by the time it will save in negotiating and subsequently using the lease.[8]

Definitions (2) Much repetition of language can be avoided by defining various terms in an interpretation clause.[9] It is sensible to indicate the existence of such a clause by placing it, or at least referring to it, at the outset.

Simple words (3) Simple and ordinary words should be used where possible. In some cases use of a specialist legal word

---

[3] See, *e.g.* on rent review clauses, para. 6–07 below.

[4] *Levermore v. Jobey* [1956] 1 W.L.R. 697 at 708.

[5] See para. 4.2 of the *Commercial Property Leases Code of Practice* (para. 1–06 below).

[6] The principles are drawn largely from the admirable work of Stanley Robinson, *Drafting: Its Application to Conveyancing and Commercial Documents* (1980).

[7] The traditional form is: the date; the parties; recitals (if any); the clause describing and leasing the premises and stating the premium if any; the term granted; the rent reserved; the tenant's covenants; the landlord's covenants; the provisos; any schedules; and the attestation clause.

[8] Modern word processing programs are now capable of generating such tables of contents automatically.

[9] Definitions should, however, be carefully considered in relation to all the provisions of the lease.

may achieve precision or brevity, but there seems little to justify much legal language other than tradition.[10]

Punctuation (4) Properly used punctuation is an aid to readability and can avoid ambiguity. However, whereas strong punctuation marks such as the full stop, colon and semi-colon seldom give rise to ambiguity, the comma can. Commas are often used non-directionally, and where several occur in a sentence it can be difficult to decide how they are paired. Thus care is required by the draftsman, and if the accidental omission of a comma could seriously affect the meaning of a sentence he should consider whether some other way of expressing the meaning without using such punctuation could be found.

Simple clauses (5) Each clause should be kept as simple as possible, so that it embodies only one concept. Complex clauses should be broken down into sub-clauses if they become overloaded. In particular, there is a danger of over-complexity during the course of negotiation: the tenant's solicitor may seek a concession by adding to a clause the words "provided that" followed by lengthy wording (which may become even more lengthy as a result of amendment by the landlord's solicitor). This technique is often ungrammatical, and (more seriously) may result in ambiguity. For example it may be unclear whether the "proviso" forms a qualification to the main clause, or creates an independent covenant capable of enforcement in its own right.[11] Careful consideration should be given to the exact status of the "proviso," which should then be located accordingly, either as a covenant, or as a sub-clause to which the main clause is made subject.

Paragraphing (6) Clarity can often be achieved, and ambiguity avoided,[12] by breaking down a clause into a number of paragraphs and even sub-paragraphs, provided a consistent scheme of indentation and numbering is used.

Schedules (7) The flow of the document as a whole can be improved by the suitable use of schedules. Lengthy and self-contained provisions, for example as to rent review, service charge, and the property and its appurtenant rights, are often placed in separate schedules.

Particulars clause (8) It may be helpful to collect together a number of important particulars[13] in a clause set out at the beginning of the lease. This technique can avoid the need to fill in such details being overlooked where the various items are scattered throughout the lease: it can also provide the parties with a summary of the most important details which is accessible at a glance.

---

[10] See, *e.g. Holicater Ltd v. Grandred Ltd* [1993] 1 EGLR 135 (use of the word "said").

[11] See *Great Northern Railway Co v. Harrison* (1852) 12 C.B. 576; *Adler v. Upper Grosvenor Street Investment Ltd* [1957] 1 W.L.R. 227.

[12] Particularly in the case of long lists of conditions or requirements—here paragraphing can avoid ambiguity as to whether the requirements are cumulative or alternative.

[13] For instance, names of parties, commencement date, term, rent, rent commencement date, review dates, redecoration dates, permitted user.

1–03 Length of leases

The advent of new technology, in particular the word processor, has made a significant impact upon drafting practice. Office precedents can be easily updated and adapted, and the reproduction of lengthy drafts becomes painless. The result has tended to be longer documents, and a modern commercial lease, together with its schedules, can easily run to 60 pages or more. However, criticism simply on the ground of length may be misplaced. A lease of 60 pages set out in an attractive and open-textured way, with appropriate paragraphing, spacing, and sideheadings, may be far more readable than a 30-page lease containing the same provisions closely typed and without breaks. Also, the length and sophistication of some provisions can be justified if the object **Unsuitable** is to avoid uncertainty or to counter difficulties demonstrated **provisions** by reported cases. What can, and should, be criticised is length caused by unnecessary verbosity or by the incorporation of unsuitable provisions. Precedents stored electronically have a tendency to accumulate further provisions over the years, rather like barnacles on the hull of a man-of-war. A provision may be entirely appropriate when added in the context of a particular transaction, but it should not necessarily always be applied thereafter. Discrimination in the use of precedents is vital in keeping documents as short as possible.

1–04 Standard forms

It is sometimes argued that the length and cost of commercial leases could be reduced by the adoption of standard forms. In the first edition of this book it was suggested that "the task of producing standard provisions capable of applying generally and of commanding universal acceptance would appear to be an impossible one. No standard form can hope to cover all the variations possible between different types of property, **Law Society's** lengths of term, etc. ...". In 1991 the Law Society introduced **forms** two standard forms of commercial lease (one for a whole building; the other for part of a building), drafted in modern language, evenly balanced between landlord and tenant, and commendably short. As anticipated in the first edition, these forms of lease appear to be little used in practice, perhaps because they are even-handed between the parties, and therefore do not sufficiently resemble the standard institutional lease traditionally produced by a landlord's solicitor, which is frequently intended (so far as permitted by the market at the time) to pass as much risk and expenditure as possible onto the tenant. A more rewarding path would appear to be the promulgation of model clauses, such as the **Model clauses** Law Society/R.I.C.S. rent review clause[14] which, although not universally adopted, can act as a valuable basis for negotiation and a yardstick as to what is generally reasonable.

[14] See para. 6–37 below.

1–05   Importance of lease provisions

Priorities

Lawyers working in the field of commercial leases need constantly to remind themselves that the actual terms of a lease are not always the decisive factor for their clients. Factors such as location, rent, rates, and building design may rank far higher in the scale of priorities. The role of the lawyer is to ensure that the client understands the legal position,[15] and to improve the client's legal position where possible: but in the final analysis the legal niceties may have to take second place to commercial reality.

1–06   Commercial Property Leases Code of Practice

Improve practice

Purely voluntary

Those involved in the negotiation of leases, including lawyers and others advising both landlords and tenants, should also be aware of the *Commercial Property Leases Code of Practice*, published on December 14, 1995.[16] The Code is intended, *inter alia*, to "improve practice in the business relationships between landlords, tenants and their advisers particularly when the grant of a lease is being negotiated and at rent review". This it seeks to achieve by setting out the key issues to be borne in mind by both landlord and tenant when negotiating a new lease, and by recommending a practical approach to be adopted by the parties during negotiations. The Code is purely voluntary in its application and has no legal force. There are no sanctions prescribed for those failing to comply with the Code, which inevitably prompts some scepticism as to its likely impact, although it is possible that the Code will be used as a means of gauging the reasonableness or otherwise of the parties' conduct, and may perhaps also be used by the court when considering the terms of a new lease pursuant to Part II of the Landlord and Tenant Act 1954.[17]

---

[15] On the distinction between clauses which a solicitor is under a duty to explain and those which the client can be expected to understand for himself, see *Aslan v. Clintons* (1984) 134 L.J. 584. The duty of a solicitor to explain unusual terms in the context of a review clause was considered by the Court of Appeal in *County Personnel (Employment Agency) Ltd v. Alan R. Pulver & Co* [1987] 1 W.L.R. 916.

[16] The Code (published by R.I.C.S. Books) was produced by a working party of representatives from 10 professional bodies involved in the property industry, representing owners and users of commercial property, and the legal and surveying professions. It came about as a consequence of an investigation by the Government in 1993 into certain aspects of rent review practice which were thought to be unfairly favouring landlords. The Government concluded that legislation was not required but that, if certain terms of commercial leases did not become more "flexible", legislation would be considered (statement of Tony Baldry of the Department of the Environment, July 19, 1994). The effect of the Code is to be reviewed after three years' operation, although quite how its effect (as distinguished from other pressures) is to be measured remains to be seen.

[17] See para. 16–46 below.

2 THE RULES OF PRIVITY OF CONTRACT

2–01 Introduction

This Chapter explains the rules governing the periods during which landlords, tenants and sureties are liable to one another, and the practical consequences arising out of these rules. In the first edition of this book, this entire subject was covered in just one page of the text, together with four footnotes. However on January 1, 1996, shortly before this second edition was published, the Landlord and Tenant (Covenants) Act 1995 came into force, and practitioners have had to learn a whole new set of rules. Confusingly, however, the Act is (with important exceptions) not retrospective in effect, and leases granted before January 1, 1996, and certain leases granted on or after that date, are subject to the old rules. Practitioners therefore need to keep in mind both sets of rules, and ensure that they are applying the appropriate set to the lease in question.

Abbreviations   In this book, and particularly in this Chapter, the following abbreviations are used:

"1995 Act"	Landlord and Tenant (Covenants) Act 1995.
"new tenancy"	A tenancy which is a "new tenancy" within the meaning of the 1995 Act. The meaning of this term is explained in para. 2–02 below.
"old tenancy"	A tenancy which is not a "new tenancy". This is not a term used in the 1995 Act, but it has come into general use by practitioners.
"AGA"	Authorised guarantee agreement (see para. 2–06 below).

2–02 Which rules apply?

There are three changes effected by the 1995 Act which apply equally to both old tenancies and new tenancies and these are explained below.[1] Otherwise the provisions of the 1995 Act apply only to new tenancies.

---

[1] See para. 2–12 below.

Meaning of "new tenancy"

The 1995 Act provides[2] that any lease granted on or after January 1, 1996 creates a new tenancy, other than in the following circumstances:

- A lease granted pursuant to an agreement for lease or order of the court[3] made before that date.[4]
- A lease granted pursuant to an option or a right of first refusal conferred before that date.[5] The date of the exercise of the right is not relevant.
- An overriding lease granted to a former tenant or his surety pursuant to section 19 of the 1995 Act in reversion to a lease which is an old tenancy (following the payment by such person of sums due under the terms of the old tenancy).[6]

A lease granted on or after January 1, 1996 by reason of an intended variation taking effect as a deemed surrender and regrant is expressly stated to be a new tenancy.[7]

Identifying a new tenancy

It is good practice to include in every lease granted on or after January 1, 1996 a clause stating whether or not the lease creates a new tenancy and, if not, the reason why not. This will ensure that in the future anyone reading the lease will know immediately whether it is the rules relating to old tenancies or the rules relating to new tenancies which apply to that lease.

2–03 Anti-avoidance provisions

The 1995 Act contains wide-ranging anti-avoidance provisions: any attempt to exclude, modify or otherwise frustrate the operation of any provision of the 1995 Act is void, as is any provision providing for the termination or surrender of the tenancy, or the imposition of any penalty or liability on the tenant, in the event of the operation of any provision of the 1995 Act.[8] It is immaterial whether the provision having this effect is contained in the lease or not (it might, for example, be contained in a licence to assign), and whether it is made before the creation of the tenancy.

Certain kinds of agreement are however expressly authorised and will not be invalidated by the anti-avoidance provisions. These are absolute or qualified prohibitions against assignment[9] and authorised guarantee agreements.[10]

---

[2] Section 1(3).
[3] Generally under Landlord and Tenant Act 1954, s.29.
[4] 1995 Act, s.1(3).
[5] 1995 Act, s.1(6) and (7).
[6] See para. 2–12 below.
[7] 1995 Act, s.1(5).
[8] 1995 Act, s.25(1).
[9] *ibid.*, s.25(2).
[10] *ibid.*, s.25(3), see para. 2–06 below.

2–04 The liability of the tenant

The original tenant

Old tenancies By reason of privity of contract, the original tenant remains liable under the covenants in the lease throughout the term, whether or not he is the tenant in occupation at the time of any default. Thus the original tenant runs the risk of default or breach by the immediate and any subsequent assignees.[11] But the tenant will not be liable for obligations created by variations to a lease after he

Variations

has assigned it, for variations to which he was not a party cannot retrospectively alter the relationship between the original landlord and the original tenant.[12] However, it is still possible for an original tenant to be liable for a rent which had been increased by a review subsequent to his assignment of the lease, or for a rent which is higher by reason of improvements carried out by a subsequent assignee, if on the construction of the lease the tenant had agreed to this.[13]

The tenant is therefore effectively in the position of a surety to the subsequent tenants, but it is not a surety relationship and the tenant has none of the means of escape available to a surety where the terms of the principal contract are varied.[14]

Continuation under 1954 Act

The original tenant will not be liable for a default arising where the lease has been assigned and the assignee is continuing in occupation under Part II of the Landlord and Tenant Act 1954,[15] nor will he be liable for interim rent under that Act.[16] However in each case it is open to the parties to extend the tenant's liability to include such obligations, and this is frequently encountered in practice.[17]

Disclaimer

Where the lease has not been assigned and is disclaimed, the tenant's liability is at an end.[18] However, where the lease has been assigned and a subsequent tenant's liquidator

---

[11] *Baynton v. Morgan* (1888) 22 Q.B.D. 74; *Thames Manufacturing Co Ltd v. Perrotts (Nichol & Peyton) Ltd* (1984) 50 P. & C.R. 1.

[12] *Friends' Provident Life Office v. British Railways Board* [1996] 1 All E.R. 336.

[13] *Centrovincial Estates plc v. Bulk Storage Ltd* (1983) 46 P. & C.R. 393; *GUS Property Management Ltd v. Texas Homecare Ltd* [1993] 27 E.G. 130; *Selous Street Properties Ltd v. Oronel Fabrics Ltd* (1984) 270 E.G. 643, 743 (as explained in *Friends' Provident Life Office v. British Railways Board* (n. 12 above).

[14] *Selous Street Properties Ltd v. Oronel Fabrics Ltd* (n. 13 above); see para. 3–15 below. Only three defences are available to the original tenant: that he has performed; that another person has performed; or that some operation of law, such as surrender, has put an end to the contractual obligations under the lease: see *Allied London Investments Ltd v. Hambro Life Assurance Ltd* (1985) 50 P. & C.R. 207; see also *Milverton Group Ltd v. Warner World Ltd* [1995] 32 E.G. 70. In *Deanplan Ltd v. Mahmoud* [1993] Ch. 151, the original tenant was held to have been released when the current tenant settled with the landlord, but that case was not followed in *MMC Investments Ltd v. Bossevain*, October 7, 1993, C.A. (unreported).

[15] *City of London Corporation v. Fell* [1993] Q.B. 589; for the Landlord and Tenant Act 1954 see para. 16–24 below.

[16] *Herbert Duncan Ltd v. Cluttons* [1993] Q.B. 589; for interim rent see para. 16–31 below.

[17] By the extension of the definition of "the term" to include any statutory period of continuation under the Landlord and Tenant Act 1954, and the definition of "rent" to include interim rent.

[18] *Hindcastle v. Barbara Attenborough Associates Ltd* [1996] 1 All E.R. 737. Any guarantor however remains liable: see para. 3–15 below.

disclaims the lease, the original tenant is still liable in spite of the disclaimer.[19] The landlord owes no duty to the original tenant, when granting consent to assignment, to ensure that the assignee is financially able to comply with the terms of the lease.[20]

Subsequent tenants A subsequent tenant under the lease is liable to his landlord during the time of his occupation, by virtue of the doctrine of privity of estate. However, liability under privity of estate lasts only so long as the tenant remains in the direct landlord and tenant relationship with the landlord. Accordingly, for old tenancies, it is normal practice for a landlord to require an assignee of a lease to enter into a direct covenant with him to observe the provisions of the lease during the residue of its term.[21] Such a direct covenant does not release the original tenant from his ongoing liability: the result is merely that the assignee as well as the original tenant will be liable for the duration of the term.[22] Where a lease is assigned several times during its term, the landlord may be able to pursue a number of people who were tenants successively, and their guarantors.

New safeguards for former tenants With effect from January 1, 1996, however, a landlord who wishes to pursue a party who is not the current tenant or the guarantor of the current tenant is not permitted to do so unless he has, within six months of the sum in question falling due, served notice in a prescribed form on that party.[23] Furthermore, a former tenant or guarantor will not be liable for sums which fall due as a result of a variation to the lease after its assignment.[24] Full details of these procedures are set out below.[25] The parties cannot contract out of these provisions.[26]

New tenancies The concepts of privity of contract and privity of estate have no place in new tenancies. The tenant is liable from the grant of the lease, or from its assignment to him, until he is released by virtue of the 1995 Act.[27]

---

[19] The original tenant remains liable as if the lease continues to exist, at least until the landlord takes any action—such as re-entering the premises—which demonstrates that he is no longer treating the original tenant as bound: *Hindcastle v. Barbara Attenborough Associates Ltd* [1996] 1 All E.R. 737 at 748 *per* Lord Nicholls. However, the original tenant will have no right to occupy the premises unless a vesting order is made by the court under the Insolvency Act 1986, s.181(2).

[20] *Norwich Union Life Insurance Society v. Low Profile Fashions Ltd* [1992] 1 EGLR 86.

[21] The direct covenant need not expressly specify that the assignee will be liable for the residue of the term: it is sufficient to refer to the lease, in which this is stated. *Estates Gazette Ltd v. Benjamin* [1995] 1 All E.R. 129. See para. 12–14 below.

[22] *J. Lyons & Co Ltd v. Knowles* [1943] 1 K.B. 366.

[23] 1995 Act, s.17.

[24] 1995 Act, s.18.

[25] See para. 2–12 below.

[26] See para. 2–03 above.

[27] 1995 Act, s.3(1), (2).

2–05 Release of the tenant

Old tenancies The tenant may be released from his

Surrender and regrant

obligations either expressly or by operation of law. Where a lease is varied to such an extent that it takes effect as a deemed surrender and regrant, the original tenant will no longer be liable under the original lease, as it has been surrendered.[28] Where a landlord grants a lease of premises to a new occupier where a former occupier is currently negotiating a surrender, it has been held that both leases cannot subsist at the same time, and the earlier of them must have been forfeited, so ending the liability of the first tenant.[29]

New tenancies A tenant is liable under the tenant's covenants in a lease while he is the tenant, but he is released automatically on an assignment of the whole of the premises comprised in the lease.[30] The tenant will also be released by implication on a deemed surrender and regrant, as explained in the paragraph above.

However, the tenant is not released automatically where the assignment is in breach of a covenant in the tenancy, or an

Excluded assignments

assignment by operation of law. In such a case (defined as an "excluded assignment"[31]), the tenant is not released on that assignment, but is released on the next following assignment which is not an excluded assignment. Until then, the tenant is jointly and severally liable with the assignee.[32]

2–06 Authorised guarantee agreements (AGAs)

Old tenancies There is no concept of an AGA for old tenancies.

New tenancies A landlord may require a tenant to act as

Lawfully implied condition

guarantor to his assignee, by means of an AGA.[33] The landlord may require this where the assignment cannot be effected without his consent, and he gives his consent subject to a condition (lawfully imposed) that the tenant is to enter into an AGA.[34] There are thought to be two circumstances where it may be lawful for the landlord to impose such a condition:

---

[28] *Friends' Provident Life Office v. British Railways Board* [1996] 1 All E.R. 336.
[29] *Redleaf Investments Ltd v. Talbot* [1995] BCC 1091.
[30] 1995 Act, s.5(2). Where only part of the premises are assigned, the tenant is released from the covenants to the extent that they relate to the part assigned: *ibid.*, s.5(3).
[31] *ibid.*, s.11(1).
[32] *ibid.*, s.13(1). He may also be required to enter into an AGA: see s.16(6).
[33] *ibid.*, s.16.
[34] *ibid.*, s.16(3).

- where the lease contains a provision that the tenant must provide an AGA before consent is given for an assignment.[35]
- where it is otherwise reasonable for the landlord to require an AGA.[36]

An AGA may not impose on the tenant a requirement to guarantee any person's liability other than the assignee, or impose upon him any liability after the assignee is released from his covenants by virtue of the 1995 Act.[37] To the extent that the AGA creates any liability in excess of that permitted, it is unenforceable.

Permitted obligations

The obligations which may be imposed by an AGA are limited by the 1995 Act.[38] An AGA may impose either primary or secondary liability, and it may require the guarantor to accept a new lease in the event of the current lease being disclaimed, so long as the new lease is for the residue of the original term, and imposes no more onerous covenants on the tenant than the disclaimed lease. The form of a typical AGA will not differ greatly from the standard forms of guarantee used by commercial property lawyers. The 1995 Act specifically provides that all the rules of law relating to guarantees will apply to an AGA.[39]

Where a tenant has guaranteed the obligations of his assignee under an AGA, the landlord cannot recover any sums from the tenant unless he has, within six months of the sum falling due, served notice in a prescribed form on him.[39a]

2–07 The liability of a guarantor

Old tenancies The duration of a guarantor's liability was a matter for agreement between the parties, but conventionally the liability of the guarantor was co-extensive with that of the tenant. Thus a guarantor at the start of the term would guarantee the obligations of the tenant for the time being throughout the term granted; similarly a guarantor of a subsequent assignee of the lease would guarantee the obligations of the tenant for the time being throughout the residue of the term granted.

Negotiated release

Guarantors were sometimes able to negotiate contractual arrangements by which they would be released on a subsequent assignment, either unconditionally, or if the covenant of the assignee was of a specified quality, or if a

---

[35] By section 22 of the 1995 Act, which amended section 19(1) of the Landlord and Tenant Act 1927, landlords and tenants may now agree conditions to be satisfied before consent to assignment need be granted: see para. 12–12 below for full details.

[36] See para. 12–13 below for a discussion of what a landlord is entitled to require on assignment generally.

[37] 1995 Act, s.16(4); a well-drafted AGA will provide for the tenant to remain liable until the assignee is released under the 1995 Act, rather than until the assignee himself assigns, to cover the possibility of the assignment by the assignee being an excluded assignment (see para. 2–05 above).

[38] *ibid.*, s.16(5).

[39] *ibid.*, s.16(8).

[39a] *ibid.*, s.17. See para. 2–12 below.

substitute guarantor was provided. A guarantor will also be released if the principal contract is varied without his consent, so as to make it likely that his liability is increased.[40]

A guarantor will also be released where the lease is surrendered by reason of a deemed surrender and regrant.[41] A guarantor will not be released on the lease being disclaimed.[41a]

Guarantors of former tenants

Since January 1, 1996, the landlord cannot recover sums from a person who guaranteed the obligations of a former tenant unless he has, within six months of the sum falling due, served notice in a prescribed form on that person.[41b] Furthermore, a former guarantor will not be liable for sums which fall due as a result of a variation to the lease after its assignment by the person whose liabilities were being guaranteed.[41c] Full details of these procedures are set out below.[41d] The parties cannot contract out of these provisions.[41e]

New tenancies   The 1995 Act provides that the liability of the guarantor cannot exceed that of the tenant; when the tenant is released from any obligations under the lease, the obligations of any guarantor are also released to the same

Release of guarantor

extent.[42] However, there is some doubt about the effect of the 1995 Act in this instance, and there is a school of thought which maintains that on a strict interpretation of section 24(2) it is still possible to take a covenant from a guarantor which will survive the release of each successive tenant. The alternative view is that such a covenant would be void by reason of the anti-avoidance provisions in section 25(1) of the 1995 Act. It is submitted that this second view is the one more likely to be adopted by the court.[43]

Guarantors and AGAs

The 1995 Act is also unclear as to whether the guarantor of an outgoing tenant can be called upon to enter into an AGA.[44] Again, there is a possibility that this would be void by reason of the anti-avoidance provisions in section 25(1).[45] If this view is correct, then it would no longer be advisable for a landlord to accept as a tenant a company with a poor covenant, relying instead on the substantial covenant of a guarantor. The reason for this is that, on assignment, the best that the landlord could achieve is an AGA in respect of the

---

[40] See para. 3–15 below.
[41] See para. 18–26 below.
[41a] See para. 3–15 below.
[41b] 1995 Act, s.17.
[41c] *ibid.*, s.18.
[41d] See para. 2–12 below.
[41e] See para. 2–03 above.
[42] 1995 Act, s.24(2).
[43] This second view was certainly the intention of the draftsman of the 1995 Act.
[44] See para. 2–06 above.
[45] The argument for this is that section 16, which validates an AGA, is in the nature of a limited exception to the fundamental rule laid down in section 5 and section 24(2) that a tenant and guarantor respectively should not be liable following assignment, and that the reference in section 16(1) is to the "tenant" alone, and not to any guarantor of the tenant. See R. Potterton and S. Cullen, "Must a Surety Guarantee an AGA?" [1996] 19 E.G. 118.

liability of the next assignee, given by the former tenant: the substantial covenant of the guarantor would no longer be available. For the time being, landlords are proposing to draft guarantee clauses in leases so that they include not just a guarantee of the tenant's covenants in the lease, but also the tenant's covenants in any AGA.[45a] Whether this will be effective is open to doubt. For absolute certainty, pending a decision by the court, the proposed guarantor should be required to accept the lease jointly with the tenant, but whether in practice this will be acceptable is not yet clear.

The guarantor will also be released in the same circumstances as under an old tenancy: express release; variation of the principal contract without his consent, so as to make it likely that his liability is increased[45b]; or where the lease is surrendered by reason of an implied surrender and regrant.[45c]

2–08 The liability of the landlord

Old tenancies Under the doctrine of privity of contract, the original landlord is liable to the original tenant throughout the term of the lease, even after the landlord has assigned his reversion. The original landlord is rarely liable under privity of contract to subsequent tenants, as it is not usual for a landlord to give a direct covenant to subsequent tenants, in the same way as subsequent tenants give such a covenant to the landlord in a licence to assign. Subsequent landlords virtually never give covenants to tenants. Where a landlord has given no covenant to a tenant, he is liable so long as he is landlord under the doctrine of privity of estate, but is not liable after he has assigned his interest.

Privity of contract

In practical terms the continuing liability of landlords seldom causes a problem, as it is rarely necessary for a tenant to enforce a covenant against a former landlord: he can usually obtain satisfaction, where necessary, from the current landlord. The theoretical risk remains, however, and the landlord's insurance covenant possibly causes the greatest concern.

New tenancies Under new tenancies a landlord is not automatically released from his covenants in the same way as a tenant is; instead he may apply to be released either on his assigning his interest[46] or when any subsequent landlord assigns his interest.[47] The landlord must give notice to each tenant in the prescribed form,[48] either before the assignment, or within four weeks after it. The tenant may either object to the release within four weeks of service of the landlord's

Landlord may apply for release

[45a] This is the approach recommended in A. Riley and P. Rogers, *Privity of Contract, a practitioner's guide*, (1995).

[45b] See para. 3–15 below.

[45c] See para. 18–26 below.

[46] 1995 Act, s.6.

[47] *ibid.*, s.7.

[48] Landlord and Tenant (Covenants) Act 1995 (Notices) Regulations 1995 (S.I. 1995 No. 2964) Form 3; Form 5 in the case of an assignment of part.

notice, or consent to it; if he fails to object within four weeks he is deemed to agree to the release. If the tenant objects to a release and fails to withdraw the objection, the landlord may apply to the county court for a declaration that it is reasonable for him to be released.[49] Where a release occurs, it is backdated to the time of the relevant assignment.[50]

Where a landlord is not released on assignment, he is permitted to apply to his tenant for release on each subsequent assignment of the reversion.[51] In practice, it is unlikely that a former landlord will hear of a subsequent assignment of the reversion in time to serve a further notice on the tenant.

Effect of release One of the effects of the landlord's being released is that he ceases to be entitled to the benefit of the tenant covenants,[52] which would include, for example, the right to demand a service charge. There is no mechanism within the 1995 Act for a landlord to stipulate that he wishes to be released in relation to either all the leases in a multi-occupied building, or none of them, and so there is a theoretical risk to a landlord that, following assignment of his interest, he might later be required by a tenant to comply with his covenants requiring expenditure, and yet be unable to recover the costs of doing so from certain tenants where a release has taken place. For this reason, landlords of multi-occupied buildings may prefer not to seek releases from their tenants on assignment. At the date of going to press, a market practice had not yet developed.

Under the rules relating to new tenancies, landlords other than the original landlord have a greater liability than under the rules relating to old tenancies. Under old tenancies, such landlords are liable only while they are the landlords, by reason of privity of estate. Under new tenancies, they are **Landlords trying** liable until they are released. It has been suggested that it **to limit their** might be possible for the lease to stipulate that the landlord **liability** will be liable only for as long as the reversionary interest is vested in him, but this is almost certainly void as a result of the anti-avoidance provisions.[53]

2–09 Effect of release of landlords and tenants

Old tenancies Where a party is released from a covenant, this is normally expressed not to affect any liability for any

---

[49] 1995 Act, s.8.
[50] *ibid.*, s.8(3).
[51] 1995 Act, s.7(2); the prescribed form is Form 4 (whole of premises) or Form 6 (part of premises).
[52] *ibid.*, s.6(2)(a), s.7(4).
[53] *ibid.*, s.25(1), see para. 2–03 above. See C. J. Mackenzie-Grieve, "Releasing the Landlord's Shackles", *Legal Times*, December 18, 1995, p. 19.

prior breaches of that covenant. Even where this is not expressed, it is normally implied.[54]

Party remains liable **New tenancies**   Where a party is released from a covenant by virtue of the 1995 Act, he remains liable for any breach of covenant that he committed before the release.[55] As a corollary, where a person ceases to be entitled to the benefit of a covenant, this does not affect any rights to sue for any breach of that covenant which occurred before that entitlement ceased.[56]

2–10   Rights of indemnity between successive tenants

Old tenancies   On an assignment of a lease for value, covenants of indemnity are implied by the assignee in favour of the assignor, that the assignee will observe and perform the covenants on the part of the tenant in the lease, and

Implied indemnity   indemnify the assignor in respect of any breach.[57] Even without the statutory indemnity, there is an implied indemnity under common law.[58]

Express indemnity   In practice it is conventional for express covenants of indemnity to be incorporated into the Deed of Assignment or Land Registry Transfer.[59]

A tenant cannot be compelled to enforce such an indemnity; so where T1 had assigned the lease to T2, who assigned it to T3, and T2 became insolvent, T1 could not compel the administrators of T2 to enforce the indemnity against T3.[60]

Indemnity now unnecessary   **New tenancies**   The statutory covenants of indemnity do not apply to assignments of new tenancies.[61] As the assignor ceases to be liable to the landlord on an assignment, no covenant of indemnity from the assignee is needed.

Exceptions   The two exceptions are where the assignor is entering into an authorised guarantee agreement[62] with the landlord, in respect of the assignee's obligations, or where the assignment is an excluded assignment.[63] In such a case, the assignor is

---

[54] *Blore v. Giulini* [1903] 1 K.B. 356. Possibly the inclusion of wording to the effect that the lease "is void and of no effect" could remove the right to sue for past breaches—*Porter v. Shephard* (1796) 6 Term. Rep. 665; *Stait v. Fenner* [1912] 2 Ch. 504—but the distinction has been doubted (see Woodfall §1–17.296, n. 54).

[55] 1995 Act, s.24(1)(a).

[56] *ibid.*, s.24(4).

[57] Law of Property Act 1925, s.77(1)(c) and (d); Land Registration Act 1925, s.24(1)(b).

[58] *Moule v. Garrett* (1872) L.R. 7 Ex. 101.

[59] See para. 18–18 below.

[60] *RPH v. Mirror Group (Holdings) Ltd* [1993] 13 E.G. 113 (this concerned the indemnity implied under s.24(1)(b) of the Land Registration Act 1925); similarly in *Stanhope Pension Trust Ltd v. Registrar of Companies* [1993] 2 EGLR 118 the Court refused to order a company to be restored to the register as this would prejudice assignees who had given indemnities.

[61] 1995 Act, s.30.

[62] See para. 2–06 above.

[63] See para. 2–05 above.

likely to require an indemnity from the assignee, and will have to take an express indemnity. Alternatively the assignor could rely upon the common law implied indemnity in *Moule v. Garrett*,[64] or ask the court to make an order for contribution in relation to the parties' joint liability.[65]

2–11 Assignments of part

The situation where part only of the property comprised in a lease is assigned is comparatively rare: most commercial leases will contain an absolute prohibition on assignments of part,[66] and it is usual in such cases to proceed by way of underlease.

The rules relating to the respective liability of the assignor and the assignee differ considerably between the assignment of part of an old tenancy and that of part of a new tenancy. This is too complex a topic to justify a lengthy explanation in this work.[67]

2–12 New safeguards for former tenants

The 1995 Act introduced three new provisions intended to reduce the burden on former tenants and their guarantors who retain liability. They all came into effect on January 1, 1996, and are effectively retrospective, applying both to new tenancies and to old tenancies.

Persons affected The new provisions will benefit a former tenant (and a guarantor of a former tenant, if such is possible) who is liable under an AGA,[68] and any person who remains liable under any tenancy. This includes both a former tenant and a former guarantor under an old tenancy, and a former tenant and a former guarantor under a new tenancy, where there has been no release following an excluded assignment.[69]

Notice of intention to recover from a former tenant A landlord is not entitled to recover certain sums from a former tenant or his guarantor unless he has, within six months of the sum becoming due, served notice on that person in the prescribed form.[70] If no notice is served, the sum cannot be recovered from that person.[71] This procedure does not affect the liability of the current tenant and any current guarantor. Landlords should bear in mind that service of such a notice on a former tenant (or his guarantor) will entitle that person

---

[64] (1872) L.R. 7 Ex. 101.
[65] By section 13, where in consequence of the 1995 Act two or more persons are bound by the same covenant, they are jointly and severally liable, and the court may provide for contribution between them in accordance with the Civil Liability (Contributions) Act 1978.
[66] See para. 12–07 below.
[67] See Woodfall §§1–16.134, *et seq.*
[68] See para. 2–06 above.
[69] See para. 2–05 above.
[70] Form 1 of the Landlord and Tenant (Covenants) Act 1995 (Notices) Regulations 1995 (S.I. 1995 No. 2964). See S. Elvidge and P. Williams, "Keeping tabs on former tenants", [1996] 24 E.G. 140.
[71] 1995 Act, s.17(2).

to settle the outstanding sums and then call for the grant to him of an overriding lease,[72] resulting in a new relationship between the landlord and the former tenant (or guarantor) and the loss of the covenant of the current tenant. In many cases the landlord is likely to have a difficult choice to make.[72a]

Fixed charges
These provisions apply only to any "fixed charge", defined as rent, service charge[73] and any amount payable under a covenant providing for the payment of a liquidated sum in the event of a failure to comply with it.[74] Specific provision is made for the position where the final amount due is unknown at the time of service of the notice: the landlord must inform the tenant in the initial notice that his liability may subsequently be determined to be for a greater amount, and a subsequent notice must be served within three months of the final sum being determined.[75] There is no sanction for serving a notice which refers to a sum which is not within the definition of "fixed charge" and in case of doubt the landlord would be wise to serve a notice to protect his position.[76]

Sums due on January 1, 1996
Where any sums falling within section 17 of the 1995 Act fell due before January 1, 1996, they were treated as falling due on January 1, 1996 and hence the landlord had six months from that date to serve a notice on those former tenants and their guarantors.[77] No notice needed to be served where proceedings for recovery of such sums had been instituted against a former tenant before January 1, 1996.[78]

Address for service
Section 23 of the Landlord and Tenant Act 1927 applies in relation to notices served under section 17.[79]

Variation of tenancy following assignment A former tenant, or his guarantor, is not liable to pay any amount under a lease to the extent that the amount is referable to a variation of the tenant's covenants in the lease made on or after January 1, 1996, and at a time after the former tenant had assigned the lease.[80] This provision applies only where the

Right to refuse variation
variation was one which the landlord had an absolute right to

---

[72] See below.

[72a] It will also require the landlord to maintain careful records of sums demanded from and paid by his tenants.

[73] Within the meaning of section 18 of the Landlord and Tenant Act 1985, and so including insurance premiums.

[74] 1995 Act, s.17(6).

[75] 1995 Act, s.17(4): the relevant prescribed form for the subsequent notice is Form 2 of the Landlord and Tenant (Covenants) Act 1995 (Notices) Regulations 1995 (S.I. 1995 No. 2964). It is arguable that this procedure is unnecessary in most cases, as leases typically provide that any such balancing payments are due as separate sums in their own right.

[76] But paragraph 7.2 of the *Commercial Property Leases Code of Practice* (see para. 1–06 above) contains a recommendation that the landlord should take reasonable steps to ensure that the current tenant does not accumulate excessive liabilities before notifying former tenants, and that all defaults of the current tenant should be notified to former tenants within the same timescale as is provided in section 17 of the 1995 Act.

[77] 1995 Act, s.17(5).

[78] *ibid.*

[79] See para. 16–25 below.

[80] 1995 Act, s.18.

refuse[81] and cannot be excluded by agreement between the parties.[82]

The importance of this new provision is lessened as a result of the Court of Appeal decision of *Friends' Provident Life Office v. British Railways Board*[83] which was made after the 1995 Act had been passed, but before it came into effect.

Former tenant's right to be granted an overriding lease It has always seemed unjust that a former tenant (or his guarantor) who paid sums due from the current tenant did not then become entitled to take over the tenancy once again.[84] The 1995 Act has instituted a new procedure to remedy this injustice. Where a former tenant (or his guarantor) has paid in full any sum mentioned in a notice under section 17,[85] he is entitled to call upon the landlord to grant him an overriding lease of the premises.[86] The overriding lease is to be granted for a term equal to the remainder of the term of the current lease, plus three days[86a] and with certain exceptions will contain the same terms as those in the current lease.[87] In this way the former tenant (or guarantor) will become the landlord of the current (defaulting) tenant, and, if that tenant defaults again, will be able to forfeit the current lease,[88] in order to retake possession, or to assign the premises with vacant possession. Stamp duty and land registry fees at the usual rates[89] will have to be paid on the overriding lease, which may be a significant expense; additionally the tenant will be responsible for the landlord's reasonable costs in connection with the grant[90] and will become responsible for complying with the landlord's covenants in the current lease. The former tenant will therefore have to consider carefully whether he wishes to take on these liabilities.

To seek the grant of an overriding lease, the former tenant must apply to the landlord in writing within a year of making

Side notes:

Former tenant may call for lease

Landlord's costs

---

[81] 1995 Act, s.18(4); or where the landlord would have had such a right but the lease has since been varied to remove it.

[82] See para. 2 03 above.

[83] [1996] 1 All ER 336, see para. 2–04 above. It had been thought that a tenant was liable under privity of contract for any variation to a lease after he had assigned it, but in *Friends' Provident* the court decided that this was a misunderstanding, and did not represent the law. By the date of that decision, section 18 of the 1995 Act, although not yet in force, had already been enacted. See Variations in leases—an escape route for tenants and guarantors (L. Harrison) [1995] 49 E.G. 117.

[84] See the Law Commission's Report No 174 (1988): *Landlord and Tenant Law—Privity of Contract and Estate* which formed the original proposals for the reform of the law of privity of contract which was ultimately achieved by the 1995 Act in a somewhat different manner. See also comments made in the preface to this second edition.

[85] See above.

[86] 1995 Act, s.19(1). For an explanation of the concept of the overriding lease (sometimes called a concurrent lease) see Woodfall §1–6.018.

[86a] Or where the landlord is himself a tenant, the longest period (less than three days) that will not wholly displace his reversion.

[87] 1995 Act, s.19(2).

[88] The default in paying the sum which was the subject of the section 17 notice cannot be used as the basis for forfeiture as by then that sum will have been paid by the former tenant, and will no longer be due.

[89] See para. 18–11 below.

[90] 1995 Act, s.19(6)(b).

the payment that entitles him to the lease, specifying that payment.[91] Any such request will need to be protected by registration as a land charge or as a notice or caution at H.M. Land Registry.[92] There may be more than one person entitled to call for an overriding lease. Priority is given to the first person to apply for such a lease.[93] Where the landlord receives two applications on the same day, preference is given to a former tenant over a guarantor, and as between former tenants, to the one whose liability commenced earlier.[94]

Order of priority

All overriding leases must state that they have been granted under section 19 of the 1995 Act, and also whether or not they are new tenancies.[95] Where a former tenant under a new tenancy exercises his right to claim an overriding lease, then that overriding lease is itself a new tenancy; conversely where the former tenant held under an old tenancy, the overriding lease is an old tenancy, despite being granted after January 1, 1996.[96]

Whether or not new tenancies

---

[91] *ibid.*, s.19(5).
[92] *ibid.*, s.20(6); a caution does not confer any priority: see para. 18–07.
[93] *ibid.*, s.19(7).
[94] *ibid.*, s.19(8).
[95] *ibid.*, s.20(2). For a lease which has to be registered at H.M. Land Registry the prescribed wording is contained in the Land Registration (Overriding Leases) Rules 1995 (S.I. 1995 No. 3154).
[96] *ibid.*, s.20(1).

3 THE PARTIES

3–01 Introduction

The names, addresses and descriptions of the parties to a lease should be stated in that part of the lease known as the premises.[1] Every lease must have a landlord and a tenant. A surety or guarantor is frequently required as a third party to a commercial lease. The particular points requiring care in relation to each party are considered in turn below.

THE LANDLORD

3–02 Generally

The landlord may be an individual or a number of individuals; a company or a corporation; trustees of a settlement or a charity; the Crown; or a local authority or development corporation. Analysis of the detailed rules as to the capacity to grant a lease of the different types of person is beyond the scope of this book, and the reader should turn to more detailed works for assistance in this regard.[2] What will be considered here are the cases where the landlord is an individual or number of individuals or a company.

3–03 Definition of landlord

A preliminary point to note is that leases have traditionally defined the landlord as including (where the context so admits) the landlord's successors in title or the person for the time being entitled to the immediate reversion. A distinction must however now be drawn between the definition of landlord, and its resulting implications, in old tenancies following enactment of the Landlord and Tenant (Covenants) Act 1995 (essentially those leases granted prior to January 1, 1996) and the position under new tenancies under the 1995 Act (essentially those granted on or after January 1, 1996).[3]

Old tenancies In the case of old tenancies, it could be argued that, so far as the covenants in the lease are concerned, it is unnecessary to widen the definition of the landlord to include successors in title, as this is already done **Touch and** by statute.[4] In any event, covenants which touch and concern **concern** the land will automatically run with the reversion under old

---

[1] This section also contains a description of the parcels, any exceptions and reservations, the operative words of demise, and any recitals: Woodfall, *Landlord and Tenant*, § 1–5.011.
[2] *e.g.* Woodfall, *Landlord and Tenant*, Vol. 1, Chap. 2.
[3] See paras. 2–01 and 2–02 above for detailed definitions of old tenancies and new tenancies.
[4] Law of Property Act 1925, ss.78, 79.

tenancies.[5] Where the definition of the landlord may have some effect is in relation to covenants which do not touch and concern the land; but in the light of conflicting decisions[6] the effect is unclear. Certainly it would seem that an extended definition of landlord will not allow a successor in title to rely on section 56 of the Law of Property Act 1925,[7] which can only operate where an instrument purports to grant to, or make a contract with, an identifiable person.[8] The real benefit of inserting such a definition in the lease is the avoidance of doubt where the word "landlord" is used in contexts such as giving approval to alterations or assignments, certifying service charges, serving notices, appointing experts, and the like.

New tenancies In the case of new tenancies, the benefit and burden of both landlord covenants and tenant covenants will be transmitted by virtue of section 3(1) of the Landlord and Tenant (Covenants) Act 1995, save for four exceptions. The exceptions are as follows:

Exceptions
(1) where the covenant is expressed to be personal to one person, in which case it will not be enforceable by or against any other person;[9]
(2) where the covenant has ceased to be binding on the assignor prior to the assignment;[10]
(3) where the covenant relates to any part of the premises which is not included in the assignment;[11]
(4) where the covenant would otherwise be unenforceable as a result of a failure to register it under the Land Registration Act 1925 or the Land Charges Act 1972.[12]

It follows that, in the case of a new tenancy, there is no need to define the landlord as including successors in title. Sections 78 and 79 of the Law of Property Act 1925 do not apply to new tenancies.[13]

---

[5] Law of Property Act 1925, s.142 and see, *e.g. Caerns Motor Services Ltd v. Texaco Ltd* [1995] 1 All E.R. 247 (a covenant which touches and concerns the land will run with the reversion even if there is no mention of successors in title, unless there are clear words to show that successors are to be excluded).

[6] See, *e.g. Re Distributors & Warehousing Ltd* [1986] 1 EGLR 90; *Coastplace v. Hartley* (1987) New L.J. 243. However, in the light of *P. & A. Swift Investments v. Combined English Stores Group plc* [1988] 2 All E.R. 885, it appears that *Re Distributors & Warehousing Ltd* can no longer be regarded as good law.

[7] Which provides that a person may take the benefit of a covenant, though not named as a party to the conveyance.

[8] *Re Distributors & Warehousing Ltd* [1986] 1 EGLR 90, 94 (but see n. 6 above); *Beswick v. Beswick* [1968] A.C. 58; *Pinemain Ltd v. Welbeck International Ltd* (1984) 272 E.G. 1166; *Sacher Investments Pty. Ltd v. Forma Stereo Consultants Pty. Ltd* [1976] 1 N.S.W.L.R. 5. But see *Shaw's Application* (1995) 68 P. & C. R. 591.

[9] 1995 Act, s.3(6)(a).

[10] 1995 Act, s.3(2)(a)(i), s.3(3)(a)(i).

[11] 1995 Act, s.3(2)(a)(ii), s.3(3)(a)(ii).

[12] 1995 Act, s.3(6)(b).

[13] 1995 Act, s.30(4).

3–04 Landlord a single individual

Death of landlord   Few problems will arise here. The landlord may die during the term of the lease, but the reversion will vest in his personal representatives who may then consent to the vesting of the reversion in anyone who is entitled to it, whether beneficially or in the capacity of trustee or personal representative.[14] If however the landlord dies intestate, or if either at the time of his death or at any time before probate is granted there is not or there ceases to be an executor with power to obtain probate, the reversion vests in the Public Trustee. In the former case the reversion vests in the Public Trustee until the grant of administration[15] and in the latter case until the grant of representation.[16] The personal representative may sue for arrears of rent due or in respect of breaches of covenant occurring both before and after the landlord's death.[17]

3–05 Landlord a number of individuals

Covenant joint or joint and several   The most important question here is whether the covenants in the lease are made with the landlords jointly, or jointly and severally. In most cases this will be resolved by section 81 of the Law of Property Act 1925, which provides that a covenant made with two or more persons after 1925 "shall be construed as being also made with both of them", *i.e.* jointly and severally.[18] The section may be excluded by a contrary intention expressed in the lease,[19] but in practice most modern leases will contain an express provision that any covenants made by more than one person are made jointly and severally.

3–06 Landlord a company

Group companies   Scope for confusion can occur where the landlord is one of a group of companies. Care should be taken to ensure that the company purporting to grant the lease is the company which actually owns the property; otherwise serious difficulties may occur.[20] Where the landlord is to undertake substantial obligations under the lease, such as the provision of services,

---

[14] Administration of Estates Act 1925, s.36.
[15] Administration of Estates Act 1925, s.9(1) (as substituted by the Law of Property (Miscellaneous Provisions) Act 1994, s.14).
[16] *ibid.*, s.9(2).
[17] See Woodfall, *Landlord and Tenant*, §§ 1–2.151, 1–2.152.
[18] Thus any of them can bring an action without joining the others; on death, rights pass to the estate of the deceased rather than the survivors; a defence against one does not operate against all; a release by one does not bind the others.
[19] Law of Property Act 1925, s.81(3).
[20] Though such difficulties may to some extent be overcome by tenancy by estoppel or by the equitable rules relating to agreements for leases: *Industrial Properties (Barton Hill) Ltd v. Associated Electrical Industries Ltd* [1977] Q.B. 580.

the tenant should ensure that the landlord named is a company of substance. If it is not, the tenant should consider requesting a guarantee for the landlord's obligations from a company of substance within the landlord's group. Such comfort is, however, rarely achieved in practice.

THE TENANT

3–07   Definition of tenant

As with the landlord, it has become common practice to define the tenant as including the successors in title, and sometimes the personal representatives,[21] of the tenant. A distinction must however now be drawn between the definition used in old and new tenancies.

Old tenancies   As mentioned above in relation to the landlord,[22] it may be doubtful whether such a definition actually confers any new rights or obligations, but it can help to avoid doubt in some parts of the lease, for example a provision allowing "the tenant" to serve notice to determine the lease, or a proviso for re-entry on the insolvency of "the tenant".

New tenancies   The definition of tenant need not include any reference to successors in title since the benefit and burden of the tenant's covenants will run by virtue of section 3(1) of the 1995 Act, subject to the exceptions set out above.[23]

Categories of tenant   The tenant of business premises is likely to be either a company or one or more individuals; in particular, where a number of individuals, it may be a partnership. Whatever the case, the landlord will face the risk that the tenant may cease to exist or become insolvent during the term. The second risk has become an increasingly sharp one in recent years. The problems posed by the different types of tenant and their possible solutions will be considered in turn.

3–08   Tenant an individual

Death of tenant   Leases of small business premises are frequently granted to single individuals. The risk is that the tenant may die or become insolvent, leaving outstanding obligations under the lease. On death, the lease will devolve upon the tenant's personal representatives, and this will not constitute a breach of the standard covenant against assignment.[24] The personal

---

[21] Whether this is necessary is debatable—it appears that successors in title can include involuntary assignees: *Re Wright* [1949] Ch. 729 (trustee in bankruptcy).

[22] See para. 3–03 above.

[23] See para. 3–03 above.

[24] *Crusoe d. Blencowe v. Bugby* (1771) 3 Wils. K.B. 234, *Seers v. Hind* (1791) 1 Ves. Jun. 294.

representatives are potentially liable to the landlord in two capacities: as representatives of the tenant and personally as assignees of the term. In the former capacity they are only liable to the extent of the deceased's assets, and the landlord is not entitled to any priority over other creditors.[25] It appears that the personal representatives will only be personally liable as assignees where they enter upon the premises, by taking possession or some equivalent act.[26] Even in cases of personal liability, the personal representative is entitled to limit his liability for rent (but not for other obligations under the lease) to the actual yearly value of the premises,[27] which may be important where the passing rent of the premises is above the market rent.

Effect on covenants

Old tenancies Where the deceased was the original tenant, the tenant's estate will remain liable on the covenants throughout the term.[28] The landlord can be more vulnerable where the deceased was an assignee of the lease, rather than the original tenant.[29] There, the liability of the estate for any future breaches can be discharged by an assignment of the lease, even to a pauper.[30] Whilst the usual clause against assignment would prevent an assignment proper, it may not prevent an assent or assignment giving effect to the terms of the will or the intestacy rules, to a beneficiary who might be a man of straw.[31] Somewhat strangely, modern leases do not seem to guard against this risk, apart from the usual surety provisions or the prohibition in the alienation covenant of any parting with possession of the demised premises, though it appears that there are a number of ways in which they might do so. The assignment clause could be extended to cover an assent or assignment by the personal representatives,[32] though in order to be fair to the tenant it would need to be a qualified rather than an absolute covenant. There could be a requirement that the personal representatives offer to surrender the lease, though this could lead to complications under the Landlord and Tenant Act 1954.[33]

---

[25] Administration of Estates Act 1925, s.34, Sched. 1, Pt. I; *Shirreff v. Hastings* (1877) 6 Ch.D. 610.

[26] *e.g* paying rent due and accruing due after the death of the tenant: *Rendall v. Andreae* (1892) 61 L.J.Q.B. 630; *Youngmin v. Heath* [1974] 1 W.L.R. 135 at 137; *Re Owers* [1941] Ch. 389 at 390.

[27] *Rubery v. Stevens* (1832) 4 B. & Ad. 241; *Hornidge v. Wilson* (1840) 11 Ad. & El. 645; *Re Bowes Earl of Strathmore v. Vane* (1888) 37 Ch.D. 128.

[28] See para. 2–04 above. The statutory procedure of the Trustee Act 1925, s.26, which allows administration of the estate to proceed in these circumstances, does not prejudice the rights of the landlord: s.26(2).

[29] Unless a direct covenant relating to compliance with the tenant's covenants throughout the residue of the term was given by the deceased on taking the assignment. See para. 2–04 above and para. 12–14 below.

[30] *Pitcher v. Tovey* (1692) 4 Mod. 71. Indeed, the duty of the personal representative is to assign as soon as possible: *Rowley v. Adams* (1839) 4 Myl. & Cr. 534.

[31] *Fox v. Swann* (1655) Sty. 482; *Crusoe d. Blencowe v. Bugby* (1771) 3 Wils. 234; *Doe d. Goodbehere v. Bevan* (1815) 3 M. & S. 353. But *cf.* (1963) 27 Conv. (N.S.) 159 (D. G. Barnsley) suggesting that assent is a breach and will certainly breach a covenant against parting with possession.

[32] *Parry v. Harbert* (1539) 1 Dyer. 45b; *Lord Windsor v. Burry* (1582) 1 Dyer 45b.

[33] See para. 12–15 below.

New tenancies Where the tenancy is a new tenancy, the tenant's estate will remain liable until an assignment of the lease which is not an excluded assignment.[34] It seems that an assent or assignment by personal representatives to a beneficiary under a will or a person entitled on intestacy will not be an excluded assignment unless it constitutes a breach of a covenant in the lease, which (as mentioned above) is not usually the case.

Bankruptcy of tenant The bankruptcy of the tenant has the effect of vesting the lease as part of the bankrupt's estate in the trustee in bankruptcy.[35] As with death, a covenant against assignment will not be broken by such an involuntary vesting.[36] Essentially, the choice facing the trustee in bankruptcy is between disposing of the lease, or disclaiming it. If he chooses to dispose of it, he will be bound by a covenant in the lease restricting assignment.[37] Disclaimer is provided for by sections 315 to 321 of the Insolvency Act 1986.[38]

Disclaimer Onerous property as defined by the 1986 Act may be disclaimed by the trustee giving the prescribed notice.[39] The effect of disclaimer is to determine the lease where the only person interested in the lease is the original tenant; but where the bankrupt is an assignee of the lease, disclaimer will not release the original tenant from liability.[40] The landlord can obtain some measure of protection against bankruptcy of the tenant by the combination of a covenant against assignment, a proviso for re-entry extending to bankruptcy orders[41] and other acts of individual insolvency under the 1986 Act,[42] and the statutory right to prove for loss or damage as a bankruptcy debt if injured by disclaimer.[43]

3–09 Joint tenants

Joint or joint and several liability Where two or more persons hold a lease as joint tenants, the death of one will leave the estate vested in the survivor or survivors. However, the landlord will no doubt wish to ensure that he can sue the estate of the deceased for breaches of covenant, as well as the survivor. At common law, this certainly used to be impossible, since the liability of a joint debtor passed on his death to the surviving joint debtors.[44] It is arguable that this rule has now been abrogated, either by

[34] 1995 Act, s.11(2). See also para. 2–05 above.
[35] Insolvency Act 1986, s.306. This would fall within the expression "excluded assignment": see para. 2–05 above.
[36] *Re Riggs, ex p. Lovell* [1901] 2 K.B. 16.
[37] See *Re Wright* [1949] Ch. 729 (a case under the Bankruptcy Act 1912).
[38] See also Insolvency Rules 1986 (S.I. 1986 No. 1925) Chap. 14.
[39] s.315(1). On what constitute onerous covenants, see *Eyre v. Hall* [1986] 2 EGLR 95. See also *M.E.P.C. plc v. Scottish Amicable Life Assurance Society; Neville Richard Eckley (Third Party)* [1993] 36 E.G. 133.
[40] *Hindcastle Ltd v. Barbara Attenborough Associates Ltd* [1996] 1 All E.R. 737. See also para. 3–15 below.
[41] Insolvency Act 1986, s.264(2).
[42] Insolvency Act 1986, ss.252(1) (interim order), 253(1) (voluntary arrangement), 273(2) (appointment of insolvency practitioner).
[43] Insolvency Act 1986, s.315(5).
[44] *Cabell v. Vaughan* (1669) 1 Wms. Saund. 288.

the prevalence of equity, or by statute.[45] However, any sensible landlord will put the matter beyond doubt by providing that liability of the tenants is joint and several, which is commonly done in practice.[46]

Bankruptcy Where one joint tenant becomes bankrupt and his trustee in bankruptcy wishes to disclaim his interest, it should be noted that under certain circumstances the court has power to vest the interest of the bankrupt in any person who is liable (whether alone or jointly with the bankrupt) to perform the lessee's covenants in the lease.[47]

3–10 Partnerships

Since a lease may not be granted to more than four persons as tenants,[48] in many cases it will not be possible for all the members of a partnership to be the tenants. In that case the partners holding the lease will do so for the purposes and benefit of the partnership,[49] provided that the lease was acquired as partnership property.[50]

Who should hold lease It is probably to the advantage of the partnership to have more than one partner holding the lease. Should a single partner holding the lease die, arrangements would have to be made to vest the lease in another partner, which might well require the consent of the landlord; whereas if a number of partners hold the lease as joint tenants, the doctrine of survivorship will operate upon the death of one of them. Furthermore, having the lease held jointly by two or more persons will bring into play the provisions of section 41A of the Landlord and Tenant Act 1954, which can considerably simplify the service of notices and other procedures under Part II of that Act.[51] A joint tenancy can also provide a degree of protection against a single tenant behaving irrationally or maliciously, *e.g.* refusing to reply to a section 25 notice served by the landlord.[52]

The main concern of the landlord will probably be to gain adequate rights against all members of the partnership, not merely those holding the lease. To some extent this is

---

[45] G.H. Treitel, *The Law of Contract* (9th ed., 1995) pp. 615, 616.

[46] This also has the advantage that the landlord can sue one of the tenants without having to join all the others as parties.

[47] Insolvency Act 1986, ss.320, 321(3).

[48] Law of Property Act 1925, s.34(2).

[49] Partnership Act 1890, s.20(1).

[50] See *Gian Singh & Co. v. Nahar* [1965] 1 W.L.R. 412.

[51] *e.g.* dispensing with the need for retired partners to be parties to any application for a new tenancy.

[52] See *Harris v. Black* (1983) 46 P. & C.R. 366—there is jurisdiction to compel a recalcitrant partner to take the necessary steps, but the court has a discretion to refuse relief. But contrast the position in relation to periodic joint tenancies: *Hammersmith and Fulham L.B.C. v. Monk* [1992] 1 A.C. 478 (held that in the absence of an express provision to the contrary a periodic joint tenancy is determinable by notice to quit given by one tenant without the consent of the other); *Crawley B.C. v. Ure* [1995] 3 W.L.R. 95 (held that consultation was not required before one of two joint tenants gave notice of her intention to quit).

Liability of partners

achieved by section 9 of the Partnership Act 1890, which provides that every partner is jointly liable for all debts and obligations of the firm incurred whilst a partner; and that the estate of each partner is severally liable for such debts and obligations. However, it may be preferable from all points of view for all partners to be made parties to the lease where practicable, with those who are not tenants being made sureties. The landlord can then expressly make all partners jointly and severally liable.

Changes in partnership

The partners will wish to avoid any difficulty with the landlord when the composition of the partnership changes. A covenant against assignment applies to assignments to the tenant's partners,[53] but the admission of new partners will not necessarily constitute an assignment.[54] It has been held that a covenant against parting with possession does not prevent one joint tenant giving up sole possession to another,[55] but it seems that difficulties could occur under such a covenant if possession were given up to partners who were not entitled to possession under the lease.[56] A covenant allowing only personal occupation by the tenant could have similarly disastrous effects upon death, retirement, or other partnership changes.[57] Therefore, the provisions relating to assignment and user need to be scrutinised carefully, and an attempt should be made to negotiate some relaxation to allow partnership changes to proceed without difficulty.

3–11 Companies

Liquidation and disclaimer

Like a trustee in bankruptcy, the liquidator of a company may disclaim a lease.[58] Alternatively, the liquidator may assign the lease, but in doing so he will be subject to any covenant against assignment in the lease.[59] The proviso for re-entry will usually include the liquidation of a tenant company among the conditions upon which it becomes operative, thereby providing an additional safeguard for the landlord.[60]

Changes in control of company

A rather different problem which can face the landlord where the tenant is a company is the possibility of prejudicial changes in the control of the company. For example, the success of a small company may be largely dependent upon the efforts of one man, who may cease to be a shareholder or director; or an unprofitable company may be jettisoned from

---

[53] *Varley v. Coppard* (1872) L.R. 7 C.P. 505; *Langton v. Henson* (1905) 92 L.T. 805.

[54] *Gian Singh & Co. v. Nahar* [1965] 1 W.L.R. 412—the other partners could occupy as beneficiaries, licensees, or have no rights at all; see also *Lord Hodson v. Cashmore* (1972) 226 E.G. 1203.

[55] *Corporation of Bristol v. Westcott* (1879) 12 Ch.D. 461.

[56] The danger will be greater if the covenant prohibits sharing possession.

[57] See *Lord Hodson v. Cashmore* (1972) 226 E.G. 1203.

[58] Insolvency Act 1986, ss.178–182; also Insolvency Rules 1986 (S.I. 1986 No. 1925) Chap. 15.

[59] *Re Farrow's Bank Ltd* [1921] 2 Ch. 164.

[60] But the tenant should be aware that unless qualified, such a proviso will extend to voluntary liquidation for the purposes of corporate reconstruction: *Horsey Estate Ltd v. Steiger* [1899] 2 Q.B. 79; *Fryer v. Ewart* [1902] A.C. 187.

the group of which it forms part. Various stratagems can be devised to meet such risks, *e.g.* providing that change of control of the company shall be deemed an assignment of the lease, or taking additional guarantees which are expressed to operate upon such a sale of shares. In practice, however, such provisions are rarely seen.

Company number   It is good practice to include the company's registered number as well as its name in the lease, in case of a subsequent change of name.

THE SURETY

3–12 Reason for surety

The risks posed to a landlord by the financial failure of an individual or corporate tenant have been outlined above. It is now standard practice, where there is any doubt as to the tenant's covenant strength, to require a tenant to provide one or more sureties to guarantee performance of the tenant's covenants and obligations and to indemnify the landlord in the event of breach.

However, there are dangers in adopting this approach in relation to a tenancy which is a "new tenancy" under the Landlord and Tenant (Covenants) Act 1995. The reason for this is that it is currently uncertain whether it is permissible for a surety of a tenant also to guarantee the obligations of that tenant under an authorised guarantee agreement. A **Risk of losing benefit of guarantee** landlord who grants a lease after January 1, 1996 to an insubstantial tenant, coupled with a guarantee from a more substantial person, is at risk of losing the benefit of the guarantee as soon as the tenant assigns the lease.[60a] A possible solution is for the landlord to require the proposed surety to enter into the lease jointly with the tenant, so that both parties would enter into an authorised guarantee agreement on an assignment of the lease. However, this course may not be acceptable to the proposed surety and, even if it is, it seems that the anti-avoidance provisions of the 1995 Act prevent the landlord taking a guarantee which will subsist beyond the second assignment of the lease.[60b]

3–13 Guarantee or indemnity

It is important to make the extent of a surety's obligation clear. A guarantee is essentially a contractual promise that the tenant will perform his obligations under the lease: thus the guarantor's obligation is to see to it that the tenant performs.[61] Default by the tenant will place the guarantor in

---

[60a] This issue is considered in greater detail in para. 2–07 above.
[60b] *i.e.* a guarantee of the lease until the first assignment, and a guarantee of the authorised guarantee agreement—if this is permitted at all—until the second assignment: see para. 2–07 above.
[61] See *Moschi v. Lep Air Services Ltd* [1973] A.C. 331 at 348.

Tenant's liability

breach of his contractual obligations and give rise to an obligation to pay damages.[62] What is important is that the liability of the guarantor is dependent upon the liability and default of the tenant.[63] Such an obligation is conceptually distinct from an indemnity, in which the surety agrees to make good the landlord's loss as an obligation independent of any default by the tenant.[64] Whether the obligation is a guarantee or an indemnity will be a question of construction, depending on the words used.[65]

Traditionally, the obligation of a surety in a lease has two limbs: a covenant that the tenant will pay the rent and perform the other covenants, and a covenant that the surety will make good the landlord's loss if he does not. Taken overall, this looks like a covenant of guarantee, and it has been judicially suggested that "an indemnity is hardly an appropriate arrangement in the circumstances of a lease, where the normal arrangement is that of a guarantee."[66]

Primary liability

It is submitted that the question of whether the surety has undertaken primary liability can only be answered by reference to the actual words used.[67] It is clear that as a matter of law a lease may provide expressly that the surety is to be jointly and severally liable with the tenant and is to be considered a principal as if named as tenant in the lease[68] and this is commonly found in modern commercial leases. The surety should consider carefully whether such provisions are appropriate. For one thing, such primary liability may not be appropriate in the case of obligations such as repair, user and compliance with statutory requirements, where the surety is not in a position to perform these obligations himself. Where the surety is capable of exercising control over the tenant, for example, where the tenant is a wholly-owned subsidiary of the surety or control is exercisable by virtue of the relationship of the companies to one another in the group, this concern can probably be overcome, although even here the surety must consider its liability should the companies cease to be within the same group, or when the lease is assigned.[69] Secondly, primary liability will preclude the defences usually available to a guarantor, which are considered below. Finally, if assuming primary liability for obligations such as rent, the surety will need to ensure that he has the same safeguards and defences

Group companies

---

[62] *ibid.*, at 351, 357, 359.
[63] *Halsbury's Laws of England* (4th ed.) Vol. 20, paras. 101, 108. For the application of this principle see *Associated Dairies Ltd v. Pierce* (1982) 265 E.G. 127 at 129.
[64] *Halsbury's Laws of England* (4th ed.) Vol. 20, para. 305; *Guild & Co. v. Conrad* [1894] 2 Q.B. 885 at 896.
[65] See, *e.g. Western Credit Ltd v. Alberry* [1964] 1 W.L.R. 945; *Stadium Finance Co. Ltd v. Helm* (1965) 109 S.J. 471; *Goulston Discount Co. Ltd v. Clark* [1967] 2 Q.B. 493. A guarantee can itself take various forms: see *Moschi v. Lep Air Services Ltd* [1973] A.C. 331 at 344–345.
[66] *Associated Dairies Ltd v. Pierce* (1981) 43 P. & C.R. 208 at 215, Judge Stabb Q.C. (affirmed on other grounds: see n. 67 below).
[67] *Associated Dairies Ltd v. Pierce* (1982) 265 E.G. 127, where the Court of Appeal found that the surety's liability was primary—the covenant was that the lessee *or the surety* would pay the rent and perform the covenants.
[68] See, *e.g. Hastings Corporation v. Letton* [1908] 1 K.B. 378.
[69] See para. 2–04 above.

as are available to the tenant, for example the benefit of a suspension of rent clause.

3–14 Advising the sureties

Directors as sureties

The practice of requiring sureties can create difficulties for the solicitor advising the tenant, where that solicitor is also expected to advise the sureties. For example, a solicitor may be instructed to act on behalf of company X in connection with a lease which that company is proposing to take. The solicitor may receive his instructions from, and conduct his correspondence with A, a director of X. The landlord may require not only A, but also B and C, two other directors of X, to execute the lease as sureties. In such circumstances it may not be adequate simply to report on the terms of the lease to A. There is the risk that B and C, should they suffer liability as sureties, might allege negligence against the solicitor for failure to advise them of the effect of the surety provisions.[70] There is the risk that A might misrepresent the effect of the surety provisions to B and C, either intentionally or inadvertently.[71] If the solicitor does advise B and C, there still remains the question of conflict of interest, and whether B and C should receive independent advice: the interest of the tenant company may diverge from the interests of those standing surety.[72] All that can be said is that the solicitor should be alert to such risks and should ensure that the scope of his retainer is as clear as possible.

The law of guarantors and sureties can, when combined with the law of landlord and tenant, provide many pitfalls both for the landlord and for the surety. Some of these are considered below.

3–15 Suretyship provisions from the point of view of the landlord

Construction

The first matter of which the landlord should be aware is that such provisions will be construed strictly against the landlord in the event of ambiguity:

> "The claim as against a surety is *strictissimi juris*, and it is incumbent on the plaintiff to show that the terms of the guarantee have been strictly complied with."[73]

---

[70] In *Cornish v. Midland Bank plc* [1985] 3 All E.R. 513, a creditor who gave wrong advice to the guarantor of a mortgage was held to owe a duty of care.

[71] This might have the effect of vitiating the guarantee: see *Kingsnorth Trust Ltd v. Bell* [1986] 1 W.L.R. 119; *Coldunell Ltd v. Gallon* [1986] 2 W.L.R. 466. See also *Midland Bank plc v. Shephard* [1988] 3 All E.R. 17; *Barclays Bank plc v. O'Brien* [1993] 4 All E.R. 417; *C.I.B.C. Mortgages plc v. Pitt* [1993] 4 All E.R. 433; *Massey v. Midland Bank plc* [1995] 1 All E.R. 929; *TSB Bank plc v. Camfield* [1995] 1 All E.R. 951.

[72] Though the risk is less where the sureties are actively involved in the running of the company.

[73] *Bacon v. Chesney* (1816) 1 Stark. 192 at 193, *per* Lord Ellenborough.

However, it has more recently been stated that this rule of construction is "very much a matter of last resort". Words used in a surety covenant must be fairly construed in accordance with their proper meaning and in this regard the surety is in no more favourable position than any other contracting party.[74]

A covenant by the surety which is construed as extending only to the contractual term of the lease will afford the landlord no help when the tenant holds over under the Landlord and Tenant Act 1954.[75] The covenant should therefore be extended beyond the contractual term by the use of words such as "or any statutory continuation thereof".[76]

Extension to holding over

Variation of lease   On general principles, any change in the principal contract to which the surety does not consent and which will prejudice the surety will have the effect of discharging the surety from liability. So, for example, the surety of a lease might be released by a surrender of part of the premises,[77] or by an agreement to allow structural alterations to the premises,[78] or by an alteration in the user clause[79] or by an agreed increase in rent, but probably not if made under a rent review clause embodied in a lease, since such a change would be in accordance with, and contemplated by, the terms of the principal contract. Similarly, a surety may be discharged by any act of indulgence by the creditor to the debtor, made or given without the surety's assent: even where beneficial to the surety.[80] A repudiatory breach of the principal contract by the creditor may have the same effect, if accepted by the debtor.[81] The landlord should guard against these risks by providing that the surety is not to be released by any act, neglect, forbearance[82] or delay on the part of the landlord, nor by the landlord's refusal to accept rent from the tenant in circumstances where the landlord's right of entry has become exercisable (so as to

Surety not to be released

---

[74] *Johnsey Estates Ltd v. Webb* [1990] 19 E.G. 84 *per* Millett J. But see *West Horndon Industrial Park Ltd v. Phoenix Timber Group plc* [1995] 20 E.G. 137 (where it was held that ambiguities in the surety's covenant should be resolved in favour of the surety).

[75] *Junction Estates Ltd v. Cope* (1974) 27 P. & C.R. 482; *A. Plesser & Co. Ltd v. Davis* (1983) 267 E.G. 1039. But the landlord may have a remedy against the surety if the tenant holds over unlawfully, since the surety will be liable to guarantee performance of the covenant to deliver up possession: *Associated Dairies Ltd v. Pierce* (1982) 265 E.G. 127.

[76] Of course this greatly increases the risks for the surety, giving rise to indeterminate liability. The surety might attempt to persuade the landlord to rely on his right to call for a surety on the grant of any new lease: see *Cairnplace Ltd v. C.B.L. (Property Investment) Co. Ltd* [1984] 1 W.L.R. 696. Alternatively the term itself should be described as including any statutory continuation: see para. 5–01 below.

[77] *Holme v. Brunskill* (1877) 3 Q.B.D. 495.

[78] *Selous Street Properties Ltd v. Oronel Fabrics Ltd* (1984) 270 E.G. 643.

[79] *Howard de Walden Settled Estates Ltd v. The Pasta Place Ltd* [1995] 22 E.G. 143; *West Horndon Industrial Park Ltd v. Phoenix Timber Group plc* [1995] 20 E.G. 137.

[80] *Polak v. Everett* (1876) 1 Q.B.D. 669.

[81] *National Westminster Bank plc v. Riley* [1986] BCLC 268. On ordinary principles, covenants in leases are independent, so that compliance by the landlord is not a prerequisite to enforcement by him.

[82] See *Selous Street Properties Ltd v. Oronel Fabrics Ltd* (1984) 270 E.G. 643 at 747 for discussion as to the possible meanings of the different words.

allow the landlord to avoid waiver of a breach of covenant), nor by any variation of the lease,[83] nor by anything other than an express release given under seal by the landlord. To avoid argument over rent reviews it might also be prudent to provide that the surety is not to be absolved by any irregularity in operating the review procedures and that the surety is to join in signing each memorandum of the reviewed rent.[84]

Surety of a former tenant   The position of the surety of a former tenant under both old and new tenancies is altered by the 1995 Act.[85] Where a lease is varied following an assignment by the tenant whose obligations the surety is guaranteeing, and the variation does not serve to discharge the surety from liability, the surety will not be liable to pay any amount under the lease to the extent that it relates to that variation.[86] The effect of the 1995 Act is limited however by the recent decision in *Friends' Provident Life Office v. British Railways Board*[87] in which it was held that a tenant could not be held liable as a result of a variation in the terms of the lease which was effected after the assignment of the lease and which was not contemplated by the original lease. It follows therefore that the position of the surety cannot be prejudiced in these circumstances.[88]

Liability outside terms of leases   The usual surety provision provides a guarantee of the tenant's obligations under the lease. Such a guarantee would probably not be construed as applying to other types of liability, such as torts committed by the tenant.[89] To avoid any doubt, the guarantee should be extended to cover expressly sums due from the tenant under any compromise made between the landlord and tenant, and sums payable by the tenant as a condition of relief against forfeiture.

Death or insolvency of surety   The landlord should also anticipate the death, insolvency or liquidation of the surety. The most sensible provision is one requiring the tenant to notify the landlord of any such event within a stipulated

---

[83] See *West Horndon Industrial Park Ltd v. Phoenix Timber Group plc* [1995] 20 E.G. 137 (where the words "or any act or thing whereby but for this provision the Guarantor would have been released" were insufficient).

[84] The problems posed by rent reviews are discussed more fully in para. 3–16 below.

[85] s.18(3).

[86] See para. 2–12 above. The variation must take place on or after January 1, 1996, and must be one which the landlord had an absolute right to refuse.

[87] [1996] 1 All E.R. 336.

[88] This appears to have been the rationale for the decision in *Metropolitan Properties Co. (Regis) Ltd v. Bartholomew* [1996] 11 E.G. 134 (decided shortly after the *Friends' Provident* case) where the landlord agreed a concession with the assignee of the lease. This was held not to release the guarantors of the assignor, as the liability of the assignor—and hence the liability of the guarantors—was unaffected by the concession, which took effect from the date of the assignment.

[89] *Associated Dairies Ltd v. Pierce* (1981) 43 P. & C.R. 208 at 216; but, *cf.* the approach of the Court of Appeal at (1982) 265 E.G. 127.

period, and, at the landlord's request, to provide an acceptable substitute. The temptation to require the provision of a substitute within a very short period should be avoided, since failure to do so will constitute a once-and-for-all breach, which the landlord may easily waive.

Disclaimer Another area requiring some foresight is the possibility of the lease being disclaimed.[90] Prior to the House of Lords's decision in *Hindcastle v. Barbara Attenborough Associates Ltd*,[91] there existed a fundamental inconsistency in the law relating to a surety's liability following disclaimer of a

Earlier conflicting decisions lease. This arose out of the conflicting, and arguably irreconcilable, decisions in *Hill v. East & West India Dock Company*[92] and *Stacey v. Hill*.[93] The effect had been that on disclaimer of a lease which was still vested in the original tenant, the liability of the surety was terminated along with that of the original tenant; however where the lease had been assigned prior to disclaimer, the liability of the original tenant, and hence of any surety for the original tenant, had remained. In *Hindcastle* the House of Lords overruled *Stacey v. Hill*, but nevertheless ruled that the lease was determined by the disclaimer. Accordingly the surety, whether of the original tenant or any subsequent tenant, remains liable as if the lease continues to exist, at least until the landlord takes any action (such as re-entering the premises) which demonstrates that he is no longer treating the surety as bound.[93a] However, the surety will have no right to occupy the premises unless a vesting order is made by the court.[93b]

Covenant to take a new lease As a result of the now-overruled decision of *Stacey v. Hill*, under which the surety of a disclaimed lease was released, it is common to find—in addition to the guarantee—a covenant by the surety to take a new lease for the unexpired residue of and on the same terms as the original lease, if required to do so by the landlord within a specified period (frequently three months) from disclaimer.[94] As a result of *Hindcastle* this appears no longer to be strictly necessary, but still has advantages.[94a] A number of important points should be borne in mind by the landlord in relation to this. It is important from the landlord's point of view to provide that the new lease is to take effect from the date of disclaimer, as opposed to the

---

[90] See paras. 3–08 and 3–11 above.
[91] [1996] 1 All E.R. 737.
[92] (1884) 9 App. Cas. 448.
[93] [1901] 1 Q.B. 660.
[93a] *per* Lord Nicholls in *Hindcastle v. Barbara Attenborough Associates Ltd* [1996] 1 All E.R. 737 at 748.
[93b] *i.e.* under the Insolvency Act 1986, s.181(2).
[94] *Murphy v. Sawyer-Hoare* [1993] 27 E.G. 127 (where such a covenant was described as giving the landlord the right "to force the surety to enter into a new lease which will create a direct contractual nexus between them").
[94a] It may suit a landlord (particularly one intending to sell his interest) to create a new lease between himself and the surety, rather than relying on the rather nebulous concept of the surety remaining liable as if the disclaimed lease was still in existence.

date on which it is granted.[95] By re-entering the premises in order to enable the new lease to be granted, the landlord will be taken as demonstrating that he regards the original lease as terminated in all respects and will consequently lose whatever rights he had against any former tenants or sureties under that lease. Having required the surety to take up the new lease, the landlord must ensure that the lease is completed within a reasonable time since an unreasonable delay might relieve the surety of its obligation to enter into the lease.[95a] Such a covenant has been held to be ancillary to the guarantee obligations, and therefore subject to discharge by the same events.[96] It has also been held that such a covenant touches and concerns the land and the benefit will pass to an assignee of the landlord's reversion without the need for an express assignment.[97] Sometimes the covenant is further extended to allow the landlord who does not require the surety to take a new lease to recoup from the surety the rent (and possibly service charge) which would have been due under the lease but for disclaimer from the date of disclaimer until the premises are re-let. After *Hindcastle* this no longer seems appropriate.

Change of landlord   Difficulties can also arise where the identity of the landlord changes, as on a sale of the freehold. Where a contract of guarantee is one involving personal confidence, it may be revoked by a change in the identity of the creditor or debtor.[98] However, it seems unlikely that such a principle would apply to a covenant of guarantee in a lease, where it must be within the contemplation of the parties that the landlord might change, and since the obligations of the tenant and guarantor are the same whoever is the landlord, the identity of the landlord is immaterial.

A more serious problem is whether an express assignment of the benefit of a surety covenant is required on a transfer of the reversion. It was formerly believed that an express assignment was essential if the benefit was to pass to an assignee of the reversion.[99] It is however now clear that in the absence of any express assignment a surety's covenant is

[in margin: Unreasonable delay]

[in margin: Transmission of benefit]

---

[95] It is thought that such a covenant is probably an option on the part of the landlord to require the tenant to take the lease, so any lease granted pursuant to it will be an old tenancy if the earlier lease was granted before January 1, 1996: 1995 Act, s.1(6).

[95a] In *Xey SA v. Abbey Life Assurance Co. Ltd* [1994] EGCS 190 the surety obtained such a declaration by the court where the surety was at all material times willing to execute the new lease but where the landlord was guilty of extreme delay amounting to nine months.

[96] *Selous Street Properties Ltd v. Oronel Fabrics Ltd* (1984) 270 E.G. 643 at 747.

[97] *Coronation Street Industrial Properties Ltd v. Ingall Industries plc* [1989] 1 W.L.R. 304.

[98] *First National Finance Corporation Ltd v. Goodman* [1983] BCLC 203. Assignment of the lease causes no problem, since the identity of the principal debtor, the original tenant, remains unchanged.

[99] See *Pinemain Ltd v. Welbeck Engineering Ltd* (1984) 272 E.G. 1116; *Re Distributors & Warehousing Ltd* [1986] 1 EGLR 90 (but see para. 3–03, n. 6 above); *Pinemain v. Tuck* (unreported); all holding that the benefit does not run with the reversion. *Cf. Coastplace Ltd v. Hartley* [1987] New L.J. 243, March 13.

capable of being enforced by a purchaser of the reversion on the basis that the covenant touches and concerns the legal estate vested in the assignee of the reversion.[1]

Duty of care owed to surety   The landlord should also be alert to the potential for the existence of a duty of care owed to the surety in the way in which the landlord enforces the provisions of the lease.[2] It is not clear how this potential duty of care might relate to the principle that a creditor can proceed against the surety without making any claim or demand against the debtor.[3] Therefore it would be sensible for the landlord to reserve expressly the right to proceed against the surety without first proceeding against the tenant; where the tenant is known to be insolvent this would be a waste of time and money, and if the tenant is solvent the surety can always join him as a third party.

Alternatives to suretyship   Before leaving the question of problems for the landlord, mention should be made of the possibility of the landlord taking out insurance to cover the insolvency of the tenant. Such a policy may in some cases prove an acceptable substitute for a surety, and avoid some of the difficulties mentioned above. The provision of a rent deposit[4] by the tenant can also obviate the need for a surety.

3–16   Suretyship provisions from the point of view of the surety

Many of the concerns of the surety will be the mirror-image of the problems for the landlord outlined above. For example, the surety should be wary of attempts to prolong his liability beyond the term of the lease, or to preserve his liability in the face of major changes to the provisions of the lease. The matters treated below are those which appear to be of particular concern to sureties.

Old tenancies   One aspect of his obligations which may

Continuing
liability of surety
greatly perturb a surety under an old tenancy is the continuing liability of the original tenant, which the surety has guaranteed.[5] Many sureties are horrified to learn that they are guaranteeing performance not only by the known tenant, but also performance by unknown future assignees throughout the residue of the term (and even during any statutory continuation if the definition of "term" has been thus extended).

In an old tenancy, the tenant will (unless the lease provides otherwise) be under a continuing contractual liability throughout the term and the surety's guarantee will continue

---

[1] *P.&A. Swift Investments v. Combined English Stores Group plc* [1988] 2 All E.R. 885; *Kumar v. Dunning* [1989] Q.B.193; *Coronation Street Industrial Properties Ltd v. Ingall Industries plc* [1989] 1 W.L.R. 304.
[2] *Standard Chartered Bank Ltd v. Walker* [1982] 1 W.L.R. 1410.
[3] *Wright v. Simpson* (1802) 6 Ves. Jun. 714 at 734.
[4] See para. 6–05 below.
[5] See para. 2–04 above.

throughout that period. This can be limited, and frequently is, by express provision in the lease. For example, many sureties insist that their liability is limited to the period during which the lease remains vested in the particular tenant whose obligations they are guaranteeing. Although in one case such a limitation was described as a "curious feature" of the guarantee,[6] such limitations have become increasingly common in recent years.

It has been held that where a surety has guaranteed an original tenant's obligations "so long as the term hereby granted is vested in the tenant", the surety's obligation determined when the term ceased to be vested in the original tenant, despite "the tenant" being defined to include the tenant's successors in title where the context so admitted and the lease including qualified rights for the tenant to assign its interest.[7]

New tenancies   Once the tenant under a new tenancy has assigned the whole of the premises let to him, he is released from liability for any breach of the tenant covenants occurring after the date of assignment and his surety is likewise released.[8] The surety would not however be released if either the assignment was an excluded assignment,[8a] or the tenant had entered into an authorised guarantee agreement[9] where the surety covenant in the lease had been drafted expressly to include the tenant's obligations under that agreement.[10]

Notification of arrears   Another danger for the surety is that arrears of rent or other breaches could accumulate to his prejudice without his knowledge.[11] This problem can easily be solved by a requirement on the landlord to notify the surety of any breaches known to him and to forward copies of any notices served upon the tenant. The 1995 Act[12] provides relief for the sureties of former tenants, under both old tenancies and new tenancies, by providing that a landlord cannot recover certain sums from a former tenant or his guarantor unless notice of those sums in a prescribed form has previously been served

---

[6] *Re Distributors & Warehousing Ltd* [1986] 1 EGLR 90 at 91 (but see para. 3–03, n. 6 above).

[7] *Johnsey Estates Ltd v. Webb* [1990] 19 E.G. 84.

[8] 1995 Act, s.24(2).

[8a] See para. 2–05 above.

[9] See para. 2–06 above.

[10] In the absence of any express provision, a surety covenant will not be taken to extend to the tenant's liability under an authorised guarantee agreement. Indeed, it is considered by many commentators that any attempt to extend the surety's liability to cover an authorised guarantee agreement may well be void as a result of s.25(1) of the 1995 Act. See also para. 2–07 above on the question of whether or not a surety can, notwithstanding the 1995 Act, extend his liability to cover the acts or defaults of the tenant's successors in title and whether a guarantee of the tenant's obligations under an authorised guarantee agreement is permitted under the 1995 Act.

[11] There is no obligation to give notice of default to the surety: *Carter v. White* (1883) 25 Ch. D. 666. Nor is a surety discharged by the creditor's failure to protect his own interests by allowing arrears to build up: *Bank of India v. Trans Continental Commodity Merchants Ltd, The Times,* October 22, 1981. But note the approach advocated by the Commercial Property Leases Code of Practice: see para. 1–07 above.

[12] 1995 Act, s.17.

on any such person within six months of the sum falling due.[13]

Overriding lease The surety should consider requiring a provision entitling him to take an overriding lease in the event of serious breaches. This would at least give the surety control which he would not otherwise have to prevent the situation worsening by enforcing the defaulting tenant's covenants. A surety of a former tenant (but not a current tenant) may now be entitled to require the grant to him of an overriding lease pursuant to section 19 of the 1995 Act in the event that he is required to pay, and does pay, certain sums owed by the current tenant.[14]

Rent reviews Rent reviews can be another source of grievance to a surety. An increase in the rent can radically affect his actual or potential liability, but in cases where he is not closely connected with the tenant he may have no say in the negotiations.[15] The best solution from the surety's point of view is to provide that the surety is only liable for the rent initially reserved. If the landlord is not prepared to accept this, it is possible to provide that the surety is to be a party to any agreement as to a revised rent,[16] but again the landlord and the tenant may object that this would add procedural complications and expense to each review. The surety can however argue with some force that he agreed to stand surety for rent to be determined on the basis of the provisions in the lease, and should at least be entitled to see that the correct procedures are followed and formulae applied, even if he takes no active part in negotiations.[17] The position is clearly more complicated where the tenant whose obligations the surety had guaranteed has assigned the lease but the surety remains liable.

Like the landlord, the surety should be aware of the possibility of mitigating his risks by a policy of indemnity insurance.

3–17 Suretyship provisions from the point of view of the tenant

The parties most likely to be concerned with provisions as to suretyship are the landlord and the surety. But the tenant should also be aware of their implications, in particular from

---

[13] See para. 2–12 above.
[14] See para. 2–12 above.
[15] For an illustration, see *Torminster Properties Ltd v. Green* [1983] 1 W.L.R. 676.
[16] See *Cressey v. Jacobs*, October 14, 1977 (unreported) but cited as Case No. 17 in R. Bernstein and K. Reynolds, *Handbook of Rent Review.* See also (1982) 2/1 R. R. 250; also [1980] L.S. Gaz. 786 (T.M. Aldridge), suggesting that the tenant could appoint the surety his attorney for rent review purposes.
[17] Though even this would be inconsistent with the usual clause providing that variation of the terms of the lease shall not release the surety: see para. 3–15 above.

Covenant to procure sureties on assignment

the point of view of the marketability of the lease. For example, leases frequently contain a covenant by the tenant to procure that on assignment to a company guarantees shall be provided by at least two directors of that company. Any such undertaking if expressed in absolute terms could make it extremely difficult, if not impossible, for the tenant to dispose of the lease. The tenant should therefore seek to insist that this should be subject to a requirement of reasonableness. Also, where it is impracticable to provide for two directors to act as guarantors, the tenant should be permitted to assign to an assignee who can provide reasonably acceptable alternative security, for example, a rent deposit.

4 THE DEMISED PREMISES AND ANCILLARY RIGHTS

4–01 Defining the premises

Need for careful definition

It is important that the lease should define the demised premises adequately and accurately. The precision with which the premises are defined assumes particular importance in the case of a lease, since many important aspects of the relationship between the parties may turn on the extent of the demise. For example, the tenant's repairing obligations may well be phrased with reference to the property demised.[1] In addition, the property demised will often form part of a larger building, and clearly more care is required to achieve precisely defined boundaries in such cases than on the sale of a free-standing property.

4–02 Description and plan

Whether a plan is necessary

The first point to consider is whether a plan should be used to identify the premises. Where the leasehold title is to be registered, and forms only part of the superior title, a plan must normally be provided,[2] sufficient to enable the demised premises to be identified on the filed plan.[3] The plan should be executed by the parties in the same manner as they would execute the lease. In other cases, those advising the parties should consider whether a plan is necessary or would be helpful: if no suitable plan exists, would the delay and expense involved in producing one be justified?[4]

Need for plan to be adequate

Where it is thought that a plan would be helpful, cheap half-measures are best avoided: it is better to have no plan at all than one which is misleading. Thus any plan should be accurate and to scale, and relate to the physical features of the

---

[1] Similarly, the extent of the demise may affect rent review, the ability to carry out alterations, and the extent of service charge and insurance obligations.

[2] Land Registration Rules 1925, r. 113(1) (unless a verbal description allows adequate identification).

[3] A scale of 1:1250 is normally required for built-up areas.

[4] Whether the tenant can compel the landlord to produce a plan is unclear. *Re Sansom and Narbeth's Contract* [1910] 1 Ch. 741 suggests a purchaser can require a plan in all simple cases where a plan would assist. *Re Sharman and Meade's Contract* [1936] Ch. 755 suggests this is so only where a plan is necessary because a verbal description is an insufficient or unsatisfactory means of identifying the premises. Whichever is correct, different considerations may apply to leases, where the landlord is under no obligation to deduce title, although in practice will often do so.

property in a recognisable way.[5] It should also be sufficiently large scale: in the context of sales of part of a residential property, use of an Ordnance Survey map on a scale of 1:2500 has been said to be worse than useless.[6] The plan should be securely bound into the lease, and incorporated by reference in the parcels clause.

Relationship of plan and description

If a plan is used, the lease should make clear whether the verbal description or the plan is to prevail in case of conflict. It is suggested that the plan should only be expressed to prevail where the parties are satisfied beyond any reasonable doubt that it is accurate and that the scale is adequate. In such cases, words such as "more particularly delineated (or described) on the plan" should be used to indicate that the plan is to prevail.[7] Otherwise, the plan should be expressed to be "for the purposes of identification only", in which case the plan can be used where the verbal description is inadequate, but will give way in case of conflict.[8]

4–03 Description of part of building

Problems in defining demise

In the case of a building let in parts, great care is needed to establish the precise extent of each demise. For example, the demise of premises bounded by an outside wall prima facie includes both sides of the wall;[9] thus the landlord may be unable to prevent the tenant fixing objects to the outside of the wall.[10] Similarly, the lease of the top floor of a building prima facie includes the airspace above it,[11] at least so far as is necessary for ordinary use and enjoyment.[12] This may

---

[5] See *Jackson v. Bishop*, C.A., 1979 (unreported, but noted at [1982] Conv. 324) where it was suggested that a property developer/vendor of residential property may be under a duty of care as to the accuracy of the plans by which he sells. It does not seem too far-fetched to suggest that the same principle could apply to a developer/landlord of commercial property. See also *Wright Davies v. Marler* (unreported) but noted at [1995] 10 C.L. 122 (a defective plan which did not accurately indicate the extent of land subject to an easement).

[6] *Scarfe v. Adams* [1981] 1 All E.R. 843 at 845.

[7] *Eastwood v. Ashton* [1915] A.C. 900. See also *A. J. Dunning & Sons (Shopfitters) Ltd v. Sykes & Son (Poole) Ltd* [1987] 2 W.L.R. 167, where the Court of Appeal considered a conflict between a plan and a reference to property comprised within a particular title number. No explicit indication was given of which was to prevail, but the majority held the plan to be the effective and dominant description. Sir John Donaldson M.R. dissented on the basis that when dealing with registered land, it was natural and desirable to treat the registered parcel as the primary unit.

[8] *Wigginton & Milner Ltd v. Winster Engineering Ltd* [1978] 1 W.L.R. 1462; *Spall v. Owen* (1981) 44 P. & C.R. 36.

[9] *Hope Bros. Ltd v. Cowan* [1913] 2 Ch. 312; *Carlisle Cafe Co. v. Muse Brothers & Co.* (1897) 67 L.J. Ch. 53; *Sturge v. Hackett* [1962] 1 W.L.R. 1257.

[10] See para. 11–03 below.

[11] *Kelsen v. Imperial Tobacco Co. (Great Britain and Ireland) Ltd* [1957] 2 Q.B. 334; it may be relevant here to consider the extent of the repairing obligations in the lease as indicative of the extent of the demise: *Straudley Investments Ltd v. Barpress Ltd* (1987) 282 E.G. 1124.

[12] *Lord Bernstein of Leigh v. Skyviews and General Ltd* [1978] Q.B. 479.

mean that the tenant of the top floor finds himself responsible for the maintenance of the entire roof of the building;[13] it may also mean that the landlord is unable to extend the building upwards or carry out other activities which impinge upon the airspace whereas the tenant will be able to.[14] Also, it has been said that the general expectation, based upon "almost invariably conveyancing practice", is that the tenant of part of a building severed horizontally is acquiring the space between the floor of his premises and the underside of the floor of the premises above.[15] Thus the demise may include the voids above or below any false ceiling or floor.[16] This question may assume considerable significance in the case of modern office premises, where the tenant may wish to make use of such voids for cables and trunking for telecommunications and electronic equipment, or where the void contains material such as asbestos which may need to be stripped out.

Buildings let in parts   Thus where a building is demised in parts, the leases of each part should adopt a consistent approach as to where the exact boundaries lie. One approach is to provide that all internal dividing walls and floors are severed medially with mutual rights of support,[17] and leave each tenant responsible for such external parts of the building as fall within his demise. However, in most cases it will be far better for the structural and common parts of the building to remain with the landlord, and for his expenditure on maintaining them to be recouped from the tenants. Therefore the practice has grown of demising only the decorative finishes of the surfaces bounding the premises, and the space enclosed by them, and excluding all load bearing structures (such as steel columns) within that space.[18] Between the two extremes lies a large number of possible variations, and the only safe advice must be to adopt the approach which is best suited to the design and construction of the building and the type of letting.

[13] Although this will depend upon the description of the demise and the wording of the repairing covenant. See *Cockburn v. Smith* [1924] 2 K.B. 119.

[14] *Davies v. Yadegar* [1990] 9 E.G. 67 (a demise of a first floor flat which included the roof and roof-space was held to include the airspace above it and consequently the tenant's proposed loft conversion was not a trespass); see also *Haines v. Florensa* [1990] 9 E.G. 70 (applying *Davies v. Yadegar*, on similar facts).

[15] *Graystone Property Investments Ltd v. Margulies* (1983) 269 E.G. 538 at 540; see *Rothschild v. Moser* [1986] N.P.C. 46.

[16] As in *Graystone Property Investments Ltd v. Margulies, ibid.* The position might be different if the existence of a false ceiling was not obvious at the time of the grant.

[17] In Inner London, the position is presently governed by Pt. VI of the London Building Acts (Amendment) Act 1939, though the Act will not apply to all party floors: see s.4(1) (definition of "party structure"). At the time of going to press the Party Wall Bill is before Parliament. This provides for a similar regime to the London Building Acts to apply to the whole of England and Wales.

[18] *City Offices (Regent Street) Ltd v. Europa Acceptance Group* [1990] 5 E.G. 71 (an internal non-structural demise amounted to an "eggshell" enclosing airspace, and removal of that eggshell by the landlord and its replacement with something different constituted reconstruction of the demise).

Floor areas There are arguments in favour of agreeing the floor area demised at the outset, and stating the figure in the lease. Such a practice can prevent the need for independent calculations as to floor space at each rent review, with the resultant likelihood of dispute between the parties. However, the practice has its own problems. Many subtle variations exist in measuring practice, and in the case of a complex building reaching initial agreement may be a slow, or even impossible, task. Secondly, it may not be enough simply to state the total floorspace: to avoid future disputes it may have to be broken down between different floors, and between different parts of the premises.[19] Thirdly, useable floorspace areas may change over time, either through structural alterations or changes in internal partitioning. For these reasons the floor area of the premises is rarely mentioned in practice.

Agreed statement of floor area

4–04 More than one parcel of land

A single lease may demise more than one parcel of land or one building which do not have to be, but usually would be, proximate to one another. Careful consideration of the rights, exceptions and covenants should be given in such cases and a single lease may not be appropriate for more complicated lettings. In addition, extreme care should be taken by the landlord when seeking to determine the lease as it may be construed as having created more than one tenancy. In such a case the landlord will have to ensure that any notice served pursuant to section 25 of the Landlord and Tenant Act 1954 takes this into account.[20]

4–05 Fixtures

The usual practice is to provide that the demise includes all landlord's fixtures, whether already affixed at the time of the grant or affixed later during the term. This seems to add nothing to the position at common law, but it can prevent doubts arising in relation to matters such as rent review and repairing and insuring obligations. The question of fixtures is discussed more fully elsewhere.[21]

4–06 Appurtenant rights

Easements, etc.

The tenant's advisers must ensure that the lease contains the appropriate easements and other appurtenant rights to enable the tenant to make effective use of the demised premises

---

[19] So as to distinguish unproductive parts such as corridors and areas with lifts opening directly on to them: see *Kings Reach Investments Ltd v. Reed Publishing Holdings Ltd*, C.A. 1984 (unreported but cited in R. Bernstein and K. Reynolds, *Handbook of Rent Review*, at D.C. 186/1).

[20] *Moss v. Mobil Oil Co.* [1988] 6 E.G. 109. See para. 16–26 below.

[21] See para. 11–10 below.

during the term. Some of the most important matters are considered below.

4–07 Access

The means of access will obviously vary according to the type of the premises; in some cases rights may be needed over an estate road, in others the right to use stairs or a lift. Where by accident the lease omits to provide any means of access, an easement of necessity may be implied, but the implication will not extend to actually including the means of access within the demise.[22]

Defining extent of rights

From the landlord's point of view it is desirable to define the tenant's rights precisely. The landlord may wish to restrict rights of access to certain times for security reasons, or to prevent excessively heavy traffic which might damage a road. Furthermore, where the landlord retains control of the means of access, he may be liable to a tenant who is affected by the excessive or unlawful use of other tenants.[23] The general principle is that the extent of a right of way is to be judged in the light of the reasonable needs of the premises concerned and the contemplated use or range of uses of those premises.[24] The lease of a factory would therefore carry the right to bring heavy traffic onto the roadway.[25] Similarly, in an Australian case,[26] it was said that the tenant of business premises who is given the right to use a lift may use the lift for the carriage of such passengers and goods as may be reasonably necessary for the conduct of the type of business contemplated by the parties when the premises were let. Thus it would be sensible for the landlord either to attempt to define what type of loads may be carried in the lift, or alternatively take a covenant from the tenant not to overload the lift.

Ancillary rights

A right of way will, unless there is any wording to indicate otherwise, carry with it the ancillary rights necessary for the reasonable enjoyment of the right of way.[27] For example, in the absence of any specific restriction vehicles may remain on the roadway for a reasonable time to allow loading and unloading.[28] This could prove a considerable annoyance to other tenants, particularly where loading areas are specifically provided elsewhere, and therefore the landlord should consider expressly negating the right to load and unload otherwise than in those designated areas. At the same time the landlord should make clear whether the rights conferred upon

---

[22] *Altmann v. Boatman* (1963) 186 E.G. 109.

[23] *Hilton v. James Smith & Sons (Norwood) Ltd* (1979) 251 E.G. 1063.

[24] *Graham v. Philcox* [1984] Q.B. 747.

[25] *Cannon v. Villars* (1878) 8 Ch.D. 415 at 421; *Bulstrode v. Lambert* [1953] 1 W.L.R. 1064.

[26] *Dikstein v. Kanevsky* (1947) V.L.R. 216.

[27] See *V. T. Engineering Ltd v. Richard Barland & Co. Ltd* (1968) 19 P. & C.R. 890 (right to space above road, but not lateral space for manoeuvre); *Hayns v. Secretary of State for the Environment* (1977) 36 P. & C.R. 317 (no right to visibility splays).

[28] *Bulstrode v. Lambert* [1953] 1 W.L.R. 1064; *McIlraith v. Grady* [1968] 1 Q.B. 468.

the tenant are exclusive or are enjoyed in common with other tenants.[29] There is however no implied right for the tenant to park on a right of way and the tenant should therefore ensure that adequate parking rights are expressly granted by the lease.[30]

    The lease should also deal with the question of maintaining the means of access. The normal principle is that the owner **Maintenance of** of the servient tenement is under no obligation to expend **means of access** money to enable or facilitate enjoyment of the easement by the dominant owner.[31] An exception to this general principle has developed in the case of essential common parts, such as staircases and lifts. Here an implied obligation rests upon the landlord to keep such means of access safe and in working order.[32] In most modern leases, the most practical solution will be for the landlord to covenant to maintain such facilities, with the ability to recoup his expenditure as part of a service charge.[33]

4–08 Service media

The tenant should obtain an express grant of the right to use the drains, cables and other such facilities serving the premises.[34] This should be extended not only to those in existence at the date of the grant, but also those provided within a specified perpetuity period.[35] It is likely that any such future rights must be exercised in such a way as to cause minimum loss, annoyance and disturbance to the servient tenement.[36]

4–09 Parking

The right to park vehicles can be dealt with in a variety of ways. A specific parking area exclusive to the tenant may be **Various methods** included within the demise. An exclusive right to park vehicles **of granting** in a defined area may be granted by licence; or alternatively **rights** the licence may confer the right to park in common with other tenants in a larger area. Also, the right to park anywhere

---

[29] *Spon Engineering Co. Ltd v. Kossman Manufacturing Co. Ltd* (1965) 195 E.G. 645. A right granted exclusively to a tenant is akin to including the right within the demise.

[30] *Handel v. St. Stephen's Close Ltd* [1994] 5 E.G. 159. See also para. 4–09 below.

[31] *Holden v. White* [1982] Q.B. 679 at 683; *Duke of Westminster v. Guild* [1985] Q.B. 688 at 700.

[32] *Dunster v. Hollis* [1918] 2 K.B. 795; *Liverpool City Council v. Irwin* [1977] A.C. 239; *De Meza v. Ve-Ri-Best Manufacturing Co. Ltd* (1952) 160 E.G. 234.

[33] See para. 8–02 below.

[34] s.62 of the Law of Property Act 1925 only applies if the easement is in use at the time of the grant, and does not apply to "latent rights" over facilities in existence but not yet used: *Sovmots Investments Ltd v. Secretary of State for the Environment* [1979] A.C. 144.

[35] The period can be up to 80 years: Perpetuities and Accumulations Act 1964, s.1(1).

[36] *Taylor v. British Legal Life Assurance Co. Ltd* [1925] 1 Ch. 395.

in a defined area on a non-exclusive basis may be made the subject of an easement.[37]

The draftsman should adopt whichever method or combination of methods best suits the demise in question, *e.g.* in the case of a city office block with a limited number of parking spaces beneath it, individual spaces may need to be allocated precisely; for a unit on an industrial park it may be appropriate to include a small parking area within the demise, and give further non-exclusive rights over a common area.

An attempt is sometimes made to prevent the parking of large commercial vehicles by confining the right to park to "private cars." In the context of a lease of a residential flat this expression has been held to mean only cars used for personal or domestic as opposed to business purposes.[38] It seems unlikely that the same approach would be adopted in the case of a lease of business premises, but in the absence of clear authority, use of the word "private" is probably best avoided.

VAT and parking rights
Any price payable for a separate grant of parking rights on property not included within the demise is subject to VAT. The landlord should be alert to this possibility and should provide for the tenant to pay any VAT chargeable on the grant.[39]

4–10 Use of sanitary and other facilities

Communal facilities
If lavatory and washing facilities do not form part of the demise, the tenant should seek the right to use any communal facilities within the building; otherwise he may well encounter difficulties with legislation requiring the provision of such facilities for employees.[40] The right to use such facilities can be conferred by licence, which may be construed as irrevocable if the effect of revocation would be to derogate from the landlord's grant.[41] Alternatively an easement to use the facilities in common with other tenants may be granted.[42]

4–11 Signs and advertisements

Need to obtain right to exhibit signs
The right to advertise his business may be of crucial importance to the tenant particularly if he is a retailer or service provider. Generally there will be no problem as to signs fixed to property forming part of the demise, though the fixing of such a sign may constitute breach of a covenant

[37] *Newman v. Jones*, Ch.D., March 22, 1982, (unreported, but noted in Megarry and Wade, *The Law of Real Property* (5th ed. 1984) p. 840).
[38] *Bell v. Alfred Franks & Bartlett Co. Ltd* [1980] 1 W.L.R. 340.
[39] See para. 19–09 below. Chap. 19 below contains a detailed discussion of the application of VAT on property dealings.
[40] See para. 7–04 below.
[41] *Creedon v. Collins* (1964) 191 E.G. 123.
[42] *Miller v. Emcer Products Ltd* [1956] Ch. 304. The supply of hot water cannot be the subject of an easement: *Regis Property Co. Ltd v. Redman* [1956] 2 Q.B. 612. However, the free running of such water can be protected as an easement: see *Rance v. Elvin* (1985) 50 P. & C.R. 9.

against alterations to the fabric[43] or appearance[44] of the premises. However, the tenant who wishes to exhibit signs on part of the building not demised to him (*e.g.* a name plate at street level, in a lift lobby or on a common signboard on a retail park) must obtain an express grant of the right to do so.[45] This may be by way of licence[46] or easement.[47] In either event it should be made clear whether the right extends simply to signs presently displayed, or to variations in future.[48] The landlord may also wish to confine the signs to those advertising the tenant's business carried on at the premises, and possibly exercise some control over the size and nature of signs displayed.

4–12   Access to adjoining property

The tenant should also consider whether or not rights of access to adjoining property, such as other parts of the building of which the demise forms part, are required, for example in order to enable the tenant to comply with his repairing covenant. Whilst it may be open to the tenant in any event to argue that such rights would constitute an easement of necessity in the absence of any express provision, the risk of dispute is removed by the grant of express rights by the lease itself where the landlord is also the owner of the adjoining land or premises.

Access to Neighbouring Land Act

The tenant may alternatively be able to secure access to adjoining property, whether or not owned by the landlord or occupied by another tenant, pursuant to the Access to Neighbouring Land Act 1992.[49] The court will grant an access order in respect of adjoining land or premises where it is satisfied that the works to be carried out are reasonably necessary for the preservation of the whole or any part of the demised premises and where those works cannot be carried out, or would be substantially more difficult to carry out, without access to that land.[50] The types of work which fall within the scope of the 1992 Act include the repair or maintenance of a building and the clearance, repair or renewal

---

[43] *London County Council v. Hutter* [1925] Ch. 626; *cf. Joseph v. London County Council* (1914) 111 L.T. 276.
[44] *Heard v. Stuart* (1907) 24 T.L.R. 104.
[45] *Frederick Berry Ltd v. Royal Bank of Scotland* [1949] 1 K.B. 619; but see also para. 4–13 below.
[46] *Wilson v. Tavener* [1901] 1 Ch. 578.
[47] *Moody v. Steggles* (1879) 12 Ch.D. 261. *William Hill (Southern) Ltd v. Cabras Ltd* (1986) 281 E.G. 309 (right to exhibit signs held to be easement; also suggested that an easily detachable sign could not be regarded as a physical appurtenance in the sense of part of the demised premises). See also para. 4–13 below.
[48] *Barbeque (Leicester Square) Ltd v. Berkeley Laboratories (London) Ltd* (1964) 190 E.G. 1055.
[49] 1992 Act, s.1(1). In *Dean v. Walker* [1996] NPC 78, a party wall was held to be land for the purpose of the 1992 Act.
[50] 1992 Act, s.1(2).

of drains and cables.[51] Once granted, access orders will be binding on the landlord's successors in title and those deriving title under him.[52]

4–13 Negating implied grants

Wheeldon v. Burrows and section 62

A potentially serious problem for landlords is that on the grant of a lease, appurtenant rights previously enjoyed on a precarious basis may become easements, either under the rule in *Wheeldon v. Burrows*[53] or by virtue of section 62 of the Law of Property Act 1925.[54] The landlord may therefore attempt to provide that the demise shall not operate to convey any rights except those specifically granted. However, it appears that such provisions will be construed against the landlord on the principle of non-derogation from grant, so that considerable care will be required in drafting if the desired result is to be produced.

The problems which can arise are well demonstrated by the decision of the Court of Appeal in *William Hill (Southern) Ltd v. Cabras Ltd.*[55] Tenants of first-floor premises were held entitled to retain illuminated signs affixed at street level to a part of the building not within the demise, on the basis that a new lease specifically included within the demise "appurtenances", which could be read as including the right to maintain the signs. A general clause negativing the implied grant of rights was held effective to exclude section 62, but was overridden by the specific reference to "appurtenances". According to Kerr L.J., the same result could have been reached on the basis of assurances given by the landlord's solicitors that the tenant could retain the signs. However, the implication of an easement from a qualified covenant against the exhibition of signs was rejected as "novel and unorthodox".

Subject to contrary intention

4–14 Exceptions and reservations by landlord

The landlord may need to except certain parts of the property from the grant to the tenant, *e.g.* common areas and structural parts of the building. In addition, the landlord may wish to reserve certain rights against the demised property. It is important to note that whereas the grant of rights in favour

---

[51] 1992 Act, s.1(4): described as "basic preservation works". The permitted works can include incidental alterations or improvements where it is, in the court's opinion, fair and reasonable in all the circumstances to regard those works as reasonably necessary for the preservation of land: s.1(5). It will therefore not extend to works of development or redevelopment.

[52] 1992 Act, s.4(1). The order must however be registered against the adjoining owner's title in accordance with the Land Registration Act 1925 or the Land Charges Act 1972, as appropriate. The tenant might also be afforded rights of entry to adjoining premises for the purpose of carrying out work in respect of a party wall pursuant to clause 8 of the Party Wall Bill (see n. 17 above).

[53] (1879) 12 Ch.D. 31.

[54] *Goldberg v. Edwards* [1950] Ch. 247; *Graham v. Philcox* [1984] Q.B. 747.

[55] (1986) 281 E.G. 309.

Needs to expressly reserve rights

of the tenant may be fairly readily implied on the principles mentioned above, the general rule is that the landlord will not be permitted to derogate from his grant by relying on impliedly reserved rights.[56] Thus any such rights must be reserved expressly.[57]

4–15 Rights of access

Fire exits

Where the premises include a means of access serving other property, the appropriate rights of access for the landlord and his other tenants should be reserved. The comments made above in relation to the grant of access rights apply equally here. Even where the obvious means of access does not form part of the demise, the landlord should consider whether any rights need to be reserved in relation to irregular means of egress, such as fire escapes and emergency exits.

4–16 Rights to use service media

Conduits, etc.

The landlord will need to reserve the right to make use of any drains, cables and other service media passing through the demised premises and serving other property. The right should be extended to cover similar facilities provided in the future, specifying a suitable perpetuity period, and should, if required, be expressed to include rights of entry to lay new service media in addition to a right to replace or repair the existing ones.[58]

4–17 Rights of entry

The landlord may need to reserve rights of entry for various purposes, *e.g.* viewing the state of repair of the premises and carrying out repairs,[59] affixing a letting sign at the end of the term, complying with covenants in a superior lease, and carrying out repairs or other work to adjoining premises.[60]

Tenant's consideration

The general principle is that such rights must be exercised reasonably, but that the landlord will not be forced to adopt a more expensive means of carrying out work in order to minimise the inconvenience to the tenant.[61] The tenant's

---

[56] *Wheeldon v. Burrows* (1879) 12 Ch.D. 31; *Re Webb's Lease* [1951] 1 Ch. 808.

[57] There are the limited exceptions of easements of necessity and easements clearly intended, such as mutual rights of support. But it will be very difficult to establish such easements: see *Re Webb's Lease* at 829; *Aldridge v. Wright* [1929] 2 K.B. 117 at 130–131.

[58] *Trailfinders v. Razuki* [1988] 30 E.G. 59.

[59] See para. 9–24 below. The landlord has an implied right of entry where he has covenanted to repair.

[60] *Regional Properties Ltd v. City of London Real Property Co. Ltd* (1980) 257 E.G. 64; *Rothschild v. Moser* [1986] N.P.C. 46 (right of access for repairs did not allow landlord to enter to carry out improvements).

[61] *Matlodge Ltd v. Miller* (1973) 227 E.G. 2247 (landlord not forced to use scaffolding in order to avoid placing supports for cradle on balcony of tenant's flat).

adviser should seek some explicit protection against unreasonable exercise of such rights by providing that rights of entry can only be exercised on notice (except in cases of emergency), at reasonable hours, and subject to the landlord making good any damage caused to the premises and causing as little interruption to the tenant's trade or business carried on there as is reasonably practicable by the exercise of the right.

4–18 Right to develop adjoining and neighbouring premises

Need to reserve rights

If the landlord contemplates developing other property nearby during the term of the lease, it will be wise to make some express provision for this. Otherwise the landlord could find his development plans thwarted by the rights of the tenant. For example, the proposed development may constitute interference with the tenant's rights of light,[62] or rights of way[63] or with some ancillary right such as the display of a sign.[64] Or it may only be possible by trespassing on the tenant's airspace,[65] or by erecting scaffolding which constitutes an actionable derogation from grant.[66]

Thus the landlord should reserve the right to develop any adjoining or neighbouring[67] premises even though the passage of light and air to the demised premises may be affected. The landlord may also wish to reserve the right to affix scaffolding or otherwise carry out works even though access to the premises may be obstructed or made less convenient. Striking a fair balance with such reservations is not easy. Certainly the

Protecting the tenant

tenant should seek to avoid the position whereby the development makes the premises unfit for his purposes (*e.g.* serious obstruction to the light of a drawing office) or where the work constitutes a serious, albeit temporary, interference with the tenant's business (*e.g.* dust and vibrations affecting a delicate process, or scaffolding obstructing public access to a shop for a long period). Much will depend on the nature of the tenant's business and the type of development which can be foreseen, but it is suggested that it should at least be provided that the development should not be such as to render the premises unfit for the purpose for which demised. It would also seem fair to distinguish between work carried out to benefit the demised

---

[62] Such rights may be negatived by clear intention, as where the landlord's intention to develop is obvious, *e.g.* where the property forms part of a comprehensive scheme: *Birmingham, Dudley & District Banking Co. v. Ross* (1888) 38 Ch.D. 295.

[63] *Overcom Properties v. Stockleigh Hall Residents Management* [1989] 14 E.G. 78 (substantial interference with the tenant's rights of way was permissible under the terms of the lease provided that reasonable access to the tenant's property remained).

[64] As in *William Hill (Southern) Ltd v. Cabras Ltd* (1986) 281 E.G. 309.

[65] *Kelsen v. Imperial Tobacco Co. (Great Britain and Ireland) Ltd* [1957] 2 Q.B. 334.

[66] *Owen v. Gadd* [1956] 2 Q.B. 99.

[67] To counter any argument that the right is confined to physically contiguous buildings: see *White v. Harrow* (1902) 86 L.T. 4.

Reasons for the works

Compensation for disturbance

premises (*e.g.* repairs to a roof) and work purely for the landlord's benefit (*e.g.* adding another lettable part to a building). In the latter instance, there seems no reason why the landlord should not compensate the tenant for the temporary inconvenience (any dispute as to the amount being referred to an arbitrator or valuer) nor why permanent depreciation caused by the work should not be reflected in a reduction in rent. Another approach, where very substantial development is likely, could be to give the tenant the option to terminate the lease, the landlord paying compensation for disturbance to the tenant's business. An analogy with compensation payable under the Landlord and Tenant Act 1954, s.37 might be drawn here. Under that section, compensation is payable if the landlord obtains possession in order to develop the premises, and there seems no reason why the position should be different where development of adjoining premises makes the demised premises unusable. The tenant might therefore argue for the adoption of the section 37 level of compensation,[68] and it might be appropriate to adapt part of section 31A(1)(a) to define the circumstances in which the option to terminate could be exercised, *i.e.* that the work will interfere to a substantial extent or for a substantial time with the use of the premises for the purposes of the business carried on by the tenant.[69]

---

[68] See para. 16–50 below.
[69] See para. 16–40 below.

5 THE TERM

5–01 Introduction

The term for which a lease is granted is customarily stated in that part of the lease known as the habendum.[1] Although a lease of business premises may be granted by way of a periodic tenancy or tenancy at will,[2] such leases are almost invariably granted for a fixed term of years. Two matters must be made clear by the lease, or at least be capable of being rendered certain before the lease takes effect. They are the maximum duration of the contractual term and the date upon which it commences.[3]

5–02 Length of term

The decision as to the length of the term is one which will probably be based upon commercial rather than legal considerations. An awareness of the underlying legal principles can, however, form an essential contribution to the decision-making process. In practice this is often not the case, since a solicitor may not become involved until the major decisions of principle, including the term of the lease, have been negotiated.

Landlord's considerations   In deciding what term to offer, the landlord is likely to have in mind the creation of a secure investment with an adequate rate of return. This will argue for a lengthy term, and it may also mean that the precise length of the term is governed by the period between succeeding rent reviews. The landlord may feel that he can achieve tighter control over future rents by a stringent rent review clause inserted in a long lease than by leaving the rent to be determined by the court under the Landlord and Tenant Act 1954, when a short lease comes to an end and the tenant seeks a new lease. On the other hand, the landlord may envisage redevelopment of the property at some future date, which will require the grant of a short term

[1] That part beginning "to hold unto", or "to have and to hold": Woodfall, *Landlord and Tenant*, 1–5.063.
[2] See para. 16–22 below for a discussion of tenancies at will.
[3] Without a term the maximum length of which is capable of being ascertained, there can be no lease: see *Lace v. Chantler* [1944] 1 All E.R. 305 (a lease until the end of the second world war was held to be void); *Prudential Assurance Co. Ltd v. London Residuary Body* [1992] 3 W.L.R. 279 (a lease until the landlord required the land for road widening was void); also see *Onyx (U.K.) Ltd v. Beard* [1996] EGCS 55 (an arrangement which provided for an indefinite period of occupation until determined by one of the parties could not be a lease, whatever else the arrangement was). It has become increasingly common in commercial leases to define the term as also including any statutory continuation of the tenancy. Without this wording, the original tenant's liability will cease on expiry of the contractual term, where the lease has been assigned, and the original tenant will not be liable during any statutory continuation by an assignee. See *City of London Corporation v. Fell* [1993] Q.B. 589 and *Willison v. Cheverell Estates Ltd* [1995] EGCS 111.

and possibly careful co-ordination to ensure that where the landlord is granting or has granted more than one lease, all such leases will fall in at the same date.[4]

Length of underlease Where the landlord is himself a lessee and is proposing to grant an underlease, the length of his own term must obviously be a material consideration.[5] Less obvious perhaps is the fact that unless the sublessor reserves a reversion of at least 14 months he will not be the "competent landlord" for the purposes of Part II of the Landlord and Tenant Act 1954, with possible adverse consequences.[6]

Tenant's considerations The tenant's prime concern will be to obtain a term suitable to his business needs. This may mean that long-term secure accommodation is required; on the other hand the tenant may want flexibility and wish to avoid the commitment of a lengthy term. This will especially be the case with new or fast-developing firms. It should not be forgotten that in some cases flexibility can also be achieved by options to renew and to determine leases.[7] In the case of certain types of premises, such as "starter units", an enlightened landlord may be willing to allow easy surrender to enable a tenant to "trade up" to larger premises in the same development. A long term may be needed if the tenant plans to incur substantial expenditure on the property or raise money on the security of the lease.

One highly significant factor in the case of tenancies which are not "new tenancies",[8] and one of which many prospective **Continuing liability** tenants were unaware when negotiating the term, is the continuing liability of the original tenant under the covenants of the lease for the duration of the term.[9] In the case of new tenancies,[10] however, where the original tenant will not generally remain liable following an assignment,[11] it is unlikely that the prospect of continuing liability will be a determining factor for the tenant when negotiating the term of the lease.[11a]

The full implications of the length of term chosen may only be appreciated when the detailed provisions of the lease are seen, *e.g.* a lengthy term may be tolerable for the tenant if the user clause and provisions for assignment are liberally drafted.

---

[4] This may also be achieved by the use of break clauses: see para. 16–05 *et seq.* below.
[5] The landlord should retain a reversion of at least one day since the grant of an underlease with a term equal to or exceeding the landlord's reversion will be construed as an assignment of the reversion. See *Lewis v. Baker* [1905] 1 Ch. 46; *Milmo v. Carreras* [1946] K.B. 306; *Averbrian v. Willmalight* (unreported but noted at [1994] C.L.Y. 2799). See para. 18–21 below.
[6] See para. 16–25 below.
[7] See paras. 16–05 and 16–10 below.
[8] See para. 2–02 above.
[9] See para. 2–04 above.
[10] See para. 2–02 above.
[11] Except where it is an excluded assignment: see para. 2–05 above.
[11a] Tenants under a "new tenancy" will, however, need to remember that they may be asked to act as guarantor of their assignee in an authorised guarantee agreement (see para. 2–06 above), and that they may therefore retain liability for as long as their assignee remains the tenant. In certain circumstances, e.g. where the assignee then enters into an excluded assignment, the tenant may remain liable even after that assignee assigns on the lease: see para. 2–05 above.

Stamp duty

Land Registry fees

The stamp duty payable on the lease (which will be paid by the tenant) rises in steps where the term exceeds seven, 35 and 100 years respectively.[12] A lease granted for a term of more than 21 years will require registration under the Land Registration Act 1925 and again this will involve fees for the tenant.[13]

5–03 The commencement date

If no date for commencement of the term is specified, it is usually taken to commence from the date of delivery of the lease. This could involve an unacceptable degree of chance and uncertainty, and may well not accord with the wishes of the parties, *e.g.* where the date inserted in the lease does not coincide with the date of delivery, or where delivery is in escrow; or where the date does not accord with the provisions as to rent.[14] Therefore it is usual to insert a certain commencement date.

A common method of specifying the date is by use of the word "from". This will generally mean that the term commences at midnight at the end of the day specified.[15] However, this inference can be displaced by clear evidence of contrary intention, for example the dates upon which rent is payable.[16] Alternative methods which can be used where it is desired to include the day specified within the term are "commencing on" or "from and including", and for the sake of certainty these phrases are to be preferred.[17]

Distinction between grant and commencement date

It is often the case that the commencement date specified will be different from the date of execution of the lease. It is essential here to appreciate the difference between the date on which the legal term of years is granted to the tenant and the date used for reckoning the length of the term and possibly various obligations arising under the lease. The distinction stems from the fact that a lease as well as being a grant is also a contractual document. A lease cannot operate to vest any term in the tenant until it is executed.[18] Nor will it normally render any act or omission prior to the date of execution a

---

[12] Stamp Act 1891, Sched. 1. The rates for terms in excess of a year are determined by the average rent and length of the lease and are calculated broadly as follows: terms not exceeding 7 years or indefinite—1% of the rent; terms not exceedings 35 years—2%; terms not exceeding 100 years—12% and terms not exceeding 100 years—24%. Rent in excess of £100 is for these purposes rounded up to the nearest £50. Schedule 1 should be checked for the exact rate payable in each case. For full details see Chapter 19 of R. Maas, *Tolleys Property Taxes 1995* (1996). See also para. 18–11 below.

[13] Land Registration Act 1925, s.22 or s.123, as amended by the Land Registration Act 1986. See para. 18–11 below.

[14] *Sandill v. Franklin* (1875) L.R. 10 C.P. 377.

[15] *Ackland v. Lutley* (1839) 9 A. & E. 879; *Meggeson v. Groves* [1917] 1 Ch. 158 at 164.

[16] *Ladyman v. Wirral Estates Ltd* [1968] 2 All E.R. 197. See also *Whelton Sinclair v. Hyland* [1992] 2 EGLR 158.

[17] *Meadfield Properties Ltd v. Secretary of State for the Environment* [1994] EGCS 144; *Trane (U.K.) Ltd v. Provident Mutual Life Association* [1994] EGCS 121.

[18] *Earl Cadogan v. Guinness* [1936] Ch. 515.

breach of covenant.[19] However, a date other than that of execution can be used as a point from which to reckon the termination date of the lease and other dates, such as those upon which rent review provisions become operable, or upon which options or break clauses may be exercised. Nor is any such date necessarily only a "unit of calculation."[20] The parties may if they wish create obligations which bind from some date before or after the date of execution: whether they have done so will depend on the construction of the words used.[21] Thus rent may be made payable in respect of a period prior to the execution of the lease as, for example, where the tenant goes into occupation before the grant.

Antecedent commencement date

There are various reasons for specifying a commencement date prior to execution. It may be convenient from the landlord's point of view to synchronise the rent review and termination dates of all his properties. Alternatively, the tenant may have gone into occupation of the premises prior to the formal grant of the lease. If the second alternative is the case, there can be little objection to the tenant being made liable for rent, insurance, service charges and the like from the commencement date. But in other cases, the tenant's solicitor should be alert to ensure that such obligations run only from the date of execution, and the wording of the lease should be scrutinised with this in mind. He should also be aware that specifying an earlier commencement date may result in his client obtaining a somewhat shorter term than may have been agreed.

Subsequent commencement date

It is possible to specify a commencement date subsequent to the date of execution. The period after which the term is stated to take effect should not exceed 21 years, otherwise the term will be void.[22] In practice, a letting which is to commence at some future date is usually dealt with by way of an agreement for lease.[23] A common example is the agreement to grant a lease upon certification of practical completion of the building.[24] This course has some advantages over the grant of a reversionary lease. It allows the rights of the parties in the interim to be clearly defined (e.g. if the building should be destroyed whilst in the course of construction), and certainty as to the terms of the lease to be granted can be achieved by annexing the form of lease to the agreement. The lease can then, if necessary and by agreement between the parties, be updated immediately prior to grant to

Advantages of agreement for lease

---

[19] *Shaw v. Kay* (1847) 1 Exch. 412; *Bradshaw v. Pawley* [1980] 1 W.L.R. 10.

[20] *Bradshaw v. Pawley* [1980] 1 W.L.R. 10.

[21] *Bradshaw v. Pawley* [1980] 1 W.L.R. 10.

[22] Law of Property Act 1925, s.149(3). A lease where the grant precedes the commencement date of the term is called a reversionary lease. Care should be taken when granting both current and reversionary leases of the same premises to the same tenant to ensure that the term granted by the reversionary lease is taken into account on any rent review under the current lease: *Toyota (G.B.) Ltd v. Legal and General Assurance (Pensions Management) Ltd* [1989] 42 E.G. 104. The two leases may be registered at H.M. Land Registry as one title: Land Registration Rules 1925, r. 47.

[23] See para. 18–07 below.

[24] *Brilliant v. Michaels* [1945] 1 All E.R. 121; *Canada Square Corporation Ltd v. Versafood Services Ltd* [1980] 101 D.L.R. (3d.) 743.

take into account any changes during the construction period. It also prevents any argument over the date from which rent is to be payable and avoids the rather confusing status of a tenant under a reversionary lease, whose estate is vested in interest but not in possession.

6 RENT AND RENT REVIEW

RENT

6-01 Reservation of rent and covenant to pay

Rent has been described as "a payment which a tenant is bound by his contract to pay to the landlord for the use of his land".[1]

Under a modern lease there will invariably be both a reservation of rent and an express covenant by the tenant to pay. While a covenant to pay will be a sufficient reservation, and a reservation will imply a covenant to pay, until the advent of the Landlord and Tenant (Covenants) Act 1995, an express covenant to pay was desirable from the point of view of the landlord in order to give continuing contractual rights against the original tenant.[2]

The lease should make clear the amount of rent,[3] when the rent is payable,[4] and whether it is payable in advance or in arrear.[5]

6-02 Rent-free periods

It has become almost the norm for the landlord to offer an initial rent-free period of occupation to the tenant, either as an inducement to take the lease, or to allow a period for fitting out the premises or sometimes both. It is occasionally the practice to reserve the rent of a peppercorn (if demanded) for such periods, but in fact this is not necessary, since,

[1] *United Scientific Holdings Ltd v. Burnley Borough Council* [1978] A.C. 904 at 935, *per* Lord Diplock. This concept of a contractual payment has overtaken the medieval idea of rent as an incident of a feudal relationship issuing out of the land. According to Lord Diplock the only surviving relic of the medieval concept is the remedy of distress. See also *C. H. Bailey Ltd v. Memorial Enterprises Ltd* [1974] 1 W.L.R. 728; *Bradshaw v. Pawley* [1980] 1 W.L.R. 10.
[2] But it seems that a mere reservation is itself enough to create continuing contractual rights: *Royton Industries Ltd v. Lawrence* [1994] 20 E.G. 151.
[3] However, it is not necessary for the amount to be ascertained until due—thus the rent may be subject to review during the term: see *C. H. Bailey Ltd v. Memorial Enterprises Ltd* [1974] 1 W.L.R. 728.
[4] The traditional practice is to make rent payable in advance on the usual quarter days which are March 25, June 24, September 29 and December 25. Rent is not in arrear until the end of the day on which it is payable. Rent can be made payable on a Sunday: *Child v. Edwards* [1909] 2 K.B. 753. However, a tenant cannot be compelled to pay rent on Good Friday or Christmas Day, or on a Bank Holiday (including December 26, and December 27 when December 26 falls on a Sunday): Banking and Financial Dealings Act 1971, s.1(4) and Sched. 1. In such cases payment is due on the next proper day. Despite many businesses closing down for a protracted Christmas holiday, few difficulties appear to be encountered in practice by continuing to make Christmas Day a rent payment day.
[5] Clear words are required to make the rent payable in advance.

contrary to popular belief, reservation of a rent is not necessary to constitute a lease.[6] The tenant should ensure that under the lease he obtains the full rent-free period agreed; in particular where the term granted is expressed to commence from some past date, linking the rent-free period to that date may deprive the tenant of part of the period.

6–03 Payment of rent

Unless otherwise agreed, payment of rent must be in legal currency, though it appears that if payment by other means, such as cheque or standing order, has been accepted in the past by the landlord, this will be regarded as effective until the landlord gives notice that he withdraws acceptance of that method.[7] A distinction must be drawn between tender of rent and payment of rent: a tender may provide the tenant with certain defences, but an unaccepted tender does not amount to payment or discharge of rent due. Nor is the landlord under any implied obligation to accept rent when tendered.[8] Perhaps surprisingly it is not the practice for leases to require the landlord to give a receipt for the rent.[9]

6–04 Other payments reserved as rent

It is common to reserve other types of payment, notably service charges and insurance premiums, as rent. By doing so, the landlord increases his range of remedies available if the tenant defaults.[9a] A well drawn lease will also reserve as rent interest on late rent and other late payments and, where appropriate, Value Added Tax on payments due under the lease.[10]

6–05 Rent deposits

In some cases a landlord may demand a rent deposit as a safeguard against default, particularly where there are no sureties to the lease.[11] In such cases the rent deposit deed should provide for the tenant to keep the amount of the

---

[6] See Woodfall, § 1–7.003; *Beer v. Bowden* [1981] 1 W.L.R. 522 and *Ashburn Anstalt v. Arnold* [1988] Ch. 1. However, without a lease there can be no rent: *Hizzett v. Hargreaves* [1986] C.A.T. No. 419; noted [1987] 3 C.L. 56b.

[7] *Tankexpress A/S v. Compagnie Financiere Belge des Petroles S.A.* [1949] A.C. 76 at 103–104.

[8] *Preston v. Lindlands Ltd* (1976) 239 E.G. 653 (but the tenant can obtain a declaration that the lease is not subject to forfeiture).

[9] A receipt can be important if the lease is assigned: see para. 18–16 below.

[9a] See Chap. 14.

[10] See Chap. 19.

[11] But see *Jaskel v. Sophie Nursery Products Ltd* [1993] EGCS 42 for an example of the need for clear drafting where any surety under the lease is also to guarantee the tenant's obligations under a separate rent deposit deed.

Sum deposited

deposit "topped-up" according to the current level of rent, with a proviso for forfeiture on default. While some older forms of deposit provide that the money should belong to the landlord, but is only applicable for specified purposes, more modern forms contain a charge by the tenant of the moneys in favour of the landlord, redeemable when the moneys are repaid.[12] The parties should deal with the question of interest on the fund, and the return of any balance to the tenant on assignment or termination of the lease. In the case of tenancies which are not "new tenancies" under the Landlord and Tenant (Covenants) Act 1995,[13] an obligation to return the deposit will not run with the landlord's reversion so as to bind a purchaser,[14] and therefore the tenant should require either that the deposit is returned upon sale of the reversion by the landlord, or that the landlord procures that the purchaser covenants directly with the tenant to comply with the landlord's obligations under the rent deposit deed. Under a "new tenancy"[15] however, the purchaser will be bound by all of the terms of the rent deposit deed including the obligation to return the deposit to the tenant.[16]

Interest on and return of deposit

6–06   Interest

Interest may be recoverable on unpaid rent as from the date it falls due,[17] but the award of interest lies with the discretion of the court which must be exercised judicially.[18] The landlord should therefore include an express covenant as to the payment of interest: this will carry the remedy of forfeiture and allow the landlord rather than the court to control the rate of interest. The interest rate must, however, be justifiable by reference to the actual damage to the landlord; otherwise it will constitute a penalty.[19]

Express covenant

RENT REVIEW

6–07   Generally

Rent review provisions are of central importance in the law of commercial leases. The practice of reserving variable rents is

---

[12] Where the tenant is a company this charge should be registered under Companies Act 1985, s.395.

[13] See para. 2–02 above for the meaning of "new tenancy".

[14] *Hua Chaio Commercial Bank Ltd v. Chiaphua Industries Ltd* [1987] 2 W.L.R. 179.

[15] See para. 2–02 above for the meaning of "new tenancy".

[16] By virtue of s.3(3) of the Landlord and Tenant (Covenants) Act 1995, which provides that the benefit and burden of all landlord covenants will pass on an assignment of the reversion. The "landlord covenants" will include those contained in any agreement which is collateral to the lease, such as a rent deposit deed, regardless of whether it was entered into before or after the date of the lease: 1995 Act, s.28(1).

[17] Supreme Court Act 1981, s.35A; County Courts Act 1984, s.89(1); *Allied London Investments Ltd v. Hambro Life Assurance plc* [1985] 1 EGLR 45.

[18] *ibid.*, at 46.

[19] Interest is usually expressed to be so many percentage points (up to 4% is common) above one of the clearing banks' base rates.

by no means a modern one, but since the 1960s it has attained prominence and universality in the context of commercial property. Rent review clauses have engendered a great body of case-law, which can only be fully considered in the specialist works on the subject.[20] Here it is only possible to highlight those areas which are particularly contentious or which require the most careful scrutiny. Those drafting and operating rent review clauses will need to consider how the process of review is to be initiated, the procedure it is to follow, and the basis upon which the new rent is to be assessed. But before turning to these matters, a few preliminary points may be disposed of.

A specialist area

6–08 Preliminary considerations

A great deal has been written about the object and purpose of reserving variable rents,[21] but essentially there would appear to be two related but not identical purposes. One is to adjust the rent to take account of general inflation. The other is to reflect changes in the market value of the particular property concerned.[22] (A third possible purpose which may sometimes be relevant is as a means of allowing a landlord to participate in the profits of a tenant, often referred to as a "turnover rent").[22a] The object of keeping pace with inflation may be achieved by some form of indexation, but this method is too blunt an instrument to take account of specific changes in property values, which may be influenced by local or individual factors. Thus the method of varying rent which has come to eclipse all others in this country is periodic review based, to varying degrees, on the market rent. It is upon this method that this Chapter will primarily concentrate, though other methods will be considered briefly by way of conclusion.

Purpose of rent review provisions

Indexation

Preliminary matters to be decided by the parties are the frequency of periodic reviews, whether the rent should be capable of review in both directions or upwards only, and whether the tenant should have any right to terminate the lease after the amount of the new rent is known.

Frequency of review

As to frequency, the once traditional period of seven years has now given way to five-yearly or in some cases three-yearly reviews.[22b] Whatever period is chosen, care must be exercised over how the review dates are defined in the lease. Defining them by reference to the date of the lease can be dangerous, because doubts can arise as to whether the period runs from the date of actual execution or the date expressed in the lease

---

[20] R. Bernstein and K. Reynolds, *Handbook of Rent Review*; D. N. Clarke and J. E. Adams, *Rent Reviews and Variable Rents* (3rd ed., 1991).

[21] See R. Bernstein and K. Reynolds, *Handbook of Rent Review*, para. 1–1; D. N. Clarke and J. E. Adams, *Rent Reviews and Variable Rents* (3rd ed. 1991) Chaps. 1 and 2.

[22] For a useful judicial summary see *British Airways plc v. Heathrow Airport plc* [1992] 19 E.G. 157 (Mummery J.).

[22a] See para. 6–39 below.

[22b] With low inflation, it will be interesting to see if rent review periods become longer again.

for the commencement of the term.[23] Better practice is to insert the actual date of the first review when the lease is executed, and to define all future review dates by reference to that, or to specify the actual dates of review (although this places the onus on the parties' solicitors to remember to insert the relevant dates).[24,25] In very long leases it may be sensible to insert some provision for reviewing the review

"Eleventh hour" reviews period. The landlord may also consider inserting a rent review at the end of the lease, on the assumption that should the tenant remain in occupation under Part II of the Landlord and Tenant Act 1954, rent obtainable on review is likely to exceed the interim rent which the landlord could obtain on making an application under section 24A of the Act.[26] Against this the tenant can argue that a section 24A rent would be fairer, in more accurately reflecting the uncertainty as to renewal under the 1954 Act.

Either-way or upwards only The purpose of a rent review clause can be seen as an attempt to preserve the original bargain of the parties against external pressures.[27] If this is correct, then logically a review should be capable of reducing as well as increasing the rent, if justified by economic circumstances and the property market. However, for many landlords the predominant purpose of rent review is to provide a secure return on their investment, and in practice there is strong resistance to the possibility of a rent review actually diminishing that return. Thus, despite the considerable pressures on landlords as a result of the recent

Upwards only remains the norm recession to agree either way reviews, upwards only reviews have generally remained the norm, considerations of logic and fairness notwithstanding. The Law Society/R.I.C.S Model Form of rent review clause[28] provides alternative forms of wording to cover each type of clause. The first edition of this book warned of the risk tenants run in accepting an upwards only clause which may result in the passing rent substantially exceeding the market rent: this warning has proved to be justified. Leases have in these circumstances proved unsaleable, or only saleable upon payment of a reverse premium. Nevertheless, while new tenants have been able to enjoy substantial rent-free periods or other inducements, the inclusion of an either-way review is still rare.[29]

If an upwards only clause is agreed, care should be taken by the landlord that this is effectively embodied in the actual wording used. There is no presumption in favour of

---

[23] See *Beaumont Property Trust v. Tai* (1982) 265 E.G. 872. Where time runs from the term commencement date this can effectively deprive the tenant of the benefit of a full period at the initially agreed rent.

[24,25] For a case of professional negligence stemming from such an omission, see *Costa v. Georghiou*, C.A., 1984 (unreported but noted at (1985) 276 E.G. 148).

[26] See para. 16–32 below.

[27] D. N. Clarke and J. E. Adams, *Rent Reviews and Variable Rents* (3rd ed. 1991), pp. 6–9.

[28] See para. 6–37 below.

[29] There is still no reported case of a court in renewal proceedings under ss.24–28 of the Landlord and Tenant Act 1954 ordering an either-way review where the former lease contained an upwards only clause. See *Forbuoys v. Newport Borough Council* [1994] 24 E.G. 156 (upwards and downwards in the renewal, but no review in previous lease).

construing a clause so as to make it upwards only.[30] One possible danger to be considered by the landlord is that the rent payable immediately before review may have been reduced on an ad hoc basis or under a suspension of rent clause to reflect damage to the property.

Break clause   One safeguard for the tenant against unacceptable increases in rent on review is a clause giving the tenant the option to determine the lease.[31] Once quite rare, but now much more frequently seen, especially with leases of 15 years and upwards, such clauses may have the effect of making time of the essence in provisions as to the activation of the rent review.[32]

6–09 Activating the review provisions

Perhaps the simplest form of rent review clause procedurally is one providing for the rent to be reviewed on a certain date, either by agreement of the parties, or in the absence of agreement by some third person on the application of either party (this approach is adopted by the Law Society/R.I.C.S. Model Form). If this is the case, no obligation will be implied on either party to set the process in motion,[33] or to negotiate.[34] Thus the conduct of the negotiation is left to the discretion of the parties, which may make an amicable settlement more likely, but on the other hand may lead to confusion and delay. The tenant should ensure that the power to refer the decision to a third party is available to him and does not rest solely in the hands of the landlord.[34a] It is also in the interests of both parties that the clause should provide for the new rent to be evidenced in writing, usually by a rent review memorandum signed by both landlord and tenant (and any surety for either party)[35] and either endorsed on or otherwise affixed to both lease and counterpart.

Determination by agreement

---

[30] *Bodfield Ltd v. Caldew Colour Plates Ltd* [1985] 1 EGLR 110 at 112; *Philpots (Woking) Ltd v. Surrey Conveyancers Ltd* [1986] 1 EGLR 97 at 98. But *cf. Brimican Investments Ltd v. Blue Circle Heating Ltd* [1995] EGCS 18 where the rent review clause was not upwards only but the landlord succeeded in his claim that it did not reflect the parties' intentions when the lease was entered into and was granted rectification.

[31] For break clauses generally, see paras. 16–05 to 16–09 below. Ideally the option should be expressed to be exercisable within a prescribed period after agreement as to or determination of the revised rent thus giving the tenant the opportunity to decide on the basis of that rent whether or not to determine the lease. An option exercisable on the review date itself is of less value to the tenant since it is rare that the revised rent is actually known by then; properly advised, the tenant should, however, have a reasonable idea of what the new rent might be.

[32] See para. 6–10 below.

[33] *Edwin Woodhouse Trustee Co. Ltd v. Sheffield Brick Co. plc* (1984) 270 E.G. 548.

[34] *Essoldo Ltd v. Elcresta Ltd* (1972) 23 P. & C.R. 1; *Wrenbridge Ltd v. Harries (Southern Properties) Ltd* (1981) 260 E.G. 1195.

[34a] See *Harben Style Ltd v. Rhodes Trust* [1995] 17 E.G. 125 and *Royal Bank of Scotland plc v. Jennings* [1995] 35 E.G. 140 for conflicting decisions where the landlord alone could initiate reference to a third party.

[35] See para. 3–16 above.

6–10 Notice to review

Many leases, particularly older ones granted in the 1970s and early 1980s, contain provisions which attempt to formalise the review process. By providing the parties with a definite procedure to follow, the task of arriving at the new rent may be conducted more efficiently. The procedures are capable of infinite variation, but a common method is for a notice to be served requesting review, followed by a time during which the parties may reach agreement, after which the matter may be referred to a third party for determination. The questions to be considered here are:

(1) who may serve the initial notice;
(2) must it be served at any specific time;
(3) what will be the consequences of failure to adhere to any time provisions; and
(4) what form should the notice take?

Who may initiate review? Often the lease will provide that only the landlord may initiate the review process. The tenant, who may be very happy to continue paying the old rent as long as possible, may regard that as acceptable. However, the situation may arise where a speedy review is in the interests of the tenant, because he wishes to assign the lease or because he wishes to know with certainty what his future rent will be[36]; or, in the rare cases where the rent can go down as well as up at review, to enable the tenant to take advantage of a fall in the market.[36a] Thus the tenant should argue where possible for the right to initiate the review himself, or at least to do so in the event of delay by the landlord.

Time provisions It is common to provide that the notice is to be served a certain time before the review date, in order to give time for negotiation (commonly three or six months),[37] although there are many leases which allow a landlord to call for a review at

---

[36] Most modern leases also oblige the tenant to pay interest, sometimes at a penal rate, on the difference between the old rent and the new rent when ascertained. Any delay could therefore prejudice the tenant.

[36a] For two decisions (producing different results) where, because rents had fallen and the leases contained either-way review provisions, the landlords were (understandably) refusing to operate the rent review machinery, see *Harben Style Ltd v. Rhodes Trust* [1995] 17 E.G. 125 and *Royal Bank of Scotland plc v. Jennings* [1995] 35 E.G. 140 (see also para. 6–14 below).

[37] *e.g. Samuel Properties (Developments) Ltd v. Hayek* [1972] 1 W.L.R. 1296. See also *Supasnaps Ltd v. Bailey* [1995] EGCS 89 where, in relation to a review clause where time was expressly of the essence, the landlord had to serve a trigger notice "before the beginning of a clear period of two quarters . . . immediately preceding the review date". The review date was June 23, 1992 and the landlord served the notice on October 9, 1991, $8\frac{1}{2}$ months before the review date. The Court of Appeal held that the period ending on June 23 was a clear quarter, preferring a sensible construction to a literal construction which produced a nonsensical result (*cf.* the Court of Appeal's decision on a tenant's break clause in *Mannai Investment Company Ltd v. Eagle Life Star Life Assurance Company Ltd* at para. 16–06 below).

any time up to the end of the review period in question.[38] It is also advisable to specify a date before which notice may not be served. A question which has given rise to a great deal of litigation is the effect of failure to comply with any time limits stated in the lease. It is now authoritatively decided that in general such time stipulations are not of the essence, and that failure to comply with them does not deprive the landlord of the right to have the rent reviewed.[39] However, time may be of the essence if an intention to that effect appears from the words of the lease or from surrounding circumstances.[40] Thus there is nothing to prevent the parties using express words to

Time of the essence

make time of the essence,[41] though it will be advisable to use very clear and unequivocal language,[42] and one can discern a tendency of the courts to avoid if possible making time of the essence in respect of the date by which the determination must be made.[43] However, the courts are so far divided on whether providing that a particular step is a "condition precedent" to determining the new rent makes time of the essence.[44] Where the timetable appears in a rent review clause makes no difference. Whether time is of the essence is a matter of substance rather than form.[45] It is also important to be clear whether time is of the essence for all steps or only for some.[46] If time is expressly made of the essence for one step, that is an indication that it is not intended to be of the essence for others[47]and a general stipulation that time is not to be of the essence in relation to the review process will take precedence over a later provision which appears to impose a strict time limit.[48]

---

[38] See *Maraday v. Sturt Properties Ltd* [1988] 46 E.G. 99 and *Holicater Ltd v. Grandred Ltd* [1993] 23 E.G. 129. Some leases give the landlord the right to choose a date subsequent to the specified date by, say, a month's notice. This can be beneficial to the landlord where rents are depressed at the specified review date.

[39] *United Scientific Holdings Ltd v. Burnley Borough Council* [1978] A.C. 904.

[40] *ibid.*, p. 930, *per* Lord Diplock.

[41] *Weller v. Akehurst* [1981] 3 All E.R. 411. See also *Darlington Borough Council v. Waring & Gillow (Holdings) Ltd* [1988] 45 E.G. 102.

[42] *Touche Ross & Co. v. Secretary of State for the Environment* (1983) 46 P. & C.R. 187; *Thorn E.M.I. Pension Trust Ltd v. Quinton Hazell plc* (1984) 269 E.G. 414 ("in any event not later than"—time not of the essence); and *cf. Drebbond v. Horsham District Council* (1978) 37 P. & C.R. 237 (reference to a third party was to be by a particular date "but not otherwise"—time was of the essence).

[43] *King (Estate Agents) Ltd v. Anderson* [1992] 5 E.G. 166 and *Shuwa Ashdown House Corporation v. Graygrigg Properties Ltd* [1992] 46 E.G. 108. But see *Art and Sound Ltd v. West London Litho Ltd* [1992] 14 E.G. 110 where a reference that "time to be of the essence of these provisions" was held to mean that, whether by agreement or arbitration, the rent had to be ascertained prior to the review date.

[44] *North Hertfordshire District Council v. Hitchin Industrial Estate Ltd* [1992] 37 E.G. 133 (time not of the essence); *cf. Chelsea Building Society v. R&A Millett (Shops) Ltd* [1994] 9 E.G. 182 (time was of the essence).

[45] *Pembroke St Georges Ltd v. Cromwell Developments Ltd* [1991] EGCS 43.

[46] *C. Bradley & Sons Ltd v. Telefusion Ltd* (1981) 259 E.G. 337.

[47] *Amherst v. James Walker Goldsmith and Silversmith Ltd* (No. 1) (1980) 254 E.G. 123.

[48] *Panavia Air Cargo v. Southend-on-Sea Borough Council* [1988] 22 E.G. 82. Such a provision is contained in the Law Society/R.I.C.S. Model Form and is almost always included in modern leases.

Inter-relationship with break clause

The inter-relationship between the timetable for rent review and a provision giving the tenant the right to terminate the lease may also have the effect of making any stipulations as to time contained in the former of the essence: otherwise the tenant's right to break if the reviewed rent is unacceptably high could be rendered nugatory.[49] It appears from *Legal and General Assurance (Pension Management) Ltd v. Cheshire County Council*[50] that possible prejudice to the tenant is not necessary and that the inter-relationship can appear from the form and language of the provisions and the coincidence of dates. In that case time was of the essence, even though as the clause stood the landlord could have served notice at the very last moment, making the informed exercise of the tenant's break clause impossible. However, the right to review was not lost in *Metrolands Investments Ltd v. J. H. Dewhurst Ltd*[51] (where the tenant's right to break was exercisable after the date by which the rent should have been determined). Although the Court of Appeal seemed to suggest that the rationale for construing time as of the essence is that the parties intended the tenant to be able to exercise the break clause with knowledge of the new rent, it was also stated that time is less likely to be of the essence if the event required is not within the full control of the landlord, for example, as here, the actual obtaining of an arbitrator's decision. The court was also influenced by the fact that the tenant could have initiated the review procedure himself.[51a] Nevertheless, the fact that either party could invoke the review machinery did not prejudice the tenant in *Central Estates Ltd v. Secretary of State for the Environment*,[51b] where the landlord's late notice meant that the tenant had no time to evaluate the effect of the new rent.

Notice to make time of the essence

Where time is not of the essence it may be possible, according to one first instance decision,[52] for a party adversely affected by delay to serve notice on the other making time of the essence. However, such a remedy will not be available where its exercise would cause unfairness: in particular where other procedural steps are available to expedite the process.

Delay by landlord

Even where time is not of the essence, the question can arise as to whether unreasonable delay on the part of the landlord in serving notice may result in the right to review being lost. It appears that unreasonable delay of itself will not have this effect.[53] However, there is some authority to suggest

---

[49] *C. Richards & Son Ltd v. Karenita Ltd* (1972) 221 E.G. 25 (applied in *Central Estates Ltd v. Secretary of State for the Environment* [1995] EGCS 110); *Al Saloom v. Shirley James Travel Services Ltd* (1981) 42 P. & C.R. 181.

[50] (1984) 269 E.G. 40. Followed in *Stephenson v. Orca Properties Ltd* [1989] 44 E.G. 81 (which also illustrates the dangers of serving notices at the last minute).

[51] [1986] 3 All E.R. 659.

[51a] See also *Edwin Woodhouse Trustee Co. Ltd v. Sheffield Brick Co. plc* (1983) 270 E.G. 548, where the landlord did not lose his right to review where there was no date by which application for third party determination was to be made.

[51b] [1995] EGCS 110.

[52] *Factory Holdings Group Ltd v. Leboff International Ltd* (1986) 282 E.G. 1005.

[53] *Amherst v. James Walker Goldsmith and Silversmith Ltd* (No. 2) [1983] Ch. 305.

that long delay may amount to evidence of abandonment of the right to review.[54] This suggestion has been criticised *obiter* by members of the Court of Appeal,[55] on the basis that a right to rent review cannot be lost by unilateral abandonment, but only by estoppel[56] or consensual variation. A dictum of Lord Salmon in *United Scientific Holdings Ltd v. Burnley Borough Council*[57] suggests that delay which causes hardship to the tenant may destroy the right to review, but this has been subsequently doubted.[58] The uncertainty surrounding this area is further reason why the tenant should not leave operation of the review machinery solely in the hands of the landlord.

Form of notice   Another question is what form the notice initiating the review should take. Certainly it should be in writing, though it is an open question whether such a requirement would be construed as being of the essence.[59] Often it is provided that the notice shall contain a proposed figure for the new rent, but there are conflicting decisions as to whether failure to insert the figure will invalidate the notice.[60] What is clear is that the notice must, on a fair reading, convey to the reader that it is intended to set in motion the review procedure.[61]

Reference to   The question may also arise as to what constitutes an
arbitration   effective reference to arbitration or to an expert as part of the review process. It has been held that a reference may be genuine even if made for the purpose of safeguarding the applicant's position and in the hope that continuing

---

[54] *Accuba Ltd v. Allied Shoe Repairs Ltd* [1975] 1 W.L.R. 1559; *Telegraph Properties (Securities) Ltd v. Courtaulds Ltd* (1981) 257 E.G. 1153.

[55] *Amherst v. James Walker Goldsmith and Silversmith Ltd* (No. 2) [1983] Ch. 305 at 315–316, *per* Oliver L.J., Lawton L.J. agreeing. *Telegraph Properties Ltd v. Courtaulds Ltd* (n. 54 above) was said to have been wrongly decided on that basis.

[56] The decided cases suggest that estoppel will be very difficult to argue successfully in this context: see *James v. Heim Gallery (London) Ltd* (1980) 41 P. & C.R. 269; *Accuba Ltd v. Allied London Shoe Repairs* [1975] 1 W.L.R. 1559; *London & Manchester Assurance Co. Ltd v. G.A. Dunn Ltd* (1983) 265 E.G. 39 at 131.

[57] [1978] A.C. 904 at 956.

[58] *Amherst v. James Walker Goldsmith and Silversmith Ltd* (No. 2) [1983] Ch. 305 at 316, 320, *per* Oliver, Lawton L.JJ.; *London & Manchester Assurance Co. Ltd v. G. A. Dunn Ltd* (1983) 265 E.G. 39 at 135, *per* Slade L.J.

[59] *Dean and Chapter of Chichester Cathedral v. Lennards Ltd* (1978) 35 P. & C.R. 309 at 314, *per* Lord Russell.

[60] *ibid.*, where the absence of a figure did not invalidate the notice. But *cf.*, *Commission for the New Towns v. R. Levy & Co.* [1990] 28 E.G. 119 where the notice was to "specify the yearly rent which the Commission proposes"—this was held to be a mandatory requirement and the failure to specify the proposed rent invalidated the notice. However, where a tenant's counter-notice failed to specify the rent the tenant was willing to pay *R. Levy & Co.* was itself distinguished; *Patel v. Earlspring Properties Ltd* [1991] 46 E.G. 153. Note that a discrepancy between the words and the figures will not invalidate a notice: *Durham City Estates v. Felicetti* [1990] 3 E.G. 71.

[61] *Norwich Union Life Assurance Society v. Sketchley plc* [1986] 2 EGLR 126 at 128 (Scott J.). But *cf.*, *Norwich Union Life Assurance Society v. Tony Waller Ltd* (1984) 270 E.G. 42 at 43, where Harman J. suggested that the notice should refer to the clause and to the procedure to be followed. Scott J. in the later case distinguished the decision of Harman J., even though the clause and the letter in each case were substantially identical, on the basis that the letter in the earlier case was expressed to be "without prejudice"; but that does not appear to have been the main ground of Harman J.'s decision.

negotiations may render arbitration or determination by an expert unnecessary.[62]

6–11 Default notices

"Trigger notice"

A variant on the procedure described above, often somewhat blandly described as a "trigger notice", is to provide that the landlord may serve notice specifying a figure for the new rent and that failure to respond by the tenant shall result in the landlord's figure becoming the new rent. It will be appreciated that this type of provision can result in considerable prejudice to the tenant, and such clauses need to be approached and operated with care.[63] Fortunately, they rarely appear in more modern leases.

Form of landlord's notice

To be effective, the landlord's notice must constitute an unequivocal invocation of the procedure in the lease,[64] although in *Royal Life Insurance v. Phillips*[65] the landlord's notice (expressed to be given "in accordance with the terms of the lease") was held to be valid despite being marked "subject to contract" and "without prejudice". However, unless the lease so provides, the landlord is under no obligation to use any particular method for calculating the figure in his notice, or to warn the tenant of the consequences of failure to reply.[66]

Tenant's counter-notice

For a tenant faced with a notice of this type, two questions are of paramount importance if he is to avoid being fixed with the possibly unrealistic and inflated figure stated in the notice: what form of counter-notice should he serve, and must he serve it within a particular time? Both questions can only be answered fully in the light of the exact wording of the lease, but from the reported cases it is possible to extract a number of general points.

Often the clause will provide that the new rent is to be that stated in the landlord's notice, or as agreed between the parties, or, at the election of the tenant, determined by an expert or arbitrator. A series of cases going back to 1979 shows that this wording can prove a trap for the unwary

---

[62] *Staines Warehousing Co. Ltd v. Montagu Executor & Trustee Co. Ltd* [1986] 1 EGLR 101, also holding that the application was not invalidated by failure to enclose the fee required by the R.I.C.S. guidance notes or to notify the other party.

[63] See *Cordon Bleu Freezer Food Centres Limited v. Marbleace Ltd* [1987] 2 EGLR 143 for a case where the amount in the tenant's counter-notice became the revised rent when the landlord failed to apply to the R.I.C.S. in time.

[64] *Shirlcar Properties Ltd v. Heinetz* (1983) 268 E.G. 362 (a landlord's notice headed "subject to contract" ineffective). See also *Norwich Union Life Assurance Society v. Sketchley plc* [1986] 2 EGLR 126 at 128, where Scott J. suggested that a more stringent attitude may be applied to notices requiring action by the recipient.

[65] [1990] 43 E.G. 70. The fact that the tenant responded to the notice appears to have satisfied the court that she understood its effect.

[66] *Taylor Woodrow Property Co. Ltd v. Lonrho Textiles Ltd* [1985] 2 EGLR 120 at 122. See also *Amalgamated Estates Ltd v. Joystretch Holdings Ltd* (1980) 257 E.G. 489 (no obligation for landlord's figure to be a bona fide and genuine estimate of market rental).

Form of counter-notice

tenant. Following these cases, in order to avoid the figure in the notice, the tenant must unequivocally elect for determination by a third party,[67] although where the tenant said he considered the landlord's figure to be excessive, it was held to be a plain indication that the tenant did not agree with the landlord's proposal.[68] Other more recent decisions[69] suggest a more liberal approach: that provided the counter-notice makes the tenant's intention to exercise his right for independent determination clear, it need not be unequivocal. Nevertheless, great care should still be taken to ensure that the counter-notice is properly drafted.

Another question is whether any time limits apply for service of the counter-notice, and if so whether time is of the essence. A time limit of three months is commonly inserted, and often landlords attempt to provide that time shall be of the essence. The tenant should be wary of accepting a provision making time of the essence expressly,[70] but even if time is not expressly made of the essence, the structure of the clause may indicate an intention to make it so. In particular, the clause may provide that if the tenant fails to serve a counter-notice within the prescribed time he shall be deemed to have accepted the landlord's figure. Such provisions have provoked a clash of authority in the Court of Appeal,[71] and

Time limits for counter-notice

---

[67] *Bellinger v. South London Stationers Ltd* (1979) 252 E.G. 699; *Amalgamated Estates Ltd v. Joystretch Holdings Ltd* (1980) 257 E.G. 489; *Edlingham v. MFI Furniture Centres Ltd* (1981) 259 E.G. 421.

[68] *Barrett Estate Services Ltd v. David Grieg (Retail) Ltd* [1991] 36 E.G. 155. Similarly in *Glofield Properties Ltd v. Morley* [1988] 2 E.G. 62 where the tenant's letter requesting the landlord to "accept this letter as formal objection and counter-notice" was sufficient despite not specifically requiring reference to an independent surveyor.

[69] *Nunes v. Davies, Laing & Dick Ltd* [1986] 1 EGLR 106; *British Rail Pension Trustee Co. Ltd v. Cardshops Ltd* (1986) 282 E.G. 331 (where the tenant's counter-notice was headed "subject to contract"); *Patel v. Earlspring Properties Ltd* [1991] 46 E.G. 153 (where the tenant failed to specify the rent he could pay, but merely said he could not meet the landlord's figure); and *Prudential Property Services Ltd v. Capital Land Holdings Ltd* [1993] 15 E.G. 147, where the tenant's response to the landlord's trigger notice did not specifically call for determination by an independent surveyor as the lease required, but made sufficiently clear the tenant's disagreement with the landlord's proposed rental figure.

[70] See *Amalgamated Estates Ltd v. Joystretch Holdings Ltd* (1980) 257 E.G. 489 at 493, *per* Templeman L.J.: "I think it is a great pity that any landlord should require, or any tenant should accept, a provision making time of the essence when the consequences are so onerous."

[71] *Henry Smith's Charity Trustees v. AWADA Trading & Promotion Services Ltd* (1983) 269 E.G. 729 (2:1 majority that time of the essence where the landlord failed to apply for a third party determination); *Mecca Leisure Ltd v. Renown Investments (Holdings) Ltd* (1984) 271 E.G. 989 (2:1 majority that time not of the essence where the tenant failed to apply). See also *Greenhaven Securities Ltd v. Compton* [1985] 2 EGLR 117 (where the court felt that to allow a late application after both parties had failed to apply to the President of the R.I.C.S. within 12 months after the review date would be to make a new bargain for the parties); *Phipps-Faire Ltd v. Malbern Construction Ltd* (1987) 282 E.G. 460 (where the landlord's failure to apply in time to the R.I.C.S. did not mean that the tenant's figure prevailed), and *Taylor Woodrow Property Co. Ltd v. Lonrho Textiles Ltd* [1985] 2 EGLR 120 where Deputy Judge B. A. Hytner Q.C. attempted to distinguish the

for the tenant the only safe course is to ensure that any time limits stated are rigorously adhered to. One analysis of such provisions which so far does not appear to have been considered by the courts is in terms of offer and acceptance. The landlord's notice suggesting a rental figure can be seen as an offer. Generally, it is not possible for the offeror to **Silence** stipulate that silence by the offeree constitutes acceptance,[72] **constituting** but there seems no reason why the parties cannot agree in **acceptance** advance that silence shall have that effect. Thus it would seem possible to frame the clause so that failure by the tenant to respond to the notice within a given period constitutes acceptance of the offer; a binding contract to pay the figure suggested in the notice will then result, and there will be nothing left to agree or arbitrate about.

Where the tenant does fail to comply with the time limit for serving a counter-notice then, providing the rent review procedure envisages arbitration rather than determination by **Extension of** an expert,[73] it may still be possible to make an application to **time by court** the High Court under section 27 of the Arbitration Act 1950 for extension of the period. It has been decided by the Court of Appeal that the section may be used where the right to refer to arbitration is unilateral.[74]

However, in order to succeed, the tenant must show that **Undue hardship** undue hardship would result from the period not being extended, and this may be difficult in cases where the delay has been long, prejudicial to the landlord, or arises from the fault of the tenant.[75] No application will be possible where the timetable for activating the review itself (as opposed to activating the arbitration procedure) is not adhered to since there is no dispute about which to arbitrate.[76]

Section 27 is not the exclusive preserve of tenants. In a

---

two Court of Appeal decisions by considering whether the deeming provision was capable of operating in favour of both parties or of one only, and expressed a preference for the decision in *Mecca* if the two cases were really in conflict. In *Mammoth Greeting Cards Ltd v. Agra Ltd* [1990] 29 E.G. 45, Mummery J. decided that reference to the rent being "conclusively fixed at the amount in the lessor's notice" was sufficient to displace the usual presumption that time is not of the essence, whereas in *Bickenhall Engineering Company Ltd v. Grandmet Restaurants Ltd* [1995] 10 E.G. 123 the Court of Appeal held that the absence of a time limit within the default clause itself meant time was not of the essence, even though there was a time limit in a separate clause.

[72] *Felthouse v. Bindley* (1863) 11 C.B. (N.S.) 869.

[73] *Fordgate (Bingley) Ltd v. Argyll Stores Ltd* [1994] 39 E.G. 135.

[74] *Pittalis v. Sherefettin* [1986] Q.B. 868, overruling *Tote Bookmakers Ltd v. Development & Property Holdings Co. Ltd* [1985] Ch. 261.

[75] See *The Aspen Trader* [1981] 1 Lloyd's Rep. 273 at 279; *Chartered Trust plc v. Maylands Green Estate Co. Ltd* (1984) 270 E.G. 845. In *Pittalis v. Sherefettin, ibid.*, the tenant's claim failed because of these factors and because he was unable to show that the landlord's figure was grossly inflated. See also *Patel (Bhanubhai) v. Peel Investments (South) Ltd* [1992] 30 E.G. 88 where the tenant's hardship, despite his delay, for which there was no good reason, coupled with the amount at stake, persuaded the court to grant an extension but on the basis that the amount in dispute was paid into a joint account pending the determination.

[76] *Ricehurst Ltd v. Pimenta* [1993] 1 W.L.R. 159.

recently reported decision[76a] the landlord was granted an extension where it had failed to apply for the appointment of an arbitrator in accordance with the time limits of the lease, albeit on terms that the landlord should pay the cost of proceedings and the tenant would not be liable for interest on any shortfall in the rent from the review date to the date of judgment.

6–12 Determining the new rent

In most cases the new rent will either be agreed between the parties or fixed by a third party, either as an expert or an arbitrator. So far as agreement is concerned, the lease should provide that any agreement is to be in writing, and correspondence written in the course of negotiation should be marked "without prejudice" in order to prevent it being used as evidence should arbitration become necessary.[77] The privilege extends to all documents so marked and forming part of negotiations, whether or not offers or "opening shots". An exchange of correspondence, where the landlord's opening letter was marked "subject to contract" and "without prejudice" but the tenant's letter of acceptance was not so marked, was nevertheless held not to give rise to a binding contract.[78]

"Without prejudice"

6–13 Arbitrator or expert?

A question to be considered in drafting the review clause is whether determination of the rent in default of agreement should be by an arbitrator or by an independent expert. The distinction is far from easy to draw in practice,[79] though the essential difference is that an arbitrator fulfils the judicial function of deciding a dispute on the evidence and submissions of the parties, whereas an expert may reach a decision purely on his own knowledge and experience.[80] This of itself is a simplification, as experts may, and frequently do, solicit evidence from the parties; and arbitrators may use their

Distinction between arbitrator and expert

[76a] *Fordgate (Bingley) Ltd v. National Westminster Bank plc* [1995] EGCS 97. The likely hardship to the landlord, the fact that it was his agent who had overlooked the time limit for appointing an arbitrator rather than the landlord himself and the fact that the tenant was not prejudiced all weighed in favour of the landlord's application succeeding.

[77] *South Shropshire District Council v. Amos* [1986] 1 W.L.R. 1271.

[78] *Henderson Group Ltd v. Superabbey Ltd* [1988] 39 E.G. 87.

[79] See D. N. Clarke and J. E. Adams, *Rent Reviews and Variable Rents* (3rd. ed. 1991), pp. 179–182.

[80] *Palacath Ltd v. Flanagan* [1985] 2 All E.R. 161; *North Eastern Co-operative Society Ltd v. Newcastle upon Tyne City Council* (1987) 282 E.G. 1409.

own special knowledge (within certain constraints)[81] and experience in evaluating the parties' evidence. But if the arbitrator introduces other evidence the parties must have the chance to comment.[82] This appears to be a departure from the earlier, less stringent, position.[83] The lease should always make clear in which capacity the third party is to act.[84]

Advantages of arbitrator

The main advantage of appointing an arbitrator rather than an expert is that the formal framework of the Arbitration Acts 1950 and 1979 will be invoked. This will provide a means of resolving a number of problems which might occur: for example the appointment of a new arbitrator should the appointed one die or become unfit to act; the determination by the court of questions of law arising during the arbitration; the compelling of witnesses by *subpoena* to give evidence or produce documents (of increasing importance given the tendency of one or other of the parties to require the outcome of the review to be kept confidential); and the award and taxation of costs. In addition, misconduct or unfairness on the part of an arbitrator can be more easily controlled than such conduct by an expert.

Advantages of expert

The main advantage of appointing an expert is probably that the cost of determination is likely to be less than by way of arbitration. However, whether this is in fact so will largely depend on how the determination is conducted in practice. There may be little advantage in terms of cost if each party retains his own surveyor to make submissions to the expert; and the costs of arbitration can be kept down by confining submissions to documentary evidence only. Another possible advantage of determination by an expert is finality: there is no statutory procedure for appealing the decision. However, ever since the 1982 decision in *The Nema*,[85] the opportunities for challenging an arbitrator's decision have been considerably curtailed. Unlike an arbitrator, an expert will have no immunity against an action in negligence,[86] which might be

---

[81] *Fox v. P.C. Wellfair Ltd* (1982) 263 E.G. 589. See also *Secretary of State for the Environment v. Reed International plc* [1994] 6 E.G. 137.

[82] *Unit Four Cinemas Ltd v. Tosara Investment Ltd* [1993] 44 E.G. 120 where the court was of the view that the arbitrator had effectively given evidence to himself by adopting a different valuation method from that used by the landlord's valuer.

[83] *Temple Crook Ltd v. Capital and Counties Property Co. Ltd* [1990] 38 E.G. 118 where the arbitrator's valuation approach was upheld and *Lex Services Ltd v. Oriel House B.V.* [1991] 39 E.G. 139 where the court held that valuation not being an exact science requiring slavish adherence to comparables meant that the arbitrator could use his own expertise and reach conclusions without giving the parties the right to object.

[84] *Fordgate (Bingley) Ltd v. Argyll Stores Ltd* [1994] 39 E.G. 135, where the judge commented that the exercise of determining the rent was particularly suitable for expert procedures.

[85] See para. 6–19, n. 34 below.

[86] *Palacath Ltd v. Flanagan* [1985] 2 All E.R. 161. The immunity of the arbitrator has been expressly preserved by the Supply of Services (Exclusion of Implied Terms) Order (No. 1) 1985 (S.I. 1985 No. 1) against the Supply of Goods and Services Act 1982, which might be thought to have removed it.

regarded as a reason in favour of appointing an expert. However, negligence will not be easy to establish,[87] and hardly provides a satisfactory remedy against a bad decision.

Factors in choosing arbitrator or expert

Thus the choice will to some extent be governed by the type of property in question. Valuation by an expert, with its informality of procedure, may be preferable for low-value properties, or where the valuation issues are likely to be straightforward. But where the sums of money at stake are likely to be considerable, or where the property raises difficult valuation problems by its special nature or lack of comparables,[88] there is a great deal to be said for arbitration. Even then, tenants in particular might consider that the expert is more likely to be pragmatic in dealing with complex situations (especially where he is not required to give reasons for his decision) and it should not be overlooked that, whatever the lease provides, it will be open to the parties on review to agree upon a different method of determining the rent. Thus where a simple valuation has become complicated by changes in the locality, or by unforeseen issues of law, it may be advisable to agree on arbitration. However, any surety to the lease will need to be consulted and give his agreement to such a variation, otherwise he will not be bound by the new rent.[89]

6–14 Appointing the third party

The usual method of appointing an arbitrator or expert is for the parties to agree, or in the absence of agreement for the appointment to be made by the President of the Royal Institution of Chartered Surveyors,[90] on the application of either party, although some leases, frequently of shops in a parade or shopping centre, will confer the right to apply on the landlord alone, so he can better control the timing of any

---

[87] *Belvedere Motors Ltd v. King* (1981) 260 E.G. 813 (negligence only if the expert failed to take matters into account, took wrong matters into account, failed to use accepted procedures, or to exercise care and skill held out as possessing—the correctness or otherwise of the decision will only be relevant in extreme cases). See also *Zubaida v. Hargreaves* [1995] 9 E.G. 320 where Hoffmann L.J. pronounced "Valuation is not an exact science; it involves questions of judgment on which experts may differ without forfeiting their claim to professional competence." (The valuer had considered neighbouring retail premises in determining the value of a restaurant where the lease prohibited non-restaurant use).

[88] For a series of picturesque examples, such as castles used as museums, sports stadia and motorway service stations, see D. N. Clarke and J. E. Adams, *Rent Reviews and Variable Rents* (3rd ed. 1991), pp. 191–192.

[89] See para. 3–15 above.

[90] Arguments as to whether the President should make an appointment cannot be raised by seeking an injunction to restrain the appointment: the non-applicant party may still seek a declaration that the appointment is void however: *United London Co-operatives Ltd v. Sun Alliance & London Assurance Co. Ltd* (1986) 282 E.G. 91.

awards.[90a] The R.I.C.S. Guidance Notes[90b] deal fully with the
position where the proposed arbitrator has a connection with
the property or either party, or where other circumstances
exist which might give rise to the appearance of bias. It may
be possible for one party to proceed straight to a request for
the appointment of an arbitrator without going through the
other steps envisaged by the lease.[91]

6–15 Arbitration procedure

Preliminary
meeting
Directions

After his appointment, the arbitrator will usually hold a
preliminary meeting, to allow the parties to make
representations as to the procedure to be followed. The
arbitrator will then give directions which should deal with the
following matters:

(1) whether the arbitration is to be conducted by a hearing,
    or on the basis of documents and written submissions;[92]
(2) agreement if possible as to a plan and description of the
    property and the basis for measuring floor-space;
(3) agreement if possible as to comparables;
(4) how any points of law arising are to be dealt with. Such
    matters can be dealt with by agreement excluding any
    appeal to the court (Arbitration Act 1979, s.3), by
    reference to the court or counsel as a preliminary point,
    by authorising the arbitrator to take legal advice, by
    appointing a legal assessor, or by the arbitrator making
    alternative awards based on the different assumptions;
(5) the timetable for serving each party's statement of case
    and proofs of evidence;
(6) length and venue of hearing, if any;
(7) the arbitrator's fees.[93]

[90a] The landlord being able to frustrate the operation of the review
machinery, by refusing to apply for the appointment of an arbitrator, can
have serious consequences for a tenant. See *Harben Style Ltd v. Rhodes
Trust* [1995] 17 E.G. 125 where the court refused to imply an obligation
on the landlord to make the application, on the basis that the lease made it
clear that the existing rent would remain payable should there be no
review. Compare, however, *Royal Bank of Scotland plc v. Jennings* [1995] 35
E.G. 140 where the judge distinguished *Harben* and granted an injunction
to compel the landlord to apply to the president of the R.I.C.S.

[90b] The R.I.C.S. Guidance Notes for surveyors acting as arbitrators or as
independent experts in rent reviews are reproduced in R. Bernstein &
K. Reynolds, *Handbook of Rent Review.*

[91] *Wrenbridge Ltd v. Harries (Southern Properties) Ltd* (1981) 260 E.G. 1195;
Laing Investment Co. Ltd v. G. A. Dunn & Co. Ltd (1982) 263 E.G. 879.
As to what constitutes a valid application, see para. 6–10, n. 62 above.

[92] If one party requests an oral hearing the arbitrator must hold one unless
the rent review clause provides otherwise; *Henry Southeran v. Norwich
Union Life Assurance Society* [1992] 31 E.G. 70.

[93] In *K/S Norjal AS v. Hyundai Heavy Industries Co.* [1991] 3 W.L.R. 1025
the Court of Appeal held that a request by an arbitrator for a commitment
fee was not misconduct on his part although the parties did not have to
pay it. Similarly in *Turner v. Stevenage B.C.* [1996] 14 E.G. 94 there was
no misconduct when an arbitrator asked for an interim fee which only one
party was willing to pay.

Discovery

One matter which may be of importance at this stage is discovery. An arbitrator has power to make orders for the production of relevant documents within the possession or power[94] of the parties to the arbitration.[95] Thus, the parties should consider whether an order for discovery could usefully aid their case; for example by bringing to the arbitrator's attention a structural survey of the building, or details of other rents agreed by the landlord, or a report on valuation on the purchase of the building. The use of discovery in this context has grown, but it has been cogently suggested that it should not be necessary if surveyors adequately understood their role as expert witness and overriding duty to the arbitrator.[96]

Privilege

Certain documents will be privileged against discovery: those marked "without prejudice" and written in the course of negotiation;[97] all correspondence between a legal adviser and his lay client, and all correspondence produced in contemplation or for the purpose of the arbitration. This leaves vulnerable correspondence between the client and his non-legal professional advisers before the arbitration was contemplated, for example correspondence between the surveyor and landlord as to the initial rent to be suggested. But even where a document is not privileged, discovery remains at the discretion of the arbitrator: important criteria will be the relevance and helpfulness of the document[98] and the prejudice which would be caused to the party producing it. Since arbitrations are held in private, arguments based on confidentiality may not carry much weight. Where rent is based on an "open market" or similar formula, there is authority for the argument that only such documents as would be available to the hypothetical negotiating parties should be disclosed. Thus the tenant's trading accounts may not be admissible except in so far as they would be available to the public under company law.[99]

---

[94] The power does not extend to documents in the possession of a subsidiary company: *Lonrho Ltd v. Shell Petroleum Ltd* [1980] 1 W.L.R. 627.

[95] Arbitration Act 1950, s.12(1).

[96] See *Urban Small Space Ltd v. Burford Investment Co. Ltd* [1990] 28 E.G. 116 where the Vice-Chancellor noted that what is a discoverable document is not restricted to documents which are admissible in evidence, and that all information which may be used either in supporting or defeating a case must be disclosed.

[97] *South Shropshire District Council v. Amos* [1986] 1 W.L.R. 1271 and see also the House of Lords' statement of the law in *Rush & Tompkins Ltd v. GLC* [1989] 3 W.L.R. 939 to the effect that the "without prejudice" rule is based on the desirability of encouraging litigants to settle their differences rather than litigating to a finish.

[98] See *W. J. Barton Ltd v. Long Acre Securities Ltd* [1982] 1 W.L.R. 398 (trading accounts of tenant not relevant in the circumstances).

[99] *Cornwall Coast Country Club Ltd v. Cardgrange Ltd* (1987) 282 E.G. 1664 which was distinguished in *Electricity Supply Nominees Ltd v. London Clubs Ltd* [1988] 34 E.G. 71 where the tenant's actual accounts, while generally inadmissible, were relevant here because of the wording of the lease itself, which provided for the production of actual accounts to the arbitrator. In *Ritz Hotel (London) Ltd v. Ritz Casinos Ltd* [1989] 46 E.G. 95 it was held the arbitrator could take into account the turnover or accounts of a company within the tenant's group if that information would be available in the market, provided he put out of his mind anything he might learn about the actual tenant's turnover or accounts.

Procedure hearing   Where there is a hearing, the procedure to be followed is largely a matter for the arbitrator, subject to an overriding duty to act fairly. However, in practice arbitrators tend to follow the procedure recommended by the R.I.C.S. Guidance Notes, the party who initiated the proceedings (the claimant) opening and calling his witnesses, followed by the respondent, and with final addresses by the respondent and claimant. Cross-examination and re-examination is allowed, following the rules adopted in court proceedings. Particular care is needed where one party is represented by a surveyor who also acts as an expert witness: confusion can easily arise if it becomes unclear in which capacity the surveyor is acting at any time. The arbitrator will invariably inspect the property.

Inspection of property   He may do so alone, but should not do so accompanied by only one party nor should he use the visit as an opportunity of gathering new evidence which he does not put to the parties.[1]

Award   There are no formal requirements for the arbitrator's award, though the R.I.C.S. Guidance Notes contain recommendations as to matters which should be included. Unless required by the rent review provisions, an arbitrator is not obliged to give reasons for his decision, and indeed if the question is purely one of valuation, little point will be served in doing so.[2] However, it is possible for either party to make an application to the court for an order that the arbitrator give reasons.[3] This procedure may be useful where the arbitrator's

Points of law   award is based on a contested point of law. However, the order may only be made if notice was given to the arbitrator requiring a reasoned award before the award was made, or if there is some special reason why such notice was not given.[4] Thus a party who perceives that a possibly important question of law has arisen during the course of the arbitration[5] should preserve his position, either by persuading the other party to join him in requesting a reasoned decision (in which case the R.I.C.S. Guidance Notes say the arbitrator should comply with the request), or by giving unilateral notice requiring reasons.[6]

6–16 Procedure on valuation by an independent expert

There are very few constraints on the procedure to be followed by an independent expert, except the fear of a possible action in negligence. The R.I.C.S. Guidance Notes

---

[1] See *Fairmount Investments Ltd v. Secretary of State for the Environment* [1976] 1 W.L.R. 1255 (a planning case).

[2] The Guidance Notes recommend that arbitrators should give reasons when both parties request it.

[3] Arbitration Act 1979, s.1(5); *Trave Schiffahrtsgesellschaft mbH & Co. KG v. Ninemia Maritime Corp.* [1986] Q.B. 802.

[4] Arbitration Act 1950, s.1(6).

[5] Assuming the question has not been dealt with already: see para. 6–13 above.

[6] If there is no point of law or no point of principle which is likely to recur on future reviews then the Notes suggest the arbitrator need not give reasons where one party objects to his doing so.

suggest that it is desirable to invite the parties to make known any relevant factual information, but that whether to invite representations, in the absence of directions in the rent review clause, is a matter for the expert's discretion. Any evidence or representations put forward by one party should of course be made available to the other. The expert and parties will need

Points of law to consider how to deal with any difficult point of law which arises. It may be dealt with by agreement, by a declaration from the court, by the expert deciding the point and making alternative awards, by the expert taking legal advice, or by the expert acting as an arbitrator.[7] Unless so required by the terms of his appointment, the expert is not bound to give reasons for his decision, nor to set out the basis of his calculations.

6–17 Evidence and comparables

It is impossible to do justice to this subject in a short paragraph,[8] but it is possible to highlight some of the main points of difficulty. Clearly evidence must be relevant and reliable in order to have weight attached to it, but the

Rules of evidence question also arises as to how far the formal rules of evidence applied in court are applicable to arbitrations. The strict legal position is by no means free from doubt,[9] but in a number of cases concerning rent reviews it has been taken for granted that the ordinary rules of evidence apply.[10]

Hearsay evidence One of the most important rules of evidence is the hearsay rule: this rule can have a considerable constraining effect on the evidence which may be put forward by an expert as to comparables. In the important case of *Land Securities plc v. Westminster City Council*[11] Hoffmann J. ruled as hearsay, and therefore inadmissible, the award of another arbitrator relating to a different but comparable property. Further, if that other arbitrator were called as an expert witness, his evidence of the comparables on which his award was based would also be inadmissible. Similarly, a witness may not put forward evidence of comparables gleaned second-hand from other surveyors, or from professional journals, however reputable the source.[12] However, such evidence will become admissible if no objection is taken to it at the time, either by the

---

[7] See R.I.C.S. Guidance Notes.

[8] More detailed treatment may be found in the *Handbook of Rent Review*, paras. 7–5 to 7–9, and in D. N. Clarke and J. E. Adams, *Rent Reviews and Variable Rents* (3rd ed. 1991), Chap. 7.

[9] See D. N. Clarke and J. E. Adams, *Rent Reviews and Variable Rents* (3rd ed. 1991), pp. 228–231.

[10] *Town Centre Securities Ltd v. Wm. Morrison Supermarkets Ltd* (1982) 263 E.G. 435; *Segama N.V. v. Penny Le Roy Ltd* (1984) 269 E.G. 322.

[11] [1992] 44 E.G. 153.

[12] *English Exporters (London) Ltd v. Eldonwall Ltd* [1973] 1 Ch. 415 at 421–423.

arbitrator or the other party:[13] but even if admissible, its hearsay nature will mean that the arbitrator may give little weight to it.

Civil Evidence Act 1995

The position is however set to change once the Civil Evidence Act 1995 comes into force, when hearsay evidence will become admissible as of right in civil proceedings. The weight to be attached to any such evidence will however be a matter for the judge's or arbitrator's direction.[13a]

Post-review date evidence

The other main question relating to evidence is that of evidence arising after the review date. It will often be the case that the arbitration will occur some time after the review date. The lease will probably require the rent to be assessed as at the review date[14] and the question will arise as to how far evidence of transactions after that date can be used as evidence. In *Duvan Estates Ltd v. Rossette Sunshine Savouries Ltd*[15] Robert Goff J. expressed the view that in general an arbitrator should not have regard to facts and events existing after the review date: however the contrary point of view appears not to have been argued. More detailed consideration of the question occurred in *Segama N.V. v. Penny Le Roy Ltd*,[16] where Staughton J. concluded that such evidence was admissible, but that the greater the lapse of time between the review date and the evidence, the less reliable the evidence would become.[17] The judgment also suggests that political or economic changes, as well as lapse of time, could render the evidence suspect. Evidence of events occurring after the review date and causing changes in property values (unless perhaps confirming a trend evident at the review date) will not be relevant, since what has to be ascertained is the value which would have been placed on the premises at the review date, without the benefit of foresight.[18]

Methods of valuation

Finally, as to the method of valuation to be adopted, it has been said that valuation is basically a matter of applying the valuer's personal expertise and experience to the property to be valued, and that too much stress should not be placed upon nice distinctions between methods of valuation.[19]

---

[13] *Town Centre Securities Ltd v. Wm. Morrison Supermarkets Ltd* (1982) 263 E.G. 435.

[13a] However, the rule that an arbitration award relating to a different property is not admissible might still stand, on grounds of public policy (another reason mentioned for the rule by Hoffmann J.).

[14] But *cf. Parkside Knightsbridge Ltd v. The German Food Centre Ltd* [1987] NPC 10 where the valuation date was taken to be the date of the trigger-notice.

[15] (1981) 261 E.G. 364.

[16] (1984) 269 E.G. 322.

[17] *ibid.*, at 326.

[18] *Industrial Properties (Barton Hill) Ltd v. Associated Electrical Industries Ltd,* Official Referee, April 7, 1976 (unreported but cited at D.C. 317, *Handbook of Rent Review*); *Ponsford v. H.M.S. Aerosols Ltd* Ch. D. February 3, 1976 (unreported but cited at D.C. 497, *Handbook of Rent Review*).

[19] *Regent Jewellers (London) Ltd v. C.H. (Bournemouth) Ltd* (1968) 207 E.G. 629, *per* Buckley J., *cf. Janes (Gowns) Ltd v. Harlow Development Corporation* (1980) 253 E.G. 799, where the "zoning method" of valuation was discussed and approved. See also *Lex Services Ltd v. Oriel House B.V.* [1991] 39 E.G. 139 (valuation is not an exact science).

6–18 Costs

An arbitrator has the discretion to award and apportion costs, and the matter should be dealt with in his award.[20] Unlike litigation, rent review arbitrations tend not to produce a clear winner and loser, so that it is impracticable to make costs **Punitive costs** follow the event. However, the arbitrator may make an adverse award of costs against a party who caused delay, or was guilty of unreasonable or obstructive behaviour, or who incurred unreasonable costs by overloading his evidence.

With an expert, his power to award costs depends on the terms of the contract which appointed him. Most modern leases (and also the Model Forms) oblige the parties to bear the costs of the expert equally, with each party bearing his own costs.

A party who is willing to compromise can and should protect himself as to costs by a so-called "Calderbank **Offers to** letter":[21] a written offer to compromise at a certain figure, **compromise** marked "without prejudice" but reserving the right to draw the letter to the arbitrator's attention on the issue of costs.[22]

In the case of arbitration, either party may apply to the **Taxation** court for taxation of an arbitrator's fees, unless such fees have been fixed by written agreement.[23]

6–19 Challenging arbitrator's decision

There are three bases upon which it may be possible to attack an adverse award: application to the High Court to remit the award to the same or a different arbitrator under section 22 of the Arbitration Act 1950, misconduct by the arbitrator and **Remission** error of law. Application to remit, while generally regarded as a lesser remedy, has nevertheless been used more frequently of late because of the difficulties of appealing against an award on an error of law. It is used, for example, where the arbitrator admits a mistake or there has been a procedural irregularity not amounting to misconduct as such. For example, in *Land Securities plc v. Westminster City Council* (No. 2)[23a] the case was remitted where the arbitrator proceeded on the basis that there were significant differences between the subject property and the main comparable, when the parties had already agreed there were no real differences. Significantly, the judge also ruled that so long as there has been a procedural misconduct or mishap that has led to an incorrect finding by the arbitrator, either party can apply for reconsideration under section 22 without having to obtain leave to appeal under section 1 of the Arbitration Act 1979.

[20] Arbitration Act 1950, s.18. The costs are not only the arbitrator's own fees and expenses but also the costs of the parties. The practice is for the arbitrator to issue an interim award dealing with the rent review determination itself and subsequently a final award which deals with costs. When the interim award is made the arbitrator will rarely know if either party has made an offer as to costs.
[21] After *Calderbank v. Calderbank* [1976] Fam. 93.
[22] *Cutts v. Head* [1984] Ch. 290.
[23] Arbitration Act 1950, s.19.
[23a] [1995] 1 EGLR 245.

Misconduct by arbitrator

The second means of challenge is provided by section 23 of the Arbitration Act 1950, which provides that where an arbitrator has misconducted himself or the proceedings, he may be removed by the court or his award set aside. The application must be made within 21 days of publication of the award.[24] This appears to mean the date of notification by the arbitrator that the award is ready to be taken up.[25] Matters which may justify remitting or setting aside an award are obvious misconduct such as acceptance of bribes, inconsistency or ambiguity in the operative parts of the award,[26] failure to allow a party a reasonable or proper opportunity to put forward his case,[27] departure from the parties' agreed statement of facts without further reference to the parties[28] and use by the arbitrator of his own knowledge or other evidence without giving the parties the opportunity to comment on it.[29] However, an error of fact or law will not constitute "misconduct"[30], and it is not enough for the court to suspect that there might have been an injustice: it is necessary to be satisfied that there has been an actual injustice.[30a] Accordingly, in the absence of evidence to the contrary, the court must assume that, if an issue of fact is properly before the arbitrator, he had acted properly in addressing it.

Removal of arbitrator

One of the parties (or both) can apply to the court for the removal of an arbitrator (or expert) once appointed before his determination is made. The grounds of objection must be well founded, however; mere suspicion of partiality will not suffice.[31] Where there has been significant delay in the arbitration process, one party can apply to the court to bring it to an end.[32]

Error of law

Appeal against an award on a question of law is provided for by the Arbitration Act 1979, s.1. The appeal may be made by the consent of all parties, or otherwise the court must be

---

[24] R.S.C. Ord. 73, r. 5(1).

[25] *South Tottenham Land Securities Ltd v. R. & A. Millett (Shops) Ltd* [1984] 1 W.L.R. 710. See also *Learmonth Property Investment Co. Ltd v. Amos Hinton & Sons plc* [1985] 1 EGLR 13.

[26] *Moran v. Lloyd's* [1983] 1 Q.B. 542.

[27] *ibid.*

[28] *Techno Ltd v. Allied Dunbar Assurance plc* [1993] 22 E.G. 109.

[29] *Top Shop Estates Ltd v. C. Danino* [1985] 1 EGLR 9; *Zermalt Holdings S.A. v. Nu-Life Upholstery Repairs Ltd* [1985] 2 EGLR 14; *Unit Four Cinemas Ltd v. Tosara Investment Ltd* [1993] 44 E.G. 120; and *Mount Charlotte Investments plc v. Prudential Assurance Company Ltd* [1995] 10 E.G. 129 (where the arbitrator had, contrary to his own directions, visited other properties which it was held must have affected his decision). However in *Turner v. Stevenage Borough Council* [1996] 14 E.G. 94 there was no misconduct when an arbitrator asked for an interim fee which only one party was willing to pay.

[30] *Moran v. Lloyd's* [1983] 1 Q.B. 542.

[30a] See for example *Broadgate Square plc v. Lehman Brothers Ltd* (No. 2) [1995] 33 E.G. 89 where the judge rejected the tenant's contention that the arbitrator was guilty of technical misconduct on the basis that his reasoning for not discounting the rent (because the rent review provisions which would be imported into the notional lease were unduly onerous) was misfounded.

[31] *Moore Stephens & Co. v. Local Authorities Mutual Investment Trust Ltd* [1992] 4 E.G. 135.

[32] *Secretary of State for the Environment v. Euston Centre Investments Ltd* [1994] 1 W.L.R. 563.

satisfied that the determination of the question of law could substantially affect the rights of one or more parties to the arbitration.[33] In a leading shipping case, Lord Diplock drew a distinction between questions as to the construction of standard term contracts, where certainty by judicial decision

Standard and "one-off" provisions

is desirable, and questions arising from clauses of a "one-off" nature, where leave to appeal should only be given if the interpretation of the arbitrator is undoubtedly and obviously wrong.[34] Since on one view most rent review clauses are of a "one off" rather than a standard nature, this distinction could have been taken as severely restricting the ability to appeal arbitrations on issues of law, with serious consequences given that the same review clause may operate not once, but several times, during the term of a lease.[35] In *Ipswich Borough Council v. Fisons plc*[36] Lord Donaldson M.R. said that leave would more readily be given if the relevant clause was in common use so that other persons in addition to the parties would benefit from a definitive ruling.[37] In other words, save in the case of the last review before the end of the lease, where the strict test of Lord Diplock would apply, a rent review clause will operate several times during the life of the lease, and it may be treated as a "standard contract" so that it will not be necessary to show that the arbitrator was obviously wrong. Nevertheless, as to whether leave to appeal should be granted, Lord Donaldson made it clear that the court has to be

Strong prima facie case of error

satisfied "that there was a more or less strong prima facie case for thinking the arbitrator had erred on a question of law".[37a] The *Fisons* decision followed a series of first instance cases which had decided that where the same point of law would regulate future reviews a more liberal approach was justified[38] and that leave should be given if there was merely a real doubt whether the arbitrator was right in law, so as to enable the law relating to the future relationship of the parties to be authoritatively determined. These cases can no longer be relied upon, however. Furthermore, leave will not be given on

---

[33] s.1(3), (4).

[34] *Pioneer Shipping Ltd v. B.T.P. Tioxide Ltd, The Nema* [1982] A.C. 724 at 737.

[35] It is now established that issue estoppel can apply on arbitration: *Arnold v. National Westminster Bank plc* [1991] 2 A.C. 93. However, in exceptional circumstances an arbitrator will be allowed to re-open an issue which was previously decided upon by a court in proceedings relating to an earlier rent review under the same lease. It is not sufficient for a party who has lost on a point of law merely to say, to avoid issue estoppel, that, in the light of other decisions, the previous decision might have been wrong. A request to re-open the decision must be made in good time: *Arnold v. National Westminster Bank plc* [1993] 1 E.G. 94.

[36] [1990] 1 All E.R. 730.

[37] *ibid.* at 734. Leave would also be more likely if (1) the arbitrator were not a lawyer and the dispute was over a difficult question of law and (2) the alleged error would have especially serious consequences for one party or the other.

[37a] Followed in *Euripides v. Gascoyne Holdings Ltd* [1995] EGCS 119 where the Court of Appeal said that "the real doubt as to whether the arbitrator was right in law" test was misplaced; there must be a strong prima facie case of error.

[38] *Lucas Industries plc v. Welsh Development Agency* [1986] Ch. 500; followed in *Warrington and Runcorn Development Corporation v. Greggs plc* (1986) 281 E.G. 1075.

over-ingenious points of law with little chance of success, or on what are essentially findings of fact[39] or matters concerning the way the arbitrator weighed the expert valuation evidence.[40]

A slightly different question is what test should be applied to questions not directly related to the interpretation of the rent review clause (such as the correct analysis and treatment of comparables or the arbitrator's approach to the method of valuing the premises).[41] Such questions may not be relevant on future reviews, but may affect the rent reviews of other properties owned by the same landlord and proceeding at the same time—in that sense they may be regarded as more than "one-off" questions.[42]

6–20   Challenging expert's decision

Final and binding

There is no statutory framework for challenging the conduct or decision of an expert. However, it has been held that where the parties have agreed to the final and conclusive judgment of an expert, then unless the expert has not performed the task assigned to him (*e.g.* by answering the wrong question) the courts will not undo his decision.[43] Whether or not the expert got the answer right is immaterial, even where the issue in dispute consists of how to construe a rent review clause or necessarily involves the solution to such a question. Earlier authority had also suggested that such challenges will be far from easy to sustain.[44]

Seeking guidance from the court

It should be noted, however, that it is possible for either party to apply to the court for a declaration as to the interpretation of disputed wording before the expert gives his determination, even where that determination is to be final and binding.[45] Reconciling the decision in *Postel Properties v. Greenwell*[46] with the subsequent Court of Appeal ruling in *Norwich Union Life Insurance Society v. P & O Property Holdings Ltd*[47] is not easy, however. There the court would not allow one party to by-pass the expert determination provisions by applying to the court for a ruling on a legal issue arising

---

[39] *My Kinda Town Ltd v. Castlebrook Properties Ltd* [1986] 1 EGLR 121; *Fine Fare Ltd v. Kenmore Investments Ltd* [1989] 1 EGLR 143.

[40] *Tesco Holdings Ltd v. Jackson* [1990] 10 E.G. 71.

[41] *Temple & Crook Ltd v. Capital and Counties Property Co. Ltd* [1990] 38 E.G. 118.

[42] In *Warrington and Runcorn Development Corporation v. Greggs plc* [1986] 281 E.G. 1075, Warner J. applied the more liberal test, but gave leave to appeal against his decision as a question of general importance.

[43] *Nikko Hotels (U.K.) Ltd v. MEPC plc* [1991] 28 E.G. 86 applying *Jones v. Sherwood Computer Services Ltd* [1992] 1 W.L.R. 277 (decided on December 8, 1989 but not reported in full until 1992).

[44] *A. Hudson Pty Ltd v. Legal & General Life of Australia* [1986] 2 EGLR 130 (Privy Council); but see also *J. T. Sydenham & Co. Ltd v. Enichem Elastomers Ltd* [1986] NPC 52 where a successful challenge to a "speaking determination" was made on a point of law.

[45] *Postel Properties Ltd v. Greenwell* [1992] 47 E.G. 106.

[46] *ibid.*

[47] [1993] 1 EGLR 164.

from the dispute. It could only do so with the other party's agreement.[48]

6–21 Evidencing the review

Memorandum of review

It is good practice to evidence the varied rent, whether arrived at by agreement or determination by a third party, by a written memorandum. The memorandum should include the arbitrator's award or expert's determination, if any, and can either be endorsed on the lease if space permits, or prepared as a separate document and kept with the lease. It is advisable from the landlord's point of view for any surety to sign the memorandum.[49]

6–22 Payment of reviewed rent and interest

Statutory controls on rent

The lease should deal with the question of the date from which the new rent becomes payable and the date on which it should actually be paid (this can be especially important where the rent is determined after the review date).[50] Provision should also be made for the payment of interest where the new rent is agreed or determined late.[51] A final eventuality to consider is the possibility of statutory controls over commercial rents, as happened between 1972 and 1975, and some provision is commonly inserted to ensure that the landlord's interests are prejudiced as little as possible by such controls.[52]

---

[48] The difference would appear to be that in *Norwich Union* it was the construction of the development agreement itself that the expert had to decide upon and neither of the parties, having elected for determination by an expert, could unilaterally look to the court to provide the answer. This decision has itself been distinguished in *Mercury Communications Ltd v. Director General of Telecommunications* [1996] 1 W.L.R. 48 where the House of Lords accepted that Mercury could apply for a declaration even when the expert (the Director General) had already given his decision. In *Mercury*, however, there was no provision that the Director General's decision was to be "final and binding".

[49] See para. 3–16 above.

[50] *South Tottenham Land Securities Ltd v. R. & A. Millett (Shops) Ltd* [1984] 1 W.L.R. 711; *Parry v. Robinson Wylie Ltd* [1987] NPC 18 (Apportionment Act 1870 applies where lease assigned).

[51] *Shield Properties & Investments Ltd v. Anglo Overseas Transport Co. Ltd* (No. 2) [1986] 2 EGLR 112. Note that interest should not be at a penal rate but rather be so as to compensate the landlord for the delay in receiving the full rent. Further it should properly be payable on each quarterly instalment of rent from the particular quarter day when that instalment fell due and not on the whole of any shortfall from the review date.

[52] *e.g.* provisions that the rent review is to operate immediately restrictions are lifted, or that the effect of restrictions be ignored on review. (It is of course possible that any legislation controlling rents would provide that such provisions would not be valid.)

6–23 Basis on which new rent to be assessed

Importance of accurate wording

Over the years, rent review clauses have come to deal in increasing detail with the basis upon which rent should be assessed on review. The semantic scrutiny to which rent review clauses are subjected has also intensified, so that it has been said that:

> " . . . precise and comprehensive draftsmanship has become essential to avoid one party or the other rushing to court and successfully arguing for his imaginative and plainly unintended interpretation of otherwise innocuous phrases."[53]

Clauses now usually provide on what basis and assumptions the rent is to be assessed, and what matters are to be disregarded.

Interpreting the clauses

As with any commercial contract, the usual canons of construction apply.[54] Accordingly, the rent review provisions must be considered in the context of the lease as a whole and where there is no ambiguity in the words used, effect must be given to them notwithstanding the adverse consequences for one party or the other. However, over the last 10 years or so, as a result of a plethora of cases demonstrating both the wide variety of clauses used and how complex some now are (with quite minor variations in wording producing significant differences) coupled with the ingenuity (not always reflecting commercial reality) of draftsmen to think up yet more possibilities, two distinct guiding principles have emerged. First, the courts will, wherever possible, look to the commercial purpose behind the provisions and, secondly, in so doing, they will favour the interpretation that results in the premises being valued having regard, so far as possible, to the actual circumstances—the so-called "presumption of reality".

Commercial purpose and presumption of reality

The presumption of reality is well demonstrated in a series of cases where the passing rent was expressed to be a percentage of the market rent. To have the notional lease[55] also contain a discount would produce some strange results and the courts have opted for reality.[56] Similarly, where the lease reserved an additional rent, this too was ignored for rent review purposes.[57] The presumption of reality has also meant that neither party should receive a windfall as a result of a particular provision. This has been most forcibly

---

[53] (1986) 277 E.G. 919 (S. Fogel and P. Freedman); *cf.*, (1986) 277 E.G. 807 (C. N. G. Arding and P. G. Plumbe). In *General Accident Fire & Life Assurance Corporation plc v. Electronic Data Processing Co. plc* (1986) 281 E.G. 65, Harman J. described such proceedings as "part of the daily bread of the Chancery Division these days".

[54] See Chap. 17.

[55] See paras. 6–26 *et seq.*

[56] *Prudential Assurance Co. Ltd v. 99 Bishopsgate Ltd* [1992] 1 EGLR 119.

[57] *Guys 'N' Dolls Ltd v. Sade Brothers Catering Ltd* [1983] 269 E.G. 129 and *Buffalo Enterprises Inc. v. Golden Wonder Ltd* [1991] 24 E.G. 171.

demonstrated in the so-called "headline rent" cases[58] where, despite the obvious intention of the draftsman in each case to **Headline rent** give the landlord the highest possible rent, in only one did he succeed, the Court of Appeal dealing deftly (but, some have contended, unconvincingly) with the subtle differences in the language of the clauses to deny the landlord more than the market rent.

Use of mathematical formulae   Where rent is to be assessed according to a complex formula, it is worth considering whether greater precision and clarity could be achieved by expressing the formula algebraically rather than verbally.[59]

6–24   Basis of valuation

The starting point for valuation will usually be market value in some form. However, this basic concept may be expressed and amplified in many subtly different ways, each with possibly important consequences from a valuation point of view.

Market rent   It has been said that where the words "market rent" are used, little purpose is served by adding words such as "open" or "rack".[60] However, the expression "yearly rent" is better avoided: the intention is probably to denote a rent payable annually, but it could possibly carry overtones of a yearly tenancy, which would depress the rent.

Where adequate comparables exist, ascertaining a market rent should be relatively straightforward, assuming the property and the terms of the letting are adequately defined. However, two possible situations may give rise to difficulties. The first is where the market rent is driven up by the **Exceptionally** existence of an individual bidder willing to pay an unusually **high bids** high rent for the premises, *e.g.* the owner of adjacent premises who is in urgent need of further accommodation. Should the fortuitous existence of such a bidder be taken into account?[61] One way of excluding such exceptional or freak rents might

---

[58] *Scottish Amicable Life Assurance Society v. Middleton Potts & Co; Co-operative Wholesale Society Ltd v. National Westminster Bank plc; Prudential Nominees Ltd v. Greenham Trading Ltd;* and *Broadgate Square plc v. Lehman Brothers Ltd* [1995] 1 E.G. 111. See para. 6–31 below.

[59] *London Regional Transport v. Wimpey Group Services Ltd* (1980) 280 E.G. 898. See also *Standard Life Assurance Co. v. Oxoid Ltd* [1986] 1 EGLR 123.

[60] See R. Bernstein and K. Reynolds, *Handbook of Rent Review*, para. 4–22 and cases cited therein.

[61] Support for the argument that all possible bidders should be taken into account can be found in *Daejan Investments Ltd v. Cornwall Coast Country Club* (1984) 50 P. & C.R. 157 at 162–163 and *Royal Exchange Assurance v. Bryant Samuel Properties (Coventry) Ltd* [1985] 1 EGLR 84 at 86. But see also *Baptist v. Masters of the Bench and Trustees of the Honourable Society of Grays Inn* [1993] 42 E.G. 287 where for the purposes of s.34 of the Landlord and Tenant Act 1954 "open market" was held not to include a higher rent which might be paid by a potential lessee with a special interest.

be to use the words "fair" or "reasonable",[62] but these expressions carry their own ambiguities which could give rise to far greater difficulties.[63] Certainly it would appear that the expression "best rent" would require consideration of such exceptional rents, even to the exclusion of more moderate bids, and therefore the use of such wording should be resisted by tenants.

"Best rent"

Conversely, it can be argued that the special bidder would only need to pay a small amount over the next best bid to secure the premises. Where "best rent" is coupled with "reasonably obtainable" it is generally considered that this does not penalise the tenant.

Market weak

The second possible difficulty is where at the date of review the market for the property is weak, so that it cannot be shown that the landlord would have been able to let the property on the open market at all or there are insufficient transactions in the market to provide comparables. It would appear that a formula relying on market rent or a hypothetical letting requires the assumption of the existence of willing parties, even if an examination of the actual market shows no willing lessee at any rent.[64] This may not be the case where the clause provides that the premises are merely assumed to be available for letting, although an upwards only clause will provide a measure of protection here for the landlord.

Tenant among bidders

Another difficulty in such situations is whether the existing tenant can be assumed to be among the hypothetical bidders; in *F. R. Evans (Leeds) Ltd v. English Electric Co. Ltd*,[65] Donaldson J. thought not although in *British Airways plc v. Heathrow Airport Ltd*[66] it was held that it was for the independent surveyor, not the court, to say who was likely to be a bidder and whether the actual tenant might bid. Moreover, an assumption of vacant possession does not of itself mean that the existing tenant must be taken to have vacated and joined the market in competing for the property.[67] The problem might be avoided by the use of wording requiring an assumption that the tenant is in the market "with others."

Negativing subjective factors

Assessing a market rent is essentially an objective exercise. Review clauses often emphasise this by referring to a willing lessor and willing lessee, thus isolating the assessment from subjective considerations of the parties, such as cash flow difficulties, changing accommodation requirements and the like.[68] Difficulties can occur where the clause attempts to water down the importance of the market by wording such as

---

[62] In *Ponsford v. H.M.S. Aerosols Ltd* [1979] A.C. 63 Viscount Dilhorne (at 77) and Lord Fraser (at 83) took the view that the words would have this effect; but *cf.*, Lord Keith at 85.

[63] See below.

[64] *Dennis & Robinson Ltd v. Kiossis Establishment* (1987) 54 P. & C.R. 282, *cf.*, *F. R. Evans (Leeds) Ltd v. English Electric Co. Ltd* (1977) 36 P. & C.R. 184.

[65] (1977) 36 P. & C.R. 184.

[66] [1992] 19 E.G. 157; see also *First Leisure Trading Ltd v. Dorita Properties Ltd* [1991] 23 E.G. 116.

[67] *Cornwall Coast Country Club Ltd v. Cardgrange Ltd* (1987) 282 E.G. 1664.

[68] *F. R. Evans Ltd v. English Electric Co. Ltd* (1977) 36 P. & C.R. 184. However, what the actual tenant might be prepared to bid cannot be ignored; see *First Leisure Trading* (n. 66 above).

"having regard to the market rent". This leaves the valuer in doubt as to how much weight to attach to the market rent and begs the question as to what other factors, if any, are also relevant.

"Reasonable rent" Also capable of giving rise to doubt is the expression "reasonable rent". This could be taken as meaning an objectively reasonable rent, *i.e.* the rent which would be agreed by a reasonable landlord and reasonable tenant; or it could mean the rent which it is reasonable for the particular tenant to pay to the particular landlord. This problem taxed the House of Lords in *Ponsford v. HMS Aerosols Ltd*[69] where, by a bare majority, it was decided that the objective meaning was correct. Accordingly, individual circumstances making it fair that the tenant should pay less than the open market rent were ignored. It follows from that case that if the parties wish subjective factors to be taken into account, they should so provide expressly, using wording such as "reasonable for the parties to agree".[70] Assessment on the basis of an objectively reasonable rent for the premises may be useful where the premises are of such a nature that no comparables are likely to be available.

6–25 When are the premises to be valued

Valuation date Almost invariably, the review clause will specify that the premises are to be valued at the particular review date and, where the wording is unclear, the courts will, where possible, choose the review date.[71]

6–26 What is to be valued

Ascertainment of a market rent cannot take place in the abstract, and the lease must make clear the premises and the nature of the interest to be valued. Defining the premises is relatively straightforward, as the lease will invariably contain a description. However, three areas require some attention.

Tenant's improvements First, how tenant's alterations and improvements are to be dealt with must be identified. If no guidance is given, the premises are valued as they stand.[72] Secondly, it should be

---

[69] [1979] A.C. 63.
[70] See *Lear v. Blizzard* [1983] 3 All E.R. 662.
[71] *London & Manchester Assurance Co. Ltd v. G.A. Dunn Ltd* (1983) 265 E.G. 39. But *cf. Prudential Assurance Co. Ltd v. Gray* (1987) 283 E.G. 648 where "date of review" was held to be the later date of actual determination. In *Glofield Properties Ltd v. Morley* (No. 2) [1989] 32 E.G. 49 "at the time of . . . determination" was to be construed as the review date even where the actual determination was several years later due to a dispute between the parties.
[72] *Ponsford v. H.M.S. Aerosols Ltd* [1979] A.C. 63 and see more particularly para. 11–14 below.

Fixtures and ancillary rights

made clear whether the valuation is to include fixtures.[73] In many situations (especially specialist buildings) it would certainly assist the independent valuer if the parties listed in the lease which items were to be rentalised and which were not. Thirdly, whether rights ancillary to the property granted otherwise than by the lease (*e.g.* a licence to park vehicles) are to be included in the valuation. It may be possible to cure an omission which would make the clause unworkable by implying a term that the absence of certain rights be disregarded.[74]

Terms of existing lease

Defining the interest to be valued is more difficult. The usual starting point is the assumption of a letting on the terms of the existing lease and consequently any onerous terms in the lease will also be contained in the notional lease, and will have an effect on the rent accordingly.[75] For example, in *Norwich Union Life Insurance Society v. British Railways Board*[76] the tenant's covenant to rebuild resulted in a $27\frac{1}{2}$ per cent reduction in the rent. The length of the term (150 years) and the state of repair of the premises were such that rebuilding during the term was very likely.

It remains to be seen how the assumption will operate in relation to a tenancy which is not a "new tenancy"[76a] in the light of the Landlord and Tenant (Covenants) Act 1995. As noted above,[76b] whatever its term, the notional lease will usually be valued as though granted on the relevant review date. It follows therefore that where the review date falls on or after January 1, 1996 the notional lease will be a new tenancy, under which the hypothetical tenant would arguably be

Effect of Landlord and Tenant (Covenants) Act 1995

prepared to pay a higher rent on the basis that there is no longer the spectre of continuing liability post assignment. Furthermore, to compound the actual tenant's disadvantage, applying the assumption that the terms of the notional lease will be those of the actual lease, these will almost certainly include an alienation covenant which will be less onerous than

---

[73] See *Young v. Dalgety plc* [1987] 1 EGLR 116 (regarding light fittings and floor coverings) and *Ocean Accident & Guarantee Corporation v. Next plc*; *Commercial Union Assurance Company plc v. Next plc* [1995] EGCS 187. The question of fixtures and rent review is discussed below: see para. 11–14.

[74] *Jefferies v. O'Neill* (1983) 46 P. & C.R. 376. See also *British Airways plc. v. Heathrow Airport plc* [1992] 19 E.G. 157.

[75] See *Scottish & Newcastle Breweries plc v. Sir Richard Sutton's Settled Estates* [1985] 2 EGLR 130 at 134–135 where that construction was preferred to a hypothetical lease based upon the usual covenants or contemporary lettings. But the language used may indicate that an assumed letting on the existing terms would not be appropriate: see *Basingstoke and Deane Borough Council v. Host Group Ltd* [1986] 2 EGLR 107 and *Prudential Assurance Co. Ltd v. Salisbury's Handbags Ltd* [1992] 23 E.G. 117. The dangers of making no comprehensive reference to the terms of the lease are illustrated by *General Accident Fire & Life Assurance Corporation plc v. Electronic Data Processing Co. plc* (1986) 281 E.G. 65 (standard reddendum assumed in hypothetical lease, but not rent review provisions); see also *Sheerness Steel Co. plc v. Medway Ports Authority* [1992] 12 E.G. 138 where the review clause was silent on the terms of the notional lease: the Court of Appeal decided the wording of the review clause showed a clear intention to override the usual commercial expectation that the willing tenant takes on a lease containing the same terms as the actual lease.

[76] (1987) 283 E.G. 846 above.

[76a] See para. 2–02 above for the meaning of "new tenancy".

[76b] See para. 6–25 above.

the equivalent covenant in a new tenancy where the landlord can, and inevitably will, exercise a greater degree of control over any proposed assignment.[76c] The tenant will surely argue that to value the notional lease as a new tenancy with a comparatively lenient alienation covenant would be to stray too far from reality and would produce an unjustly inflated rent. A realistic and more even-handed approach would be to assume that the notional lease is effectively granted pursuant to the actual lease which is thus to be construed as an agreement for lease entered into prior to commencement of the 1995 Act, with the result that the notional lease should accordingly be construed as an old tenancy. It is inevitable that this issue will be the subject of litigation before too long.

Where there are supplemental licences or deeds of variation, these too should be incorporated in the notional **Supplemental** lease in the absence of express conditions to the contrary.[77]
deeds Of course, this assumption could raise questions about the precise construction of any part of the lease, but the provisions which have given rise to most litigation are user covenants and rent review provisions themselves, both of which may have a profound effect on the market rent.

6–27 Rent review provisions in hypothetical lease

As to rent review provisions, it has become common practice (possibly from "conveyancing overcaution")[78] to provide that the assumed letting is not to include the rent payable under the existing lease: hardly surprising in view of the purpose of the review clause. Otherwise it might be contended that the open market rent should be tempered by reference to the former rent, as with the interim rent provisions under section 24A of the Landlord and Tenant Act 1954.[79] However, in a number of cases[80] landlords have successfully argued that such wording requires the provisions for rent review themselves to be disregarded, thereby entitling the landlord to an uplift in the reviewed rent (in some cases as much as 20 per cent) to reflect the artificial assumption of no future reviews. These decisions[81] caused considerable consternation and uncertainty, but helpful guidance as to the approach to

---

[76c] See para. 12–12 below.

[77] *Lynnthorpe Enterprises Ltd v. Sidney Smith (Chelsea) Ltd* [1990] 3 E.G. 93 and see also *Orchid Lodge (UK) Ltd v. Extel Computing Ltd* [1991] 32 E.G. 57 and *Commercial Union Life Assurance Company plc v. Woolworths plc* [1994] EGCS 191.

[78] *Lister Locks Ltd v. T.E.I. Pension Trust Ltd* (1981) 264 E.G. 827 at 828.

[79] See para. 16–32 below.

[80] *e.g. Pugh v. Smiths Industries Ltd* (1982) 264 E.G. 823; *National Westminster Bank plc v. Arthur Young, McLelland Moores & Co.* [1985] 1 EGLR 61; *Equity & Law Life Assurance plc v. Bodfield Ltd* [1985] 2 EGLR 144 (on appeal (1987) 281 E.G. 1448).

[81] The last two cases cited at n. 80 above gave rise to particular concern, since they went further than the earlier cases in (1) applying the strict construction even though the clause could fairly be said to be susceptible to a more moderate construction; and (2) applying that construction to a common form of wording in use in many clauses.

adopt in construing such provisions was subsequently provided by Sir Nicholas Browne-Wilkinson V-C, in *British Gas Corporation v. Universities Superannuation Scheme Ltd.*[82] The suggested approach is as follows:

(1) words which require all provisions as to rent to be disregarded produce a result so manifestly contrary to commercial common sense that they cannot be given literal effect. This would require the valuation to ignore the covenant to pay rent, the proviso for re-entry for non-payment, and payments such as service charge and insurance premiums reserved as rents;[83]

(2) clear words requiring the rent review provisions (as opposed to all provisions as to rent) to be disregarded must be given effect to, however wayward the result;[84]

(3) subject to (2), in the absence of special circumstances it is proper to give effect to the underlying commercial purpose of a rent review clause and to construe the words so as to require future rent reviews to be taken into account in fixing the open market rental.[85] Any distinction based on whether the wording refers to the *amount* of rent or *provisions* as to rent was rejected as unduly semantic.[86]

Where the assumptions and disregards are unduly one-sided it might be thought that this could adversely affect the rental value. However, in *Broadgate Square plc v. Lehman Brothers Ltd.* (No. 2)[87] the court upheld the arbitrator's finding that it would be "double-counting" to reduce the rent as a result of an onerous assumption.

---

[82] [1986] 1 W.L.R. 398; and see also *General Accident Fire & Life Assurance Corporation plc v. Electronic Data Processing Co. plc* (1986) 281 E.G. 65 at 67; also *Equity & Law Life Assurance plc v. Bodfield Ltd* (1987) 281 E.G. 1448 at 1451, where the guidelines were approved, subject to certain caveats.

[83] See also *M.F.I. Properties Ltd v. B.I.C.C. Group Pension Trust Ltd* [1986] 1 All E.R. 974 at 976.

[84] For examples of such wording, see *Pugh v. Smiths Industries Ltd* (1982) 264 E.G. 823 ("disregarding the provisions of this clause"); *Securicor Ltd v. Postel Properties Ltd* [1985] 1 EGLR 102 ("there being disregarded this clause"). See also *M.F.I. Properties Ltd v. B.I.C.C. Group Pension Trust Ltd* [1986] 1 All E.R. 974, where it was said that a provision cannot be ignored simply because it is counterfactual or has no immediately obvious commercial justification.

[85] This approach has been followed in *Electricity Supply Nominees v. F.M. Insurance Co. Ltd* [1986] 1 EGLR 143; *Amax International Ltd v. Custodian Holdings Ltd* [1986] 279 E.G. 762 and *British Home Stores Ltd v. Ranbrook Properties Ltd* (1988) 16 E.G. 80. But *cf.* the result in *Equity & Law Life Assurance plc v. Bodfield Ltd* [1986] 2 EGLR 111, although significantly, in more recent cases involving the determination of either the full rental value less a discount or a base rent coupled with an additional rent, the courts have preferred the interpretation which reflected reality and therefore assumed future reviews: see *Prudential Assurance Co. Ltd v. 99 Bishopsgate Ltd* [1992] 1 EGLR 119 and *Buffalo Enterprises Inc. v. Golden Wonder Ltd* [1991] 1 EGLR 171.

[86] [1986] 1 W.L.R. 398 at 403.

[87] [1995] 33 E.G. 89. The valuer was to assess the rent after the willing tenant had had the benefit of all rent-free periods available in the open market, and not just a period for fitting out.

Problems concerning the rent review provisions can also occur where the interval between reviews is longer than that typically to be found in lettings at the time of the review. It may be possible to argue that this should result in an uplift in rent, since a landlord willing to let on a basis of long review periods would be likely to require an increased initial rent to reflect the advantage to the tenant and the greater likelihood of prejudice to the landlord from inflation. It is suggested that this is essentially a question of valuation, and that there is nothing in the usual form of rent review clause to prevent regard being had to this question.[88]

Long review intervals

6–28 User clause in hypothetical lease

Another difficult area is the relationship between the user clause in the lease and assessment of the rent on review. As a general rule, it would seem logical that the stricter the user clause and the fewer the potential uses of the property, the lower the rent it should command on the open market. Indeed, this logic is reflected in the fact that landlords are much less attracted to tight user provisions than once was the case.[89] Where the lease contains an absolute limitation on user, *i.e.* one which does not provide for the possibility of the limitation being relaxed, it has been held by the Court of Appeal that the possibility of the landlord relaxing the restriction should not be taken into account so as to increase the rent payable on review.[90] However, it has also been said that where the lease expressly contemplates that other forms of user might be authorised, the way is open for that possibility to be taken into account,[91] even though in the absence of express words to the contrary the landlord would be entitled to act arbitrarily in refusing any relaxation.[92] Where the lease provides that the landlord may not unreasonably withhold his consent to change of use, this should certainly be taken into account.[93] It would seem logical that it must also be considered whether an application to widen the clause would be likely, since the landlord cannot widen it unilaterally. However, in *Tea Trade Properties Ltd v. CIN Properties Ltd*[94] the judge allowed the landlord to assume

---

[88] See *Handbook of Rent Review*, para. 6–5. So far as the decision in *Lear v. Blizzard* [1983] 3 All E.R. 662 suggests otherwise it appears unsound.

[89] See para. 10–01 below. Witness also the unsuccessful attempts by some landlords unilaterally to widen user clauses to secure an uplift: *C & A Pensions Trustees Ltd v. British Vita Investments Ltd* (1984) 272 E.G. 63.

[90] *Plinth Property Investments Ltd v. Mott Hay & Anderson* (1978) 38 P. & C.R. 361. Lord Denning M.R. and Shaw L.J. based their decision on the ground that it would be too uncertain an exercise, Brandon L.J. on the principle that it is to be assumed that all rights and obligations under the lease will be enforced and observed. The decision has been subject to much criticism, but was followed in *London Scottish Properties Ltd v. Council for Professions Supplementary to Medicine*, C.A., November 8, 1977 (unreported but cited at D.C. 391, *Handbook of Rent Review* (1985)).

[91] *Forte & Co. Ltd v. General Accident Life Assurance Co. Ltd* (1987) 54 P. & C.R. 9.

[92] See para. 10–09 below.

[93] *Forte & Co. Ltd v. General Accident Life Assurance Co. Ltd* (1987) 54 P. & C.R. 9.

[94] [1990] 22 E.G. 67.

that the whole of the premises could be used as offices since he had obtained planning permission for such use. The fact that the tenant did not so use the premises and had not requested a change of use was not relevant.

Use confined to tenant only

The principle that the stringency of the user clause must be taken into account may break down where the clause is such as to negate the chosen means of valuation for review. Thus in *Law Land Co. Ltd v. The Consumers' Association Ltd*,[95] the user clause effectively restricted use to the activities of one named tenant, but the review was to be on the basis of an open market rental valuation because of an assumption of vacant possession. The Court of Appeal held that in order to make the review clause workable, the user clause must be read as permitting use for the business of any hypothetical lessee, the name of such lessee being substituted for that of the original tenant.[96] The somewhat paradoxical result is that so long as the valuer is expressly directed to value on an open market basis, adopting the more stringent type of user restriction may favour the landlord in rent review terms. However, it should not be forgotten that the effect of such a provision is likely to make the lease non-assignable, and this in itself is likely to have a serious effect on rent.

Similarly, where the rent review clause envisaged that the parties were to have regard to "rental values then current for property let for 125 years . . . for industrial purposes" but the user clause permitted special steel making and rolling purposes only, the Court of Appeal allowed the valuation to be on the wider basis. Note, however, there was no direction in the lease as to the form of the notional lease.[97]

Disregard of user restrictions

Given the significant valuation consequences of user provisions,[98] it is not surprising that landlords sometimes attempt to obtain the best of both worlds by providing that any user restrictions are to be disregarded in assessing the market rent. A fairer solution would be to provide that restrictions on user are to be disregarded to the extent that they are actually modified or relaxed during the term.[99] This formulation also has the advantage that it probably implies

---

[95] (1980) 255 E.G. 617.

[96] Followed in *Sterling Land Office Developments Ltd v. Lloyds Bank plc* (1984) 271 E.G. 894 and in *Orchid Lodge U.K. Ltd v. Extel Computing Ltd* [1991] 32 E.G. 57 (where a planning permission personal to the tenant was assumed to be available to the hypothetical tenant (but no one else)) and *Post Office Counters Ltd v. Harlow District Council* [1991] 36 E.G. 151 (where the open market and vacant possession assumptions allowed the arbitrator effectively to re-draft the user clause restricting use to that of the hypothetical tenant); but distinguished in *James v. The British Crafts Centre* (1987) 282 E.G. 1251, where the user clause allowed use by a named tenant in addition to a general use.

[97] *Sheerness Steel Co. plc v. Medway Ports Authority* [1992] 12 E.G. 138.

[98] For examples, see *Duvan Estates Ltd v. Rossette Sunshine Savouries Ltd* (1981) 261 E.G. 364; *U.D.S. Tailoring Ltd v. B.L. Holdings Ltd* (1981) 261 E.G. 49.

[99] A nonsensical provision was construed as having this effect in *Pearl Assurance plc v. Shaw* [1985] 1 EGLR 92. See also *Lynnthorpe Enterprises Ltd v. Sidney Smith (Chelsea) Ltd* [1990] 8 E.G. 93, where the judge, applying the presumption of reality, held that the terms of the notional lease should reflect variations to the lease itself (unless the variations were personal to the actual tenant).

that the possibility of the clause being relaxed, as opposed to actual relaxation, is to be ignored.

6–29 The length of the term to be assumed

The lease should make clear the length of the term which is being valued on review. Prior to the introduction of the now common formula of the longer of a term equal to the unexpired residue of the actual term and some set period (usually 10 or 15 years), there were two main alternatives: **Original term or unexpired residue** either a term equivalent to the term originally granted may be assumed (so that, for example, on each rent review under a 20 year lease, a new 20 year term is assumed), or a term equal to the unexpired residue of the original term at the date of review. Where the first alternative is intended, the lease must so provide in express terms. Otherwise the court is likely to infer that "a term of years equal to the said term" began when the original term commenced.[1] The second alternative favours the tenant, since the length of the assumed lease will diminish with successive reviews, although it should be remembered that the possibility of renewal under Part II of the Landlord and Tenant Act 1954 can be taken into account.[2] Similarly, the Court of Appeal have held that a reversionary lease may be taken into account.[3]

Where the lease contains no express indication of the length of the term to be assumed, a court is likely to favour the approach most in accordance with reality; that is, review on the basis of the unexpired residue of the term.[4]

Both approaches still have their adherents. The "unexpired **Merits of** residue" approach may seem superficially closer to reality **approaches** (and, indeed, comparables with terms equal in length to the original "whole term" may be hard to find) but supporters of the "whole term" approach argue that it accords more accurately with the purpose of a rent review clause, which is to review the rent reserved under the original lease in the light of market changes. In fact, a number of years ago it was recognised that neither approach was fully satisfactory.

---

[1] *Lynnthorpe Enterprises Ltd v. Sidney Smith (Chelsea) Ltd* [1990] 8 E.G. 93. Followed in *Tea Trade Properties Ltd v. C.I.N. Properties Ltd* [1990] 22 E.G. 67 and *British Gas plc v. Dollar Land Holdings plc* [1992] 12 E.G. 141.

[2] *Pivot Properties Ltd v. Secretary of State for the Environment* (1980) 41 P. & C.R. 248.

[3] *Toyota (G.B.) Ltd v. Legal & General Assurance (Pensions Management) Ltd* [1989] 42 E.G. 104.

[4] As in *Norwich Union Life Insurance Society v. Trustee Savings Bank Central Board* [1986] 1 EGLR 136; *Ritz Hotel (London) Ltd v. Ritz Casino Ltd* [1989] 46 E.G. 95; *Tea Trade Properties Ltd v. CIN Properties Ltd* [1990] 22 E.G. 67 and *British Gas plc v. Dollar Land Holdings plc* [1992] 12 E.G. 141. But *cf. Prudential Assurance Co. Ltd v. Salisbury's Handbags Ltd* [1992] 23 E.G. 117 where the court rejected this approach since otherwise the notional lease would have been for over 80 years without any reviews, resulting in an undeserved windfall for the landlord. In *Dennis & Robinson Ltd v. Kiossis Establishment* [1987] 1 EGLR 133, it was held, *obiter*, that the hypothetical term should run from the original date of the term; this is clearly contrary to what the parties intended, but seems to be based upon the fact that the reviews under the hypothetical lease were to operate in specified years all falling during the original term.

Attempting to value a short letting on the basis of repairing covenants appropriate to a 20 or 25 year lease can result in an unduly depressed rent; but so can the assumption of a 20 or 25 year letting of a building which in reality is nearing the end of its useful life. Therefore many modern precedents attempt the compromise mentioned above, namely directing that a term be assumed of the unexpired residue or of some specified period (usually 10 or 15 years), whichever is the longer. The Law Society/R.I.C.S. and I.S.V.A. Model Forms take this approach.

Occasionally, and usually in a ground lease, the review clause provides that the length of the term should be such as would produce the highest rent at review or as would be most likely in the prevailing market conditions.[5]

6–30 Letting with vacant possession

Vacant possession

The clause will often provide that the assumed letting is to be with vacant possession and as a whole. The effect of a direction as to assuming vacant possession is that the tenant is to be deemed to have moved out or never to have occupied the premises.[6] Thus any "sitting tenant" considerations are excluded, as is any effect on rent flowing from the tenant's occupation. The direction also requires any sub-tenancy to be ignored, which could potentially favour either party; *e.g.* subletting of part on a protected residential tenancy could considerably depress the rent, but a non-protected residential letting of a separate part at a high rent might substantially increase it. Whether this extends to sub-leases granted prior to the lease will turn on the particular wording used and the surrounding facts.[7] It will be sensible to provide expressly for the position where sub-leases exist or are envisaged: *e.g.* the landlord may wish to assume that any parts capable of subletting are sub-let.

If no mention is made of vacant possession, a disregard of the tenant's occupation might assist to produce the same result.[8]

The assumption of vacant possession is capable of producing some very startling adverse consequences for the

[5] See for example *Prudential Assurance Co. Ltd v. Salisbury's Handbags Ltd* [1992] 23 E.G. 117 and *Millshaw Property Company Ltd v. Preston Borough Council* [1995] EGCS 186.

[6] *F. R. Evans (Leeds) Ltd v. English Electric Co. Ltd* (1977) 36 P. & C.R. 184. See also *Australian Mutual Provident Society v. Overseas Telecommunications Commission (Australia) Ltd* [1972] 2 N.S.W.L.R. 806 (requirement to assume lease discharged and premises put out to tender).

[7] Compare *Avon County Council v. Alliance Property Co. Ltd* (1981) 258 E.G. 1181 (sub-leases subject to which lease granted not taken into account) and *Hill Samuel Life Assurance Co. Ltd v. Preston Borough Council* [1990] 36 E.G. 111 (rent to be assessed on what an investment lessee would pay for the premises with vacant possession by reference to what he would hope to receive from sub-tenants) with *Scottish & Newcastle Breweries plc v. Sir Richard Sutton's Settled Estates* [1985] 2 EGLR 130; *Forte & Co. Ltd v. General Accident Life Assurance Ltd* [1986] 2 EGLR 115 and *Laura Investments Ltd v. London Borough of Havering* [1993] 8 E.G. 120 (subleases taken into account).

[8] *Hill Samuel Life Assurance Co. Ltd v. Preston Borough Council* [1990] 36 E.G. 111.

landlord. For example, in the celebrated case of *99 Bishopsgate Ltd v. Prudential Assurance Co. Ltd*[9] the Court of Appeal held

Fitting out period assumed

that the assumption required notice to be taken of the fact that on a letting with vacant possession, the incoming tenant would be likely to require a rent free period for fitting out. Similarly, the tenant may be assumed to have removed all his tenant's fixtures by the review date, which may have a depressing effect on rent.[10] The landlord should take care to counter these adverse effects by providing that the premises are to be assumed to be fit for immediate occupation[11] or that, in fixing the rent, no reduction is to be made to take account of any rental concession which might be granted on a new letting with vacant possession in respect of a fitting out period.[12]

This whole area has become something of a minefield over recent years. In *Orchid Lodge (U.K.) Ltd v. Extel Computing Ltd*[13] the Court of Appeal decided that an acknowledgment by the assignee in a licence to assign that for rent review

Fit for use and occupation

purposes "the . . . premises are fit for use and occupation" did not mean valuing the premises on the assumption that they were fitted out to a better standard than they actually were.

In *Iceland Frozen Foods Ltd v. Starlight Investments Ltd*[14] the assumption was "that the premises remain in existence and are ready for immediate occupation and use". The landlord

Ready for immediate occupation and use

argued that this meant use for any purpose and in any condition that the willing tenant would want them to be in, but the Court of Appeal, in rejecting this approach, said that "ready for immediate occupation and use" amplified the immediately preceding words so that although the premises were to be valued as more than in a shell condition (that is with the basic structural works completed but no wiring, plumbing, etc.) they were not to be valued as in such a condition as would enable the tenant to walk in and start trading straightaway. Subsequently, in *Pontsarn Investments Ltd*

Fit for immediate occupation and use

v. Kansallis–Osake-Pankki[15] the assumption of "vacant but fit for immediate occupation and use" was held not to mean fitted out (again, with the connotation of the tenant being able to start trading staightaway) but rather that the premises were ready to take the tenant's fitting out works. Specifically, "fit" meant "free from defects" rather than fitted out. The judge felt this interpretation was consistent with the subsequent disregard of the tenant's improvements. Why expect a tenant to pay rent assuming the presence of notional fixtures and fittings when he did not have to pay rent for his

---

[9] [1985] 1 EGLR 72.

[10] *New Zealand Government Property Corp. v. H.M. & S. Ltd* [1982] 1 Q.B. 1145.

[11] See the Law Society/R.I.C.S. Model Form. But there may be other reasons for rental concessions, for example reinstatement of premises in disrepair, or simply as an inducement to take the lease.

[12] Great care needs to be taken in drafting such an assumption; see *Prudential Nominees Ltd v. Greenham Trading Ltd* [1995] 1 E.G. 111 (para. 6–31 below).

[13] [1991] 32 E.G. 57.

[14] [1992] 7 E.G. 117.

[15] [1992] 22 E.G. 103.

actual fitting out works? In other words, this assumption is directed not at what is to be valued but rather when. This also appears to be the basis of the Court of Appeal's decision in *London & Leeds Estates Ltd v. Paribas*[16] so that while, at first instance, the judge had embarked on an almost metaphysical analysis of what fitting out works the notional tenant might have required and who would have carried them out, the Court of Appeal adopted a much more straightforward approach and held that the assumption was there to stop the actual tenant from arguing for a lower rent because the premises were not fitted out.[16a]

6–31 Rent-free periods as inducements

In the mid to late 1980s draftsmen recognised that a "fit for use and occupation" assumption might not on its own be enough in cases where the rent-free period offered to the tenant reflected not only the period estimated for fitting out but also an inducement to take the lease. When the recession of the early 1990s hit and rental values fell by 50 per cent or more (with office buildings in the City of London being particularly affected), rent-free periods of up to three years were not uncommon and tenants were also offered capital sums to pay for the costs of fitting out, or simply as an inducement to persuade them to sign up. Often, there was a combination of the two. The simple monetary effect on what rent the tenant pays is relatively easily calculated, but surveyors have found it less easy to explain the effect of such concessions on rental values when establishing the market rent. For example, where the rent is £100,000 per annum for the first five years of the term and the tenant enjoys a year's rent-free period (say two months to fit out and the balance as an inducement), is the rental value £100,000 per annum or £80,000 per annum given that the total rent paid over the five year period is £400,000?[17] To protect the landlord, an assumption started to appear in leases that no reduction was to be made to reflect the fact that in the open market tenants were enjoying extended rent-free periods or receiving other inducements. A series of cases (the so-called "headline rent" cases) on the point were heard in 1993 and 1994, four of which were consolidated into a single appeal.[18] The Court of Appeal, in a relatively brief judgment given the imaginative arguments used in the lower courts, decided that in only one case, *Broadgate Square plc v. Lehman Brothers Ltd* did the

---

[16] [1993] 30 E.G. 89.
[16a] The judge in *Ocean Accident & Guarantee Corporation v. Next plc*; *Commercial Union Assurance Company plc v. Next plc* [1995] EGCS 187 also decided that an assumption that the premises had been "fully fitted out and equipped" did not mean that tenant's or trade fixtures were to be rentalised.
[17] In practice, of course, the calculation is more complex as a result of discounting the value of future income.
[18] *Scottish Amicable Life Assurance Society v. Middleton Potts & Co*; *Co-operative Wholesale Society Ltd v. National Westminster Bank plc*; *Prudential Nominees Ltd v. Greenham Trading Ltd*; and *Broadgate Square plc v. Lehman Brothers Ltd* [1995] 1 E.G. 111.

Headline rents

draftsman of the lease succeed in achieving his aim of disregarding all rent-free periods available to tenants at the review date and not just a rent-free fitting out period; he did this by stipulating that the revised rent would be that payable "after the expiry of any rent free period". In each of the other three cases heard at the same time, the Court of Appeal picked its way through similar wording but was able to identify subtle differences so as to deny the landlord any element of a windfall gain, although the Court recognised the fairness of the proposition that the willing tenant (and therefore the real tenant) should not enjoy the benefit of a further (genuine) rent-free period within which to fit out, on the reasonable basis that the actual tenant would almost certainly have already enjoyed this benefit when he first took on the lease. By emphasising the commercial purpose of rent reviews, the Court of Appeal made it clear that, unless there are very clear words to show that the valuer should take the rent after the rent-free period had expired or after the tenant

No windfall for the landlord

had received any other inducement available, then the landlord should not enjoy any windfall profit.[19] This principle can, it is suggested, be applied with equal force to other assumptions and disregards which fly in the face of reality and result in either party enjoying some unwarranted benefit to the detriment of the other party.

Disregard of rent-free periods, etc.

Although at first blush there may appear to be no difference between an assumption that the willing tenant has enjoyed the benefit of a rent-free period and a direction to disregard such a concession, the decision in *City Offices plc v. Bryanston Insurance Co. Ltd*[20] also well demonstrates the pitfalls in this area. The rent review provisions required not only an assumption that the rent would be that which would be payable after the expiry of any rent-free period, but also that other inducements available to tenants in the open market should be disregarded. The judge decided that to give effect to this disregard, the willing tenant would reduce his bid on the basis that he was no longer to enjoy what other prospective tenants in the market were being offered. Accordingly, such a disregard is better avoided.

6–32   Letting as a whole

Sometimes the review clause directs that the property is to be valued on the assumption that it is let as a whole. This may have important consequences in the case of a large building which would be marketable if sub-divided, but where the market for letting as a whole is poor.[21] An assumed letting as a whole may produce a significantly lower rental figure than

Sub-lettings

the sum of sub-lettings of separate parts, although in the context of an investment lease, a willing tenant may still take

---

[19] In practice such clear wording is very rarely found; and after this judgment tenants would be most unwilling to accept it in new leases.

[20] [1993] 11 E.G. 129.

[21] See *F. R. Evans (Leeds) Ltd v. English Electric Co. Ltd* (1977) 36 P. & C.R. 184; *99 Bishopsgate Ltd v. Prudential Assurance Co. Ltd* [1985] 1 EGLR 72.

into account the prospect of receiving rents from occupational tenants, notwithstanding the direction "let as a whole".[22]

Alternatively, the rent review clause might direct that the open market rent to be agreed or determined on review is to be whichever is the greater of the rent achievable on a letting of the property as a whole and the aggregate of the rents at which the constituent parts of the property could be let. This formula is however commonly rejected by tenants on the basis that the valuation should reflect the terms on which the property is actually let.

6–33   Planning permission and development potential

Permitted use and licences

In practice, the value of an interest in property will vary considerably depending on the permitted use for planning purposes, or whether any licences necessary to use the property for particular purposes (*e.g.* gaming or the sale of liquor) are forthcoming. It is therefore important to indicate how far such considerations should be taken into account on rent review.[23]

Assumption as to lawful use

In one case a direction to value the premises on the basis of letting for certain purposes was held to carry with it the implication that the premises could lawfully be so used.[24] However, it would be unwise to treat the case as laying down any rule of general application; each case must turn on its own facts, and in some instances the correct approach may be to assess the prospects of permission for lawful use being obtained, rather than assume permission already exists.[25]

Terms of permission

Even where planning permission has been granted, close regard should be paid to the terms of the permission and to any conditions, which may effectively nullify an increase in rental value attributable to an unconditional permission.[26]

---

[22] *Hill Samuel Life Assurance Co. Ltd v. Preston Borough Council* [1990] 36 E.G. 111.

[23] For a striking example concerning gaming licences, see *Cornwall Coast Country Club Ltd v. Cardgrange Ltd* (1987) 282 E.G. 1664. See also *Parkside Clubs (Nottingham) Ltd v. Armgrade Ltd* [1995] 48 E.G. 104 (where an assumption that "the Tenant" had obtained all necessary licences was held to refer only to the actual tenant under the lease and not the hypothetical tenant). See also *Tea Trade Properties Ltd v. CIN Properties Ltd* [1990] 22 E.G. 67 where the existence of a planning permission (granted on the landlord's application) to use an entire property as offices meant the premises could be valued on that basis.

[24] *Bovis Group Pension Fund Ltd v. G. C. Flooring & Furnishing Ltd* (1984) 269 E.G. 1252; *cf., Hill v. Harris* [1965] 2 Q.B. 601, para. 18–05 below. For a case involving the need to carry out works before the premises could be lawfully used; see *Exclusive Properties Ltd v. Cribgate Ltd* [1986] 2 EGLR 123.

[25] See *Daejan Investments Ltd v. Cornwall Coast Country Club* [1985] 1 EGLR 77 at 80–81. Development potential may be taken into account if proven: *Rushmoor Borough Council v. Goacher* [1985] 2 EGLR 140. *cf., Railstore Ltd v. Playdale* [1988] 35 E.G. 87 where the likelihood of planning permission was small.

[26] See, *e.g.*, *Wolff v. London Borough of Enfield* (1987) 281 E.G. 1320 (permission limited to one named occupant).

6–34   Matters to be assumed

Performance of tenant's covenants

Some of the common assumptions made on review have already been mentioned above. A further assumption which is frequently required is that the tenant has complied with all the covenants under the lease. Thus no reduction in rent will be made because of the dilapidated state of the premises, if that state results from the tenant's failure to repair in accordance with the covenants in the lease. It would appear that the same result may be reached in the absence of any express provision on the basis of the principle that no man should take advantage of his own wrong.[27] The argument that this allows double recovery to the landlord seems misplaced: if the landlord subsequently attempted to recover damages for breach of covenant the damage to the reversion would be cushioned by the effect of the rent review clause and damages reduced accordingly.

It is therefore important to consider the effect of all parts of the lease in order to appreciate fully the import of the rent review provisions: *e.g.* a tenant who has covenanted to repair and renew as necessary all parts of the building may find that if a serious defect manifests itself he must not only rectify it at his own expense, but also do so without any compensating abatement in rent.[28] In this connection, the repairing standard required by the tenant's covenant is determined by the parties' expectation at the time the lease was granted before any possible defects are discovered.[29]

Landlord's covenants

A difficult question is how far failure by the landlord to comply with his obligations may be taken into account in reducing the rent on review. Objectively, a properly-advised tenant should not accept a provision requiring performance by the landlord to be assumed, but even so there may be some scope for argument that performance should be assumed as an implied term, on the basis that the tenant has remedies to enforce the landlord's covenants and it may be assumed that he will make use of them. However, it seems unlikely that such an argument could prevail against both the actual state of the premises[30] and the principle that the landlord should not derive a benefit from his own wrong.[31] Nor is the tenuous ability to obtain redress by litigation any remedy for the interference with occupation which may be caused by the

---

[27] *Harmsworth Pension Funds Trustees Ltd v. Charringtons Industrial Holdings Ltd* [1985] 1 EGLR 97; *Family Management Ltd v. Gray* (1979) 253 E.G. 369.
[28] But see *Norwich Union Life Insurance Society v. British Railways Board* (1987) 283 E.G. 846 where the rent was reduced by $27\frac{1}{2}$% as a consequence of the lease containing a tenant's covenant to rebuild.
[29] *Sandhu v. Ladbroke Hotels Ltd* [1995] 39 E.G. 152.
[30] See *Fawkes v. Viscount Chelsea* [1980] Q.B. 441 at 454, 457 (a lease renewal where the court ordered a lower rent until the landlord had carried out various repairs).
[31] See n. 27 above.

landlord's neglect.[32] Given that it appears impossible[33] to award a differential rent (one varying according to the state of the premises) on review in the absence of some express power to do so, the fairest solution would appear to be to value the premises as they stand, taking account of the landlord's failure to repair, but with some allowance to reflect the possibility of the landlord being forced to put the premises into repair in future.

Rebuilding and reinstatement

An assumption generally considered fair between the parties is that if the premises are damaged or destroyed, they are to be assumed to have been rebuilt or restored (see Model Forms; despite the possible overlap with the "fit for occupation and immediate use" assumption, draftsmen usually include both). The possible relationship between the assumption and the provisions relating to insurance and suspension of rent[34] should be carefully considered. Where the letting is of part of a building or in a shopping development it is not uncommon for the assumption to extend to the building or development as a whole.

VAT status of the tenant

Since the Finance Act 1989 allowed VAT to be charged on rent,[35] landlords have sometimes sought to include an assumption to the effect that all willing tenants can recover VAT so as not to exclude those tenants, mainly in the financial sector (insurance companies and brokers, banks, etc.), which can recover none or only a very small part of VAT paid. This departure from reality was strongly resisted by tenants, who argued that the landlord should take the market as he found it. It has consequently become comparatively rare in practice to include such an assumption and, where included in a draft lease, its deletion is generally accepted by the landlord.

Nothing done to diminish rental value

Another common assumption is that no work has been carried out that might diminish rental value (see Model Forms). Landlords may give consent to alterations or a change of use which, because of the need to comply with fire regulations and the like, cut down on the lettable area of the premises. The effect of the assumption is to require the valuer to ignore any consequential reduction in the rent and can sometimes help a landlord mitigate the effect of the disregard of tenants' improvements. For example, a retail tenant who has improved access to the first floor of his demise by enlarging the staircase will almost certainly have reduced the net lettable area on the ground floor and the assumption is designed to ensure that that reduction is ignored. The fact that the first floor may now be more valuable in rental value terms is unlikely to benefit the landlord because of the disregard of tenants' improvements, and certainly if the

---

[32] *Handbook of Rent Review*, para. 4–56. Where that interference is temporary (for example, there are disrepairs which the landlord has in hand as part of a rolling programme of works) it would be unfair on the landlord to value the premises in their then state. Rather the valuer should assume the works had been completed. The Model Forms recognise the difficulty but fail to come down on one side or the other.
[33] *Clarke v. Findon Developments Ltd* (1984) 270 E.G. 426.
[34] See para. 13–17 below.
[35] See Chap. 19.

landlord is looking both to benefit from the increase in the rental value of the first floor, and at the same time to rentalise the space taken up by the enlargement to the staircase on the ground floor, then the wording will have to be unambiguous on the point. Otherwise, following the headline rent cases,[36] the court is likely to deny the landlord the prospect of a windfall profit. As a consequence, when shop units are let in shell condition, it is not uncommon for the rent review clause to contain an assumption that a staircase of a particular size has been constructed between ground and first floors either by the landlord at its own expense or by the tenant but in pursuance of an obligation to the landlord, thereby negativing the disregard of tenants' improvements in this respect.

6–35 Disregard of tenant's occupation and goodwill

It is usual to direct that the fact that the tenant has been in occupation of the premises shall be disregarded.[37] This avoids the argument that a sitting tenant would be willing to pay a rent above the market rate to avoid the disruption and

Effect of disregard of occupation

inconvenience of moving or to preserve the occupation of premises especially adapted to his purpose;[38] but it may also have the effect of negating any concessions which a landlord might be willing to offer to a good sitting tenant (for example, the anchor tenant in a shopping centre). In some cases it may be desirable for the tenant to require that his occupation of other premises also be disregarded, for instance where he occupies as a single unit a number of adjacent properties held under different leases.[39] The tenant should also always try to ensure that the disregard extends to any permitted sub-tenant's occupation and, possibly, the occupation of any group companies if the sharing of occupation is permitted.

Goodwill

Rather similar is the usual disregard of any goodwill attaching to the holding by reason of the business carried on by the tenant or his predecessor in title.[40] It is probably the case that the disregard is inserted on the basis of convention rather than strict logic,[41] and no doubt in many cases it will prove extremely difficult to isolate the element of rental value attributable to goodwill. But so long as landlords continue to

---

[36] See para. 6–31 above.
[37] See also Landlord and Tenant Act 1954, s.34(1)(a).
[38] *Harewood Hotels Ltd v. Harris* [1968] 1 W.L.R. 108 at 114–115.
[39] See *First Leisure Training Ltd v Dorita Properties Ltd* [1991] 23 E.G. 116 (where it was held that the arbitrator need not assume that the tenant, as occupier of adjoining premises, would not be one of the bidders) and *Secretary of State for the Environment v. Reed International plc* [1994] 6 E.G. 137 (where it was reasonable for an arbitrator to determine, using his valuation experience, that the hypothetical tenant would have made a small overbid of £1 per sq ft faced with a potential active bidder (*i.e.* the Department of the Environment) as occupier of the adjoining office block).
[40] See also Landlord and Tenant Act 1954, s.34(1)(b).
[41] D. N. Clarke and J. E. Adams, *Rent Reviews and Variable Rents* (3rd ed. 1991) pp. 452, *et seq.*

be willing to incorporate the disregard of goodwill, tenants should certainly not reject it.[42]

6–36　Disregard of improvements

Meaning of "improvements"

Probably the most important matter to be disregarded is any improvement made to the property by the tenant or any sub-tenant.[43] The injustice of requiring the tenant to pay a substantially increased rent as a result of his own work or expenditure is obvious,[44] but the exact definition of what improvements should be disregarded is much more difficult. As to the meaning of "improvement", no comprehensive definition exists at present, though decisions on the Landlord and Tenant Act 1927[45] may provide some guidance, and it would appear that the provision of items which constitute landlord's fixtures can be regarded as an improvement.[46] It has also been said that "improvement" connotes some alteration or addition to an existing building, and that modifications to the design of a building in the course of construction, so as to be part of the building as originally constructed, are not improvements.[47]

By whom improvement carried out

The first point to consider is whether improvements must have been carried out by any particular person in order to be disregarded. Limiting the disregard to improvements carried out by the tenant carries two dangers. The first is that improvements carried out by some third party, such as the tenant's predecessor in title or a sub-tenant, would not fall to be disregarded. This could not only allow the landlord to enjoy a windfall gain, but also prejudice a tenant who had given some consideration for the work.[48] The disregard should therefore be extended to improvements by the tenant's predecessors in title and persons deriving title through the tenant. However, the requirement that work be carried out by the tenant does not necessarily mean that the tenant must have physically carried out the work. The requirement will probably be satisfied if the work is carried out by some third

---

[42] See *Prudential Assurance Co. Ltd v. Metropolitan Estates Ltd* [1993] 32 E.G. 74 where the disregard of the tenant's occupation in a lease of a public house was held to imply that goodwill be disregarded too.

[43] See below for the risks when there are sub-leases.

[44] A striking example of the injustice which can occur if no provision is made is *Ponsford v. H.M.S. Aerosols Ltd* [1979] A.C. 63. See also *Sheerness Steel Co. plc v. Medway Ports Authority* [1992] 12 E.G. 138 where the court found there were clear words to override the normal commercial expectation that the tenant's own improvements would not be rentalised.

[45] See para. 11–05 below.

[46] *New Zealand Government Property Corp. v. H.M. &. S. Ltd* [1982] Q.B. 1145. See further para. 11–14 below.

[47] *Scottish & Newcastle Breweries plc v. Sir Richard Sutton's Settled Estates* [1985] 2 EGLR 130 at 137; see also *Panther Shop Investments Ltd v. Keith Pople Ltd* (1987) 282 E.G. 594, where a rear extension and storage building built by the tenant under a previous lease without any obligation to the landlord to do so had become part of the premises under the new lease and so were no longer to be disregarded.

[48] See *Laura Investment Co. Ltd v. London Borough of Havering* [1992] 24 E.G. 136 where the tenant had to pay rent for buildings created by his sub-tenants even though under the sub-leases the buildings were to be disregarded for rent review purposes.

party at the tenant's cost and at his request.[49] The second potential problem is that the disregard could be construed as limited to improvements carried out by the tenant as tenant, thus possibly excluding work carried out under a previous tenancy,[50] or as a licensee prior to the grant of the lease. The courts are likely to attempt to include such improvements in the disregard where carried out in clear contemplation of a lease being granted or with the encouragement of the landlord.[51] It is suggested that where improvements have been carried out under a previous lease, or are to be carried out before the tenancy is granted, for example under an agreement for lease, the clause should expressly provide for the appropriate disregard to be made.[52]

Improvements prior to grant of lease

The second point to consider is whether the improvement must have been carried out with any necessary consent in order to be disregarded (both the Law Society/R.I.C.S. and the I.S.V.A. Model Forms require prior consent). If not qualified, such a requirement could be read as extending not only to the consent of the landlord, but also to any necessary planning or building regulation consents. The requirement of consent has been held to prevail over the usual assumption that the tenant has complied with all his obligations in a case where no consent was obtained.[53] Nor, it would appear, will the requirement be modified in cases where the landlord's consent is unreasonably withheld, either by an implied term or by the general principle that no man should take advantage of his own wrong.[54] Tenants should therefore qualify the clause by inserting wording along the lines of "or without landlord's consent where such consent has been unreasonably withheld".

Whether consent obtained to improvement

Thirdly, it is common to exclude from the disregard improvements carried out pursuant to an obligation to the landlord. This carries a number of hidden dangers for the tenant:

Improvements under obligation to landlord

(1) it would exclude from the disregard any works carried out by the tenant under an obligation in the lease, *e.g.* fitting out works;

---

[49] *ibid.* Tenants should be wary of expressions such as "at the tenant's sole expense" since otherwise a contribution, however small, from the landlord, towards the cost of the works might mean the loss of the disregard.

[50] See *Re "Wonderland," Cleethorpes* [1965] A.C. 58 (now modified by statute in the context of the 1954 Act); *Brett v. Brett Essex Golf Club Ltd* [1986] 1 EGLR 154—the improvement must be to the premises as demised by the lease. Followed in *Panther Shop Investments* (see n. 47 above).

[51] *Hambros Bank Executor & Trustee Co. Ltd v. Superdrug Stores Ltd* [1985] 1 EGLR 99 at 101; *Scottish & Newcastle Breweries Ltd v. Sir Richard Sutton's Settled Estates* [1985] 2 EGLR 130 at 137. But *cf., Euston Centre Properties Ltd v. H. & J. Wilson Ltd* (1982) 262 E.G. 1079 where there was no enforceable agreement for a lease until the work was done; and also *Panther Shop Investments* (see n. 47 above).

[52] For evidential purposes it is important that a careful record of the scope of the improvements should be retained with the title deeds, including (if relevant) the licence granted pursuant to the previous lease.

[53] *Hamish Cathie Travel England Ltd v. Insight International Tours Ltd* [1986] 1 EGLR 244.

[54] *Hamish Cathie Travel England Ltd, ibid.*

(2) it could exclude works carried out pursuant to an obligation contained in some other document, most notably a licence for alterations or an agreement for lease. It will usually be possible to construe a licence not as imposing an obligation to carry out the work but as laying down the way in which the work is to be done if the tenant chooses to do it,[55] but this will not necessarily be the case in an agreement for lease;

(3) when read in conjunction with the usual covenant that the tenant will comply with all statutory requirements,[56] it could have the effect of preventing the disregard of improvements carried out to meet health or fire safety regulations.[57] Many leases, including the Model Forms, recognise this danger by excluding obligations that require compliance with statutes or directions from local authorities or other bodies exercising power under statute or Royal Charter. Some landlords will in turn qualify this exclusion in relation to works necessary to comply with statutes which result from the tenant's own voluntary improvements.

Obligation to reinstate
Finally, it may be noted that a disregard of improvements may lead to the conclusion that any obligation by the tenant to reinstate the premises to their original condition at the end of the term should also be disregarded: if the benefit from the temporary improvement is disregarded, it is illogical to include the burden of reinstatement.[58]

How improvements are to be disregarded Some provisions require only the effect of the improvements on rental value to be disregarded; others require the improvements themselves to be disregarded. Each formulation has its own uncertainties and in practice the distinction may be more apparent than real.[59] Valuable general guidance as to methods of valuation to be adopted is contained in *GREA Real Property Investments Ltd v. Williams*[60] and *Estates Projects Ltd v. Greenwich London Borough*.[61] In the former case,

---

[55] *Ridley v. Taylor* [1965] 1 W.L.R. 611 at 616; *Godbold v. Martin the Newsagents Ltd* (1983) 268 E.G. 1202. See also *Historic Houses Hotels Ltd v. Cadogan Estates* [1995] 11 E.G. 140 where a direction that the premises should be deemed to have been let in their altered state *ab initio* did not mean that the tenant's improvements should be rentalised and, *cf.*, *Ivory Gate Ltd v. Capital City Leisure Ltd* [1993] EGCS 710 where the licence made clear the works should not be disregarded.
[56] See para. 7–04 below.
[57] *Forte & Co. Ltd v. General Accident Life Assurance Ltd* [1986] 2 EGLR 115.
[58] See *Pleasurama Properties Ltd v. Leisure Investments (West End) Ltd* [1986] 1 EGLR 145 at 147 (also based on the ground that a tenant for whose benefit the licence was given should not derive further benefit from having the obligation to reinstate taken into account).
[59] Where, say, the tenant has built an extension, to disregard its presence could allow the landlord to argue that the willing tenant might pay more because of the ability to extend the demise. To disregard the effect on rent of the extension would deny this approach since, with the extension already constructed, there would be no room to extend. And see D. N. Clarke and J. E. Adams, *Rent Reviews and Variable Rents* (3rd ed. 1991) p. 416.
[60] (1979) 250 E.G. 651.
[61] (1979) 251 E.G. 851.

Intention of parties

Forbes J. regarded the paramount consideration as being that any method of valuation adopted should properly reflect the intention of the parties as expressed in the lease, interpreted in the surrounding circumstances. The intention essentially is that the rental should keep pace with inflation[62] and that from such rent should be eliminated the rental equivalent (itself affected by inflation) of the tenant's works. Comparables by way of unimproved but otherwise equivalent property may be relevant and in particular the cost and the value of the work must be distinguished.[63]

Incorporation of the disregard in the Landlord and Tenant Act 1954, s.34   Section 34 contains a number of disregards to be made on assessing the rent for a tenancy granted under the Act.[64] This includes a disregard of improvements. Older leases frequently incorporated the statutory disregards by reference, but few modern leases do so. Incorporation of the section can give rise to the following uncertainties, and for that reason may be better avoided:

Dangers of incorporating s.34

(1) Is the disregard incorporated in its original form or as amended by the Law of Property Act 1969? If the former, then the tenant will not be able to have improvements made under an earlier tenancy disregarded.[65] On the facts of *Brett v. Brett Essex Golf Club Ltd*[66] the Court of Appeal held that the clause used in that case referred to the section in its original form.

(2) Even if reference is to the section as amended, only improvements made within the last 21 years will be disregarded, and since the section dates the 21 years from the application for a new tenancy, there is considerable doubt as to how it might apply to a rent review clause.

(3) The section refers to the rental value of "the holding", a statutory concept.[67] There could be difficulty in applying the concept consistently with any assumptions contained in the rent review clause as to vacant possession and letting as a whole.

(4) The section only applies to improvements carried out by a person who at the time it was carried out was the tenant. This could cover improvements by a predecessor in title of the tenant, but might not cover improvements by a sub-tenant or licensee.

6–37   Model Forms of clause

As well as the many rent review clause precedents provided in the standard works, two forms of model clause have been

---

[62] But *cf.*, para. 6–08 above.
[63] For the practical problems which can occur in identifying the improvements when accurate records have not been kept or have been lost, see *Young v. Dalgety plc* [1987] 1 EGLR 116.
[64] See para. 16–47 below.
[65] *Re "Wonderland," Cleethorpes* [1965] A.C. 58.
[66] [1986] 1 EGLR 154.
[67] See para. 16–41 below.

Law Society/
R.I.C.S. Form

produced and promulgated by professional bodies. The first of these to appear was the Law Society/R.I.C.S. Model Form, first published in 1979,[68] and currently in an edition produced in Law Society/R.I.C.S. Form 1985.[69] The form comprises three variants, to cover determination by an arbitrator, by an expert, or by an arbitrator or expert at the landlord's option. Within each variant there is the option for upwards only or upwards and downwards reviews. It is possible to criticise certain aspects of the Model Form, notably the somewhat convoluted nature of some of the drafting,[70] but generally the clause provides a fair balance between the parties (e.g. either party may initiate the procedure), and deals with many of the points of difficulty mentioned in this Chapter. Improvements by the tenant pursuant to an obligation to comply with statutory requirements can be disregarded; no reduction is to be made to take account of a notional rent-free period[70a]; and the length of the term to be assumed is dealt with in detail.

I.S.V.A. Form

The other Model Form is that published by the Incorporated Society of Valuers and Auctioneers.[71] The layout of the clause is simpler and easier to follow than the Law Society/R.I.C.S. version, and again the clause attempts to reach a fair compromise between the interests of the landlord and tenant and takes into account many of the decided cases on the subject. The aspect of the clause which has attracted the most attention[72] is sub-clause 1.3 (G), relating to tenant's improvements, which provides that "a fair allowance" shall be made in respect of such improvements. The rationale is that it is easier and more realistic for a third party to value the premises as they are and then to make a fair allowance, than to attempt to value premises in a hypothetical condition with the actual improvements, or their effect on rental value, being ignored.

Use of Model
Forms

The Forms have not been used in practice to any large extent although, in areas of dispute, they have on occasions been used as a touchstone representing a fair balance. In any event, as with all precedents, the Model Forms should be used as servants rather than masters, and will doubtless need modification in many cases to suit the particular circumstances. In particular, it should be remembered that no rent review clause can or should cover every eventuality, and it is vital to draft other documents governing the landlord and

---

[68] [1979] L.S. Gaz. June 6, 564; [1980] L.S. Gaz. March 26, 326.
[69] [1985] L.S. Gaz. December 18, 3664. For an appraisal see (1986) 277 E.G. 604 (S. Fogel and P. Freedman), also at [1986] L.S. Gaz. February 12, 430.
[70] See [1986] L.S. Gaz. January 22, 165 (M. Rakusen).
[70a] However this is almost certainly ineffective to create a headline rent, in the light of *Prudential Nominees Ltd v. Greenham Trading Ltd* [1995] 1 E.G. 111: see para. 6–31 above.
[71] First published in 1984; see *Precedents for the Conveyancer* 5–89. There are two forms, of which Form A will be best suited to a lease of commercial property at a rack rent. See (1984) 272 E.G. 57 (R. Finch), 496, 618 (S. Fogel and P. Freedman), 1274 (R. Finch); also at [1984] L.S. Gaz. November 14, 3169, [1985] L.S. Gaz. January 16, 110.
[72] See the references in n. 71 above, and also (1984) 272 E.G. 119 (L. W. Melville), 231 (P. Freedman), 375 (R. Goldberg).

tenant relationship, such as licences for alterations, with the rent review implications in mind.

6–38 Indexed rents

Problems with indexation

Though legally possible,[73] indexation of rent has never attained popularity in this country. One problem is that there is no official index specifically reflecting changes in property prices.[74] Nor would any index be able to reflect fully changes in the value of a particular property. Despite this, there is something to be said for combining indexation with traditional periodic rent reviews as a means of keeping rent constantly adjusted to the general level of inflation.[75]

Space forbids any comprehensive treatment of index-linked rents,[76] but the following matters will need to be provided for in any lease adopting the method: it should be clear what index is to be used; at what intervals the revalorisation is to occur; how changes in the reference base of the index are to be dealt with;[77] and what is to happen if the publication of the index is delayed, or if the index is discontinued.

6–39 Turnover rents

The possibility of linking rent to the profit derived from the land by the tenant is a well-established one, but as with index-linking, except for certain large shopping centres and specialist uses, has failed to take root in modern commercial property practice. A few reported cases on such rents can be found.[78]

Drafting considerations

Again, only the barest outline of the matters to be considered in drafting such provisions is possible.[79] The landlord will usually wish to protect himself by specifying a minimum rent, below which the rent cannot fall, or which can be substituted for the turnover rent at the landlord's option. Not only the percentage, but the base upon which the percentage is calculated, must be provided for, *i.e.* gross receipts, net receipts, or profits.[80] Provision may be needed for interim payments before the base figure is fully known.

---

[73] *Blumenthal v. Gallery Five Ltd* (1971) 220 E.G. 31.

[74] The Retail Price Index does not—but there are various commercially-prepared indices which do: see D. N. Clarke and J. E. Adams, *Rent Reviews and Variable Rents* (3rd ed. 1991), pp. 559–568.

[75] For an interesting example, see *Bissett v. Marwin Securities.* (1987) 281 E.G. 75.

[76] For full discussion, see D. N. Clarke and J. E. Adams, *Rent Reviews and Variable Rents* (3rd ed. 1991), Chap. 20.

[77] This problem has been considered in the context of indexation of a service charge: *Cumshaw Ltd v. Bowen* (1987) 281 E.G. 68.

[78] *Bramhall Tudor Cinema Properties Ltd v. Brennan's Cinemas Ltd* (1955) 166 E.G. 528; *Naybr v. Uttoxeter Urban District Council* (1974) 231 E.G. 619; *Tucker v. Granada Motorway Services Ltd* [1979] 1 W.L.R. 683.

[79] See D. N. Clarke and J. E. Adams, *Rent Reviews and Variable Rents* (3rd ed. 1991), Chap. 17 for details.

[80] For the difficulties which can arise, see *Bramhall Tudor Cinema Properties Ltd v. Brennan's Cinemas Ltd* (1955) 166 E.G. 528.

The landlord will need to reserve sufficient rights to allow him to verify the figures upon which the rent is based, and close attention will need to be paid to other provisions of the lease, such as user and assignment, which could affect rent levels.

6–40   Geared rents

Calculation of rent

Finally, attention may be directed to a type of provision which is in regular use, particularly in building leases, namely rent which is fixed by reference to rents received under sub-leases. This enables the landlord to share in the profits and rental value accruing from the completed development.[81] It will be crucial to have a clear definition of how the rent is to be calculated, and this will usually be on a percentage basis of rents either receivable or received from sub-leases.[82] The tenant will no doubt wish to deduct from the sub-lease rents his own outgoings as sub-lessor, and provision should be made to cover the possibility of sub-leases being granted on a premium basis, and parts of the property remaining unoccupied, or occupied by the tenant.[83] The landlord will doubtless wish to exercise some control over sub-lettings as the ultimate source of his rent, and provision will be needed to allow the landlord to verify sub-lease terms and rent levels.[84] The possibility of the tenant carrying out improvements at his expense which enhance the rental income from the sub-leases should be foreseen and provided for.

Synchronisation of reviews

Similarly, the tenant should ensure that the rent review provisions of the sub-leases are not more favourable to the undertenants than the provisions under the headlease are to the tenant.[85] Extreme care is also needed in synchronising any

---

[81] See *Handbook of Rent Review*, para. 4–7; D. N. Clarke and J. E. Adams, *Rent Reviews and Variable Rents* (3rd ed. 1991), pp. 601–609, *et seq.*, (1983) 267 E.G. 229 and 328 (D. Wood and R. Finch).

[82] For an example of the potential problems in calculation, see *Freehold & Leasehold Shops Properties Ltd v. Friends' Provident Life Office* (1984) 271 E.G. 451. The distinction between rents received and rents receivable is very important. The former allows deductions for unpaid rent, the latter does not. Moreover, rents "receivable" means rents actually receivable by the tenant, so if premises are occupied by the tenant himself, no rent can be said to be receivable during that period: *Fraser Pipestock v. Gloucester City Council* [1995] 36 E.G. 141. In that case, given the tenant's occupation, the landlord argued for a "fair market rent" but the court refused to imply the necessary machinery.

[83] See *British Railways Board v. Elgar House Ltd* (1969) 209 E.G. 1313.

[84] See *Power Securities (Manchester) Ltd v. Prudential Assurance Co. Ltd* (1986) 281 E.G. 1327. Note also Landlord and Tenant Act 1927, s.19(1)(b) whereby the tenant under a building lease for more than 40 years can assign or underlet without consent until the last seven years of the term unless the landlord is a government department, local or public authority or statutory or public utility company. This provision does not apply to assignments of leases which are "new tenancies" under the Landlord and Tenant (Covenants) Act 1995: see para. 2–02 above.

[85] See *Laura Investment Co. Ltd v. Havering L.B.C.* [1992] 24 E.G. 136 where buildings erected by the sub-tenants were to be rentalised in the headlease even though the sub-leases disregarded such buildings. Fortunately the tenant's plight was remedied in *Laura Investment Co. Ltd v. Havering L.B.C.* (No. 2) [1993] 8 E.G. 120 where the court decided that the headlease review should operate on the basis that the property was to be valued subject to the sub-leases existing at the time.

provisions for rent review in the lease with those in the sub-leases; failure in this regard could potentially lead to a time-lag between rental increases under the sub-leases and receipt of the benefit of those increases by the head landlord.[86] It is far simpler not to attempt synchronisation, but simply to provide that the rent shall be a percentage of the sub-lease rents as they vary from time to time.

---

[86] See *Co-operative Insurance Society Ltd v. Centremoor Ltd* (1982) 266 E.G. 1027.

7 RATES AND STATUTORY REQUIREMENTS

7–01 Introduction

The ownership and occupation of real property can involve considerable financial burdens, not least those arising as a result of statutory requirements. Consequently, commercial leases invariably impose an obligation on the tenant not only to pay all rates, taxes and outgoings relating to the demised premises but also to comply with all statutory requirements affecting them or their use.

Statutory financial burdens

The most obvious example of such a financial burden is the liability for uniform business rates. Water and sewerage charges may also be payable. While specific charges for paving, lighting and similar matters are no longer so common as they were a century ago, modern legislation contains many provisions by which the owner or occupier of property can be compelled to spend considerable sums on the property. It will be of prime concern to landlord and tenant that the lease should allocate such liabilities between them, or provide some mechanism for apportionment. Effective provision can only be made against the background of some knowledge of the various statutes imposing such liabilities.

7–02 Uniform business rates

The general principle of rating law[1] is that rates are imposed upon the occupier of land, provided that the four ingredients of rateable occupation are present, namely that the occupation must be actual, exclusive for the occupier's purposes, of some value to the occupier, and for not too transient a period.[1a]

Tenant usually liable for rates

Thus the rating authority will usually look to the tenant for rates due,[2] even where the landlord and tenant have agreed that the former shall be liable, or where the tenant has paid the rates to the landlord for payment on to the authority.

---

[1] Preserved by Local Government Finance Act 1988, s.65(2) (see also s.43 as to liability for rates).

[1a] See *Hampson (t/a Abbey Self Storage) v. Newcastle-upon-Tyne C.C.* [1996] EGCS 4.

[2] In *Royal Borough of Kingston-upon-Thames v. Marlow* [1996] 17 E.G. 187 the tenant had vacated the premises in response to forfeiture proceedings commenced by his landlord, thus accepting the forfeiture. The rating authority nonetheless pursued a claim against the tenant for unpaid rates, arguing that the tenant remained liable until he could produce an order of the court terminating his tenancy. This was rejected by the court, which held that the tenant ceased to be liable for rates on vacating the premises and accepting forfeiture of his lease.

Unoccupied property The provisions of section 45 of the Local Government Finance Act 1988 and the Non-Domestic Rating (Unoccupied Property) Regulations 1989[3] can give rise to problems for both landlords and tenants. Their effect is that the "owner"[4] of unoccupied property may be rated for a proportion of the occupied rate: the proportion of the rates payable for unoccupied property, currently 50 per cent of the occupied property rate, is set by the Secretary of State for the Environment. There is however an exemption from liability for rates for properties which are unoccupied for no more than three months.

In *Camden London Borough Council v. Bromley Park Gardens Estates Ltd*[5] a tenant vacated premises before the end of the lease, taking advantage of a three-month period of grace[6] to avoid paying rates. When the lease came to an end, the landlord was held to be liable for unoccupied rates on the basis that there was only one rate-free period, commencing when the property became unoccupied; the termination of the lease did not entitle the landlord to a fresh three-month

Implications for landlord

period. Thus there is a danger to a landlord that the tenant may, by going out of occupation, deprive the landlord of a useful rate-free period in which to re-let the property. The danger can be mitigated by a covenant by the tenant not to leave the property unoccupied without the landlord's consent, and also a covenant to indemnify the landlord against any liability for rates caused by breach of the covenant. The tenant should however resist giving any such covenants.

Implications for tenant

The tenant may need to be aware of the possible implications of the 1988 Act and the 1989 Regulations both at the commencement of and during the term. In some cases, the tenant will be unable to go into occupation immediately, and will not wish to pay rates until he does so. The problem is that in one case[7] the Court of Appeal held that the period during which the building was unoccupied ran from the date upon which the building was completed, not the date upon which the new rating hereditament was carved out by the grant of the lease. Therefore the tenant may find that he is liable for rates immediately the lease is granted, even if the premises are not ready for occupation.[8] A further problem is that a "completion notice" may be served by the rating authority on the owner of a building in the course of

[3] S.I. 1989 No. 2261.
[4] See Local Government Finance Act 1988, s.65(1). The "owner" is the person entitled to possession of the property since clearly liability for rates for unoccupied property cannot depend upon occupation. If the unoccupied property is subject to a lease or tenancy, the tenant will be the owner for rating purposes.
[5] [1985] 2 EGLR 179.
[6] Then available under the General Rate Act 1967.
[7] *Brent London Borough Council v. Ladbroke Rentals Ltd* [1981] R A 153.
[8] Where there is work to be done which is customarily done after the building has been completed, *e.g.* partitioning, the period reasonably required in which to carry out such work may be added to the date on which the building was completed so as to defer the final date of completion: *Ravenseft Properties Ltd v. London Borough of Newham* [1976] Q.B. 464; *Drake Investments Ltd v. London Borough of Lewisham* (1983) 133 New L.J. 746; *London Merchant Securities plc v. London Borough of Islington* [1988] 3 W.L.R. 173.

construction, specifying a date upon which the building is to be regarded as completed.[9] Such a notice can be served in relation to the whole or part of the building. Thus in the case of leases or agreements for leases of buildings in the course of construction, the tenant should enquire whether a completion notice has been served, and impose obligations on the landlord not to agree with the rating authority a completion date without the tenant's consent and to inform the tenant of any future notices so that they can be appealed if necessary. The tenant should also have the relevant rating provisions in mind when going out of occupation during the course of the lease, in particular when going out of occupation to allow the landlord to carry out work to the premises.

7–03   Water charges

Water charges are generally payable by the occupier of premises, except where the owner is liable by statute or by agreement with the water undertaker.[10] Doubt may arise as to whether a covenant to pay rates includes water charges.[11] Therefore the covenant should be extended by use of the word "outgoings" or a specific covenant to pay water charges should be inserted. In cases where the landlord provides the water supply as part of his services, he should ensure that water charges can be recovered under the service charge.

Shared facilities   The tenant who shares the use of common facilities such as lavatories should be wary of the potential liability to water charges. A covenant to pay such charges can operate even if the premises have no direct water supply.[12] Even quite slender rights to use such facilities can result in substantial liability, and unfairness may result if there is no provision for the apportionment of liability between the various users.[13] Similar problems can arise in respect of charges for sewerage services, which may be levied not only on premises connected to a public sewer, but also on premises having the benefit of facilities which drain to a public sewer.[14]

7–04   Statutes requiring capital expenditure

There is a large and confusing body of authority on the question of whether covenants to pay rates and other impositions and outgoings can oblige a tenant to pay sums of

---

[9] Local Government Finance Act 1988, s.46A and Sched. 4A, as amended by Local Government and Housing Act 1989, Sched. 5, para. 36. The date specified must not be more than three months from the date of service of the notice.

[10] Water Industry Act 1991, s.144.

[11] See *Direct Spanish Telegraph Co. Ltd v. Shepherd* (1884) 13 Q.B.D. 202; *Bourne & Tant v. Salmon & Gluckstein Ltd* [1907] 1 Ch. 616; and *cf. Badcock v. Hunt* (1888) 22 Q.B.D. 145.

[12] See *Drieselman v. Winstanley* (1909) 53 S.J. 631; *King v. Cave-Brown-Cave* [1960] 2 Q.B. 222.

[13] See *West Pennine Water Board v. Jon Migael (North West) Ltd* (1975) 73 L.G.R. 420 at 424, *per* Scarman L.J.

[14] Water Industry Act 1991, s.144(1)(b).

a capital nature for the improvement of the premises. One line of cases stressed the prime importance of the width of the words used,[15] whereas another line suggested that the width of such words could be qualified by the circumstances surrounding the lease, *e.g.* the type of charges which the parties had in contemplation at the time of the grant.[16] The distinction will rarely be of importance today, because as mentioned above modern leases usually contain a separate covenant by the tenant to comply with all statutes, regulations and bye-laws affecting the property.[17] Brief details of the main provisions by which expenditure may be required are considered in turn.

Whether covered by covenant to pay rates and outgoings

Fire precautions   Under the Fire Precautions Act 1971,[18] a fire certificate may need to be obtained before the premises can be used. Conditions may be imposed upon the issue of the certificate, *e.g.* as to the provision of fire escapes and fire-fighting equipment, the carrying out of structural alterations, and the keeping of log books of equipment checks. Generally the occupier of the premises is responsible for compliance with the terms of the certificate,[19] but an important exception applies in the case of factories, offices and shops forming part of a building in single ownership: there the onus of compliance lies with the owner.[20]

Conditions on issue of fire certificate

Other provisions may also be relevant. Special rules apply to certain specified premises, where the processes or uses carried out there give rise to particular fire risks.[21] By section 71 of the Building Act 1984, a local authority can require the owner of a building of public resort[22] to execute work to fire exits; and by section 72 of the same Act the provision of fire escapes can be required for hotels, hospitals

---

[15] *Payne v. Burridge* (1844) 12 M. & W. 727; *Thompson v. Lapworth* (1868) L.R. 3 C.P. 149; *Aldridge v. Fearne* (1886) 17 Q.B.D. 212; *Foulger v. Arding* [1902] 1 K.B. 700; *Farlow v. Stevenson* [1900] 1 Ch. 128; *Lowther v. Clifford* [1927] 1 K.B. 130; *Villenex Co. Ltd v. Courtney Hotel Ltd* (1969) 20 P. & C.R. 575.

[16] *Tidswell v. Whitworth* (1867) L.R. 2 C.P. 326; *Valpy v. St Leonard's Wharf Co. Ltd* (1903) 67 L.T. 402; *Mile End Old Town (Vestry) v. Whitby* (1898) 78 L.T. 80; *Allum v. Dickinson* (1882) 9 Q.B.D. 632; *Wilkinson v. Collyer* (1884) 13 Q.B.D. 1.

[17] Nonetheless, since the two covenants may overlap, care should be taken to ensure that they are consistent: *Arding v. Economic Printing and Publishing Company Ltd* (1898) 79 L.T. 622.

[18] s.1. The Act applies to premises used for purposes designated by the Secretary of State, *e.g.* factories and offices and shops by S.I. 1989 No. 76. The Act may apply even though only a small proportion of a building is being used for such purposes: *Oxfordshire County Council v. Chancellor Masters and Scholars of Oxford University, The Times,* December 10, 1980.

[19] s.6(5).

[20] Fire Precautions Act 1971, Sched. 2 (as inserted by Fire Safety and Safety of Places of Sport Act 1987, s.16). More may be required of the owner than simply imposing a covenant to comply with the Act upon the tenant. By s.25 the owner must prove he "took all reasonable steps and exercised all due diligence" to avoid the commission of an offence.

[21] Fire Certificates (Special Premises) Regulations 1976 (S.I. 1976 No. 2003).

[22] Defined in s.24, *e.g.* theatres, restaurants, shops.

and certain premises with sleeping accommodation for employees on upper floors.[23]

Factories   The Factories Act 1961 imposes many onerous obligations as to matters such as the sound construction of floors, passages and stairs, and the provision of drinking water and sanitary facilities. Generally, it is the occupier who is liable,[24] though some provisions apply to the owner of a **Common** "tenement factory",[25] or the owner who provides common **facilities** facilities.[26]

Offices and shops   The Offices, Shops and Railway Premises Act 1963[26a] contains obligations as to a range of matters: overcrowding, temperature, ventilation, lighting, sanitary and washing facilities, and the state of floors, stairs and passages. Again, primary responsibility falls upon the occupier,[27] but the owner may be liable in the case of **Common parts** common parts or conveniences.[28]

Health and safety at work   By section 2 of the Health and Safety at Work, etc. Act 1974 it is the duty of every employer to ensure, so far as is reasonably practicable, the health, safety and welfare of all his employees. This duty can extend to the maintenance of places of work in a safe condition,[29] and to non-employees using the premises as a place of work or using plant there.[30]

Public health   Work may be required under the Public Health Acts 1936 and 1961, *e.g.* the provision of satisfactory drainage, the repair of drains and sewers and the repair of dilapidated or ruinous buildings.

Building standards   The Building Act 1984, s.1 authorises the making of building regulations which may impose continuing obligations on owners and occupiers. Inner London is governed by the London Building Acts

---

[23] Not applicable to Inner London: see Sched. 3, Pt. II, para. 5. But provisions as to means of escape from fire are to be found in Pt. V of the London Building Acts (Amendment) Act 1939 and the Building (Inner London) Regulations 1985 (S.I. 1985 No. 1936) as amended by S.I. 1986 No. 452, S.I. 1987 No. 798, S.I. 1991 No. 2768.

[24] Factories Act 1961, s.155.

[25] *ibid.*, s.121; defined by s.176.

[26] *ibid.*, s.122.

[26a] In relation to railway premises, other requirements will now be relevant for premises which are subject to the access regime of the Railways Act 1993, but this is beyond the scope of this work.

[27] Offices, Shops and Railway Premises Act 1963, s.63.

[28] *ibid.*, s.42.

[29] Health and Safety at Work, etc. Act 1974, s.2(2)(d).

[30] *ibid.*, s.4; and see *Westminster City Council v. Select Management Ltd* [1984] 1 W.L.R. 1058. Note also the provisions relating to premises in the Disability Discrimination Act 1995, *e.g.* s.6 (employer's duty to make adjustments to the premises to accommodate disabled people) and s.21 (similar duty imposed upon providers of services). Both landlords and tenants should also be aware of the duties relating to health and safety imposed on those carrying out *inter alia* works of repair, alteration and decoration by the Construction (Design and Management) Regulations 1994 (S.I. 1994 No. 3140).

(Amendment) Act 1939 and also, since January 6, 1986, the Building Regulations.

Environmental legislation The tenant may also be liable, as a result of a covenant generally requiring compliance with statutes, to shoulder substantial expense for works under environmental legislation: for example the costs of cleaning up contaminated land which forms part of the demise. See Chapter 20 below for a detailed discussion of the environmental considerations for both parties.

7–05 Apportionment of costs

It will be appreciated that such statutory requirements can lead to the premises being improved considerably at the tenant's expense. In such circumstances, the tenant may feel with some justification that he should be entitled to a contribution from the landlord. Many of the statutes mentioned above provide a procedure to allow the party required to carry out work to apply to court[31] on the basis that all or part of the expense ought to be borne by someone **Power of court** else having an interest in the premises; the court is given **to apportion** powers to apportion the expense, and in some cases to modify **expenditure** the terms of the lease.[32] The degree of discretion conferred upon the court varies between the different provisions, but most require the court to have regard to the terms of the lease. Some require other factors to be considered: *e.g.* the Building Act 1984, s.102 requires regard to be had to the nature of the work and to the degree of benefit to be derived from the work by the different persons concerned. In *Watney Combe Reid & Co. Ltd v. Westminster City Council*[33] the Court of Appeal held that the landlord could be said to have derived benefit from the installation of a fire escape by the tenant, in that otherwise the landlord would have had to do the work, even though the landlord derived no benefit in terms of cash or increased rent; also that the court was entitled to have regard to the rental history of the premises and their likely imminent demolition.

From the tenant's point of view, a cause for concern is that the apportionment provisions are piecemeal rather than comprehensive, and it may be largely a matter of chance whether the tenant is able to apply for apportionment, depending on the type of premises and the Act under which the work is required. The tenant may therefore wish to see **Express** some equivalent provision for apportionment written into the **provision as to** lease in order to provide fuller protection. **apportionment** To the landlord, such provisions represent a substantial threat to the "clear lease" philosophy.[33a] Given that most of

[31] Usually the county court.
[32] *e.g.* the Fire Precautions Act 1971, s.28(3) and s.28(A); the Building Act 1984, s.102; the London Building Acts (Amendment) Act 1939, s.107; the Factories Act 1961, s.170; the Offices, Shops and Railway Premises Act 1963, s.73(2); the Public Health Act 1936, s.290.
[33] (1970) 214 E.G. 1631.
[33a] See para. 8–01 below.

the apportionment provisions require that regard be given to the terms of the lease, there is some scope for reducing the risk of an adverse apportionment order. In *Monk v. Arnold*[34] Channell J. suggested that if the lease specifically placed the burden of expenses under the provision in question on one party it would not be just or equitable to vary that agreement; but that there was a discretion if the work was covered only by "some general expression in the covenant." On the other hand, Lord Alverstone C.J. thought that the court, while having regard to the terms of the contract, was not bound by it and that factors such as the length of the term unexpired were also relevant. Channell J.'s view was followed by Lawrence J. in *Munro v. Lord Burghclere*[35]; and in *Horner v. Franklin*,[36] Vaughan Williams L.J. thought that there was no discretion to overthrow the terms of the bargain embodied in the lease. However, in *Horner v. Franklin*, Romer L.J. rejected the view that the question of apportionment should be determined solely by the terms of the lease. Thus the possibility remains open that the landlord may by clear drafting lessen the risks of apportionment; but success cannot be guaranteed.

7–06   Statutory improvements and rent review

Improvements to the premises required by statute may also be relevant in the context of rent review. This issue is discussed elsewhere.[37]

---

[34] [1902] 1 K.B. 761.
[35] [1918] 1 K.B. 291.
[36] [1905] 1 K.B. 479.
[37] See para. 6–36 above.

8 SERVICES AND SERVICE CHARGES

8-01 Introduction

The use of service charge provisions is now standard in commercial leases. This is partly due to the shift towards the development of properties in which communal services are desirable, if not essential, such as office blocks, industrial and retail parks and indoor shopping centres. Another factor militating towards comprehensive service charge provisions is the requirement of landlords and investors for "clear leases", namely leases under which all conceivable expenditure relating to the property can be passed on to the tenant or tenants.[1]

Effects of recession
One of the effects of the recession at the end of the 1980s was to ensure that tenants of commercial premises paid even greater attention to service charge demands and accounts than was previously the case. Whilst landlords and investors continue to press for "clear leases", tenants have become more inclined to challenge service charge demands and, in the case of negotiation of new leases, to require substantially more involvement in the administration and calculation of service charges, resulting in considerable amendment to the standard institutional lease. Whilst this approach has inevitably led to differences of opinion between landlords and tenants, there have been attempts to deal with those differences. A guide promoted by, amongst others, the British Property Federation and entitled *Service Charges in Commercial Properties* was published at the beginning of 1995[2] and, whilst having no legal or statutory status, was intended " ... to promote good administrative and business practice between owners and occupiers in the management of services in commercial properties ..." and " ... to encourage a good working relationship ... through consultation and communication about what services are required, their quality and costs ...".[3] Initiatives of this nature, if adopted in practice, could reduce the scope for disputes, both in the negotiation and subsequent interpretation of commercial leases.

It is neither practicable nor desirable to draw up a standard service charge clause, as every building will be managed

---

[1] For a judicial consideration of the concept of a "clear lease" see *O'May v. City of London Real Property Co. Ltd* [1982] 2 A.C. 726 and para. 9–02 below.

[2] *Service Charges in Commercial Properties—A Guide to Good Practice*, produced in conjunction by the British Council of Shopping Centres, British Property Federation, British Retail Consortium, Incorporated Society of Valuers and Auctioneers, Property Managers Association, the Royal Institution of Chartered Surveyors, and the Shopping Centre Management Group.

[3] Aims quoted in the Guide mentioned at n.2 above.

Matters needing consideration

differently, but it is, nonetheless, possible to isolate the various factors which will need to be considered and covered by the clause. These are:

(1) the obligation on the landlord to provide services;
(2) to what services and expenditure the clause extends;
(3) how the expenditure is to be apportioned between the various tenants;
(4) the procedure for certifying the expenditure and the apportionment;
(5) when and by what means the service charge is payable;
(6) whether any provision should be made for the creation of a reserve fund for major items of non-recurrent expenditure.

8–02   Obligation on landlord to provide services

Which matters are to be the responsibility of the landlord is a question to be decided on the individual circumstances of each lease. Standard items include repair, insurance, heating and hot water, air conditioning, maintenance of common parts, and the provision of staff to service the development.

Importance of covenant by landlord

In order to minimise disputes and ensure the provision of services, the tenant should ensure that, in respect of those services which the tenant regards as vital, the landlord should covenant expressly to perform them. It should not be assumed that an obligation by the tenant to pay for such matters necessarily places a correlative obligation on the landlord.[4] Similarly, a covenant by a third party, commonly a management company, to provide services would not necessarily imply a covenant that the landlord would provide the services if the third party failed to do so.[5] An unequivocal covenant to provide services, or to procure their provision by a third party, is desirable to avoid the argument that performance by the landlord is merely a condition precedent of the tenant's obligation to pay.[6] Conversely, it is possible to phrase the landlord's obligation so as to make payment of the

---

[4] Such an obligation was implied in *Barnes v. City of London Real Property Company Ltd* [1918] 2 Ch. 18 and *Edmonton Corporation v. W. M. Knowles & Son Ltd* (1961) 60 L.G.R. 124: but neither case was followed by the Court of Appeal in *Duke of Westminster v. Guild* [1985] Q.B. 668; and see also *Concorde Graphics Ltd v. Andromeda Investments S.A.* (1982) 265 E.G. 386. However, an obligation to keep essential services, such as a lift, in order may be implied on the basis of necessity: *Liverpool City Council v. Irwin* [1977] A.C. 239; *De Meza v. Ve–Ri–Best Manufacturing Co. Ltd* (1952) 160 E.G. 364.

[5] *Hafton Properties Ltd v. Camp; Camp v. Silchester Court (Croydon) Management Co. Ltd* [1994] 3 E.G. 129. Tenants should consequently obtain an express covenant from the landlord to procure that the third party's services are performed. The transmission of the benefit of covenants by third parties, such as management companies, contained in "new tenancies" is governed by the Landlord and Tenant (Covenants) Act 1995, s.12.

[6] *Westacott v. Hahn* [1918] 1 K.B. 495. For an example of an express covenant where specific performance was ordered, see *Posner v. Scott-Lewis* [1986] 3 W.L.R. 531 (covenant to employ resident porter to keep premises clean, operate heating and remove rubbish).

service charge a condition precedent, but whether this is so will depend on the intentions of the parties as gathered from the lease as a whole and surrounding circumstances, and clear language will be necessary.[7] Certainly a tenant will wish to avoid this and to secure an unconditional obligation.

Qualified obligation

Where the landlord is willing to enter into an obligation to provide services, he will often seek to qualify it in some way, since otherwise he will not be excused if performance becomes impossible.[8] One way is to covenant only to use best or reasonable endeavours to supply the service,[9] or to covenant to provide the service only so far as is practicable. Another is to exclude liability in certain events, such as mechanical failure, replacement or maintenance of equipment, or shortage of fuel or labour.[10] In these situations it is both usual and reasonable for the tenant to seek a covenant from the landlord to keep the period of disturbance to a minimum; to provide an alternative service (wherever possible), and to reinstate the original service as soon as reasonably practicable.

Variation of services

Quite frequently, the landlord reserves the right to vary the services provided. Such provisions are perhaps primarily aimed at variations of detail, or adding additional services as circumstances dictate, but if unqualified their effect might be to allow the landlord to withdraw such vital facilities as repairs, heating and security. The tenant should seek to provide that specific key services may not be withdrawn or varied, and also that any variation in the services must be in the interests of the tenants as a class. The tenant should also consider whether or not he requires the ability to request that additional services be provided by the landlord from time to time.

Standard of provision

The standard to which services such as cleaning, heating and repairs are provided may be a matter of great dissatisfaction to tenants. In some cases, such as heating, it is possible to specify the standard required in some detail,[11] but in others only quite general expressions can be used, trusting

---

[7] *Yorkbrook Investments Ltd v. Batten* [1985] 2 EGLR 100.

[8] See *Yorkbrook Investments Ltd v. Batten, ibid.* (the landlord was not excused from performance of a covenant to supply hot water and heat by the fact that the heating system was antiquated and unreliable).

[9] A "reasonable endeavours" obligation imports a lower standard than "best endeavours", whilst "all reasonable endeavours" is probably a middle position somewhere between the two: *UBH (Mechanical Services) Ltd v. Standard Life Assurance Co., The Times*, November 13, 1986; and see para. 18–17 below.

[10] It is questionable how far such provisions may be affected by the Unfair Contract Terms Act 1977. The Act does not apply to any contract so far as it relates to the creation or transfer of any interest in land: Sched. 1, para. 1(b); and see *Precedents for the Conveyancer*, para. 5–48 (notes). See also *Electricity Supplies Nominees Ltd v. I.A.F. Group Ltd* [1993] 37 E.G. 155 where it was held that the exclusion of the Act set out at Sched. 1, para. 1(b) applied to the whole of any contract relating to the creation or transfer of an interest in land and not just the part of it effecting the creation or transfer: consequently in this case the reasonableness test imposed by s.3 of the Act was held not to apply to a provision in a lease which excluded the tenant's right of set-off.

[11] It may be important to specify whether the duty is merely to lay on a supply of heat to the boundary of the demised premises, or to arrange for the distribution of heat within the premises: see *UBH (Mechanical Services) Ltd v. Standard Life Assurance Co., The Times*, November 13, 1986.

to the courts to fill in the gaps should disputes arise.[12] Thought should also be given to the hours during which services are to be provided and to whether any additional charge is to be levied where services are provided outside normal business hours, as stated in the lease (and, if so, how this is to be apportioned between the various tenants). Where the landlord can be said to be supplying the service in the course of a business, terms will be implied that the service will be carried out with reasonable care and skill and (unless the lease makes provision to the contrary) within a reasonable time.[13] However, it is easy to foresee that difficult questions could arise over the precise standard of care required of the landlord by these implied terms. For example, does the implied term as to care and skill effectively make the landlord the guarantor of the competence of any contractor he engages to carry out the service, or can the landlord discharge his duty by taking proper care in selecting and supervising the contractor?

Reasonable care and skill

8–03 The expenditure covered by the service charge

The aim of the service charge from the point of view of the landlord should be to afford him complete reimbursement of his expenditure in servicing and maintaining the building.[14] There is no presumption that a service charge will cover all those matters which the landlord has covenanted to perform,[15] and therefore the landlord should ensure that the landlord's covenants and the service charge items correspond. A common way of doing this is to provide that the service charge covers all expenditure under the landlord's covenants and also a list of other specific items, often set out in a schedule to the lease. However, it is now fairly common also to see identified in the service charge schedule those works or services the cost of which will not be recoverable from the tenant in any circumstances.[16] The services specified will vary

Clause should be comprehensive

[12] See, *e.g. Quennell v. Salaman* (1955) 165 E.G. 285 (landlord covenanted to keep a staircase "well and sufficiently lighted"; held that this meant that there must be a degree of illumination sufficient for normal use of the staircase by persons of normal vision, and that the lighting must not provide an optical illusion or trap for any normally-sighted person).

[13] Supply of Goods and Services Act 1982, ss.13, 14.

[14] Modern commercial leases will provide not only for reimbursement of sums actually expended by the landlord but also sums which the landlord is obliged to pay and which, at the end of the financial year, he has not in fact paid. See *Capital & Counties Freehold Equity Trust Limited v. BL plc* (1987) 283 E.G. 563 (use of, and difference between, the words "expended", "become payable" and "incurred" in relation to a landlord's service charge expenditure).

[15] See *Rapid Results College Ltd v. Angell* [1986] 1 EGLR 53 at 55, *per* Dillon L.J. However, it may be possible for the landlord to claim for his expenditure on the basis of quasi-contract or an implied term: see *Rance v. Elvin* (1985) 50 P. & C.R. 9 at 17, 18.

[16] These might include the cost of putting right defects in the original construction or design of the premises and the service costs attributable to vacant units or those let on non-standard leases. Similarly, items of expenditure relating to the initial provision of, for example, equipment used in the provision of the services should be excluded.

"Sweeping-up" provisions

according to the nature of the building, but the objective of the draftsman should be to provide a comprehensive list, with a "sweeping-up" provision to cover any expenses regarded by the landlord in future as desirable,[17] or alternatively power for the landlord to vary the services from time to time.[18] In one instance, a clause allowing the landlord to extend or vary services referred to as specific items in a schedule to the lease was held not to permit the recovery of expenditure on a completely different item; the clause was construed as merely giving the landlord the right to vary the specified works.[19]

Secondary expenditure

Secondary expenditure should not be overlooked: for example, clauses are frequently included which enable the landlord to recover the cost of providing staff to service the building, which landlords will submit should include insurance and state pension contributions, the cost of providing working clothes and equipment, the provision of facilities such as canteens and staff rooms, and in some cases accommodation.[20] However, the recoverable cost of providing these items should be restricted to the reasonable and proper cost incurred by the landlord and where it is incurred in the interests of the tenants as a whole.

One item which can cause particular difficulty is repair and maintenance of the building and the extent to which the landlord can recover the costs incurred in such repair and maintenance, and care in drafting is needed on both sides.[21]

---

[17] A tenant should ensure that the "sweeping up" provision does not inadvertently render him liable to reimburse expenditure which has been negotiated out of the list of express items he is to pay, as mentioned above.

[18] The onus will be on the landlord to show that the expenditure falls within the provision, and this may sometimes be difficult: see *Boldmark Ltd v. Cohen* [1986] 1 EGLR 47; *Mullaney v. Maybourne Grange (Croydon) Management Co. Ltd* [1986] 1 EGLR 70; *Reston v. Hudson* [1990] 37 E.G. 86 (window frames not within demise therefore cost of replacement recoverable via the service charge). The tenant should ensure that some control is reserved by a provision that such expenditure may only be incurred where the landlord reasonably deems it desirable for reasons of good estate management or efficiency: but the relationship between such provisions and the certification procedure (see below) should be considered. More sophisticated safeguards are possible; for example requiring advance notice of or consent to any change, with reference to an independent expert should a specified proportion of tenants object.

[19] *Jacob Isbicki & Co. Ltd v. Goulding & Bird Ltd* [1989] 1 EGLR 236.

[20] The landlord should seek to recover notional rent where he provides the accommodation himself, though such an expense may also be included in a "sweeping-up" clause: see *Avagil Investments Ltd v. Corner*, C.A., October 3, 1975, (unreported). Another example of secondary expenditure, held to be recoverable under a general "sweeping-up" clause, is the provision of a fixed track and cradle system for window-cleaning: *Sun Alliance & London Assurance Co. Ltd v. British Railways Board* [1989] 2 EGLR 237.

[21] Reference should be made to the chapter on repairing obligations for the potential problems. In *Rapid Results College Ltd v. Angell* [1986] 1 EGLR 53, the landlord could not recover expenditure on a parapet since it did not form part of the exterior of the premises. In *Mullaney v. Maybourne Grange (Croydon) Management Co. Ltd* [1986] 1 EGLR 70, the landlord was not entitled to recover expenditure on replacing windows—the work went beyond "repair" and the new windows could not be regarded as an "additional amenity" within the service charge provisions. Contrast this with *Reston v. Hudson* (see above at n. 18). The parties should have particular regard to the question of inherent or latent defects and costs relating to their remedy or incurred in making good damage caused by them.

Management expenses

Some provision is also desirable from the landlord's point of view for recovering the expenses of managing the development; either the cost of employing managing agents, or a management charge where the landlord manages the development himself. It is usual for the tenant to attempt to impose some ceiling on such expenses, perhaps by reference to a stated percentage of the service charge. In the past some leases followed the practice of securing to the landlord a disguised profit by apportioning the service charge so that the sum of the proportions payable by each tenant exceeded the total cost of providing the services. This practice should not be regarded as acceptable, and tenants should be alert to guard against it. One way of achieving this is to provide that the landlord must include in the certificate of expenditure, provided at the end of each service charge year, a note of the proportions payable by each of the tenants of the building.[22]

Area covered and unlet units

One final matter requiring care is the geographical area over which the services are provided. In, say, a shopping centre development, the tenants may not wish to reimburse the landlord for expenditure in maintaining the car parking areas on the basis that such expenditure should be covered by the car parking tariffs, and that accordingly costs relating to these areas should expressly be excluded from the items of expenditure which fall within the service charge. On the other hand, it may be that at some time in the future the landlord will wish to extend the centre, and the service charge should allow expenditure on maintaining (though not of course erecting) such extensions to form part of the service charge payable by all tenants.[23] The service charge should also anticipate the position if units remain unlet. The fairest provision is for the landlord to contribute from his own resources the proportion of the service charge relating to such units.

8–04 Apportionment of the cost

Need for simplicity

Some provision must be made for apportioning the total expenditure between the tenants.[24] The problem is that no single method of apportionment will produce a fair result for all services. The use made of the various services will differ according to many factors: the number of employees of each tenant where common facilities such as lavatories are provided; the type of business of each tenant with regard to services such as security and refuse collection; the number of clients or customers of each business as to wear and tear on the common parts, and the location of each tenant within the

---

[22] See para. 8–04 below for a discussion of methods of apportionment of costs between tenants.

[23] Changes in apportionment may be required as a result (see para. 8–04 below).

[24] If not in the original lease, such a provision may well be inserted on the grant of a new lease under Part II of the Landlord and Tenant Act 1954: *Hyates v. Titan Properties Ltd* (1972) 24 P. & C.R. 359.

development with regard to facilities such as lifts.[25] A further complication with service charges in shopping centres is the potential difficulty caused by some tenants opening for Sunday trading, while others decide not to do so.[25a] This fact has to be recognised, and attempts to produce highly sophisticated and complex apportionment provisions to cover every variation are likely to be misguided: they may be far more costly and troublesome to operate than is justified by the marginal increase in fairness which they produce. It is probably sensible to adopt one of the usual methods of apportionment set out below.

Fixed proportion   In many ways this is the simplest basis of apportionment: merely allocating a fixed percentage of the service charge to each unit at the outset.[26] However, it is not without its difficulties. The main one is that the original proportions can become unfair as circumstances change.[27]

Periodic review   Thus some provision is desirable for periodic review of the apportionment, or for adjustment by the landlord from time to time, although a revised arrangement can be difficult without the consent of all the tenants, some of whom will undoubtedly have to pay higher contributions as a result.

Floor space   Another method of apportionment is based on the floor-space ratios between the different units in the development. If this method is adopted, it is important to avoid disputes occurring every year as to the precise amount of floor space in each unit. This can be done by stating the amount of floor space per unit at the outset in the lease, but this will not take account of changes occurring as a result of sub-division of units, structural alterations, etc. and consequently is rarely seen in practice.

The other problem with apportionment based on floor-space is that it may unduly favour tenants of small units at the **Weighted floor** expense of tenants of large units, whose demands on services **space** do not increase proportionately with the size of their premises. A solution which goes a long way towards meeting this objection is that of "weighted floor space", that is attributing a certain proportion of the service charge to the first 1,000 square feet of space, a different proportion to the next 1,000, and so on, the proportion decreasing for each segment. The main disadvantage of this approach is that the tenants of the smaller units are wont to feel that the larger tenants are not paying their due proportion, which can lead to a sense of injustice. This approach is, for this reason, very rarely seen in practice.

Use of services   No doubt an apportionment calculated every year on the basis of the actual benefit derived from each

---

[25] Ground floor tenants are notoriously reluctant to contribute to the cost of maintaining lifts although it is submitted that they should, in fairness, contribute their share.

[25a] See para. 10–07 below.

[26] See, *e.g. Adelphi (Estates) Ltd v. Christie* (1983) 269 E.G. 221, a case indicating that care is needed in underletting when this method is used.

[27] *e.g.*, the addition of further units (see *Pole Properties Ltd v. Feinberg* (1981) 43 P. & C.R. 121), or changes in the services provided.

service by each tenant would be the fairest method. However its uncertainty, difficulty, complexity and scope for dispute mean that it is likely to be inappropriate for any but the most straightforward of services, *e.g.* requiring contributions to the upkeep of a road according to use. However, what can be

Discretion of landlord   useful is a provision allowing the landlord to depart from the fixed basis of apportionment in respect of any items where application of that basis would produce an unfair result, *e.g.* where one tenant requests the provision of extra services solely for his benefit. However, the unrestricted use of such a provision could undermine the certainty desirable in service charge provisions; therefore it may be advisable to specify the circumstances in which the discretion can be exercised more definitely than simply by reference to unfairness.

Fair proportion   The lease could alternatively provide that the tenant's service charge contribution will be a fair proportion of the landlord's total expenditure. That proportion would be calculated by, say, the landlord's surveyor. This approach clearly lacks the certainty of any prescribed formula for determining the tenant's contribution but has the advantage of flexibility, enabling all relevant factors to be taken into account. The tenant should however ensure that he has the opportunity to challenge the apportionment, something which will be unattractive to the landlord given the potential for delay in the administration and collection of the service charge.[28]

8–05   Certification of expenditure and apportionment

Some clear agreed procedure for certification of the landlord's expenditure (and possibly the means of apportionment) is desirable, both to protect the tenant and to prevent disputes. In general the courts will imply a term that costs incurred are to be fair and reasonable.[29] The most usual method is to

Certified or audited accounts   provide that the landlord shall produce certified or audited accounts as soon as practicable after the end of the financial year in question. The tenant may wish to reserve the right to call for a more detailed breakdown in addition and to inspect receipts, vouchers and the like in order to check the accuracy of the service charge statements or accounts. Any time limit for delivery of the account will not be of the essence unless expressed to be so.[30] The issue of a proper certificate is likely

---

[28] See para. 8–05 below for a discussion of challenges to the service charge certificate.

[29] *Finchbourne Ltd v. Rodrigues* [1976] 3 All E.R. 581. But even so the landlord will probably retain considerable discretion: see *Manor House Drive Ltd v. Shahbazian* (1965) 195 E.G. 283 (landlord entitled to replace zinc roof rather than periodically patch up old one).

[30] *West Central Investments Ltd v. Borovik* (1977) 241 E.G. 609.

to be construed as a condition precedent of the tenant's liability to pay.[31]

Who is to certify account

Questions of practical importance are who is to certify or audit the account and to what extent the certified account may be challenged, either in whole or as to specific items. The usual practice is for certification to be carried out by a surveyor or accountant, and where the landlord is a large company or corporation, the landlord may intend to use an "in-house" surveyor for this purpose. If so, the landlord should be advised expressly to stipulate for this in the lease, otherwise such certification may be invalid.[32] The tenant in turn should stipulate that the person certifying is to be appropriately qualified professionally, either as a surveyor or an accountant: at least the tenant will then be entitled to expect a degree of independent professional judgment.[33]

Challenges to certificate

In the interests of finality, the landlord may be tempted to provide that the certificate shall be conclusive and not open to challenge. However, any attempt to make the certificate conclusive as to matters of law may be void as an attempt to oust the jurisdiction of the court.[34] It also appears that the provision will in such cases be void *in toto*, so that the certificate will not be conclusive as to matters of fact either. Thus the certificate should be expressed to be conclusive only as to matters of fact, though this may still leave the difficult borderline questions of mixed fact and law. Even then, it seems doubtful whether challenge to obvious errors can be precluded, for example where figures are added up wrongly.[35]

Challenge

What the landlord will be most eager to prevent are challenges on the basis that the expenditure on services is

---

[31] *Finchbourne Ltd v. Rodrigues* [1976] 3 All E.R. 581. In *Concorde Graphics Ltd v. Andromeda Investments S.A.* (1982) 265 E.G. 387 at 390, Vinelott J. left open the possibility that the court could settle the amount. It may be unfair if one bad item in the accounts prevents the landlord recovering the uncontested items; an express provision allowing the landlord to recoup expenditure on uncontested items even where other sums are in dispute may be advisable. The problem may be avoided altogether by the lease providing for advance payments (see below).

[32] In *Finchbourne Ltd v. Rodrigues* [1976] 3 All E.R. 581, certification was to be by the landlord's managing agents acting as experts. In fact certification was by a firm of which the landlord was the sole proprietor. The Court of Appeal held that "expert" entitled the tenant to assume an independent expert would be used; nor could the firm be said to be the "agent" of the landlord.

[33] See *Concorde Graphics Ltd v. Andromeda Investments S.A.* (1982) 265 E.G. 387 at 389. See also *New Pinehurst Residents Association (Cambridge) Ltd v. Silow* [1988] 1 EGLR 227 (where it was held that although the managing agents comprised shareholders/directors of the landlord company, they were clearly separate legal persons from the landlord and, distinguishing *Finchbourne v. Rodrigues, ibid.*, that the managing agents' independence could not be challenged on the basis that some of their members were also tenants of the subject premises). In some cases it may be sensible to stipulate for certification by the landlord's auditors, where the landlord is a public company.

[34] *Re Davstone Estates Ltd's Lease, Manprop Ltd v. O'Dell* [1969] 2 Ch. 378. But see *Nikko Hotels (U.K.) Ltd v. M.E.P.C. Ltd* [1991] 2 EGLR 103.

[35] See *Dean v. Prince* [1954] Ch. 409 at 427, *per* Denning L.J., quoted by Cairns L.J. in *Finchbourne Ltd v. Rodrigues* [1976] 3 All E.R. 581 at 586. The tenant should remove any such doubt by providing that where the certificate is to be conclusive, it is conclusive save in the case of manifest error.

extravagant, or that particular services could have been provided more cheaply elsewhere. To this end, service charges often expressly preclude challenge on this ground. It is no doubt irksome for a landlord to have to justify every decision, but on the other hand it is a potentially harsh step to prevent a tenant with a valid objection from raising it. Compromises can be suggested, such as a time limit for challenge, or challenge only being effective if made by a specified number of tenants, but what should be appreciated is that the ability to challenge expenditure in retrospect represents a very significant threat to the clear lease policy, as it may result in the landlord spending considerable sums of money which he later finds cannot be recouped. Tenants should therefore not be surprised to encounter considerable resistance to such

Arbitration proposals. If challenge is to be by way of reference to an arbitrator or expert, then the person to whom it is referred should be independent of the landlord, and certainly not the same person who certified the expenditure initially.[36]

A different kind of safeguard for the tenant is provided by a requirement that proposed expenditure be notified to the

Advance notice tenant, together with estimates, giving an opportunity to object in advance. Such provisions are comparatively rare in commercial leases, and where they are inserted the landlord should be careful to comply with them, since submission of the details is likely to be a condition precedent of the tenant's liability to pay.[37]

8–06   Method of payment

The landlord will wish to use income from the service charge to meet expenditure as it falls due; otherwise he will have to meet the expenditure from his own resources or borrowing.[38] The usual method of meeting this problem is as follows: the lease defines the financial year in respect of which the service charge is payable, and the certificate as to the total charge is

Interim issued after the end of that year; however during the year
payments interim payments are made, usually quarterly, based upon a certified estimate of the expenditure made at the start of the period. Adjustment is made when the final charge is known, either by the tenant paying the difference, or by the landlord making an allowance. The tenant should insist either on any allowance being made against the next service charge payment or, alternatively, he could require that the landlord pays over the difference between the actual and estimated service charge together with interest. Landlords will however resist any

---

[36] *Concorde Graphics Ltd v. Andromeda Investments S.A.* (1982) 265 E.G. 387, noted at [1983] Conv. 94 (J.E.A.).

[37] *CIN Properties Ltd v. Barclays Bank plc* [1986] 1 EGLR 59. See also *Northway Flats Management Co. (Camden) Ltd v. Wimpey Pension Trustees Ltd* [1992] EGCS 63.

[38] And in the absence of a clear provision, the landlord will not be entitled to recover interest on the borrowing; *Boldmark Ltd. v. Cohen* [1986] 1 EGLR 47. Any such provision should allow for interest on notional as well as actual borrowing: *ibid.*, at 50, *per* Slade L.J. See also *Capital & Counties Freehold Equity Trust v. BL plc* (1987) 283 E.G. 563.

obligation to repay any excess service charge, let alone interest on that excess.

Reservation as rent

A different question is whether the service charge should be reserved as rent, or whether the tenant should simply covenant to pay it. Reservation as rent will give the landlord the potentially very powerful remedy of distress,[39] but on the other hand where forfeiture is sought for non-payment the tenant will have greater rights to apply for relief.[40]

Distress

8–07 Replacement and reserve funds

In the ordinary course of events, the expenditure required on the building is likely to vary considerably from year to year. One cause of this is the need for periodic maintenance: redecoration will be required every few years, heating systems will need to be serviced, and so on. Such expenditure is both regular in occurrence and predictable in amount. However, another possible cause of fluctuation is an unpredictable structural or mechanical failure, or a requirement to comply with newly-introduced legislation, the cost of which cannot be foreseen.

Regular expenditure

In the case of the regular and foreseeable items of expenditure, it is clearly prudent to make provision for allocating the cost between the service charge each year, rather than imposing it all on the charge for the year in which the expenditure happens to fall. The reserve will be held by the landlord for only a relatively short time, and should be placed in a separate interest-bearing account, with interest (net of tax) being credited to the service charge account.

Provision for irregular expenditure

Provision for major irregular contingencies is a very different matter. A very considerable financial reserve will be needed in order adequately to cover matters such as replacement of a roof or a heating system, and the reserve may need to be held for a long period of time. These factors mean that the tenants will probably require their position to be safeguarded by the funds being held on trust either by the landlord or by independent trustees.[41] This raises legal difficulties as to whether a non-charitable trust for the maintenance of a building can be valid,[42] and also potentially serious tax problems. The former difficulties are perhaps

Fund held on trust

[39] Though not where the amount is unascertained or in dispute: see *Concorde Graphics Ltd. v. Andromeda Investments* S.A. (1982) 265 E.G. 387. See also *Escalus Properties Ltd v. Robinson* [1995] 4 All E.R. 852, where a service charge was held to be rent where the lease provided that it was to be deemed to be due by way of additional rent.

[40] See para. 14–06 below and Chap. 19 for a discussion of the VAT treatment of service charges.

[41] It is possible for a trust to arise by implication: *Re Chelsea Cloisters* (1980) 41 P. & C.R. 98. But clearly an express provision is preferable: see *Frobisher (Second Investments) Ltd v. Kiloran Trust Co. Ltd* [1980] 1 W.L.R. 425, where Walton J. declined to find a trust in a commercial setting in the absence of necessity. The situation could be governed by contract (see *Conservative and Unionist Central Office v. Burrell* [1982] 1 W.L.R. 522), but a trust is desirable to protect the funds from creditors of the landlord in the event of insolvency.

[42] See *Re Denley's Trust Deed* [1969] 1 Ch. 373; *Re Lipinski's Will Trusts* [1976] Ch. 235.

theoretical rather than real, and can easily be outweighed by the practical advantages of a reserve fund, but there is little doubt that the tax implications have discouraged many landlords from creating such funds.[43]

Points requiring attention

Where such a fund is to be created, it is suggested[44] that the following points need to be considered and provided for. A suitable perpetuity period should be specified, *i.e.* a period of 80 years, or a shorter period where appropriate.[45] The beneficiaries of the trust will need to be specified: often the beneficiaries will be the tenants from time to time contributing to the fund, but there are also reasons in favour of specifying the tenants immediately before the expiry of the perpetuity period.[46] The uses to which the fund may be put should be clearly specified. The amount of contributions to the fund should be assessed each year by a suitably qualified professional. The landlord should contribute in respect of any unlet parts of the building. Interest earned should accrue to the fund, and any tax payable should be met from the fund. The accounts of the fund should be audited annually. A formal trust deed giving powers of investment and appointment of trustees may well be desirable, though it appears to be rare in practice. Provision should be made for the landlord to account to the fund for any capital allowances received when work is carried out. If the landlord is trustee of the fund, he should be required to transfer the fund to any

Sale of reversion

purchaser should he sell the reversion. And finally, some provision should be made for distribution of the fund among the beneficiaries in the event that no expenditure is required, *e.g.* where the landlord terminates all the leases and carries out some comprehensive scheme of redevelopment.

---

[43] Reserve funds have also not found favour with a number of tenants, particularly the multiple retailers, who prefer to have the use of such funds, and pay the proportion properly demanded on an "as and when demanded" basis. For a detailed consideration of the tax implications of reserve funds see Murray Ross, *Drafting and Negotiating Commercial Leases* (4th ed., 1994) pp. 254–260.

[44] These suggestions are based largely on the advice offered by the Joint Sub-Committee of the Law Society and Royal Institution of Chartered Surveyors on Model Clauses in Commercial Leases: "Service Charge Clauses" (1986) L.S.Gaz. 1056.

[45] Perpetuities and Accumulations Act 1964, s.1.

[46] K. Lewison, *Drafting Business Leases* (5th ed., 1996) p. 178.

9 REPAIRS, REDECORATIONS AND DILAPIDATIONS

9-01 Introduction

Types of covenant

The traditional practice in drafting commercial leases is to insert: first, a covenant on the part of the tenant to repair the premises during the term and to yield them up in repair at the end or on earlier determination of the term; secondly, a further covenant to repair within a specified period if required by the landlord; and thirdly a separate covenant by the tenant to redecorate the premises periodically. Considerable care needs to be taken both in drafting the provisions as to repair and in applying them to the infinite variety of events which may overtake the fabric of a building. This Chapter falls into three parts. The first considers repair and the second redecoration. The third deals with claims and remedies in respect of breaches of these covenants.

Law Commission proposals for reform

Before considering the present law, it should be noted that the Law Commission has recommended[1] that certain aspects of the law relating to repair and maintenance of leased property be reformed. The most important features of the Law Commission's recommendations, for the purpose of this book, are the need for specific allocation of the responsibility for repair; improvement of the effectiveness of the remedies for enforcing repairing obligations; and the abolition of the law of waste as it applies to tenancies.

The specific recommendations can be summarised as follows:

(1) there should be implied into every lease (subject to certain limited exceptions which are not relevant for the purpose of this book) a landlord's covenant to keep the demised premises in repair[1a] and likewise any common parts of the building of which the demise forms part, where disrepair of such premises would affect the tenant's enjoyment of them or the demised premises[1b];

---

[1] Law Com. No. 238 "Landlord and Tenant: Responsibility for State and Condition of Property", December 13, 1995. If enacted, the main changes would however apply only to leases granted after the new provisions took effect.

[1a] The implied repairing obligation would be an obligation both to put and keep the premises in repair.

[1b] The implied covenant would be negatived by any express repairing obligation, where the parties had expressly contracted out of the implied covenant or where the landlord was subject to a repairing obligation by virtue of any other statute. The implied covenant could be excluded or modified by the parties in the lease itself or any collateral agreement, *e.g.* a licence, made before or after the grant of the lease. The intention wold be that it should no longer be possible for a lease to be granted which does not allocate to one party or the other the responsibility for repair.

(2) there should be a discretionary remedy of specific performance in respect of breach of a repairing obligation[1c]; and

(3) the law of waste[1d] as it applies to tenancies should be abolished and replaced by an implied statutory covenant by the tenant to take proper care of the demised premises, to make good any wilful damage to the premises and not to carry out any alterations or other works which would, or would be likely to, destroy or alter the character of the premises to the landlord's detriment.

At the time of going to press, the Government has not responded to this report. Realistically, there is unlikely to be Parliamentary time for its implementation in this session of Parliament.

REPAIRS

9–02   The allocation of liability

Landlord's implied obligations

It is possible for a lease to make no provision whatsoever as to repair. The parties would then be subject only to such terms as are implied at common law or by statute. As to the landlord, the common law implies no general covenant that the premises are fit for use or that the landlord will carry out repairs,[1e] although exceptional circumstances may justify a departure from the general principle.[2] The statutory implied terms as to fitness for habitation and repairing obligations found in the Housing Act 1985[3] have no application to leases of business premises. However, the landlord who has an express or implied right to enter the premises to carry out maintenance or repairs[4] may, by virtue of the Defective Premises Act 1972, s.4(4), fall under an obligation to take such care as is reasonable to ensure that all persons who might reasonably be expected to be affected by defects in the state of the premises are reasonably safe from personal injury or damage to their property. The duty is owed if the landlord either knows or ought in all the circumstances to have known of the defect[5] and can extend to the tenant as well as to third

---

[1c] For these purposes a "repairing obligation" would be defined as a covenant to repair, maintain, renew, construct, or replace any property.

[1d] See para. 11–04 below.

[1e] *Hart v. Windsor* (1844) 12 M. & W. 68; *Sleafer v. Lambeth B.C.* [1960] 1 Q.B. 43; *Duke of Westminster v. Guild* [1985] Q.B. 668; *Tennant Radiant Heat Ltd v. Warrington Development Corp.* [1988] 11 E.G. 71. Compare the position as to licences to occupy land, where in *Western Electric Ltd v. Welsh Development Agency* [1983] 1 Q.B. 796 a warranty as to sound construction was implied. However no such obligation was implied in the later case of *Morris-Thomas v. Petticoat Lane Rentals Ltd* (1987) 53 P. & C.R. 238. But note the Law Commission's recommendation that an implied covenant be included in commercial leases (see para. 9–01 above).

[2] See *Liverpool City Council v. Irwin* [1977] A.C. 239, discussed above at para. 4–07 (n. 32) and para. 8–02 (n. 4).

[3] ss.8, 11.

[4] See para. 4–06 above.

[5] Defective Premises Act 1972, s.4(2).

parties.[6] It will only be of assistance where the defect is of a type which may cause personal injury or property damage, and even then the landlord may well satisfy the duty by steps short of actual repair.

Tenants' implied obligations

All tenants have an implied obligation to use the premises in a tenant-like manner, which involves abstaining from acts of wilful or negligent damage and also carrying out routine acts of minor maintenance such as cleaning windows and chimneys.[7] There is authority to suggest that a tenant for a term of years is liable for permissive waste, which can be seen as imposing an obligation to do such repairs as may reasonably be required to prevent the structure of the building falling into a state of premature decay.[8] However, the exact nature and boundaries of the tort of permissive waste remain unexplored in modern property law and considerable doubt exists as to whether a tenant for years would be held liable for permissive waste if the matter were thoroughly litigated today.[9]

Because of the sparseness and uncertainty of the implied obligations as to repair, a commercial lease will invariably contain express provisions. In drafting such obligations, the

Which party is to repair

first and most fundamental question to be settled is upon which party liability should be placed. In practice the answer is dictated by the state of the market, the length of the term and the type of property concerned.

Landlords of commercial property frequently aim to achieve a "clear lease" by imposing upon the tenant all or part of the

Clear leases

burden of repair. The reasoning behind the clear lease was stated succinctly by Lord Hailsham L.C. in the celebrated case of *O'May v. City of London Real Property Co. Ltd*:[10] "to render the income derived from the rent payable by tenants as little subject to fluctuation in respect of outgoings as may be possible." On this basis sums expended on the repair and maintenance of the property, whether regular upkeep or necessitated by some unforeseen event, are regarded as outgoings to be made the tenant's responsibility so far as possible. The tenant may reasonably ask why he should be required to assume a risk so disproportionate to his limited interest in the property.[11] To this the answer (at least in a landlord's market) is likely to be that such leases have passed into the realm of standard practice and that if the tenant thinks he can find premises with a more lenient landlord he is welcome to try. Faced with that stark choice, often the most

---

[6] *Smith v. Bradford City M.B.C.* (1982) 44 P. & C.R. 171.

[7] *Warren v. Keen* [1954] 1 Q.B. 15. But note the Law Commission's recommendation that this obligation be replaced by a new implied covenant (see n. 1 above and para. 10–37 of the Law Commission's report).

[8] See W. A. West, *The Law of Dilapidations* (9th ed., 1988) p. 14.

[9] See Woodfall, *Landlord and Tenant*, § 1–13.124, where the authorities are reviewed. For voluntary waste see para. 11–04 below. The Law Commission has recommended that the law of waste as it applies to tenancies be abolished (see para. 9–01 above). The Law Commission's report contains a useful discussion at Part X of the law of waste as it currently applies between landlord and tenant.

[10] [1982] 2 A.C. 726 at 737.

[11] *ibid.*, at 749, *per* Lord Wilberforce.

that can be done is to try and negotiate some protection for the tenant against the most potentially crippling risks, as discussed later in the chapter.

Nature of the property

The other significant factor in determining liability for repairs is the nature of the property. Where the lease is of a single, self-contained building let to one tenant the landlord may wish to impose a direct obligation for all repairs on the tenant. Such a simple solution is unlikely to be feasible in the case of leases of parts of a building, such as a floor in an office block, or where the tenants are reliant upon common areas and services, as with units in a modern shopping centre. To place separate repairing obligations on each tenant in such situations would be to invite the risk of chaos and acrimony, probably with the landlord being drawn in as an unwilling referee. The landlord may therefore accept direct repairing obligations as to the main structure and common parts of the building, whilst still achieving a clear lease by recouping his expenditure through a service charge or similar provisions.[12] This solution, unless the landlord undertakes to repair all parts of the building, will involve differentiating between those parts which are the landlord's and those which are the tenant's responsibility. As will be seen below,[13] this demands careful drafting.

9–03 The tenant's covenant to repair

Where the tenant covenants to repair, the landlord's solicitor will need to ensure that the covenant is comprehensive and that its language leaves the tenant with no scope for denying liability as to a particular item of disrepair. The tenant's solicitor ought to be alert to the full implications of the covenant in the light of the premises to be demised. It is suggested that four fundamental matters should be clear from the covenant, read in the context of decided cases: first, the timing of repairs; secondly, the spatial extent of the covenant; thirdly, the types of defect covered by the covenant; and fourthly, the standard of work required.

9–04 The timing of the obligation

Put, keep and yield up in repair

A repairing covenant can be expressed in three main ways: to put the premises in repair; to keep them in repair, and to leave or yield them up in repair at the end of the term. Frequently the words are used in conjunction. The central obligation of keeping the premises in repair in fact comprehends the other two, since it creates a continuing obligation upon which the tenant is liable throughout the

---

[12] Service charges are discussed in Chap. 8.
[13] At para. 9–03 below.

term.[14] If the premises are not in repair at the start of the term, then a covenant to keep them in repair imports a prior obligation to put them into repair.[15] Nonetheless, it does no harm to insert an express obligation to put into repair. It could be regarded as good practice to do so, thereby avoiding any misconception on the part of the tenant as to the full extent of his obligation. It is common practice to include a separate obligation as to yielding up and leaving the premises in repair, and indeed in exceptional cases such as very short leases this may be the only obligation. The obligation should be expressed to bite "at the expiry or sooner determination" of the term, so as to avoid argument that it does not apply where the lease is surrendered, forfeited, or terminated by a break clause.[16] The tenant should be aware that repairing obligations may survive the expiration of the lease, as where the premises are burnt down on the last day of the term. There the tenant would be under an obligation to reinstate within a reasonable time, provided the landlord were willing to allow him access to do so.[17]

Yield up and leave in repair

9–05 The spatial extent of the obligation

Problems can occur where the extent of the property covered by the covenant is left undefined, or is wider or narrower than might be expected. The most straightforward situation occurs where there is a demise of the whole of a building with the tenant covenanting to repair all parts. But even there, the landlord should consider a number of matters. First, there is the question of whether the repairing obligation should extend to facilities such as drains and roadways serving the demised premises exclusively, if indeed these are not already part of the demise. Secondly, there is the question of whether the covenant should expressly be extended to cover buildings subsequently erected.[18] And thirdly, the landlord will wish to ensure that repairing obligations extend to landlord's fixtures within the premises. By this term is meant items affixed by way of addition to the property, rather than forming part of the original structure, and fixed either by the landlord, or by the tenant in such circumstances as not to be legally removable by him.[19]

Demise of whole building

---

[14] *Luxmore v. Robson* (1818) 1 B. & Ald. 584.
[15] *Proudfoot v. Hart* (1890) 25 Q.B.D. 42. This however will not mean that a tenant will be liable to remove an inherent defect; the case has been interpreted as confined to the situation where the condition of the premises has deteriorated from a former better condition: *Post Office v. Aquarius Properties Ltd* [1987] 1 All E.R. 1055 at 1063, 1064, 1065.
[16] *Dickinson v. St. Aubyn* [1944] 1 K.B. 454.
[17] *Matthey v. Curling* [1922] 2 A.C. 180.
[18] A general covenant to repair will cover such buildings but a covenant to repair applied in its terms to existing buildings will not be extended to cover new buildings: *Smith v. Mills* (1899) 16 T.L.R. 59; *Field v. Curnick* (1926) 95 L.J.K.B. 756. Extensions to existing buildings would appear to be covered, however.
[19] See para. 11–11 below.

Demise of part of building

Far more complex problems arise in the case of a series of lettings within a single building. The difficulties of accurately defining the extent of each demise have already been discussed,[20] and these difficulties should always be borne in mind when drafting and considering a repairing covenant. In the case of internal walls dividing two tenants vertically, the question may arise as to which of the two is liable to repair and whether any contribution may be claimed from the other. The same problem may arise as between tenants divided horizontally by a party floor. In the absence of excluding words a demise will include the whole of the outside wall abounding it,[21] so that each tenant would be solely responsible for his part of the external walls of the building. By contrast, the tenant of the top floor of the building could find himself responsible for the whole of the roof,[22] and the tenant of the ground floor for the foundations.[23] Such disasters can only be avoided by careful drafting, and by reading the repairing obligation together with the definition of the demised premises.

The best solution will usually be for the landlord to assume responsibility for repairing those parts of the building which it would be impracticable for the tenants to maintain individually or in conjunction. One method of achieving this is to exclude from the tenant's repairing covenant certain

"Structure," "exterior", etc.

parts of the building, for example "the structure," "the exterior," and "foundations, load-bearing walls and timbers and roof". Both parties need to be wary when this method is used, since some expressions are imprecise in meaning, and others may lead to unexpected results when applied to the actual method of construction of the premises.

Structure

It is easy to categorise certain parts of a building as being part of the structure, for example the main walls and roof.[24] Other parts may give rise to serious debate and possibly litigation. Examples are ornamental features such as balconies and cornices,[25] non-load-bearing internal walls and partitions, the various components of wooden floors, and windows.[26] Where the expression "structural repairs" is used further

---

[20] See para. 4–03 above.

[21] *ibid.*

[22] *ibid.*

[23] *ibid.*

[24] *Granada Theatres Ltd v. Freehold Investments (Leytonstone) Ltd* [1958] 1 W.L.R. 845 at 849; [1959] Ch. 592.

[25] *Blundell v. Obsdale* (1958) 171 E.G. 491.

[26] In *Boswell v. Crucible Steel Company* [1924] 1 K.B. 119, large plate glass windows of 7 feet 6 inches high, resting on brick walls 2 feet 6 inches high and constituting most of the frontage of two walls of the premises were held to be part of the structure. In *Holiday Fellowship Ltd v. Hereford* [1959] 1 W.L.R. 211 ordinary wooden framed windows were not regarded as part of the main walls and inferentially not part of the structure. *Cf. Irvine v. Moran* (1991) 24 H.L.R. 1 where it was held, albeit in the context of a "dwelling house", that the structure consists of those elements which give it its essential appearance, stability and shape but which are not necessarily load-bearing; in particular, windows and window frames were held to form part of the structure. In the case of a modern building utilising large areas of glass in its construction it would clearly be unsafe to leave the point vague.

problems can arise, since it is not entirely clear whether the adjective refers to the part of the building requiring repair or the nature of the work required.[27]

Exterior

Use of the expression "the exterior" can be similarly unhelpful. One has to ask: the exterior of what? Reference to the exterior of the demised premises will produce a very different obligation from a reference to the exterior of the building, since for example a roof may not necessarily be regarded as the exterior of top floor premises.[28] In the case of a modern building, constructed of a steel and reinforced concrete framework, with walls of concrete panels with an external cladding of stone, the cladding would no doubt be part of the "exterior," but it is by no means clear that the concrete panels and framework would be regarded as such.

More precision might be achieved by a list of different parts of the building, such as "roof," "foundations" and "main or load-bearing walls." However, there is a risk that some significant part of the building may be inadvertently omitted from the list. Conversely, the repair of one part of the building may involve work to another part not on the list, as in *Smedley v. Chumley and Hawke Ltd,*[29] where the landlord in repairing the walls of the building was also required to carry out major works to the foundations. And again, care must be taken to ensure that the words used are appropriate to the type of building. It would be nonsense to speak of "timbers" in relation to a modern steel and concrete structure: and in fact the external walls of such a building may not be load-bearing but simply built upon a load-bearing skeleton.

Demise of space only

Perhaps partly as a result of the problems outlined above, an alternative solution has emerged in conveyancing practice. This involves restricting the demise to the space enclosed by the abounding walls, floors and ceilings, the internal surfaces of such walls, floors and ceilings,[30] and all landlord's fixtures and services exclusively serving the demised premises. Internal non-load-bearing walls within the area could be included, but any internal structural columns or walls running through the area would need to be specifically excluded, apart from their external finishes. The repairing covenants in the lease can then simply be related to the demise, the tenant undertaking liability for the demised premises and the landlord for all other parts of the building. This approach has a great deal to commend it, though it may have unwelcome implications for

---

[27] *Cf., Granada Theatres Ltd v. Freehold Investments (Leytonstone) Ltd* [1958] 1 W.L.R. 845 with *Blundell v. Obsdale* (1958) 171 E.G. 491.

[28] *Rapid Results College Ltd v. Angell* [1986] 1 EGLR 53; *cf. Campden Hill Towers Ltd v. Gardner* [1977] Q.B. 823 and *Douglas-Scott v. Scorgie* [1984] 1 W.L.R. 716, where in the context of the Housing Act 1961, s.32 the Court of Appeal took a broad and robust view of the meaning of "exterior".

[29] (1981) 44 P. & C.R. 50.

[30] *i.e.* plaster surfaces of walls or wall finishes, plaster work of ceilings or ceiling tiles or finishes (excluding any space above suspended ceilings), floor boards or floor coverings, or possibly floor screed, door frames and doors, and possibly window frames. A similar demise was described in *City Offices (Regent Street) Ltd v. Europa Acceptance Group* [1990] 5 E.G. 71 as amounting to airspace enclosed in an "eggshell".

the tenant who would like to make use of or carry out alterations to the structural parts of the building.[31]

9–06   The defects covered by the covenant

There is a very substantial body of case-law as to the meaning of the word "repair".[32] Nonetheless, considerable difficulty can arise in deciding whether the work required to rectify a defect is to be regarded as a repair. Consequently, draftsmen frequently attempt elucidation and expansion of the expression in the repairing covenant.

Distinction between repair and renewal

One difficulty is the distinction between repair and renewal, put as follows by Buckley L.J. in *Lurcott v. Wakely and Wheeler.*[33]

> "Repair is restoration by renewal or replacement of subsidiary parts of a whole. Renewal, as distinguished from repair, is reconstruction of the entirety, meaning by the entirety not necessarily the whole but substantially the whole."

It follows from the distinction that where the work required is so extensive as to amount to complete or substantial rebuilding of the premises it will be regarded as going beyond "repair."[34] On the other hand, replacement of a part of the whole, such as a wall or roof, may involve very considerable work and expense yet still constitute a repair.[35] The landlord may therefore attempt to extend the tenant's obligation by words such as "renew" and "rebuild," referring specifically to the whole as well as to every part of the demised premises.[36] The tenant may seek to resist such words on the basis that he should not be obliged to give to the landlord a building superior to that demised, but again his chances of success will depend on the strength of the landlord's market position. A more constructive approach is to consider what factors may lead to the need for such drastic rebuilding, *e.g.* age in an old

---

[31] See para. 11–03 below. Similarly, the voids below raised floors or above suspended ceilings which are commonly used as cable routes.

[32] See, *e.g. Lister v. Lane* [1893] 2 Q.B. 212; *Ravenseft Properties Limited v. Davstone (Holdings) Ltd* [1980] Q.B. 12. The Law Commission in its report on the law governing repair (see para. 9–01 above), whilst recognising the present scope for disputes over the meaning of "repair", doubted that any statutory definition would achieve greater certainty and concluded that its meaning should continue to be a matter for judicial interpretation (see para. 2–15 of the report).

[33] [1911] 1 K.B. 905 at 924.

[34] *Lister v. Lane* [1893] 2 Q.B. 212; *Torrens v. Walker* [1906] 2 Ch. 166. One important qualification to this principle is damage by fire: see para. 9–17 below.

[35] *Lurcott v. Wakely and Wheeler* [1911] 1 K.B. 905; *Elite Investments Ltd v. T.I. Bainbridge Silencers Ltd* [1986] 2 EGLR 43.

[36] The landlord should however be aware of the potentially adverse effects of such an extensive repairing covenant on rent review; *Norwich Union Life Insurance Society v. British Railways Board* [1987] 283 E.G. 846; see para. 6–26 above.

building, construction or design defects in a new building, subsidence in certain areas, and accidents such as fire. Thought can then be given as to how the tenant is best protected against the particular risk.

Old buildings   Where the building to be demised is old and dilapidated, tenants often assume that they will not be liable for putting it into any better condition. Such an assumption would be dangerous. There is clear authority to suggest that a repairing covenant must be construed in the light of all the surrounding circumstances, including the state of the building at the date of the lease.[37] But it is also clear that a covenant to repair can involve putting into repair premises which were out of repair at the time of the demise.[38] The words of Fletcher Moulton L.J. in *Lurcott v. Wakely and Wheeler*[39] may be cited as sounding a suitable note of caution:

> "We must bear in mind that while the age and the nature of the building can qualify the meaning of the covenant, they can never relieve the lessee from his obligation. If he chooses to undertake to keep in good condition an old house, he is bound to do it, whatever be the means necessary for him to employ in so doing. He can never say: 'The house was old, so old that it relieved me from my covenant to keep it in good condition'."

The most obvious precaution is for the tenant to have the building surveyed before entering into the lease. If defects are found, then the possibility of limiting the repairing obligation
Schedule of   by reference to an agreed schedule of condition annexed to
condition   the lease should be considered. However, to be of any use the schedule will need to be sufficiently detailed, preferably including photographs of the areas of obvious disrepair.[40]

Another possibility, though rarely used except occasionally
"Fair wear and   in the case of short leases, is the formula "fair wear and
tear excepted"   excepted". Such words would at least protect the tenant from being required to rectify dilapidations caused by ordinary and reasonable use and the ordinary operation of natural forces,[41] although there would still be an obligation to make good such dilapidations if this were necessary to prevent further damage.[42]

---

[37] *Brew Bros. Ltd v. Snax (Ross) Ltd* [1970] 1 Q.B. 612 at 640; *Wainwright v. Leeds City Council* (1984) 82 L.G.R. 657. It could be argued that this factor is more relevant to the standard of finish required than to the type of defect covered.

[38] *Proudfoot v. Hart* (1890) 25 Q.B.D. 42, approved on this point by Harman L.J. in *Brew Bros. Ltd v. Snax (Ross) Ltd* [1970] 1 Q.B. 612.

[39] [1911] 1 K.B. 905 at 916.

[40] The practice is developing of using video recordings for the purpose of schedules of condition. This can however present evidential problems where the video is mislaid, not being annexed to the lease. Photographic and video evidence may be hearsay, although *Phipson on Evidence* (14th ed. 1990) states (at para. 21–19) that it probably is not.

[41] *Haskell v. Marlow* [1928] 2 K.B. 95; *Manchester Bonded Warehouse Co. v. Carr* (1880) 5 C.P.D. 507.

[42] *Regis Property Co. Ltd v. Dudley* [1959] A.C. 370.

9–07 Design and construction defects

A different problem is that of want of repair arising from
defects in the design or construction of the building, a
problem which has frequently come before the courts in
recent years and one which is now invariably addressed in
modern commercial leases.

The first point to consider is whether any such defect has
given rise to disrepair. If the defect does not lead to damage,
so that the building remains in the same condition as when
demised, the tenant is not liable, since there is no disrepair.[43]

Defects and Not every defect will lead to damage, *e.g.* inadequate
damage foundations would constitute a defect and might or might not
distinguished lead to damage in the form of cracked or bowed walls. An air-
conditioning system which is badly designed and inefficient
could be said to be defective, but not damaged.[44] Thus under
a covenant simply to repair, a landlord might find himself
unable to compel a tenant to rectify a discovered defect
which, while seriously affecting the capital and letting value of
the premises, had not yet manifested itself in physical damage.
Such a situation could be covered by a covenant upon the
tenant "to rectify any apparent defect in the premises whether
or not resulting in physical damage".[45]

9–08 Whether work is "repair"

If however a defect does give rise to damage, the work of
rectification required may have to be carried out under the
repairing covenant. Until the case of *Ravenseft Properties Ltd v.
Davstone (Holdings) Ltd*[46] it was sometimes suggested that a
covenant to repair could not extend to rectifying such
"inherent" or "radical" defects, or their consequences.[47] In
Ravenseft Forbes J. rejected any such absolute rule:[48]

Question of "It is always a question of degree whether that which the
degree tenant is being asked to do can properly be described as
repair, or whether on the contrary it would involve giving
back to the landlord a wholly different thing from that
which he demised."

---

[43] *Post Office v. Aquarius Properties Ltd* [1987] 1 All E.R. 1055 (weak areas of
concrete made basement prone to flooding but caused no damage); *Quick
v. Taff-Ely B.C.* [1986] Q.B. 809 (badly-designed window-frames caused
condensation but no disrepair); *Stent v. Monmouth D.C.* (1987) 282 E.G.
705 (defective external door).

[44] *Jackson v. Mumford* (1904) 52 W.R. 342.

[45] However, as Slade L.J. commented in *Post Office v. Aquarius Properties Ltd*
[1987] 1 All E.R. 1055 at 1066, such an obligation is not one which a
tenant under a commercial lease might reasonably be expected readily to
undertake.

[46] [1980] Q.B. 12.

[47] *Lister v. Lane and Nesham* [1893] 2 Q.B. 212 at 216, 218; *Collins v. Flynn*
[1963] 2 All E.R. 1068 at 1070; *Brew Bros. Ltd v. Snax (Ross) Ltd* [1970]
1 Q.B. 612 at 646.

[48] [1980] Q.B. 12 at 21. The statement was approved by the Court of Appeal
in *Quick v. Taff-Ely B.C.* [1986] Q.B. 809.

The controversial work in *Ravenseft* was remedial work to stone cladding which had begun to come away from the exterior of the building because of faulty tying-in and the lack of expansion joints. The work to rectify the defective construction and to insert expansion joints together amounted to £55,000. The value of the building at the time was £3,000,000. Forbes J. held the tenant responsible for the cost of the work, which he said did not change the character of the building.

Since this decision, a number of other cases have considered similar defects. Whilst each case must be decided on its own facts, it is possible to extract some factors which seem to have weighed in interpreting a repairing covenant in such circumstances:

"Wholly different thing"

(1) whether the work required will render the property a wholly different thing to that demised.[49] Thus the state of the premises at the time of the demise is relevant, but one case suggests that what must be regarded is the premises not as they actually were, but as they were contemplated by the parties[50];

Substantial nature of work

(2) how physically substantial the work required is[51];

(3) the cost of the work required relative to the value of the premises or the cost of a new building, and the rent reserved by the lease[52];

(4) the lease as a whole and the commercial relationship between the parties[53];

(5) whether the work is necessary in order to avoid work clearly within the repairing covenant from being rendered abortive[54];

(6) the work required should be looked at in its totality rather than as a series of component parts[55];

(7) whether the work is a long-term improvement, looking to the future rather than the present[56];

[49] *Ravenseft Properties Ltd v. Davstone (Holdings) Ltd* [1980] Q.B. 12; *Hilliard Property Co. Ltd v. Nicholas Clarke Investments Ltd* (1984) 269 E.G. 1257; *Elmcroft Developments Ltd v. Tankersley-Sawyer* (1984) 270 E.G. 140; *Quick v. Taff-Ely B.C.* [1986] Q.B. 809.

[50] *Smedley v. Chumley & Hawke Ltd* (1981) 44 P. & C.R. 50 at 56. However, this cannot be taken as requiring rectification of defects which have caused no disrepair: see n. 43 above.

[51] *Post Office v. Aquarius Properties Ltd* [1985] 2 EGLR 105 (Hoffmann J., affirmed on other grounds at [1987] 1 All E.R. 1055).

[52] *Ravenseft Properties Ltd v. Davstone (Holdings) Ltd* [1980] Q.B. 12; *Hilliard Property Co. Ltd v. Nicholas Clarke Investments Ltd* (1984) 269 E.G. 1257; *Elmcroft Developments Ltd v. Tankersley-Sawyer* (1984) 270 E.G. 140; *Biddor Building Co. Ltd v. Tricia Guild Associates Ltd*, Q.B., January 25, 1985 (unreported). In *Elite Investments Ltd v. T.I. Bainbridge Silencers Ltd* (1986) 280 E.G. 1001 at 1008, Deputy Judge P.V. Baker Q.C. suggested that if the cost of a new building and the value of the premises were seriously divergent, regard should be had to the former.

[53] *Post Office v. Aquarius Properties Ltd* [1985] 2 EGLR 105; affirmed on other grounds at [1987] 1 All E.R. 1055.

[54] *Ravenseft Properties Ltd v. Davstone (Holdings) Ltd* [1980] Q.B. 12; *Smedley v. Chumley & Hawke Ltd* (1981) 44 P. & C.R. 50; *Elmcroft Developments Ltd v. Tankersley-Sawyer* (1984) 270 E.G. 140.

[55] *Brew Bros. Ltd v. Snax (Ross) Ltd* [1970] 1 Q.B. 612 at 641, 645, but *cf.* Harman L.J. at 631.

[56] *Mullaney v. Maybourne Grange (Croydon) Management Co. Ltd* [1986] 1 EGLR 70.

(8) work is not necessarily precluded from being a repair simply because it takes advantage of modern materials,[57] or, it would appear, methods.

Ordinary speaker of English

It has been said that the test is essentially whether the ordinary speaker of English would regard the work as "repair".[58]

To avoid the possibility of argument over building defects, many leases are now drafted as to leave no doubt that such defects fall within the tenant's repairing obligations.

9–09 Exclusion of liability for inherent defects

Conversely, the tenant faced with an ordinary repairing covenant may wish to exclude inherent defects from its ambit.[59] The question is how such objectives are best achieved. At the simplest level, a proviso may be added to the tenant's repairing covenant stating that the tenant is to repair notwithstanding that such repair may be rendered necessary by inherent defects, or alternatively that nothing shall be construed as obliging the tenant to carry out such repairs.[60] However, such provisions would leave many important matters unclarified. The term "inherent defect" is an imprecise one, which could refer to defects existing when the building was erected, or those existing at the time of the lease.[61] Similarly, whether a defect is "latent" can only sensibly be decided with reference to a point in time, which should be specified in the lease. Where liability for inherent defects is excluded, the precise scope of the exclusion should be carefully considered. For example, do the parties intend to extend the tenant's exclusion of liability for inherent defects

Specific provisions as to design and construction defects

"Inherent" and "latent" defects

---

[57] *Elite Investments Ltd v. T.I. Bainbridge Silencers Ltd* [1986] 2 EGLR 43.

[58] *Post Office v. Aquarius Properties* [1985] 2 EGLR 105 (Hoffmann J.); affirmed on other grounds, [1987] 1 All E.R. 1055, and cited with approval by Deputy Judge P.V. Baker Q.C. in *Elite Investments Ltd v. T.I. Bainbridge Silencers Ltd* [1986] 2 EGLR 43.

[59] Although some solicitors advising tenants may feel diffident on this point, believing that the landlord is unlikely to countenance any such exclusion, the market does vary and some landlords are more flexible than others. A compromise may be in the interests of both parties, since few landlords wish to have disgruntled and resentful tenants. A landlord who wishes to retain the building as a long-term investment may paradoxically be more flexible than one who wishes to sell the reversion quickly, since the latter will be concerned that lease terms be acceptable to institutional investors.

[60] In this case a corresponding obligation should be placed on the landlord: see para. 9–19 below.

[61] In *Brew Bros. Ltd v. Snax (Ross) Ltd* [1970] 1 Q.B. 612 at 640, Sachs L.J. thought that the term could not be limited to defects existing when the building was erected. It is suggested that if the parties wish to confine the term to that meaning they should use the term "original defects." In *Elite Investments Ltd v. T.I. Bainbridge Silencers Ltd* [1986] 2 EGLR 43, failure to paint galvanised roof sheeting at the outset was held not to constitute an inherent defect.

beyond those in the structure of the building? If not, then the exclusion should be limited appropriately. Otherwise the tenant might refuse to carry out decorative repairs where these become necessary because of bad workmanship or unsuitable materials.[62] The question of damage caused partly by inherent defects and partly by natural causes might also be considered.[63] The effects of naturally occurring subsidence might be worsened by inherent weaknesses in the walls of the building. One solution might be for the tenant's liability to be abated to the extent that the inherent defect contributed to the damage.

Where the tenant is to be made liable in respect of inherent defects, it is suggested that those defects should be defined in the lease. One means of definition is by reference to the origin **Definition of** of the defect, for example, "defects due to the design, **inherent defects** materials, components or construction of the property, or to defective workmanship or supervision during its construction". Where the tenant is to be excused from liability for inherent defects, a similar formula may be used, or alternatively the defects may be defined as those in respect of which the landlord has a cause of action in contract or tort against a third party.[64]

9–10 Other similar obligations

Covenants to keep drains cleansed, etc.

It is possible to envisage other defects where the word "repair" would be unsuitable. Many leases contain a covenant by the tenant to keep drains cleansed and free from obstruction, since a blocked drain or pipe will not constitute disrepair.[65] Similarly, landlord's fixtures such as heating and air-conditioning equipment will need to be kept not only in repair but in working order, and perhaps periodically replaced with more efficient or modern units. The tenant's covenant in relation to such fixtures may reflect this by requiring the tenant to maintain the fixtures in good condition and efficient working order and to replace such fixtures as may become unusable, obsolete or otherwise in need of replacement.[66] The tenant who is forced to accept such an obligation should ensure that the equipment is in a sound condition before the

---

[62] *e.g.*, peeling wall finishes or loose decorative tiles.

[63] As in *Brew Bros. Ltd v. Snax (Ross) Ltd* [1970] 1 Q.B. 612.

[64] See para. 9–12 below for the question of liability for negligence by third parties.

[65] Though it may constitute a breach of the implied obligation to use in a tenant-like manner (para. 9–02 above). See also *Wycombe Area Health Authority v. Barnett* (1984) 47 P. & C.R. 394; and *cf. Bishop v. Consolidated London Properties Ltd* (1933) 102 L.J.K.B. 257.

[66] For construction of a covenant to keep premises (a radio broadcasting station) "modern and up-to-date" see *Gooderham and Worts Ltd v. Canadian Broadcasting Corporation* [1947] A.C. 66. In *Delronne v. Clohesy-Mart* [1975] C.L.Y. 1850 it was held that a covenant to keep landlord's fixtures in repair required the tenant to replace whole machines when they wore out, and that the resulting replacements were the landlord's property.

commencement of the lease, and if not either require the landlord to rectify any defects or agree a schedule of condition limiting the tenant's liability.

9–11 Desirability of a survey

Even where the tenant is compelled to accept a lease making him liable for inherent defects, there may still be means of minimising the risks.

Survey by tenant One obvious precaution is for the tenant to have the building surveyed before entering into the lease. This may prove practicable in the case of a lease of a whole building to a single tenant, but difficulties may arise in other cases. A survey of the part to be demised may give little help in assessing the state of the vital structural parts of the building, and it may be impossible to inspect other parts which have already been demised unless an appropriate right of entry has been reserved.

Another problem is the cost of a structural survey of the whole building by the intending tenant of a small part. This **Use of landlord's** could to some extent be alleviated by the landlord making **survey** available to the tenant for copying the documentation relating to the construction of the building, or, where the landlord himself purchased the building, a copy of the landlord's survey.[67]

9–12 Tenant's rights against third parties

The tenant should also consider whether or not he will have any right of action against those involved in the construction of the building, e.g. a negligent builder, structural engineer or architect. Since usually there will be no direct contractual relationship between the tenant and such persons, any cause of action would have to be founded on tort. However, following the decision of the House of Lords in *D. & F. Estates Ltd v. Church Commissioners for England*,[68] the only claim which would succeed would be one in respect of personal injury or damage to other property, namely property other than the building itself. The tenant would not therefore be able to recover costs which he had incurred in making good an inherent defect or the damage caused by it from those involved in the construction of the building, even if their

---

[67] Though this would not necessarily give the tenant any cause of action against the surveyor unless he knew the use to which the landlord was going to put the survey: *Yianni v. Edwin Evans & Sons* [1982] Q.B. 438; *Shankie-Williams v. Heavey* [1986] 2 EGLR 139.

[68] [1989] A.C. 177. Followed in *Murphy v. Brentwood District Council* [1991] 1 A.C. 398; *Department of the Environment v. Thomas Bates & Son Ltd* [1991] 1 A.C. 499.

negligence could be proved. Such costs, described as "pure economic loss", would consequently be irrecoverable.[69]

Assignment One way of attempting to circumvent these problems is for the landlord to assign any cause of action he has to the tenant. However, the landlord may be understandably reluctant to do this, particularly where a number of tenants are involved and the landlord has retained responsibility, for example, for repair of the structure or common parts of the building. If the landlord does agree to assign any available cause of action to the tenant, thus affording the tenant a contractual remedy, the assignment must be made strictly in accordance with the terms of the principal contract, for example, the building contract or a professional's appointment, since failure to do so will render the purported assignment ineffective.[70]

The tenant may however still have a remedy in the event that the landlord has either ineffectively transferred any accrued rights of action or has refused to enter into any such assignment, following the decision of the House of Lords in *Linden Gardens Trust Ltd v. Lenesta Sludge Disposals Ltd.*[71] In that case, defects were found in a major development which necessitated extensive remedial works, and by which stage the property had been sold by the first plaintiff to the second

Ineffective plaintiff, together with a purported, but ineffective,
assignment assignment of the benefit of the building contract. Both plaintiffs sued the building contractor for breach of covenant in relation to the defects in the development. The second plaintiff was found to have no right of action against the building contractor on the basis that the purported assignment of the benefit of the building contract was ineffective, being made in breach of its terms. The first plaintiff, the original party under the building contract and by whom the property had been sold during the course of construction, was however held entitled to recover substantial damages from the building contractor, notwithstanding the fact that the property had been sold prior to discovery of the defects and that the first plaintiff had apparently suffered no loss as a result of those defects. The first plaintiff's entitlement to damages was based on the premise that the parties were to be treated as having entered into the building contract on the basis that the first plaintiff would be entitled to enforce contractual rights against the building contractor for the benefit of those who had suffered as a result of the contractor's defective performance but who, under the terms

---

[69] The tenant would be able to sue for economic loss resulting from an inherent defect caused by another's negligence only where he could establish that the relationship between himself and the tortfeasor was as close and akin to a contractual relationship as that existing in *Junior Books Ltd v. Veitchi Co. Ltd* [1981] 1 A.C. 520. This relationship and the scope of the duty of care arising from it was however described by Lord Bridge in *D. & F. Estates Ltd v. Church Commissioners for England* [1989] A.C. 177 as unique and the court's decision so dependent upon that uniqueness that it "cannot be regarded as laying down any principle of general application in the law of tort or delict".

[70] *Linden Gardens Trust Ltd v. Lenesta Sludge Disposals Ltd; St. Martins Property Corporation Ltd v. Sir Robert McAlpine Ltd* [1994] A.C. 85.

[71] *ibid.*

of the building contract, could not acquire any rights against the contractor for breach.

    This important case constitutes one of the few exceptions to the general rule that a plaintiff who no longer owns property as at the date of the breach is entitled to recover at **"No loss"** most only nominal damages—the "no loss" argument.[71a] It **argument** should however be noted that this exception, and consequently the entitlement to more than nominal damages, will only apply where there are no other legal remedies available against the defaulting contractor. The exception would not therefore apply where a tenant had obtained collateral warranties from the building contractor and the professional team on entering into the lease, since the tenant would then have a direct contractual remedy.[72]

    Furthermore, if the tenant is to rely upon the protection afforded by *Linden Gardens*, he must ensure that he is in a position to require the landlord to pursue whatever rights of action the landlord may have against those involved in the design and construction of the building and either to account to the tenant for any sums recovered or to off-set those sums against the tenant's liability for making good the defect in question or any damage caused by it.[73] Clearly, without any such obligation, there will be little or no incentive for the landlord to pursue any claim where liability for the defect in question can be passed straight onto the tenant at no cost to the landlord.

9–13 Subrogation

It might be argued that the circumstances of a clear lease represent a situation where the equitable doctrine of subrogation could provide a solution. The tenant who accepts liability for inherent defects effectively becomes the landlord's insurer of the integrity of the building: in such circumstances could not the tenant claim to be subrogated to the landlord's contractual rights against the negligent builder or architect? If it is accepted that subrogation is a wide principle not confined to existing categories,[74] the application of the remedy would be a bold, but not impossible, step. It would also appear to be

---

[71a] But see *Darlington B.C. v. Wiltshier Northern Ltd* [1995] 3 All E.R. 895, where a plaintiff was permitted to recover damages even after assignment of the building contract, on the basis that it had clearly been entered into for the benefit of another person whose loss was foreseeable.

[72] See para. 9–14 below.

[73] Any agreement between the landlord and tenant whereby the landlord can be required to take any such action should also deal with the conduct of any resulting proceedings, *i.e.* at whose cost and by whom they will be conducted. Consideration should also be given to the possibility of the landlord's action failing and an order for costs being made against him. If the action was commenced at the tenant's instigation and for his benefit, the tenant should be liable for the costs awarded against the landlord.

[74] See *Orakpo v. Manson Investments Ltd* [1978] A.C. 95 at 110, 112; R. Goff and G. Jones, *The Law of Restitution* (4th ed., 1993) p. 601, *et seq.*; R. P. Meagher, W. M. C. Gummow, J. R. F. Lehane, *Equity: Doctrines and Remedies* (3rd ed., 1992) paras. 952–959.

Rare in practice possible for a right of subrogation to be reserved expressly in the lease.[75, 76] It is however rare in practice for a tenant to rely upon a right of subrogation in order to mitigate his liability for inherent defects, preferring instead to extract an obligation from the landlord to pursue whichever rights he may have against those responsible for the defects in question or alternatively by entering into a direct contractual relationship himself with those involved in the design and construction of the property.

9–14 Collateral warranties

It is now common practice for tenants entering into leases of new premises to obtain from those involved in the design and construction of the premises, usually the building contractor, architect, structural engineer and mechanical and electrical **Duty of care** engineer, a duty of care deed, or "collateral warranty". The building contractor or relevant professional will warrant that he has used, and if appropriate will continue to use, all reasonable skill and care in carrying out his duties in relation to the development.

It is however by no means certain that if a defect comes to light the tenant will be able to recover under the warranty since its value will depend almost entirely upon the warrantor's solvency at the time the claim is brought and **Risk of lack of** upon the warrantor having adequate professional liability **insurance** insurance in place at that time. Whilst the collateral warranty will invariably require the warrantor to effect and maintain insurance, the tenant's greatest risk is that insurance is not in fact effected or, once effected, lapses or is vitiated for any reason. Furthermore, the true value of collateral warranties has yet to be tested in the courts and whilst a full set of warranties would, ostensibly at least, afford the tenant some protection if he has accepted liability for inherent defects, the better route from the tenant's point of view is to ensure that inherent defects are expressly excluded from his repairing covenant and that liability for such defects is expressly assumed by the landlord.

9–15 Other possible solutions

The tenant who is worried about the extent of repairing **Short lease** obligations could attempt to negotiate a short lease. A sinking fund could be used to provide a reserve to cover heavy repair **Sinking fund** costs, thus avoiding unfairness to the tenant who happens to hold the lease when repairs become necessary.[77] Finally, in a **Insurance** few cases insurance against inherent defects may prove to be

[75, 76] *Orakpo v. Manson Investments Ltd* [1978] A.C. 95 at 119.
[77] Though there are difficulties, discussed in connection with service charges at para. 8–07 above.

the solution.[78] Such insurance is not usually available for completed buildings or those already under construction (so that the underwriters can be satisfied as to the standard of construction); nor will it necessarily cover the whole term of a 20 or 25–year commercial lease.[79]

9–16 The standard of repair required

Relevant factors Considerably less doubt exists in relation to this question. Regard must be paid to the age, character and locality of the property, and to the requirements of a reasonably-minded tenant of the class who would be likely to take it.[80] The class of tenant who would be likely to take the premises is to be judged as at the commencement rather than the expiry of the term, so that any changes occurring during the term are of no account.[81] There might be some difficulty in applying the concept of "class of tenant," formulated in relation to residential leases in a more class-conscious age than our own, to commercial leases, where the tenant is likely to be a company, and where in an age of rapid technological innovation the requirements of tenants may change very rapidly. Would the class be defined by reference to the size and financial strength of the likely tenant, or by reference to the type of business? These questions await a definitive answer by the courts, but the landlord who wishes to achieve a greater degree of control over the standard of repair work could do so by stipulating that repairs are to be carried out to specifications provided by the landlord, or to the satisfaction of the landlord or his surveyor.[82] If the stipulation is that repairs are to be carried out to the satisfaction of the landlord's surveyor, the landlord should be aware that the

---

[78] For a comprehensive survey, see Latent Defects in Buildings: An Analysis of Insurance Possibilities; Report prepared by Atkins Planning for the Building Economic Development Committee (N.E.D.O., 1985). See also [1991] 11 E.G. 102 (R. Grover).

[79] The current period covered by such insurance is usually 10 years, based on the French model (decennial cover). But as the Atkins Report, n. 78 above, para 2.4, points out some defects, such as failure of cladding, may take up to 30 years to manifest themselves, while others may take up to 15 years—for example, failure of reinforced concrete, or corrosion of metallic structures. In addition, such insurance normally excludes from the property covered electrical or mechanical services, such as air conditioning. See also Chap. 11 of "Constructing the Team" published in July 1994 by Sir Michael Latham, the final report of the Government/Industry Review of Procurement and Contractual Arrangements in the U.K. Construction Industry. The Latham Report recommended that legislation be enacted requiring compulsory latent defects insurance for a period of ten years from practical completion of all new commercial buildings. This recommendation has been backed by a Government chaired working party, the Constructors' Liaison Group, but at the time of going to press no legislation dealing with compulsory latent defects insurance is proposed.

[80] *Proudfoot v. Hart* (1890) 25 Q.B.D. 42 at 52.

[81] *Anstruther-Gough-Calthorpe v. McOscar* [1924] 1 K.B. 716; *Sandhu v. Ladbroke Hotels* [1995] 39 E.G. 152.

[82] Very few landlords seem to do this, and it would be surprising if any tenant was prepared to accept any such stipulation.

appointment of the surveyor may be regarded as a condition precedent to the tenant's liability to repair.[83]

9–17 Insured risks

Excepting insured risks

An important exception to the rule that a covenant to repair does not require renewal of the whole of the premises[84] occurs where the premises are destroyed by fire or natural disaster. There the tenant will be liable to rebuild, regardless of whether or not the destruction was due to his negligence.[85] It is therefore important that the tenant ensures that he is not liable to repair or rebuild the premises at his own cost where there is insurance money available to do so. The usual formula for achieving this is a proviso excepting from the repair covenant damage caused by insured risks, unless the insurance policy has been invalidated by, or the insurance monies are irrecoverable as a result of, the act or default of the tenant. The landlord may wish to provide that the tenant is only excused to the extent of insurance monies actually received, should those monies be inadequate to cover the cost of reinstatement.[86]

9–18 Covenant to repair on notice

Right of entry by landlord in default

As mentioned above,[87] leases frequently contain a separate covenant to repair within a specified period (traditionally three months) of being given notice of want of repair by the landlord.[88] Sometimes the covenant is coupled with a right for the landlord to enter and do the work himself and to recoup his expenditure from the tenant, should the tenant fail to comply with the notice.[89] The tenant who fails to repair within the three month period will be exposed to the risk of forfeiture. A more common approach, and arguably a fairer one, is for the tenant to covenant to commence the works within a shorter period and thereafter to proceed with them expeditiously.[90]

9–19 The landlord's covenant to repair

A covenant by the landlord to repair is becoming something of a rarity in commercial leases, except where the building is

---

[83] *Cannock v. Jones* (1849) 3 Ex. 233; *Hunt v. Bishop* (1853) 3 Ex. 675.
[84] See para. 9–06 above.
[85] *Bullock v. Dommitt* (1796) 6 T.R. 650; *Matthew v. Curling* [1922] 2 A.C. 180; *Sturcke v. S.W. Edwards Ltd* (1971) 23 P. & C.R. 185.
[86] For further discussion of the problem, see para. 13–13 below.
[87] See para. 9–01 above.
[88] Such provisions appear to have been in use for well over 150 years: see *Horsfall v. Testar* (1817) 7 Taunt. 385.
[89] The effects of these, and similar, provisions are further discussed in the context of landlord's remedies, below, para. 9–24.
[90] Rather than giving a set period, it might be preferable to provide that the work shall commence as soon as appropriate in the circumstances.

let to a number of different tenants who will reimburse the costs incurred by the landlord in carrying out repairs. The rules stated above as to the construction and extent of a covenant to repair will apply equally where the landlord is the covenantor.[91] However, there are a number of additional problems to be considered.

Express covenant needed   An express covenant is required to oblige the landlord to repair.[92] Therefore in the case where the lease contains provisions allowing the landlord to recoup expenditure on repairs the tenant should not assume that the landlord will be bound to keep the premises in repair. An express covenant should be insisted upon.

Secondly, where the landlord has expressly covenanted to keep the demised premises, as distinguished from any retained parts of the property, in repair he will not be in breach of his **Notice of** obligation until he has received notice of any disrepair.[93] If **disrepair** however the landlord's covenant to keep in repair extends beyond the particular demise and applies, for example, to other parts of the building of which the demise forms part, no such notice of disrepair need be served and the landlord will be in breach of his repairing obligations immediately a defect occurs.[94] Consequently, landlords will often seek to qualify their repairing covenant to provide expressly that they will only be liable for disrepair once notice has been given by the tenant.

Spatial extent of   Thirdly, the tenant should consider carefully whether the **covenant** landlord's covenant covers all the necessary parts of the building, including services, access and common parts. A term may be implied that the landlord will use reasonable care to keep essential facilities in a fit condition,[95] but only in

---

[91] See, *e.g. New England Properties plc v. Portsmouth New Shops Ltd* [1993] 23 E.G. 130; *Credit Suisse v. Beegas Nominees Ltd* [1994] 11 E.G. 151.

[92] *Westacott v. Hahn* [1918] 1 K.B. 495. See also *Tennant Radiant Heat v. Warrington Development Corp.* [1988] 11 E.G. 71 where it was held that there is no general principle whereby as a matter of business efficacy a landlord's covenant to repair will be implied. But note the Law Commission's recommendations referred to in para. 9–01 above, which would import a statutory implied covenant to repair on the part of the landlord, if the parties did not include any express allocation of repairing liability.

[93] *O'Brien v. Robinson* [1973] A.C. 912; *McGreal v. Wake* (1984) 269 E.G. 1254. But note that constructive notice may suffice under s.4(2) of the Defective Premises Act 1972.

[94] *Bishop v. Consolidated London Properties Ltd* (1933) 102 L.J.K.B. 257. In *British Telecom plc v. Sun Life Assurance Society plc* [1995] 3 W.L.R. 622 it was held that the rule in *O'Brien v. Robinson* (n. 93 above) was an exception to the general rule that a landlord is liable under his repairing covenant immediately there is any disrepair; the exception in *O'Brien* applies only to disrepair within the demised premises and for which the landlord is liable, as opposed to disrepair affecting any premises retained by the landlord. But note that the decision in this case dealt solely with a landlord's covenant to keep premises in repair and merely queried whether or not the position might be different where the landlord had covenanted simply to repair, which Nourse L.J. suggested was a rarity in modern leases. Similarly, Nourse L.J. queried, but did not decide upon, whether or not a further exception to the general rule should be made where the defect was caused by circumstances wholly outside the landlord's control.

[95] *Liverpool City Council v. Irwin* [1977] A.C. 239 (service facilities in a residential block of flats).

exceptional circumstances.[96] In the absence of an express covenant, the landlord will not be liable to the tenant for damage caused to the tenant's property by the dilapidated state of the common parts unless negligence can be shown on his part.[97]

Inherent defects

It should also be considered whether or not the landlord is to be required expressly to accept liability for inherent defects, both those affecting the demised premises and any arising elsewhere in property of which the demise forms part. The tenant should ensure that where he has excluded from his own repairing obligations liability relating to inherent defects, the landlord has assumed a corresponding obligation to deal with any such defects, with a further provision that the cost of so doing should not form any part of the service charge[98] and should not by any other means be passed back to the tenant.

"Best endeavours"

Fourthly, the landlord may attempt to modify and circumscribe his obligations to repair. He may quite legitimately exclude liability for wants of repair caused by the wilful acts or negligence of the tenant, and also obligations in respect of unauthorised alterations carried out by the tenant. Less acceptable are attempts to limit the obligation to the use of "best endeavours" or some similar phrase. This could seriously weaken the tenant's position should the need arise to compel the landlord to repair.[99] Landlords also sometimes attempt to limit their obligations to such repairs as are necessary for the reasonable use of the demised premises. The tenant should treat such limitations with extreme caution since the value and marketability of his leasehold interest may be seriously prejudiced by the state of the remainder of the building, even if it does not physically affect the demised premises or the use made of them.

Duties to third parties and to tenant

Two final points may be mentioned briefly. Where the landlord has covenanted to repair his duty will extend beyond the tenant to others whose person or property may be harmed by the state of the premises.[1] Also the landlord who has played some part in the construction of the premises may be liable to the tenant in respect of defects resulting from the landlord's negligence.[2]

---

[96] *Duke of Westminster v. Guild* [1985] Q.B. 668 (no obligation on landlord to clear drain serving demised premises). See also *Cluttenham v. Anglian Water Authority*, *The Times*, August 14, 1986, (no obligation on owner of access road to clear rutted ice and snow).

[97] *Kiddle v. City Business Properties Ltd* [1942] 1 K.B. 269; *A. Caselton & Co. Ltd v. Jack* (1950) 155 E.G. 478; *W. H. Smith & Son Ltd v. Daw*, C.A., March 31, 1987 (unreported).

[98] See para. 8–03 above.

[99] See para. 8–02 above and para. 18–17 below for discussion of such obligations.

[1] Defective Premises Act 1972, s.4. See para. 9–02 above.

[2] Defective Premises Act 1972, ss.1–3; *Rimmer v. Liverpool City Council* [1985] Q.B. 1; *D. & F. Estates Ltd v. Church Commissioners for England* [1989] A.C. 177. See also *Optilon v. Commission for the New Towns* [1993] 35 E.G. 125 in which it was held that the landlord's obligations relating to construction of the premises pursuant to an agreement for lease survived completion of the lease itself even though the tenant had accepted a full repairing obligation under the lease.

REDECORATION

9–20 Specification of work

General formula

The tenant will usually covenant to decorate the interior, and sometimes the exterior, of the premises.[3] The work required of the tenant should be specified in detail, with regard to the type of materials suitable to the premises, or to developments in decorating materials and finishes. It is suggested that either the specification should be drafted with the actual premises in mind, or alternatively that some general formula should be used, such as "with appropriate high quality materials and in a proper and workmanlike manner" or "to the satisfaction of the landlord". The landlord might also consider inserting a requirement that the colours to be used be approved by him in writing, at the very least when redecorating during the last year of the term.

9–21 Timing of work

Redecoration in specified years

The timing of the work is also customarily specified. There is invariably an obligation to redecorate in the last year of the term, however determined. However, the tenant should seek to avoid wording which could oblige him to redecorate in consecutive years, as for instance where the lease is surrendered in the year following the last decoration.[4] Usually the lease will provide for redecoration at specified intervals during the term.[5] In practice such covenants are often broken with impunity, since a covenant to decorate in a specified year of the term will, if not complied with, result in a once-and-for-all breach which may be waived when the landlord next accepts rent.[6] Thus the landlord may need to carry out systematic monitoring to ensure compliance with the covenant, and the tenant may be resentful at being required to redecorate in a particular year when he may perceive no real

---

[3] It is sensible to insert such a covenant because of doubts as to whether the obligation to repair would import a duty to decorate: cf. *Proudfoot v. Hart* (1890) 25 Q.B.D. 42 and *Crawford v. Newton* (1886) 36 W.R. 54. It could be argued that a covenant to repair should not extend to minimal repairs such as plaster cracks and nail holes in walls: *Perry v. Chotzner* (1893) 9 T.L.R. 488.

[4] In *Bairstow Eves (Securities) Ltd v. Ripley* [1992] 32 E.G. 52 the tenant's breach of a similar covenant invalidated his exercise of an option to renew the lease, which was conditional upon compliance with the tenant's covenants. Compliance with the obligation to redecorate during the last year of the term was strictly construed, even though the premises were in a good state of decoration and it was arguable that only nominal damages might be recoverable.

[5] Customarily every third year for external decoration and every fifth for internal. But regard should be had to the nature of what is required rather than following tradition slavishly. For example, work such as cleaning stonework may only need doing every ten years, or at longer intervals.

[6] See para. 14–05 below.

need to do so.[7] A possible solution would be for the covenant to oblige the tenant to redecorate only when required to do so in writing by the landlord. The tenant should ensure that the landlord may only serve notice when redecoration is reasonably necessary or at not less than specified intervals.

9–22 Redecoration after repairs

Landlord's responsibility

The question of redecoration may also arise after repairs have been carried out to the property. In two cases it has been held that a landlord's obligation to repair carries with it an obligation to make good the decorative state of the premises so far as affected by the repair work.[8] In view of these decisions, the landlord might consider an express provision placing the responsibility for such work on the tenant, or at least relieving the landlord.

9–23 Miscellaneous provisions relating to condition

As well as redecoration, other obligations relating to the condition of the premises may be placed upon the tenant. Some or all of the following may be relevant, depending on the nature of the premises:

(1) to keep the premises clean and tidy (and possibly to maintain a contract for periodical cleaning with a contractor approved or nominated by the landlord);
(2) to maintain, clean and when necessary replace carpets;
(3) to clean windows periodically, often once a month;[9]
(4) to clean and unblock when necessary pipes and sanitary equipment;[10]
(5) to clean external stonework and brickwork;
(6) to make regular inspections of the premises and to inform the landlord of any defects or wants of repair;[11]
(7) to cultivate open spaces and keep them free of weeds or rubbish;

---

[7] It should be noted that the court has jurisdiction in certain circumstances to relieve a tenant from liability for internal decorative repairs where in all the circumstances the landlord's requirements are unreasonable: Law of Property Act 1925, s.147.

[8] *McCreal v. Wake* (1984) 269 E.G. 1254; *Bradley v. Chorley B.C.* (1985) 275 E.G. 801. In the latter case the Court of Appeal thought it irrelevant as to liability that the tenant was in breach of his own obligations to decorate, though possibly relevant to quantum.

[9] With large buildings it might be sensible for the landlord to undertake this, at least as to outside surfaces; indeed, arrangements by the tenant for cleaning the windows from the inside could contravene the Health and Safety at Work, etc. Act 1974: *Sun Alliance & London Assurance Co. Ltd v. British Railways Board* [1989] 2 EGLR 237.

[10] See *Starrokate Ltd v. Burry* (1983) 265 E.G. 871.

[11] Such inspections may be important in helping to detect any failure of structural parts of the building but are commonly resisted by tenants.

(8) to keep electrical and other equipment in working order and replace it when necessary.[12]

DILAPIDATIONS AND REMEDIES

A number of special rules apply to breaches of repairing covenants and may conveniently be discussed at this stage.[12a]

9–24   Breach of tenant's repairing obligations

Forfeiture   The first step in forfeiting a lease for breach of a repairing covenant will be service by the landlord of a notice under section 146 of the Law of Property Act 1925.[13] If the lease falls within the scope of the Leasehold Property (Repairs) Act 1938,[14] namely a lease for a term of seven years or more, of which three or more are unexpired on service of the notice, and the notice relates to breach of a covenant or agreement to keep or put the property in repair[15] then the notice must, in order to be valid, contain a statement of the tenant's right to serve a counter-notice claiming the benefit of the 1938 Act.[16] The tenant may within 28 days serve a counter-notice on the landlord to the effect that he claims the benefit of the Act.[17] The effect of the counter-notice is that the landlord can take no further action by way of proceedings or otherwise to re-enter or forfeit the lease, without the leave of the court.[18] To obtain leave the landlord must prove[19] that one of the following grounds exists:[20]

Leasehold Property (Repairs) Act 1938

Tenant's counter-notice

   (1) that the immediate remedying of the breach is requisite for preventing substantial diminution in the value of the reversion, or that the value has already been substantially diminished by the breach;

---

[12] See para. 9–10 above.

[12a] Note also the Law Commission's recommendations with regard to the remedies for breach of a repairing obligation (see para. 9–01 above and Part IX of the Law Commission's Report).

[13] See para. 14–06 below.

[14] s.7(1).

[15] It has been held not to cover a covenant to cleanse the premises: *Starrokate Ltd v. Burry* (1983) 265 E.G. 871, nor to a covenant to lay out insurance monies on reinstating the premises: *Farimani v. Gates* (1984) 271 E.G. 887.

[16] s.1(4). The statement must be in characters not less conspicuous than those used in the rest of the notice and contain details of the time within which and the manner in which the counter-notice may be served and specifying the name and address for service. On these requirements, see *Sidnell v. Wilson* [1966] 2 Q.B. 67; *Middlegate Properties Ltd v. Messimeris* [1973] 1 W.L.R. 168; *B.L. Holdings Ltd v. Marcolt Investments Ltd* (1978) 249 E.G. 849.

[17] s.1(1).

[18] s.1(3).

[19] The requisite standard of proof was held by the House of Lords in *Associated British Ports v. C. H. Bailey plc* [1990] 2 A.C. 703 to be proof on the balance of probabilities.

[20] s.1(5).

Grounds under the 1938 Act

(2) that the breach must be remedied immediately to comply with any act, bye-law or other statutory provision, or any court order made thereunder;

(3) where the tenant is not in occupation of the whole of the premises that the breach must be remedied immediately in the interests of the occupier of the premises or of part of them;

(4) that the breach could be remedied immediately at relatively small expense compared with the probable cost of postponing the work;

(5) special circumstances which in the opinion of the court render it just and equitable to give leave.

In refusing or granting leave, the court can impose such conditions on either party as it thinks fit.[21] Should leave be given and the landlord proceed to enforce his right of re-entry or forfeiture, the tenant can apply for relief in the usual way.[22]

Landlord's notice

Damages The Act also applies to claims for damages against tenants for breach of repairing covenants under leases falling within the scope of the Act.[23] Where three years or more of the lease remain unexpired when an action for damages is commenced, the action must be preceded by a notice of not less than one month under section 146 of the Law of Property Act, specifying the matters mentioned above.[24] Again, the tenant can serve a counter-notice,[25] with the effect that leave of the court is required before the landlord can proceed with an action for damages.[26]

Tenant's counter-notice

Problems for landlord

It will be appreciated that the effect of the 1938 Act procedure may be to cause substantial delay to a landlord seeking to enforce repairing obligations against his tenant. In one case[27] a landlord who acted quickly to carry out repairs for which the tenant was responsible, in order to avoid danger to passers-by, was held unable to recover his expenditure from the tenant, on the basis that under the 1938 Act service of a section 146 notice was an essential first step to recovery and that such a notice could not be served in respect of a breach which had already been rectified, albeit by the landlord.

Reliance on express right of entry

In the case just mentioned the landlord could, instead of simply carrying out the work, have relied on the usual provision contained in the lease allowing the landlord to give notice of disrepair, to remedy the disrepair himself in the absence of compliance by the tenant and to recoup the expenditure.[28] Any claim to recover the expenditure under

---

[21] s.1(6).

[22] Law of Property Act 1925, s.146(2). See para. 14–06 below.

[23] See above.

[24] s.1(2), (4). See n. 16 above. The notice must also comply with section 146 by specifying the breach, requiring its remedy (if capable of remedy), and requiring compensation in money for the breach: see para. 14–06 below.

[25] s.1(1).

[26] s.1(3). The grounds for leave are set out above.

[27] *S.E.D.A.C. Investments Ltd v. Tanner* [1982] 1 W.L.R. 1342. Possibly this case would be decided differently after *Jervis v. Harris* (see n. 29 below).

[28] See para. 9–18 above, though that course would have involved considerable delay.

such a provision will constitute a claim for debt rather than damages and so escape the requirements of the 1938 Act.[29]

When drafting such rights of entry in new leases, a distinction should be drawn between a clause (a) giving the landlord the right to enter only after a period of notice requiring the work to be done has expired; and (b) giving the landlord the right to enter at any time when a breach of the repairing covenant exists.[30] It appears that there are at least four advantages to be gained from using such provisions. First, there is the advantage of speed where emergency works are required. This will only be achieved by the use of a clause of the second type and by dispensing with notice in advance.[31] However, such situations are likely to occur only comparatively rarely. Secondly, there is the advantage that the contractual nature of the landlord's right to enter onto the premises and carry out repairs which the tenant has failed to do places the right of entry outside the scope of section 1 of the 1938 Act.[32] Thirdly, the landlord's claim for his expenditure is something other than a claim for damages, being a claim for debt, and consequently the restrictions imposed by section 18 of the Landlord and Tenant Act 1927 on damages recoverable will not apply.[33] Both this and the second advantage are obtainable by either type of provision. Fourthly, the landlord retains full control over the work carried out and its cost. This advantage can only be fully obtained by a provision allowing the landlord to enter without notice, otherwise the tenant would have the option of complying with the notice and carrying out the work himself. Finally, it should not be forgotten that the insertion of such provisions may have serious implications for the liability of the landlord to third parties for injury caused by the state of the premises.[34]

Advantages of such express rights

---

[29] See *Jervis v. Harris* [1996] 1 All E.R. 303, where the Court of Appeal held that the landlord's claim was not a claim for compensation for breach of the tenant's repairing covenant but for reimbursement of sums actually spent by the landlord in carrying out the repairs himself, having entered the premises to do so under a power contained in the lease. The Court of Appeal overruled the earlier contrary decision in *Swallow Securities Ltd v. Brand* (1981) 45 P. & C.R. 328 (where the landlord's claim in similar circumstances was held to be a claim for damages) and approved the decision in *Hamilton v. Martell Securities Ltd* [1984] Ch. 226.

[30] In *Colchester Estates (Cardiff) v. Carlton Industries plc* [1986] Ch. 80, the provision relied upon allowed the landlord to enter only where the tenant had not complied with three months' notice to repair. In *Hamilton v. Martell Securities Ltd* [1984] Ch. 266, the language of the provision appeared to allow the landlord to enter without any notice, but was treated by agreement as allowing entry only after three months' notice.

[31] Though one possibility suggested in *S.E.D.A.C. Investments Ltd v. Tanner* [1982] 1 W.L.R. 1342, was service of a section 146 notice requiring immediate action.

[32] *Jervis v. Harris* [1996] 1 All E.R. 303.

[33] See para. 9–25 below.

[34] By s.4(4) of the Defective Premises Act 1972 (para. 9–02 above) the landlord falls under a duty from the time when he first is, or by notice can put himself, in a position to exercise his right of entry. Thus if the right of entry is immediate the landlord is liable as soon as he is aware of the defect. If the right of entry arises only after three months' notice he is liable when the notice would have expired had he served it at the earliest opportunity.

Costs and expenses of proceedings

The landlord's costs and expenses in or in contemplation of proceedings can be made recoverable expressly by the lease, and will not be regarded as falling within the ambit of the 1938 Act.[35]

9–25 Measure of damages

By section 18 of the Landlord and Tenant Act 1927 the damages recoverable for breach of the tenant's repairing covenant may in no case exceed the amount by which the value of the reversion is damaged by the breach; and in particular no damages are recoverable for breach of a covenant to put or leave premises in repair at the end of the lease, if it is shown that the premises were at that time destined for demolition or for such structural alterations as would render any repairs valueless.[36]

Limitation on damages

Measure of damages

The measure to be used has been described as the difference in value between the reversion in its actual state of repair and the state it would have been in had the covenant been complied with.[37] It will frequently be difficult in practice to apply this measure due to lack of reliable comparable evidence of premises in a state of similar disrepair.[38] Therefore the cost of putting the premises into repair (where the work is actually done or is to be done immediately the term ends[39]) "is relevant evidence and will very often be prima facie evidence, or at any rate the starting point, from which the amount of the diminution in the value of the reversion may be deduced".[40] The fact that repairs may be carried out by an incoming tenant rather than the landlord would appear to be irrelevant.[41]

It should be noted that sums recoverable under the lease where the landlord enters to carry out repairs on default by the tenant are not restricted by section 18.[42] Similarly an agreement by the tenant to expend a specified sum each year on repairs is not caught by that section.[43]

---

[35] Law of Property Act 1925, s.146(3). See also *Bader Properties Ltd v. Linley Property Investments Ltd* (1968) 19 P. & C.R. 620; *Middlegate Properties Ltd v. Gidlow-Jackson* (1977) 34 P. & C.R. 4.

[36] The wording of this part of the section is somewhat opaque and has given rise to difficulties. See *Salisbury v. Gilmore* [1942] 2 K.B. 38; *Keats v. Graham* [1960] 1 W.L.R. 30; *Hibernian Property Co. v. Liverpool Corporation* [1973] 1 W.L.R. 751.

[37] *Smiley v. Townsend* [1950] 2 K.B. 311. Where the reversion is itself a lease, see *Lloyds Bank Ltd v. Lake* [1961] 1 W.L.R. 884; *Family Management Ltd v. Gray* (1979) 253 E.G. 369; *Culworth Estates Ltd v. Society of Licensed Victuallers* [1991] 2 EGLR 54.

[38] The price realised if the premises are sold later may not be reliable if price changes have intervened: *Smith v. Mulvihill*, C.A., May 10, 1985 (unreported).

[39] *Palmer v. Pronk, Davis & Rusby Ltd* (1954) 164 E.G. 608.

[40] *Drummond v. S & U Stores Ltd* (1980) 258 E.G. 1293, *per* Glidewell J.

[41] *Haviland v. Long* [1952] 2 Q.B. 80; *Drummond v. S & U Stores* (1980) 258 E.G. 1293; *Mather v. Barclays Bank plc* [1987] 2 EGLR 254.

[42] See n. 29 above.

[43] *Moss' Empires v. Olympia (Liverpool) Ltd* [1939] A.C. 544.

Need for co-operation between professional advisers

In conclusion, the importance of close co-operation between the professional advisers of the landlord in a dilapidations claim should be noted. If the claim is to be effectively pursued, the landlord's solicitor and surveyor will need to ensure that they are advising and acting in a co-ordinated fashion.

9–26 Injunction

Possibility of remedy by injunction

It is often said that a landlord may not enforce a tenant's covenant to repair by means of a mandatory injunction.[44] However, there is no modern authority to that effect,[45] and it is now clear that a landlord's covenant to repair may be enforced in this way. In exceptional circumstances therefore, a landlord might legitimately apply for such relief.[46] It seems unlikely that an injunction would be granted where the work to be done could not be specified simply, or where some other adequate remedy was available to the landlord.

9–27 Breach of landlord's repairing obligations

Measure of damages

Damages   The principles governing a claim for damages for breach of a landlord's repairing covenant are those generally applicable to the measure of contractual damages. The object is to restore the tenant to the position he would have been in had there been no breach.[47] Thus, in a case involving damages for the disrepair of residential property,[48] it has been said that damages recoverable may include the cost of reasonable alternative temporary accommodation if rendered necessary by the state of disrepair, the cost of any repairs paid for by the tenant, damages for the vexation of living in seriously defective premises, and (where to the knowledge of the landlord the premises were acquired with the intention of assignment or subletting) the diminution in the market value

---

[44] Usually based on *Hill v. Barclay* (1810) 16 Ves. Jun. 402 at 405, *per* Lord Eldon L.C.; and apparently accepted as correct by Rougier J. in *U.B.H. (Mechanical Services) Ltd v. Standard Life Assurance Co.*, The Times, November 13, 1986.

[45] In *Regional Properties Ltd v. City of London Real Property Co. Ltd* (1980) 257 E.G. 65 at 66, Oliver J. suggested that what was maybe only a dictum in *Hill v. Barclay* (1810) 16 Ves. Jun. 402, had been logically much weakened, but was supported by the text-books.

[46] *e.g.*, in cases of emergency, as in *S.E.D.A.C. Investments Ltd v. Tanner* [1982] 1 W.L.R. 1342 at 1349, where it was suggested that a mandatory injunction might have been sought or threatened. The recent Law Commission Report on repairing obligations (see para. 9–01 above, n. 1) contains a useful summary of this area of the law and concludes that there is no reason in principle why an injunction should not be granted to a landlord.

[47] *Calabar Properties Ltd v. Stitcher* [1984] 1 W.L.R. 287.

[48] *ibid.*

of the premises. Each case will turn on its own facts, and different items may well be recoverable in the case of a lease of business premises.[49]

Enforcement by injunction

Specific performance and mandatory injunctions   It is now clear that specific performance can in some circumstances be granted to enforce a landlord's obligations to repair and maintain the property.[50] In cases of extreme urgency and hardship to the tenant, even interlocutory relief may be granted.[51]

Appointment of a receiver   By section 37(1) of the Supreme Court Act 1981, the court has jurisdiction to appoint a receiver in all cases where it appears just and convenient to do so. In a number of cases this jurisdiction has been used where a landlord was failing to comply with repairing obligations.[52] The receiver may collect the rents and any service charge due and apply them in accordance with the terms of the lease on repair and maintenance.[53]

Functions of receiver

Set-off and deduction from rent   Another possible remedy is the ancient one of the tenant carrying out the work of repair himself and deducting the expenditure from rent.[54] However, this remedy is hedged with a number of qualifications[55] and its parameters are not exactly clear, so it should be exercised with some caution.

A similar, and possibly more extensive, remedy is an equitable set-off of damages against rent.[56] Most modern commercial leases however expressly exclude any right of set-off on the part of the tenant and similarly any right to

---

[49] *e.g.*, the loss of trade or goodwill caused by the state of the premises or damage to stock. In particular, where the lease permits underletting it might be argued that the practice of underletting surplus portions of commercial property is so common that no specific notice of an intention to underlet need be given to render any diminution in value of the premises recoverable if the tenant is prevented from underletting at full market value. Such a loss might be regarded as one arising in the ordinary course of events: see *Hadley v. Baxendale* (1854) 9 Exch. 341; *Victoria Laundry (Windsor) Ltd v. Newman Industries Ltd* [1949] 2 K.B. 528.

[50] *Francis Cowcliffe Ltd* (1977) 33 P. & C.R. 368; *Peninsular Maritime Ltd v. Padseal Ltd* (1981) 259 E.G. 860; *Parker v. Camden L.B.C.* [1986] Ch. 162. Note the Law Commission's recommendations concerning the availability of specific performance as a remedy for any party's breach of a repairing obligation: see para. 9–01 above.

[51] *Parker v. Camden L.B.C.* [1986] Ch. 162.

[52] *Hart v. Emelkirk Ltd* [1983] 1 W.L.R. 1289, *Daiches v. Bluelake Investments Ltd* [1985] 2 EGLR 67; *Clayhope Properties Ltd v. Evans* [1986] 2 EGLR 34.

[53] However, the remedy has its problems; if the assets in the form of rent receipts are insufficient to meet the expenses of the receiver, these cannot be recouped from the landlord: *Evans v. Clayhope Properties Ltd* [1987] 1 W.L.R. 225.

[54] *Lee-Parker v. Izzet* [1971] 1 W.L.R. 1688; *Melville v. Grapelodge Developments Ltd* (1978) 39 P. & C.R. 179; *Asco Developments v. Gordon* (1978) 248 E.G. 683.

[55] Such as prior notice to the landlord and the work not being excessive.

[56] *British Anzani (Felixstowe) Ltd v. International Marine Management (U.K.) Ltd* [1980] Q.B. 137.

withhold rent. This has been held not to fall within the ambit of the Unfair Contract Terms Act 1977.[57] A covenant by the tenant to pay rent "without deduction" will not exclude a right of set–off.[57a]

---

[57] *Electricity Supplies Nominees Ltd v. I.A.F. Group plc* [1993] 37 E.G. 155. See para. 8–02, n. 10 above.
[57a] *Connaught Restaurants Ltd v. Indoor Leisure Ltd* [1994] 1 W.L.R. 501.

10 PROVISIONS AS TO USE

10–01 Introduction

Most commercial leases will contain provisions as to the use to be made of the premises. However, in drafting such provisions, the landlord's solicitor should remember that the imposition of tighter control than is necessary or justified by **Effect on rent** the circumstances is likely to have a severely depressing effect on the rent obtainable on review.[1] It may be possible to protect the landlord's interests adequately without confining the tenant too narrowly. Depending on the circumstances, one or more of the following types of provision may be used.

10–02 Nuisance and annoyance

A covenant by the tenant not to use the premises so as to cause a nuisance will usually be desirable. The law appears to be moving increasingly towards a position whereby a landlord may be liable for the acts of his tenant which constitute a nuisance, either because he expressly or impliedly authorised those acts, or because he failed to take steps to restrain them.[2]

"Annoyance" The covenant may be widened by prohibiting any "annoyance" by the tenant: this is a wider term than nuisance, and has been said to extend to any thing which disturbs the reasonable peace of mind of the ordinary sensible Englishman.[3]

Another type of covenant aimed at the prevention of **"Offensive** nuisance is the prohibition of any "offensive trade," **trade"** sometimes amplified in older leases by a picturesque list of specific offensive trades.[4] The question of whether a trade is offensive will depend on the nature of the business, the locality in which it is situated, and the manner in which it is carried on.[5]

In certain cases, for example the letting of premises to be used as a place of entertainment, it may be sensible for the

---

[1] See para. 6–28 above.

[2] *Hilton v. James Smith & Sons (Norwood) Ltd* (1979) 251 E.G. 1063; *Tetley v. Chitty* [1986] 1 All E.R. 663. See also para. 20–05 below.

[3] *Tod-Heatly v. Benham* (1888) 40 Ch.D. 80 at 98. See also *Our Boys' Clothing Company Ltd v. Holborn Viaduct Land Co. Ltd* (1896) 12 T.L.R. 344; *Errington v. Birt* (1911) 105 L.T. 373; *D.R. Evans & Co. Ltd v. Chandler* (1969) 211 E.G. 1381; *National Schizophrenia Fellowship v. Ribble Estate* [1994] 3 E.G. 132.

[4] For a striking modern example see *Bovis Group Pension Fund Ltd v. G.C. Flooring & Furnishing Ltd* (1982) 266 E.G. 1005, where a lease granted in 1972 contained a list of prohibited trades running to 136 words and including scavenger, nightman, farrier, fellmonger, melter of tallow, maker of grease for carriages, and flayer of horses, followed by a provision that in particular the premises were only to be used as professional offices.

[5] *Duke of Devonshire v. Brookshaw* (1899) 81 L.T. 83.

Noise   avoidance of doubt to insert a covenant not to create a
nuisance or annoyance by way of noise or the playing of
music.[6] Such a covenant may also be appropriate in modern
shopping centres with open-fronted units, where the over-
enthusiastic provision of "background" music within one shop
can be a source of annoyance for other tenants and for
shoppers. The landlord should not overlook the fact that in
certain circumstances he may be held responsible for noise
nuisance emanating from the premises.[7]

10–03 Restrictions affecting the reversion

It may be that the landlord is himself under restrictions as to
the user of the premises, either because of a restrictive
covenant affecting the freehold, or because of covenants in a
superior lease. If so, the landlord will need to ensure that the
tenant complies with such obligations, and the soundest way
of doing this is probably to take a covenant from the tenant to
comply with the restrictions, setting them out fully in a
schedule to the lease. This ensures that any assignee of the
lease will take with full notice of such restrictions.[7a]

10–04 Planning

The landlord will wish to ensure that the tenant does not, by
Possible effects   changing the use of the premises, prejudice the use permitted
of changes of use   for planning purposes, and thereby the value of the reversion.
It has been held that a planning permission, once
implemented, may become "spent": thus if the use of
premises is changed from that authorised by a planning
permission it may be impossible to revert to that use without
a fresh permission.[8] A covenant by the tenant not to make or
implement any planning application without the landlord's
consent is sometimes inserted, but this still leaves open the
risk that the tenant may make some lawful change of use for
which planning permission is not required.[9] What the
landlord has to balance in each case is to what extent such
protection justifies the reduction in the rental value of the
premises resulting from tight restrictions on changes of use.[10]
The importance to an intending tenant of checking the
planning position is discussed elsewhere.[11]

[6] *Hampstead & Suburban Properties Ltd v. Diomedous* [1969] 1 Ch. 248 (such
a covenant held sufficiently certain).

[7] *R. v. London Borough of Southwark* (noted in [1986] Environmental Data
Services Report No. 132 at 17). See also paras. 20–04 and 20–05 below.

[7a] Although in many cases a tenant or undertenant will be subject to
restrictions contained in the freehold interest or a superior title whether or
not he has notice: see paras. 18–08 and 18–22 below.

[8] *Cynon Valley Borough Council v. Secretary of State for Wales* (1986) 53
P. & C.R. 68; [1986] J.P.L. 760.

[9] As by moving between Use Classes as permitted by the General
Development Order.

[10] An alternative might be to require the tenant to indemnify the landlord
against any loss resulting from a change of use undertaken without the
landlord's consent.

[11] See para. 18–05 below.

10–05 Uses requiring specific licences

Covenant to preserve licences

Some uses may require a licence by the local authority or some other body.[12] Where the licence attaches to the premises rather than the person carrying on the business, the landlord will be concerned to ensure that the value of the premises is not diminished by the licence being lost. Therefore the landlord should insert a covenant by the tenant to obtain and renew the licence as necessary, to comply with any conditions or requirements attached to it, and not to do anything to jeopardise it.

10–06 Preventing the premises falling vacant

Covenant to trade

In the case of shop premises, the landlord may wish to ensure that the tenant trades from the premises during normal hours and does not leave the premises vacant. Vacant premises in a shopping development can impose serious security problems and, particularly in the case of an anchor tenant, can have an adverse effect on other premises within the development and consequently their rental values. In such cases a covenant to keep the premises open during normal working hours can be valuable to the landlord. Breach of the covenant could give a rise to a claim by the landlord for damages or, where damages would be an inadequate remedy, an order for specific performance. The courts have traditionally been reluctant to grant mandatory injunctions requiring people to carry on business[13] but the Court of Appeal has held[14] that although the practice of the courts is not to enforce "keep open" covenants in leases relating to retail premises if, in all the circumstances, an award for damages would be unlikely to compensate the landlord fully, an order for specific performance would be granted.[15] The landlord should however weigh against the advantages of a keep open covenant

---

[12] See also para. 20–02 below.

[13] *Braddon Towers Ltd v. International Stores Ltd* [1987] 1 EGLR 206; *F.W. Woolworth plc v. Charlwood Alliance Properties Ltd* [1987] 1 EGLR 53; *Costain Property Developments Ltd v. Finlay & Co. Ltd* [1989] 1 EGLR 237.

[14] *Co-operative Insurance Society Ltd v. Argyll Stores (Holdings) Ltd* [1996] 9 E.G. 128 (where the tenant closed the demised premises, an anchor supermarket unit in a shopping centre, in breach of a "keep open" covenant).

[15] The Court of Appeal (Millett L.J. dissenting) was influenced by the fact that the terms of the covenant were clear and intelligible to the tenant and that consequently the court was in a position to tell the tenant what was expected of it. The court sought by its decision to achieve a sense of fair dealing in a case where it appeared that the tenant had deliberately run the risk of a claim for damages being brought rather than comply with its obligation to keep the demised premises open, which clearly was not the intention of the covenant. Millett L.J., adopting what he described as the courts' usual "pragmatic approach", expressed a "fundamental objection" to the grant of an order for specific performance, namely that "if granted for any length of time or for an indefinite period [the order] was oppressive". In his view, the potentially large and unquantifiable losses to which the tenant would be exposed by the grant of specific performance were out of all proportion to the loss which his breach had caused to the landlord. Leave to appeal to the House of Lords has been granted.

its potentially adverse effect on rent review. In any event, the tenant may be unwilling to enter into any such covenant given its implications where the premises become surplus to the tenant's requirements or cease to be profitable.[16]

10–07   Sunday trading

Normal business hours

Where a lease was entered into before August 26, 1994 and contains an obligation to keep the premises open during normal business hours, it will not be regarded as requiring the tenant to open the premises on Sunday, unless specifically provided otherwise.[17] Tenants taking new leases of premises of a type which would commonly be open for business on Sundays, *e.g.* DIY centres or certain other retail premises, should consider whether or not they are prepared to accept an obligation to open on Sundays and, if not, should expressly qualify any reference to normal business hours accordingly.

The tenant should on the other hand ensure that there is no restriction imposed upon the hours or days during which the premises may be used, particularly where the tenant's business operates on a twenty-four hour basis. This may however result in an increased service charge liability for the tenant.[18]

10–08   Restriction to specified use

By making use of the types of provision mentioned above, there may be no need to restrict the tenant to a specified use. However, in some cases such restriction is necessary, either because the landlord wishes to ensure that all units within a development are used for similar purposes (*e.g.* offices or light industrial units) or because he wishes to secure a balance of different types of use, for example units within a shopping centre,[18a] or simply because he wishes to retain strict control over the tenant's use of the premises.

A covenant to use premises for the business of a specific retail purpose will not however require retail sales to be carried on from the actual premises demised; it is sufficient for the premises to be used as ancillary to such use carried on elsewhere.[19]

"Permitting" and "suffering"

It is common to extend the tenant's covenant so as to restrain the tenant from permitting or suffering a prohibited use. To "permit" means either to give leave for an act to be done, or to abstain from taking reasonable steps within the

[16] Particularly in the light of the *Argyll Stores case*, nn. 14 and 15 above.
[17] Sunday Trading Act 1994, s.3.
[18] See para. 8–04 above.
[18a] See *Chelsfield M.H. Investments Ltd v. British Gas plc* [1995] N.P.C. 169 (where the landlord was granted an interlocutory injunction requiring the tenant to comply with its restrictive user covenant pending the main hearing relating to breach of the user covenant: the court was influenced by the landlord's cogent evidence of its tenant-mix policy).
[19] *Montross Associated Investments S.A. v. Moussaieff* [1992] 1 EGLR 55.

power of the covenantor to prevent it.[20] There is some authority[21] to suggest that the word "suffer" has a wider meaning than "permit"; but the distinction seems far from clear.

Sub-letting

The object of widening the user covenant in this way is usually to prevent the tenant sub-letting the premises for some unauthorised use. However, doubt exists as to whether the mere act of sub-letting would constitute a breach of such a covenant.[22] Also the failure to embark upon litigation against a sub-tenant might well not constitute a breach of the covenant, especially where the outcome of the litigation would be uncertain.[23] Thus the landlord who wishes to protect himself fully should consider imposing a covenant that any underlease shall contain a covenant to comply with the covenants in the headlease, and also a provision that the tenant will enforce the sub-tenant's covenant.

Use of planning use classes

Great care is needed in defining the specific use permitted if a workable and sufficiently certain definition is to be produced. In some cases all that may be needed is restriction in generic terms, *e.g.* "office," "retail shop," "warehouse," "research laboratory," and so on. In such cases it is quite common to incorporate by reference a definition from the Town and Country Planning (Use Classes) Order 1987,[24] if a suitable one exists. This has the advantage of incorporating the detailed definitions provided by the 1987 Order (and probably also any judicial authority on the meaning of the expressions)[25] and thereby providing greater precision than simply stating the generic use. However, this technique could give rise to its own difficulties, particularly if the 1987 Order is amended after completion of the lease to alter the scope of the various Use Classes. The lease must therefore be clear as to whether or not the user clause refers to the 1987 Order in its original form or as amended from time to time.[26]

The decision in *Brewers' Company v. Viewplan plc*[27] suggests that where a lease provides for the premises to be used for a purpose within a specified Class of an Order, a change in the Uses Classes will not necessarily alter the meaning of the user clause. In that case, the permitted use included any use falling within Class III of the Town and Country Planning (Use

---

[20] *Berton v. Alliance Economic Investment Co. Ltd* [1922] 1 K.B. 742; *Sefton v. Tophams Ltd* [1967] A.C. 50; *Commercial General Administration Ltd v. Thomsett* (1979) 250 E.G. 547.

[21] *Roffey v. Bent* (1867) L.R. 3 Eq. 759; *Barton v. Reed* [1932] 1 Ch. 362.

[22] The majority judgments in *Sefton v. Tophams Ltd* [1967] A.C. 50 suggest it is not a breach, as does the decision in *Prothero v. Bell* (1906) 22 T.L.R. 370. But *cf. A. Lewis & Co. (Westminster) Ltd v. Bell Property Trust Ltd* [1940] Ch. 345 at 351.

[23] *Berton v. Alliance Economic Investment Co. Ltd* [1922] 1 K.B. 742. But *cf. Atkin v. Rose* [1923] 1 Ch. 522.

[24] S.I. 1987 No. 764.

[25] *e.g., R v. Thurrock B.C., ex.p. Tesco Stores Ltd* [1993] 3 P.L.R. 114 on whether a "warehouse club" is a "shop" for the purposes of Class A1 of the 1987 Order.

[26] Since the 1987 Order came into force on June 1, 1987, there have been various amendments to the Use Classes.

[27] [1989] 2 EGLR 133.

Variations to the Use Classes Order

Classes) Order 1972. Class III having been replaced by Class B1(c) of the 1987 Order and the 1987 Order providing that use changes within the same Class would not generally be taken to involve the development of land and would not therefore require planning permission, the landlord sought to argue that the user clause should be read as containing a reference not to Class III or simply to new Class B1(c) but to Class B1 as a whole. This meant that the permitted use was wider, which was in turn relevant for the purposes of rent review. It was held however that because the relevant part of the user clause referred only to Class III of the 1972 Order, without reference to any future statutory modifications, the permitted use was restricted to Class III. If the user clause were to be construed as referring to the Class as defined from time to time, some very capricious results could occur and in the interests of certainty it is advisable to incorporate any definition from the Order by setting it out verbatim. That way, not only is certainty secured, but the parties can see the permitted use set out fully in the lease, and those negotiating the lease will have to consider how appropriate the definition really is.

Specified trade

In some cases more than a generic description of the permitted use is required. The most common instance is the lease of a shop, where the landlord wishes to restrict the use to a particular type of trade. This can be done in positive terms, stating that only one type of business may be carried on; or in negative terms, prohibiting certain types of trade.[28] It can also be done by referring to a particular type of trade or shop (*e.g.* baker, grocer, toy shop) or by referring to particular types of goods (*e.g.* fruit and vegetables, shoes, alcoholic liquor). One problem of trying to define a particular trade is that it may be possible to carry on activities ancillary to that trade, whilst remaining within the permitted use.[29] To what extent a use is ancillary to a particular business is largely a matter of degree.[30] Another problem is that terms used in retailing may change their meaning over time, and accordingly the degree of precision required may be difficult to achieve in the context of a developing economic pattern.[31] In particular the draftsman should beware of adopting outdated expressions, such as "hosier", "haberdasher" and "fancy goods".[32] It should also be remembered that the words used will fall to be construed in the sense which they bore at the date of the

Outdated expressions

---

[28] Sometimes the techniques are combined, but this can give rise to dangerous uncertainty: see *Appleby Developments Ltd v. Holloway* (1962) 183 E.G. 861.

[29] *e.g.: Stuart v. Diplock* (1889) 43 Ch.D. 343 (covenant not to carry on business of ladies' outfitter not broken by hosier selling items of underwear); *A. Lewis & Co. (Westminster) Ltd v. Bell Property Trust Ltd* [1940] Ch. 345 (covenant against carrying on trade of tobacconist not broken by sale of cigarettes in teashop); *Bier v. Danser* (1951) 157 E.G. 552 (covenant to carry on trade of hairdresser broken by sale of jewellery but not by sale of contraceptives).

[30] *St Marylebone Property Co. Ltd v. Tesco Stores Ltd* [1988] 2 EGLR 40.

[31] *Burgess v. Hunsden Properties Ltd* (1962) 182 E.G. 373.

[32] *ibid.* (although it is difficult for the draftsman to anticipate when a particular expression may in the future become outdated).

lease.[33] Another problem is that some words, such as "supermarket", may convey no precise meaning except to someone experienced in the retail trade; thus expert evidence may be necessary in order to determine whether a breach of covenant has occurred.[34] In general, it appears that greater precision may be obtained by reference to specific goods rather than a type of trade,[35] though again uncertainty can occur where the goods are described generically.[36] Often the best solution may be to restrict the use of the premises to a specific type of business and to provide in addition that certain types of goods must not be sold.[37]

"Allied trades"

Occasionally a user clause may be widened by permitting a particular business and "other allied trades". This technique is capable of giving rise to considerable uncertainty and is consequently best avoided. For example, is the allied nature of the trade to be judged by the type of processes involved, by the end product, or by some other test?[38]

"High class"

In other cases, a use may be narrowed by describing the business to be carried on as "high class" or "first class", *e.g.* a "high class restaurant". It has been said that what is high class will depend on the location of the premises, and also that the expression cannot be defined with precision but may be useful in preventing use in a way which is palpably not "high class".[39]

10–09 Consent to change of use

Absolute prohibition

Where the user clause absolutely prohibits any change of use, the landlord will be under no obligation to give consent to any change, and may act as unreasonably as he wishes in refusing consent.[40]

No implied proviso against unreasonableness

Similarly, where the clause provides that the use may be changed with the landlord's consent, no proviso will be implied to the effect that consent is not to be unreasonably withheld.[41] Thus the tenant should always seek to obtain such a proviso when the lease is being negotiated. The landlord will then be prevented from refusing consent to a change of use in

---

[33] *Rother v. Colchester Corporation* [1969] 1 W.L.R. 720; *Texaco Antilles Ltd v. Kernochan* [1973] A.C. 609; *Westminster City Council v. Duke of Westminster, The Times,* April 15, 1992.

[34] *Calabar (Woolwich) Ltd v. Tesco Stores Ltd* (1977) 245 E.G. 479; *Basildon Development Corporation v. Mactro Ltd* [1986] 1 EGLR 137.

[35] See *Labone v. Litherland U.D.C.* [1956] 1 W.L.R. 522; *Buckle v. Fredericks* (1890) 44 Ch.D. 244; also the cases cited at n. 29 above.

[36] *e.g. Stevenage Development Corporation v. Baby Carriages & Toys (Stevenage) Ltd* (1968) 207 E.G. 531 ("nursery goods" held not to include baby clothes).

[37] As in *Basildon Development Corporation v. Mactro Ltd* [1986] 1 EGLR 137.

[38] See *Fox Chemical Engineering Works Ltd v. Martin* (1957) 169 E.G. 297, where Upjohn J. based his decision on the processes used.

[39] *Rossi v. Hestdrive Ltd* [1985] 1 EGLR 50 at 52.

[40] Of course the increase in rent achievable by widening the permitted user may be a powerful inducement to consent.

[41] *Guardian Assurance Co. Ltd v. Gants Hill Holdings Ltd* (1983) 267 E.G. 678; *cf.* in other circumstances, *Cryer v. Scott Brothers (Sunbury) Ltd* (1986) 55 P. & C.R. 183 (see para. 11–06, n. 26 below) and *Price v. Bouch* [1986] 2 EGLR 179.

order to secure to himself collateral advantages.[42] So for example, he might be unable to put forward the wish to prevent competition with a business of his as a reason for refusing consent, where the user covenant was originally framed with some other object in mind. In the case of a qualified covenant against change of use where the proposed change does not involve any structural alteration of the premises, the landlord may not require payment of a fine, whether in the nature of increased rent or otherwise, for his licence or consent.[43] Also, in the case of a qualified covenant against change of user, if consent is withheld by the landlord the burden of proof as to whether or not such consent has been unreasonably withheld lies with the tenant.[44]

10–10 Effect of user provisions on alienability

A potentially serious effect of a strict user clause is the effect it may have should the tenant wish to assign the lease or grant an underlease. The user clause should therefore be read in conjunction with the provisions in the lease as to alienation. The relationship is considered in more detail in the context of restrictions on assignment.[45]

10–11 Protecting the tenant's use of the premises

Quiet enjoyment and derogation from grant

Every tenant will to some extent be protected against interference with his business by the landlord's covenant for quiet enjoyment and the principle that the landlord should not derogate from his grant.[46] Therefore acts by the landlord, and possibly by other tenants, which render the premises unfit or unsuitable for the purpose for which they were let may constitute a breach of either obligation.[47] However, there are limits to the protection afforded by these principles. The covenant for quiet enjoyment does not constitute a warranty by the landlord that the premises are fit for the tenant's

---

[42] *Anglia Building Society v. Sheffield City Council* (1982) 246 E.G. 311.
[43] Landlord and Tenant Act 1927, s.19(3). A reasonable sum may be required in respect of damage to the reversion or to the landlord's neighbouring premises and the legal and other expenses of the licence. In *Barclays Bank plc v. Daejan Investments (Grove Hall) Ltd* [1995] 18 E.G. 117 the landlord's requirement that, in consideration of his consenting to the proposed change of use, he be granted a right to break (and thus take the benefit of the profit rent payable under a proposed underletting of the premises) was held to constitute a demand for a fine. The tenant's claim however fell foul of s.19(3) since the proposed change of use involved structural alterations to the premises.
[44] *Tollbench Ltd v. Plymouth City Council* [1988] 23 E.G. 132. The Landlord and Tenant Act 1988 (see para. 12–08 below) does not apply to covenants relating to user.
[45] See para. 12–14 below.
[46] See para. 16–03 below.
[47] *Shaw v. Stenton* (1858) 2 H. & N. 858; *Sanderson v. Berwick-on-Tweed Corporation* (1884) 13 Q.B.D. 547; *Aldin v. Latimer Clark, Muirhead & Co.* [1894] 2 Ch. 437; *Hilton v. James Smith & Sons (Norwood) Ltd* (1979) 251 E.G. 1063.

intended purpose, either legally or physically.[48] Nor does the protection extend to uses by the tenant not contemplated by the landlord at the time of the grant.[49] Finally, quiet enjoyment and non-derogation from grant will not prevent the landlord from doing acts which affect the tenant's business economically but do not directly interfere with the tenant's use of the premises.[50] Thus in the absence of any express provision to the contrary the landlord will be free to compete with the tenant's business or to grant a lease of nearby premises to a competitor.[50a]

Direct covenant from landlord
There are two main ways of protecting the tenant against such competition. One is to take a direct covenant from the landlord not to let other premises to a competing business. The area covered by the restriction must of course be carefully defined. Such a covenant will give a direct cause of action in damages against the landlord,[51] and will allow the tenant to restrain by injunction any proposed unlawful letting.[52] However, it will not give any direct cause of action against the competing tenant once the lease has been granted.[53] Nor would such a covenant oblige the landlord to take steps to restrain any prohibited use of the other premises once the lease had been granted.[54] As with a covenant restricting the tenant's use of the premises, great care is required in defining the prohibited or permitted use. Such covenants are to be construed strictly since they tend towards restraint of trade, and a covenant against letting for a specified trade will not necessarily prevent competition from another trade which to some extent deals in the same goods as the prohibited trade.[55]

Letting scheme
The other way in which the tenant may be protected against competition is the creation of a letting scheme in which all the tenants are subject to similar restrictions which they can mutually and directly enforce.[56] The leading case in English law where such a scheme was found to exist is *Newman v. Real Estate Debenture Corporation Ltd.*[57] However, the case has been described as a "high-water mark",[58] and in a number of cases attempts to establish the existence of such

---

[48] *Dennett v. Atherton* (1872) L.R. 7 Q.B. 316; *Newby v. Sharpe* (1877) 8 Ch.D. 39; *Molton Builders Ltd v. City of Westminster L.B.C.* (1975) 30 P. & C.R. 182.

[49] *Robinson v. Kilvert* (1889) 41 Ch.D. 88.

[50] *Port v. Griffith* [1938] 1 All E.R. 295.

[50a] *Romulus Trading v. Comet Properties* [1996] N.P.C. 52.

[51] *Stanley v. Kenneth Properties Ltd* (1957) 170 E.G. 133. A collateral assurance by the landlord may have the same effect: *Conns Water Properties Ltd v. Wilson* (1986) 16 *Chartered Surveyor Weekly*, September 25, 928 (Northern Ireland High Court of Justice).

[52] *Brigg v. Thornton* [1904] 1 Ch. 386.

[53] *ibid.*

[54] *Kemp v. Bird* (1877) 5 Ch.D. 974.

[55] *Rother v. Colchester Corporation* [1969] 1 W.L.R. 720.

[56] For an example of such a scheme in a shopping precinct, see *Re Spike and Rocca Group Ltd* [1979] 107 D.L.R. (3d.) 62.

[57] [1940] 1 All E.R. 131. See also *Fitz v. Iles* [1893] 1 Ch. 77 where the issue went by default, and *Stuart v. Diplock* (1889) 43 Ch.D. 343, where the ability of one tenant to enforce the covenant against another was assumed with some doubt.

[58] *Kelly v. Battershell* [1949] 2 All E.R. 830 at 841 (Cohen L.J.).

a scheme have failed.[59] It appears that very clear and consistent language would be needed to create a scheme and establish the necessary intention. One difficulty in proving such a scheme in a leasehold context is that similar restrictions on user could be explained by the wish of the landlord to exercise control and management rather than the intention to create mutually enforceable obligations between the tenants.[60] Thus the ability of the landlord to consent to changes of use from time to time is inconsistent with the existence of such a scheme.[61]

10–12   Attacking user restrictions

Restraint of trade   It appears that the doctrine of restraint of trade is capable of applying to restrictions contained in leases.[62] However, on the basis of the test propounded by the majority of the House of Lords in *Esso Petroleum Ltd v. Harper's Garage (Stourport) Ltd*[63] the doctrine would not be applicable to restrictions imposed on the grant of a lease allowing the tenant to trade from premises where he could not do so before. The doctrine must therefore be regarded as affording very little scope for a tenant to challenge the validity of user restrictions.

Similarly, restrictive practices legislation is potentially capable of applying to provisions in leases, but the occasions where it may directly be brought to bear will be highly exceptional.[64]

Modification by Lands Tribunal   In the case of long leases[65] the Lands Tribunal has jurisdiction to modify or discharge user restrictions on certain specified grounds.[66] However, any application for discharge is unlikely to succeed where the covenant still secures a substantial advantage to the landlord by allowing him to exercise control and estate management.[67]

---

[59] *Kemp v. Bird* (1877) 5 Ch.D. 974; *Ashby v. Wilson* [1900] 1 Ch. 66; *Browne v. Flower* [1911] 1 Ch. 219.

[60] *Levene v. Clapham Super Market Ltd* (1958) 171 E.G. 719.

[61] *Pearce v. Maryon-Wilson* [1935] 1 Ch. 188.

[62] *Amoco Australia Pty. Ltd v. Rocca Bros. Motor Engineering Co. Pty. Ltd* [1975] A.C. 561; *Alec Lobb (Garages) Ltd v. Total Oil (Great Britain) Ltd* [1985] 1 W.L.R. 173.

[63] [1968] A.C. 269 at 298, 309, 316. See also *Alec Lobb (Garages) Ltd v. Total Oil (Great Britain) Ltd* [1985] 1 W.L.R. 173.

[64] *Re Ravenseft Properties Ltd.'s Application* [1978] 1 Q.B. 52 (partly because of the lack of a "trading nexus" between the parties and the subject-matter of the agreement and partly because of the adoption of the "new opportunity" test of *Esso Petroleum Ltd v. Harper's Garage (Stourport) Ltd* [1968] A.C. 269).

[65] The lease must have been granted for a term of 40 years or more of which at least 25 have expired: Law of Property Act 1925, s.84(12).

[66] Law of Property Act 1925, s.84(1).

[67] See *Memvale Securities Ltd's Application* (1975) 233 E.G. 689.

11 IMPROVEMENTS, ALTERATIONS AND FIXTURES

IMPROVEMENTS AND ALTERATIONS

11–01 Generally

In order to maximise the usefulness of the premises to himself, a tenant may wish to carry out alterations to their physical structure. The first question to be answered is whether the proposed work is permitted by the lease, or whether the landlord's consent must be sought. This involves consideration of any express covenants in the lease, the extent of the demise and the law of waste.

11–02 Express covenants against alterations

Covenant against cutting and maiming structure

Most leases will contain some restriction on the tenant's ability to carry out structural alterations. However, the exact wording used can differ significantly, with important effects on the type of work covered. Older leases sometimes contain a covenant against cutting or maiming the main walls and timbers. Such a covenant may prevent relatively minor operations, such as cutting or drilling small holes to support a sign,[1] or notching joists to receive air conditioning pipes[2] but conversely it will not prevent alterations to the appearance of the building which have no impact upon the fabric.[3] Also difficulties may arise in deciding what constitutes the main walls and timbers, *e.g.* would cutting doorways in internal and non-load-bearing walls give rise to a breach?[4]

Covenant against alterations

The more usual modern covenant not to make alterations to the premises has been interpreted as referring to permanent alterations affecting the form and structure of the premises, and it has been said that it should not be construed so as to prevent a tradesman from doing those acts which are convenient and usual for the ordinary and reasonable conduct of his business.[5] This leaves a great deal of uncertainty.

---

[1] *London County Council v. Hutter* [1925] Ch. 626.
[2] *Hagee (London) Ltd v. Co-operative Insurance Society Ltd* [1992] 7 E.G. 122.
[3] *Joseph v. London County Council* (1914) 111 L.T. 276.
[4] See *Lilley & Skinner Ltd v. Crump* (1929) 73 S.J. 366 (apparently not in that case).
[5] *Bickmore v. Dimmer* [1903] 1 Ch. 158 at 167 (erection of clock outside watchmaker's shop held not to be breach of covenant).

"Additions"

Clearly the covenant would prevent substantial works of demolition and reconstruction by the tenant. Equally clearly it would not prevent minor works incidental to the tenant's business, such as the erection of shelves in a shop or a reasonably-proportioned sign advertising the tenant's business. But many types of works can be envisaged which could be regarded as falling on either side of the line: for example, the erection of office partitioning, the installation of a new shop front, and so on. Even if not "alterations", such works might be regarded as "additions", which are also forbidden by many modern leases. Where such doubts arise under an existing lease, they will have to be resolved by agreement, or failing that, a court declaration. In drafting new leases, it may be possible to avoid such doubts by the exercise of some forethought. For example, the tenant may know that he is likely to wish to install partitioning or a lift: if so, there is no reason why such works should not be expressly exempted from the general covenant subject to certain conditions as to how the work is carried out and providing for reinstatement at the end of the term. Conversely, a landlord may be anxious that no alterations are made to the air-conditioning or heating system without his consent, and a specific covenant to that effect could be inserted.

Covenant against altering external appearance

Another type of covenant sometimes encountered is one against making alterations to the external appearance of the premises. Such a covenant could have capricious consequences, preventing quite minor changes such as the fixing of an advertisement,[6] but allowing major structural alterations which preserve the facade of the building.

Absolute and qualified covenants

An important distinction must be drawn between covenants absolutely forbidding alterations, and those prohibiting alterations except with the landlord's consent. The significance of the distinction will appear later, but for present purposes it should be emphasised that the tenant should always resist an absolute prohibition and seek to replace it with a covenant in qualified form.

It should also be noted that whether the covenant against alterations is absolute or qualified, the tenant will not be liable for a breach of the covenant where the acts which constitute the breach are carried out by an independent contractor acting contrary to the tenant's instructions and without the tenant's knowledge.[7]

Covenant against waste

As well as a covenant against alterations, older leases sometimes also contain a covenant against acts of waste.[8] Care is needed here, since a covenant allowing alterations with the landlord's consent could potentially be nullified by an absolute prohibition of waste. However, it seems likely that in such cases of conflict, the covenant against waste would be

---

[6] *Heard v. Stuart* (1907) 24 T.L.R. 104; *cf. Gresham Life Assurance Society v. Ranger* (1899) 15 T.L.R. 454 (covenant not broken by tenant keeping down shop blind for legitimate trade purposes).

[7] *Hagee (London) Ltd v. Co-operative Insurance Society Ltd* [1992] 7 E.G. 122.

[8] Waste is discussed at para. 11–04 below.

regarded as overridden by the more specific provisions as to alterations.[9]

11–03 The extent of the demise

In considering whether a proposed alteration may be carried out, there may be a tendency to refer only to the relevant covenant in the lease. However, attention should also be directed to the definition of the demised premises,[10] since clearly the tenant will have no right to carry out works to parts of the building not within the demise unless such a right has been expressly or impliedly granted.[11]

11–04 The law of waste

Scope of tort of waste

Structural alterations to the premises may in some circumstances constitute use of the premises in an untenant-like manner and the tort of waste.[12] However, the precise scope of the tort remains unclear.[12a] The Court of Appeal has considered the applicability of the law of waste to a situation where the tenant of premises used for a chemical business installed extractor fans,[13] an operation which involved cutting through the brickwork and cladding of which the premises were constructed. The fans were removed by a subsequent occupier of the premises, leaving the holes open. One member of the Court of Appeal was of the opinion that the installation of the fans did not constitute waste, since it was not so inconsistent with the terms of the lease and the permitted user of the premises as to be used in an untenant-like manner.[14] Another member[15] thought that making the holes and installing the fans was an act of waste. Similarly, the court was divided over whether removing the fans and failing to make good the holes constituted waste.[16] Doubt also exists over whether an action in waste can lie where the act is covered by an express covenant, or whether the landlord may elect to sue in contract under the covenant or in tort for waste.[17]

---

[9] See *F. W. Woolworth & Co. Ltd v. Lambert* [1937] Ch. 37 at 60, 65.
[10] *Davies v. Yadegar* [1990] 1 EGLR 71 and *Haines v. Florensa* [1990] 1 EGLR 73 (in each case a loft conversion did not involve trespass into airspace since the airspace above the roof formed part of the demise).
[11] *Tideway Investments and Property Holdings Ltd v. Wellwood* [1952] Ch. 791.
[12] *Hyman v. Rose* [1912] A.C. 623; *Marsden v. Edward Heyes Ltd* [1927] 2 K.B. 1.
[12a] The Law Commission has recommended abolition of the law of waste as it applies to tenancies and its replacement with an implied duty on a tenant to take reasonable care of the premises (see para. 9–01 above).
[13] *Mancetter Developments Ltd v. Garmanson Ltd* [1986] 2 W.L.R. 871.
[14] *ibid.*, at 881–882, *per* Kerr L.J.
[15] *ibid.*, at 880, *per* Sir George Waller.
[16] Dillon and Kerr L.JJ. thought so: see at 877–878 and 882. Sir George Waller thought not: see at 880.
[17] Compare Dillon L.J. at 876 and Kerr L.J. at 881–882. The Law Commission Report referred to at para. 9–01 above contains a useful discussion of the law of waste (see Part X).

Waste and express provisions

Another question which remains unsatisfactorily unclear is how the tort of waste relates to the express provisions of the lease governing alterations. It would probably be difficult for a landlord to argue that acts expressly permitted or contemplated by the lease constitute waste. However, to what extent can the tort be impliedly qualified? For example, if a lease contains a covenant against making structural alterations to the exterior of the premises, can the tenant assume that he is free to alter the interior, or would he run the risk of an action for waste in doing so? To avoid such doubts the lease could provide expressly that the landlord's sole remedy in respect of alterations shall be under the covenants in the lease, and that no action shall be brought under the common law of waste. Such provisions are very rarely seen in practice, not least because they serve to draw to the landlord's attention the alternative remedies available to him.

11–05   Consent to alterations and improvements

Absolute prohibition

Even where the prohibition on alterations is absolute, it is always open to the tenant to attempt to persuade the landlord to give permission for the proposed work. The landlord will however be under no obligation to consent to the works and, if minded to do so, will be at liberty to impose whatever conditions he thinks fit upon the carrying out of the works. If the landlord refuses to consent to the works, however, the tenant is not, contrary no doubt to the belief of many landlords, left without any means of redress.

Landlord and Tenant Act 1927

The tenant's redress may be found in the provisions of Part I of the Landlord and Tenant Act 1927, under which a business tenant may obtain the authority of the court to make improvements to the demised premises notwithstanding any restriction upon or prohibition of such works in the lease.[18] The relevant procedures which must be followed by the tenant in order to obtain the court's authorisation are discussed later in this Chapter[19] in the context of the tenant's entitlement to compensation for certain improvements on quitting the premises at the end of the term. The point to note here is the court's power to override what on the face of the lease appears to be an absolute prohibition upon alterations.[20]

---

[18] Landlord and Tenant Act 1927, s.3(4).

[19] See para. 11–07 below.

[20] The Law Commission Report referred to at n. 32 below also considered the revision, and simplification, of the authorisation procedure in s.3(4) of the 1927 Act but concluded that the effect of s.3(4) should be retained. The Law Commission noted at para 4.1 of their Report that although s.3 of the 1927 Act is not frequently relied upon in court, it is often used by tenants in negotiations with their landlords, presumably as a means of leverage.

It may also be possible to override an absolute prohibition where the work is necessary to comply with some statutory requirement.[21]

Qualified covenant

Implied proviso that consent not be unreasonably withheld

Where the covenant prohibits the making of improvements[22] without the consent of the landlord, section 19(2) of the Landlord and Tenant Act 1927 deems the covenant to be subject to a proviso that such consent is not to be unreasonably withheld, notwithstanding any express provision to the contrary. The subsection is expressly stated not to preclude the landlord's right to require as a condition of giving consent the payment of a reasonable sum for damage to or diminution in the value of the premises or any neighbouring premises belonging to the landlord or payment of the legal or other expenses properly incurred by the landlord in connection with such consent; nor does it preclude the right, where the improvement does not add to the letting value of the premises and where such a requirement would be reasonable, to require an undertaking to reinstate the premises.

In order to fall within section 19(2) the work proposed need not constitute an "improvement" to the premises in the sense of improving their value. The test of an improvement has been said to be whether it improves the comfort, convenience and beneficial use of the premises from the point of view of the tenant.[23] However, it is also arguable that the improving effect of the work must be judged in the light of the premises demised, and that work which has the effect of destroying the identity of the subject-matter demised cannot be regarded as an improvement to that subject-matter.[24]

Grounds for refusal

A landlord's refusal of consent to proposed alterations may be based on many grounds: aesthetic or historic objections to what is proposed; diminution in either rental or market value of the premises (or possibly neighbouring premises); even

---

[21] See for example, Factories Act 1961, s.169, Offices, Shops and Railway Premises Act 1963, s.73(1); Fire Precautions Act 1971, s.28(2). When in force, the Telecommunications Act 1984, s.96 may provide a remedy where the landlord refuses permission for alterations to install or connect a telecommunications system. See also the Disability Discrimination Act 1995 under which a tenant, being an employer or trade organisation, will be entitled to carry out alterations in order to comply with the duties imposed by the Act, notwithstanding any prohibition on alterations in the lease or any provision imposing conditions upon the carrying out of alterations. In these circumstances the lease will be construed as though permitting the relevant alteration subject to the landlord's prior consent, which must not unreasonably be withheld but which may be granted subject to reasonable conditions: ss.6, 15 and 16. Similar provisions apply where the tenant supplies goods or services to the public or a sector of it: ss.19(2), 21, 27. The provisions of the Act relating to premises had not been implemented as at May 31, 1996.

[22] The section applies to all covenants having the effect of preventing alterations: *F. W. Woolworth & Co. Ltd v. Lambert* [1937] Ch. 37 at 49; *Lambert v. F. W. Woolworth & Co. Ltd* [1938] Ch. 883 at 909.

[23] *F. W. Woolworth & Co. Ltd v. Lambert* [1937] Ch. 37 at 49, 50 (but *cf.* Greene L.J. at 63). *Lambert v. F. W. Woolworth & Co. Ltd* [1938] Ch. 883 at 901, 910.

[24] See [1938] Ch. 883 at 901, *per* Slesser L.J. (this will involve looking at how the premises are described in the lease). See also [1938] Ch. 883 at 896 (Greer L.J.) and [1937] Ch. 37 at 64 (Greene L.J.) (both dissenting judgments); also *Hesketh Estates Ltd v. Cohen* (1948) 151 E.G. 465.

sentimental reasons.[25] By analogy with covenants as to assignment and changes of use, it is likely that a court would not allow the landlord to refuse consent in order to obtain some collateral advantage not secured by the terms of the lease.[26] Tactically, it is better for the landlord to make his objections clear at the outset, and also, if he requires compensation for the works, to suggest a figure. The onus will then be on the tenant to show that the grounds or the sum demanded are unreasonable.[27]

11–06   Conditions of consent

Where the landlord is willing to consent to the alterations, he will wish to retain some control over how the work is done and possibly provide for reinstatement at the end of the term. Traditionally this has been done by means of a formal licence for alterations, though as leases grow more sophisticated it is increasingly common to find such provisions anticipated in the lease.

Typical conditions   Typical conditions relate to approval of plans and specifications by the landlord[28]; compliance with such plans by the tenant; an obligation on the tenant to ensure that all necessary planning and building consents are obtained; that the work is carried out without causing a nuisance or annoyance to other occupiers, expeditiously and in a good and workmanlike manner[28a]; that all damage is made good, and an indemnity against all damage or liability on the part of the landlord caused by the works. The landlord should also reserve a right to enter to view the works to ensure compliance with any conditions. Another typical condition prohibits the tenant from applying for or implementing a planning permission without landlord's consent. The tenant should ensure that in all such conditions the landlord's

---

[25] See [1938] Ch. 883 at 907, 910; also *Dowse v. Davis* (1961) 179 E.G. 335 where refusal on the ground that the consent of the superior landlord had not yet been obtained was held reasonable.

[26] See para. 10–09 above and para. 12–13 below. See also *Cryer v. Scott Brothers (Sunbury) Ltd* (1986) P. & C.R. 183 and *Barclays Bank plc v. Daejan Investments (Grove Hall) Ltd* [1995] 18 E.G. 117 (an application for consent to a change of use, in return for which the landlords required, inter alia, a break clause in their favour which could produce a financial advantage in the form of rent receivable under a proposed underletting—held to constitute a fine).

[27] Compare the result in the two Woolworth cases, n. 23 above. In the first the landlord demanded £7,000 which the tenant could not show was an unreasonable sum. In the second the landlord did not name any sum, and accordingly could not argue refusal to compensate on the part of the tenant.

[28] It may be possible to imply a term that such approval shall not be unreasonably withheld: *Cryer v. Scott Brothers (Sunbury) Ltd* (1986) P. & C.R. 183; especially where the capricious refusal of consent would render the whole procedure nugatory; *Dallman v. King* (1837) Bing. N.C. 105. See also *Clerical General and Medical Life Assurance Society v. Fanfare Properties Ltd* Ch.D., June 2, 1981 (unreported).

[28a] The landlord should also require the tenant to carry out the works in compliance with the Construction (Design and Management) Regulations 1994 (S.I. 1994 No. 3140) whenever the regulations apply to the works in question.

consent is not to be unreasonably withheld or delayed as these words will not necessarily be implied.[29]

Requirement to re-instate

Where the work proposed is such that the landlord may wish to recover possession of the premises in their original condition at the end of the lease,[30] an obligation by the tenant to re-instate the premises if the landlord so requires should be secured. If omitted it will not be implied, since the general rule is that a tenant is under no obligation to remove buildings erected by him unless erected in breach of some stipulation in the lease.[31]

11–07 Compensation for improvements

Statutory right to compensation

By section 1 of the Landlord and Tenant Act 1927, a tenant of business premises may be entitled, upon quitting at the end of the tenancy, to obtain compensation from the landlord for an improvement which at the termination of the tenancy adds to the letting value of the holding.[32] The Act provides some safeguards against abuses of this provision. In order to obtain compensation, the tenant must serve notice of his intention to make the improvement upon the landlord.[33] The landlord may within three months object to the improvement, in which case it will be for the tenant to convince the court that the improvement is such as should be certified as a "proper improvement".[34] In order to be so certified, the improvement must be of such a nature as to be calculated to add to the letting value of the holding at the termination of the tenancy, reasonable and suitable to its character, and not such as to diminish the value of any other property belonging to the

---

[29] See, *e.g. Pearl Assurance plc v. Shaw* [1985] 1 EGLR 92.

[30] *e.g.* where the work does not add to the letting value but is done to further the tenant's possibly idiosyncratic enjoyment of the premises. A good example is *Pleasurama Properties Ltd v. Leisure Investments (West End) Ltd* [1986] 1 EGLR 145 where shop premises in Oxford Street were converted into a dolphinarium.

[31] *Never-Stop Railway (Wembley) Ltd v. British Empire Exhibition (1924) Incorporated* [1926] 1 Ch. 877. In practice such an obligation is normally put in the lease at the outset.

[32] The Law Commission recommended in a Report dated March 14, 1989 entitled *Landlord and Tenant Law: Compensation for Tenants' Improvements* (Law Com. No.178) that the statutory scheme in Part I of the Landlord and Tenant Act 1927 for compensating business tenants for their improvements to the premises should be abolished. The Report concludes that the compensation procedure is not much used and summarises at para 3.5 the reasons for such disuse as being "the impact of Part II of the Landlord and Tenant Act 1954; the complexity of the 1927 Act procedure and the impracticality of retaining the necessary records; the procedure's unsuitability in the case of particular types of property; the prevalence of contractual arrangements to exclude compensation; the short life-span of some improvements; and ignorance of the statutory requirements". The Government announced in July 1994 that it proposed to implement the Law Commission's recommendations but a draft Bill had not been presented as at May 31, 1996.

[33] s.3(1), (5).

[34] s.3(1).

landlord or any superior landlord.[35] The tenant may not obtain a certificate that improvements are proper for the payment of compensation after the improvements have been completed.[36] Also, the landlord may prevent certification as a proper improvement by offering to carry out the improvement himself in consideration of a reasonable increase in rent.[37]

Avoiding obligation to compensate   It is not possible to contract out of the compensation provisions,[38] but arguably some protection can be obtained under section 2(1)(b) of the 1927 Act. This provision[39] states that a tenant is not entitled to compensation in respect of any improvement "which the tenant or his predecessors in title were under an obligation to make in pursuance of a contract entered into . . . for valuable consideration". Two elements are necessary here: a contractual obligation to carry out the improvement; and valuable consideration. As to the first, any such obligation will usually be found in the licence for alterations.[40] However, there will need to be an obligation to carry out the work, and not merely (as is usually the case) conditions as to how the work should be carried out should the tenant choose to do so.[41] The second requirement is that the obligation be supported by some valuable consideration. In practice, reliance is often placed on the granting of consent itself as the consideration. However, it has been suggested that only relaxation of an absolute covenant would constitute such consideration, and that relaxation of a qualified covenant would not. Thus in such cases the insertion of some consideration in the licence would appear prudent from the landlord's point of view, although it must of course be genuine consideration.

11–08   Improvements and rent review

It is of vital importance for the tenant that his improvements, and particularly any made pursuant to a statutory requirement (such as the installation of a sprinkler system), will have no effect on the rental value of the premises so as to lead to an increase in the rent payable on review. This question is discussed fully in the chapter dealing with rent review provisions.[42]

---

[35] s.3(1) (but see also s.48(1) of the 1954 Act). An improvement can be legitimate even if including demolition and rebuilding or if carried out to enable the building to be used for some other purpose: *National Electric Theatres Ltd v. Hudgen* [1939] 1 Ch. 553.

[36] *Hogarth Health Club v. Westbourne Investments* [1990] 2 E.G. 69.

[37] s.3(1).

[38] s.9 (which must now be read in conjunction with s.49 of the 1954 Act).

[39] As supplemented by s.48(1) of the 1954 Act.

[40] An obligation to a third party will suffice: *Owen Owen Estate Ltd v. Livett* [1956] Ch. 1. In practice a well-advised tenant would be unwilling to accept such a covenant, both for this reason and in case it prevents the effect of his works being disregarded on rent review (see also para. 6–36 above).

[41] *Godbold v. Martin the Newsagents Ltd* (1983) 268 E.G. 1202.

[42] See para. 6–36 above.

11–09 Other implications of improvements

Increase in rates and insurance

There are a number of other possible implications of improvements which should not be overlooked. The first is that improvements may lead to an increase in the rateable and insurable values of the property.[43] This will usually be of little concern to the landlord, since the tenant will be responsible for rates and insurance premiums either directly or by way of reimbursing the landlord.[44] However, in those rare cases where the landlord is responsible for these outgoings, it should be expressly stipulated that the tenant is to reimburse the landlord for any extra liability resulting from the improvements.[45]

Deemed premium

In the case of a lease for a term of 50 years or less which obliges the tenant to carry out work on the premises (other than repairs and maintenance), the amount by which the reversion is thereby enhanced in value is deemed a premium and may be taxed in the landlord's hands accordingly.[46] It seems unlikely that improvements required subsequently under a licence could be regarded as deemed premiums.[47]

Value Added Tax

There are potentially serious VAT consequences for the tenant relating to improvements carried out in certain circumstances. These are considered at Chapter 19 below.[48]

FIXTURES

11–10 Generally

As well as altering the physical structure of the premises, the tenant may wish to install plant or equipment in order to further his business. A question of prime importance is whether such items may be removed by the tenant at the end of the term. This depends on whether the item in question has become a fixture or remains a chattel, and, if a fixture, whether it is a landlord's or a tenant's fixture.

11–11 Fixture or chattel

Degree and purpose of attachment

The test for distinguishing between a fixture and chattel is well-known. First the degree of attachment to the land must be considered, and then the purpose of attachment, whether to improve or make better use of the land, or merely to

---

[43] As to the possible effect of partitioning on rateable value, see *Lewis Vintners t/a Smokey Joe v. Speight* (1984) 272 E.G. 1177.

[44] If the landlord arranges the insurance, the tenant will need to inform him of the increased insurable value.

[45] Landlord and Tenant Act 1927, s.16 is a similar provision but only applies to an improvement "executed under" the Act.

[46] Income and Corporation Taxes Act 1988, s.34(2), (3).

[47] *ibid.*, s.34(5). Such works are not "sums payable" within the sub-section; nor are they given as "consideration for the variation or waiver" of any term of the lease—see *Pleasurama Properties Ltd v. Leisure Investments (West End) Ltd* [1986] 1 EGLR 145 at 146.

[48] See para. 19–15 below.

facilitate enjoyment of the object itself.[49] It is not necessary for an object to be substantially fixed to the premises in order to become a fixture. Thus in one Canadian case[50] a fitted carpet in a hotel was held to be a fixture, though easily removable. The intention in laying it was to facilitate the better use of the hotel, and it was envisaged that it would be undisturbed so long as it served that purpose.

11–12   Landlord's or tenant's fixture

Even if an object is regarded as a fixture, it may still be removable by the tenant in certain circumstances. Such fixtures are often known as tenant's fixtures.[51] The most important category of tenant's fixtures in the context of commercial leases is that of trade fixtures, those attached by the tenant for the purpose of his trade or business, but which do not become part of the structure itself.[52] Items which do become part of the structure of the building, such as a new shop front, doors or windows, are certainly not tenant's fixtures, and are not accurately described as fixtures at all.[53] Also it is probably the case that an item affixed to replace one originally provided by the landlord may not be removed; unless possibly the tenant has preserved the original item and can re-install it.[54] In order to be regarded as a tenant's fixture, the item in question must be removable without rendering it unusable elsewhere.[55] So for example, air-conditioning plant which could be dismantled, removed and re-assembled elsewhere would be a tenant's fixture, but plasterboard

Trade fixtures

[49] See Megarry and Wade, *The Law of Real Property* (5th ed., 1984) pp. 732–734 and cases cited on those pages and *TSB Bank plc v. Botham* [1995] EGCS 3. A special provision applies to gas fittings lent or let for hire by a public gas supplier, which shall not be deemed to be landlord's fixtures, notwithstanding their degree of annexation; Gas Act 1986, Sched. 5, para. 19(1)(b). See also Electricity Act 1989, Sched. 6, para. 9 and Water Industry Act 1991, s.179(4) for provisions relating to electricity and water fittings or apparatus.

[50] *La Salle Recreations Ltd v. Canadian Camdex Investments Ltd* (1969) 4 D.L.R. (3d.) 549. Compare *Young v. Dalgety plc* [1987] 1 EGLR 116, where carpeting fixed to a screeded floor by gripper rods and pins was held to be a tenant's fixture; and *TSB Bank plc v. Botham* [1995] EGCS 3 where carpeting fixed in the same manner in a residential flat was also held to be a fixture (this case has been criticised by commentators).

[51] See Woodfall, *Landlord and Tenant*, § 1–13.141. The term "landlord's fixtures" can encompass items fixed by the landlord, and also those fixed by the tenant or a third party and which the tenant has no right to remove.

[52] *Poole's Case* (1703) 1 Salk. 368; *New Zealand Government Property Corp. v. H.M. & S. Ltd* [1982] Q.B. 1145 at 1157.

[53] *Boswell v. Crucible Steel Co.* [1925] 1 K.B. 119. But the distinction can be elusive: Lord Denning, M.R. in *New Zealand Government Property Corp. v. H.M. & S. Ltd* [1982] Q.B. 1145 described such items as landlord's fixtures. Items such as internal partitioning or a false ceiling could be regarded as falling on either side of the line.

[54] This would appear to be the reasoning behind Lord Denning's example of a new safety curtain as a landlord's fixture in *New Zealand Government Property Corp. v. H.M. & S. Ltd* [1982] Q.B. 1145. It seems improbable that such an item would be regarded as part of the structure of the building if it were introduced as a completely new item by the tenant.

[55] *Webb v. Frank Bevis Ltd* [1940] 1 All E.R. 247; *Smith v. City Petroleum Ltd* [1940] 1 All E.R. 260; *Young v. Dalgety plc* [1987] 1 EGLR 116.

partitioning which would be broken up in the course of removal would not.

The fact that an object is placed on the premises pursuant to a contractual obligation to the landlord will not necessarily make it a landlord's fixture. Where the obligation relates simply to installation of the object with no provision as to ownership or permanent attachment, the status of the object will be decided on ordinary principles.[56]

11–13   Removal of tenant's fixtures

The tenant may remove tenant's fixtures during the term or, after the term ends, during such period as he remains in possession in such circumstances that he is entitled to suppose himself still a tenant.[57] In cases where the tenancy is terminable by such short notice that there is inadequate time to remove the fixtures, a further reasonable period will be allowed for removal.[58] Where an existing lease expires or is surrendered and is followed immediately by another lease to the same tenant remaining in possession, the right to remove fixtures will not be lost, but will be exercisable during the new tenancy.[59]

The right to remove tenant's fixtures can be excluded by clear language.[60]

Making good on removal
The removal of items which the tenant is not entitled to remove will clearly constitute waste. But it appears that even where the tenant is entitled to remove a fixture, he may be liable if he fails to make good the premises to the extent of leaving them in a reasonable condition,[61] or in such a state as to be most beneficial or useful to the landlord or to those who might next take the premises.[62] Therefore, a majority of the Court of Appeal has held[63] that removal of extractor fans, which left holes in the external fabric of the premises, was actionable, either as an excess of the right of removal,[64] or as an act of voluntary waste by leaving the premises in a damaged state.[65] It appears that the obligation to make good extends only to the structure of the building and not to matters of mere decoration.[66]

---

[56] *Mowats Ltd v. Hudson Bros. Ltd* (1911) 105 L.T. 400; *Young v. Dalgety plc* [1987] 1 EGLR 116.
[57] *Weeton v. Woodcock* (1840) 7 M. & W. 14; approved in *New Zealand Government Property Corp. v. H.M. & S. Ltd* [1982] Q.B. 1145.
[58] *Smith v. City Petroleum Ltd* [1940] 1 All E.R. 260.
[59] *New Zealand Government Property Corp. v. H.M. & S. Ltd* [1982] Q.B. 1145.
[60] *Re British Red Ash Collieries Ltd* [1920] 1 Ch. 326; *cf. Lambourn v. McLellan* [1903] 2 Ch. 268.
[61] *Mancetter Developments Ltd v. Garmanson Ltd* [1986] 2 W.L.R. 871 at 877, *per* Dillon L.J.
[62] *Foley v. Addenbroke* (1844) 13 M. & W. 174 at 196, 198.
[63] *Mancetter Developments Ltd v. Garmanson Ltd* [1986] 2 W.L.R. 871.
[64] *ibid.,* at 877, *per* Dillon L.J.
[65] *ibid.,* at 882, *per* Kerr L.J.; *cf.* Sir George Waller at 880, who thought that since the wall was already holed before the equipment was removed, no damage was caused by removal.
[66] *ibid.,* at 878, *per* Dillon L.J.; *Re De Falbe* [1901] 1 Ch. 523 at 542. However, this line may be very difficult to draw in practice.

11–14 Fixtures and rent review

Tenant's fixtures

The question of whether fixtures are to be taken into account in assessing the rent on review can only be answered fully in the light of the wording of the relevant parts of the lease. However, in the case of tenant's fixtures, it is likely to be possible to make out a good case for ignoring them. If the rent is assessed by reference to the "demised premises," then it can be argued that tenant's fixtures, being inherently removable, do not form part of the premises.[67] Furthermore, if the notional lease to be valued includes an assumption as to vacant possession, this may involve making the assumption that all tenant's fixtures have been removed.[68]

Landlord's fixtures

Whether the value attributable to landlord's fixtures originally provided by the tenant is to be disregarded depends on the terms of the review clause. There is no reason why an express disregard of all items originally affixed by the tenant should not be incorporated into the clause, but if this is not the case, the tenant will have to rely on the fixture being classed as an "improvement" under the standard disregard.[69] The decision in *New Zealand Government Property Corp. v. H.M. & S. Ltd*[70] provides some support here, since all the members of the Court of Appeal regarded "improvements" within section 34 of the Landlord and Tenant Act 1954 as including improvements made by the tenant which are landlord's fixtures.[71]

11–15 Compensation for fixtures

The statutory right to compensation for improvements made to the holding and which add to the letting value of the holding[72] does not extend to "a trade or other fixture which the tenant is by law entitled to remove".[73] From this it may be inferred that compensation is available for improvements constituting irremovable fixtures.

11–16 Capital allowances

Capital expenditure on plant or machinery for the purposes of a trade can confer an entitlement to capital allowances.[74]

---

[67] *New Zealand Government Property Corp. v. H.M. & S. Ltd* [1982] Q.B. 1145; *Young v. Dalgety plc* [1987] 1 EGLR 116. See also *Ocean Accident & Guarantee Corporation v. Next plc; Commercial Union Assurance Co. plc v. Next plc* [1995] EGCS 187.
[68] See para. 6–30 above.
[69] See para. 6–36 above.
[70] [1982] Q.B. 1145
[71] *ibid.*, at 1160, 1161, 1165.
[72] Landlord and Tenant Act 1927, s.1(1); see para. 11–07 above.
[73] *ibid.*, s.1(1).
[74] Capital Allowances Act 1990, s.22. For further consideration of this topic see Newbold and Wilson, *Practical Capital Allowances* (1995).

Capital Allowances Act 1990

Where capital expenditure is incurred on plant or machinery which becomes a fixture and the person incurring the expenditure has an interest in the relevant land, the fixture is to be treated for material purposes as belonging to the person incurring the expenditure.[75]

Recent attempts to ensure, by the use of retention of title or similar clauses, that ownership of plant or machinery remained with the contractor installing it even though it was fixed to the land, have failed.[76] Once the equipment in question has become a fixture, it belongs to the owner of the land to which it is affixed and "the terms agreed . . . between the fixer of the chattel and the owner of the land cannot affect the determination of whether, in law, the chattel has become a fixture and therefore in law belongs to the owner of the soil".[77]

---

[75] *ibid.*, s.52(1). See *Melluish (HMIT) v. BMI (No. 3) Ltd* and related appeals [1995] 3 W.L.R. 630.

[76] *Melluish (HMIT) v. BMI (No. 3) Ltd* [1995] 3 W.L.R. 630; *Aircool Installations v. British Telecommunications plc*, April 26, 1995 (unreported).

[77] *Per* Lord Browne-Wilkinson at pp. 637–638 in *Melluish (HMIT) v. BMI (No. 3) Ltd.*

12 ALIENATION

12–01 Introduction

It is rare to find a commercial lease without any restraint upon the freedom of the tenant to dispose of his interest in the property. However, the stringency with which such provisions are drafted can vary, influenced for example by factors such as the length of the term or the suitability of the premises for sub-division.

The position at common law is that unless restrained by the lease the tenant has freedom of disposition. Essentially there are three variable factors which the parties should consider: the nature of the disposition restricted; whether the restriction extends only to the disposition of the whole of the premises or also to the disposition of parts; and whether the restriction absolutely prohibits disposition or allows it subject to the landlord's consent. As with restrictions on user,[1] the landlord should consider whether the protection offered by such **Effect on rent** restrictions outweighs their possible depressing effect upon the rent obtainable on review.

12–02 Construction generally

In drafting and construing such covenants it should be remembered that the various restrictions do not form watertight compartments and can overlap in effect.[2] Also the landlord's adviser should bear in mind that a court is likely to construe such provisions strictly against the landlord, on the **Forfeiture** basis that breach may give rise to forfeiture.[3] Thus clear and unambiguous language is vital.

Where a lease contains a restriction on disposition, a disposition in contravention of it is effective but as mentioned above it may render the lease liable to forfeiture.[4]

12–03 Covenant against assignment

Matters not covered by covenant The effect of such a covenant is to prohibit the tenant's parting with the whole of his term of years by way of legal assignment. Thus, of itself, it will not protect the landlord

---

[1] See para. 10–01 above.
[2] *Marks v. Warren* [1979] 1 All E.R. 29.
[3] *ibid.*; *Russell v. Beecham* [1924] 1 K.B. 525.
[4] See *Commissioners of Works v. Hull* [1922] 1 K.B. 205. In the case of an underletting in breach of covenant, the court in *Hemingway Securities Ltd v. Dunraven* [1995] 9 E.G. 322 granted to the landlord a mandatory injunction requiring the immediate surrender of the underlease which had been granted by the defaulting tenant. In the case of an unauthorised assignment, the landlord should serve his s.146 notice on, and issue his proceedings against, the assignee: *Old Grovebury Manor Farm v. Seymour Plant Sales & Hire* (No. 2) [1979] 1 W.L.R. 263.

against the tenant underletting the premises,[5] mortgaging them, or declaring a trust of them.[6] Nor will the restriction catch involuntary assignments, as on death or bankruptcy.

12–04   Covenant against underletting

Such a covenant will prevent the tenant granting an underlease, but not granting a licensee the right to occupy the premises.[7] However, since the decision of the House of Lords in *Street v. Mountford*[8] it would be a risky exercise to attempt to circumvent the covenant in this way, unless the circumstances of the arrangement are such that the licensee is clearly not entitled to exclusive possession. It is an open question whether a covenant against underletting is broken by assignment.[9]

A covenant against underletting could prevent the tenant mortgaging or charging his interest.[10] Thus where the tenant's interest could provide potential security for a loan, express **Provision for** provision should be made allowing the tenant to charge the **charging** lease, subject possibly to the landlord's consent.[11]

The usual covenant against underletting will not prevent further sub-letting by an underlessee, even where the tenant's consent is necessary to such sub-letting.[12]

12–05   Covenant against parting with possession

A covenant against parting with possession is only broken by **Scope of** an arrangement under which the tenant entirely excludes **restriction** himself from possession of the premises in favour of a newcomer who enters for his own purposes.[13] Thus the covenant will not be broken by the tenant sharing possession, occupying the premises by an agent, or granting rights to use the premises falling short of complete possession.

[5] At least in the case of a genuine underletting for part of the term: *Langford v. Selmes* (1857) 3 K. & J. 220; *Milmo v. Carreras* [1946] K.B. 306.

[6] *Gentle v. Faulkner* [1900] 2 Q.B. 267.

[7] *Edwardes v. Barrington* (1901) 85 L.T. 650.

[8] [1985] A.C. 809; see para. 16–22 below.

[9] *Marks v. Warren* [1979] 1 All E.R. 29.

[10] Law of Property Act 1925, ss.86(1), 87(1) and *Serjeant v. Nash, Field & Co.* [1903] 2 K.B. 304. This is certainly the case if the mortgage is by sub-demise. The position where the mortgage is by charge is less clear: *Re Good's Lease* [1954] 1 W.L.R. 309 at 312; *Grand Junction Co. Ltd v. Bates* [1954] 2 Q.B. 160 at 168.

[11] Such consent may not be unreasonably withheld: Law of Property Act 1925, s.86(1) (sub-demise); Landlord and Tenant Act 1927, s.19(1) (charge). Commercial leases will usually contain a complete prohibition upon the charging of part only of the demised premises.

[12] *Mackusick v. Carmichael* [1917] 2 K.B. 581 (underlessee not an "assign" within covenant). The solution is to provide that any underlease must contain a provision against underletting without the landlord's consent, and for the tenant of the headlease to covenant with the landlord to enforce that provision.

[13] *Jackson v. Simons* [1923] 1 Ch. 373; *Stening v. Abrahams* [1931] 1 Ch. 470; *Lam Kee Ying Sdn. Bhd. v. Lam Shes Tong* [1975] A.C. 247 at 256.

Assignment or underletting

It is important to note (particularly for the tenant's adviser) that assignment or underletting can constitute a breach of a covenant against parting with possession. Thus the covenant may have the effect of filling some of the gaps mentioned above in covenants against assignment and underletting.

12–06 Covenant against sharing possession

Meaning of "possession"

Such a covenant is wider than one against parting with possession.[14] In this context "sharing possession" has been construed as meaning sharing the use or occupation of the premises.[15] Such a covenant therefore imposes potentially very onerous restrictions on the use of the property by the tenant[16] and accordingly should only be accepted where the circumstances justify an unusually strict degree of control by the landlord. The tenant should in any event ensure that he and his successors are entitled to share possession of the premises with any company or companies which are members of the same group as the tenant.[17]

12–07 Alienation of whole or part

It can be a vitally important question whether a prohibition extends only to dispositions of the whole of the demised premises, or whether a disposition of part can constitute breach. Fragmentation of the occupation of various parts of the premises between different persons can be highly undesirable from the landlord's point of view: it may result in a number of different tenants having rights under Part II of the Landlord and Tenant Act 1954[18] and it can make the covenants in the lease difficult to enforce effectively.

Therefore it should be stated expressly that covenants against assignment, underletting[19] and parting with possession[20] extend to such acts in relation to any part of the premises as well as to the whole.

It is common in practice to distinguish between dispositions of part and dispositions of the whole, prohibiting the former absolutely, while allowing the latter subject to the landlord's consent.

[14] *Tulapam Properties Ltd v. De Almeida* (1981) 260 E.G. 919.
[15] *ibid.*
[16] *e.g.*, preventing the tenant from allowing a neighbouring occupier to park on the premises.
[17] This is usually accepted by landlords on condition that no relationship of landlord and tenant is created by the sharing arrangement and that the arrangement ends immediately the companies cease to be members of the same group.
[18] See para. 16–15 below.
[19] A covenant against underletting prima facie only prevents underletting of the whole: *Wilson v. Rosenthal* (1906) 22 T.L.R. 233; *Cook v. Shoesmith* [1951] 1 K.B. 752; *Chatterton v. Terrell* [1923] A.C. 578 (underletting of whole by a number of separate underleases held to be breach).
[20] Such a covenant can, it seems, be broken by underletting of a part: *Abrahams v. Macfisheries Ltd* [1925] 2 K.B. 18: but *cf. Russell v. Beecham* [1924] 1 K.B. 525.

12–08 Absolute and qualified covenants

An absolute prohibition on disposition leaves the tenant in a weak position: he can attempt to persuade or induce the landlord to relax the covenant, but lacks any legal leverage to do so.[21]

Statutory proviso as to reasonableness

Where a disposition is prohibited without the consent of the landlord, the covenant is subject to a statutory proviso that consent shall not be unreasonably withheld.[22] The proviso may not be excluded, but does not preclude the right of the landlord to require payment of reasonable legal and other expenses in connection with the grant of consent.

A similar proviso is usually expressly stated in leases,[22a] and from the tenant's standpoint is an essential requirement.

"Respectable and responsible person"

Where such a proviso is subject to the qualification that consent shall not be unreasonably withheld in the case of a "respectable and responsible person", the effect of such a qualification has been said to be either to release the tenant from the covenant where the person proposed meets those criteria or to form a covenant by the landlord not to withhold consent in such a case: either way the landlord cannot argue that he can reasonably withhold consent to a disposition to such a person.[23] In this context "person" can include a company and a company is capable for this purpose of being regarded as "respectable".[24] "Responsible" refers to the ability of the person proposed to undertake liability for the rent and other obligations contained in the lease.[25]

12–09 No fine to be payable for consent

Where a lease prohibits a disposition without licence or consent, statute provides that unless the lease contains an express provision to the contrary no fine or sum of money is payable for such licence or consent.[26] Doubt can arise as to what constitutes a "fine". It appears that a returnable deposit to secure performance of obligations is not a fine,[27] nor is the demand for a direct covenant by the assignee to pay rent and

Meaning of "fine"

[21] One exception is where the landlord's refusal is based upon racial or sexual discrimination against, or discrimination on the grounds of some disability of, the proposed assignee or underlessee: Sex Discrimination Act 1975, s.31; Race Relations Act 1976, s.24; Disability Discrimination Act 1995, s.22.

[22] Landlord and Tenant Act 1927, s.19(1)(a). Different provisions apply in relation to building leases under s.19(1)(b) but see para. 12–12, n. 46 below in relation to "new tenancies".

[22a] The Commercial Property Leases Code of Practice (see para. 1–06 above) recommends in para. 4–2 that leases should expressly include (*inter alia*) a proviso that the landlord's consent cannot be unreasonably withheld, even though it is implied by statute.

[23] *Moat v. Martin* [1950] 1 K.B. 175.

[24] *Willmott v. London Road Car Company* [1910] 2 Ch. 525.

[25] *ibid.*; see also *Re Greater London Properties Ltd's Lease* [1959] 1 W.L.R. 503.

[26] Law of Property Act 1925, s.144. As with the Landlord and Tenant Act 1927, s.19(1), the statutory proviso does not preclude the right to require a reasonable sum for legal or other expenses incurred in connection with the licence or consent.

[27] *Re Cosh's Contract* [1897] 1 Ch. 9.

observe the covenants in the lease.[28] But a demand for increased rent, even if ostensibly to compensate the landlord for damage caused by the assignment, will be a fine.[29]

12–10   Effect of unreasonable refusal of consent

Landlord and Tenant Act 1988

The Landlord and Tenant Act 1988 came into force on September 29, 1988. Before that date, in the absence of an express covenant by the landlord not to withhold consent unreasonably, unreasonable refusal to a disposition did not give rise to an action in damages.[30] The tenant had the choice of proceeding with an assignment or underletting on the basis that consent had been unreasonably withheld, or seeking a declaration from the court as to the landlord's unreasonableness. Neither option was satisfactory from the point of view of the tenant, who was unlikely to have any real ability to persuade the landlord to deal with the application speedily.[31]

Tenancies to which the Act applies

The 1988 Act applies where the terms of a tenancy (whether made before or after the 1988 Act came into force) include a covenant not to assign, underlet, charge or part with possession of the whole or any part of the premises without the consent of the landlord and the covenant is subject to the qualification that the landlord's consent is not to be unreasonably withheld.[32]

If a breach of a duty imposed by the 1988 Act occurs, the tenant may claim damages in civil proceedings in the same manner as any other claim in tort for breach of a statutory duty.[33]

Duties imposed by the Act

The duties which the 1988 Act imposes arise where a person who may consent to a disposition receives a written application by the tenant for such consent and can be summarised as follows:

---

[28] *Waite v. Jennings* [1906] 2 K.B. 11.

[29] *Jenkins v. Price* [1907] 2 Ch. 229. See also *Barclays Bank plc v. Daejan Investments (Grove Hall) Ltd* [1995] 18 E.G. 117 (para. 10–09, n. 43 above).

[30] See *Ideal Film Renting Co. v. Nielson* [1921] 1 Ch. 575. A proviso, whether express or implied, that consent to a disposition will not be unreasonably withheld does not create a covenant by the landlord that he will not unreasonably withhold such consent. The 1988 Act applies only in relation to alienation covenants so that where a landlord's consent to other matters is required, it may be appropriate for the tenant to require an express covenant from the landlord that he will not unreasonably withhold such consent.

[31] *29 Equities Limited v. Bank Leumi (U.K.) Limited* [1987] 1 All E.R. 108.

[32] Landlord and Tenant Act 1988, s.1(1). The Act applies whether the qualification is express, as the result of specific words in the lease, or implied, for example, by s.19(1) of the Landlord and Tenant Act 1927.

[33] 1988 Act, s.4.

(1) to give consent within a reasonable time, except in a case where it is reasonable not to give consent;[34]

(2) to serve on the tenant written notice of his decision within a reasonable time specifying, if the consent is subject to conditions, those conditions, or if the consent is withheld the reasons for withholding it;[35]

(3) to pass on applications within a reasonable time to others from whom it is believed consent is required.[36]

Giving consent subject to a condition which is not a reasonable condition does not satisfy the duty imposed by the 1988 Act, and for the purposes of the 1988 Act it is only reasonable to refuse consent where, if the consent was withheld, the tenant would be in breach of covenant if he completed the proposed transaction.[37]

Similar duties are imposed where application is made to a landlord (or another person whose consent is needed) seeking consent to a relevant disposition by a sub-tenant.[38]

Consent to the proposed disposition must, as mentioned above, be given within a reasonable time unless it is reasonable to refuse consent. The question then arises as to **When time** when that "reasonable time" starts to run. It was argued in **starts to run** *Dong Bang Minerva (U.K.) Ltd v. Davina Ltd*[39] that the reasonable time for considering the tenant's application did not start to run until an undertaking for the landlord's costs had been given. Whilst the court did not actually decide that point it did indicate that if a request for an undertaking as to costs could prevent the "reasonable time" starting to run against the landlord until the requisite undertaking was received, it could only do so where the sum for which the undertaking had been requested was reasonable. Landlords would be well advised, at least until the matter is considered further by the courts, not to delay their consideration of a tenant's application for licence until a satisfactory costs undertaking is received.[40]

It will be for the person who owes the duty under the 1988 Act to demonstrate that he has satisfied it. The 1988 Act **Burden of proof** therefore reverses the burden of proof at common law, where the burden was generally upon the tenant to show that his landlord was acting unreasonably.[41]

---

[34] The courts considered what is a reasonable time in *Midland Bank v. Chart Enterprises* [1990] 2 EGLR 59 and *Dong Bang Minerva (U.K.) Ltd v. Davina Ltd* [1995] 5 E.G. 162.

[35] 1988 Act, s.1(3). See, *e.g. Kened Ltd v. Connie Investments Ltd* [1995] EGCS 87 (where it was held that if a landlord failed to provide a written reason for withholding his consent, doubt was cast on the weight to be attributed to that reason).

[36] 1988 Act, s.3.

[37] 1988 Act, s.1(4) and (5).

[38] 1988 Act, s.3.

[39] [1995] 5 E.G. 162.

[40] As to construction of undertakings for costs in these circumstances see *Goldman v. Abbott* [1989] 48 E.G. 151.

[41] The landlord need not however justify as "facts" the matters upon which he was relying provided that a reasonable person in his position could have reached the same conclusion: *Air India v. Balabel* [1993] 30 E.G. 90.

12–11   Timing of reasons for refusal

It seems that the relevant date for determining whether or not the landlord's refusal of consent is reasonable is the date at which consent is refused.[42]

Where the tenant takes proceedings challenging the landlord's refusal the landlord may rely on reasons other than those originally given to the tenant. However, it must be **Considerations** shown that at the relevant time such considerations were **in the mind of** present in the mind of the landlord and grounded his refusal. **the landlord** In *C.I.N. Properties v. Gill*[43] the court refused the landlord's application to have admitted in evidence, to support his contention that consent to an assignment had been reasonably withheld, accounts for an assignee company relating to a period after consent had been refused, as well as details of an order for the winding up of the assignee company which had also been made after that date.

12–12   Incorporating conditions for assignment into the lease

It has been held that a landlord cannot curtail the effect of section 19(1)(a) of the Landlord and Tenant Act 1927 by stipulating the circumstances in which reasons for refusing consent will be deemed reasonable or by stipulating that in specified circumstances he may withhold his consent.[44]

"New tenancies" However, in relation to new tenancies under the Landlord and Tenant (Covenants) Act 1995,[45] section 19(1) of the Landlord and Tenant Act 1927 has been amended by the 1995 Act in relation to assignments but not other dispositions.[46]

The amendment[46a] permits landlords and tenants to agree[47] upon the circumstances in which the landlord may withhold consent to an assignment or any conditions subject to which

---

[42] *C.I.N. Properties Ltd v. Gill* [1993] 37 E.G. 152.
[43] *ibid.*
[44] *Re Smith's Lease* [1951] 1 All E.R. 346; *Creery v. Summersell and Flowerdew & Co. Ltd* [1949] Ch. 751.
[45] See para. 2–02 above for the meaning of "new tenancy".
[46] New sections 19(1A) to 19(1E) have been inserted by s.22 of the Landlord and Tenant (Covenants) Act 1995. The new sections also apply in relation to building leases which are "new tenancies".
[46a] The amendment of s.19(1) was the result of a negotiated deal between the British Property Federation and the British Retail Consortium, as part of the discussions leading to the abolition of the doctrine of privity of contract. Landlords were concerned that unless they were permitted greater control over the identity of assignees, they would be at risk of the value of their investments being devalued when a blue-chip tenant was replaced by a tenant with a lesser covenant.
[47] The agreement may be contained in the lease or elsewhere and may be made at any time before the application for landlord's licence is made: Landlord and Tenant Act 1927, s.19(1B).

consent may be granted.[47a] If a landlord refuses to allow an assignment in those circumstances or will consent only subject to those conditions, he will not be regarded as acting unreasonably.[48]

Some circumstances or conditions will be objectively verifiable[49] but where the landlord has a discretion to consider whether a particular state of affairs exists, the tenant is afforded the protection of a requirement that the circumstances or the conditions cannot be framed by reference to any matter that falls to be determined by the landlord or a third party unless the power to make that determination has to be exercised reasonably or the tenant has an unrestricted right to have any such determination conclusively reviewed by an independent third party.[50]

12–13 Criteria for judging reasonableness of refusal

A considerable body of case law has built up as to the factors which can justify refusal of consent to assignment or underletting, which will continue to be relevant in relation to both old tenancies and new tenancies[51,52] (subject to any express requirements in relation to assignment as outlined in para. 12–12 above), where there is an express or implied proviso that the landlord's consent to a disposition will not be unreasonably withheld or delayed. The authoritative summary of the principles to be applied remains that of Balcombe L.J. (with whose judgment Fox and Mustill L.JJ. agreed) in *International Drilling Fluids Ltd v. Louisville Investments (Uxbridge) Ltd:*[53]

[47a] Landlords had intended to impose stringent conditions upon the identity and quality of potential assignees, but became concerned that this would be considered as onerous on rent review, and started to moderate their demands. A working party set up by the Association of British Insurers has produced a set of model conditions which are reproduced in [1996] 7 E.G. 54; however it is too soon to be able to say whether the model conditions have found favour either with landlords or with tenants. However two consistent themes are now emerging: (1) all landlords will be requiring an AGA (explained in para. 2–06 above) from an outgoing tenant as a matter of course; and (2) whichever conditions for assignment are being included in leases, there will invariably be a "sweeping-up" provision, enabling the landlord to withhold consent in any case where it is reasonable to do so, even where the conditions are satisfied.

[48] Section 1 of the Landlord and Tenant Act 1988 is to have effect subject to those amendments. Strictly the use of careful drafting would have permitted pre-conditions to operate prior to the Landlord and Tenant (Covenants) Act 1995 coming into force and may still be effective in relation to covenants governing underletting, which are not affected by the 1995 Act: see *Bocardo S.A. v. S & M Hotels Ltd* [1980] 1 W.L.R. 17.

[49] *e.g.* specific financial tests such as a requirement that the assignee must have pre-tax profits in excess of three times the current annual rent under the lease. See also n. 62 below.

[50] Landlord and Tenant Act 1927, s.19(1C).

[51,52] See para. 2–02 above for the meaning of "new tenancy".

[53] [1986] Ch. 513 at 519–521.

Landlord protection

(1) the purpose of a qualified covenant against assignment is to protect the landlord from having his premises used or occupied in an undesirable way, or by an undesirable tenant or assignee;

"Uncovenanted advantage"

(2) therefore, a landlord is not entitled to refuse consent on grounds which have nothing whatever to do with the relationship of landlord and tenant in regard to the subject-matter of the lease.[54] Put slightly differently, this means that the landlord may not object on grounds extraneous to the intention of the parties when the covenant was granted and accepted, so as to gain some "uncovenanted advantage"[55];

Standard of proof

(3) it is not necessary for the landlord to prove that the conclusions which led him to refuse consent were justified, if they were conclusions which might be reached by a reasonable man in the circumstances[56];

Use by assignee

(4) it may be reasonable to refuse consent on the ground of the purpose for which the proposed assignee intends to use the premises, even if that purpose is not expressly forbidden by the lease[57];

Disproportionate harm to tenant

(5) while a landlord need usually consider only his own relevant interests in deciding whether to refuse consent, there may be cases where a refusal of consent will cause disproportionate harm to the tenant compared with the resulting benefit to the landlord. In such cases refusal may be unreasonable[58];

Question of fact

(6) subject to these propositions, the reasonableness or otherwise of refusal is in each case a question of fact, dependent upon all the circumstances.

The propositions above were set out by Balcombe L.J. in relation to covenants against assignment. However, there seems no reason why they should not be equally applicable to a covenant against underletting or parting with possession. The crucial question will be to consider the object and purpose of the covenant. Thus it may be reasonable to refuse consent to a sub-letting of part which would have the effect of creating a Rent Act protected tenancy and so prejudice the landlord's ability to recover possession, or change the nature of the premises from commercial to mixed use.[59] On the other **Underletting** hand, where the lease itself recognises the possibility of underletting part, it would be difficult to base a refusal of

[54] *Houlder Bros. & Co. Ltd v. Gibbs* [1925] Ch. 575.

[55] *Bromley Park Gardens Estates Ltd v. Moss* [1982] 1 W.L.R. 1019. This would seem to preclude the landlord relying on general reasons of estate management unless those reasons can be related to the original policy of the covenant: *cf. dicta* in *Viscount Tredegar v. Harwood* [1929] A.C. 72 at 81 and *Rayburn v. Wolf* (1985) 50 P. & C.R. 463 at 466. It is submitted that a reason aimed at preventing harm to the landlord's interests is more likely to be reasonable than one made with the object of improving the landlord's position.

[56] *Pimms v. Tallow Chandlers Co.* [1964] 2 Q.B. 547 at 564.

[57] See further para. 12–14 below. And see *Warren v. Marketing Exchange for Africa Ltd* [1988] 2 EGLR 247.

[58] This proposition was formulated in an attempt to reconcile divergent streams of authority.

[59] See *West Layton Ltd v. Ford* [1979] Q.B. 593.

consent simply on the ground that such an underletting would make the premises more difficult to manage from the landlord's point of view.[60] The most satisfactory safeguard if the landlord is concerned about such difficulties is to prohibit absolutely the underletting of part.

12–14   Common reasons for refusal of consent

It may be useful to refer to some of the more usual grounds employed by landlords in refusing consent to dispositions.

Status of assignee

A frequent reason for refusal is the status of the proposed assignee. Objections may be made on the basis of the reputation, lack of business experience,[61] or financial standing[62] of the proposed assignee. A landlord may refuse consent on the ground that insufficient information has been given to assess these matters,[63] or that the information given is unsatisfactory.[64] With certain types of premises, such as hotels, where the profitability of the business may affect the rent obtainable on review, the landlord may be justified in demanding to see a proposed assignee's previous trading accounts.[65]

Lack of information

Status of assignee compared with tenant

A slightly different question is whether the landlord can object on the basis that the proposed assignee is satisfactory, but not so attractive a tenant as the existing one: if so, a lease to a very substantial tenant, such as a government department or international corporation, could be regarded as assignable only to a body of similar status. It would appear that such a reason will only be acceptable where the assignment is likely to result in real damage to the landlord's interests—the apprehension of a diminution in the paper value of the reversion with no practical adverse consequences for the landlord will not be sufficient, particularly if substantial

---

[60] See *Rayburn v. Wolf* (1985) 50 P. & C.R. 463.

[61] *Re Tydeman's Lease* (1961) 177 E.G. 259; *Air India v. Balabel* [1993] 30 E.G. 90.

[62] See *British Bakeries (Midlands) Ltd v. Michael Testler & Co. Ltd* [1986] 1 EGLR 64. A commonly used rule of thumb, not challenged in that case, is that the accounts of the assignee should show a pre-tax profit of not less than three times the rent payable under the lease. It has also been said (albeit in 1959, when a more relaxed attitude to such matters prevailed) that the matter is to be approached from a practical and realistic standpoint, and not with regard to "a point which might be taken by a pedantic chartered accountant": *Re Greater London Properties Ltd's Lease* [1959] 1 W.L.R. 503 at 507, *per* Danckwerts J.

[63] *Isow's Restaurants Ltd v. Greenhaven (Piccadilly) Properties Ltd* (1969) 213 E.G. 505.

[64] *Rossi v. Hestdrive Ltd* [1985] 1 EGLR 50 (where the information furnished led to reasonable doubts as to how the assignee might conduct the business). References relating to the past performance of a proposed assignee do not necessarily indicate that he can safely undertake increased responsibilities: *British Bakeries (Midlands) Ltd v. Michael Testler & Co. Ltd* [1986] 1 EGLR 64; *Ponderosa International Development Inc. v. Pengap Securities (Bristol) Ltd* [1986] 1 EGLR 66. The prudent tenant should provide all the information he thinks the landlord will need to reach his decision as soon as possible in order to avoid doubt as to when the "written application" has been made for the purposes of the Landlord and Tenant Act 1988.

[65] *City Hotels Group Ltd v. Total Property Investments Ltd* [1985] 1 EGLR 253.

detriment would accrue to the tenant from refusal of consent.[66] However, the situation may be different where the assignment would have practical consequences for the landlord (for instance where the landlord needs to sell the reversion in the near future) and the harm to the tenant can be minimised by the tenant underletting rather than assigning.[67] Such an objection may also be relevant in the case of a turnover rent linked to the trading achievements of the tenant.[68]

No duty to tenant

Where a lease requires the landlord's consent to assignment, there is no implied term that the landlord owes the original tenant a duty to take reasonable care in approving an assignee to ensure that the assignee is of sufficient financial strength to be able to pay the rent and perform the tenant's covenants under the lease.[69]

Requirement of direct covenants

In some cases a landlord may seek to make it a condition of consent to assignment that the assignee enters into direct covenants with the landlord to pay the rent and perform and observe the covenants in the lease.[70] There is some authority, albeit *obiter*, to suggest that such a requirement is reasonable in the case of an assignment.[71] However, it is submitted that the landlord who makes such a demand is seeking an uncovenanted advantage collateral to the real purpose of the assignment clause. What the landlord is seeking is in effect two continuing guarantors of the tenant's obligations, the original tenant and the proposed assignee, rather than simply the original tenant. This may give the landlord additional security, but has little to do with the qualifications of the proposed assignee.[72] If the proposed assignee does not appear to be of sufficient substance to undertake the obligations of the lease, a direct covenant from him will not alter this fact. If he is of sufficient substance, the demand for a direct covenant appears to go beyond what the landlord is legitimately entitled

[66] *International Drilling Fluids Ltd v. Louisville Investments (Uxbridge) Ltd* [1986] Ch. 513 at 521. See also the reasoning of Deputy Judge E. Nugee, Q.C. at first instance: [1985] 2 EGLR 74 at 79.

[67] *Ponderosa International Development Inc. v. Pengap Securities (Bristol) Ltd* [1986] 1 EGLR 66, where the argument that the landlord would still have the benefit of the original tenant's personal covenant was discounted on the basis that the market would place less reliance on it than would a lawyer. One issue which arises out of the changes to the rules as to privity of contract is the extent to which the court will now have regard to the loss of the covenant of the outgoing tenant on the assignment of a "new tenancy". Logically, if the existence of his covenant in the past was discounted (as in *Ponderosa*, above), then the loss of the covenant should make little difference (particularly where the former tenant has in fact entered into an authorised guarantee agreement in relation to the liability of the assignee).

[68] See *Angus Restaurants Ltd v. Day*, August 19, 1982, Falconer J. (unreported) but noted by E. Nugee Q.C. in the judgment at [1985] 2 EGLR 74 at 79. See also para. 6–39 above.

[69] *Norwich Union Life Insurance Society Ltd v. Low Profile Fashions Ltd* (1991) 64 P. & C.R. 187.

[70] The requirement may be inappropriate for "new tenancies" as defined in the Landlord and Tenant (Covenants) Act 1995.

[71] *Balfour v. Kensington Gardens Mansions Ltd* (1932) 49 T.L.R. 29.

[72] Although in *Venetian Glass Gallery Ltd v. Next Properties Ltd* [1989] 30 E.G. 92 the availability of a guarantor and the original tenant's continuing liability was taken into account by the court.

to demand. In practice, landlords continue to demand direct covenants and assignees continue to provide them as being the line of least resistance.

The position may be different where the lease expressly provides for a direct covenant being given by the assignee. It has been held, in the context of a building lease, that the proviso to a covenant by the tenant not to assign or part with possession without the landlord's consent which required that upon any assignment the tenant was to obtain an acceptable guarantor for the assignee and a direct covenant with the landlord was not struck down by section 19(1)(b) of the Landlord and Tenant Act 1927.[73]

Status of underlessee
Objections relating to the identity and status of a proposed underlessee need to be considered rather differently. Unlike an assignee, the underlessee will enter into no direct relationship with the landlord, and it has been held unreasonable to demand that he do so by direct covenant as a condition of consent.[74] It could therefore be argued that provided the proposed underlessee does not appear likely to use or abuse the premises in such a way as to harm the landlord's interests, his ability to pay the rent reserved by the headlease is of no relevance. However, such an argument could be dangerously over-simplistic. If the tenant does not receive adequate income from the underlessee to pay the landlord the rent due under the headlease, the landlord could be severely prejudiced. Furthermore, the operation of Part II of the Landlord and Tenant Act 1954 or the Law of Property Act 1925 could ultimately have the effect of bringing the landlord and underlessee into a direct relationship.[75] Finally, the grant of an underlease at a high premium and low rent could seriously depreciate the value of the landlord's interest.[76] Thus the landlord should in granting consent to a proposed underlease have regard to the terms proposed, to the ability of the underlessee to comply with those terms, and should also consider whether ultimately he would be happy to see the underlessee as a direct tenant.[76a]

It is becoming increasingly common to require a covenant

[73] *Vaux Group plc v. Lilley* [1991] 4 E.G. 136 (where it was held that the requirements of the proviso, *e.g.* obtaining a guarantor for the assignee's obligations, were not conditions precedent to the assignment being effected—Knox J. was not as a result prepared to nullify the bargain which the parties had struck on the basis of s.19(1)(b)).

[74] *Balfour v. Kensington Gardens Mansions Ltd* (1932) 49 T.L.R. 29. But a direct covenant may be justified in exceptional circumstances, *e.g.* if the landlord occupies premises in the same building and is concerned as to how the demised premises will be used: *Re Spark's Lease* [1905] 1 Ch. 456.

[75] *e.g.* if the landlord is the competent landlord in relation to the underlessee and the underlessee applies for a new tenancy; or if the landlord forfeits the headlease and the underlessee applies for relief under the Law of Property Act 1925, s.146(4).

[76] This could justify refusal of consent: *Re Town Investments Ltd's Underlease* [1954] Ch. 301; see also *Kaye v. Shop Investments Ltd* (1966) 198 E.G. 1091, where the refusal of consent to underletting unless the total rents amounted to three times the ground rent under the lease was held reasonable.

[76a] Note also the effect of the Law of Distress (Amendment) Act 1908 which, in certain circumstances, permits a superior landlord to look to an undertenant for rent due under the headlease.

Requirement of underlease at full value

by the original tenant not to underlet save at full rack rental value. Such a provision carries dangers for both parties. It could be construed as preventing the landlord objecting to a full value underletting even if reasonable grounds for objection exist;[77] therefore it should be expressly stated that the requirement of full value is additional to that of consent and not in substitution for it. The covenant could also cause a great deal of difficulty for the tenant, either because he is unable to find an underlessee willing to take the premises at a rack rent, or because a dispute arises with the landlord over what is the rack rental value. Even more problematic for the tenant in a falling market is a clause which requires that the underlease rent will be no less than the rent passing under the headlease (or the relevant proportion of it). Where market rents have fallen since the last rent review under the headlease it may be impossible to agree an underletting at a rent which satisfies this requirement.[78]

Proposed use

Another very frequent type of objection relates to the use to which the proposed assignee or underlessee intends to put the premises. The validity of such objections may in some cases turn on the provisions in the lease relating to user, but such provisions will not always be conclusive.[78a] Where the disposition itself will necessarily constitute breach of the user provisions of the lease it seems that consent may be reasonably refused on that basis. An example is where the lease contains a positive covenant to use the premises only for the particular purposes of the named tenant.[79] Similarly, where the terms of a proposed underlease would oblige the underlessee to use the premises in a manner inconsistent with restrictions in the headlease, the landlord may legitimately object.[80] However, objection may be unreasonable where a proposed assignee could use the premises in a lawful manner, but the landlord apprehends that a breach of user provisions is likely: here it can be said that the landlord will still be entitled to enforce the user provisions to prevent any such use.[81] Such an argument may not always be conclusive,

---

[77] See *Moat v. Martin* [1950] 1 K.B. 175.

[78] Various schemes have been suggested to enable an underlease to be granted in these circumstances: these generally involve an underlease being granted at the full passing rent coupled with an agreement by the tenant to repay to the undertenant a part of the rent each quarter so that the net rent paid equates to what the undertenant was originally willing to pay. There is a severe risk that this sort of arrangement will constitute a sham (see para. 16–22, n. 19 below) and for that reason it is not recommended.

[78a] In a recent case (not yet reported, but mentioned in *Property Week*, April 25, 1996, p. 6), the Crown Estate Commissioners were held to have acted reasonably in withholding consent to a proposed assignment by their tenant Signet plc on the basis that the assignee's proposed use of the premises would conflict with their estate management policy, even though that policy was not expressly stated in the lease.

[79] *Granada T.V. Network Ltd v. Great Universal Stores Ltd* (1963) 187 E.G. 391. See also *Falgor Commercial S.A. v. Alsabahia S.A.* [1986] 1 EGLR 41.

[80] *The Packaging Centre Ltd v. The Poland Street Estate Ltd* (1961) 178 E.G. 189.

[81] *Killick v. Second Covent Garden Property Co. Ltd* [1973] 1 W.L.R. 658; *British Bakeries (Midlands) Ltd v. Michael Testler & Co. Ltd* [1986] 1 EGLR 64. Query if the same would be true of a proposed underlease, where the landlord's rights of enforcement are more tenuous.

however. In one first-instance decision,[82] the tenant of a large store in a shopping centre ceased trading in breach of a covenant to keep the store open, and refused to say whether the proposed assignee intended to resume trading. The landlord's refusal of consent was held reasonable: he had good grounds for apprehending that the breach would continue, to the detriment of other properties in the centre. Also he had not been told the true nature of the transaction to which he was asked to assent.[83]

Uses not forbidden by lease
A landlord can refuse consent on grounds of the proposed use, even though that use is not forbidden by the lease.[84] For example, the lease might forbid the premises being used as a fried-fish shop, but this does not imply that the landlord could have no reasonable objection to proposed use as a nightclub. However, where the user clause in the lease is so restrictively drawn as to permit use for one specified purpose only, it is not reasonable to refuse consent on grounds of user where the proposed use is the only one permitted by the lease, at least where the result will be that the property is left vacant and the landlord is fully secured for payment of the rent.[85] It has been held reasonable to object to a proposed

Competing use
assignment on the basis that the proposed use would be a business competing with that of the landlord,[86] or that of neighbouring tenants.[87] However, it is submitted that these decisions must be read as subject to the proposition that refusal cannot be based on grounds extrinsic to the relationship of landlord and tenant or the original purpose of the relevant provisions.[88] If the tenant can show that the original purpose of the relevant provisions did not include protection against competition, then logically the landlord's refusal on such a ground should be unreasonable.

Subsisting breaches
A final reason for refusing consent to assignment or underletting is that there are subsisting breaches of covenant on the part of the tenant. Where the breaches of covenant are serious a landlord may be justified in refusing consent until they are rectified,[89] though it could be argued that in the case of a continuing breach the landlord will still have a remedy after assignment against the assignee.[90] Objection on the basis

---

[82] *F.W. Woolworth plc v. Charlwood Alliance Properties Ltd* (1986) 282 E.G. 585.
[83] See *Fuller's Theatre and Vaudeville Company Ltd v. Rofe* [1923] A.C. 435, P.C., at 440.
[84] *International Drilling Fluids Ltd v. Louisville Investments (Uxbridge) Ltd* [1986] Ch. 513.
[85] *ibid.*
[86] *Whiteminster Estates Ltd v. Hodges Menswear* (1974) 232 E.G. 715.
[87] *Premier Confectionery (London) Co. Ltd v. London Commercial Sale Rooms Ltd* [1933] Ch. 904; *Coopers & Lybrand v. William Schwarz Construction Co.* (1980) 116 D.L.R. (3d.) 450.
[88] See n. 55 above. See also *Anglia Building Society v. Sheffield City Council* (1982) 266 E.G. 311. But *cf.* the decision relating to the Crown Estate Commissioner's property mentioned in n. 78a above.
[89] *Goldstein v. Sanders* [1915] 1 Ch. 549.
[90] Difficulties of enforcement will be greater in the case of an underletting, which may justify a stricter approach. It certainly would seem prudent and unobjectionable to require a tenant to discharge any arrears of rent and service charge before assignment, since such sums could not be recovered from the assignee.

of trivial or minor breaches is likely to be regarded as "sour grapes" and unreasonable.[91]

Tenant's option to determine
Where the lease contains a tenant's option to determine which may be exercised only by the original tenant, the landlord will not be acting unreasonably if he refuses to permit an assignee to reassign to the original tenant who intends to operate the break clause.[92]

12–15 Offer-to-surrender clauses

A provision which is occasionally encountered in connection with restrictions on assignment is the so-called "offer-to-surrender" or "offer-back" clause. Such clauses commonly provide that if the tenant wishes to assign he must first make an irrevocable offer to the landlord to surrender the lease and will only be entitled to assign if the landlord does not accept that offer. A timetable for acceptance of the offer will usually be incorporated, and the clause may provide either that the surrender is to be for no consideration, or (more commonly) for a consideration equal to the premium which the tenant could obtain in the open market.[93]

Purpose of such provisions
The main objective behind such provisions is to allow the landlord extra control, free from considerations of reasonableness, over who is to be his tenant.[94] Surrender-back clauses are however very unattractive from a tenant's point of view since they can seriously affect the marketability of the lease, particularly where the tenant has found a prospective assignee who may lose interest whilst the landlord decides whether or not to accept the tenant's offer to surrender.

Another serious problem is how such clauses are affected by statute. It has been held by the Court of Appeal[95] that such provisions are not invalidated by section 19 of the Landlord and Tenant Act 1927, discussed above. However, in the case of a lease protected by Part II of the Landlord and Tenant Act **Agreement to surrender void** 1954, it has been held that the agreement to surrender formed when the tenant's offer is accepted is void under section 38(1) of that Act, since it has the effect of precluding the tenant from applying for a new lease.[96] The effect of the

---

[91] *Cosh v. Fraser* (1964) 189 E.G. 421 (minor alterations in breach of covenant); *Beale v. Worth* [1993] EGCS 135 (dispute over repairs).

[92] *Olympia & York Canary Wharf Ltd v. Oil Property Investments Ltd* [1994] 2 E.G. 121. The rent payable under the lease was well in excess of the market rent likely to be obtained on a reletting of the premises. The parties proceeded on an agreed assumption that the original tenant was still entitled to break the lease, which must be doubtful now in the light of the Court of Appeal's decision in *Max Factor Ltd v. Wesleyan Assurance Society* (see para. 16–06 below).

[93] The open market value of the lease will usually be determined either by agreement between the parties or, in the absence of agreement, by a third party, acting as expert or arbitrator. Alternatively the tenant might be required to produce evidence of an actual offer made by a prospective assignee.

[94] See [1985] L.S. Gaz. 1704, June 12 (S. Tromans).

[95] *Bocardo S.A. v. S & M Hotels Ltd* [1980] 1 W.L.R. 17.

[96] *Allnatt London Properties Ltd v. Newton* [1984] 1 All E.R. 423. The decision can be criticised as having ignored the more relevant s.24(1) of the 1954 Act.

two decisions is to produce a potentially unproductive stalemate: the tenant may not assign without making the offer to surrender; if he does the lease may well be subject to forfeiture; if an offer to surrender is made and accepted the landlord cannot enforce it, but depending upon the wording of the provision,[97] the tenant may still not be free to assign.[98]

Possible solution

One, as yet untested, answer to this conundrum may lie in the power of the court to authorise an agreement for the surrender of the tenancy on the joint application of the landlord and tenant.[99] However, any provision obliging the tenant to concur in making such an application could itself arguably be void under section 38(1), so the usefulness of this approach remains in doubt.[1]

In view of these problems, the use of surrender-back provisions is not recommended: the tenant will be little better off than under an absolute prohibition on assignment,[2] with the added disadvantage for both parties of a complex and uncertain legal position.

---

[97] The clause may state merely that the tenant is obliged to make an offer; on the other hand it may state that the tenant can only assign if the offer is not accepted. Clearly in this case the tenant should ensure that the landlord is deemed to have rejected the offer if he fails to accept it within a prescribed period.

[98] These propositions are derived from the first instance judgment of Megarry V.-C. in *Allnatt London Properties Ltd v. Newton* [1981] 2 All E.R. 290, which covers the issues more fully than that of the Court of Appeal.

[99] Landlord and Tenant Act 1954, s.38(4)(b). See (1985) 273 E.G. 151 at 455, 568.

[1] See (1985) 273 E.G. 351 at 567, 927, and [1986] L.S. Gaz. 1704 (S. Tromans).

[2] Since the landlord will not be obliged to accept the tenant's offer to surrender, such clauses offer no guarantee that the tenant can escape from an onerous lease.

13 INSURANCE, REINSTATEMENT AND SUSPENSION OF RENT

13–01 Introduction

Every well-drawn lease must make provision for damage to the property by fire or other catastrophe. The terms of the lease should be such as to ensure that the premises are adequately insured, and should also provide for what is to be done if damage does occur.

INSURANCE

13–02 Matters to be covered

A covenant to insure is likely to deal with the following matters:

(1) what is to be insured;
(2) who is to insure;
(3) with which insurer;
(4) in whose name;
(5) against what risks;
(6) for what sum.

It may well be inadvisable to specify the answers to some of these questions too precisely over a 20 or 25 year term, and the clause should aim to strike a balance between providing sufficient guidance and protection for the parties, whilst preserving the element of discretion necessary to adapt the cover to changing circumstances.

13–03 What is to be insured

It is of fundamental importance that the obligation to insure relates to all the premises which the tenant has covenanted to repair; in addition it should extend to all other premises of which the demised premises are an integral part, whether structurally, operationally or economically.[1] Any tenant's fixtures, although removable at any time by the tenant[2] are,

---

[1] *e.g.* in the case of a shopping centre the tenant would wish the insurance and the landlord's obligation to reinstate any damage to extend to the entire centre.
[2] See para. 11–12 above.

until removed, vested in the landlord, and should therefore be included in the property to be insured.[3]

Insurance for loss of rent

The lease should also provide for the insurance against loss of rent in the event of the premises becoming unusable or incapable of being accessed. It is important for the landlord to ensure that the period for which cover is being obtained is the same as the period during which the tenant's obligation to pay rent is suspended following an insured event.[4]

Plate glass insurance

Leases of shops (and frequently—but incorrectly—leases of other types of buildings) often contain a tenant's covenant to insure the plate glass in the premises (which constitutes the shop windows, and perhaps the doors). This is a misunderstanding on the part of lawyers: in nearly every instance plate glass will actually be included within the items which are covered by the landlord's insurance policy, making this covenant inappropriate.[5]

13–04 Who is to insure

Factors determining who insures

The frequently-used term "F.R.I. lease" (full repairing and insuring) assumes that it is the tenant who will insure. However, the general practice is for the landlord to covenant to insure and to recover his expenditure from the tenant by way of insurance rent or as an item under the service charge provisions. Premiums recoverable by the landlord are frequently expressed to be payable as rent so as to confer upon the landlord all the remedies available in the case of rent arrears.[6] Alternatively they may be recovered under service charge provisions[7], though it may be preferable to separate insurance premiums from other service charge expenditure so as to enable the landlord to recoup his expenditure immediately.

Landlord to insure

The decision as to which party is to insure will often be dictated by the nature of the building. Clearly a building occupied by a number of different tenants with shared parts and facilities is best insured as a whole by the landlord. Insurance by the tenant will be a more practicable proposition with a building in single occupation,[8] but even there the landlord may prefer to insure himself rather than relying on the tenant to do so.[9] In the remainder of this Chapter, for

---

[3] If the insurance is effected by the landlord, he will require details of the value of the tenant's fixtures, or their reinstatement cost (see para. 11–09, n. 44 above).

[4] See para. 13–17 below.

[5] In any event, many tenants are given letters from their landlords waiving the obligation to insure plate glass, and it is likely that in most other cases no cover is ever taken out in spite of the obligation in the lease. Where tenants do have such cover, there is probably double insurance, as explained at para. 13–04 below.

[6] See para. 6–04 above.

[7] See Chap. 8.

[8] *e.g.* where the landlord receives only a nominal rent, or where a particular type of tenant (*e.g.* a supermarket operator) is in a position to obtain cover at an advantageous rate.

[9] The landlord need then not worry that the tenant might let the policy lapse, or that the tenant's insurers might repudiate liability on the basis of non-disclosure or misrepresentation by the tenant (see para. 13–10 below).

convenience, the text assumes that the insurance is to be obtained by the landlord (unless the converse is expressly stated), but the comments in this Chapter will apply in whichever party's name the cover is taken.

Importance of keeping to bargain

Whatever the eventual decision, the parties should be careful to adhere to it. In *Argy Trading Development Co. Ltd v. Lapid Developments Ltd*[10] the tenant covenanted to insure warehouse premises. After discussion, the landlord insured the premises under a block insurance policy covering other buildings. The tenant did not take out any insurance. Unfortunately, the landlord was taken over by another company, which decided not to renew the block policy and failed to inform the tenant of this decision. The premises were gutted by fire while uninsured. The tenant's claims against the landlord, based on breach of contract, estoppel and negligence, all failed.

Double insurance

On the other hand, insurance by both parties can sometimes lead to difficulties. Where the landlord covenants to insure, a covenant is often inserted into the lease prohibiting the tenant from taking out any further insurance cover. The draftsman's fear is that, if the tenant does insure, the landlord may not receive a full indemnity under its insurance policy. In the case of genuine double insurance (as this is termed), the concern of the insured will be that part of the proceeds may be paid to another party, who may not be able to make it available for reinstatement of the property because either or both of the policies contains a rateable contribution clause,[11] or a provision stating that the insurer is not liable for any loss covered by any other policy.[12] However, merely because two parties effect insurance over the same property does not of itself create double insurance. For there to be double insurance, the insurances must be in respect of the same interest in the property: where the landlord and the tenant have each insured their own interest, no question of double insurance can arise.[13]

Proof of insurance

The party not insuring will wish to be able to satisfy himself from time to time that the premises are insured. This can be achieved by insuring the premises in joint names,[14] or by the party not insuring having its interest noted on the policy. It is normal for the party insuring to covenant to produce the policy and the last premium receipt on demand, subject often to a proviso that production may not be required more than once a year, or upon a disposition of the lease or reversion. However, the landlord may not always wish the tenant to have the right to see the whole policy (perhaps because the policy may cover other premises and include details such as the amount of rent insured), in which case the obligation may be

---

[10] [1977] 1 W.L.R. 444.

[11] Although it has been held that he may be compelled to account for it to the person with the reinstatement obligation: *Reynard v. Arnold* (1875) L.R. 10 Ch. 386.

[12] As in *Portavon Cinema Co Ltd v. Price* [1939] 4 All E.R. 601; note however that where both policies contain such wording the clauses have been held to cancel one another out: *National Employers Mutual General Insurance Association Ltd v. Haydon* [1980] 2 Lloyd's Rep. 149.

[13] *Portavon Cinema Co Ltd v. Price* [1939] 4 All E.R. 601.

[14] See para. 13–07 below.

merely to produce evidence that the premises are insured in accordance with the terms of the lease, by way of extracts from the policy or by other means. From the tenant's point of view this is unsatisfactory. The landlord should preferably be required to produce a copy of the insurance policy, and to advise the tenant from time to time of any material proposed change in the ambit, quantum or terms of the cover.

13–05 With which insurer

Whoever is to insure, both parties will be concerned that the cover is obtained on suitable terms from an insurer of adequate standing and substance. Apart from this, their aims may well diverge. The landlord may wish to use a particular insurer who covers other property owned by the landlord, and thereby obtain a discount or commission. The tenant, as the party ultimately paying the premium, is likely to be concerned to obtain the cheapest adequate cover. Where the tenant is to

Tenant insuring insure, the landlord will often require the insurance to be taken out with a named company, or one nominated by the landlord from time to time.[15] Such a clause deprives the tenant of the power to "shop around", and an amendment should be sought allowing insurance with any company approved in writing by the landlord, such approval not to be unreasonably withheld. The provision that approval may not be unreasonably withheld must be inserted, as otherwise no term as to reasonableness will be implied.[16]

Where the landlord is to insure, the only restriction usually
Landlord inserted is that he insure with a "reputable" office.[17] The
insuring tenant should be aware that in such a case the landlord will be under no implied obligation to minimise the tenant's burden by seeking the cheapest insurance.[18] It is difficult to suggest any way of dealing with this problem fully. Clearly it is not always wise to change insurers every year for the sake of a few pounds, but on the other hand it is not obvious why the tenant should pay a higher premium than necessary in order that the landlord can insure with a company which will pay him a higher commission. The prudent tenant should seek to provide that the insurance is effected at reasonable rates of

---

[15] In such a case, changing insurers without the landlord's agreement will be a breach of covenant: *John Lyons Charity v. Haysport Properties Ltd* [1995] EGCS 171.

[16] *Viscount Tredegar v. Harwood* [1929] A.C. 72.

[17] There appears to be no ready definition of "reputable," though similar expressions have been considered in the context of assignment provisions: see *Willmott v. London Road Car Co. Ltd* [1910] 2 Ch. 525; *Re Greater London Properties Ltd's Lease* [1959] 1 W.L.R. 503. A more precise formula might be "a publicly-quoted insurance company or with Lloyd's underwriters."

[18] *Bandar Property Holdings Ltd v. J.S. Darwen (Successors) Ltd* [1968] 2 All E.R. 305; *Havenridge v. Boston Dyers* [1994] 49 E.G. 111 (premiums were "properly paid" even if they were higher than the tenant could have obtained).

Landlord to account for commission

premium, having regard to rates available from time to time in the London insurance market, and perhaps that the landlord should account to the tenant, or share with the tenant, any commission received from the insurer.[19]

13–06 Subrogation

Rights against third parties

The doctrine of subrogation places the insurer in the position of the insured. Therefore if the insurer makes a payment for loss suffered by the insured, it becomes entitled to all the rights and remedies of the insured which relate to the subject matter of the insurance policy, as against third parties.[20] In the case of *Mark Rowlands Ltd v. Berni Inns Ltd*,[21] the Court of Appeal considered the doctrine of subrogation in the context of negligence by the tenant which had caused the damage. The relevant lease contained the common provision that the landlord should insure and reinstate the premises in case of damage; the premium was reimbursed by the tenant. The court held that it must have been the intention of the parties that the insurance should enure for the benefit of the tenant as well as the landlord, and that the landlord should be indemnified against damage by the policy, and would have no claim against the tenant for such damage, even if caused by negligence.[21a] Consequently the insurer had no right of subrogation against the tenant.[22]

13–07 Insurance in joint names

Joint names impracticable

Both parties should consider at the drafting stage of the lease whether insurance in joint names is desirable, since if the lease provides that insurance is to be in the name of only one party the addition of the name of the other party may constitute a breach of covenant.[23] In some cases insurance in joint names will be impracticable: *e.g.* where the landlord insures under a single policy a large building occupied by many tenants. Here the tenant should consider requesting that a note of his interest be endorsed on the policy, and that a written waiver of subrogation rights be obtained from the

---

[19] In reality, many commercial leases contain a provision entitling the landlord to retain such discount or commission.

[20] For further details of the doctrine of subrogation, see M. A. Clarke, *The Law of Insurance Contracts* (2nd ed., 1994), Chapter 31.

[21] [1986] Q.B. 211.

[21a] See also *Lambert v. Keymood Ltd* [1996] N.P.C. 58 (where the tenant's conduct in lighting a bonfire too close to the building was held to be reckless: in this case there was no common intention that the landlord's insurance should benefit the tenant).

[22] The position might be different if the damage was deliberately caused by the tenant.

[23] *Penniall v. Harborne* (1848) 11 Q.B. 368.

insurer.[24] In this way some, though not all, of the benefits of insurance in joint names can be obtained.

13–08 Against what risks

List of insured risks

Even in modern commercial leases, the insurance provisions rarely reflect contemporary insurance practice in their definitions of "insured risks". Many leases still look fondly back to the Victorian era by referring to insured risks as being fire and "such other risks as the landlord in his absolute discretion deems appropriate". Other leases are even worse, defining insured risks as being "such of the following risks as the landlord shall from time to time insure against". Neither formulation accords with the wording of typical modern insurance policies. In practical terms, however, it is clear that leases are likely to continue to contain provisions of this kind, and from the point of view of the tenant it is advisable for the list of risks against which insurance is to be obtained to be as wide as possible. There are two main reasons for this. First, it is customary for the tenant's repairing covenant not to apply to damage by insured risks,[25] and secondly the tenant's liability to pay rent will customarily only be suspended where there has been damage by insured risks.[26] As it is usually the tenant who ultimately pays the insurance premium, the landlord is unlikely to object to a tenant's request to widen as much as possible the list of risks against which the landlord is to insure.

Exclusions, limitations and excesses

Nevertheless, the party who covenants to insure would be prudent to provide that the covenant is subject to such cover being available and to any excesses, limitations and exclusions imposed by the insurance company. The tenant will wish to ensure that there are as few exclusions and limitations as possible, and a fair compromise would be a reference to such exclusions and limitations as are standard in the London insurance market from time to time.

Damage caused by terrorism

Since January 1, 1993, special arrangements have applied for damage caused by acts of terrorism,[27] following the refusal of international reinsurers to cover this risk.[28] The new arrangements provide for additional premiums to be payable for cover against acts of terrorism, which are paid via the

[24] Typical wording might be "In the event of a claim arising under this policy, the Insurer agrees to waive any right, remedy or relief to which it might become subrogated against the Insured's tenants of the insured premises unless the loss has been occasioned by or contributed to by fraudulent or criminal or malicious acts of such tenants".

[25] See para. 9–17 above.

[26] See para. 13–17 below.

[27] Defined by the Association of British Insurers as activities directed towards the overthrowing or influencing of any government *de jure* or *de facto* by force or violence.

[28] This followed the IRA bombing of the Baltic Exchange in April 1992, but before the explosions in Bishopsgate in April 1993 and in Docklands in February 1996. Co-incidentally this last explosion took place on the weekend during which this Chapter was being updated for the second edition of this book, and one of the buildings most severely damaged housed the offices of the publishers of this book.

insurance company to a mutual insurance company Pool Reinsurance Company.[29] The first £100,000 of each loss is to be borne by the insurer; the second layer is covered by Pool Re; if that company's funds become exhausted, the insurers will make a further contribution of 10 per cent of the premiums which have been passed to Pool Re, and the Government will bear any additional loss.[30]

13–09 The sum insured

Bases of insurance

Given the speed at which construction costs and property values can change, it would clearly be inadvisable to stipulate the sum to be insured over a period of 20 or 25 years, as was sometimes the case in the past. At the simplest level, damage to real property can be insured on one of three bases: (1) the market value of the property; (2) the cost of providing an equivalent modern replacement building; (3) reinstatement of the original building.[31] While the maximum amount of cover stated in the policy will provide a ceiling to the sum recoverable, ultimately the insurer will only be bound to pay a sum reflecting the actual loss of the insured, which may largely depend upon the way in which the insured intends to deal with the property. Thus if no real intention to reinstate exists, only market value may be recoverable.[32] Therefore if the parties to the lease intend that the premises should be reinstated in the event of destruction the lease should clearly state that insurance is to be effected on that basis. A formula which is frequently used, and which has the advantage of

"Full reinstatement value"

prior judicial interpretation, is "full reinstatement value". This has been held to mean the cost of reinstatement at the time when the work actually takes place,[33] which may be a considerable time after the insurance is effected. It is therefore essential that the parties make a realistic estimate of the time which reinstatement (including the obtaining of any necessary planning or other consents) is likely to take.

Reinstatement or replacement

Depending on the type of the building demised, the parties may prefer to see it replaced with an equivalent modern building rather than exactly reinstated in the event of it being destroyed.[34] If that is the case, then insurance to full reinstatement value is likely to represent a waste of money. To avoid this, the insurance covenant and the provisions in the lease as to reinstatement obligations should be drafted so as to reflect the true intention of the parties.

---

[29] Known colloquially as "Pool Re".

[30] The authority for the Government to act as insurer of last resort derives from the Reinsurance (Acts of Terrorism) Act 1993. See "Insurance against terrorism" (W. Gloyn) *Gazette*, June 9, 1993 p. 20; "Terrorism and leases" (S. Fogel and S. Pinkerton) [1993] 7 E.G. 74; "Latest changes in ratings" (A. McFarlane) [1993] 27 E.G. 113; "Picking up the pieces" [1996] 7 E.G. 41.

[31] Set out by Forbes J. in *Reynolds v. Phoenix Assurance Co. Ltd* [1978] 2 Lloyd's Rep. 440 at 446.

[32] *Leppard v. Excess Insurance Co. Ltd* [1979] 1 W.L.R. 512.

[33] *Gleniffer Finance Corpn. Ltd v. Bamar Wood & Products Ltd* [1978] 2 Lloyd's Rep. 49.

[34] See para. 13–14 below.

Whatever the basis of insurance chosen, the cover should include ancillary costs such as site clearance and shoring-up, the professional fees incurred in obtaining planning permission and rebuilding, any VAT payable, and costs such as planning application fees. In view of *Pleasurama Ltd v. Sun Alliance and London Insurance Ltd*,[35] it might be prudent to provide for insurance on the basis that such sums shall be recoverable if expended whether rebuilding eventually takes place or not. Accordingly, the lease should provide that those items are to be included in the insurance.

13–10 Invalidation of the insurance policy

Mere negligence on the part of the insured, or any other person, will not invalidate an insurance policy;[36] indeed, the deliberate act of any person (other than the insured) will not have this effect. However the lease should provide for the

Tenant's activity possibility of the insurance policy becoming invalidated. The lease may allow for this possibility in a number of ways:

(1) a proviso that the landlord's obligation to insure and keep the premises insured ceases to the extent that the policy is invalidated by the act or default of the tenant;
(2) a proviso that the landlord is not bound to rectify damage caused by an insured risk where the policy is so invalidated;
(3) a proviso that the tenant's covenant to repair (usually excluded in relation to damage by insured risks) applies to damage where the policy is so invalidated;
(4) a covenant by the tenant to pay to the landlord any sums rendered irrecoverable by the invalidation of the policy;
(5) a proviso that rent shall not be suspended where the policy is invalidated.

From the tenant's point of view four comments may be made upon provisions of this kind. The first is that non-

Policy voidable disclosure and misrepresentation do not make a policy void, but give the insurer the right to avoid it. Therefore, such provisions should be worded so as to operate only where the election to avoid the policy is made. Secondly, the landlord will often attempt to extend such provisions to cases where

Sub-tenant the policy is avoided by reason of the act or default of a sub-tenant. This is in accordance with the general expectation of landlords that a tenant will take responsibility for the acts of his sub-tenant; but it could undoubtedly operate harshly against the tenant.[37] Thirdly, the tenant should remember that

Fault of landlord a policy may also be rendered voidable by the fault of the

[35] [1979] 1 Lloyd's Rep. 389.
[36] *Shaw v. Robberds* (1837) 6 Ad. & El. 75.
[37] The tenant must ensure that equivalent provisions appear in the underlease.

Copy of policy

Disclosure of relevant matters

Misrepresentation

Use of premises

Non-invalidation clause

landlord, *e.g.* where the landlord makes a misrepresentation or fails to disclose a material fact. Finally, in order to ensure compliance with the terms of the policy, the tenant will need to see a copy, which should be requested as soon as possible: a summary is insufficient.[38]

It is possible for a policy to be vitiated by matters not connected with the tenant's use of the premises, for example failure to disclose a criminal conviction.[39]

Representations are statements made during negotiations, prior to the acceptance of an offer. There is no special principle of insurance law which requires answers in proposal forms to be read as importing promises as to future conduct,[40] but an incomplete answer may be capable of amounting to a misrepresentation.[41] In the normal position where a landlord insures, the tenant will not be completing a proposal form and will not be making any reprsentations: however, the landlord should ensure that any information obtained from the tenant required for the completion of the form is obtained in writing, in case there should be any later dispute.

Often the landlord will take the added precaution of a covenant by the tenant not to use the premises in such a way as to jeopardise the insurance policy[42] or cause the premium to be increased.[43] Such a covenant can be enforced by injunction.[44]

It is in the interests of both landlord and tenant that the insurance policy contain a non-invalidation clause which will, typically, provide that the insurance will not be invalidated by any act or omission or by any alteration unknown to or beyond the control of the insured, whereby the risk of damage or destruction is increased, so long as the insured informs the insurer immediately he is aware of it, and pays any reasonable additional premium which the insurer requires.

---

[38] See para. 13–04 above.

[39] *Woolcott v. Sun Alliance and London Insurance Ltd* [1978] 1 W.L.R. 493. Insurance contracts are contracts of utmost good faith, and non-disclosure of any material facts known, or which ought to have been known, by the insured enables the insurer to avoid the contract.

[40] See, *e.g. Hussain v. Brown, Times L.R.*, December 15, 1995 (no continuing warranty that a burglar alarm would remain operational); *Hair v. Prudential Assurance Co Ltd* [1983] 2 Lloyd's Rep. 667 (no continuing warranty that premises would remain occupied).

[41] See, *e.g. Western Assurance Co v. Harrison* (1903) 33 S.C.R. 473 (insured failed to mention two out of three previous fires).

[42] A typical fire policy permits the insurer to avoid liability if the risk of damage is increased. This was held to be the case in *Farnham v. Royal Insurance Co. Ltd* [1976] 2 Lloyd's Rep. 437, where a barn was used for the repairing of metal containers requiring the use of arc-welding equipment; however, in *Exchange Theatre Ltd v. Iron Trades Mutual Insurance Company Ltd* [1984] 1 Lloyd's Rep. 149 a policy was not avoided merely because a petrol generator and petrol were taken into a bingo hall.

[43] A tenant would be well-advised not to accept this provision, and instead agree to pay any increased premium, to maintain flexibility in his use of the premises.

[44] *Chapman v. Mason* (1910) 103 L.T. 390, where the tenant was restrained from keeping highly inflammable materials on the premises.

REINSTATEMENT

13–11 Generally

It is important to ensure that insurance moneys intended for reinstatement are applied accordingly. Apart from one statutory exception,[45] the insurer's liability is to pay money to the insured.[46] Protection may be obtained by the insurance being carried out in joint names,[47] or by relying on a finding that the insurance had been effected for the joint benefit of both parties.[48] However, the best protection for the non-insuring party is an express covenant to apply the insurance moneys[49] to the reinstatement of any damage to the premises.[50] The matters which the covenant may deal with are set out below.[50a]

13–12 Time of reinstatement

Receipt of monies

Neither party will wish to come under an obligation to spend money until the insurance monies have been received, and it is usual for the obligation to be worded so as to bite only upon receipt of such monies. It is likely to be a condition of the insurance policy that the insurer be notified immediately. Provisions requiring the landlord to make a claim on the policy are rarely seen in leases, but in any event it has been held (at least where the tenant has paid the insurance premiums) that there is an implied obligation on the landlord to make such a claim.[51]

Specified period for reinstatement

Where it is the tenant who covenants to reinstate, the landlord may be tempted to require the work to be completed within a specified period. Both parties should be wary of such a provision. It is easy for the work to take longer than expected through the fault of no-one, and failure to complete on the due date would be a once-and-for-all breach, easily

---

[45] Section 83 of the Fire Prevention (Metropolis) Act 1774, which has been held to apply to the whole of England and Wales, enables in the case of damage by fire a non-insuring party with an interest in the property to require the insurer to apply the insurance moneys to reinstatement, rather than paying them over to the insured, so long as notice is given to the insurer within the prescribed period, and before the claim is paid out. The Act does not apply to policies with Lloyd's (which is not an insurance office).

[46] *Rayner v. Preston* (1881) 18 C.L.D. 1.

[47] See para. 13–07 above.

[48] As in *Mumford Hotels Ltd v. Wheler* [1964] 1 Ch. 117.

[49] Excluding moneys in respect of loss of rent (see para. 13–03 above).

[50] The obligation should ideally apply in relation to any damage by an insured risk, not just where the premises are as a result of the damage incapable of use and occupation: see *Vural Ltd v. Security Archives Ltd* (1989) 60 P. & C.R. 258. Ideally the obligation on the insuring party should be as extensive as in any agreement whereby one party agrees to carry out works for another (*e.g.* as to the quality of workmanship, the requirement to obtain collateral warranties (see para. 9–14 above) etc.), but in practice it is conventional for the covenant to state simply that the party will reinstate the relevant building as speedily as is reasonably possible.

[50a] See paras. 13–12 to 13–16 below.

[51] *Vural Ltd v. Security Archives Ltd* (1989) 60 P. & C.R. 258.

waived by the landlord. It has been held that where no date is expressed, an obligation to reinstate within a reasonable time will be implied and that failure to comply is a once-and-for-all breach.[52] An alternative solution may be to require the tenant to commence the work within a specified period and thereafter to proceed with all reasonable speed.[53]

Requirement to reinstate expeditiously

Where the landlord is to reinstate, the tenant should ensure that there is some obligation to carry out the work expeditiously; uncertainty as to the time when the premises will be ready for occupation is likely to have more serious consequences for the tenant than for the landlord, since the tenant will need to find alternative premises while the damage is being made good (normally the period of rent cesser).

"Forthwith"

In *S. Turner (Cabinet Works) Ltd v. Young*[54] the landlord covenanted to lay out on reinstatement insurance monies received "forthwith". Pearce J. held that this meant that reinstatement must take place within a reasonable time in all the circumstances, bearing in mind that a reasonable landlord should be aware of the fact that the tenant is likely to be suffering more than he is. He went on to say that though the duty only arose on receipt of the monies, the reasonable time allowed was to be judged on the basis that the landlord would have known of the problem for some time before that, and therefore should have been prepared to act expeditiously.

13–13   Shortfall in insurance monies

Express obligation to make up shortfall

Should the insurance monies prove insufficient[55] for the work required, the question will arise as to whether either party should be liable to make up the shortfall. A covenant merely to lay out monies received would not create such an obligation, which should therefore be expressly stated. The fairest solution is probably for the party who insures to make up the shortfall, since it will probably have arisen as a result of under-insurance on his part.

13–14   Standard of reinstatement

Careful thought should be given at the drafting stage to the standard of reinstatement required. Exact replacement may be very costly and unnecessary, especially in the case of an old

---

[52] *Farimani v. Gates* (1984) 271 E.G. 887.
[53] See *Precedents for the Conveyancer*, para. 5–88A.
[54] (1955) 165 E.G. 632.
[55] Most policies will contain an "average" clause, providing that if, at the time the loss occurs, the value of the subject matter of the insurance exceeds the sum insured, the insured is his own insurer for the difference. Thus, in the case of a total loss, the insurer will pay no more than the sum insured, and in the case of a partial loss, the insurer will pay only such proportion of the loss as the sum insured bears to the value of the subject matter of the insurance.

Equivalent or exact replacement

building.[56] The landlord who covenants to reinstate may wish to see his obligation limited to the provision of accommodation which is equally commodious and convenient and reasonably equivalent to the demised premises, though not necessarily identical. In practice leases do not seem to contain such provisions as often as one would expect.

13–15 Where reinstatement is impossible

In a few cases, restoration of the premises may prove impossible, perhaps because planning permission cannot be obtained. Though in theory a lease can be terminated by the doctrine of frustration, such cases are likely to occur only very rarely.[57] Accordingly, it may be in the best interests of both parties to insert a reciprocal right to terminate the lease after the end of the rent cesser.

Division of insurance moneys

Whether the lease is terminated or not, the question of which party is entitled to the insurance money may arise. In *Re King*[58] the majority of the Court of Appeal held that despite insurance having been effected in joint names the monies belonged to the tenant, who had paid the premiums. Lord Denning M.R. dissented, holding that the monies belonged to both parties proportionately to their respective interests. In *Beacon Carpets Ltd v. Kirby*[59] reconstruction of the premises was possible, but the parties agreed that it should not take place and that the lease should be surrendered. Inexplicably, they failed to agree how the insurance monies should be apportioned. The Court of Appeal held that both parties had an interest in the monies, which the parties appeared to be treating as standing in place of the building: the tenant by virtue of his liability to repair and pay the premiums, the landlord by virtue of his obligation to reinstate. Their respective interests were to be calculated by valuing the freehold with vacant possession and the leasehold immediately prior to the fire and apportioning the insurance fund rateably according to the respective values of the interests. An express provision could provide a greater degree of sophistication and avoid the difficulty of attempting to infer the parties' intentions from the terms of the lease and their subsequent actions, *e.g.* specifying whether the tenant's statutory rights of renewal are to be taken into account;

Need for express provision

---

[56] See *Camden Theatre Ltd v. London Scottish Properties Ltd* (unreported, 1984; K. Lewison, *Drafting Business Leases*, (5th ed., 1996), p. 156) where Nicholls J. held that the repainting with gold paint of mouldings originally covered with gold leaf was a breach of covenant; also *Vural Ltd v. Security Archives Ltd* (1989) 60 P. & C.R. 258, in which a landlord was required to replace a factory floor with wood block flooring rather than cheaper linoleum, as the tenant's business of garment making required this.

[57] *National Carriers Ltd v. Panalpina (Northern) Ltd* [1981] A.C. 675; *Biddor Building Co. Ltd v. Tricia Guild Associates Ltd*, Q.B.D., January 25, 1985 (unreported). The position where the premises consist of upper storeys and are totally destroyed remains obscure: see *Izon v. Gorton* (1839) 5 Bing. (N.C.) 501, and Megarry and Wade, *The Law of Real Property* (5th ed., 1984) p. 692.

[58] [1963] 1 Ch. 459.

[59] [1985] Q.B. 755.

specifying the date at which the interests should be valued; adjustments to cover sums expended in preparation for rebuilding and any shortfall in the insurance monies; and the provision of arbitration machinery. It must be admitted, however, that such provisions are rarely encountered in practice at present.

13–16 Where the landlord does not wish to reinstate

Right to terminate lease

Destruction of the premises may provide the landlord with a useful opportunity for redevelopment; alternatively reinstatement may simply be uneconomic. To cover such eventualities, the landlord may wish to reserve a right to terminate the lease. Alternatively, the landlord may reserve the right to elect not to reinstate the premises, the tenant then having the right to surrender the lease.[60]

In the unlikely event of the tenant being willing to accept such a provision, he should at least attempt to obtain a fair proportion of the insurance monies, perhaps by providing that he is to obtain the full market value of his leasehold interest. This is more akin to a surrender than to an apportionment approach, reflecting that destruction of the premises is in a sense merely fortuitous. It should be made clear whether the tenant's interest is to be valued as immediately before the damage, or afterwards; the tenant should, of course, argue strongly for the former approach. On the other hand, the tenant could argue that the situation is analogous to the landlord successfully opposing a new tenancy on ground (f) under section 30(1) of the Landlord and Tenant Act 1954,[61] and that he should receive equivalent compensation to that provided for by section 37 of that Act.[62]

SUSPENSION OF RENT

13–17 Proviso for suspension of rent

No implied cesser of rent

At common law, the tenant's obligation to pay rent continues even though the premises may have become unusable. As mentioned above,[63] cases where the tenant will be able to argue successfully that he is released from his obligation to pay rent by frustration of the lease will be rare. Nor will the tenant be excused from the obligation to pay rent by other clauses in the lease, for example those excusing the tenant from repairing premises damaged by fire,[64] or giving the landlord the right to insure against loss of rent (unless,

---

[60] See *Precedents for the Conveyancer*, § 5–58.
[61] See para. 16–40 below.
[62] See para. 16–50 below. The 1954 Act may of course continue to apply to the lease, if the tenant's cessation of occupation is only temporary: see para. 16–16 below.
[63] See para. 13–15 above.
[64] *Hare v. Groves* (1796) 3 Anst. 687; *Belfour v. Weston* (1786) 1 T.R. 310.

possibly, the landlord has exercised his right to do so at the tenant's expense).[65]

Express proviso

For these reasons, the tenant will require some provision suspending the rent, or some proportion of it, where the premises become totally or partially unfit for occupation or the means of access is unusable. Provisos for suspension of rent tend in practice to be drafted in a very standardised way. They invariably and reasonably provide that the rent is not to be suspended where the tenant has caused the insurance policy to be vitiated.[66] They usually provide for arbitration as to the proportion of rent to be abated where the premises are not totally destroyed by some formula such as "a fair proportion having regard to the nature and extent of the damage". They almost always restrict suspension to cases of damage by insured risks. Usually it is only rent which is suspended, though the tenant might argue that the proviso should be extended to cover service charges in addition, *e.g.* where the tenant's part of the building is destroyed but other parts remain in operation.

13–18 Length of period of suspension

Loss of rent insurance

The length of the suspension will be crucial to the tenant. The usual provision is for suspension until the premises are again fit for occupation, or for a period corresponding to that covered by loss of rent insurance (often five years in a modern office building, or three years for retail premises), whichever is the shorter. The risk to be faced by the tenant is that rent may become payable again before the premises are fit for use, with potentially ruinous consequences. Provisions are frequently seen enabling the tenant to terminate the lease if the premises are not capable of occupation after the expiry of the period for which the landlord is obliged to insure against loss of rent, although from the point of view of the landlord they have the serious disadvantage that they may lose their tenants after a substantial proportion of the reinstatement may already have been completed.

---

[65] *Cleveland Shoe Co. Ltd v. Murrays Book Sales (King's Cross) Ltd* (1973) 227 E.G. 987.
[66] See para. 13–10 above.

14 PROVISIONS AS TO FORFEITURE

14–01 Generally

The ability to forfeit a lease provides the landlord with his most powerful sanction for breaches of covenant by the tenant. However, the remedy will only be available where the lease is drafted appropriately. This means that the tenant's obligations must be expressed as conditions, or, more commonly, the lease must contain a suitably-worded forfeiture clause.

14–02 Conditions

It is possible by suitable wording to make the continuance of a lease conditional upon the due performance by the tenant of his obligations.[1] In such a case, the effect of a breach is to make the lease voidable at the option of the landlord.[2] In practice, however, such wording is rarely used and a commercial lease will instead almost invariably contain a forfeiture clause.

14–03 Forfeiture clauses

Form of proviso for re-entry
A forfeiture clause in a lease will usually take the form of a proviso by which the landlord reserves to himself a power of re-entry upon certain stated events, upon which the term granted by the lease will determine.

It is important to note that if the lease merely reserves to the landlord a right to forfeit, rather than a right to re-enter, the landlord may be limited to a right to commence proceedings for possession. This is clearly of limited value to the landlord and should be avoided by clear drafting in the forfeiture clause.

Breach of covenant
It is also important for the landlord to ensure that the wording of the clause is adequate to cover breaches of both positive and negative obligations. It appears that the expression "non-performance" can apply to things done in breach of negative covenants as well as things left undone in

---

[1] *e.g.*, if the lease is granted "upon condition that" or "provided that" the covenants are performed.
[2] *Doe d. Henniker v. Watt* (1828) 8 B. & C. 308.

breach of positive covenants,[3] but to avoid any doubt it may be sensible to use a less ambiguous expression such as "breach" or "non-observance".

Forfeiture on insolvency

The right of re-entry will also frequently be expressed to be exercisable upon the tenant becoming bankrupt or having an administration order made (or even upon presentation of a petition for the order), being wound up or having a receiver appointed, making any composition arrangement with creditors, or upon any goods on the premises being taken in execution. The landlord's wish to be able to forfeit the lease in the event of the tenant becoming insolvent is understandable, but the tenant should be conscious of the possible difficulties of such provisions. First, the proviso should be modified so as not to apply on the liquidation of a solvent tenant company for the purpose of amalgamation or reconstruction. Secondly, the right of the landlord to determine the lease upon the tenant becoming insolvent could seriously prejudice any mortgagee of the tenant's interest, thereby reducing the possibility of the tenant using the lease as security for a loan. This is particularly important where the tenant is paying the landlord a premium for the lease and has raised the premium by way of a loan. A mortgagee has a measure of statutory protection against forfeiture. The Law of

Protection for mortgagee

Property Act 1925, s.146(4) allows the mortgagee to apply for relief on his own account, and section 146(10) effectively gives a period of grace of 12 months to find an acceptable purchaser of the term.[4] However, the use of section 146(4) presents many problems,[5] section 146(10) does not cover all the circumstances in which a right of forfeiture for insolvency might be expressed to be exercisable,[6] and both routes involve potentially costly court applications. Therefore, where the mortgageability of the lease is important to the tenant, the tenant's solicitor could attempt to negotiate some express provision based on section 146(10) and offering any prospective mortgagee some assurance of security. Thirdly, the proviso for re-entry may sometimes be extended not only to the insolvency of the tenant but also the insolvency of any surety. Here the tenant's solicitor should seek to avoid any such extension but at the very least should propose a further provision allowing the tenant to provide a substitute surety acceptable to the landlord (the landlord's consent not to be unreasonably withheld) and thereby avoid forfeiture.

Rent arrears

The proviso for re-entry should also cover arrears of rent. In particular, the landlord should provide that re-entry can be made when the rent is a specified number of days in arrear,[7] whether formally demanded or not. This avoids the exceedingly technical common law requirements as to a

---

[3] *Harman v. Ainslie* [1904] 1 K.B. 698, contrary to suggestions in a number of earlier cases.

[4] See *Harry Lay Ltd v. Fox* (1963) 186 E.G. 15.

[5] See para. 14–06 below.

[6] *e.g.*, appointment of a receiver, making a composition agreement, or the taking in execution of goods.

[7] Often 14 days.

proper formal demand before the landlord can proceed to forfeiture.

14–04   Exercising the right of forfeiture

Where the circumstances entitling the landlord to forfeit the lease have arisen, the landlord must elect either to exercise this right or to treat the lease as continuing. Once there has been some unequivocal act, making clear to the tenant the landlord's forfeiting of the lease, the landlord is no longer entitled to treat the lease as continuing if the tenant decides not to challenge the landlord's action[8] or to apply for relief from the forfeiture.[9]

The landlord may exercise his right of re-entry and forfeiture either by physically re-entering the premises or by commencing proceedings for possession.

Peaceable re-entry

The first method should be exercised with caution: although forfeiting a lease of non-residential premises in this way is not of itself an offence, threats or actual violence used in order to do so may be.[10] The re-entry must be such as to establish unequivocally the landlord's intention to determine the lease. Entry merely in order to make vacant premises secure will not be sufficient,[11] nor will an arrangement with a sub-tenant for payment of rent direct to the landlord[12] nor will the landlord retaining the keys to the premises for a short period.[13] The previously held view that forfeiture by re-entry would bar any claim by the tenant for relief, thus giving the landlord a tactical advantage, is no longer correct, and the tenant may apply for relief under section 146(2) of the Law of Property Act 1925.[14]

Possession proceedings

The second method of effecting forfeiture is by the issue and service of a writ claiming possession.[15] Since the landlord's intention to forfeit must be communicated to the tenant, it is the service of the writ, and not merely its issue, which effects the forfeiture. However, unless the tenant accepts the forfeiture,[16] until judgment for possession is given

---

[8] *G.S. Fashions Ltd v. B. & Q. plc* [1995] 9 E.G. 324; *Royal Borough of Kingston-upon-Thames v. Marlow* [1996] 17 E.G. 187. But see *Hynes v. Twinsectra Ltd* [1995] 35 E.G. 136 in which the Court of Appeal held that where forfeiture proceedings were dismissed, here by consent, the lease was restored to its full existence, as if no such proceedings had been brought.

[9] See para. 14–06 below.

[10] Criminal Law Act 1977, s.6.

[11] *Relvok Properties Ltd v. Dixon* (1972) 25 P. & C.R. 1.

[12] *Ashton v. Sobelman* [1987] 1 W.L.R. 177. Compare the position where a new lease is granted direct to the sub-tenant or to a stranger: *London and County (A. & D.) Ltd v. Wilfred Sportsman Ltd* [1971] Ch. 764; *Redleaf Investments Ltd v. Talbot* [1995] BCC 1091. Also a s.146 notice must be served before re-entering: see para. 14–06 below.

[13] *Proudreed v. Microgen Holdings* [1996] 12 E.G. 127 (taking of the keys by the landlord during negotiations with the insolvent tenant's sureties for the grant to them of a lease of the premises was not in itself evidence of a surrender since there was no other indication that the landlord intended to take possession of the premises).

[14] *Billson v. Residential Apartments Ltd* [1992] 2 W.L.R. 15.

[15] *Canas Property Co. Ltd v. K.L. Television Services Ltd* [1970] 2 Q.B. 433.

[16] *G.S. Fashions Ltd v. B. & Q. plc* [1995] 9 E.G. 324; *Royal Borough of Kingston-upon-Thames v. Marlow* [1996] 17 E.G. 187.

and there is no outstanding application for relief, it cannot be said that the lease is determined beyond hope of revival. During the intervening "twilight period" the position of the parties under the lease is unfortunately far from clear.[17] Where the breach by the tenant consists of some positive and continuing action, *e.g.* breach of a user covenant, the landlord may be tempted to combine possession proceedings with an application for an injunction to restrain the unlawful conduct. Such a course needs to be pursued with extreme caution, because the inclusion of the alternative claim could result in the possession proceedings not being a sufficiently clear election to determine the lease.[18]

14–05 Waiver

What constitutes waiver

The right to forfeit a lease may be lost by the landlord waiving the relevant breach of covenant. Waiver will occur where the landlord, with knowledge of the circumstances constituting the relevant breach,[19] does some unequivocal act recognising the continued existence of the lease.[20] Perhaps the most common act constituting waiver is the acceptance of rent payable in respect of the period after the cause of forfeiture.[21] A demand for rent has been regarded as having

---

[17] *Peninsular Maritime Ltd v. Padseal Ltd* (1981) 259 E.G. 860; *Meadows v. Clerical Medical and General Life Assurance Society* [1981] Ch. 70; *Associated Deliveries Ltd v. Harrison* (1984) 50 P. & C.R. 91; *Liverpool Properties Ltd v. Oldbridge Investments Ltd* [1985] 2 EGLR 111; *Hynes v. Twinsectra Ltd* [1995] 35 E.G. 136.

[18] *Calabar Properties Ltd v. Seagull Autos Ltd* [1969] 1 Ch. 451.

[19] Knowledge by the landlord's agent can also suffice: *Metropolitan Properties Co. Ltd v. Cordery* (1979) 251 E.G. 567. But see *Chrisdell Ltd v. Johnson and Tickner* (1987) 283 EGLR 1553, in which the landlords were held not to have waived their right to forfeit where they had decided not to take proceedings on the strength of statements made in correspondence by the tenant and his solicitors to the effect that there had been no breach of, in this case, the alienation covenant. The landlords, having acted on the basis that a court might accept the tenant's explanation of events and being unsure whether or not that explanation was true, could not later be said to know all necessary facts to establish a breach. See also *Cornillie v. Saha* [1996] EGCS 21 (where it was held that for there to be a waiver the landlord need not know all of the facts but only sufficient facts either to show that there had been a breach or which point to a breach or which put the landlord on enquiry as to the nature of the breach).

[20] Service of a s.146 notice, being an essential pre-requisite to forfeiture, has been held not to constitute an act of waiver: *Church Commissioners for England v. Nodjoumi* (1986) 51 P. & C.R. 155. Nor does the entering into and continuation of "without prejudice" negotiations between landlord and tenant: *Re National Jazz Centre Ltd* [1988] 38 E.G. 142, provided that rent is neither demanded nor accepted during such negotiations purportedly without prejudice to the right to forfeit: *Expert Clothing Service and Sales Ltd v. Hillgate House Ltd* [1986] Ch. 340.

[21] *Green's Case* (1582) Cro. Eliz. 3; *Ward v. Day* (1863) 4 B. & S. 337, 358; *Price v. Worwood* (1859) 4 H. & N. 512. Rent payable in respect of a period before the breach occurred can be accepted provided care is taken not to acknowledge the payer as tenant in the receipt.

the same effect.[22] Where rent has been demanded or accepted as such it is probably not open to the landlord to argue that waiver has not occurred,[23] but where other acts are involved the court is free to look at all the relevant circumstances to decide whether the acts, considered objectively, are consistent only with the continued existence of the tenancy.[24]

Effect of waiver

Waiver will extend only to the particular breach in question; and in relation to that breach it will be important to determine whether the breach is a completed or a continuing one. Waiver of a single completed (or once-and-for all) breach will preclude any further forfeiture proceedings in respect of that breach. Examples include a breach of covenant against assignment or sub-letting,[25] failure to lay out insurance monies on reinstatement within a reasonable time,[26] failure to erect buildings by a certain date,[27] failure to pay rent on the due date[28] and the carrying out of unauthorised alterations.[29] By contrast, waiver of a continuing breach will not prevent the landlord bringing forfeiture proceedings in respect of the breach should it continue after the waiver. Examples of continuing breaches are failure to observe a covenant to repair[30] and use of the premises for an unauthorised purpose.[31]

Irremediable breaches

Confusion frequently arises between once-and-for-all and irremediable breaches,[32] although the two concepts are in fact

---

[22] *Expert Clothing Service and Sales Ltd v. Hillgate House Ltd* [1986] Ch. 340 at 359, but see *In re A Debtor* (No. 13A–10–1995) [1995] 1 W.L.R. 1127 where it was held that the demand for rent which had accrued prior to the event which gave rise to the right to forfeit, in this case a further non-payment of rent, did not constitute a waiver.

[23] But see *John Lewis Properties plc v. Viscount Chelsea* [1993] 34 E.G. 116 where the landlord's bankers had accepted rent cheques and credited them to the landlord's account but the money paid had in each case subsequently been returned to the tenant by the landlord with letters clearly stating that rent would not be demanded or accepted because of the alleged breach of covenant. It was held that this did not constitute a waiver. See also *In re A Debtor*, n. 22 above.

[24] *Expert Clothing Service and Sales Ltd v. Hillgate House Ltd* [1986] Ch. 340 at 359, at 360. See also *Cardigan Properties Ltd v. Consolidated Property Investments Ltd* [1991] 7 E.G. 132, in which it was held that where the tenant failed in breach of covenant to produce an insurance policy, the commencement and continuation by the landlord of proceedings for its production constituted a waiver of the landlord's right to forfeit.

[25] *Scala House and District Property Co. Ltd v. Forbes* [1974] Q.B. 575.

[26] *Farimani v. Gates* (1984) 271 E.G. 887.

[27] *Stephens v. Junior Army and Navy Stores Ltd* [1914] 2 Ch. 516; but compare *John Lewis Properties plc v. Viscount Chelsea* [1993] 34 E.G. 116 (obligation held to be frustrated following listing of the building by the Secretary of State).

[28] *Church Commissioners for England v. Nodjoumi* (1986) 51 P. & C.R. 155.

[29] *Iperion Investments Corporation v. Broadwalk House Residents Ltd* [1992] 2 EGLR 235, in which it was held that once a landlord had knowledge of a breach of covenant caused by the carrying out of works, subsequent completion of those works did not create a further breach.

[30] *Coward v. Gregory* (1866) L.R. 2 C.P. 153. See also *Greenwich London Borough v. Discreet Selling Estates* [1990] 48 E.G. 113 in which it was held that where notice of forfeiture for breach of a repairing covenant was served on a tenant and rent was subsequently accepted, no fresh notice was required if the condition of the premises either remained the same or had deteriorated since service of the original notice.

[31] *Doe d. Ambler v. Woodbridge* (1829) 9 B. & C. 376.

[32] See para. 14–06 below.

quite separate. A breach of covenant not to assign or sub-let without landlord's consent falls into both categories,[33] but each has a different consequence. The once-and-for-all nature of the breach is relevant to the question of waiver; the fact that it is irremediable affects only the necessary contents of any section 146 notice, *i.e.* any such notice need not require the tenant to remedy the breach.

It is easy for waiver to occur unintentionally through clerical error or other accident,[34] and therefore landlords **Attempts to** sometimes attempt to exclude the doctrine by inserting a **exclude doctrine** proviso to the effect that acceptance of rent shall be deemed not to constitute waiver, or that a breach shall not be waived other than in writing. There is authority to suggest that the doctrine of waiver may not be modified in this way,[35] but in any event such provisions should not normally be acceptable to the tenant, at least without being watered down considerably. They may protect the landlord against inadvertent waiver, but they could also allow the landlord to behave with wilful equivocation toward the tenant, accepting rent for a prolonged period and then seeking forfeiture when it serves his purpose. It should, in addition, be noted that a landlord cannot avoid waiver by purporting to demand or accept rent "without prejudice".[36]

14–06 Statutory requirements and relief against forfeiture

No attempt will be made here to provide a comprehensive account of the law relating to forfeiture proceedings and relief against forfeiture. The following brief summary is offered merely as an aide memoire to the practitioner.

Before enforcing a right of re-entry or forfeiture (whether by actual re-entry or by proceedings) for any breach other than non-payment of rent, the landlord must serve on the **Section 146** tenant[37] a notice complying with section 146(1) of the Law of **notice** Property Act 1925. The notice must specify the breach,[38]

---

[33] *Scala House and District Property Co. Ltd v. Forbes* [1974] Q.B. 575.

[34] *e.g. Central Estates (Belgravia) Ltd v. Woolgar* (No. 2) [1972] 1 W.L.R. 1048 (where the demand for and acceptance of rent through agents with knowledge of a breach effected a waiver of the right to forfeit).

[35] *R. v. Paulson* [1921] 1 A.C. 271.

[36] *Central Estates (Belgravia) Ltd v. Woolgar* (No 2) [1972] 1 W.L.R. 1048; *Expert Clothing Service and Sales Ltd v. Hillgate House Ltd* [1986] Ch. 340.

[37] In the case of joint tenants, all must be served: *Wilson v. Hagon* [1959] C.L.Y. 1787 (C.C.). Note also the extent of the application of s.146 as demonstrated in *Hill Street Investments Ltd v. Bellshore Property Investments Ltd* [1996] N.P.C. 20 where it was held that the Act's definition of a "lessee" was not exhaustive and that an equitable assignee (who had failed to register the transfer to it) was entitled to apply for relief.

[38] The breach must be sufficiently specified to enable the tenant to know what is required of him, but detailed instructions as to how it is to be rectified need not be given: *Fox v. Jolly* [1916] 1 A.C. 1.

require the breach to be remedied if it is capable of remedy,[39] and require the tenant to make monetary compensation for the breach.[40] A reasonable time must be allowed for compliance with the notice:[41] even where the breach is irremediable a short time must be allowed for the tenant to consider what action he should take.[42]

Relief   The law as to relief against forfeiture is complex and technical. A distinction must be drawn between relief against forfeiture for non-payment of rent and for other types of breach.

As regards non-payment of rent, relief may be granted by the High Court under both statutory[43] and equitable[44]

---

[39] The landlord need not require the tenant to remedy a breach which is incapable of being remedied. The distinction between a remediable and an irremediable breach does not lie in whether the covenant is positive or negative or in whether the breach is a once-and-for-all or continuing breach, but in whether the harm done to the landlord by the breach is for practical purposes capable of being retrieved within a reasonable time: *Expert Clothing Service and Sales Ltd v. Hillgate House Ltd* [1986] Ch. 340 at 355, 358. See also *Savva v. Houssein* [1996] N.P.C. 64 where it was held that a breach of covenant is only incapable of remedy where compliance with the s.146 notice together with payment of appropriate monetary compensation would not remedy the harm suffered or likely to be suffered by the landlord: furthermore there was nothing in the Law of Property Act 1925 which required the court to differentiate between positive and negative covenants. A breach which has the effect of giving the premises a bad reputation is likely to be regarded as irremediable: *Rugby School Governors v. Tannahill* [1935] 1 K.B. 87 and *British Petroleum Pension Trust Ltd v. Behrendt* [1985] 2 EGLR 97 (premises used for immoral purposes); *Ali v. Booth* (1969) 199 E.G. 641 (breaches of food and drugs regulations by tenant of restaurant). However, it is not always possible to characterise even breaches of this sort as irremediable with absolute certainty: see *Burfort Financial Investments Ltd v. Chotard* (1976) 239 E.G. 891; *Re Koumoudouros and Marathon Realty Co. Ltd* (1978) 89 D.L.R. (3d.) 551. Thus the safest course is to require the breach to be remedied if capable of remedy: see *Class v. Kencakes Ltd* [1966] 1 Q.B. 611. The Court of Appeal has held that breach of a covenant against subletting is irremediable, but some of the reasoning used seems suspect: *Scala House and District Property Co. Ltd v. Forbes* [1974] 1 Q.B. 575.

[40] Despite the apparently clear wording of s.146 it has been held that the landlord need not ask for monetary compensation if he does not want it: *Rugby School Governors v. Tannahill* [1935] 1 K.B. 87.

[41] See *Bhojwani v. Kingsley Investment Trust Ltd* [1992] 39 E.G. 138 in which it was held that a re-entry which would have been unlawful because it was effected too soon after service of a s.146 notice complaining of breach of the repairing covenant was nevertheless lawful because the rent was in arrear.

[42] In *Scala House and District Property Co. Ltd v. Forbes* [1974] 1 Q.B. 575, 14 days was held sufficient for this purpose. In *Billson v. Residential Apartments Ltd* [1991] 3 W.L.R. 264 the court held that the landlord, in peaceably re-entering 14 days after service of a section 146 notice requiring the tenant to remove unauthorised alterations, had allowed sufficient time, since the tenant had made it clear that he had no intention of remedying the breach. See also *Bhojwani v. Kingsley Investment Trust Ltd* [1992] 39 E.G. 138 and *Cardigan Properties Ltd v. Consolidated Property Investments Ltd* [1991] 7 E.G. 132. A separate but related point is the opinion expressed in *Iperion Investments Corporation v. Broadwalk House Residents Ltd* [1992] 2 EGLR 235, that whether or not a reasonable time has elapsed since service of a s.146 notice is irrelevant to the question of waiver.

[43] Supreme Court Act 1981, s.38(1), applying where there is an action for forfeiture proceeding in the High Court. See also the Common Law Procedure Act 1852, s.212, allowing the tenant to obtain a stay of proceedings, but not relief, by payment of arrears.

[44] The jurisdiction is significantly restricted by the Common Law Procedure Act 1852, ss.210, 211.

jurisdictions. A procedure for relief is also available where the landlord is proceeding to enforce a right of forfeiture by a county court action.[45]

In the case of other types of breach, relief may be sought in the High Court, provided the landlord is proceeding, by action or otherwise, to enforce a right of forfeiture.[46] Whether the inherent equitable jurisdiction to grant relief against forfeiture for non-payment of rent extends to other kinds of breach remains a difficult open question,[47] as does the extent to which that jurisdiction can be regarded as having been superseded by the more recent statutory power to grant relief.[48] The statutory jurisdiction to grant relief is also available in the county court where the landlord is proceeding by way of county court action, or where he is proceeding to enforce the forfeiture otherwise than by action and the rateable value of the premises is within the county court limit.[49]

14–07 Underlessees and mortgagees

Forfeiture of a lease will involve the destruction of all subordinate interests created out of it. Thus underlessees and mortgagees are vulnerable. Both have quite substantial, if unnecessarily complex, rights to apply for relief, although it can be difficult to predict the terms upon which such relief

---

[45] County Courts Act 1984, s.138. The section has been amended by the Administration of Justice Act 1985, s.55 to extend the power to grant relief to a period of 6 months from when the landlord obtained possession: see S.I. 1986 No. 1503. See also the County Courts Act 1984, s.139(2) giving jurisdiction to grant relief on an application by the tenant where the landlord has enforced a right of re-entry without court action and the rateable value of the premises is within the county court limit.

[46] Law of Property Act 1925, s.146(2). In order to qualify for relief where the landlord is seeking possession by court action, the tenant must apply before the landlord has obtained judgment and entered into possession pursuant to that judgment. If the landlord has peaceably re-entered the premises without first obtaining a court order, the tenant may still apply for relief, although in deciding whether to grant relief the court will take into account all the circumstances, including delay on the part of the tenant: *Billson v. Residential Apartments Ltd* [1992] 2 W.L.R. 15. An application may be made once a s.146 notice has been served: *Pakwood Transport Ltd v. 15 Beauchamp Place Ltd* (1977) 36 P. & C.R. 112.

[47] Compare *Wadmam v. Caloraft* (1804) 10 Ves. Jun. 67; *Sanders v. Pope* (1806) 12 Ves. Jun. 283; *Shiloh Spinners Ltd v. Harding* [1973] A.C. 691; *Billson v. Residential Apartments Ltd* [1991] 3 W.L.R. 264.

[48] Compare *Abbey National Building Society v. Maybeech Ltd* [1985] Ch. 190 and *Smith v. Metropolitan City Properties Ltd* [1986] 1 EGLR 52. See also the majority decision of the Court of Appeal in *Billson v. Residential Apartments Ltd* [1991] 3 W.L.R. 264, which held that except in cases involving fraud, accident or mistake, the court's equitable jurisdiction to grant relief against forfeiture in the case of a wilful breach of covenant (other than non-payment of rent) does not apply where there is a landlord and tenant relationship, in which case the provisions of section 146 of the Law of Property Act 1925 will prevail. This aspect of the decision was not discussed when the case went to appeal before the House of Lords.

[49] Law of Property Act 1925, s.146(13), added by County Courts Act 1984, Sched. 2, Pt. II, para. 5.

Warning of forfeiture

will be granted.[50] One serious problem is that such persons may not know that steps are being taken to forfeit the lease until it is too late to apply for relief.[51] This problem has to some extent been alleviated by changes to High Court and County Court Rules[52] by which a landlord issuing proceedings for forfeiture is obliged to send a copy of the writ to, or file a copy of the particulars of claim for service on, any

Notification of mortgagees and underlessees

underlessee or mortgagee of whom he is aware. However, this will not help a mortgagee or underlessee whose existence is unknown to the current landlord, nor in cases where forfeiture occurs by peaceable re-entry. One solution is for the mortgage to contain an obligation by the tenant to inform the mortgagee of any section 146 notice or other step towards forfeiting the lease.[53]

14–08 Law Commission recommendations

The Law Commission recommended in 1993[54] abolition of the present law of forfeiture and its replacement by a statutory scheme under which a lease could only be terminated, in the absence of agreement between the parties, by court order.

Statutory termination scheme

Under the statutory scheme proposed by the Law Commission, if a "termination order event" occurs, basically comprising a tenant's breach of covenant or insolvency, the landlord will have a right to apply for an order terminating the lease, a "termination order". This would be a statutory right and consequently no provision relating to it need be made in the lease.[55]

If a termination order was granted, the tenancy would end on the date ordered by the court. In the meantime the tenancy would continue. The court could alternatively make a remedial order, which would only bring the lease to an end if

---

[50] *Hill v. Griffin* (1986) 282 E.G. 85. In *Escalus Properties v. Robinson* [1995] 3 W.L.R. 524, the Court of Appeal granted relief retrospectively in four cases to a mortgagee by sub-demise, holding that the class of applicant under s.146(2) could not be limited to those in privity of contract or estate with the landlord. In *Bank of Ireland Home Mortgages Ltd v. South Lodge Developments* [1996] 14 E.G. 92 a mortgagee was granted relief even though the landlord had granted a new lease of the premises at a premium: relief was given by way of the grant of a lease in reversion upon the new lease, with the landlord required to pay the premium it had received to the mortgagee.
[51] *Egerton v. Jones* [1939] 2 K.B. 702.
[52] Rules of the Supreme Court (Amendment No. 2) Order 1986 (S.I. 1986 No. 1187) rr. 2, 3; County Court (Amendment No. 2) Rules 1986 (S.I. 1986 No. 1189), r. 2.
[53] For example, 14 days' arrears of rent, service of a s.146 notice, forfeiture proceedings, or re-entry.
[54] Law Com No 221, *Landlord and Tenant Law: Termination of Tenancies Bill* dated December 6, 1993. The Report incorporates, with modifications, the Law Commission's earlier recommendations relating to landlords' termination orders contained in their 1985 Report, *Forfeiture of Tenancies* (Law Com No 142). A draft Bill to implement the Law Commission's proposals was annexed to the Report but as at May 31, 1996 the Law Commission's recommendations had not been implemented.
[55] The landlord's right to commence proceedings could however be excluded by express provision.

the tenant failed to take the remedial action required by the court within a specified period.

Derivative interests

Where a lease is terminated under this statutory procedure, all derivative interests, both sub-tenancies and mortgages, will automatically be terminated, as under the present law. The derivative interests may however be preserved on the application of either the landlord or the person holding the derivative interest.

The Report also considers the question of waiver, the Law Commission describing the current law as unsatisfactory. Under the new scheme, the landlord would only be regarded

Waiver

as having waived an event which would trigger his right to apply for a termination order where his conduct after learning of that event would lead a reasonable tenant, and has led the actual tenant, to believe that he will not apply for an order on the basis of that event.

15 MISCELLANEOUS PROVISIONS

15–01 Introduction

It is possible to categorise most of the important provisions in a lease as dealing with matters such as rent, repair, outgoings, insurance, user, alienation, and so forth. However, a number of covenants and provisos are sometimes encountered which cannot be so categorised, and which are dealt with in this Chapter.

COVENANTS

15–02 Protection of easements

Problems for the tenant

A covenant by the tenant to preserve all easements which benefit the premises is common. Such a covenant could require the tenant to take steps by litigation or otherwise in order to prevent encroachments on the rights of light, air or access of the premises. Two points may be made here. First, the covenant could operate harshly against a tenant under a short lease, who could find himself forced into expensive and time-consuming disputes in order to protect the landlord's long term interests. In such cases an amendment merely requiring the tenant to inform the landlord of any known encroachments should be proposed. If this amendment is unacceptable to the landlord, the tenant should at least ensure that he is only obliged to take such steps as are reasonably required by the landlord and then at the landlord's expense. Secondly, the effect of the covenant could be to prevent the tenant having any recourse against the landlord for interference with the rights of the demised premises by other tenants.[1] It would seem logical that since the landlord will usually be in a better position than the tenant to restrain the excesses or unreasonable behaviour of other tenants, an exception should be made to the covenant to cover encroachments by other tenants of the same landlord. However, the covenant is rarely qualified in this way in practice.[2]

15–03 Refuse and effluent

The disposal of refuse and effluent can be a major consideration in retail and industrial developments, and

---

[1] *e.g.* interference with the tenant's rights of access. See para. 4–07 above.
[2] It should be noted in any event that one tenant cannot acquire by prescription rights over land occupied by another tenant of the same landlord: *Kilgour v. Gaddes* [1904] 1 K.B. 457. The one exception to this rule is in respect of rights of light: *Morgan v. Fear* [1907] A.C. 425.

proper disposal can constitute a quite considerable expense of running a business.[3] The landlord will often require the tenant to covenant to dispose of refuse in a proper and regular manner, possibly using the facilities provided by the landlord, and not to allow refuse to accumulate on the premises or elsewhere on the development. Consideration should be given as to how to secure compliance with the legal requirements concerning the proper disposal of industrial and commercial waste under section 34 of the Environmental Protection Act 1990 and regulations issued under it.[3a] The duty of care and documentation requirements of this provision will apply to the tenant as waste producer, but may also apply to a landlord who undertakes to arrange disposal and is thereby regarded as a broker in relation to the waste.[3b] A landlord who undertakes to dispose of the tenant's waste should obtain appropriate advice as to his own legal duties relating to such disposal. They may include the requirement to register as a broker of waste.[3c] In the case of industrial premises, the proper disposal of effluent will to some extent be covered by the covenant to comply with statutory requirements,[4] but it is quite common

Liquid trade effluent

to encounter a covenant by the tenant not to discharge deleterious matter into the drains serving the premises.[5] The tenant should consider whether rigid enforcement of such a covenant would cause problems of waste disposal, particularly if the relevant sewerage undertaker is willing to consent to the discharge,[6] and it may be necessary to define the types of effluent prohibited more narrowly in order to protect the tenant.

15–04 Overloading of floors and wiring

With certain types of premises, such as factories and warehouses, there is a risk that the premises may be damaged by heavy equipment. Similarly, electrical installations may be damaged or made unsafe by overloading. A covenant against such overloading is consequently often seen in modern commercial leases.[7]

[3] See also Chap. 20 below for a discussion of the environmental considerations for both landlord and tenant.
[3a] The Environmental Protection (Duty of Care) Regulations 1991 (S.I. 1991 No. 2839): see also Department of the Environment Circular 19/91 explaining the requirements.
[3b] A landlord could, for example, find himself liable if a tenant places unsuitable or difficult waste in a container designed and intended to receive ordinary commercial waste, which is then consigned to a facility which is not licensed to receive it. The landlord could safeguard against such a situation to some extent by stipulating that only normal office waste is to be placed in such containers and that it is the tenant's own responsibility to dispose lawfully of any other types of waste arising on the demised premises.
[3c] See the Waste Management Licensing Regulations 1994 (S.I. 1994 No. 1056), reg. 20 and Circular 11/94, Annex 8.
[4] See para. 7–04 above.
[5] See Public Health Act 1936, s.27.
[6] Under the Water Industry Act 1991, Pt. IV, Chap. III.
[7] The tenant should seek details of the floor loading limits by way of a preliminary enquiry.

15–05 Planning and other compensation

A lease will sometimes contain a covenant by the tenant to make such provision as is just and equitable for the landlord to receive his due proportion of any planning or other compensation payable in respect of the premises. The tenant should clearly limit his liability to payment out of sums received rather than those payable. Although there seems no reason why the landlord should not be required to covenant in similar terms to cover the possibility, albeit remote, that he may receive compensation some of which is attributable to the tenant's interest in the property, such covenants are rarely seen in practice.

15–06 Statutory notices and planning applications

Problems for tenant

The tenant will often covenant to inform the landlord of any statutory or rating notices or communications received in respect of the premises and to join with the landlord in making objections to or representations against such notices. Clearly any such obligation should be limited to notifying the landlord of receipt of the relevant notice since the covenant could otherwise place the tenant in the unenviable position of having, at his own cost, to object to or appeal against matters which may not affect his enjoyment of the premises and, even where they do, the tenant would be precluded from pursuing his own objections.

15–07 Regulations of landlord

Control of landlord's discretion

In developments such as shopping centres, business and retail parks the landlord will often reserve the power to make regulations for the future management of the development. Since all of the problems which may arise in managing a complex development cannot be foreseen and provided for at the outset, this is a valuable power. However, the tenant should beware of conferring unlimited power on the landlord in this way. Clearly, if regulations exist, the tenant should ask to see them before entering into the lease and should ensure that he is notified of any changes to them. The tenant should also limit the landlord's power to make regulations to those which may reasonably be regarded as necessary for the efficient management of the estate or in the interests of the tenants as a whole.[8]

---

[8] The tenant would ideally require the landlord to obtain the approval of all of the tenants before making or varying such regulations but clearly this could make management of the development unworkable.

15–08   Indemnity to landlord

A landlord will sometimes seek to obtain an indemnity from
the tenant against liability to third parties. Such liability could
arise under the Defective Premises Act 1972 or possibly for
breach of statutory duties, for example under the Health and
Safety at Work, etc. Act 1974.[9] The tenant should ensure that
such indemnity does not extend to liability arising from
breach of the landlord's own obligations under the lease, for
example the repair of structural or common parts.

PROVISOS

15–09   Arbitration

In the interests of both parties some means should be
provided for resolving disputes arising during the life of the
lease. It can be forcefully argued that matters relating to the
construction of the lease are best referred straight to the

**Determination
by arbitrator or
by court?**

court, rather than be determined by an arbitrator who may
not be a lawyer, given the difficulty of an appeal against an
adverse determination.[10] On the other hand, questions may
arise which are better determined by an experienced and
professionally-qualified arbitrator than by a court: *e.g.* whether
the premises are adequately insured; whether a service charge
account is fair; whether regulations are justified on good
estate management grounds; and what proportion of rent
should be suspended to reflect damage to the premises.

Two possible solutions suggest themselves. One is to
identify those provisions where determination by arbitration
would be most helpful and to set out machinery relating only
to those provisions. The other is to produce a general
arbitration clause, but to provide that in matters concerning
the construction of the lease or any issue of law[11] either party
may refer the question direct to the court. It remains however
relatively rare in practice to include arbitration provisions in
leases, save in the context of rent review and occasionally
service charges.

Questions relating to arbitration and determination by an
expert are discussed in the Chapters on rent review and
service charges.[12]

15–10   **Service of notices**

Careful consideration should be given to the manner in which
the lease is to provide for service of notices. It has long been
the practice to incorporate in leases the provisions of the Law
of Property Act 1925, section 196 in order, *inter alia,* to

---

[9] See para. 7–04 above: see also *Solomons v. R. Gerzentein Ltd* [1954] 1 Q.B.
565; on appeal [1954] 2 Q.B. 243.
[10] See para. 6–19 above.
[11] Possibly also questions of unreasonably withholding consent by the
landlord, of which the courts have considerable experience.
[12] See Chaps. 6 and 8 above.

validate the service of notices under the lease by leaving them at the demised premises.[13] Following the decision of the court in *Wandsworth Borough Council v. Attwell*,[13a] this can no longer be regarded as good practice. In that case, the court restricted the application of s.196(5) to notices "required" to be served under a lease. The court did not however attempt to clarify exactly which notices could be said to be required to be served under a lease and those which would be construed as purely voluntary. For that reason, the better practice must now be to deal expressly in the lease with the manner in which notices are to be served and how their service may be proved.

Notices required to be served

15–11 Costs

It is usual for the lease to deal with the question of the various costs which may arise. There will usually be a proviso that the tenant is to pay the landlord's costs incurred in respect of the various licences required by the lease for assignment, alterations, and so on.[14] In addition, it will often be stated that the tenant is to pay the costs incurred by the landlord in seeking to forfeit the lease (for example in preparing and serving a section 146 notice) whether or not the matter proceeds to forfeiture. Such a proviso seems unobjectionable if the reason that forfeiture does not proceed is that the tenant obtains relief by rectifying the breach. However, it is difficult to see why it should apply where the landlord's action for forfeiture was misconceived, malicious, or based upon a mistake (*e.g.* where the landlord miscalculates the amount of rent due). It is suggested therefore, although seldom seen in practice, that any such proviso should be expressly limited to cases where there is an actual breach of covenant and the forfeiture action does not proceed either because of relief being given, or because the tenant remedies the breach, or because the matter is settled by agreement.

Costs of forfeiture proceedings

[13] On the basis of s.196(5) of the Act.
[13a] [1996] 1 E.G. 100.
[14] These provision are often found in relevant tenant's covenants themselves, *e.g.* the alienation or alterations covenants, rather than in the provisos.

16 SECURITY OF TENURE

16–01 Introduction

A secure and stable base from which to operate is important for most businesses; for many it is crucial. Therefore the tenant will wish to know how secure his occupation is both during and after the term of the lease. Security during the term of the lease is provided by the landlord's covenant for quiet enjoyment—but it may also be jeopardised by the existence of a break clause allowing the landlord to terminate the lease. Additional security may be provided by an option allowing the tenant to renew the lease and, when the term ends, by the tenant's rights under Part II of the Landlord and Tenant Act 1954. Each of these matters—quiet enjoyment, break clauses, options to renew and statutory security—is considered in turn in this Chapter.

QUIET ENJOYMENT

16–02 Purposes of covenant for quiet enjoyment

The landlord's covenant for quiet enjoyment can be seen as serving two purposes. One is the protection of the tenant against eviction or dispossession. The other is the protection of the tenant in occupation against interference with his use of the premises. It is only the first aspect of the covenant which will be considered in this Chapter; the second aspect is covered in the Chapter relating to the use of the premises.[1]

16–03 Nature of the covenant

It is important to realise the limitations of the usual covenant for quiet enjoyment. The relationship of landlord and tenant will imply an undertaking by the landlord as to quiet **No warranty of** enjoyment.[2] But the implied covenant does not in any sense **title** constitute a warranty that the landlord's title is good, since it will only be broken by interruptions by the landlord himself and those claiming under him.[3] A commercial lease will usually contain an express covenant as to quiet enjoyment, thereby excluding any implied obligation. Here the extent of

---

[1] See para. 10–11 above.
[2] *Budd-Scott v. Daniell* [1902] 2 K.B. 351.
[3] *Bandy v. Cartwright* (1853) 8 Exch. 913; *Jones v. Lavington* [1903] 1 K.B. 253.

Qualifications on covenant

the obligation depends upon the words used, but the covenant will usually be qualified so as to guarantee freedom from interruptions only by the landlord and persons lawfully claiming from or under him. The main points of concern for the tenant are as follows.

Tenant to pay rent and perform covenants   The covenant is usually qualified by prefixing the words "the tenant paying the rent and performing the covenants on his part to be performed". It appears that the words do not make the covenant for quiet enjoyment a conditional one,[4] but they do

Preserve right to re-enter

preserve the landlord's right to re-enter upon breach of covenant.

Interruptions by title paramount   Should the tenant be evicted by someone with a title superior to that of the landlord, he will have no redress under a qualified covenant.

Sub-lessees

This risk can be particularly sharp for the tenant under a sub-lease whose lease may determine upon forfeiture of the headlease.[5] However, the covenant for quiet enjoyment must be read in conjunction with the rest of the lease: in some sub-leases the definition of the landlord is widened to include any superior landlord, and this may, perhaps inadvertently, have the effect of extending the covenant for quiet enjoyment to the superior landlord's acts.[6]

Rights created by predecessors in title   It has been held that a qualified covenant against interruptions by persons

"Claiming under" and "holding under"

lawfully "claiming under" the landlord does not extend to interruptions by virtue of rights granted by a predecessor in title of the landlord.[7] Such a covenant has been described as "limited"[8] and it appears that a covenant against interruptions by persons "holding under" the landlord might produce better protection for the tenant in this respect.[9] But in other respects "holding under" might be the narrower expression, e.g. it might not cover a person entitled to the benefit of an easement created by the landlord.

Lawful acts only   The covenant is generally taken as offering no protection against unlawful interruptions by persons other than the landlord. This is so regardless of

---

[4] *Taylor v. Webb* [1973] 2 K.B. 283; *Slater v. Hoskins* [1982] 2 N.Z.L.R. 541 (landlord entered cinema, changed locks and removed fuses in order to prevent tenant showing films while not licensed for fire safety; held to be breach of covenant for quiet enjoyment, but circumstances taken into account in reducing damages).

[5] See *Spencer v. Marriott* (1823) 1 B. & C. 457 (forfeiture for breach of user covenant in headlease of which sub-tenant ignorant); *Kelly v. Rogers* [1892] Q.B. 910 (forfeiture for unpaid rent due under headlease).

[6] *Queensway Marketing Ltd v. Associated Restaurants Ltd* (1984) 271 E.G. 1106.

[7] *Celsteel Ltd v. Alton House Holdings Ltd (No.2)* [1987] 1 W.L.R. 291.

[8] *ibid.*, at 296, *per* Fox L.J.

[9] *ibid.*, at 294.

whether the word "lawfully" appears in the covenant.[10]
However, a covenant against interruptions by a named person
will extend to all acts of that person, whether lawful or
unlawful, and this principle has been held to extend to a
person not named but identified by reference to his position
as superior landlord.[11]

Interruptions by named persons

Agreed incumbrances   Where the parties have agreed that
the tenant shall be subject to some specific incumbrance,
interference with the tenant caused by that incumbrance will
not be a breach of the covenant for quiet enjoyment.[12] It is
immaterial whether the lease is expressly made subject to the
incumbrance or not.[13]

Measure of damages   Where the landlord was in
permanent breach and acting violently the tenant recovered
lease premiums, conveyancing costs and (exceptionally)
damages for distress.[14] Where sub-letting the premises was
likely in the usual course of events, the tenant may recover
loss of rent and if the tenant has to leave, he can recover the
cost of alternative accommodation.[15]

16–04   Implications for leasehold conveyancing

The limited nature of the usual covenant for quiet enjoyment
is relevant to the practice of leasehold conveyancing, in
particular the importance of investigation of the landlord's
title by the tenant. This aspect of the covenant is discussed in
the Chapter on conveyancing practice.[16]

BREAK CLAUSES

16–05   Purpose of break clauses

Break clauses may serve many different purposes, for the
benefit of either or both of the parties. For example, a break
clause may be inserted to allow the tenant to escape from a
lease if the premises are destroyed and cannot be rebuilt,[17] if
the rent is raised to an intolerable level on review,[18] or simply
to allow the tenant to escape from his obligations under the
lease. In these circumstances the option to break is often

---

[10] *Williams v. Gabriel* [1906] 1 K.B. 155. Nor is the covenant broken by acts
pursuant to a court order, *e.g.* entry following an order for possession on
the ground of forfeiture: *Hillgate House Ltd v. Expert Clothing Services &
Sales Ltd* (1986) 282 E.G. 715.
[11] *Queensway Marketing Ltd v. Associated Restaurants Ltd* (1984) 271 E.G.
1106 at 1110.
[12] *Celsteel Ltd v. Alton House Holdings Ltd (No.2)* [1986] 1 W.L.R. 666 (Scott
J., affirmed on other grounds: see n. 7 above).
[13] *ibid.*
[14] *Sampson v. Floyd* [1989] 33 E.G. 41.
[15] *Mira v. Ayler Square Investments* (1990) 22 H.L.R. 182.
[16] See para. 18–08 below.
[17] See para. 13–15 above.
[18] See para. 6–08 above.

accompanied by a "penalty rent" of one or two years' rent payable to the landlord on exercise. A break clause in favour of a landlord may be included to enable him to obtain vacant possession, most probably for the purpose of redevelopment.[18a]

16–06   Requirements as to exercise

Provisions to be strictly complied with

The lease should make clear first, who is entitled to exercise the option to terminate the lease as, if the clause does not specify who may exercise it, it will be construed as exercisable by the tenant only.[19] Where a break clause is expressed to be operable only by the named original tenant it has been held that the right does not survive assignment, so that even if the lease is re-vested in the original tenant, the right to break is no longer exercisable.[20] Secondly, when the option is to be exercised should be clear. As an option to determine the term, the provisions as to exercise must be strictly complied with[21] and time is of the essence unless negatived.[22] It is therefore sensible to avoid any requirement to serve notice on or by a date calculated by reference to the commencement date of the term, or the number of years of the term; the formula "at any time after" a specified date is preferable. Finally, the means of exercising the option are important. Usually the right will be exercisable by notice in writing. Service of notice on a landlord's managing agents was held valid where there was no specific requirement to serve it on the landlord.[23] A notice purporting to exercise the right will be construed so as to be effective where possible, but as a technical document, some defects cannot be overlooked,[24] and in particular the termination date in the notice must be correct.[25] From the

---

[18a] Although the procedures under the Landlord and Tenant Act 1954 will still have to be followed: see paras. 16–26 and 16–40 below.

[19] *Dann v. Spurrier* (1803) 3 Bos. & P. 399. A literal interpretation of a break clause was rejected where this prevented a guarantor exercising the option in *William Hill (Southern) Ltd v. Waller* [1991] 1 EGLR 271. See also *Dun & Bradstreet Software Services (England) Ltd v. Provident Mutual Life Assurance Society* [1996] N.P.C. 57 (break notice validly served by a company for whom the tenant held as bare trustee: the company was held to have acted as general agent for the tenant).

[20] *Max Factor Ltd v. Wesleyan Assurance Society* [1996] EGCS 82; see also *Olympia & York Canary Wharf Ltd v. Oil Property Investments Ltd* [1994] 2 EGLR 48 (in which the court had not needed to consider the point as the parties had proceeded on an agreed construction that the right would survive assignment); and also *Brown & Root Technology Ltd v. Sun Alliance and London Assurance Co. Ltd* [1995] 3 W.L.R. 558 as to what constitutes assignment in these circumstances.

[21] *A. & J. Mucklow (Birmingham) Ltd v. Metro-Cammell Weymann* [1994] EGCS 64.

[22] Cf. *Chilton Court (Baker Street) Residents Ltd v. Wallabrook Property Co. Ltd* [1989] 43 E.G. 173.

[23] *Peel Developments (South) Ltd v. Siemens Ltd* [1992] 47 E.G. 103.

[24] *Hankey v. Clavering* [1942] K.B. 326 at 330.

[25] *Mannai Investment Company Ltd v. Eagle Star Life Assurance Company Ltd* [1995] 1 W.L.R. 1508 (notice served to determine on January 12, when it should have stated January 13, was held invalid); however contrast *Micrografix Ltd v. Woking 8 Ltd* [1995] 37 E.G. 179 (notice containing date of March 23, 1994 instead of June 23, 1995 was surprisingly held valid).

landlord's point of view the simplest course is to make the provisions as to the form and length of notice consistent with the provisions as to section 25 notices, so that a single notice can satisfy both the requirements of the lease and of the Landlord and Tenant Act.[26]

16–07 Effect of exercise

Where the tenant has the right to break, the landlord should ensure that any existing rights of the landlord will not be prejudiced by the termination. This can be done by providing that termination shall not affect the landlord's accrued rights in respect of non-payment of rent or breaches of covenant. It is increasingly common for the clause to stipulate that performance by the tenant of all his obligations is a condition precedent of the right to break[27] or may be implied by the wording of the clause.[28] There is no implication that breaches of covenant need be material to prevent the option being exercised.[29] It is a matter of construction whether the date on which there must be compliance is the date when the notice is given, or the date when it expires, or both.[30] A tenant intending to exercise a break clause must therefore consider at an early stage what action on his part may be necessary to ensure compliance with the covenants in the lease,[30a] particularly those relating to repair and decoration. The landlord will wish to ensure that obligations such as redecoration should be expressed so as to operate on termination, and not only at the end of the original term granted.[31]

Compliance with covenants in lease

Effect of termination of headlease

The exercise of a tenant's notice to quit by a headtenant in his lease has the effect of terminating an underlease,[32] and it is likely that the service of a tenant's break notice would have the same effect.

16–08 Power to break on condition

A tenant will not usually wish to give the landlord completely unfettered powers to terminate the lease, and so the landlord will frequently be restricted to termination upon specified grounds, (e.g. upon requiring the premises for redevelopment or for his own occupation). If so, a bona fide intention on the part of the landlord to use the property in the way specified

Genuine intention

---

[26] See para. 16–26 below.
[27] *Simons v. Associated Furnishers Ltd* [1931] 1 Ch. 379. See also below, nn. 57 *et seq.*
[28] *Trane (U.K.) Ltd v. Provident Mutual Life Association* [1995] 3 E.G. 122.
[29] But see *William Hill (Southern) Ltd v. Waller* [1991] 1 EGLR 271.
[30] See the comments in para. 16–13 below in relation to this issue as it relates to options to renew.
[30a] See *Reed Personnel Services Ltd v. American Express Ltd* [1996] N.P.C. 7; also *Trane (U.K.) Ltd v. Provident Mutual Life Association* [1995] 3 E.G. 122 and *Bairstow Eves (Securities) Ltd v. Ripley* [1992] 32 E.G. 52.
[31] *Dickinson v. St. Aubyn* [1944] K.B. 454; see para. 9–21 above.
[32] *Pennell v. Payne* [1995] 6 E.G. 152.

will be required before the power to terminate arises.[33] The landlord should take care that the grounds upon which he may break are wide enough to embrace his possible future plans for the premises. For example, in *Coates v. Diment*[34] a provision allowing the landlord to re-enter such land as he might require for a building site or for planting or other purposes was, when construed *ejusdem generis*, inadequate to allow the landlord to re-enter to build a sports stadium. The landlord should avoid break clauses allowing him to resume possession of part only of the premises. Such provisions can prove useless in the face of the rule that a section 25 notice under the Landlord and Tenant Act 1954 can only be served in relation to the whole of the land comprised in the tenancy.[35] The landlord should either grant a separate lease of that part of the property to which the break clause relates, or make the break clause applicable to the whole of the property upon the landlord requiring possession of the whole or any part. A clause may still be construed as effective to allow the landlord to resume possession of the whole even where only possession of part is required immediately.[36]

Notice relating to whole of land

16–09   Interaction of tenant's break notice with section 26 of the 1954 Act

In an over-rented market, it has been suggested that it may be possible for a tenant to serve a break notice and immediately serve a section 26 request[37] requesting a new tenancy to be granted at a lower rent. This would effectively give the tenant an option to renegotiate the rent. The service of either notice on its own prevents service of the other[38] but it has been suggested that section 26(2) is capable of being read in such a way that a tenant may be permitted to serve the section 26 request on its own, without a break notice being served at all.

Option to renegotiate rent

At first instance the court has considered this possibility in *Garston v. Scottish Widows Fund and Life Assurance Society*[39] and decided that this is not the manner in which the 1954 Act operates; however, it is quite likely that the issue may come before the court again, either in different circumstances, or on appeal.[40]

---

[33] *Commissioners of Inland Revenue v. Southend-on-Sea Estates Co. Ltd* [1915] A.C. 428 at 432. The contrasts with the requirement under the Landlord and Tenant Act 1954: see para. 16–40 below.

[34] [1951] 1 All E.R. 890. See also *Craddock v. Fieldman* (1960) 175 E.G. 1149 (power to determine lease in order to develop site of which premises were part held to be exercisable only where landlord intended to develop substantially whole of site; no power to break in order to develop part).

[35] *Southport Old Links Ltd v. Naylor* [1985] 1 EGLR 66 (see para. 16–26 below).

[36] *Parkinson v. Barclays Bank Ltd* [1951] 1 K.B. 368.

[37] See below, para. 16–28.

[38] 1954 Act, s.26(4).

[39] [1996] 1 W.L.R. 834. For a commentary on the case see S. Murdoch "Break notices and s.26 requests" [1996] 17 E.G. 186.

[40] At the time of going to press the tenant is appealing to the Appeal Committee of the House of Lords for leave to appeal to the House of Lords.

OPTIONS TO RENEW

16–10 Introduction

An option to renew a lease can be a very valuable right indeed. Care should therefore be exercised to ensure that it is properly drafted, protected and exercised.

16–11 Drafting

The option should deal with the time at which and the manner in which it may be exercised. The tenant should bear in mind at the drafting stage that such requirements will have to be strictly complied with. The terms of the new lease should be specified in the option.[41] Usually these will be the same as the terms of the old lease, but special care is required over two matters: rent and the option itself.

Rent under new lease

As to rent, the landlord will no doubt wish to have the opportunity of increasing the rent at the time of renewal. It is important to avoid the risk of the option being held void for uncertainty for failure to provide a means to ascertain the new rent;[42] instead provide either machinery or a formula (or both) to determine the rent.[43] Recent decisions point to the court upholding the validity of options by implying a term that the rent to be agreed be a fair rent when it was the clear intention of the parties to be bound by the option[44] or, where an option provided for a fair and reasonable rent to be agreed, by implying that this would be the reasonable open market rent.[45] Given the practice of making rent review clauses increasingly sophisticated, it would appear to be anomalous not to make use of an equally detailed formula for the determination of rent on renewal.[46] If the renewal is for anything other than a short term, the landlord should ensure that rent review clauses are provided for, since the power to fix a new rent will not necessarily carry with it the power to introduce rent reviews.[47]

[41] In some cases the court may be willing to rectify any deficiency by reference to a lease in such form as the landlord might reasonably require: *Trustees of National Deposit Friendly Society v. Beatties of London Ltd* [1985] 2 EGLR 59. In a landlord's market this may prevent the landlord obtaining such favourable terms as he might otherwise have done.

[42] *King's Motors, Oxford Ltd v. Lax* [1970] 1 W.L.R. 426 (option held void for uncertainty where there was no means for ascertaining the rent in default of agreement); doubted in *Trustees of National Deposit Friendly Society v. Beatties of London Ltd* [1985] 2 EGLR 59 and *Corson v. Rhuddlan B.C.* (1990) 59 P. & C.R. 185.

[43] See, *e.g. Brown v Gould* [1972] Ch. 53; *Sudbrook Trading Estate Ltd v. Eggleton* [1983] 1 A.C. 444. The courts appear to be willing to make such agreements work by supplying the mechanism themselves or by implying a formula.

[44] *Corson v. Rhuddlan B.C.* (1990) 59 P. & C.R. 185.

[45] *Arc v. Schofield* (1990) 38 E.G. 113.

[46] *Cf. Lear v. Blizzard* [1983] 3 All E.R. 662, where the court was able to provide guidance as to the approach to improvements by the tenant.

[47] *National Westminster Bank Ltd v. B.S.C. Footwear Ltd* (1980) 42 P. & C.R. 90; *Bracknell Development Corporation v. Greenlees Lennards Ltd* (1981) 260 E.G. 500; *Lear v. Blizzard* [1983] 3 All E.R. 662.

Excluding option from new lease Care should also be taken to exclude the option to renew itself from the new lease, otherwise the result may be a perpetually renewable lease, converted to a 2,000 year term by the Law of Property Act 1922.[48] The courts attempt to construe leases so as to avoid such a result,[49] but it will be wise to put the matter beyond doubt by the use of clear language.

Costs of renewal The tenant is normally required to pay the landlord's costs on renewal. The tenant will wish to ensure that such provision is limited to reasonable legal and surveying costs, without prejudice to the power of the court or arbitrator to make an award as to costs in the event of a dispute or if the landlord generally behaves unreasonably.

16–12 Protecting the option

In the event of the landlord selling the freehold and the purchaser refusing to honour the option, the tenant will have a remedy in damages against the original landlord who granted the option.[50] However, the tenant will also wish to ensure that the option binds any purchaser of the reversion. If **Overriding interest** title to the reversion is registered, the option will be binding as an overriding interest, provided that the tenant is in actual occupation of the property or in receipt of rents from a sub-tenant.[51] However, rather than rely on this, it seems preferable to protect the option by entry of a notice on the register of the reversionary title. If title to the reversion is **Registration of option** unregistered, the option must be registered as a Class C(iv) land charge.[52]

16–13 Exercising the option

There are potential problems for the tenant similar to those encountered in relation to options to break.[53] An option must be exercised strictly in accordance with its terms. Thus the right to exercise the option may be lost once the date for doing so has passed.[54] Equally, a notice given an unreasonable time before the time stated for exercise may be ineffective.[55]

---

[48] s.145 and Sched.15. See *Caerphilly Concrete Products v. Owen* [1972] 1 All E.R. 248.

[49] *Plumrose Ltd v. Real & Leasehold Estates Investment Society Ltd* [1970] 1 W.L.R. 52; *Majorie Burnett Ltd v. Barclay* (1980) 258 E.G. 642.

[50] See *Wright v. Dean* [1948] Ch. 686; *Kitney v. Greater London Properties Ltd* (1984) 272 E.G. 786.

[51] Land Registration Act 1925, s.70(1)(g); *Neon Rentals Ltd v. Greening* (1958) 171 E.G. 567.

[52] *Beesly v. Hallwood Estates Ltd* [1960] 1 W.L.R. 549; *Kitney v. M.E.P.C. Ltd* [1977] 1 W.L.R. 981; *Taylors Fashions Ltd v. Liverpool Victoria Trustees Co. Ltd* [1982] Q.B. 133.

[53] See para. 16–06 above.

[54] *United Scientific Holdings Ltd v. Burnley Borough Council* [1978] A.C. 904 at 929.

[55] *Band v. Kirklington and Piccadilly Estates Ltd* [1947] L.J.R. 884; *Multon v. Cordell* [1986] 1 EGLR 44, although it was hinted in *A. & J. Mucklow (Birmingham) Ltd v. Metro-Cammell Weymann Ltd* [1994] EGCS 64 that it may be valid.

What the tenant ideally requires is a period within which notice can be given, rather than a date upon which it must be given.

Breach of covenant

The other point of difficulty for the tenant can occur where he is in, or has been in, breach of covenants in the lease. Such a breach would in equity disentitle the tenant from an order for specific enforcement of an option,[56] but in any event the option will almost invariably be made conditional upon payment of rent and performance of the other covenants in the lease. The attitude of the courts to such provisions appears to be that strict compliance is required and that even relatively minor or innocuous breaches of covenant can lose the tenant the right to renew.[57] The true question has been said to be whether at the material date there are subsisting breaches of covenant, in the sense that the breach itself or a cause of action for forfeiture or damages still exists.[58] Accordingly, "spent" breaches can be ignored, but the distinction drawn between "spent" and "subsisting" breaches seems an elusive one. A breach of the covenant to decorate in the final year of the term has been held to disentitle the tenant to the right to renew[59] but last minute disrepair may not amount to breach of the covenant to repair according to Judge Cooke in *Trane (U.K.) Ltd v Provident Mutual Life Association*.[60]

Condition precedent

Where the right to renew contained a condition precedent that the parties should first agree a new business plan and business agreement, but at the time of renewal the landlord did not require such a plan and agreement and accordingly refused even to start negotiations, the court ruled that the tenant no longer needed to comply with the condition.[61]

Date of compliance

The parties may wish to make clear the date at which compliance is to be judged, *i.e.* date of notice, date of renewal or both. From the tenant's point of view it is preferable if compliance is to be judged as late as possible and if breaches which have been rectified are to be disregarded. This allows the tenant to rectify breaches existing before or at the date of the notice exercising the option. [62] This is unlikely to be satisfactory from the landlord's point of view, because it may allow a tenant who has persistently been in arrears with rent and in default of other obligations under the lease to put matters right at the last moment, and obtain a new term.[63] The most satisfactory compromise may be to provide that the

---

[56] *Job v. Banister* (1856) 2 K. & J. 374; affirmed (1856) 26 L.J. Ch. 125.
[57] *West County Cleaners (Falmouth) Ltd v. Saly* [1966] 1 W.L.R. 1485; *Kitney v. Greater London Properties Ltd* (1984) 272 E.G. 786 (where it was suggested that compliance with the terms of the lease is sufficient; no specially high standard of compliance is required).
[58] *Bass Holdings Ltd. v. Morton Music Ltd* [1987] 2 All E.R. 1001.
[59] *Bairstow Eves (Securities) Ltd v. Ripley* [1992] 32 E.G. 52.
[60] [1995] 3 E.G. 122 at 126 (a case relating to a break clause).
[61] *Little v. Courage Limited, The Times,* January 6, 1995.
[62] *Bassett v. Whitely* (1983) 45 P. & C.R. 87 (two payments of rent were withheld temporarily to bring pressure to bear on landlord to carry out repairs).
[63] *Bassett v. Whitely* (1983) 45 P. & C.R. 87 at 92, *per* Griffiths L.J.

"Reasonable performance" tenant must have "reasonably performed"[64] all the obligations and stipulations in the lease, and that reasonable performance shall be judged at the date of termination of the old tenancy with reference to the conduct of the tenant throughout the term, thus allowing the tenant some time to rectify breaches but not protecting the persistently bad tenant. A reference to performing all obligations in the lease is likely to include the payment of rent on the due date, since leases now invariably contain a covenant by the tenant to pay rent as reserved.

SECURITY OF TENURE UNDER THE LANDLORD AND TENANT ACT 1954

16–14   Introduction

Part II of the Landlord and Tenant Act 1954 provides the tenant of business premises with a considerable measure of security of tenure. Apart from a number of amendments made by the Law of Property Act 1969, the Act has remained largely unchanged, and has provided a stable background to the landlord and tenant relationship in the business sector (contrasting with the many changes and shifts of policy in the residential and agricultural sectors). The Act is generally accepted as serving its purpose well, and the following quotation is probably typical of the attitude of the property world at large:

> "It is well understood, accepted by lessors and lessees as striking a realistic balance between their interests and enables the parties to order their financial and business affairs in a workable fashion."[65]

Review of the Act The Act looks set to continue to provide such a balance in the foreseeable future. In 1988 the Law Commission published a working paper which considered the operation of the Act[66] and followed this up with a report in 1992.[67] The Law Commission concluded that the Act was working successfully and that any changes made should be broadly neutral. A number of recommendations for change were made, and reference is made to the more important ones (but by no means all of them) throughout the text which follows.[68]

The scheme of the Act needs to be studied as a whole, since it provides for security of tenure not by any general principle, but by a logical progression of procedural steps,

---

[64] This formula was used in *Bassett v. Whitely* (n. 63 above) and was held to give the court a useful degree of discretion. It might also allow the tenant to exercise the option even where a technically irremediable breach has occurred: see *Bass Holdings Ltd v. Morton Music Ltd* [1986] 280 E.G. 1435 at 1442 (Scott J.); on appeal see [1987] 2 All E.R. 1001.

[65] (1980) 255 E.G. 333 at 337 (D.T. Hoyes). See also the tribute of Diplock L.J. in *Scholl Manufacturing Co. Ltd v. Clifton (Slim-Line) Ltd* [1967] 1 Ch 41 at 49.

[66] Pt. II of the Landlord and Tenant Act 1954, Working Paper No. 111.

[67] *Business Tenancies: a Periodic Review of the Landlord and Tenant Act 1954, Pt. II*, H.C. 224. (Law Com. Rep. No. 208.)

[68] The Government has announced that it intends to implement most of the recommendations, but no date has yet been set: statement by Tony Baldry, Environment Minister, July 19, 1994.

culminating either in the landlord obtaining possession, or the tenant obtaining a new tenancy. It is impossible to review every aspect of the Act in detail in this book: concentration will therefore be placed upon those areas most frequently encountered or most likely to give rise to difficulties in practice.[69]

16–15   Scope of the Act

Tenancies covered by Act
By section 23 the Act applies to ". . . any tenancy where the property comprised in the tenancy is or includes premises which are occupied by the tenant and are so occupied for the purposes of a business carried on by him or for those and other purposes."

In the vast majority of cases the application of the section to the actual facts will present little difficulty: exclusive possession is likely to connote the existence of a tenancy,[70] and it will usually be clear whether or not the tenant is carrying on a business from the premises,[71] though of course borderline cases can occur.[72] However, certain situations can give rise to problems, and those which arise most frequently are considered below.

16–16   Occupation of the premises

The use of the word "premises" does not mean that the tenancy must include a building or other structure: a lease of open land[73] or a public open space[74] can be protected under the Act.

Meaning of "premises"
However, it has been held to exclude the grant of a right of way,[75] a lease of an advertising hoarding[76] and a lease of chattels[77] from the protection of the Act. Such rights would, however, be protected if granted as ancillary rights under a lease of business premises.

Whether the tenant is in occupation is a question of fact, depending on the degree of control and user exercised by the

---

[69] For a detailed treatment, see D.W. Williams, C.M. Brand and C.C. Hubbard, *Handbook of Business Tenancies* (1985).
[70] See para. 16–22 below.
[71] See para. 16–18 below.
[72] *Lewis v. Weldcrest* [1978] 1 W.L.R. 1107.
[73] *Bracey v. Read* [1963] Ch. 88.
[74] *Wandsworth L.B.C. v. Singh* [1991] 33 E.G. 90.
[75] *Land Reclamation Co. Ltd v. Basildon District Council* [1979] 1 W.L.R. 767; *Nevill Long & Co. (Boards) Ltd v. Firmenich and Co. Ltd* (1983) 268 E.G. 572.
[76] *Wilson v. Taverner* [1901] 1 Ch. 578; *Kewel Investments Ltd v. Arthur Maiden Ltd* [1990] 15 E.G. 58; however, see also *Taylor v. Pendleton Overseers* (1887) 19 Q.B.D. 288 where, on the facts, a lease existed.
[77] *Nuflats & Properties Ltd v. Sheckman* (1959) 174 E.G. 39.

Control by tenant tenant.[78] Thus the tenant's rights under the Act may be lost by abandoning the premises, or by handing over control to another.[79] However, the tenant will not necessarily lose his rights by ceasing to be in physical occupation, since it is possible for premises to be regarded as "occupied" even if empty for a time.[80] Thus the tenant who is forced to vacate premises damaged by fire may still be in occupation, provided he maintains an intention to resume physical possession as soon as possible.[81] However, where a business is deliberately interrupted, the "thread of continuity of business user"[82] is more likely to be broken.[83]

Sub-letting Further problems can arise where the tenant sub-lets all or part of the premises. Ordinarily this would deprive the tenant of occupation, and thereby the protection of the Act, in relation to that part. However, in certain cases it may be possible for the tenant to argue that the sub-letting is his business, and that he remains in occupation for that purpose. To succeed, however, the tenant will need to demonstrate retention of occupation in some way, *e.g.* by continued control over the premises, the provision of services, a continued physical presence by way of a manager, porter or the like, the allocation of time and resources to management of the sub-let parts, etc.[84] In the recent case of *Graysim Holdings Ltd v. P. & O. Property Holdings Ltd*[85] the House of Lords held that the operator of a market hall, who let out individual lock-up units to traders, was not in occupation for its own business: the individual traders were entitled to new leases, and once these had been granted, the market operator would have no independent business of its own.

---

[78] *Hancock and Willis v. G.M.S. Syndicate Ltd* (1983) 265 E.G. 473.
[79] *ibid.*
[80] *I. & H. Caplan Ltd v. Caplan (No. 2)* [1963] 1 W.L.R. 1247.
[81] *Morrison Holdings Ltd v. Manders Property (Wolverhampton) Ltd* [1976] 1 W.L.R. 533. In view of some dicta in this case it would seem prudent to make any such intention clear to the landlord. See also *Aireps Ltd v. City of Bradford Metropolitan Council* [1985] 2 EGLR 143 (tenant moved voluntarily into temporary accommodation; premises demolished; rights under 1954 Act lost) and *Demetriou v Robert Andrews (Estate Agencies)* (1991) 62 P. & C.R. 536 (tenant ceased occupying premises which were no longer occupiable by reason of neglect for which neither the landlord nor the tenant were liable; held he had lost his rights).
[82] *Aspinall Finance v. Viscount Chelsea* [1989] 9 E.G. 77, 79 *per* Judge Paul Baker Q.C. The expression was first used in *I. & H. Caplan Ltd v. Caplan (No. 2)* (see n. 80 above).
[83] *ibid.* In this case the tenant closed its casino and surrendered its gaming licence for use elsewhere, intending to re-open the casino when another licence could be obtained. It was held that it had ceased to occupy.
[84] For examples of cases where the control was sufficient, see *Lee Verhulst (Investments) Ltd v. Harwood Trust* [1973] 1 Q.B. 204; *William Boyer & Sons Ltd v. Adams* (1975) 32 P. & C.R. 89; *Groveside Properties Ltd v. Westminster Medical School* (1984) 47 P. & C.R. 507; *Linden v. Department of Health and Social Security* [1986] 1 W.L.R. 164. For cases where there was insufficient control, see *Bagettes Ltd v. G.P. Estates Ltd* [1956] Ch. 290; *Trans-Britannia Properties Ltd v. Darby Properties Ltd* [1986] 1 EGLR 151.
[85] [1995] 3 W.L.R. 854.

16–17 Occupation by the tenant

Occupation by agent

It is possible for the tenant to occupy premises through a manager or agent, rather than personally.[86] There are limits to how far this doctrine can be extended, and accordingly difficulties for the tenant can occur where the premises are occupied and the business run by someone who is in law a different person. For example, in *Cristina v. Selear*[87] tenants ran their business through a series of limited liability companies. The Court of Appeal held that the companies rather than the tenants were carrying on the business, despite the fact that the tenants held all the shares in, and controlled, the companies. The decision can therefore prove a trap for the individual tenant who decides to incorporate his business.

Group companies

In the case of a group of companies, it is possible for one company to occupy through another by appointing it as manager.[88] If this is not the case, the tenant may be assisted by section 42(2) of the Act, which provides that occupation and carrying on a business by one company within the group[89] shall be treated for the purposes of section 23 as equivalent to occupation or carrying on a business by the member of the group holding the tenancy. A similar provision applies to tenancies held on trust, to allow occupation or the carrying on of a business by the beneficiaries to be attributed to the trustee tenant.[90] This provision may be of particular assistance where a tenancy is held by some members of a professional partnership on behalf of the other partners.[91]

16–18 Occupation for the purposes of a business

Ancillary purposes

It should be noted that the Act does not require that the tenant must actually run his business from the premises, but simply that the premises should be occupied for the purposes of the business. This leaves some scope for the tenant to claim protection in respect of premises used for ancillary purposes, such as storage or the accommodation of staff. However, some nexus will be required between the tenant's business and the purposes for which the premises are used.[92] Thus in

---

[86] *Cafeteria (Keighley) Ltd v. Harrison* (1956) 168 E.G. 668. *Cf., Teasdale v. Walker* [1958] 1 W.L.R. 1076 (sham agreement; occupation by licensee not sufficient). See also *Dellneed v. Chin* (1986) 281 E.G. 531 where a "management agreement" was held to confer exclusive possession rather than merely a licence or right to manage.

[87] [1985] 2 EGLR 128; followed in *Nozari-Zadeh v. Pearl Assurance plc* (1987) 283 E.G. 457; see also *Pegler v. Craven* [1952] 2 Q.B. 69.

[88] *Ross Auto Wash Ltd v. Herbert* (1979) 250 E.G. 971.

[89] On the meaning of "group" see s.42(1) and Companies Act 1985, s.736.

[90] s.41(1).

[91] See *Lord Hodson v. Cashmore* (1973) 226 E.G. 1203; para. 3–10 above.

[92] In *Chapman v. Freeman* [1978] 1 W.L.R. 1298 at 1301 it was said that occupation must be for business reasons rather than reasons merely of convenience: this would seem to be an unnecessary gloss upon the words of the Act and difficult to apply. See also *Groveside Properties Ltd v. Westminster Medical School* (1983) 47 P. & C.R. 507, where on the facts the opposite conclusion was reached.

one case, the use of premises for the dumping of rubbish from another shop of the tenant's, which was being refurbished, was held not to fall within the Act.[93]

Meaning of "business"
The expression "business" is very wide-ranging, and is defined to include a trade, profession or employment and any activity carried on by a body of persons whether corporate or unincorporate.[94] This is wide enough to include almost all activities carried out for profit, or as part of an occupier's *raison d'etre*, including a teaching hospital,[95] an office occupied by civil servants[96] and the maintenance of public open space by a local authority.[97] However it appears not to extend to activities carried on as hobbies, such as keeping animals.[98]

16–19 Mixed use

Difficult questions can arise where premises are used for a number of purposes, or where the use changes over a period of time. The wording of section 23(1) leaves open the possibility of the use of premises partly for business and partly for other purposes. In the case of premises used partly for business and partly for residential purposes a business tenancy within the 1954 Act will exclude any regulated tenancy under the Rent Act 1977.[99] However, it may be a difficult question of degree whether the occupation is for the purpose of a

Residential use
business.[1] If the premises are used partly for residential purposes and are capable of being regarded as a "house," there is also the possibility that they may be covered by the Leasehold Reform Act 1967, with its rights of enfranchisement and extended lease.[2] Use for agricultural purposes may take the premises outside the 1954 Act and

Agricultural use
within the Agricultural Holdings Act 1986.[3] Changes in the use to which the premises are put during the course of the lease may have this result, though the courts would probably be reluctant to regard the tenancy as fluctuating between the different schemes of protection on anything other than strong evidence of major changes of use.[4] Since every case will turn

---

[93] *Hillil Property and Investment Co. Ltd v. Naraine Pharmacy Ltd* (1979) 252 E.G. 1013; *cf. Nuflats & Properties Ltd v. Sheckman* (1959) 174 E.G. 39 where tidying up premises was held to constitute occupation for the purposes of a business.

[94] s. 23(2).

[95] *Hills (Patents) v. Board of Governors of University College Hospital* [1956] 1 Q.B. 90.

[96] *Town Investments Ltd v Department of the Environment* [1978] A.C. 359.

[97] *Wandsworth L.B.C. v. Singh*, see n. 74 above.

[98] *Gurton v. Parrott* [1991] 1 EGLR 98.

[99] Rent Act 1977 s.24(3); 1954 Act, s.23(1); see also *Kent Coast Property Investments v. Ward* [1990] 45 E.G. 107 (property comprised corner shop with accommodation above, all of which were occupied for the purpose of the tenant's business: held that the whole demise was subject to the Act).

[1] *Cheryl Investments Ltd v. Saldanha; Royal Life Saving Society v. Page* [1979] 1 W.L.R. 1329; *Simmonds v. Egyed* [1985] C.L.Y. 1908.

[2] *Tandon v. Trustees of Spurgeon's Homes* [1982] A.C. 755.

[3] s.43(1)(a); *Wetherall v. Smith* [1980] 1 W.L.R. 1290.

[4] See *Wetherall v. Smith* [1980] 1 W.L.R. 1290; *Pulleng v. Curran* (1980) 44 P. & C.R. 58.

on its own facts, all that can be safely said is that the practitioner should be alert to detect such problems, that borderline cases will require very detailed scrutiny of the background and present use of the premises, and that to avoid disputes it is important that accurate records of changes of use be kept by the parties or their professional advisers.

16–20 Unauthorised uses

Section 23(4) of the Act provides that the tenant is not protected when carrying on a business in breach of a prohibition of use for business purposes. However, two factors should be noted as weakening substantially the protection which the sub-section might be thought to afford a landlord.

Change from one business use to another The first is that the reference to the prohibition of use for business purposes does not include a prohibition of use for the purposes of a specified business, or of use for purposes of any other than a specified business.[5] Thus the sub-section protects the landlord where the tenant is flouting a blanket ban on all business use, but not where the tenant changes from one business use which is authorised to another which is not.

Consent to use Secondly, section 23(4) will not apply where the immediate landlord or his predecessor in title has consented to the breach or the immediate landlord has acquiesced in it. The distinction drawn between consent and acquiescence is important: consent is much narrower than acquiescence and demands some affirmative or positive act, not mere tacit consent or lack of opposition.[6]

Sub-tenants Finally, it should be noted that the protection of the Act may be claimed by a sub-tenant, even where the sub-lease was granted in breach of a covenant in the headlease. In such a case a prohibition on business user in the headlease will not protect the landlord: section 23(4) will not apply since the sub-tenant will not be in breach of any restriction on user under the terms of his tenancy.[7]

16–21 Occupations excluded from the Act

A number of types of tenancy are specifically excluded from the operation of the Act. It is also possible to exclude the Act by granting a tenancy-at-will or a licence, or by agreement **Specific exclusions** authorised by the court. The specific exclusions are as follows:

(1) agricultural holdings;[8]

---

[5] s.23(4).
[6] *Bell v. Alfred Franks & Bartlett Co. Ltd* [1980] 1 W.L.R. 340. See also *Bigos v. John Rowntree Social Service Trust* (1965) 193 E.G. 1035.
[7] *D'Silva v. Lister House Development Ltd* [1971] Ch. 17. It was recognised that this could be a source of hardship to the landlord in *Dodson Bull Carpet Co. Ltd v. City of London Corporation* [1975] 1 W.L.R. 781.
[8] s.43(1)(a).

(2) mining leases;[9]
(3) service tenancies, *i.e.* a tenancy granted to the tenant by reason of an office or employment held from the landlord and terminating or terminable upon the tenant ceasing to hold that office or employment;[10]
(4) leases for a term certain not exceeding six months. But the exclusion does not apply where: (a) the tenancy contains provisions for its renewal or extension; or (b) the tenant has been in occupation for a period exceeding 12 months, including any period of occupation by a predecessor in title carrying on the business carried on by the tenant;[11]
(5) the tenant's rights under the Act may be considerably curtailed where the landlord is one of a number of specified public bodies; *e.g.* government departments, local authorities, development corporations, statutory undertakers, industrial estate corporations, the Welsh Development Agency and the Development Board for Rural Wales;[12]
(6) tenancies of premises licensed for the sale of intoxicating liquor for consumption on the premises were formerly excluded from the Act but this exclusion no longer applies.[13]

16–22 Licences and tenancies-at-will

Licence The Act will not apply to a licence to occupy business premises.[14] In theory, therefore, the grant of a licence rather than a lease provides a potential means of excluding the Act. However, since the decision of the House

Street v. Mountford

of Lords in *Street v. Mountford*,[15] such attempts must be regarded as inadvisable. In that case, the House of Lords held that the grant of exclusive possession for a term[16] and at a rent[17] would, in all but a few exceptional cases,[18] constitute

---

[9] s.43(1)(b); *O'Callaghan v. Elliott* [1966] 1 Q.B. 601 (lease for extraction of sand and gravel excluded).
[10] s.43(2).
[11] s.43(3).
[12] See ss.57, 58, 60, 60A, 60B.
[13] Landlord and Tenant (Licensed Premises) Act 1990.
[14] See *Shell Mex & B.P. Ltd v. Manchester Garages Ltd* [1971] 1 W.L.R. 612; *Manchester City Council v. National Car Parks* (1981) 262 E.G. 1297; *Matchams Park (Holdings) Ltd v. Dommett* (1984) 272 E.G. 549; *Esso Petroleum Company Ltd v. Fumegrange Ltd* [1994] 46 E.G. 199.
[15] [1985] A.C. 809.
[16] See para. 5–01 above.
[17] Reservation of a rent is not necessary in every case: in *Ashburn Anstalt v. Arnold (No. 2)* [1988] 1 EGLR 64 a vendor of property awaiting redevelopment was permitted to remain in occupation after completion rent-free pending its demolition, and was held to be a tenant, not a licensee. See also *Canadian Imperial Bank of Commerce v. Bello* (1991) 64 P. & C.R. 48.
[18] *e.g.* occupation as a service occupant, or as a purchaser pending completion—as to which see below and para. 18–31 below. It has been accepted at first instance that these exceptional cases are illustrative and not exhaustive and that the categories are not closed: *Dellneed Ltd v. Chin* (1986) 281 E.G. 531 at 539.

Exclusive possession

the grant of a lease rather than a licence. Thus the question will usually turn on whether the agreement grants exclusive possession, rather than fine consideration of whether the parties intended to grant a lease or a licence. Even where the agreement is drafted so as to provide for shared, as opposed to exclusive, possession or where the owner retains a key, there is still the danger that it could be regarded as a sham.[19] It might be argued that *Street v. Mountford* was decided in the context of residential tenancies and that an approach giving more weight to the expressed intentions of the parties could prevail in the context of business premises. However, generally such cases as have been decided subsequently in the business context do not appear to have departed significantly from the approach prescribed by the House of Lords.[20]

Possible uses for licences

In view of the courts' approach, it is suggested that the use of licences of business premises is restricted to four areas, at least on the current state of the law:

(1) a licence used in a situation where clearly and genuinely the licensee is not to have exclusive possession, *e.g.* trade concessions such as the right to sell refreshments in a theatre[21] or petrol in a service station.[22]

(2) an agreement whereby the licensee has a right to occupy parts of the premises, but the particular part is subject to variation at the licensor's option. Such an agreement, permitting the storage of equipment in a disused pottery, was held to be a licence in *Dresden Estates Ltd v. Collinson*,[23] but it must be stressed that the mere inclusion of such a provision in an agreement requiring the licensee to relocate will be of no assistance unless at the outset the parties genuinely intend that it may be operated in practice.

(3) a licence granted by a company which is not permitted by its constitution to grant a lease.[24] There are strong grounds for believing that this would be unlikely to be upheld by the court if in practice a lease had been

---

[19] See *e.g. Antoniades v. Villiers* [1990] 1 A.C. 417. A sham can be described as the position where the parties do not intend their legal relationship to be governed by the provisions of the document in question.

[20] *University of Reading v. Houghton-Johnson* [1985] 2 EGLR 113; *Smith v. East Anglian Entertainment Activities Ltd* [1985] 1 EGLR 206; *Dellneed Ltd v. Chin* (1986) 281 E.G. 531; *Ashburn Anstalt v. Arnold (No. 2)* [1988] 1 EGLR 64. Also Lord Templeman, in referring in his judgment in *Street v. Mountford* [1985] A.C. 809 at 824 to *Shell-Mex & B.P. Ltd v. Manchester Garages Ltd* [1971] 1 W.L.R. 612, applied the same test as that applying to residential tenancies.

[21] *e.g. Clore v. Theatrical Properties Ltd* [1936] 3 All E.R. 483.

[22] *Shell Mex & BP Ltd v Manchester Garages Ltd* [1971] 1 W.L.R. 612; *Esso Petroleum Company Ltd v. Fumegrange Ltd* [1994] 46 E.G. 199. See also *Hunts Refuse Disposals v. Norfolk Environmental Waste Services Ltd* [1996] N.P.C. 88.

[23] (1987) 281 E.G. 1321. The Court of Appeal suggested in that case that the attributes of residential and commercial tenancies might be different, but it seems that this is not an approach which has been followed subsequently; Woodfall comments (in § 1–1.022, n. 1) that if there is a distinction, "it is not clear what it is".

[24] *Precedents for the Conveyancer*, para. 5–1.

granted. It could be alleged that a tenancy by estoppel, or an agreement for lease, had arisen.[25]

(4) a licence to a prospective tenant to allow him into occupation pending completion. In *Street v. Mountford*, Lord Templeman instanced occupancy under a contract for sale of the land as one case where exclusive possession would not connote a lease.[26] The same reasoning would extend to occupation pending the formal grant of a lease.[27] Occupation in such circumstances can give rise to different problems, which are considered in the Chapter on leasehold conveyancing.[28]

Tenancy-at-will   A tenancy-at-will has been held not to fall within the Act, whether it arises by implication of law[29] or expressly.[30] However, it has been said that a court should look carefully at an agreement purporting to be a tenancy-at-will, to ensure that it is not really a periodic tenancy or one for a term certain merely described as a tenancy-at-will.[31] In view of this, use of a tenancy-at-will is probably best confined to the classic cases where such a tenancy is appropriate, namely holding over at the end of a term,[32] or holding pending negotiation of the terms of a lease.[33]

16-23   Excluding the Act by agreement

Generally, an agreement purporting to exclude the tenant from making an application for a new tenancy under Part II of the 1954 Act is void.[34] However, by section 38(4) an agreement to exclude the provisions of the Act as to the continuation and renewal of the tenancy may be authorised by the court. The authorisation may be given on the joint application of the persons who will be landlord and tenant in relation to a tenancy to be granted[35] for a term of years

Joint application to exclude Act

---

[25] See [1980] Conv. 112 (P.H. Pettit).
[26] [1985] A.C. 809 at 827; *Bretherton v. Paton* [1986] 1 EGLR 172.
[27] Indeed Lord Templeman gave that as the rationale for *Isaac v. Hotel de Paris Ltd* [1960] 1 W.L.R. 239, a case in a commercial setting; see [1985] A.C. 809 at 823.
[28] See para. 18–31 below.
[29] *Wheeler v. Mercer* [1957] A.C. 416.
[30] *Manfield and Sons Ltd v. Botchin* [1970] 2 Q.B. 612.
[31] *Hagee (London) Ltd v. A.B. Erikson and Larson* [1976] 1 Q.B. 209; *cf.*, the different approaches adopted by members of the Court of Appeal in *Greater London Council v. Minchin*, February 25, 1981 (unreported, but noted under Case 45 in *Handbook of Business Tenancies* (1985)).
[32] Though its use here will be limited since a tenant holding over will usually do so under the 1954 Act: see para. 16–24 below. For a case in which the tenant did not have the protection of the 1954 Act see *Dean and Chapter of Canterbury Cathedral v. Whitbread plc* [1995] 24 E.G. 148.
[33] *Javad v. Aqil* [1990] 41 E.G. 61.
[34] s.38(1).
[35] Thus it is important that the order be obtained before the lease is granted. In *Essexcrest Ltd v. Evenlex Ltd* [1988] 1 EGLR 69 the order was obtained after the lease had been granted, and the lease was accordingly held to fall within the protection of the Act. See also para. 18–31 below.

certain.[36] The agreement must be contained in or endorsed on the lease or such other instrument as the court may specify.[37]

The joint application can be made either to the High Court or to the county court. It is open to the parties to confer jurisdiction on the most convenient county court.[38]

Grounds of application

Little clear guidance exists as to the grounds on which the court may grant or refuse an application under section 38(4). In *Hagee (London) Ltd v. A. B. Erikson and Larson*[39] Lord Denning, M.R. suggested[40] that the county court inevitably approves such an agreement when made by business people, properly advised by their lawyers; and that the court has no materials (*sic*) on which to refuse it. The application should state the grounds upon which it is made,[41] and should be accompanied by the draft lease. A High Court application should be supported by an affidavit setting out the reasons why both parties do not wish the provisions of the Act to apply.[42] However, the landlord should beware of stating his reasons in a way which might give rise to estoppel against him later.[43] Certainly the affidavit should deal with the question of both parties having been separately advised.

Agreement subject to exclusion order

The landlord should always have in mind the risk, albeit remote, of the application being rejected, and should expressly reserve his position in that event, as he will probably not wish to grant a tenancy at all if it is to be protected. It is therefore prudent to make any agreement as to the terms of the tenancy subject to the court's approval to the exclusion of the Act being obtained. It has been held at first instance that an agreement conditional upon the obtaining of an order under section 38(4) will not create any legally binding tenancy protected by the Act, notwithstanding possession by the prospective tenant and the payment of rent in the interim.[44] However, the provision invariably contained in agreements for lease in these circumstances, requiring each party to use its

---

[36] This includes tenancies for terms of less than a year: *Re Land and Premises at Liss, Hants.* [1971] Ch. 986 but does not include a term for an initial fixed period and continuing thereafter from year to year: *Nicholls v. Kinsey* [1994] 16 E.G. 145. *Quaere* whether it would include a term of years determinable by a break clause, though in practice such agreements are frequently approved by the courts. However, the fact that the court approves an agreement does not indicate that it has jurisdiction to do so: *Nicholls v. Kinsey (ibid.).*

[37] s.38(4)(a). However, in *Tottenham Hotspur Football and Athletic Co. Ltd v. Princegrove Publishers Ltd* [1974] 2 Q.B. 17, where the tenant simply went into occupation following the court order without the execution of a lease, Lawton J. held the exclusion of the Act effective, on the basis that the tenant held under an agreement for a lease including a term of exclusion.

[38] County Courts Act 1984, s.18.

[39] [1976] 1 Q.B. 209.

[40] *ibid.*, at 215. The suggestion was *obiter.*

[41] C.C.R., Ord. 3, r. 4. and Ord 43, r.20. See [1986] Lit., Vol. 5, No. 7, 285 at 287 (H.H. Judge Brian Clapham).

[42] *The Supreme Court Practice*, Ord. 97/6A/1.

[43] *e.g.* an intention to demolish may affect the ability to recover damages for dilapidations: *cf. Dunns Motors Ltd v. Cashman (J.P.) & Sons Ltd*, C.A., January 11, 1982 (unreported, but cited as Case 98 in the *Handbook of Business Tenancies* (1985)).

[44] *Cardiothoracic Institute v. Shrewdcrest Ltd* [1986] 1 W.L.R. 368. There was no such agreement in *Essexcrest Ltd v. Evenlex Ltd* (see n. 35 above).

best endeavours to obtain such an order, will probably be void under section 38(1), being an agreement which will have the effect of precluding the protection of the Act.

16–24   The operation of the Act

Structure of Act's protection

The protection afforded by the Act to the tenant may be summarised as follows: at the date upon which the contractual tenancy would otherwise determine, the tenancy continues by virtue of the Act; thus continued, the tenancy may only be determined in specified ways; the tenant has a right to apply to the court for the grant of a new tenancy, and the landlord may oppose such an application on specified grounds. Within this simple structure is comprised much complex and technical detail, which can all too easily provide pitfalls for both parties.

By section 24, a tenancy to which the Act applies shall not come to an end unless terminated in accordance with the provisions of the Act. This applies to both a term certain and a periodic tenancy. The effect of the section is to prolong the existing tenancy on the same terms, subject only to the statutory variations as to the mode of termination and the ability to seek a new tenancy.[45] Such a tenancy remains an estate in land, capable (subject to its terms) of being assigned, and capable of being forfeit. Part of a tenancy cannot be continued: where the Act applies to only part of the premises comprised in a tenancy the entire tenancy continues.

Continuation of the tenancy

Determination of tenancy

Section 24(2) provides that notwithstanding section 24(1), a tenancy may be determined by a notice to quit given by the tenant,[46] by surrender,[47] or by forfeiture of the tenancy or a superior tenancy.

Where the continuation tenancy ceases to be one to which the Act applies, for example where the tenant ceases to carry on a business from the premises,[48] the tenancy does not automatically determine, but may be terminated (subject to any express terms as to termination) by not less than three nor more than six months' notice in writing given by the landlord to the tenant.[49]

---

[45] *Bolton (H.L.) Engineering Co. Ltd v. T.J. Graham & Sons Ltd* [1957] 1 Q.B. 159 at 168; *Bowes-Lyon v. Green* [1963] A.C. 420 at 434, 446. In *Willison v. Cheverell Estates Ltd* [1995] 26 E.G. 133 the court held that once the landlord had determined the lease in accordance with a break clause, he could not then purport to exercise a rent review (but the expression "term" had not been extended to include any statutory continuation, as is common in modern leases; see para. 5–01, n. 3 above).

[46] Unless the notice was given before the tenant had been in occupation under the tenancy for a month.

[47] But not where the surrender was executed before the tenant had been in occupation under the tenancy for a month, or was executed in pursuance of an agreement so made. Also the surrender must take immediate effect, as an agreement for surrender (unless sanctioned by the court in accordance with s.38(4)(b)) will be void under s.38(1) of the Act: *Tarjomani v. Panther Securities Ltd* (1983) 46 P. & C.R. 32; and see para. 12–15 above.

[48] See para. 16–18 above.

[49] s.24(3)(a).

Notice by tenant

A tenant who does not wish a fixed term tenancy to continue under the Act may prevent it doing so by serving notice that he does not wish the tenancy to continue.[50] Service of such a notice is mandatory even if the tenant wishes to vacate on or before the contractual termination date.[51] The notice must be in writing and given to the immediate landlord not less than three months before the end of the contractual term. Such notice may not be given before the tenant has been in occupation under the tenancy for a month.

A tenancy granted for a term of years certain which is continuing by virtue of the Act may be terminated on any quarter day[52] by not less than three months' notice in writing given by the tenant to the immediate landlord.[53] Again such notice may not be given before the tenant has been in occupation under the tenancy for a month.

Where the landlord and tenant agree to the grant of a new tenancy on a specified date, the current tenancy terminates on that date and the provisions of the Act cease to apply to it, thereby preventing the tenant making any application for a new tenancy.[54] Landlord means "competent landlord".[55] It is thought that this provision will apply also to an agreement between the landlord and a sub-tenant.[56]

Steps toward the grant of a new lease The continuation of the tenancy under section 24 is only the start of the process envisaged by the Act. Section 24 goes on to provide that the tenant under such a tenancy may, subject to section 29, apply to the court for a new tenancy. Two possible routes to this application are given by the section: a landlord's notice to terminate the tenancy under section 25 and a tenant's request for a new tenancy under section 26. However, before considering the two routes in detail, certain key concepts must be clarified.

16–25 Common rules and concepts under the Act

A number of rules and concepts under the Act are common to notices under section 25 and requests under section 26,

---

[50] s.27.

[51] *Long Acre Securities Ltd v. Electro Acoustic Industries Ltd* [1990] 6 E.G. 103; *Esselte A.B. v. Pearl Assurance plc* [1995] 37 E.G. 173 (both these cases have been criticised (see *e.g. Property Week*, August 3, 1994, p. 25 (K. Lewison)) and the latter one is going to appeal); also *Provident Mutual Life Assurance Association v. Greater London Employers' Association Limited* [1996] 23 E.G. 129.

[52] *Quaere* whether this means the common law quarter days or the quarter days specified in the tenancy, if different; it is submitted that if there is any divergence it means the contractual quarter days as otherwise difficulties as to apportionment would arise.

[53] s.27(2).

[54] s.28. The agreement must be a binding one: *R. J. Stratton Ltd v. Wallis Tomlin & Co. Ltd* [1986] 1 EGLR 104 (agreement held effective, though not enforceable for want of registration under Land Charges Act 1972).

[55] *Bowes-Lyon v. Green* [1963] A.C. 420. See para. 16–25 below.

[56] *ibid.*

and to the responses to each required by the Act. It is helpful
to deal with these rules at the outset, and to keep them in
mind when considering the alternative procedures.

"Landlord" The first concept is that of "the landlord".
The Act draws a distinction between "the immediate
landlord" and "the landlord". Under section 44 of the Act
"the landlord" or "competent landlord" is defined as the
owner of the reversion expectant (whether immediate or not)
upon the termination of the relevant tenancy which is either
the fee simple or is a tenancy which will not come to an end
by effluxion of time or notice within 14 months.[57] For some
purposes of the Act, notices may be served by or on the
immediate landlord.[58] But for many crucial sections of the
Act[59] it will be vital to ascertain who is the competent
landlord by reference to section 44. The effect of the section
is that for any one lease there will only be one competent
landlord, who will be the first person above the tenant in the
chain to hold a reversion of 14 months or more or, if there is
no-one in that position, the freeholder. The competent
landlord may change over time[60] and this may necessitate
action on the part of the tenant.[61]

Sub-tenancies In cases where the tenant's immediate landlord is himself a
tenant, the provisions of Schedule 6 to the Act will apply.[62]
The Schedule provides rules to govern the relationship
between the tenant, the landlord and any mesne or superior
landlords. One important consequence of these rules is that
the acts of the landlord can bind any mesne landlord, but not
any superior landlord. However, the detail and complexity of
the Schedule is such that any attempt to summarise the
provisions would be liable to mislead, and therefore reference
should be made to the actual words of the Schedule in any
case where it applies.[63]

Time limits The next point which is common to both
procedures is the use of time limits. For example, a landlord's
section 25 notice must be given not more than 12 nor less
than six months before the date of termination specified in
it.[64] The tenant is required to respond in writing to the notice
within two months after it is given stating whether or not the
tenant is willing to give up possession,[65] and where the tenant
is not willing to give up possession to apply for a new tenancy

---

[57] Sched. 6 refers to the landlord as the "competent landlord", and that
terminology is habitually used.
[58] *e.g.* ss.27(1), 27(2), 44(2).
[59] Including ss.24A, 25, 26, 28, 30.
[60] *X.L. Fisheries Ltd v. Leeds Corporation* [1955] 2 Q.B. 636.
[61] *e.g.* he will need to add the new landlord as a party to any proceedings:
Piper v. Muggleton [1956] 2 Q.B. 569. There may be some duty on a
landlord to inform a tenant of a change in competent landlord: *Shelley v.
United Artists Corp* [1990] 16 E.G. 73.
[62] s.44(3).
[63] *Handbook of Business Tenancies* (1985) provides a helpful series of precepts
derived from the Schedule: para. 2–37. See also [1983] L.S.Gaz. 1975,
(A. J. Williams).
[64] s.25(2).
[65] s.29(2).

not less than two nor more than four months from the date that the landlord's notice was given.[66] Similarly, a tenant's request for a new tenancy under section 26 must specify a commencement date not more than 12 nor less than six months after the making of the request;[67] the landlord has to reply to the notice within two months of its being made if he wishes to oppose the grant of a new tenancy;[68] and the tenant must make any application for a new tenancy not less than two nor more than four months from the date on which the request was made.[69]

Failure by professional advisers to comply with these time limits is one of the most common forms of negligence in operating the Act.[70] It is possible for one party to waive the strict observance of the time limits by the other, either expressly, or by passive encouragement with knowledge of the contravention.[71] However, reliance on such a doctrine will usually be a matter of last resort, and is no substitute for **Importance of** careful compliance with the Act's timetable. Failure by the **compliance with** tenant who has served a valid section 26 request to apply in **time limits** time to the court for a new tenancy is particularly disastrous, since the tenant will not be allowed to cure the defect by serving a new section 26 request,[72] and accordingly the tenancy will come to an end at the date specified in the first section 26 request for the new tenancy to begin.[73]

Therefore the professional adviser should possess both a clear understanding of how the time provisions operate, and a reliable system of work to ensure that they are observed in practice. The following are the main questions which can arise:

(a) From when does time run, *i.e.* at what date is the section 25 notice taken to be given, or the section 26 request **Date from which** to be made? It is generally accepted that the relevant date is **time runs** that of service of the notice or request.[74] This will usually be the date on which the notice or request was received through the post, or on which it was personally delivered.[75] If the notice was posted, there is a presumption that it was delivered in the ordinary course of the post,[76] but where the notice was sent by ordinary post the presumption can be rebutted by

---

[66] s.29(3).

[67] s.26(2). The date cannot be earlier than the date on which the current tenancy would come to an end of effluxion of time or by notice by the tenant.

[68] s.26(6).

[69] s.29(3).

[70] *Handbook of Business Tenancies*, para. 10–02.

[71] *Kammins Ballrooms Co. Ltd v. Zenith Investments (Torquay) Ltd* [1971] A.C. 850. But see *Salomon v. Akiens* [1993] 14 E.G. 97, where the court held that there had been no waiver.

[72] *Polyviou v. Seeley* [1980] 1 W.L.R. 55; *Stile Hall Properties Ltd v. Gooch* [1980] 1 W.L.R. 62.

[73] s.26(5).

[74] In a slightly different context, "given" has been treated as synonymous with "served": *Sun Alliance and London Assurance Co. Ltd v. Hayman* [1975] 1 W.L.R. 177 at 183, 185. See also *Re 88 Berkeley Rd, N.W.9* [1971] Ch. 648.

[75] The question of the different modes of service is discussed below.

[76] *Papillon v. Brunton* (1860) 5 H. & N. 518.

proof of later delivery or no delivery at all.[77] Whether posted or delivered personally, it would appear that the date of service will be the date upon which the notice or request reached the relevant destination rather than the date on which it actually came to the recipient's attention.[78]

"Month"   (b) What is meant by "month"? Time limits under the Act are defined by reference to periods calculated in months. The principle to be adopted is the "corresponding date rule", as considered by the House of Lords in *Dodds v. Walker.*[79] Under the rule a period calculated in months from a specified date will end on the corresponding day (*i.e.* that day bearing the same number) in the appropriate month.[80]

Length of period   (c) What is meant by "not less than", "not more than" and "within"? The use of the phraseology "not less than" and "not more than" means in effect that the period allowed for taking action will include the corresponding date on which the period begins and the corresponding date on which it ends.[81] In other words, an application which must be made not less than two nor more than four months from February 13, can be made at the earliest on April 13, and at latest on June 13.[82] Any reply to a section 25 notice or section 26 request must be given "within two months". A straightforward application of the corresponding date rule would tend to suggest that if (say) a section 26 request is made on February 13, the landlord's reply must be given on or before April 13. But it may be possible to argue that a reply given on April 14 is valid, on the general principle that where a particular time is given within which an act is to be done, and the time is to run from a certain date, the day of that date is excluded.[83] In practice, however, clearly no sensible adviser will wish to cut things as finely as that.

Date of notice   (d) On what date is the act required effectively done? Where the giving of a notice is required within a certain time, it would appear that to be effective the notice must be served rather than simply despatched within the period.[84] Where the act required is the making of an application to the court, an

---

[77] *Chiswell v. Griffon Land & Estates Ltd* [1975] 1 W.L.R. 1181; *cf.* the position of letters sent by the recorded delivery service: *Italica Holdings S.A. v. Bayadea* [1985] 1 EGLR 70. Use of the document exchange service may be similarly inadvisable: see *Imprint (Print and Design) Ltd v. Inkblot Studios Ltd* (1985) 129 S.J. 133.

[78] *Papillon v. Brunton* (1860) 5 H. & N. 518; *Price v. West London Investment Building Society* [1964] 1 W.L.R. 616; *Lord Newborough v. Jones* [1975] Ch. 90.

[79] [1981] 1 W.L.R. 1027.

[80] Except where the day has no corresponding date in the subsequent month (*e.g.* February 30) in which case the period will end on the last day of the month. It would appear to be immaterial that the last day is a public holiday: *Hodgson v. Armstrong* [1967] 2 Q.B. 299.

[81] *E.J. Riley Investments Ltd v. Eurostile Holdings Ltd* [1985] 1 W.L.R. 1139.

[82] See also *Hogg Bullimore & Co. v. Co-operative Insurance Society Ltd* (1984) 50 P. & C.R. 105 (landlord's s.25 notice served on April 2 specified termination date of October 2; held good since date of service was not given "less than" six months before specified termination date).

[83] *Goldsmiths' Co. v. West Metropolitan Rail Co.* [1904] 1 K.B. 1; *Stewart v. Chapman* [1951] 2 K.B. 792.

[84] The same principles as are mentioned in (a) would apply.

application posted so as to arrive on Easter day (that being the last day on which the application could have been made) has been held effective.[85]

Service of notices   The final set of common rules to be considered are those relating to service of notices under the Act. By section 23(1) of the Landlord and Tenant Act 1927[86] any notice or request served under the 1954 Act must be in writing and may be served personally, or by leaving it for the recipient at his last known place of abode in England or Wales,[87] or by sending it through the post in a registered letter[88] addressed to him there.[89] A person claiming that a recorded delivery letter was not delivered has the burden of proof against him: he must show that it was not delivered.[90] Service on the landlord's duly authorised[91] agent is expressly permitted, from which it may be inferred that a notice to be served on the tenant should be served only on him personally. The tenant can safely assume that his original landlord remains unchanged and serve notice upon him accordingly, until he receives notice to the contrary.[92]

Companies   Notice may be served on a company by leaving it at, or sending it by post to, the registered office of the company.[93] Special provisions apply to premises held by joint tenants and used for the purposes of a partnership; notice can be served on, and applications made by, simply those joint tenants actually carrying on business, so that there is no need to include former partners who still retain an interest in the premises.[94]

Service by fax   It may be possible to serve a notice by fax.[95] Rules of Court now allow service of documents by fax in certain circumstances[96] and it is likely that a court would have regard to those if a question arose.

---

[85] *Hodgson v. Armstrong* [1967] 2 Q.B. 299. However a notice to trigger a rent review sent by recorded delivery letter which could not be delivered on the final day (a Saturday) as there was no-one on the premises to receive it, and which was delivered on the following Monday, was held to be out of time: *Stephenson v. Orca Properties* [1989] 44 E.G. 81.

[86] Applied to the 1954 Act by s.66(4).

[87] This can include a place of business: *Price v. West London Investment Building Society* [1964] 1 W.L.R. 616; *Italica Holdings S.A. v. Bayadea* [1985] 1 EGLR 70.

[88] Or using the recorded delivery service: see Recorded Delivery Service Act 1962, s.1(1).

[89] The methods stated are permissive rather than mandatory, therefore other methods can be used provided the notice is actually served: *Stylo Shoes Ltd v. Prices Tailors Ltd* [1960] Ch. 396. Thus ordinary post can be used, though it will be inadvisable to do so: see the cases cited at n. 77 above.

[90] *Lex Services Ltd v. Johns* [1990] 10 E.G. 67.

[91] See *Sector Properties Ltd v Meah* (1974) 229 E.G. 1097.

[92] s.23(2) of the Landlord and Tenant Act 1927. This is subject to the rules as to the competent landlord, stated above. Also see *Shelley v. United Artists Corp* [1990] 16 E.G. 73.

[93] Companies Act 1985, s.725.

[94] s.41A; and see paras. 3–10 and 16–17 above.

[95] See *Hastie & Jenkenson v. McMahon* [1991] 1 All E.R. 255.

[96] R.S.C. Ord. 65, r. 5.

16–26　Landlord's section 25 notice

The landlord may terminate a tenancy to which the 1954 Act applies by serving a notice under section 25. The notice must be in the prescribed form[97] and must specify the date at which the tenancy is to come to an end. The date may not be earlier than the date on which the tenancy could have been determined apart from the Act or on which it would expire by effluxion of time.[98] It must be given not more than 12 nor less than six months before the specified date of

Content of notice termination.[99] The notice must require the tenant to notify the landlord within two months of the giving of the notice whether or not he will be willing to give up possession[1] and must state whether the landlord would oppose any application for a new tenancy and, if so, upon which of the grounds specified in section 30.[2] A section 25 notice may not be served so as to terminate a tenancy of part only of the holding,[3] but it may terminate more than one tenancy.[4]

It is possible to use a single notice to exercise a break clause and comply with section 25, but care is required to ensure that the notice complies with the requirements of the break clause as well as those of section 25.[5] The landlord should remember that service of a section 25 notice upon his immediate tenant may result in the landlord becoming the competent landlord as regards a sub-tenant.[6] Accordingly, where appropriate, a subsequent section 25 notice may need to be served on the sub-tenant.[7]

Where the landlord comprises more than one person, all the landlords must be named in the section 25 notice.[8] If several buildings owned by separate landlords are all comprised in one tenancy, service of one section 25 notice for each building will not be effective unless it is clear to the tenant that the notices must be treated as one.[9]

---

[97] See Landlord and Tenant Act 1954 Part II (Notices) Regulations 1983 (S.I. 1983 No. 133, Form 1), amended by the Landlord and Tenant Act 1954 Part II (Notices) (Amendment) Regulations 1989 (S.I. 1989 No. 1548). Reg. 2(2) permits a notice "substantially to the like effect" to be used but this is not recommended.

[98] s.25(3),(4). A notice expiring on the last day of the term is valid: *Re Crowhurst Park* [1974] 1 W.L.R. 583 (but is perhaps unwise, as it leaves no margin for error).

[99] s.25(2). But where at common law more than 6 months' notice to quit would be required, see s.25(3)(b).

[1] s.25(5).

[2] s.25(6).

[3] *Southport Old Links Ltd v. Naylor* [1985] 1 EGLR 66 and *Moss v. Mobil Oil Co.* [1988] 6 E.G. 109 (lease held to have created two separate tenancies, which were capable of termination separately).

[4] *Tropis Shipping v. Ibex Property Corporation* [1967] EGD 433.

[5] *Scholl Manufacturing Co. Ltd v. Clifton (Slim Line) Ltd* [1967] 1 Ch. 41.

[6] *Rene Claro (Haute Coiffure) Ltd v. Hallé Concerts Society* [1969] 1 W.L.R. 909.

[7] See *Keith Bayley Rogers & Co. v. Cubes Ltd* (1975) 31 P. & C.R. 412 where the Court of Appeal held that notices served on the tenant and sub-tenant on the same day could be presumed to have been served in the correct order.

[8] *Pearson v. Alyo* [1990] 25 E.G. 69.

[9] *M. & P. Enterprises (London) Ltd v. Norfolk Square Hotels Ltd* [1994] 14 E.G. 128.

Defective notices

Section 25 notices frequently fail to comply with one or more of the requirements mentioned above. The courts have shown a considerable willingness to overlook errors or departures from the proper form or wording, provided that the substance of the landlord's intention is clear from the notice and the notice gives the tenant adequate information to allow him to decide how to proceed.[10] In some cases, shortcomings in the notice may be cured by information given in a covering letter.[11] However, some defects will be so serious as to invalidate the notice, where their effect is seriously to mislead the tenant or leave him in total ignorance as to the landlord's intentions.[12] In particular the landlord should be wary of qualifying a section 25 notice, *e.g.* stating that he would not oppose a new tenancy of part of the holding, or provided guarantors are given. Such a notice may be construed as one indicating opposition to a new tenancy, and the landlord will then be in difficulty because no ground of opposition will have been indicated.[13]

Honest belief

It is possible that a notice given by a landlord which does not reflect his honest belief in its contents could be a nullity.[14]

A section 25 notice cannot be withdrawn.[15] If a section 25 notice is invalid, there is nothing in the Act to prevent the landlord serving a second, correct one.[16] Such a notice may include further grounds of opposition to a new tenancy.[17] It is common in such a case to serve the second notice without prejudice to the contention that the first notice was valid, to preserve the original termination date in case the first notice is declared to be valid by the court.

---

[10] *e.g. McMullen v. The Great Southern Cemetary & Crematorium Co. Ltd* (1958) 172 E.G. 855; *Lewis v. M.T.C. (Cars) Ltd* [1975] 1 W.L.R. 457; *Philipson-Stow v. Trevor Square Ltd* (1980) 257 E.G. 1262; *Morris v. Patel* (1986) 281 E.G. 419 (use of outdated form of notice did not prejudice tenant); *Bridges v. Stanford* (1991) 63 P. & C.R. 18 and *Baglarbasi v. Deedmethod* [1991] 2 EGLR 71 (form of notice prescribed by the regulations did not comply with the provisions of s.25 but tenants were not prejudiced—following these cases the regulations were amended: see para. 16–26, n. 97 above).

[11] *Stidolph v. The American School in London Educational Trusts Ltd* (1969) 211 E.G. 925 (notice unsigned); *Falcon Pipes Ltd v. Stanhope Gate Property Co. Ltd* (1967) 204 E.G. 1243 (notice undated).

[12] *e.g. Barclays Bank Ltd v. Ascott* [1961] 1 W.L.R. 717 (notice effectively said landlord would oppose a new tenancy but no ground of opposition given); *Morrow v. Nadeem* [1986] 1 W.L.R. 1381 (wrong person named as landlord); *Herongrove Ltd v. Wates City of London Properties plc* [1988] 24 E.G. 108 (notice referred only to ninth floor offices and omitted reference to basement storage areas and car parking spaces: held tenant could have been in doubt as to which premises were the subject of the notice); *Yamaha-Kemble Music U.K. Ltd v. ARC Properties Ltd* [1990] 1 EGLR 261 (notice named as landlord a company which was a subsidiary of the true landlord).

[13] *Barclays Bank Ltd v. Ascott* [1961] 1 W.L.R. 717.

[14] *Earl of Stradbroke v. Mitchell* [1991] 3 E.G. 128, a case concerning an agricultural tenancy.

[15] *Stile Hall Properties v. Gooch* [1980] 1 W.L.R. 62 (a case decided under s.26 but thought to apply to s.25). Exceptionally, Sched. 6 para. 6 permits a s.25 notice to be withdrawn where a superior landlord becomes a competent landlord, in limited circumstances.

[16] *Smith v. Draper* (1990) 60 P. & C.R. 252.

[17] *ibid.*

16–27 Tenant's response to section 25 notice

Counter-notice

A tenant who has been served with a section 25 notice and who wishes to obtain a new lease must within two months serve notice in writing upon the landlord that he will not be willing at the date of termination to give up possession of the property.[18] No particular form of notice is required, and it may be possible to spell a sufficient notice out of written negotiations for a new tenancy. Unless section 41A applies,[19] all joint tenants need to join in the notice.[20] To avoid any doubt, a clear notice should be given to the landlord well within the time limit.

Landlord's notice defective

In some cases it may appear to the tenant's advisers that the landlord's section 25 notice is defective. Any temptation to regard the notice as a nullity and ignore it should be strongly resisted, for two reasons. First, what appears to be a departure from the proper form may well turn out not to be a fatal defect. Secondly, the tenant who is aware of the defect and fails to take the point up with the landlord promptly may be held to have waived the defect.[21] The appropriate course is to serve a counter-notice as required by the Act and to go on to make an application for a new tenancy, whilst pointing out to the landlord that the right to take an objection to the section 25 notice is reserved.[22] If necessary a request for a declaration that the section 25 notice is void can be added to the application for a new tenancy.[23]

16–28 Tenant's section 26 request

Contents of request

A tenant's request for a new tenancy must be made by notice in the prescribed form[24] and must specify a date on which the new tenancy is to begin, which must be not more than 12 nor less than six months after the making of the request.[25] It must set out the tenant's proposals as to the property to be comprised in the new tenancy, the rent, and the other terms.[26] No section 26 request can be made where the landlord has already served a section 25 notice or where the

---

[18] ss.25(5), 29(2). The Law Commission has recommended that this requirement should be dispensed with—see para. 16–14, n. 67 above.

[19] See para. 3–10 above.

[20] *Lewington v. Trustees for the Protection of Ancient Buildings* (1983) 45 P. & C.R. 336; *cf. Mehmet v. Dawson* (1984) 270 E.G. 138.

[21] *Morrow v. Nadeem* [1986] 1 W.L.R. 1381 (where on the facts the defect was not known to the tenant on receipt).

[22] *Craddock v. Feldman* (1960) 175 E.G. 1149.

[23] *A.J.A. Smith Transport Ltd v. British Rail* (1981) 257 E.G. 1257; and see s.43A.

[24] s.26(3); see S.I. 1983 No. 133, Form 8.

[25] s.26(2). The date cannot be earlier than the date on which the current tenancy would come to an end by effluxion of time or by notice by the tenant.

[26] s.26(3); including the proposed length of the term: *Sidney Bolsom Investment Trust Ltd v. E. Karmios & Co. (London) Ltd* [1956] 1 Q.B. 529.

tenant has previously given notice to quit or given notice under section 27.[27]

Tactical considerations

Since the effect of a section 26 request is to terminate the existing tenancy,[28] the tenant should think seriously before making such a request, particularly where the landlord shows no inclination to serve a section 25 notice. However, there may be advantages to the tenant in serving a request in some cases. Where the landlord seems likely to serve a section 25 notice, the tenant may, by serving a section 26 request specifying a commencement date 12 months hence, retain possession under the terms of the old lease for longer than would be the case if the landlord served a section 25 notice. Secondly, service of a section 26 request may place the landlord in difficulties if he has plans for redevelopment but those plans are not sufficiently advanced to justify opposition to a new tenancy.[29]

Interaction with break clause

It has been suggested that a tenant may be permitted to exercise a break clause by service of a section 26 request and by so doing be able to retain his right to a new tenancy under the Act and so effectively negotiate a lower rent.[30]

16–29 Landlord's response to section 26 request

Landlord's counter-notice

If the landlord wishes to oppose a new tenancy, he must within two months of the section 26 request give notice to the tenant that he will oppose an application to the court for the grant of a new tenancy, and on which of the grounds under section 30 he will rest his opposition.[31] The notice is not required to be in any particular form. Careful thought must be given as to which grounds of opposition are specified, as the landlord will not be able to rely on different grounds later.[32]

16–30 Renewal of tenancy by agreement

It is likely that service of a section 25 notice or section 26 request will lead to negotiations between the parties. If the negotiations result in a binding agreement for the renewal of the tenancy, the existing tenancy will continue until the date agreed for the grant of the new tenancy, but no longer, and the Act will not apply to it.[33]

---

[27] s.26(4).
[28] s.26(5).
[29] See para. 16–40 below.
[30] See para. 16–09 above.
[31] s.26(6).
[32] s.30.
[33] s.28; see para. 16–24, n. 54 above.

16–31   Tenant's application for a new tenancy

Pending land action

Time limit for application

If agreement cannot be reached, the tenant will need to apply to the court[34] for the grant of a new tenancy. The application may be protected by registration as a pending land action to avoid the danger of an assignee of the reversion taking free of the claim.[35] The application must be made not less than two nor more than four months from the giving of the section 25 notice or the making of the section 26 request. The time limits can be extended by agreement and it is sensible to do so to allow time for a new lease to be negotiated.[36] As well as the time limits under the 1954 Act, the parties should be aware of the timetable for steps in the proceedings laid down by the High Court and County Court Rules.[37]

16–32   Interim rent

Following the giving of a section 25 notice or the making of a section 26 request, it is possible for the landlord to apply to the court for determination of a rent which it would be reasonable for the tenant to pay while the tenancy continues by virtue of section 24.[38] The landlord should always consider making such an application, particularly where the rent under the existing tenancy is low. There is no similar procedure to allow the tenant to apply for such a determination, which puts the tenant at a serious disadvantage when rents are falling.[39]

The court has a discretion whether or not to determine such a rent,[40] but where it does so the rent is to be a rent which it would be reasonable for the tenant to pay, and the court is to follow the directions of section 34 of the Act[41] as if a new tenancy from year to year had been granted to the tenant, and have regard to the rent payable under the terms of

---

[34] Either the High Court or the county court: s.63; *Norman E. Potts (Birmingham) Ltd v. Rootes Ltd* (1957) 170 E.G. 39. An application to the wrong county court is not necessarily fatal: *Sharma v. Knight* [1986] 1 W.L.R. 757.

[35] s.29(1).

[36] s.29(3). An application issued earlier than the two months' date is invalid: *Stevens & Cutting v. Anderson* [1990] 11 E.G. 70. Whether a landlord is estopped from refusing a new tenancy where the tenant has failed to comply with the time limits depends on the facts: compare *J. T. Developments Ltd v. Quinn* (1991) P. & C.R. 33 with *Salomon v. Akiens* [1993] 14 E.G. 97.

[37] The various steps are summarised in the *Handbook of Business Tenancies*, paras. 5–05, *et seq.* On the question of extension of these time limits under the County Court Rules, see *Robert Baxendale Ltd v. Davstone (Holdings) Ltd* [1982] 1 W.L.R. 1385; *Ali v. Knight* (1984) 272 E.G. 1165; *Evans Constructions Co. Ltd v. Charrington & Co. Ltd* [1983] 1 Q.B. 810. As to the jurisdiction of the county court to amend defective applications, see *Nurit Bar v. Pathwood Investments Ltd* (1987) 54 P. & C.R. 178.

[38] s.24A.

[39] The Law Commission has recommended that the tenant should be given such a right, see para. 16–14, n. 67 above.

[40] *English Exporters (London) Ltd v. Eldonwall Ltd* [1973] Ch. 415.

[41] See para. 16–47 below.

**Determination
of interim rent**

the existing tenancy.[42] In practice this means that the open market rent will be determined applying section 34 and will then be tempered by a reduction with reference to the old rent.[43] The interim rent is payable from the date on which the proceedings for determination of an interim rent were commenced[44] or from the date specified in the section 25 notice or section 26 request, whichever is the later.[45] So as not to lose any opportunity to obtain a higher rent, the

**Tactical
considerations**

landlord may wish to commence proceedings for an interim rent as soon as possible. However, against this must be weighed the fact that the comparables to be used in determining the interim rent will be those current at the date on which the interim rent period begins to run:[46] therefore by waiting before commencing proceedings, the landlord may be able to make use of more favourable comparables in a market where rents are rising sharply or where a round of rent reviews is known to be due.[47]

A claim for interim rent will survive discontinuance of the tenant's application for a new tenancy.[48]

16–33 Obtaining information under section 40

**Request for
information**

In order to comply with the requirements of the Act and to make sound tactical decisions, both parties may need information as to the interests existing in the property. For example, the tenant will need to ascertain who is the competent landlord; and the landlord may wish to find out whether the tenant occupies the whole of the premises for his business, or whether any sub- tenancies have been created. Such information may be obtained by making use of the procedures laid down in section 40. By serving notice in the prescribed form,[49] the landlord can place the tenant under a

---

[42] s.24A(3).

[43] *English Exporters (London) Ltd v. Eldonwall Ltd* [1973] Ch. 415; *Fawke v. Viscount Chelsea* [1980] Q.B. 441; *Ratners (Jewellers) Ltd v. Lemnoll Ltd* (1980) 255 E.G. 987; *Charles Follett Ltd v. Cabtell Investment Co. Ltd* (1987) 283 E.G. 195; *Conway v. Arthur* [1988] 40 E.G. 120; *French v. Commercial Union Assurance Company plc* [1993] 24 E.G. 115; however a reduction is not always appropriate: *Department of the Environment v. Allied Freehold Property Trust Ltd* [1992] 45 E.G. 156.

[44] *Stream Properties Ltd v. Davis* [1972] 1 W.L.R. 645; *Victor Blake (Menswear) Ltd v. Westminster City Council* (1978) 38 P. & C.R. 448. Note that the relevant date is that of the landlord's application under s.24A, not the tenant's application for a new tenancy. The landlord's application under s.24A can validly be made by way of answer to the tenant's application. In that case the relevant date will be that of the answer: *Thomas v. Hammond-Lawrence* [1986] 1 W.L.R. 456.

[45] s.24A(3). There is no power for the court to order an interim rent backdated prior to the issue of the application for interim rent, even if the delay in issuing the application is that of the court: *R. v. Gravesend County Court, ex p. Patchett* [1993] 26 E.G. 125.

[46] *English Exporters (London) Ltd v. Eldonwall Ltd* [1973] Ch. 415.

[47] See *Janes (Gowns) Ltd v. Harlow Development Corporation* (1980) 253 E.G. 799.

[48] *Artoc Bank & Trust Ltd v. Prudential Assurance Co. plc* [1984] 1 W.L.R. 1181; *Michael Kramer & Co. Ltd v. Airways Pension Board Trustees Ltd* (1976) 246 E.G. 911.

[49] S.I. 1983 No. 133, Form 9.

duty to notify him within a month of the position regarding the occupation of the premises, and of the existence and terms of any sub-tenancies.[50] Similarly, the tenant may demand information from anyone holding a superior interest in the property[51] or their mortgagee[52] as to the ownership of the freehold, the identity of the superior landlord, and the duration of his interest.[53] There are however no sanctions in the Act for failing to comply with these requests.[54]

16–34   Opposing the grant of a new tenancy

The landlord may oppose the grant of a new tenancy on such of the grounds set out in section 30 as have been stated in his section 25 notice or in his reply to the tenant's section 26 request. Once these grounds have been stated they cannot subsequently be amended. The landlord can also object on the basis that the tenancy is not within the Act.[55] Once the court application has been made the tenant must continue to occupy pursuant to the Act up to and including any court hearing in order to retain the protection of the Act.[56] Each of the grounds is considered below.

General points on grounds (a) to (c)   When relying on these grounds the landlord should consider whether his case might **Discovery of** be helped by an order for discovery of the tenant's accounts. **tenant's** Such an order may be of considerable assistance to the court **accounts** and should be sought if appropriate.[57] As an alternative to serving a section 25 notice and relying on one or other of these grounds, the landlord should consider the alternative **Forfeiture as an** possibility of an action for forfeiture, which if successful will **alternative** terminate the tenancy and prevent the tenant making any application for a new one.[58]

Relevant time   The relevant time to consider whether the landlord can satisfy grounds (a), (b), or (c) is the date of trial, although the court can take into account the position at the date of the landlord's section 25 notice or section 26 counter-notice.[59]

16–35   Ground (a): disrepair caused by tenant

The tenant ought not to be granted a new tenancy in view of the state of repair of the holding, being a state resulting from the tenant's failure to comply with his obligations as to repair and maintenance.

[50] s.40(2).
[51] S.I. 1983 No. 133, Form 10.
[52] *ibid.*, Form 11.
[53] s.40(3).
[54] The Law Commission has recommended that there should be an action for breach of a statutory duty, see para. 16–14, n. 67 above.
[55] See paras. 16–21 to 16–23 above.
[56] *Domer v. Gulf Oil (Great Britain) Limited* (1975) 119 S.J. 392.
[57] *Re St. Martin's Theatre* [1959] 1 W.L.R. 872.
[58] See para. 16–24 above.
[59] *Betty's Cafés Ltd v. Philips Furniture Stores* [1959] A.C. 20.

Reliance on this ground will involve consideration of the extent of the tenant's liability to repair, as well as the actual state of the holding. The leading case on the ground is *Lyons v. Central Commercial Properties Ltd.*[60] There the Court of Appeal held that the ground conferred a discretion upon the court, albeit one which should be exercised narrowly, which was not confined to consideration of the state of repair of the premises. Ormerod L.J., without attempting to define the precise limits of the discretion, thought that the judge could have regard "to the conduct of the tenant in relation to his obligations, and the reasons for any breach of the covenant to repair which has arisen". It might, for example, be reasonable for the tenant not to spend money on the premises while negotiations are proceeding which might result in the premises being demolished.

Discretion of court

16–36 Ground (b): delay in paying rent

The tenant ought not to be granted a new tenancy in view of his persistent delay in paying rent which has become due.

Again, this ground confers a discretion upon the court. In exercising its discretion the court is likely to have regard to the size of the arrears and the length of the delay. It has been said in one county court decision that neither the size nor the length of the arrears need necessarily be substantial.[61] The fact that the rent is likely to be substantially increased on renewal may also be relevant.[62] The tenant is likely to have a better chance of resisting this ground if he can offer some security for rent on the grant of a new tenancy,[63] such as a rent deposit or a surety. The tenant will also be required to explain the reasons for previous late payment of rent and to satisfy the court that there will be no recurrence.[64]

Relevant factors

16–37 Ground (c): other substantial breaches

The tenant ought not to be granted a new tenancy in view of other substantial breaches of his obligations under the current tenancy, or for any other reason connected with the tenant's use or management of the holding.

As well as the general discretion inherent in this ground, the requirement that the breaches be "substantial" gives the court considerable latitude in deciding whether or not the tenant should be granted a new lease. The court may have regard to the whole of the tenant's conduct throughout the tenancy, and is not confined to the specific matters alleged in

---

[60] [1958] 1 W.L.R. 869.
[61] *Horowitz v. Ferrand* [1956] C.L.Y. 4843.
[62] *Maison Kaye Fashions Ltd v. Horton's Estate Ltd* (1967) 202 E.G. 23.
[63] *Hopcutt v. Carver* (1969) 209 E.G. 1069.
[64] *Hurstfell v. Leicester Square Property Co.* [1988] 37 E.G. 109.

Relevant conduct

the landlord's notice.[65] Nonetheless, the landlord intending to rely on ground (c) would be sensible to arm himself with hard allegations of specific misconduct and not merely vague charges of general mismanagement. As well as breaches of the tenancy obligations, the ground entitles the landlord to rely on other reasons connected with the tenant's use of the holding, *e.g.* breaches of planning control or of the criminal law.[66] In certain cases the conduct of the tenant on land other than the holding may be taken into account, if the conduct is connected with the tenant's use or management of the holding and such conduct is likely to prejudice the landlord's interest.[67]

16–38   Ground (d): alternative accommodation

The landlord has offered and is willing to provide or secure the provision of alternative accommodation for the tenant.

The terms on which the alternative accommodation is available must be reasonable having regard to the terms of the current tenancy and other relevant circumstances. Also the accommodation and the time at which it will be available must be suitable for the tenant's requirements, including the preservation of goodwill, and having regard to the nature and class of his business and the situation, extent and facilities of the present holding. It has been held that the landlord need not make the offer of alternative accommodation before serving his section 25 notice, but that, once made, the offer must be kept open.[68] The questions of reasonableness and suitability are to be determined on the facts at the date of the hearing.[69] An offer of part of the tenant's present accommodation may suffice for this ground.[70] If the landlord satisfies ground (d) the court has no residual discretion and must refuse a new tenancy.

Timing of offer

16–39   Ground (e): property to be let as a whole

The landlord requires possession of the holding for the purpose of letting or otherwise disposing of it together

---

[65] *Eichner v. Midland Bank Executor and Trustee Co. Ltd* [1970] 1 W.L.R. 1120. It is not clear whether regard may be had to the tenant's proposed future conduct and use: *Turner & Bell v. Searles (Stanford-le-Hope) Ltd* (1977) 33 P. & C.R. 208; *cf.* Roskill L.J. at 212 and Cairns L.J. at 213. On principle and on the wording of the ground there seems no reason why this should not be taken into account.

[66] *Turner & Bell v. Searles (Stanford-le-Hope) Ltd* (1977) 33 P. & C.R. 208.

[67] *Beard v. Williams* [1986] 1 EGLR 148.

[68] *M. Chaplin Ltd v. Regent Capital Holdings Ltd*, C.C. (cited as Case 97 in D. W. Williams, C. M. Brand and C. C. Hubbard, *Handbook of Business Tenancies* (1985)).

[69] *ibid.*

[70] *Lawrence v. Carter* (1956) 17 E.G. 222, C.C. (tenant furrier offered present holding less two changing cubicles used by customers).

with other property as a whole, the rent obtainable from separate lettings of the holding and the other property being substantially less than the rent reasonably obtainable from letting as a whole, and in view thereof the tenant ought not to be granted a new tenancy.

This ground seems to be little-used in practice. An **Superior** important qualification is that it can only be used by a superior **landlords only** landlord against a sub-tenant of part of the property. It cannot therefore be used by a landlord against his immediate tenant or a sub-tenant of the whole, where the landlord feels that a better return could be obtained by re-letting the holding in conjunction with other property. It is also limited to reduction of rental income and does not extend to a diminution in capital value of the landlord's reversion. The language of the ground makes it clear that the court is invested with a discretion in determining it.

16–40 Ground (f): demolition or reconstruction

On the termination of the current tenancy the landlord intends to demolish or reconstruct the premises comprised in the holding or a substantial part of those premises or to carry out substantial work of construction on the holding or part thereof and that he could not do so without obtaining possession of the holding.

This is one of the most frequently used grounds. As the plethora of reported authority on the ground shows,[71] considerable care is needed on the part of the landlord if he is to use it successfully.

Intention of The first point to note is that the landlord must intend to **landlord** carry out one or more of the various operations outlined in the ground. An intention has been said to connote not simply contemplating a state of affairs; but rather a decision to bring about that state of affairs, together with a reasonable prospect of being able to do so.[72] A landlord can satisfy the requirement even if he has wholly delegated the practical questions of the scheme to his advisers.[73] Thus the landlord should not attempt to rely upon the ground if his attitude to redevelopment is equivocal, or if his plans for redevelopment are not fully formed, or if there are serious obstacles in the way of his carrying out those plans.[74] If the proposed reconstruction of the holding forms part of a larger scheme the landlord must demonstrate the requisite intention in relation to the scheme as a whole.[75]

---

[71] A summary of the leading authorities can be found in the *Handbook of Business Tenancies*, para. 6–49.

[72] *Cunliffe v. Goodman* [1950] 2 K.B. 237, *per* Asquith L.J.; see also *Betty's Cafés Ltd v. Phillips Furnishing Stores Ltd* [1959] A.C. 20.

[73] *P.F. Ahern & Sons Ltd v. Hunt* [1988] 1 EGLR 74.

[74] *Reohorn v. Barry Corporation* [1956] 1 W.L.R. 845 (where the landlord was still negotiating the means of carrying out the work and its ability to do so was questionable, many factors being outside its control).

[75] *Edwards v. Thompson* [1990] 29 E.G. 41.

Proof of intention Whether the landlord has the requisite intention is a question of fact to be determined at the date of the hearing;[76] therefore it may be possible for the landlord to advance his plans between service of his section 25 notice and the date of the hearing,[77] or even between the beginning and the end of the hearing. However, the landlord may lose something in credibility by last-minute changes to his proposals.[78] Where the landlord is a company, the safest way of showing a settled intention is by a board resolution to carry out the work.[79] A further resolution authorising a director to give evidence of the company's intention if necessary would be prudent. Alternatively, a director or directors could be given authority to make the decision.[80] However, it may be possible to overcome the lack of a formal resolution by evidence from directors representing the directing mind and will of the company.[81] Further weight can be added to the landlord's case by an undertaking to carry out the work proposed.[82]

Difficulties for landlord Particular instances where the landlord may fall into difficulties under ground (f) are cases where his financial arrangements for the proposed work are inadequate[83] or where the requisite planning or other consents have not been obtained.[84] However, the courts have held that the mere absence of concluded contracts for demolition or building[85] or a development agreement[86] will not of itself prevent the landlord from demonstrating the requisite intention. The question is whether a reasonable man would believe that planning permission is not needed or that there is a reasonable prospect of it being obtained.[87] It is important to attempt to foresee any such obstacles and to take the appropriate steps to surmount them.

Nature of work intended The next point to be considered is the nature of the work intended. The landlord need not intend to carry out the work personally: it can be done through building contractors or by granting a building lease.[88] However, any building lease must genuinely allow the landlord to retain control over the work, and not be simply a disguised sale of the landlord's interest.[89] Alternatively, the landlord may, after serving his section 25 notice, sell on to a developer. The developer will then be the

---

[76] *Betty's Cafés Ltd v. Phillips Furnishing Stores Ltd* [1959] A.C. 20.

[77] *Manchester Garages Ltd v. Petrofina (U.K.) Ltd* (1975) 233 E.G. 509.

[78] But *cf. A. W. Birch Ltd v. P.B. (Sloane) Ltd* (1956) 167 E.G. 283.

[79] *Espresso Coffee Machine Co. Ltd v. Guardian Assurance Co. Ltd* [1959] 1 W.L.R. 250.

[80] *Branhills Ltd v. Town Tailors Ltd* (1956) 168 E.G. 642; *David Allen Neon Displays Ltd v. Spanton* (1958) 171 E.G. 679.

[81] *H.L. Bolton (Engineering) Co. Ltd v. T.J. Graham & Sons Ltd* [1957] 1 Q.B. 159.

[82] *Chez Gerard Ltd v. Greene Ltd* (1983) 268 E.G. 575.

[83] *DAF Motoring Centre (Gosport) Ltd v. Hatfield & Wheeler Ltd* (1982) 263 E.G. 976.

[84] *Joss v. Bennett* (1956) 167 E.G. 207.

[85] *Levy (A) & Son v. Martin Brent Developments Ltd* [1987] 2 EGLR 93.

[86] *Capocci v. Goble* (1987) 284 E.G. 230.

[87] *Gregson v. Cyril Lord Ltd* [1963] 1 W.L.R. 41; followed in *Cadogan v. McCarthy & Stone Developments Ltd* [1996] EGCS 94.

[88] *Gilmour Caterers Ltd v. Governors of the Royal Hospital of St. Bartholomew* [1956] 1 Q.B. 387. See also *Spook Erection v. British Railways Board* [1988] 21 E.G. 73.

[89] *David Allen Neon Displays Ltd v. Spanton* (1958) 171 E.G. 679.

landlord and will be able to make out the necessary intention to develop at the date of the hearing.[90]

Motive for the works

Once a landlord establishes a genuine intention to carry out work under the Act it is irrelevant that his motive may be to sell the premises for a good price,[91] or that he intends to carry out the work and then to lease the property to someone else.[92]

Start of the works

Though the ground states that the landlord must intend to carry out the work on termination of the current tenancy, some latitude must be applied, so that the landlord does not have to commence work instantly, simply within a reasonable time.[93]

Nature of the work

On analysis of the ground, the work proposed may be either demolition, reconstruction, or substantial construction work. In each case it may involve all or part of the holding.[94] Whether the work does fall within any of these categories will be a question of fact, the court looking at the work as a whole.[95] However the works considered as a whole will not amount to construction if none of the items considered separately could be so regarded.[96] It is implicit that the works of construction will fall within ground (f) only if they directly involve the structure of the building. In the case of a comprehensive scheme of redevelopment, little difficulty may arise; but the landlord who wishes to refurbish a building should consider carefully whether the works are sufficiently drastic to fall within the ground. Broadly, construction requires new or additional work while reconstruction requires the demolition of the whole or part of the existing structure.[97] The Court of Appeal considered the phrase "works of reconstruction" in *Romulus Trading Co. Ltd v. Henry Smith's Charity Trustees*[98] and concluded that for works to qualify as reconstruction it must be shown that they are "works of rebuilding (including preparatory or ancillary works) involving a substantial interference with the structure of the building, but not necessarily confined to the outside or other load-bearing walls".[99]

"The holding"

Another point to be kept in mind is that only works to "the holding" are relevant under the ground. This means that the landlord cannot rely on works to parts of the building not comprised in the relevant tenancy, *e.g.* work to the common parts, or to a roof if not demised to the tenant.

Need to obtain possession

A final aspect of ground (f) to be considered is that the landlord must show that he could not reasonably do the work without obtaining possession of the holding. This has been interpreted as meaning that the landlord must require legal

---

[90] *A. D. Wimbush & Son Ltd v. Franmills Properties Ltd* [1961] Ch. 419.
[91] *DAF Motoring Centre (Gosport) Ltd v. Hutsfield & Wheeler Ltd* (1982) 263 E.G. 976.
[92] *Turner v. Wandsworth L.B.C.* [1994] 25 E.G. 148.
[93] *Method Developments Ltd v. Jones* [1971] 1 W.L.R. 168; *Livestock Underwriting Agency v. Corbett & Newson* (1955) 165 E.G. 469.
[94] Though in the case of demolition or reconstruction the part must be "substantial".
[95] *Bewley (Tobacconists) Ltd v. British Bata Shoe Co. Ltd* [1959] 1 W.L.R. 45.
[96] *Barth v. Pritchard* [1990] 20 E.G. 65.
[97] *Cook v. Mott* (1961) 178 E.G. 637.
[98] [1990] 2 EGLR 75.
[99] *ibid.*, at 77, *per* Farquharson L.J.

possession, and not simply physical possession: that is to say that the work could not be done without bringing the tenancy to an end.[1] This means that if the landlord is able to carry out the work consistently with the terms of the tenancy (*e.g.* where the lease confers upon the landlord the right to enter to carry out the work) then he will not be able to rely on this ground.[2] However,it is not only the actual undertaking of the work which is relevant here, but also the effect of the work when completed. Thus, even if the landlord is entitled to enter and do work, if the effect of that work when completed would be inconsistent with the tenancy (*e.g.* a derogation from the landlord's grant) then the landlord will need possession in the legal sense, as well as physical possession.[3]

Also relevant to this question is section 31A, which provides that the landlord shall not be held to require possession if the tenant either:

Defeating a landlord's opposition under ground (f)

(a) agrees to the inclusion in the new tenancy of terms giving the landlord access and facilities for carrying out the work and that, given that access, the landlord could reasonably carry out the work without obtaining possession and without interfering to a substantial extent or for a substantial time with the use of the holding for the purposes of the tenant's business; or

(b) is willing to accept a tenancy of an economically separable part[4] of the holding and either paragraph (a) is satisfied with respect to that part or the landlord could carry out the work on the remainder.

Tenant agreeing to entry by landlord

Paragraph (a) in particular will be useful where the lease contains no right of entry to carry out works, or the right of entry which it confers is inadequate to carry out all the work intended. However, the qualification that the work must not interfere to a substantial extent or for a substantial time with the tenant's use of the holding can prove a stumbling block to a tenant wishing to rely on the paragraph, particularly since the landlord is under no duty to formulate his plans in such a way as to minimise any interference. Authoritative guidance on the application of the paragraph may be found in the

Guidelines

judgment of Slade L.J. in *Cerex Jewels Ltd v. Peachey Property Corporation Ltd*,[5] where His Lordship deduced the following five principles:

(1) only such work as may not be carried out under any right of entry in the lease should be regarded for the purposes of the paragraph;

---

[1] *Heath v. Drown* [1973] A.C. 498.
[2] *ibid.*; see also *Price v. Esso Petroleum Ltd* (1980) 255 E.G. 243.
[3] *Leathwoods Ltd v. Total Oil (G.B.) Ltd* (1984) 270 E.G. 1083; upheld by Court of Appeal on March 21, 1985 (unreported).
[4] An economically separable part is defined by s.31A(2).
[5] [1986] 2 EGLR 65 at 68. See also *Redfern v. Reeves* (1978) 247 E.G. 991; *Price v. Esso Petroleum Ltd* (1980) 255 E.G. 243; *Mularczyk v. Azralnove Investments Ltd* [1985] 2 EGLR 141.

(2) the question of whether the works will interfere with the tenant's use of the holding is one of fact and degree;[6]

(3) the court must look simply to the physical effect of the work on the use of the holding and not to any potential interference with the goodwill of the business or the business itself;

(4) the time and extent of the interference must be assessed with reference only to the period during which the work is actually being carried out, ignoring the future of the business after the work is completed;

(5) in order to deprive the tenant of the protection of the paragraph, the work must interfere with the tenant's use of the holding both substantially and for a substantial time; in other words substantial interference for a short time or slight interference for a substantial time is not enough.

Tenancy of part   Where the tenant relies on paragraph (b), his willingness to accept a tenancy of part will not allow him to resist possession if the landlord has a bona fide intention involving the whole of the premises: the paragraph does not justify the court in considering whether the landlord's plans are reasonable or in modifying them.[7]

Section 31A has no application unless and until the landlord has established under ground (f) that it is necessary for him to obtain legal possession. The Court of Appeal has held that if the landlord succeeds on the principal question under s.30(1)(f) the court must then consider whether either paragraphs (a) or (b) of section 31A(1) are satisfied. The tenant is not required to elect between reliance upon paragraphs (a) and (b).[8]

16–41 Ground (g): landlord intends to occupy

On termination of the current tenancy the landlord intends to occupy the holding for the purposes, or partly for the purposes of a business to be carried on by him therein, or as his residence.

Intention of landlord   There are certain similarities between this ground and ground (f), in particular the requirement of the landlord's intention. The requirements of proof of intention are the same for both grounds and in both cases must be established at the date of the hearing.[9] In determining whether the landlord has established the necessary intention a practice has

---

[6] In *Blackburn v. Hussain* [1988] EGLR 77 the court held that works proposed by a landlord which would affect the tenant's use of the premises for at least 12 weeks would plainly cause substantial interference.

[7] *Decca Navigator Co. Ltd v. Greater London Council* [1974] 1 W.L.R. 748.

[8] *Romulus Trading Co. Ltd v. Henry Smith's Charity Trustees* [1991] 1 EGLR 75.

[9] Thus in *Europark (Midlands) Ltd v. Town Centre Securities plc* [1985] 1 EGLR 88, the landlord's intention was shown by minutes of board meetings, an affidavit of the property director and the obtaining of quotations for equipment to be used by the landlord on resuming possession.

grown up of the landlord offering an undertaking that he will occupy the premises if given possession. An undertaking coupled with a resolution of the board has been held to be a significant factor to be taken into account by the court.[10] The landlord who has alternative accommodation open to him can be in difficulties in relying on this ground; an attempt to "have his bun and his penny"[11] by keeping both options open may prevent him showing the requisite firm intention.

The landlord's intended occupation need not be personal; he can occupy through a manager provided the arrangement is not a sham,[12] through a company in which he has a controlling interest,[13] through a management company[14] or if he is a trustee, through the beneficiaries[15] provided that such occupation is by virtue of the beneficiaries' interest under the trust and not otherwise.[16] Whilst it may be desirable, there is no requirement that a landlord's assertion of his intention to occupy should be corroborated.[17] The ground is silent as to how long the landlord must intend to occupy for, and it has been said that an intention to occupy for as little as six months might be adequate in some circumstances.[18]

The intention must be to occupy for the purposes of the landlord's business, or as his residence. An intention to sub-let without the provision of any services or active management **Occupation for** will not be sufficient.[19] Occupation for the purposes of the **business** landlord's business can include ancillary purposes, such as storage or car parking.[20] And an intention to occupy the whole of the holding and to carry out a business on part will also be sufficient.[21]

"Holding" The use of the word "holding" in the ground has given rise to disproportionate difficulties. There are two types of case where it may be important. The first is where the landlord intends to demolish and rebuild, or carry out substantial work to, the premises before occupying them. In such

---

[10] *London Hilton Jewellers Limited v. Hilton International Hotels* [1990] 1 EGLR 112.

[11] *Espresso Coffee Machine Co. Ltd v. Guardian Assurance Co. Ltd* [1959] 1 W.L.R. 250 at 254, *per* Lord Evershed, M.R. (where the landlord was able to justify keeping both sets of negotiations on foot on the basis that he intended to occupy the holding in the short term and then move into the other premises).

[12] *France v. Shaftward Investments*, C.A., June 25, 1981 (unreported but cited as Case 77 in the *Handbook of Business Tenancies* (1985)).

[13] s.30(3).

[14] *Teeside Indoor Bowls Limited v. Stockton on Tees Borough Council* [1990] 2 EGLR 87.

[15] s.41(2). See *Frish Ltd v. Barclays Bank Ltd* [1955] 2 Q.B. 541; *Sevenarts v. Busvine* [1968] 1 W.L.R. 1929; *Morar v. Chauhan* [1985] 1 W.L.R. 1263.

[16] *Meyer v. Riddick* [1990] 1 EGLR 107.

[17] *Mirza v. Nicola* [1990] 30 E.G. 92.

[18] *Willis v. Association of Universities of the British Commonwealth* [1965] 1 Q.B. 140 at 150, *per* Lord Denning, M.R., *e.g.* where the landlord intends to pass the business on to a successor at the end of that time; but not where he intends to transfer the premises to a purchaser for cash. See also *Jones v. Jenkins* [1986] 1 EGLR 113 at 115.

[19] *Jones v. Jenkins*, and *cf.* para. 16–16 above.

[20] *Hunt v. Decca Navigator Co. Ltd* (1972) 222 E.G. 625.

[21] *Method Developments Ltd v. Jones* [1971] 1 W.L.R. 168.

circumstances it could be argued, on the strength of the much-criticised case of *Nursey v. P. Currie (Dartford) Ltd*[22] that what the landlord will occupy will no longer be the holding. However, it has been suggested that it is unlikely that the intention of the legislature in enacting ground (g) was to allow the landlord to recover possession of the holding only in a sterilised and unalterable state,[23] and the decision has been said to be confined to the demolition and replacement of existing buildings and not to apply to the construction of buildings on a vacant site.[24] It is suggested that where the landlord does intend to carry out substantial work to the holding before occupation it would be safer to add ground (f) and not rely simply on (g). Provided both intentions are genuine, it is possible for them to be used together.[25] The other problematic situation is where the landlord wishes to

Amalgamation of premises amalgamate the holding with other property and occupy them together. Another possible ratio of *Nursey v. Currie* is that in such a case the identity of the holding will have been lost and that therefore the landlord cannot be said to intend to occupy it.[26] However, the Court of Appeal in *J. W. Thornton Ltd v. Blacks Leisure Group plc*[27] preferred to rest *Nursey v. Currie* on the demolition *ratio* mentioned above, and held that a landlord who wished to enlarge his shop by incorporating into it the holding (only minor structural work being required) was entitled to rely on ground (g).

Sale of goodwill A landlord who at the start of the lease absolutely disposed of the goodwill of his business to the tenant will not be able to rely on ground (g) if he intends to carry on the same business; having assigned the goodwill to the tenant he could be restrained by injunction from carrying on the business.[28]

"Five-year rule" A final and important aspect of ground (g) is the so-called "five-year rule". By section 30(2) a landlord is not entitled to rely on the ground if his interest was purchased or created within the five years preceding the termination of the current tenancy, and at all times since the purchase or creation of the landlord's interest the holding has been comprised in a tenancy or tenancies within the Act.[29] If the landlord has held his interest for five years or more it would appear to be immaterial that the capacity in which he held it has changed over that period.[30] The rule has no application where the creation or purchase of the landlord's interest pre-dates the grant of the current tenancy.[31]

---

[22] [1959] 1 W.L.R. 273.
[23] *Cam Gears Ltd v. Cunningham* [1981] 1 W.L.R. 1011 at 1016, *per* Templeman L.J.
[24] *ibid.* See also *Leathwoods Ltd v. Total Oil (G.B.) Ltd* (1986) 51 P. & C.R. 20.
[25] *Fisher v. Taylor's Furnishing Stores Ltd* [1956] 2 Q.B. 78.
[26] This would appear to be the reasoning of Wynn-Parry J.
[27] [1986] 2 EGLR 61.
[28] *Daleo v. Iretti* (1972) 224 E.G. 61, C.C.
[29] On the question of what constitutes purchase, see *Frederick Lawrence Ltd v. Freeman, Hardy & Willis Ltd* [1959] Ch. 731.
[30] *Morar v. Chauhan* [1985] 1 W.L.R. 1263.
[31] *Northcote Laundry Ltd v. Frederick Dornelly Ltd* [1968] 1 W.L.R. 562.

16–42 Landlord's opposition successful

Termination of tenancy

If the landlord is successful in opposing the tenant's application for a new tenancy on one of the above grounds, the court may not order a new tenancy.[32] The tenancy will come to an end three months from the date on which the application is finally disposed of.[33] The tenant's advisers should remember to seek a certificate from the court under section 37(4) where the ground in question was (e), (f) or (g). This will assist in obtaining compensation from the landlord.[34]

Appeal

The tenant's advisers may also consider the possibility of an appeal against the decision. Somewhat spurious appeals are sometimes made on tactical grounds, either to gain the tenant a further period of occupation,[35] or in the hope that building costs may rise or other factors conspire to thwart the landlord's plans.[36] While often being highly effective, such tactics may come dangerously close to being an abuse of the process of the court.[37] Changes in 1993 to the Rules of the Supreme Court now provide that leave is required to appeal to the Court of Appeal in matters relating to the 1954 Act. Strict time limits apply for lodging an appeal. In considering an application for leave to appeal out of time the court will consider the length of the delay, the reasons for the delay, whether there is an arguable case on the appeal and the degree of prejudice to the other party if time is extended.[38]

16–43 Grant of a new tenancy

Where the landlord does not oppose a new tenancy, or his opposition is unsuccessful, the court must make an order for the grant of a new tenancy comprising such property, at such rent, and on such terms, as are provided by the Act.[39] It should be remembered that all the terms may be agreed between the parties without recourse to the court.[40] However, the adviser who conducts negotiations without knowledge of the terms which the court could or would be likely to order is bound to be at a disadvantage. If no agreement is reached the court is empowered to decide the terms of the new tenancy in accordance with sections 32–35.

---

[32] s.31(1).
[33] s.64(1), (2).
[34] See para. 16–50 below. In the High Court the order must state all the grounds on which a new tenancy is precluded: R.S.C., Ord. 97, r. 7.
[35] *Photo Centre Ltd v. Grantham Court Properties (Mayfair) Ltd* (1964) 191 E.G. 505.
[36] *A.J.A. Smith Transport Ltd v. British Waterways Board* (1981) 257 E.G. 1257.
[37] *ibid.*
[38] *Rawashden v. Lane* [1988] 40 E.G. 109.
[39] s.29(1).
[40] s.28. Any agreement must be in writing: s.69(2).

16–44 The property to be comprised in the tenancy

"The holding" The property to be comprised in the new tenancy is "the holding";[41] that is, the property comprised in the original tenancy, less any part not occupied by the tenant.[42] In the absence of agreement as to the extent of the holding, it is to be designated by the court with reference to the circumstances at the date of the order. Where the extent of "the holding" is less than the property comprised in the original tenancy (*e.g.* where the tenant has sub-let part) the landlord can require the tenant to take a new tenancy of the whole of the property.[43] This provides useful protection for the landlord against the perpetuation of multiple interests in the property.

Any rights comprised in the original tenancy and enjoyed by the tenant in connection with the holding are to be included in the new tenancy.[44] Thus ancillary rights such as easements or a licence to display advertisements[45] are protected. But the court has no jurisdiction to insert in the new tenancy rights not contained in the old, even if such rights have been enjoyed *de facto* by the tenant during the term.[46]

16–45 The duration of the new tenancy

In default of agreement, the duration of the new tenancy is to be such as is determined by the court as reasonable in all the circumstances, subject in the case of a term of years certain to **Relevant factors** a maximum of 14 years.[47] The court must have regard to all appropriate factors in exercising its discretion, and these will include the length of the current lease,[48] the length of time the tenant has been holding over already under section 24, hardship to either party,[49] the landlord's future plans for the property,[50] and even the relationship between the parties.[51]

Landlord's intention to redevelop A particularly important factor can be that the landlord has plans to redevelop or re-occupy the premises, but was unable to satisfy ground (f) or (g), perhaps because his plans were

---

[41] s.32(1).
[42] s.23(3).
[43] s.32(2).
[44] s.32(3).
[45] *Re No. 1 Albemarle St.* [1959] Ch. 531.
[46] *G. Orlik (Meat Products) Ltd v. Hastings and Thanet Building Society* (1975) 234 E.G. 281. But there seems no reason why the new tenancy should not constitute a conveyance for the purposes of the Law of Property Act 1925, s.62 and so pass such rights: see *Goldberg v. Edwards* [1950] Ch. 247.
[47] s.33. The Law Commission has recommended that this should be increased to 15 years (see para. 16–14, n. 67 above).
[48] *Betty's Cafés Ltd v. Phillips Furnishing Stores Ltd* [1959] A.C. 20.
[49] *Upsons Ltd v. E. Robins Ltd* [1956] 1 Q.B. 131.
[50] *ibid.*
[51] *Orenstein v. Donn*, C.A., May 5, 1983 (unreported but cited as Case 95 in the *Handbook of Business Tenancies* (1985)).

not sufficiently advanced or because he fell foul of the five-year rule.[52] An approach frequently adopted by the court in such cases is to order a short term[53] or alternatively to order the insertion of a break clause in the new tenancy.[54] This involves the delicate task of striking a balance between the conflicting interests of landlord and tenant: the policy of the Act is not to prevent redevelopment but this must be reconciled with "a reasonable degree of security of tenure" for tenants.[55] The court has shown a willingness to include a break clause if there is a real possibility (as opposed to a probability) that the premises will be required for reconstruction during the continuance of the proposed term.[56]

Tenant seeking short term

It is not always the case that the landlord seeks a shorter term than the tenant is willing to accept—occasionally the tenant's needs may be for only a short term which the landlord alleges will damage the value of his reversion.[57] Here the court must decide what is fair and reasonable in the circumstances and must weigh the hardship to the tenant in taking a long term which he may find difficult to assign against any prejudice to the landlord's reversion caused by a short-term letting.[58]

The new tenancy commences on the coming to the end of the current tenancy.[59] This will be either the date specified in the landlord's section 25 notice or tenant's section 26 request or, if proceedings have been commenced, three months from their final disposal.[60] Given the uncertainties as to when this may be, the practice which the court should follow is to stipulate the date on which the new tenancy is to expire, and not simply its length.[61]

---

[52] *Upsons Ltd v. E. Robins Ltd* [1956] 1 Q.B. 131; *Frederick Lawrence Ltd v. Freeman, Hardy & Willis Ltd* [1959] Ch. 731.

[53] *London and Provincial Millinery Stores Ltd v. Barclays Bank Ltd* [1962] 1 W.L.R. 510. The desirability of synchronising the tenancy with the termination dates of others within the landlord's scheme of redevelopment so as to avoid "leapfrogging" of term dates should not be overlooked: see *Michael Chipperfield v. Shell U.K. Ltd* (1980) 42 P. & C.R. 136.

[54] *Amika Motors Ltd v. Colebrook Holdings Ltd* (1981) 259 E.G. 243; *J.H. Edwards & Son Ltd v. Central London Commercial Estates Ltd* (1984) 271 E.G. 697.

[55] *ibid.* at 698, per Fox L.J.

[56] *National Car Parks Ltd v. Paternoster Consortium Ltd* [1990] 15 E.G. 53.

[57] *C.B.S. United Kingdom Ltd v. London Scottish Properties Ltd* [1985] 2 EGLR 125; *Charles Follett Ltd v. Cabtell Investment Co. Ltd* [1986] 2 EGLR 76 (where with the agreement of the landlord, these difficulties were overcome by ordering the term sought by the landlord subject to a break clause exercisable by the tenant); on appeal, see (1987) 283 E.G. 195.

[58] However, where a tenant agreed with his landlord during the course of the hearing that he would take a 10 year term but subsequently before the conclusion of the hearing decided that he required only a three year term, the court refused to grant the shorter term without the consent of the landlord (on the basis that there was a concluded agreement) or alternatively without the consent of the court (on the basis of a concession made to the court): *Boots the Chemist Ltd v. Pinkland Ltd* [1992] 2 EGLR 98.

[59] s.33.

[60] s.64.

[61] *Turone v. Howard de Walden Estates Ltd* (1983) 267 E.G. 440.

16–46 The terms of the new tenancy other than the rent

Exercise of discretion

In default of agreement, the other terms of the new tenancy (*e.g.* service charge) are to be determined by the court having regard to the terms of the current tenancy and to all relevant circumstances.[62] It is clear that the issues of duration and the other terms of the new tenancy have to be determined prior to a determination of the rent under section 34.[63] The court's discretion is wide but the proper approach has been considered by the House of Lords in *O'May v. City of London Real Property Co. Ltd.*[64] There Lord Hailsham L.C. said:[65]

> "I do not in any way suggest that the court is intended or should in any way attempt to bind the parties to the terms of the current tenancy in any permanent form. But I do believe that the court must begin by considering the terms of the current tenancy, that the burden of persuading the court to impose a change in those terms against the will of either party must rest on the party proposing the change and that the change proposed must, in the circumstances of the case, be fair and reasonable and should take into account, amongst other things, the comparatively weak position of a sitting tenant requiring renewal, particularly in conditions of scarcity, and the general purpose of the Act which is to protect the business interests of the tenant so far as they are affected by the approaching termination of the current lease, in particular as regards his security of tenure."

Justified changes

Thus a court will be unlikely to sanction a change to the current terms put forward by one party with no other purpose than improving his own position, at least where the change is detrimental to the other party.[66] On the other hand a change may be justified in order to modernise the lease terms and bring them into line with current practice (provided that this is fair and reasonable),[67] or because of the previous behaviour of the other party.[68] The court is able to order that a surety be provided under the new tenancy.[69]

---

[62] s.35(1). The reference to all relevant circumstances includes a reference to the operation of the provisions of the Landlord and Tenant (Covenants) Act 1995: s.35(2), inserted by the 1995 Act, Sched. 1, para. 4. See "Lease renewals after the 1995 Act" (R. Bunce and P. Williams) [1996] 15 E.G. 96.

[63] *Cardshops Ltd v. Davies* [1971] 2 All E.R. 721.

[64] [1983] 2 A.C. 726.

[65] *ibid.*, p. 740.

[66] *e.g. Gold v. Brighton Corporation* [1956] 1 W.L.R. 1291; *Cardshops Ltd v. Davies* [1971] 1 W.L.R. 591; *Aldwych Club Ltd v. Copthall Property Co. Ltd* (1963) 185 E.G. 15.

[67] *Hyams v. Titan Properties Ltd* (1972) 224 E.G. 2017; subject of course to the criteria of *O'May v. City of London Real Property Co. Ltd* [1983] 2 A.C. 726.

[68] *Re 5 Panton St., Haymarket* (1959) 175 E.G. 49 (covenant only against structural alterations as landlord had been petty over minor ones in the past; also new proviso that landlord to reply to applications for consent within 30 days).

[69] *Cairnplace Ltd v. C.B.L. (Property Investments) Co. Ltd* [1984] 1 W.L.R. 696. Where the tenants are partners, see s.41A(6).

Landlord and A tenancy granted on or after January 1, 1996 will be a
Tenant "new tenancy" as defined by the Landlord and Tenant
(Covenants) Act (Covenants) Act 1995[70] unless it was granted pursuant to a
1995 court order made before January 1, 1996.

Unless the parties agree in writing that the tenant shall pay
Costs of the new the costs of negotiating and executing the new tenancy, the
tenancy court may not use its discretion to insert a term in the new
tenancy that the tenant shall pay the landlord's costs even if
the current tenancy contains such a provision.[71]

16–47 Rent under the new tenancy

In the absence of agreement as to the new rent, section 34
provides a formula by which it is to be determined. The rent
is to be that at which, having regard to the terms of the
tenancy[72] (other than those relating to rent),[73] the holding
Matters to be might reasonably be expected to be let in the open market by
disregarded a willing lessor,[74] disregarding:

(a) any effect on rent of the fact that the tenant or his
predecessors in title have been in occupation of the
holding;
(b) any goodwill attached to the holding by reason of the
carrying on there of the tenant's business by him or a
predecessor;
(c) any effect on rent of an improvement[75] carried out by a
person who at that time was the tenant, if carried out
otherwise than in pursuance of an obligation to his
immediate landlord [76] and either carried out during the
current tenancy or completed not more than 21 years
before the application for the new tenancy was made,
provided that any part of the holding affected by the
improvement has at all times since completion been
comprised in tenancies protected by the Act and that at
the determination of each tenancy the tenant did not
quit;
(d) in the case of a holding comprising licensed premises,
any addition to its value attributable to the licence, if it

---

[70] See para. 2–02 above.
[71] Costs of Leases Act 1958; *Cairnplace Ltd v. C.B.L. (Property Investments)
Co. Ltd* [1984] 1 W.L.R. 696.
[72] *e.g.* strict user clauses or onerous repairing obligations: see *Newey & Eyre
Ltd v. J. Curtis & Son Ltd* (1984) 271 E.G. 891.The terms must of course
be fixed before the rent is determined, see para.16–46 above.
[73] See para. 6–27 above.
[74] See para. 6–12 above.
[75] Removable tenant's fixtures are not improvements, but will also be
disregarded as not forming part of the demised premises: *New Zealand
Government Property Corporation v. H.M. & S. Ltd* [1982] Q.B. 1145. See
also para. 11–14 above.
[76] As to where improvements are carried out under a licence, see para. 6–36
above.

appears that the benefit of the licence belongs to the tenant.[77]

For the purposes of section 34 an open market includes: a situation to create a market, a willing lessor and willing lessee, a reasonable period in which to negotiate the letting and the negotiations at arm's length, the property freely exposed to the market and in the market account is not to be taken of any higher rent that might be paid by a potential lessee with a special interest.[78] A market can still be an open market even though most of the persons occupying premises in that market belong to a particular profession or engage in a particular trade.[79]

Landlord and Tenant (Covenants) Act 1995   One of the matters to be taken into account by the court in determining the rent is the effect on rents of the operation of the provisions of the Landlord and Tenant (Covenants) Act 1995.[80]

Valuation   Determination of the rent will in practice be a matter for expert valuation evidence, though judges have on a number of occasions expressed their preference for an approach using the broad sword rather than exact mathematics.[81] The date at which the level of the new rent has to be determined is the date of the hearing but the court is entitled to take into account matters which could reasonably be expected to occur between this date and the date of commencement of the new term.[82] The court should bear in mind that if the tenant is given a rent substantially below market value he may be tempted to assign the tenancy at a profit.[83] The question of valuation evidence is discussed in the Chapter on rent and rent review.[84]

Rent review provisions   The new tenancy may include a rent review clause if the court thinks fit.[85] The insertion of such provisions is now standard practice if the new tenancy is to be of a substantial duration. Questions such as whether the clause should be upwards only[86] and the frequency of reviews[87] will be determined by evidence such as any provisions in the current lease and local conditions.

[77] For a case in which this disregard applied see *Ganton House Investments Ltd v. Crossman Investments Ltd*, May 19, 1993 (unreported but cited as case CC 17 in the *Handbook of Business Tenancies* (1985)).

[78] *Baptist v. Masters of the Bench and Trustees of the Honourable Society of Gray's Inn* [1993] 42 E.G. 287.

[79] *ibid.*

[80] s.34(4), inserted by 1995 Act, Sched. 1, para. 3.

[81] *e.g. Violet Yorke Ltd v. Property Holding & Investment Trust Ltd* (1967) 205 E.G. 429. See also *Oriani v. Dorita Properties Ltd* (1987) 282 E.G. 1001.

[82] *Lovely Orchard Services v. Daejan Investments (Grove Hall) Ltd* (1977) 246 E.G. 651.

[83] *McLaughlin v. Walsall Arcade Ltd* (1956) 167 E.G. 356.

[84] See para. 6–17 above. Valuation may be assisted by the power of the court to appoint an independent assessor—without charge to the parties: see (1986) 279 E.G. 492 (M. J. Russell).

[85] s.34(3).

[86] See *Janes (Gowns) Ltd v. Harlow Development Corporation* (1979) 253 E.G. 799; *Charles Follett Ltd v. Cabtell Investment Co. Ltd* [1986] 2 EGLR 76; *Amarjee v. Barrowfen Properties Ltd* [1993] 2 EGLR 133.

[87] *W.H. Smith Ltd v. Bath City Council*, C.C. (unreported but noted at (1986) 277 E.G. 822).

16–48   Costs of the proceedings

Court's discretion as to costs

Any agreement in advance that the tenant shall pay the landlord's costs in proceedings under the Act is void.[88] The general principle is that costs are at the discretion of the court,[89] although they should normally follow the event as in any other case.[90] In cases where the landlord opposes the grant of a new tenancy it will usually be obvious which party has succeeded. However, in many cases it will be impossible to point to a clear winner or loser in proceedings under the Act, but the court's discretion may be exercised against a party who has taken unjustified points or who has unreasonably refused an offer by the other party. Therefore in negotiations as to rent or other terms of the new tenancy, the parties' advisers should always consider making an offer without prejudice, but subject to the right to bring it to the court's attention on the issue of costs.[91] In one case[92] a tenant who, having obtained a new lease, then used his right under the Act to refuse to take it[93] was ordered to pay the landlord's costs.

16–49   After the order for a new tenancy

Agreement of parties

Revocation of order

The result of an order for a new tenancy is that the landlord is bound to execute or make, and the tenant to accept, a lease or agreement for a lease embodying the terms agreed or determined by the court,[94] although the Act provides no sanction if either the landlord or the tenant fails to comply. To this there are two exceptions. The first is where the landlord and tenant agree not to act on the order. The second is that the tenant may within 14 days apply to the court for revocation of the order if, for example, the terms ordered are too onerous. The court appears to have no jurisdiction either under the Act or inherently to extend this period. The current tenancy then continues until at least the date upon which it would, in any event, have been continued by virtue of sections 24 and 64 or for such longer period as may be agreed or is necessary to afford the landlord a reasonable opportunity of reletting or otherwise disposing of the premises.[95]

16–50   Statutory compensation

Where the tenant is unable to obtain a new lease and is forced to give up possession the question of compensation may

---

[88] s.38(1); *Stevenson and Rush (Holdings) Ltd v. Langdon* (1978) 37 P. & C.R. 208.
[89] *Decca Navigator Co. Ltd v. Greater London Council* [1974] 1 W.L.R. 748.
[90] *Computer Machinery Co v. Drescher* [1983] 1 W.L.R. 1379.
[91] See further para. 6–18 above.
[92] *Rom Tyre & Accessories Co. Ltd v. Crawford Street Properties Ltd* (1966) 197 E.G. 565.
[93] See para. 16–49 below.
[94] s.36(1). The tenant is bound to execute a counterpart or duplicate if required by the landlord.
[95] s.36(2).

Disturbance

become relevant. Compensation for improvements carried out by the tenant is dealt with elsewhere,[96] and of particular concern here is compensation for disturbance. This is provided for by section 37, which applies where the court is precluded from making an order for a new tenancy by any of grounds (e), (f), or (g) and not on any other ground, or where no ground other than (e), (f) or (g) has been specified in the landlord's section 25 notice or reply to section 26 request, and the tenant has either made no application for a new lease or has withdrawn his application. Thus the tenant who is faced with opposition by the landlord on one or other of those grounds (and only those grounds), and who is either willing to quit or does not feel that he can defeat the landlord, does not have to make a token application in order to obtain compensation. Where additional grounds are relied on, the tenant must make an application to preserve his rights.

Amount of compensation

The compensation payable for premises occupied solely for the purposes of a business is either the rateable value or twice the rateable value of the holding.[97] Compensation of twice the rateable value is payable where during the 14 years preceding the termination of the current tenancy,[98] the holding or premises comprised in it have been occupied for the purposes[99] of a business carried on by the occupier or for those and other purposes.[1] If at any time during those 14 years there was a change in the occupier of the premises, the person occupying after the change must have been the successor to the business carried on by the previous occupant. Thus what is essential to claim the higher compensation is the continuity of the business, not the identity of the occupier. It should be noted that it is not necessary that the whole of the holding be occupied for a business for 14 years, so long as part of it has been. Thus, a tenant who has carried on a business for 14 years, during which time the holding has become enlarged, will be entitled to compensation of twice the rateable value of the whole holding, not simply that part where the business has been carried on for 14 years.[2]

There is a possibility that an alternative method of calculation of compensation may also be available. When domestic rates were abolished in 1990, an alternative scheme for compensation for business premises containing a domestic

---

[96] See para. 11–07 above.

[97] s.37(2), (3); Local Government Planning and Land Act 1980, s.193 and Sched. 33, para. 4; Landlord and Tenant Act 1954 (Appropriate Multiplier) Regulations 1990 (S.I. 1990 No. 363). The rateable value is as at the date of the landlord's s.25 notice or the s.26(6) counter-notice; for determination of the rateable value see s.37(5) and S.I. 1954 No. 1255.

[98] The date of termination is the date specified in the section 25 notice or the date specified in the tenant's section 26 request as the day from which the new tenancy is to begin: s.37(7).

[99] s.37(3)(a). The tenant must have been in actual occupation for 14 years. Carrying out fitting out works to the premises is not occupation for this purpose: *Department of the Environment v. Royal Insurance* (1987) 54 P. & C.R. 26.

[1] s.37(3)(b).

[2] *Edicron v. William Whitely Ltd* [1984] 1 W.L.R. 59. It appears from that case that the extent of the holding is determined as at the date of the landlord's s.25 notice or s.26(6) counter-notice.

element was introduced,[3] which could if interpreted literally be applicable also to premises used solely for business purposes. In certain circumstances compensation equal to eight or 16 times the pre-April 1990 rateable value would then be payable. However the County Court has held[4] that the alternative compensation provisions do not apply to premises used solely for business premises.

Date for assessing compensation
The date for assessing compensation is the date upon which the tenant quits the premises.[5] Thus the appropriate multiplier to adopt is the one in force at that date.[6]

Exclusion of compensation
Once the right to compensation has accrued it is possible for the parties to fix the amount by agreement.[7] It is also possible to exclude or reduce the amount of compensation by prior agreement, subject to one important qualification.[8] This is that any such agreement is void where the business has been carried on on the holding or part of it over the whole five years preceding the date on which the tenant is to quit the holding.[9] Leases frequently contain a provision excluding compensation in these circumstances. In such cases the landlord should remember that where he is entitled to serve a section 25 notice less than five years after the commencement of the term, failure to serve a section 25 notice in good time may result in the tenant carrying on business for longer than five years and so render void the agreement excluding compensation.

Withdrawal of opposition by landlord
Once the landlord has stated his intention to object to a new tenancy on grounds (e), (f), or (g) he cannot escape from the liability to pay compensation by withdrawing his opposition. If he does withdraw his opposition, the tenant who has already applied for a new tenancy may either continue the application and obtain a new tenancy, or may obtain leave to discontinue the proceedings and obtain compensation: the landlord has no right both to recover the premises and avoid the payment of compensation.[10]

---

[3] Schedule 7 to the Local Government and Housing Act 1989; Local Government Finance (Miscellaneous Amendments and Repeal) Order 1990 (S.I. 1990 No 1285).
[4] *Busby v Co-operative Insurance Society Ltd* [1994] 6 E.G. 141.
[5] *Cardshops Ltd v. John Lewis Properties Ltd* [1983] Q.B. 161.
[6] The multiplier may be varied by statutory instrument: 1954 Act, s.37(8).
[7] s.38(2).
[8] s.38(3).
[9] s.38(2).
[10] *Lloyds Bank Ltd v. City of London Corporation* [1983] Ch. 192.

17 INTERPRETATION AND RECTIFICATION OF LEASES

17–01 Introduction

A commercial lease is likely to remain in operation for many years, governing the relationship between the parties long after the process of negotiation and drafting is completed. During the life of the lease, questions can arise as to the exact meaning of its terms. A knowledge of the basic rules of construction applied by the courts in interpreting commercial documents generally can be helpful in resolving those difficulties. Such knowledge can also be useful as part of the drafting process: it can point to possible areas of difficulty, and may prevent the use of language likely to cause problems in the future. In a few cases, where something has gone very seriously wrong with the drafting of a lease, it may be necessary to seek the remedy of rectification, which is also considered in this chapter.[1]

INTERPRETATION

17–02 General principles

Basic principle of construction

In *Pioneer Shipping Ltd v. B.T.P. Tioxide Ltd*[2] Lord Diplock stated that the meaning of a written contract is a question of law. He also said that the object of construing any commercial contract is to ascertain the mutual intentions of the parties as to the legal obligations each assumed by the words in which they or their advisers chose to express them: "what each would have led the other reasonably to assume were the acts that he was promising to do or refrain from doing by the words in which the promises on his part were expressed."[3]

This means that the court's attention must first be directed to the actual words used in the lease, which in the absence of

---

[1] Typographical errors or other obvious mistakes of expression can be corrected as a matter of construction provided it is clear that a mistake has been made and what is needed to put it right. See *Durham City Estates v. Felicetti* [1990] 3 E.G. 71 (inconsistency between words and figures in rent review notice—words held to prevail).

[2] [1982] A.C. 724.

[3] *ibid.* at 736; see also *L. Schuler A.G. v. Wickman Machine Tools Sales Ltd* [1974] A.C. 235 at 263, *per* Lord Simon.

Qualifications

any evidence to the contrary are to be interpreted in their strict and primary sense.[4] However, this principle needs to be qualified in a number of respects. First, the strict and literal meaning of the words may not be followed if to do so would lead to absurdity, repugnance, or inconsistency with the rest of the instrument.[5]

Construction as a whole

Secondly, a document must be construed as a whole,[6] so that the meaning of a word or phrase in one part of it may be affected by the intention of the parties as expressed in other parts.[7] This is particularly important in the case of lengthy and complex documents such as commercial leases, which are likely to contain many closely related provisions:[8] consistency in drafting is therefore vital. Thirdly, the words used may have no definite primary meaning, but may be capable of a variety of meanings. Here the approach must be to consider what the words used would have meant to commercial men at the time of the grant.[9] This may involve considering the meaning which an expression bore in the past, as opposed to its contemporary meaning.[10] It can lead to serious difficulties in the case of user covenants[11] in leases, where the activities comprehended within a particular description of business may change over time.[12]

Uncertainty

Another principle which may qualify the "literal meaning" approach, and which is potentially of great significance to commercial leases, is the unwillingness of the courts to allow a transaction to perish for uncertainty. This is particularly so for commercial documents of a continuing nature, where the parties have already acted, and continue to do so, in reliance on the validity of the transaction.[13] Thus, applying this principle, the court may give an expression in a lease a

---

[4] *Enlayde Ltd v. Roberts* [1917] 1 Ch. 109 (covenant to insure against loss or damage by fire not qualified by evidence as to risks uninsurable in practice); see also *Westacott v. Hahn* [1918] 1 K.B. 495 at 510 (evidence as to customary provision of repairing materials by landlord inadmissible).

[5] *Re Levy, ex p. Walton* (1881) 17 Ch.D. 746 at 751; *Toyota (G.B.) Ltd v. Legal and General Assurance (Pensions Management) Ltd* [1989] 42 E.G. 104.

[6] *Barton v. Fitzgerald* (1812) 15 East 530 at 541; *N.E. Railway v. Lord Hastings* [1900] A.C. 260 at 267.

[7] *Brewers' Company v. Viewplan plc* [1989] 45 E.G. 153.

[8] See, *e.g. Smedley v. Chumley and Hawke Ltd* (1981) 44 P. & C.R. 50 at 55 (effect of landlord's repairing covenant was to cut down the width of tenant's); also *White v. Harrow* (1902) 86 L.T. 4 ("adjoining premises" held to mean only physically contiguous premises since expression used elsewhere was "adjoining and neighbouring").

[9] *Earl of Lonsdale v. Att-Gen* [1982] 1 W.L.R. 887 at 900, 924.

[10] *ibid.* See also *Texaco Antilles Ltd v. Kernochan* [1973] A.C. 609, where the question was said to be one of fact.

[11] See para. 10–08 above.

[12] *Burgess v. Hunsden Properties Ltd* (1962) 182 E.G. 373. In *Calabar (Woolwich) Ltd v. Tesco Stores Ltd* (1977) 245 E.G. 479 "supermarket" was held to be a word with no definite meaning in ordinary usage, so that its meaning was settled by expert evidence as to the meaning in 1961 when the lease was granted. See also *Westminster City Council v. Duke of Westminster* [1991] 4 All E.R. 136 where an obligation to use flats for the "working classes" imposed in 1937 was held to be still capable of definition and application.

[13] *F. & G. Sykes Ltd v. Fine Fare Ltd* [1967] 1 Lloyd's Rep. 53 at 57–58; *Thomas Bates & Son Ltd v. Wyndham's (Lingerie) Ltd* [1981] 1 W.L.R. 505 at 519; *Beer v. Bowden* [1981] 1 W.L.R. 522.

meaning other than its strict legal one,[14] may imply ancillary
rights or ancillary machinery necessary to make the provisions
of the lease workable,[15] and may make use of objective
standards of reasonableness in order to prevent uncertainty.[16]
This approach can be taken a stage further by the court
seeking not only to prevent the contract from being void or
unworkable, but by construing it so as to avoid a conclusion
"Business   which "flouts business common sense".[17] The court has held
common sense"   that this does not mean

> "that one can rewrite the language which the parties have
> used in order to make the contract conform to business
> common sense. But language is a very flexible instrument
> and, if it is capable of more than one construction, one
> chooses that which seems most likely to give effect to the
> commercial purpose of the agreement".[18]

This so called "purposive" approach is gaining ground and
has found particular favour in the interpretation of highly
complex and involved rent review provisions where the court
has frequently leaned against a construction which would
distort a true market rent.[19] But this approach has its limits
and a "literal meaning" approach may be appropriate if the
language in question is unambiguous and there are not other
special surrounding circumstances[20] or where to apply a
purposive approach would involve "not simply a matter of
construction: [but] demolition and reconstruction".[21]

17–03 Extrinsic evidence

How far evidence outside the terms of lease may be used as
an aid to construction is a difficult question. It has been said

[14] *Tulapam Properties Ltd v. De Almeida* (1981) 260 E.G. 919 (covenant not to
"share possession" was meaningless if "possession" was given its strict legal
meaning since possession is indivisible—construed as prohibiting sharing
use).
[15] *Wong v. Beaumont Property Trust Ltd* [1965] 1 Q.B. 173 at 183; *Sudbrook
Trading Estate Ltd v. Eggleton* [1983] 1 A.C. 444 followed in *R. & A. Millett
(Shops) Ltd v. Leon Allan International Fashions Ltd* [1989] 18 E.G. 107.
But note the court's approach in *Fraser Pipestock Ltd v. Gloucester City
Council* [1995] 36 E.G. 141.
[16] *Sweet & Maxwell Ltd v. Universal News Services Ltd* [1964] 2 Q.B. 699;
Greater London Council v. Connolly [1970] 2 Q.B. 100.
[17] *Antaios Cia Naviera S.A. v. Salen Redevierna A.B.* [1985] A.C.191 at 201,
per Lord Diplock. See also *Miramar Maritime Corp. v. Holborn Oil Trading
Ltd* [1984] A.C. 676 at 682.
[18] *Co-operative Wholesale Society Ltd v. National Westminster Bank plc* [1995] 1
E.G. 111, *per* Hoffmann L.J. See also *Millshaw Property Co. Ltd v. Preston
Borough Council* [1995] EGCS 186.
[19] *ibid.* See also *Arnold v. National Westminster Bank plc* [1990] 1 E.G. 58, *per*
Hoffmann L.J.
[20] *Broadgate Square plc v. Lehman Brothers Ltd* [1995] 1 E.G. 111.
[21] See *Freehold Leasehold Shop Properties Ltd v. Friends' Provident Life Office*
(1984) 271 E.G. 451, *per* Oliver L.J.; also see *Philpots (Woking) Ltd v.
Surrey Conveyancers Ltd* [1986] 1 EGLR 97 (the court will avoid absurd
results but not necessarily unpredictable or capricious ones). Also, a
seemingly absurd result may be explicable by concessions granted the other
way: see *M.F.I. Properties Ltd v. B.I.C.C. Group Pension Trust Ltd* [1986] 1
All E.R. 974 at 976.

Relevant circumstances

that the time is long past " . . . when agreements, even those under seal, were isolated from the matrix of facts in which they were set and interpreted purely on internal linguistic considerations".[22] What is important is the intention which reasonable persons, placed in the situation of the parties, would have had—and therefore the court must " . . . place itself in thought in the same factual matrix as that in which the parties were".[23] This approach can involve some knowledge of the commercial purpose of the contract, the genesis and background of the transaction, the factual background known to both parties at the date of the contract, and the market context.[24] Thus in construing a lease, it will be relevant to consider the subject-matter of the letting.[25] Similarly, the state of the general law as at the date of the lease may shed light on the intentions of the parties.[26] Evidence as to the projected use of the property by one party may also be relevant,[27] though the court will probably be wary of such evidence.

Negotiations and subsequent conduct

However, there are limitations to this principle. Evidence of negotiations or of the actual intentions of one or other party will not normally be admissible. This will usually exclude evidence based on drafts of the lease, for the reason that during negotiation the intentions of each party will be in a state of evolution, and it is only the final agreement which records the actual consensus.[28] Also excluded will be evidence of the subsequent conduct of the parties,[29] unless that conduct is such as to amount to a variation of the contract or raise some form of estoppel.[30]

Parol evidence rule

Furthermore, under the so-called parol evidence rule, extrinsic evidence is not admissible other than as an aid to construing the written terms of the agreement: it cannot, so the rule suggests, be used to add to, contradict, vary or alter those terms. However, in the context of leases, this obstacle

---

[22] *Prenn v. Simmonds* [1971] 1 W.L.R. 1381 at 1383–1384, *per* Lord Wilberforce.

[23] *Reardon Smith Line Ltd v. Hansen-Tangen* [1976] 1 W.L.R. 989 at 997, *per* Lord Wilberforce.

[24] *Prenn v. Simmonds* [1971] 1 W.L.R. 1381 at 1385; *Reardon Smith Line Ltd v. Hansen-Tangen* [1976] 1 W.L.R. 989 at 995; *John Lewis Properties plc v. Viscount Chelsea* [1993] 34 E.G. 116.

[25] *Levermore v. Jobey* [1956] 1 W.L.R. 697 at 701. The length of the term may also be relevant: see *Killick v. Second Covent Garden Property Co. Ltd* [1973] 1 W.L.R. 658 at 663.

[26] *Bracknell Development Corp. v. Greenlees Lennards Ltd* (1981) 260 E.G. 500 at 502. But *cf. Henry Smith's Charity Trustees v. A.W.A.D.A. Trading & Promotion Services Ltd* (1984) 269 E.G. 729, where Sir John Donaldson M.R. regarded the device as an undesirable extension of *stare decisis*.

[27] *The Shannon Ltd v. Venner Ltd* [1965] 1 Ch. 682 (evidence of future intention for property used in ascertaining dominant tenement of right of way).

[28] *Prenn v. Simmonds* [1971] 1 W.L.R. 1381 at 1384; *Guys'n'Dolls Ltd v. Sade Brothers Catering Ltd* (1983) 269 E.G. 129. But compare *Lister Locks Ltd v. T.E.I. Pensions Trust Ltd* (1981) 264 E.G. 827, suggesting that negotiations may be valuable evidence where an exchange of letters conveniently records something which did find its way into the lease.

[29] *James Miller & Partners Ltd v. Whitsworth Street Estates (Manchester) Ltd* [1970] A.C. 583 at 603, 606, 611, 615; *L. Schuler A.G. v. Wickman Machine Tools Sales Ltd* [1974] A.C. 235 at 252, 261.

[30] See *Amalgamated Investment & Property Co. Ltd v. Texas Commerce International Bank Ltd* [1982] 1 Q.B. 84.

has frequently been outflanked by evidence showing a collateral warranty on the faith of which the lease was executed, or even a complete collateral contract.[31] Thus in *ConnsWater Properties Ltd v. Wilson*[32] a landlord was held liable for very substantial damages for breach of an oral assurance given to a prospective tenant of a restaurant in a shopping centre that he would be in a monopoly position, despite the lack of any provision to that effect in the lease.

17–04 **Other rules of construction**

Mention can finally be made of some miscellaneous rules which may be of use.

First, by section 61 of the Law of Property Act 1925, certain expressions are given certain meanings unless the context otherwise requires.[33] Redundant provisions reproducing these statutory rules are often found in leases.

Statute

Secondly, leases sometimes contain lists of items, followed by general words. A common example in older leases is a covenant by the tenant to deliver up at the end of the lease all "doors, locks, keys, wainscots, hearths, stoves and all other erections, buildings, improvements, fixtures and things which are now or which at any time during the said term shall be fixed, fastened or belong to" the demised premises.[34] A modern equivalent could be a list of items in respect of which a service charge is payable. In such cases it may be possible to identify a common genus by which the meaning of the concluding general words may be restricted—the *ejusdem generis* rule.[35] The justification for the rule is that if the meaning of the general words are not restricted the earlier particular words would be of no practical effect.

"*Ejusdem generis*" rule

Another rule which can be a trap for the draftsman is that expressed by the maxim *expressio unius est exclusio alterius*: the expression of one or more things implies the exclusion of other things of the same class which are not mentioned expressly.[36] Thus the draftsman who lists obligations to repair by reference to various parts of the building and who inadvertently omits mention of some important part could fall foul of this rule, as could the draftsman who lists a series of offensive trades which are prohibited in the premises.

"*Expressio unius*" rule

[31] *De Lasalle v. Guildford* [1901] 2 K.B. 215; *Walker Property Investments (Brighton) Ltd v. Walker* (1947) 177 L.T. 204; *City of Westminster Properties Ltd v. Mudd* [1959] Ch. 129.

[32] (1986) 16 *Chartered Surveyor Weekly*, September 25, 928 (Northern Ireland High Court of Justice).

[33] "Month" means a calendar month (as to which see para. 16–25 above); "person" includes a corporation; the singular includes the plural and vice versa; and the masculine includes the feminine and vice versa.

[34] *Lambourn v. McLellan* [1903] 2 Ch. 268.

[35] *ibid.* Compare *Wilson v. Whately* (1860) 1 J. & H. 436 where no genus could be found; and see also *Coates v. Diment* [1951] 1 All E.R. 890 (para. 16–08 above). See also *Skillion plc v. Keltec Industrial Research Ltd* [1992] 5 E.G. 162 for a discussion as to the circumstances in which the rule applies.

[36] The courts appear to apply it with some mistrust: in *Colquhoun v. Brooks* (1888) 21 Q.B.D. 52 at 65 Lopes L.J. referred to it as "a valuable servant but a dangerous master. "

"Contra proferentem" rule

Finally, there is the *contra proferentem* rule, by which doubts as to the meaning of particular phrases are resolved against the grantor or against the party relying on the term. In the context of leases, in most cases this will be the landlord: he is the grantor and most of the covenants are inserted for his benefit.[37] However, this will not necessarily be the case.[37a] Some provisions in leases, such as options for renewal, are for the benefit of the tenant; also the reservation of an easement in favour of the landlord will be construed against the tenant as a regrant with the tenant as grantor.[38] Moreover, it would be dangerous to place too much reliance on the rule: it can only operate where there is ambiguity, and in the context of a lease it can be difficult to apply.[39] It has been described as "a canon of construction of last resort" which cannot carry much weight in the case of a lease, where "its effect would in most cases be entirely arbitrary".[40]

RECTIFICATION

17–05 Generally

It is striking how many of the leading cases on rectification concern leases. The length and complexity of many leases, and the frequently protracted nature of the drafting and negotiation process, make it easy for mistakes to creep in to the final version of the document. Where this occurs, a claim for rectification may have to be considered, though such litigation is often complex and unpredictable in outcome, depending largely on the facts of each case.[41] The position is complicated because the mistake can arise in different ways: it

---

[37] *White v. Harrow* (1902) 86 L.T. 4 (covenant by tenant not to object to development ought not to be construed to permit landlord to derogate from grant in the absence of clear language); *Lambourn v. McLellan* [1903] 2 Ch. 268 (clause restricting tenant's right to remove fixtures construed against landlord); *Lee v. Railway Executive* [1949] 2 All E.R. 581 (clause excluding landlord's liability for damage construed against landlord); *Gruhn v. Balgray Investments* (1963) 107 S.J. 112 (landlord's option to determine lease construed against landlord); *Killick v. Second Covent Garden Property Co. Ltd* [1973] 1 W.L.R. 658 at 663 (clause restraining assignment construed against landlord); *Skillion plc v. Keltec Industrial Research Ltd* [1992] 5 E.G. 162 (user clause construed against landlord).

[37a] See, *e.g.* *Dukeminster (Ebbgate House One) Ltd v. Somerfield Properties Co. Ltd* [1996] EGCS 56: the court was unwilling to apply the rule where the transaction in question involved a sale and leaseback, which gave the tenant greater control over the terms of the lease.

[38] *Johnstone v. Holdway* [1963] 1 Q.B. 601; *St. Edmundsbury and Ipswich Diocesan Board of Finance v. Clark (No. 2)* [1975] 1 W.L.R. 468; for criticism see Megarry and Wade, *The Law of Real Property* (5th ed., 1984) p. 858. But see *Trailfinders Ltd v. Razuki* [1988] 30 E.G. 59.

[39] See *Credit Suisse v. Beegas Nominees Ltd* [1994] 11 E.G. 151 where it was suggested that a landlord's repairing covenant might be construed narrowly as the cost would be passed on to the tenant by way of a service charge. See also *West Horndon Industrial Park v. Phoenix Timber* [1995] 20 E.G. 137 where it was held that ambiguities in a surety's covenant should be resolved in favour of the surety.

[40] *Amax International Ltd v. Custodian Holdings Ltd* [1986] 2 EGLR 111 at 112 (Hoffmann J.). See also *Beaumont Property Trust v. Tai* (1982) 265 E.G. 872 for doubts in this respect.

[41] *Co-operative Insurance Society Ltd v. Centremoor Ltd* (1982) 266 E.G. 1027 at 1031, *per* Dillon L.J.

may have been spotted by neither party until after execution; alternatively it may have been noticed by one party who failed to draw it to the attention of the other.

17–06 Requirements for rectification

The factors which must be established to succeed in a claim for rectification are as follows:

(1) the parties had a certain and common intention as to what the terms of their agreement should be;
(2) the parties executed a document in pursuance of their agreement;
(3) the document failed to record the intention accurately;
(4) either both parties were under the mistaken impression at the time of execution that the document did reflect their true agreement, or the plaintiff alone was mistaken, and the defendant, aware of the plaintiff's mistake, did nothing to draw it to his attention;
(5) since rectification is an equitable remedy, the court must be willing in its discretion to grant it.

Each factor must be considered in greater detail.

17–07 The common intention

The intention of the parties must be common to them both, sufficiently certain, and continuing up to the time of execution of the document. It need not amount to a contract in its own right, but must be manifested by "some outward expression of accord".[42] In the context of leases, examples of evidence which may fulfil this requirement are agent's particulars,[43] correspondence between the parties,[44] travelling drafts,[45] heads of terms,[46] and any agreement for lease,[47] as well as oral evidence.

Certainty of common intention   The common intention must be sufficiently certain—in the words of one old case, the plaintiff must show "exactly and precisely to what form the deed ought to be brought".[48] Thus in one case, a claim for rectification of a curious rent review clause which had serious financial consequences for the tenant failed because, although the judge agreed that the clause was

---

[42] *Jocelyne v. Nissen* [1970] 2 Q.B. 86 at 98, *per* Russell L.J.
[43] *Central & Metropolitan Estates Ltd v. Compusave Ltd* (1982) 266 E.G. 900.
[44] *ibid.; cf. Kemp v. Neptune Concrete Ltd* [1988] E.G. 71.
[45] *Boots the Chemist Ltd v. Street* (1983) 268 E.G. 817.
[46] *Co-operative Insurance Society Ltd v. Centremoor Ltd* (1983) 268 E.G. 1027; *J. J. Huber (Investments) Ltd v. The Private DIY Co. Ltd* [1995] EGCS 112.
[47] *Thomas Bates & Son Ltd v. Wyndham's (Lingerie) Ltd* [1981] 1 W.L.R. 505; but see *London Regional Transport v. Wimpey Group Services* (1987) 53 P. & C.R. 356.
[48] *Fowler v. Fowler* (1859) 4 De G. & J. 250 at 265, *per* Lord Chelmsford L.C. Merely to show that the parties were confused as to their intention is therefore insufficient: *Cambro Contractors Ltd v. John Kennelly Sales Ltd, The Times*, April 14, 1994.

unreasonable, one could only guess at what the true intention of the parties was.[49]

Matters of detail   However, the plaintiff need not necessarily prove all the terms in every detail. In *Central & Metropolitan Estates Ltd v. Compusave Ltd*[50] rectification was given to insert into a lease a rent review clause inadvertently omitted by the landlord. All that could be shown was a common intention that reviews be five-yearly, but this was sufficient to allow rectification, and the clause could then be made to work by implication of terms that the rent should be a fair and reasonable one agreed by the parties, or fixed by the court in the absence of agreement.

17–08 Execution of a document which fails to record the intention accurately

Once a common intention has been shown, this aspect will usually cause little difficulty. However, problems can **Discrepancy** sometimes arise because the various documents in a leasehold **between** transaction do not correspond as they should. In *Co-operative* **documents** *Insurance Society Ltd v. Centremoor Ltd*[51] an error resulted in the rent review provisions in an underlease and sub-underlease failing to correspond, with the serious financial consequence that the underlessor could not participate immediately in increases in rent under the sub-underlease. Despite doubts as to whether it was the underlease or sub-underlease which was wrong, rectification was given: the important point was that they did not correspond as they should.

In *London Regional Transport v. Wimpey Group Services Ltd*[52] the problem was that a rent review formula agreed between surveyors was not accurately reproduced in the tortuous wording used in an agreement for a lease. On the grant of the lease itself, another form of wording was used which did accurately reflect the original formula, but such was the complexity of the wording that no-one noticed the discrepancies. A claim for rectification by the tenant to bring the formula in the lease into line with that in the agreement for a lease failed. Hoffmann J. suggested that the doctrine of rectification requires a mistake about the document which it is sought to rectify; here the intention was not simply that the lease should correspond with the agreement for the lease, but that it should embody the originally agreed formula. Thus the real mistake was as to the effect of the agreement for the lease.[53]

---

[49] *Pugh v. Smiths Industries Ltd* (1982) 264 E.G. 823. *Cf. Brimican Investments Ltd v. Blue Circle Heating Ltd* [1995] EGCS 18.

[50] (1982) 266 E.G. 900. See also *Thomas Bates & Son Ltd v. Wyndham's (Lingerie) Ltd* [1981] 1 W.L.R. 505.

[51] (1982) 266 E.G. 1027.

[52] [1986] 2 EGLR 41.

[53] The decision could also be based on avoiding circuitry of actions, since Hoffmann J. (*ibid.* at 42) suggested that the agreement could itself have been rectified.

Discrepancy of lease and counterpart   Another possible error is a discrepancy between the lease and counterpart, particularly where they are prepared by different parties and are not carefully checked. The ordinary rule is that in case of conflict, the lease prevails. But where the error in the lease is clear, it may be rectified to correspond with the counterpart.[54]

17–09 Mistake of both parties or known to one

Rectification can be given where both parties were mistaken, namely a common mistake.[55] It is also possible to obtain the remedy in cases of mistake by one party only, a unilateral mistake, provided the other knew that the discrepancy between intention and documentation was a mistake.[56] According to Buckley L.J. in *Thomas Bates Ltd v. Wyndham's (Lingerie) Ltd*[57] it must be shown:

Requirements for unilateral mistake

(1) that the plaintiff erroneously believed that the document contained a particular provision or alternatively that it did not contain a particular provision which, mistakenly, it did contain;[58]

(2) that the defendant was aware that the document did not, or alternatively did, in fact contain that provision and of the plaintiff's mistake;[59]

(3) that the defendant omitted to draw the mistake to the notice of the plaintiff;[60]

(4) that the mistake was one calculated to benefit the defendant.[61]

---

[54] See *Burchell v. Clark* (1876) 2 C.P.D. 88. This should rarely be a problem now that it is the practice for both parts to be prepared by the landlord's solicitor.

[55] See *e.g.*, *Equity & Law Life Assurance Society Ltd v. Coltness Group Ltd* (1983) 267 E.G. 949; *Boots the Chemist Ltd v. Street* (1983) 268 E.G. 817.

[56] *A. Roberts & Co. Ltd v. Leicestershire County Council* [1961] Ch. 555; *J. J. Huber (Investments) Ltd v. The Private DIY Co. Ltd* [1995] EGCS 112; see *Commission for the New Towns v. Cooper (Great Britain) Ltd* [1995] 2 W.L.R. 677 as to what constitutes actual knowledge in law. See also n.59 below.

[57] [1981] 1 W.L.R. 505 at 516. The case also provides useful observations on the standard of proof required.

[58] *Commission for the New Towns v. Cooper (Great Britain) Ltd* [1995] 2 W.L.R. 677 where the plaintiff's mistake was as to the construction of the document.

[59] Awareness or "actual knowledge" of the plaintiff's mistake will be inferred if the defendant wilfully shuts his eyes to the obvious or wilfully and recklessly fails to make such enquiries as an honest and reasonable man would make. Even mere suspicion of the plaintiff's mistake may be enough if the defendant intends the plaintiff to be mistaken and diverts the plaintiff's attention from discovering the mistake by making false and misleading statements: *Commission for the New Towns v. Cooper (Great Britain) Ltd* [1995] 2 W.L.R. 677.

[60] This need not amount to "sharp practice", but there must still be an element of unconscionable behaviour by the defendant: *Thomas Bates Ltd v. Wyndham's (Lingerie) Ltd* [1981] 1 W.L.R. 505 followed in *Kemp v. Neptune Concrete Ltd* [1988] 48 E.G. 71 and *Commission for the New Towns v. Cooper (Great Britain) Ltd* [1995] 2 W.L.R. 677.

[61] Eveleigh L.J. added in *Thomas Bates Ltd v. Wyndham's (Lingerie) Ltd*, *ibid*. at 521, that it would also suffice if the mistake was detrimental to the plaintiff.

17–10   Discretionary remedy

As an equitable remedy, rectification is at the discretion of the court. Thus it may be lost by delay on the part of the plaintiff in seeking the remedy once the mistake is known.[62] As a "mere equity" it will not be available against a bona fide purchaser of a legal or equitable estate for value.[63] However, a right to rectification is transmissible in favour of an assignee or purchaser of an interest in land.[64]

Negligence on the part of the plaintiff in making the mistake will not bar the remedy,[65] but it may result in the remedy only being given on terms allowing the defendant to rescind the contract,[66] or an unfavourable order as to costs.[67] Rectification will not necessarily be ruled out merely because the lease contains a clause providing that it comprises the "entire agreement" between the parties[68] or because both parties were represented by solicitors.[69]

Entire agreement

---

[62] *Beale v. Kyte* [1907] 1 Ch. 564.

[63] *Westminster Bank Ltd v. Lee* [1956] Ch. 7: *Equity & Law Life Assurance Society Ltd v. Coltness Group Ltd* (1983) 267 E.G. 949 (rectification of rent review memorandum given against gratuitous assignee of lease).

[64] *Boots the Chemist Ltd v. Street* (1983) 258 E.G. 817

[65] *Weeds v. Blaney* (1977) 247 E.G. 211.

[66] In *Central & Metropolitan Estates Ltd v. Compusave Ltd* (1982) 266 E.G. 900 rectification to insert a rent review clause was given on the basis that the tenant would have the benefit of a break clause after the review. But *cf. Riverlate Properties Ltd v. Paul* [1975] Ch. 133.

[67] *Garrard v. Frankel* (1862) 30 Beav. 445; *Boots the Chemist Ltd v. Street* (1983) 268 E.G. 817.

[68] *J.J. Huber (Investments) Ltd v. The Private DIY Co. Ltd* [1995] EGCS 112.

[69] *ibid.*

18 LEASEHOLD CONVEYANCING

18–01 Introduction

Much of this book is concerned with the contents of commercial leases and with the continuing relationship between the landlord and tenant under such leases. However, equally important is the process by which leasehold interests are created, transferred and extinguished, and the law of leasehold conveyancing is therefore put in context in this Chapter. The grant and assignment of leases, underleases, and the surrender of leases will be considered in turn. Detailed treatment of general principles of conveyancing law is beyond the scope of the Chapter, which will concentrate upon the principles and problems of particular relevance to leasehold conveyancing of commercial property. One matter which will be considered in detail at the end of the Chapter is the frequent practical problem posed by the tenant, assignee or underlessee who wishes to obtain possession of the property before conclusion of the legal formalities.[1]

GRANT OF A LEASE

18–02 Preliminary matters

The first transaction to be considered is the grant of a new lease by the owner of a freehold interest in land.

Negotiation of terms   Negotiation of the basic terms of the lease will usually be a matter for the parties and their agents or surveyors, and the solicitor on each side will often be

Amount of detail agreed   instructed only after these terms have been agreed in the "heads of terms". However, the amount of detail contained in the heads of terms can vary enormously. The parties should at least have agreed the identity of the tenant, the initial rent, the length of the term, the frequency of any rent reviews and the property to be comprised in the lease. They may have gone on to reach agreement on matters such as who is to repair and insure, whether any service charge is payable, the use to be permitted, whether guarantors will be required, whether Part II of the Landlord and Tenant Act 1954 is to be excluded, and so on.

The less detail agreed in principle, the harder will be the job of the solicitor on each side. The landlord's solicitor will

Need to consult client   need to consult his client or the client's agent on fundamental, as well as technical, issues when preparing the draft lease, and the likelihood of objections on matters of

---

[1] See paras. 18–30 *et seq.* below.

principle from the tenant's side is sharply increased. The more vague the initial agreement between the parties, the more likely it becomes that second thoughts will occur as to the agreed rent and term as the other aspects of the proposed lease come more clearly into focus. The solicitors advising each party should be alert to this possibility.

User and rent   For example, a demand by the landlord for a restrictive user clause or for the exclusion of the 1954 Act should prompt the tenant's solicitor to consider whether a proposal for reducing the agreed rent is justified. To protect the tenant's interests fully, very close liaison between the tenant's solicitor, the tenant's surveyor and the tenant himself is necessary—and if the tenant has no surveyor the solicitor should suggest to him that he seriously consider instructing one.

Code of Practice   At this stage, the solicitor should consider supplying his client with a copy of the *Commercial Property Leases Code of Practice*, if the client has not already received one. As mentioned earlier[2] the Code is voluntary rather than compulsory, but it contains useful guidance and best practice suggestions for landlords and tenants and their professional advisers. It is too soon to say whether it will be widely adopted by the property industry.

Initial contact between the solicitors   The first contact between the solicitors acting for each party will usually be a letter stating that the writer has been instructed to act for the landlord or the tenant as the case may be upon the grant of the proposed lease, and asking for confirmation that the recipient has instructions from the other side. Where the writer has to hand the details of any terms agreed, it is convenient to set them out at this stage, and this may lessen the risk of misunderstanding arising later.

Where the agreed terms of the proposed lease are set out in a letter or memorandum from the client's agent, it may be quicker simply to send a copy of that letter to the solicitor on the other side, rather than transcribe the terms into a solicitor's letter. Clearly any matters of a confidential nature should be deleted from the copy which is forwarded to the other side's solicitor.

Initial exchange of letters   The initial exchange of letters between the parties' solicitors should deal with two important matters: the status of the correspondence and ensuing correspondence under section 2 of the Law of Property (Miscellaneous Provisions) Act 1989; and the question of allocation of the costs of the transaction.

18–03   Creating a binding contract

The effect of section 2 of the Law of Property (Miscellaneous Provisions) Act 1989 is that for a contract made on or after

---

[2] See para. 1–06 above. For the Law Society's comments on the Code, see *Gazette* December 6, 1995, 28.

Section 2   September 27, 1989 for the sale or other disposition of an
interest in land[3] to be valid, it must:

- be in writing;[4]
- incorporate all the terms which the parties have
  expressly agreed in one document (or, where contracts
  are exchanged, in each document);[5] the terms may
  however be incorporated by reference to another
  document;[6]
- be signed by or on behalf of each party to the contract
  (or where contracts are exchanged, the parties may
  sign different parts).[7]

Section 2 replaced section 40 of the Law of Property Act
1925, which, unlike section 2, merely prevented an action
being brought upon a contract to buy or sell land, or to grant
a lease, unless it was made or evidenced in writing and signed
by or on behalf of the person against whom enforcement was
sought. It became customary for solicitors to mark their
correspondence "subject to contract" (or in the case of the
grant of a lease "subject to lease") to indicate that no contract
or lease should come into effect until a formal contract or
lease had been exchanged. It was originally believed that, even
after section 2 came into force, it was possible for a contract
to be made in correspondence,[8] but it is now clear that this is
no longer permitted.[9] In spite of this, letters between
solicitors continue to be marked "subject to contract" or
"subject to lease", as a precaution against either party
inadvertently becoming legally committed to the transaction
earlier than intended.

Contracts to   Section 2 does not apply to a contract to grant a lease
which Section 2   taking effect in possession for a term of three years or less at
does not apply   the best rent which can be obtained without taking a fine.[10]
Nor does it have any relevance to a contract which has been
completed.[11,12]

Side letters   It is quite common for the parties in a leasehold transaction
to agree certain matters in the form of a letter, separate from
the lease. This could be because the arrangements are
personal to that landlord and that tenant, because there were
matters which one or both of the parties wanted to keep
confidential (particularly in relation to incentives to tenants

---

[3] This includes the grant, assignment and surrender of a lease. It also
includes the variation of such a contract: *McCausland v. Duncan Lawrie Ltd*
[1996] EGCS 103.
[4] Law of Property (Miscellaneous Provisions) Act 1989, s.2(1).
[5] *ibid.*
[6] *ibid.*, s.2(2).
[7] *ibid.*, s.2(3).
[8] *Hooper v. Sherman* [1994] N.P.C. 153.
[9] *Commission for the New Towns v. Cooper (Great Britain) Limited* [1995] 2
W.L.R. 677, in which the Court of Appeal held that "exchange of
contracts" is a well-recognised expression in which each party signs a
separate but identical document, intending not to be bound until the other
party is also bound. See also *Enfield L.B.C. v. Arajah* [1995] EGCS 164.
[10] Nor to a contract made in the course of a public auction, or one regulated
by the Financial Services Act 1986: Law of Property (Miscellaneous
Provisions) Act 1989, s.2(5).
[11,12] *Tootal Clothing Ltd v. Guinea Properties Ltd* (1992) 64 P. & C.R. 452.

when rents are falling)[13] or because they reflect a last minute agreement negotiated after the main documentation had been settled and engrossed. Where a side letter accompanies a lease, then section 2 is probably not relevant, for the lease is not a contract for the disposition of an interest in land: rather, it is the disposition itself.[14] However, where the side letter accompanies a contract, then section 2 will apply, and care must be taken that either the contract is referred to in the letter, or vice versa, to ensure validity of the contract.[15]

Exclusion of Landlord and Tenant Act 1954 Part II

Where it is intended to exclude the provisions of Part II of the Landlord and Tenant Act 1954 which would otherwise protect the occupation of the tenant,[16] the landlord's solicitor should also provide that the transaction is subject to a court order being obtained to authorise an agreement to exclude the Act.[17] This will prevent the inadvertent grant of a lease in the absence of the necessary order.

18–04 Allocation of costs

The initial exchange of correspondence between the parties' solicitors should also deal with the issue of costs.

Costs

Notwithstanding any custom to the contrary, a party to a lease is not bound to pay the whole or any part of any other party's solicitor's costs of the lease, unless the parties to the lease agree otherwise in writing.[18] Until fairly recently landlords commonly, if not invariably, sought to require the tenant to pay their costs in granting the lease; today this is not so usual, although it is still encountered. Whether the tenant can resist such a request depends on the state of the market and the relative importance which each party accords to the transaction proceeding.

Limiting costs

Where the tenant has agreed to pay the landlord's solicitor's costs, the tenant's solicitor can at least seek to protect his client by agreeing only to pay "reasonable" costs or by seeking a pre-estimate or imposing some upper limit on the landlord's costs. The landlord is likely to require the tenant to pay his costs whether or not the matter proceeds to completion. Even if the tenant is forced to agree to this, there seems no reason why he should have to pay the landlord's costs if the latter

Withdrawal

decides to withdraw from the transaction for some reason unconnected with the tenant or with the negotiation of the terms of the lease; for example, if the landlord finds another tenant willing to pay a higher rent. The tenant's solicitor should make this plain.

---

[13] See for example para. 6–31 above.
[14] *Lotteryking Ltd v. AMEC Properties Ltd* [1995] 28 E.G. 104.
[15] In practice the courts have made it clear that they will not allow technical arguments over whether section 2 is satisfied to enable a party in default to escape from his obligations: for example, see *Tootal Clothing Ltd v. Guinea Properties Ltd* (1992) 64 P. & C.R. 452; *Wright v. Robert Leonard (Developments) Ltd* [1994] EGCS 69; *Record v. Bell* [1991] 4 All E.R. 470.
[16] See para. 16–23 above.
[17] See *Cardiothoracic Institute v. Shrewdcrest Ltd* [1986] 1 W.L.R. 368; para. 16–23 above.
[18] Costs of Leases Act 1958, s.1.

Undertaking as to costs

The landlord's solicitor will often refuse to proceed with the transaction until the tenant's solicitor gives an undertaking as to payment of the landlord's costs. Whether the tenant's solicitor is willing to do this will probably depend on his or her relationship with the client and possibly whether the client is willing to put the solicitor in funds in advance. Such undertakings should not be given lightly,[19] and it is submitted that it is quite justifiable to refuse to give them at all as a matter of policy: the landlord chose to open negotiations with the prospective tenant and there seems no reason why the tenant's solicitor rather than the landlord should bear the risk of the tenant breaking his promise to pay the landlord's costs. In practice, however, if the landlord refuses to proceed on any other basis, the tenant's solicitor may have to agree to provide an undertaking. This should certainly be limited to a maximum amount, to be negotiated between the two parties' solicitors.

18–05 Searches and preliminary enquiries

Upon receiving confirmation that the matter is proceeding, the tenant's solicitor will need to put in hand various searches and enquiries.

Local search

A local land charges search should be made, together with the appropriate additional enquiries of the local authority.

Planning position

Of particular significance in the case of commercial premises is the planning position. The grant by the landlord of a lease authorising premises to be used for a particular purpose does not amount to a warranty that they may lawfully be so used,[20] and neither does the usual covenant for quiet enjoyment.[21] Indeed, it is now usual for leases to exclude any warranty on the part of the landlord as to the permitted or lawful use of the premises.

Thus, in the absence of any misrepresentation of the planning position by the landlord,[22] the tenant may find himself forced to pay rent and spend money on premises which under planning law cannot be used for his intended

---

[19] See para 25.11 of the *Guide to the Professional Conduct of Solicitors* (7th ed., 1996).

[20] *Hill v. Harris* [1965] 2 Q.B. 601; *Edler v. Auerbach* [1950] 1 K.B. 359; *Stokes v. Mixconcrete (Holdings) Ltd* (1978) 36 P. & C.R. 427 (affirmed C.A. (1978) 38 P. & C.R. 488).

[21] *Dennett v. Atherton* (1872) L.R. 7 Q.B. 316.

[22] *Laurence v. Lexcourt Holdings Ltd* [1978] 1 W.L.R. 1128. Whether or not the tenant will be able to rescind the lease on the ground of mistake will depend upon the contractual allocation of risk as to the planning position: see *William Sindall plc v. Cambridgeshire C.C.* [1994] 1 W.L.R. 1016 (where the court's decision in *Laurence v. Lexcourt Holdings Ltd* was doubted by Hoffmann L.J. on the basis that it had not considered the contractual allocation of risk in that case). On the duty to disclose fully and frankly any known registered local land charges, see *Rignall Developments Ltd v. Halil* [1988] Ch. 190.

purpose.[23] To avoid this situation, some investigation of the planning history of the premises may be required.[24] Information may be gleaned from replies to the additional enquiries of the local authority and from the landlord's replies to preliminary enquiries about the past use of the premises. It may also be necessary to consult the planning registers kept by the local planning authority.[25] If serious doubts arise as to the planning position, one course which may be followed is for the tenant to make a planning application and enter into a

Conditional contract
contract for a lease conditional on planning permission being obtained.[26] The agreement should make clear whether full[26a] or outline permission is required; and also possibly the effect of the imposition of any conditions. Alternatively a lease may be executed giving the tenant an option to determine it if permission is not obtained within a specified period.[27]

Other searches
The tenant's solicitor will also make all the other searches which he would make if the property were being purchased instead of leased. In particular it may be worth making a company search on the landlord if the landlord is a company, either as part of the exercise of investigating title,[28] or if the landlord's substance is of concern to the tenant (*e.g.* where the landlord is to carry out works, or provide continuing services under the lease).

Preliminary enquiries
The tenant should also make the usual preliminary enquiries of the landlord, so far as they are applicable to the property. Though the answers to these enquiries are often so guarded and qualified as to be useless, the landlord may well be in possession of important information, such as boundary disputes or adverse claims relating to the property,[29] the past

---

[23] See *Best v. Glenville* [1960] 1 W.L.R. 1198.

[24] It is essential to establish whether at the relevant time the existing use or any operations which have taken place are lawful, *i.e.* that no enforcement action may be taken at that time in respect of them and that they do not contravene the requirements of any enforcement notice then in force: Town and Country Planning Act 1990, s.191(2) (as amended). Note that the effect of an established use certificate already in force under older statutory provisions (Town and Country Planning Act 1990, s.191 (as originally enacted)) is to make the use to which it relates immune from enforcement action and thus lawful.

[25] Register of applications for planning permission, register of enforcement and stop notices: Town and Country Planning Act 1990, ss.69 and 188 (as amended) respectively. For an example where a firm of solicitors were found to have been negligent in failing to uncover a planning condition restricting the use of premises, see *G.P. & P. Ltd v. Bulcraig & Davis* [1986] 2 EGLR 148.

[26] See, *e.g. Hargreaves Transport Ltd v. Lynch* [1969] 1 W.L.R. 215; *Richard West and Partners v. Dick* [1969] 2 Ch. 424. The agreement may contain an obligation to use best endeavours to obtain permission: see *I.B.M. United Kingdom Ltd v. Rockware Glass Ltd* [1980] F.S.R. 335.

[26a] Note however that the planning legislation does not use the term "full": the application will be either in "outline" or not.

[27] *Stokes v. Mixconcrete (Holdings) Ltd* (1978) 36 P. & C.R. 427 (affirmed (C.A.) (1978) 38 P. & C.R. 488). In this case the provision was unfortunately worded so that the tenant had the right to break if permission was refused within 12 months; in fact it was refused after 13 months and it was held that the tenant could not rely on the provision.

[28] See para. 18–08 below.

[29] This is vital given the limited nature of the landlord's covenant for quiet enjoyment: see para. 16–03 above.

Inherent defects

use of the property,[30] and the rateable value of the property. One matter which deserves some careful thought is the question of inherent defects in the physical structure of the property. As we have seen, these may cause major difficulties for a tenant under a full repairing lease.[31] It would not seem unreasonable to expect a landlord who requires a tenant to assume full responsibility for the physical structure of the building to disclose any defects of which he knows, particularly where the landlord was responsible for the original construction of the building. Any such request by the tenant is likely to be met by the stock answer that the tenant should rely on his own survey but, as we have seen,[32] such a solution may not be practicable for the tenant. Any attempt positively to mislead the tenant as to the condition of the premises will be actionable,[33] but at present the law stops short of imposing any duty of frank disclosure on the prospective landlord and as a result it is rare for a landlord to provide adverse information voluntarily.

Survey

The tenant would be wise to commission a survey of the property. As well as revealing the suitability of the premises for the tenant's requirements, and confirming that the rent agreed is reasonable (or otherwise as the case may be), the survey can indicate the extent of the tenant's likely liabilities under the lease, *e.g.* repair, likely cost of works required to the building to which the tenant may have to contribute by way of service charge, and compliance with statutory requirements such as the provision of fire escapes or lavatories.[34] It may also be necessary where there is a possibility of contamination of the site.[35] Whether the survey should be carried out before or after the terms of the lease are negotiated is a question reminiscent of the chicken and the egg. Carrying out the survey first will allow the tenant's solicitor to negotiate terms armed with full background information; on the other hand an awareness of the terms proposed by the landlord can be helpful to the surveyor carrying out the survey. No general rule applies, except that the tenant's solicitor and surveyor should keep each other fully informed at all times, and certainly the surveyor will need to see a copy of the proposed form of lease at the earliest opportunity.

At this stage the landlord will no doubt wish to make enquiries into the general and financial soundness of the tenant, and possibly any guarantors. This will usually take the

References

form of requiring financial and trade references and, where the tenant is a company, making a company search. The landlord will also ask his bank to take up a reference from the tenant's bank, although this will no doubt be given without responsibility on the part of either bank.

---

[30] Important for ascertaining the planning position: see above, and possible past contaminative uses: see Chap. 20.

[31] See paras. 9–07 and 9–09 above.

[32] See para. 9–11 above.

[33] See *Gordon v. Selico Co. Ltd* [1986] 1 EGLR 71.

[34] See para. 7–04 above.

[35] See para. 20–11 below.

18–06 Procedure for negotiating

Negotiating the draft lease

Travelling draft

The procedure for negotiating the lease usually takes the following form. The landlord's solicitor will prepare a draft lease and send two copies to the tenant's solicitor.[36] The tenant's solicitor will consider the draft, taking his client's instructions as necessary, and will return one copy to the landlord's solicitor with his amendments and additions written in red ink, or if substantial additional provisions are proposed, typed as riders. This copy then becomes the travelling draft. The landlord's solicitor, again taking instructions as necessary, will return the draft, confirming or refusing the tenant's amendments as the case may be and perhaps suggesting any consequential amendments, this time in blue or green ink. The process of passing the draft back and forth can be repeated until agreement is reached,[37] but where the points at issue have become narrowed down to manageable proportions, the solicitors on each side should consider whether progress could be assisted by a face-to-face meeting (preferably accompanied by their clients and their clients' surveyors), or if that is not practicable, a telephone conversation. It is usually harder to maintain an unreasonable and intransigent position in conversation than when distanced by correspondence.

Client's instructions

Both solicitors should be aware of the need to take instructions from their clients as negotiations proceed: ultimately many matters of principle will call for a decision from the client rather than the solicitor, however eager the client may be to leave matters to the lawyers. The tenant's solicitor should be aware of his or her duty not only to bring the terms of the draft lease and amendments to it to the tenant's attention, but also to explain the legal effect of these provisions and point out possible problems stemming from them.[38]

Mistakes in drafting

The situation can sometimes occur where one party suspects that the other may have made a mistake in drafting. For example, the tenant's solicitor may notice that the initial rent inserted in the draft lease is less than the figure which he understood the tenant had agreed. In such cases, the obvious temptation can be to shut one's eyes to the possible mistake. However, this may result in the eventual contract being set aside for mistake, if it can be proven that one party knew of the other's mistake and an element of sharp practice was

---

[36] Before the introduction of photocopiers these were a top copy and carbon. As every solicitor now has access to a photocopier, it is a mystery why the practice of supplying two copies of the draft lease has persisted.

[37] Using different colour inks on each occasion to distinguish the various revisions. This has now become rarer: it is more usual for a further draft version to be produced on the word processor, with outstanding points indicated by the use of square brackets. This eliminates the need to hand-colour the photocopies (colour photocopying still being comparatively expensive).

[38] See *Sykes v. Midland Bank Executor and Trustee Co Ltd* [1971] 1 Q.B. 113; *County Personnel (Employment Agency) Ltd v. Alan R. Pulver & Co.* [1987] 1 All E.R. 289. See also *Commercial Property Leases Code of Practice* (1995) para. 2.4.

present,[39] or possibly if on an objective standard he should have known of the mistake.[40] Another risk is a subsequent action to rectify the lease.[41]

18–07 Agreement for lease

It is not usual for the grant of a lease to be preceded by a contract. However, an agreement for a lease may be desirable in some circumstances in order to commit both parties to the transaction, and the following are the most usual occasions:

(1) works need to be carried out to the building, or the building itself has not been constructed[42];
(2) some licence or consent is required before the tenant can begin to trade[43];
(3) the tenant requires possession urgently, and an agreement for lease can be entered into more speedily than a formal lease[44];
(4) an order of the court is to be obtained to authorise the lease to be contracted out of Part II of the Landlord and Tenant Act 1954[45];
(5) consent for the grant of the lease has been sought from a superior landlord but not yet been granted.

Agreement as to form of lease It is essential in practice for the exact terms of the lease to be granted to be agreed before contracts are exchanged and that the agreed form of lease should be annexed to the agreement.[46] Technically, it would be possible to dispense with this and rely on the implied term that the lease when granted will contain "the usual covenants".[47] However, considerable doubt may arise as to whether a covenant is "usual" in the technical sense,[48] and some older authorities suggest that many covenants which today might be thought usual, if not inevitable, will not necessarily be so.[49] Therefore, in all except the simplest cases, it will be unwise to rely on the implication of the usual covenants.

[39] See, *e.g. Commission for the New Towns v. Cooper (Great Britain) Limited* [1995] 2 All E.R. 929; *J.J. Huber (Investments) Ltd v. The Private DIY Co. Ltd* [1995] EGCS 112.
[40] *Cf. Agip SpA v. Navigazione Alta Italia SpA* [1983] Comm. L.R. 170.
[41] Rectification is dealt with above: see paras. 17–05 *et seq.* above.
[42] A letting in these circumstances is often termed a "pre-let".
[43] The most usual example is planning consent but it could also be a justices' licence for the sale of alcohol or a gaming licence.
[44] It is still essential of course, for the terms of the lease to be in an agreed form before exchange of agreements (see n. 46 below).
[45] See para. 16–23 above.
[46] The obligation will be to depart from the agreed form only so far as is necessary: *Vangeen v. Benjamin* (1976) 239 E.G. 647; and see National Conditions of Sale, condition 19(1).
[47] *Propert v. Parker* (1832) 3 My. & K. 280.
[48] *Hampshire v. Wickens* (1878) 7 Ch. D. 55; *Flexman v. Corbett* [1930] 1 Ch. 672; *Charalambous v. Ktori* [1972] 1 W.L.R. 951; *Chester v. Buckingham Travel Ltd* [1981] 1 W.L.R. 96.
[49] *e.g. Church v. Brown* (1808) 15 Ves. 258 (covenant against assignment not usual). Many of these old cases may require reconsideration in the light of *Chester v. Buckingham Travel Ltd* [1981] 1 W.L.R. 96.

Lease or agreement for lease

A different question is whether the tenant should hold under a lease or an agreement for a lease. Despite the well-worn generalisation that "an agreement for a lease is as good as a lease"[50] and the fact that an agreement for a lease can confer protection under the Landlord and Tenant Act 1954, there are important differences between the tenant holding under a contract and the tenant who has been formally granted a lease.[51] In particular, the tenant under an agreement for a lease may be denied the remedy of specific performance if he is in breach of the terms of the agreement;[52] and it is doubtful whether he can seek relief against forfeiture for non-payment of rent.[53]

Protecting priority by registration

Although frequently dispensed with or overlooked, an agreement for a lease should be appropriately protected by registration, either as a Class C(iv) land charge, or by entry of a notice if the landlord's title is registered. It is good practice for the contract to require the landlord to place his land or charge certificate on deposit at the Land Registry and to inform the tenant of the deposit number.[54] Where the landlord fails to place his land or charge certificate on deposit, the tenant may protect his interest by means of a caution, but this confers no priority and is not as satisfactory as a notice.[55]

18–08 Investigating the landlord's title

By section 44(2) of the Law of Property Act 1925, in the absence of any special condition in the contract, an intending tenant is not entitled to call for the title to the freehold.[56]

Whether landlord should deduce title

However, the tenant's solicitor should always consider whether the landlord should nevertheless be required to deduce title, as the usual covenant for quiet enjoyment will afford little protection to the tenant against the landlord's title proving defective. In certain cases full deduction of title may be a justifiable request, such as where the tenant is to pay a premium for the grant, or intends or is required to spend substantial sums on the property, or intends to use the term as security for a loan. In addition, a tenant who can raise "any distinct and tangible issue as to the goodness of the title"[57]

---

[50] *Parker v. Taswell* (1858) 2 De G. & J. 559; *Walsh v. Lonsdale* (1882) 21 Ch. D. 9; *Re Maugham* (1885) 14 Q.B.D. 956 at 958.

[51] See Megarry and Wade, *The Law of Real Property* (5th ed., 1984) p. 642; see also *Ashburn Anstalt v. Arnold* [1988] 2 W.L.R. 706.

[52] *Coatsworth v. Johnson* (1886) 55 L.J.Q.B. 220; *Henry Smith's Charity Trustees v. Hemmings* (1982) 265 E.G. 383; for an example of this principle applied to a development agreement, see *Alghussein Establishment v. Eton College* [1988] 1 W.L.R. 587.

[53] *Swain v. Ayres* (1888) 21 Q.B.D. 289; *Sport International Bussum B.V. v. Inter-Footwear Ltd* [1984] 1 W.L.R. 776 at 789–790; affirmed [1984] 1 W.L.R. 790. For other breaches, see Law of Property Act 1925, s.146(5)(a).

[54] See para. 18–11 below.

[55] *Clark v. Chief Land Registrar* [1994] 3 W.L.R. 593.

[56] This provision probably also extends to title to ancillary matters, such as rights of way: see *Jones v. Watts* (1890) 43 Ch. D. 574.

[57] *ibid.*, at 584, *per* Cotton L.J. Furthermore, any representation by the landlord that he is legally in a position to grant a lease may be actionable; see *Hizzett v. Hargreaves* (1986) C.A.T. 419; noted, [1987] 3 C.L. 56b.

will not be prevented by section 44(2) from requiring that issue to be resolved.

However, even apart from these cases, some investigation of the landlord's title will usually be justified. The risk that the landlord may turn out to have no title at all is probably slight, and can often be cured by the doctrine of tenancy by estoppel, but there are three much more substantial reasons for investigating title of which the tenant's solicitor should be aware. The first is that, where the landlord's title is not registered at the Land Registry, and the lease being granted is for a term exceeding 21 years, the tenant will not be able to obtain absolute title for his lease unless he is able to deduce the landlord's title to grant the lease to the Chief Land Registrar.[58] The second reason is that the landlord's freehold may be mortgaged or charged; if so, the mortgagee's consent is likely to be required to the grant of a lease. The landlord should therefore be asked to disclose any such incumbrances, and to provide suitable evidence before completion that any requisite consents have been obtained.[59]

Charge on freehold

The third reason is that the landlord's title may be subject to restrictive covenants which could prevent the tenant from using the property for his intended purpose. The soundest practice is for the landlord to disclose all such incumbrances at the outset by inserting a covenant in the draft lease that the tenant will observe them and indemnify the landlord against any breach, the incumbrances being set out in full in a schedule to the lease. However, this is not always done, and the tenant should consider the risk posed by such covenants. The implications differ in the case of registered and unregistered titles.

Restrictive covenants affecting freehold

In the case of unregistered title, covenants pre-dating January 1, 1926 will not affect the tenant unless he has actual or constructive notice of them. Failure to stipulate for investigation of the freehold title will not fix the tenant with constructive notice for this purpose.[60] However, in the case of post–1925 covenants, where these are registered as Class D(ii) land charges, the tenant will be treated as having actual notice of them,[61] despite the fact that under section 44(2) he was not entitled to the information necessary to enable him to carry out an effective land charges search.[62] The tenant's solicitor should therefore ask the landlord to provide the names of estate owners in order to enable a search to be made, or alternatively to produce a copy of the search certificate obtained when the landlord purchased, together with confirmation that the search was made against all

Unregistered title

---

[58] See para. 18–11 below.
[59] The tenant's concern is that a lease granted in these circumstances without the mortgagee's consent will not bind the mortgagee, who may therefore sell the property free of the tenant's interest.
[60] Law of Property Act 1925, s.44(5).
[61] *ibid.*, s.198.
[62] In this respect s.198 appears to override s.44(5): see *White v. Bijou Mansions Ltd* [1937] 1 Ch. 610 at 621. Nor is the tenant entitled to compensation under the Law of Property Act 1969, s.25 for undiscoverable land charges: see s.25(9).

relevant estate owners.[63] Where this is not forthcoming, the tenant will have to obtain the landlord's confirmation in the replies to enquiries that there are no restrictive covenants which affect his proposed use.

Registered title   Where the landlord's title is registered, the tenant will be affected with notice of any restrictive covenant entered on the register.[64] As the register is now open for general inspection, the tenant's solicitor will be able himself to apply for office copies of the landlord's title if the landlord refuses to supply them.

Implied covenants for title   Prior to July 1, 1995, it was not possible for covenants for title to be implied into the grant of a lease by the use of the statutory keywords (such as "beneficial owner"), and it was not usual to incorporate any similar express covenants. Since July 1, 1995 it is now possible to incorporate the implied covenants by the use of the words "with full title guarantee" or "with limited title guarantee", in the same manner as any other conveyancing transaction. Details of the covenants thereby implied are set out later in this Chapter, in the section concerned with assignment of a lease.[65]

18–09   Pre-completion searches

Appropriate pre-completion searches are no less important to an intending tenant than to a prospective purchaser. In addition to the matters mentioned above, the tenant will wish to know of matters such as bankruptcy, winding-up proceedings or receivership affecting the landlord which could prejudice his ability to grant a valid lease.

Insolvency of landlord

Land charges search   If the title is unregistered, the tenant should make a land charges search against the name of the landlord. This will reveal any charges or mortgages registered against the landlord which the landlord has not disclosed.[65a] If the landlord is an individual it will also reveal any registered petition in bankruptcy.[66] Any order appointing a receiver which has been registered will also be apparent, as will any registered pending land actions.[67] If the tenant knows the names of former estate owners, a search should be made against them, for the reasons given above. If the landlord is a company, the tenant should make a search in the Companies Register. This is important in order to discover any floating charge created by the landlord or any land charge for securing

Company search

---

[63] The tenant can rely on such a search: see Land Charges Act 1972, ss.10(4) and 17(1).

[64] Land Registration Act 1925, s.50(2). Again s.44(5) of the Law of Property Act will seemingly offer no help to the tenant: *White v. Bijou Mansions* [1937] 1 Ch. 610.

[65] See para. 18–18 below. In practice the incorporation of implied covenants for title into leases is not yet widespread.

[65a] But a first legal mortgage protected by the deposit of title deeds does not need to be registered: Land Charges Act 1972, s.2(4).

[66] Land Charges Act 1972, s.5(1)(b).

[67] *ibid.*, s.6(1)(b). For example, a claim for relief for forfeiture by a former tenant, registration of which would bind a subsequent tenant: *Fuller v. Judy Properties Ltd* [1992] 14 E.G. 106.

money created before January 1, 1970.[68] The search will also reveal any winding-up proceedings, and any change in the landlord's name.

Registered title Where the landlord's title is registered, a single search of the Register will suffice to cover all incumbrances.[69] A search of the Companies Register to check for any winding-up proceedings and any change in the company's name is also advisable.[70]

18–10 Completion

Completion will usually consist of execution of the lease and counterpart by the landlord and the tenant respectively, followed by exchange and, if appropriate, payment of the first instalment of rent. Except for leases not exceeding three
Execution of years, the lease must be by deed.[71] Completion meetings are
deed rare nowadays, and exchange usually occurs at the office of the landlord's solicitor, usually without the tenant's solicitor present.

The landlord's solicitor should check carefully that the documents are correctly executed.[72] An individual should execute the document in the presence of a witness, who attests the signature.[73] A company should execute either by the affixing and attestation of its common seal[74] or by the signature of a director and secretary[75] of the company, with the document being expressed to be executed by the company.[76]

Execution by foreign companies used to cause difficulties, as many such companies did not have common seals. It is
Execution by now provided that a foreign company may execute a deed in
foreign the manner permitted by the laws of the territory in which the
companies company is incorporated for the execution of documents by such a company.[77] A person dealing with a company which executes a document in this way will need to be satisfied as to the local law, and will require advice from lawyers in the relevant jurisdiction.

---

[68] A land charges search does not afford adequate protection against these matters: Land Charges Act 1972, s.3(7) (as amended by the Companies Act 1989, Sched. 16).

[69] See Land Registration Rules, rr. 287 and 289.

[70] Ruoff & Roper, *The Law and Practice of Registered Conveyancing* (1991 ed.) para. 30.25 states that a company search is not required but it is still good practice to make one.

[71] Law of Property Act 1925, ss.52(1), 54(2).

[72] The document must be validly executed by the parties if it is to constitute a deed: Law of Property (Miscellaneous Provisions) Act 1989, s.1(2)(b).

[73] Law of Property (Miscellaneous Provisions) Act 1989, s.1(3). The requirement that the document be sealed was abolished by s.1(1)(b) of the 1989 Act.

[74] Companies Act 1985, s.36A(2).

[75] Or by two directors; s.36A(4).

[76] Companies Act 1985, s.36A(4). A document executed thus will take effect as though executed under the company's common seal.

[77] The Foreign Companies (Execution of Documents) Regulations 1994 (S.I. 1994 No. 950), imported into Land Registry documents by the Land Registration (Execution of Deeds) Rules 1994 (S.I. 1994 No. 1130).

Delivery and escrow

The moment at which the lease takes effect can be a matter of some obscurity. The general rule is that a deed takes effect once delivered. A deed executed by an individual will not be effective until delivered by that individual or someone authorised by him to do so.[78] In the case of execution by a company, the deed is presumed to be delivered upon execution, unless a contrary intention is proved.[79] However, where a deed is delivered conditionally, or as an escrow, it only takes effect upon the condition being fulfilled.[80] In the meantime, the deed cannot be revoked by the grantor. It seems that a distinction can however be drawn in the case of a lease, which will not be treated as having been delivered until both lease and counterpart have been exchanged. In *Longman v. Viscount Chelsea*[81] the Court of Appeal held that even though the lease had been duly executed and the conditions subject to which it was executed had been or could be fulfilled there was, in the absence of exceptional circumstances, no concluded agreement until exchange.[82] In the case of a lease executed in escrow it has been held by a majority of the Court of Appeal that once the condition is satisfied rent payable "from the date hereof" is payable by the tenant from the date of delivery, not the date of satisfaction of the condition.[83] If this is not the intention of the tenant he should ensure that express provision is made to the contrary in the lease.

Dating the lease

On completion, the landlord's solicitor will need to date the lease and counterpart and fill in any blanks, such as the date from which the term is to commence, the date from which the rent becomes payable and the dates on which the rent is to be reviewed. Care should be taken not to overlook this important matter, and it is not unknown for disagreements to arise between the parties' solicitors at the last minute as to the identity of these dates. Failure to insert the date of exchange in a lease will not necessarily imply that it is delivered in escrow or is in some way conditional; the date upon which it takes effect will be the actual date of delivery.[84]

---

[78] Law of Property (Miscellaneous Provisions) Act 1989, s.1(3)(b).
[79] Companies Act 1985, s.36A(5). Note that it must be clear on the face of the document that it is intended by the parties that it takes effect as a deed. See *Johnsey Estates (1990) Ltd v. Newport Marketworld Ltd* [1996] EGCS 87. The rebuttable presumption contained in s.36A(5) can be rebutted by stating in the testimonium that the deed is not delivered until the date of the lease.
[80] *Foundling Hospital v. Crane* [1911] 2 K.B. 367.
[81] (1989) 58 P. & C.R. 189. See also *Beesly v. Hallwood Estates Ltd* [1961] Ch. 105. What is crucial is the intention of the party delivering the deed—there is no need for the other party to concur, but the intention must be made clear in some way: see *Glessing v. Green* [1975] 1 W.L.R. 863 at 867; *Alan Estates Ltd v. W.G. Stores Ltd* [1982] Ch. 511 at 526; *Vincent v. Premo Enterprises (Voucher Sales) Ltd* [1969] 2 Q.B. 609.
[82] *cf. Venetian Glass Gallery Ltd v. Next Properties Ltd* [1989] 30 E.G. 92 (where it was held that in the absence of evidence that there was no intention to deliver it as a deed, a duly executed licence to assign was an escrow conditional only on delivery of the counterpart and payment of money, here, a rent deposit). These two cases are difficult to reconcile.
[83] *Alan Estates Ltd v. W.G. Stores Ltd* [1982] Ch. 511. For criticism, see [1982] Conv. 409 (P.H. Kenny). This does not however vest the leasehold interest in the tenant until the condition is satisfied.
[84] *Bentray Investments Ltd v. Venner Time Switches Ltd* [1985] 1 EGLR 39.

Merger of agreement in lease

Following completion of the lease, those provisions of any preceding agreement for lease then merge with the lease insofar as they relate to the same subject matter.[85] However, it is common for the parties to provide expressly that merger will not occur in relation to any obligations which remain to be complied with.[86]

18–11   Post-completion matters

Stamp duty

Stamp duty is payable on leases on an ad valorem basis depending upon the rent and the length of the term.[87] The lease should be stamped within 30 days of execution.[88] The counterpart should also be stamped, the duty being fixed at 50p.[89] Where there is a prior agreement for lease, this is itself stampable at the rates applicable to leases. The lease will not attract additional duty (although it must be presented for stamping) so long as it is in the form specified in the agreement for lease.[90] In practice the agreement need not normally be stamped until the lease is executed.[91]

A lease for a term of seven years or more (and also an agreement for such a lease) must be produced to the Inland Revenue by the tenant, who must provide the prescribed particulars of the transaction on the "Particulars Delivered" form.[92]

Where there is no prior agreement for lease, the lease must contain a certificate to this effect to be properly stamped.[93]

Registration

If the lease is granted for a term of more than 21 years from the date of delivery of the grant, registration under the Land Registration Act 1925 is compulsory, whether the superior title is registered[94] or unregistered.[95] In the latter case the lease should be delivered to the Land Registry for registration within two months of its completion.[96] The tenant should attempt to obtain registration with absolute title, although this will only be possible where either the superior title is registered or the tenant is able to deduce his landlord's

---

[85] *Leggott v. Barrett* (1880) 15 Ch. D. 306.
[86] See *e.g. Optilon Ltd v Commission for the New Towns* [1993] 25 E.G. 125 (landlord's obligation in agreement for lease to construct the premises in a good and workmanlike manner took precedence over the tenant's covenant in the lease to keep the premises in repair).
[87] Stamp Act 1891, Sched 1. And see para. 5–02, n. 12 above.
[88] Stamp Act 1891, s.15.
[89] *ibid.*, s.72 and Sched 1.
[90] Stamp Act 1891, s.75 as amended by Finance Act 1994, s.111.
[91] Finance Act 1994, s.240. Note that if the lease does not relate to substantially the same term and property as the agreement for lease, duty will be payable on both the agreement and the lease and, in respect of the duty payable on the agreement, penalties and interest will be backdated to the date of the agreement, not the lease. Accordingly where it is likely that the lease will not reflect the agreement for lease, it is sensible to stamp the agreement for lease on its execution.
[92] Finance Act 1931, s.28(1) (as amended).
[93] Finance Act 1994, s.240.
[94] Land Registration Act 1925, ss.19(2), 22(2).
[95] Land Registration Act 1925, s.123 as amended by Land Registration Act 1986, s.2(1).
[96] *ibid.*

title. In other cases the tenant will be registered with good leasehold title.[97]

As a corollary to substantive registration of the leasehold estate, notice of the lease needs to be entered on the register of the landlord's title. When applying for substantive registration of the lease, there is no need to make a separate application for this: the Chief Land Registrar will attend to it automatically.[98] However, problems can occur if the landlord refuses to produce his land or charge certificate for this purpose.[99] In the vast majority of cases the landlord will co-operate, but it would be a sensible precaution for the tenant to obtain the landlord's agreement in advance[1] to place his land or charge certificate on deposit on completion or within a specified time (usually seven days) thereafter, and to notify the tenant of the deposit number.

Entry of notice on freehold title

Registration of options

Where the lease is not subject to registration under the Land Registration Act, the tenant's solicitor should consider whether any other registration is necessary; the most usual example is where the lease contains an option to purchase the reversion or to renew the lease (an option to determine the lease early is not an estate contract and does not need to be registered). Where the landlord's title is unregistered, a C(iv) Land Charge needs to be registered against the name of the landlord.[2] Where the landlord's title is registered (but the lease is for a term of 21 years or less), then the option may be an overriding interest; if not, a notice or caution needs to be registered against the landlord's title.[3]

Custody of lease

Finally, the solicitor on each side will need to take his client's instructions as to custody of the lease or counterpart and, where relevant, the leasehold land certificate.

ASSIGNMENT OF A LEASE

18–12   Generally

Some of the features of conveyancing practice on the assignment of an existing lease are similar to those on the grant of a new lease, for example, the rules for avoiding a binding contract being concluded too soon, and the need for local searches and enquiries.[4] But there are significant

---

[97] See Ruoff and Roper, *The Law and Practice of Registered Conveyancing* (1991 ed.) paras. 12.06, 12.07.

[98] Land Registration Rules 1925, r. 46; and see Ruoff and Roper, *The Law and Practice of Registered Conveyancing* (1991 ed.) para. 21.12.

[99] See Land Registration Act 1925, s.64(1), and especially s.64(1)(c). See also *Strand Securities Ltd v. Caswell* [1965] Ch. 958; Land Registration Rules, rr. 46, 298; Ruoff and Roper, *The Law and Practice of Registered Conveyancing* (1991 ed.) para 21.14.

[1] This is often achieved in practice by way of an undertaking to do this given by the landlord's solicitor.

[2] See para. 18–07 above.

[3] See para. 18–07, n. 55.

[4] Obviously, different preliminary enquiries will need to be made; for example, as to the level of any past service charge (see *Heinnemann v. Cooper* (1987) 284 E.G. 1237), whether the lease is a "new tenancy" under the Landlord and Tenant (Covenants) Act 1995 (see para. 2–02 above) and as to the position under Part II of the Landlord and Tenant Act 1954.

Special considerations

differences between the two transactions. The assignment of an existing lease is invariably preceded by a contract.[5] The landlord's consent to the assignment will normally have to be obtained. The assignee will wish to know what the terms of the lease are, and whether it may be at risk of forfeiture for breach of covenant. The terms of the deed of assignment itself, and the obligations which it places upon the assignor and the assignee, will also be important. This section of the Chapter will consider these particular issues, in the context of the assignment of the whole of the premises comprised in a lease.[6]

18–13 Printed conditions of sale

Standard Conditions

National Conditions

Two sets of printed conditions are commonly incorporated into contracts for the sale and purchase of commercial leases. They are the National Conditions (20th edition) and the Standard Conditions of Sale (3rd edition). Both have their disadvantages. The Standard Conditions were originally designed for residential transactions, as part of the TransAction scheme. They are gradually being introduced into commercial transactions, but are not yet in widespread use;[7] even when they are used, extensive amendments are often made to them, making it difficult to comment upon their effect generally. The National Conditions (20th edition), although 15 years old and out-of-print, are still widely used for commercial transactions. Relevant provisions of each set of printed conditions are mentioned in the following text, but it must be borne in mind that they are frequently modified by special conditions.

18–14 Title

Relevant factors as to whether title to be deduced

As to the title of the assignor, the proposed assignee of a lease will wish to be satisfied of three matters: that the lease was validly granted; that it is now vested in the assignor; and that the property is not subject to any restrictive covenants which could prevent the assignee carrying on his intended business. In practice, the extent to which title is deduced will depend on a number of variables: whether the title of the landlord was investigated when the lease was granted; how long ago the lease was granted; whether the leasehold title is registered or will need to be registered on completion of the assignment;[8] and the importance which the assignee attaches to obtaining a sound title (depending on whether a premium is to be paid,

---

[5] Except where the parties are connected, such as members of the same group of companies.
[6] Assignments of parts of leasehold premises are rarely met in practice. For details see, *e.g.* Woodfall, §§ 1–16.134, *et seq.*
[7] See, *e.g.* Standard Conditions, *Gazette*, October 4, 1995 (L. Heller and G. White).
[8] See para. 18–20 below.

the length of the unexpired residue of the term, whether the
term is intended as security, and so on).

Freehold title

So far as the landlord's title is concerned, section 44(2) of
the Law of Property Act 1925 provides that in the absence of
any special condition in the contract the intending assignee is
not entitled to call for the title to the freehold. Thus the title
will commence with the lease. By section 45(2) of the Law of
Property Act 1925 the assignee must assume unless the
contrary appears that the lease was duly granted. Neither set
of printed conditions attempts to modify this position, so that
any right of the assignee to deduction of the freehold title
must be dealt with by a special condition.

**Restrictive
covenants**

The assignee who does not investigate the freehold title
should be aware of the risk that it may be subject to prior
restrictive covenants registered against the names of former
owners of the freehold. This problem is discussed above in
connection with the grant of leases.[9] There will be no
problem where the assignor is registered with absolute
leasehold title, but there is a risk of such incumbrances
binding the assignee where the title is good leasehold.[10] In
such cases, where the landlord's title is now registered with

**Conversion of
title**

absolute title, the possibility of an application to have the title
converted to absolute leasehold should not be overlooked.[11]

**Non-disclosure
of known defects**

The assignor is under an obligation to make full and frank
disclosure of any known defects in title, and in the absence of
such disclosure may be unable to enforce the contract by
specific performance.[12]

Title of assignor

As well as the freehold title and the validity of the grant of
the lease, the assignee will be concerned with the title of the
assignor. In the absence of any special condition, the assignee
will be entitled to see the lease itself, no matter how long ago
it was granted,[13] an assignment at least 15 years old (if there
is one), and any subsequent assignments. Thus in the case of
leases granted more than 15 years ago there will be no right
to call for a complete chain of assignments from the original
tenant to the assignee.[14] Neither set of printed conditions of
sale attempts to modify this position.

18–15   Terms of the lease

The purchaser of a leasehold interest will obviously be
concerned as to the terms of the lease. Misrepresentation of
its terms by the assignor may result in specific performance

---

[9] See para. 18–08 above. Of course there is little that can be done to rectify
this where the title was not investigated on the grant of the lease, unless
the landlord's title is registered, or the landlord is prepared to co-operate.

[10] Land Registration Act 1925, s.10; Ruoff and Roper, *The Law and Practice
of Registered Conveyancing* (1991 ed.) para. 5.12.

[11] Land Registration Act, s.77(1) as amended by Land Registration Act 1986,
s.1(1).

[12] *Faruqi v. English Real Estates Ltd* [1979] 1 W.L.R. 963. Alternatively the
assignee can repudiate the contract: *Heywood v. Mallalieu* (1883) 25 Ch. D.
357.

[13] *Frend v. Buckley* (1870) L.R. 5 Q.B. 213.

[14] *Williams v. Spargo* [1893] W.N. 100. But a known defect can be raised if
sufficiently specific: *Re Scott and Alvarez's Contract* [1895] 1 Ch. 596.

Onerous covenants

against the assignee being refused.[15] Further, the assignee will not be bound to accept the lease if it contains onerous covenants of an unusual character unless they were disclosed before contract, or the assignee was given a fair opportunity of ascertaining the terms of the lease.[16] Thus prima facie the onus of disclosure lies with the assignor.[17] This duty of disclosure will not be negatived by a contractual term as to the acceptance of title by the assignee; where such conditions are employed the assignee has the right to assume that the assignor has disclosed what it is his duty to disclose.[18] In practice these rules cause little difficulty: the assignor can fulfil his obligation of disclosure either by giving express notice of such covenants as are unusual and onerous, or by

Opportunity to inspect lease

providing the assignee with an opportunity of inspecting the lease before contracts are exchanged. Given the difficulty of deciding what provisions are sufficiently unusual to warrant disclosure,[19] and the ease with which a lease can be photocopied, it is hardly surprising that assignors invariably opt for the latter alternative.[20]

18–16 Compliance with the terms of the lease

The assignee will also wish to know that the covenants in the lease have been performed, otherwise he could be purchasing an estate liable to forfeiture. Two distinct but related questions arise here: what proof is the assignee entitled to demand that the covenants have been performed; and if a breach occurs after exchange of contracts but before completion, does responsibility for rectifying it lie with the assignor or the assignee?

The answer to the first question is to be found in section 45(2) of the Law of Property Act 1925, which provides that on production of the receipt for the last payment of rent due before the actual date of completion, the assignee shall

Evidence of performance of covenants

assume, unless the contrary appears, that all the covenants and provisions of the lease have been duly performed and observed up to the date of actual completion. The limitations of the section should be noted. First, the receipt is not

Receipt not conclusive

conclusive evidence, and therefore it is open to the assignee to take objection to breaches of covenant which he can prove.[21]

---

[15] *Charles Hunt Ltd v. Palmer* [1931] Ch. 287 (leasehold shops described as "valuable business premises"; in fact use restricted by lease to one kind of business only).

[16] *Reeve v. Berridge* (1888) 20 Q.B.D. 523; *Flexman v. Corbett* [1930] 1 Ch. 672.

[17] *Re White and Smith's Contract* (1896) 1 Ch. 637; *Molyneux v. Hawtrey* [1903] 2 K.B. 487.

[18] *Re Haedicke and Lipski's Contract* [1901] 2 Ch. 666; *Re Davis and Cavey* (1888) 40 Ch. D. 601.

[19] See para. 18–07 above.

[20] This practice is recognised by the sets of printed conditions of sale: see National Condition 11(2) and Standard Condition 8.1.2. An express obligation to supply a copy of the lease means that an accurate copy must be supplied and the obligation will survive completion: *Feldman v. Mansell* (1962) 184 E.G. 331.

[21] *Re Highett and Bird's Contract* [1903] 1 Ch. 287.

However, it would be open for the contract to provide that a receipt should be conclusive evidence of performance.[22]

Secondly, it is arguable that the provision will not extend to **Continuing breaches** continuing breaches of covenant, since even after acceptance of rent the lease may still be subject to forfeiture.[23] Thirdly, there is old authority to suggest that even a stipulation that a receipt is to be conclusive evidence of compliance with the **Later breaches** terms of the lease will not preclude objections to breaches committed by the assignor between contract and assignment.[24]

Problems over the receipt can also arise where there is **To whom rent** doubt as to whether the person to whom the rent was paid **paid** was the person entitled to receive it.[25] Both the sets of printed conditions guard against this problem by providing that the purchaser is to assume without proof that the person giving the receipt was the person entitled to the rent, or that person's authorised agent.[26]

As to the second question (i.e., who is responsible for **Responsibility** rectifying known breaches of covenant) the answer must be **for rectifying** prima facie the assignor. An unrectified breach of covenant **breaches** which renders the lease liable to forfeiture means that the assignor cannot show good title. It would appear to make no difference that the assignee knew of the defect at the time of the contract, and obtained a lower price as a result of it.[27] As well as putting right past breaches, the assignor is under an obligation not to commit new breaches of covenant: he must keep the title unimpeached until actual completion, unless completion is delayed by some act of the assignee.[28]

However, it is possible to exonerate the assignor from **Sale subject to** liability for existing breaches of covenant by means of express **existing breaches** stipulations, and this should be done whenever the bargain between the parties is that the assignee is to take subject to existing breaches. The effect of such a stipulation is that the assignee cannot require the assignor to remedy the breach as an incident of making title.[29] The most common type of

---

[22] *Lawrie v. Lees* (1880) 14 Ch. D. 249; *Re Taunton and West of England Perpetual Benefit Building Society and Roberts' Contract* [1912] 2 Ch. 381 at 385. Neither set of printed conditions attempts to do this. Nor would it be advisable for the assignor to attempt to preclude objection to a breach of which he knows unless he discloses it: see *Beyfus v. Lodge* [1925] 1 Ch. 350.

[23] See J.T. Farrand, *Contract & Conveyance* (4th ed., 1983) p. 139. Also see *Re Martin* (1912) 106 L.T. 381.

[24] *Howell v. Kightley* (1856) 21 Beav. 331 at 336.

[25] It must be paid to such a person in order to justify the assumption that the covenants have been performed: *Re Higgins and Percival* (1888) 57 L.J. Ch. 807. Doubt as to whom the rent should be paid will justify the refusal of specific performance: *Pegler v. White* (1864) 33 Beav. 403 (it also appears from that case that in general the assignor need not deduce title to show who is entitled to the rent).

[26] National Condition 11(3); Standard Condition 6.6.

[27] *Re Highett and Bird's Contract* [1903] 1 Ch. 287. This can perhaps be explained on the basis that the breach is a removable defect so that knowledge of it by the assignee does not necessarily imply acceptance of it.

[28] *Palmer v. Goren* (1856) 25 L.J. Ch. 841. This can of course be onerous where completion is unexpectedly delayed for some reason, such as difficulty in obtaining licence to assign.

[29] See *Re King* [1962] 1 W.L.R. 632 at 655, *per* Buckley J.

Conditions of sale breach to which an assignee will agree to take subject is failure to repair. This is covered by a general condition in both the sets of printed conditions, to the effect that the purchaser purchases with full knowledge of the actual state and condition of the property and shall take the property as it stands.[30] However, there is some doubt as to whether such a general provision is adequate to preclude objections to disrepair amounting to breach of covenant;[31] therefore to avoid doubt a special condition might be inserted expressly providing that the assignor shall not be required to carry out any work to the property even where necessary in order to remedy a breach of covenant or comply with statutory requirements. The statutory requirements point would cover the possibility of a public authority requiring work to be carried out between contract and assignment. Failure to carry out such work might itself constitute a breach of covenant.[32]

18–17   Obtaining landlord's consent

Invariably the landlord's consent to the assignment will be required.[33] Four questions can arise here: what duty is placed upon the assignor to obtain the necessary consent; what corresponding duty rests upon the assignee with regard to the provision of references and the like; what constitutes consent; and what is to happen if consent cannot be obtained?

Duty of assignor to seek consent The position under an open contract is that the assignor must use all reasonable efforts to obtain the consent of the landlord.[34] Thus the assignor will not be required to embark on litigation against the landlord to obtain consent,[35] nor to allow the assignee an opportunity of approaching the landlord.[36] This obligation is also contained in the Standard Conditions.[37] The National Conditions go further, and provide that the assignor is to use his best endeavours to obtain the licence.[38] It has been said that best endeavours " . . . are something less than efforts which go beyond the bounds of reason, but are considerably more than casual and intermittent activities. There must at least be the doing of all that reasonable persons reasonably could do in the

---

[30] National Condition 13(3); Standard Condition 3.2.1.
[31] cf. *Lockharts v. Bernard Rosen & Co.* [1922] 1 Ch. 433 (condition sufficient) and *Re Englefield Holdings Ltd and Sinclair's Contract* [1962] 1 W.L.R. 1119 (words of general condition insufficiently clear to exonerate assignor).
[32] See para. 7–04 above.
[33] On this see generally Chap. 12 above.
[34] *Lehmann v. McArthur* (1868) L.R. 3 Ch. 496.
[35] *ibid.*
[36] *Lipmans Wallpaper Ltd v. Mason and Hodghton Ltd* [1969] 1 Ch. 20.
[37] Standard Condition 8.3.2(a). The similar expression "all reasonable endeavours" was considered in *Baring Securities Limited v. D.G. Durham Group plc* [1993] EGCS 192.
[38] National Condition 11(5).

circumstances".[39] It is submitted that such an obligation might at least require the assignor to attempt to rebut by correspondence grounds put forward by the landlord for refusing consent which appear factually or legally unsound but it has been held that it does not require the assignor to take proceedings against the landlord for unreasonably withholding consent.[40]

Costs　　It has been held that there is no implied obligation that the tenant will pay the landlord's legal costs in relation to the application for a licence which is unsuccessful,[41] although in practice it is common nowadays both for the lease to contain an express clause to this effect, and for the landlord's solicitors to request an undertaking from the tenant's solicitors to be responsible for their costs whether or not the licence is granted.[42]

Duty of assignee　　As to the assignee, he is under an implied obligation to use his best endeavours to satisfy the reasonable requirements of the landlord for references and other information.[43] Both sets of printed conditions attempt to incorporate this obligation. The Standard Conditions do so clearly, providing that "the buyer is to provide all information and references[44] reasonably required".[45] The National Conditions are unfortunately oblique and ambiguous: they provide that "the purchaser supplying such information and references,[46] if any, as may reasonably be required of him, the vendor will use his best endeavours to obtain such licence . . . ."[47] In *Shires v. Brock*[48] Goff and Buckley L.JJ. held that this condition imposes no positive obligation on the assignee, but merely qualifies the assignor's obligation. But in the same case, Scarman L.J. suggested that the condition did impose or recognise as a contractual term an obligation on the assignee to provide "full, honest and truthful information and proper, credible

---

[39] *Pips (Leisure) Productions Ltd v. Walton* (1980) 43 P. & C.R. 415 at 420 (Sir Robert Megarry V–C). The case also suggests that the obligation might be qualified by facts being known to the assignor which might make the task more difficult but not disclosed to the assignee. See also *Terrell v. Mabie Todd and Co. Ltd* [1952] 2 T.L.R. 574; *I.B.M. United Kingdom Ltd v. Rockware Glass Ltd* [1980] F.S.R. 335; *Alghussein Establishment v. Eton College* [1988] 1 W.L.R. 587; and *cf.* the expression "reasonable endeavours" which it appears is less onerous: *UBH (Mechanical Services) Ltd v. Standard Life Assurance Co.*, The Times, November 13, 1986, para. 8–02, n. 9 above.

[40] *Fischer v. Toumazos* [1991] 48 E.G. 123.

[41] *Goldman v. Abbot* [1989] 48 E.G. 151.

[42] In *Dong Bang Minerva (UK) Ltd v. Davina Ltd* [1995] 5 E.G. 162 the court had to consider whether this was reasonable in the light of the Landlord and Tenant Act 1988: see para. 12–10 above.

[43] *Scheggia v. Gradwell* [1963] 1 W.L.R. 1049 at 1062, *per* Harman L.J.; *Shires v. Brock* (1977) 247 E.G. 127. In the latter case Goff L.J . said (at p. 131) that regard must be had both to whether the landlord was being reasonable and to the circumstances and conduct of the assignee.

[44] Query if this would oblige the assignee to do more than give information and provide references; *e.g.* submit to an interview: see *Elfer v. Beynon Lewis* (1972) 222 E.G. 1955

[45] Standard Condition 8.3.2 (b).

[46] See n. 44 above.

[47] National Condition 11(5).

[48] (1977) 247 E.G. 127.

references about the true state of his financial position".[49] If the view of the majority in *Shires v. Brock* is correct, it is still arguable that the assignee remains under his common law obligation not to frustrate the contract by not supplying information.[50] In addition, it has been held that the assignee may not do anything which would cause the landlord to withhold his licence.[51]

What action constitutes consent

Consent from the landlord is normally given in the form of a licence under seal, but consent in the form of a letter is not uncommon. It has been held that once a corporate landlord has sealed the licence, his consent has been given and cannot then be rescinded.[52]

Position on refusal of consent

Where the landlord refuses his consent to assignment, apparently unreasonably, it is possible for the parties to proceed with the assignment and either seek a declaration as to the unreasonableness of the landlord[53] or claim damages for breach of the landlord's statutory duty not unreasonably to withhold consent.[54] Under an open contract, refusal of consent will allow either party to rescind the contract, since the assignor cannot show good title. The assignee could claim return of any deposit, subject presumably to his not being in breach of the obligation to co-operate in obtaining consent.[55]

Rescission

However, the right to rescind will only arise at the date of completion, since the obtaining of consent is a matter of conveyance, and can be achieved at any time before completion.[56] Furthermore, careful consideration will need to

What constitutes refusal

be given as to whether consent has actually been refused. An intimation that the landlord is willing to consent in principle may suffice, even if expressed to be subject to the preparation of a formal licence.[57] Also it has been held that a demand by the landlord for a deposit from the assignor against dilapidations, which the assignor is willing to pay, will not justify the assignee in rescinding.[58]

---

[49] *ibid.* p. 133. See also *Elfer v. Beynon-Lewis* (1972) 222 E.G. 1955, where Plowman J. appeared to be of the same view.

[50] See *Shires v. Brock* (1977) 247 E.G. 127 at 133, *per* Buckley L.J.

[51] *Jebco Properties Ltd v. Mastforce Ltd* [1992] N.P.C. 42.

[52] *Venetian Glass Gallery Ltd v. Next Properties Ltd* [1989] 30 E.G. 92 (compare with *Longman v. Viscount Chelsea* [1989] 58 P. & C.R. 189 where a lease sealed in such circumstances was held not to be irrevocable). See para. 18–10 above.

[53] *Young v. Ashley Gardens Properties Ltd* [1903] 2 Ch. 112; *Theodorou v. Bloom* [1964] 1 W.L.R. 1152. This is a dangerous step for a tenant to take where the lease is a new tenancy under section 1(3) of the 1995 Act, as if the landlord is held to have acted reasonably it will result in an excluded assignment and the tenant will not be released from his covenants. See para. 2–05 above.

[54] Landlord and Tenant Act 1988, s.4: see para. 12–10 above.

[55] Law of Property Act 1925, s.49(2).

[56] *Property & Bloodstock Ltd v. Emerton* [1968] Ch. 94; *Milner v. Staffordshire Congregational Union (Incorporated)* [1956] 1 Ch. 275; *Ellis v. Lawrence* (1969) 210 E.G. 215 (time extended beyond completion date where assignee went into occupation, the purchase money being placed in a joint account); *cf. Smith v. Butler* [1900] 1 Q.B. 694 at 699, where Romer L.J. suggested four cases where a refusal of consent may justify immediate recission.

[57] *Rutter v. Michael John Ltd* (1960) 201 E.G. 299; *Bader Properties Ltd v. Linley Property Investments Ltd* (1967) 19 P. & C.R. 620.

[58] *Re Davies' Agreement* (1969) 21 P. & C.R. 328.

Standard Condition 8.3.4 provides that if consent is not granted three working days before the contractual completion date, or is subject to any condition to which the purchaser reasonably objects, either party may rescind the contract by notice to the other. The National Conditions of Sale provide[59] that if licence cannot be obtained, the vendor may rescind the contract on the same terms as if the purchaser had persisted in an objection to title which the vendor was unable to remove.[60] The operation of this condition was considered by Warner J. in *Bickel v. Courtenay Investments (Nominees) Ltd.*[61] He considered that the condition was intended to afford the assignor a quick remedy and a means of escape from litigation and delay. Accordingly, the assignor may make use of the condition to rescind even if doubt exists as to whether the landlord's refusal of consent is reasonable or not. All that the assignor needs to show is that under the lease the landlord's consent is necessary, that the assignor has used his best endeavours to obtain it and that it cannot be obtained. It has been held, however, that this does not permit the tenant to require the assignee to vacate immediately, if the contract provides for the assignee to vacate after seven days.[62]

However, the Court of Appeal has held that the condition does not require the licence to assign to have been obtained by the completion date.[63] The question is whether at the date of purported recission it can be said as a matter of fact and common sense that the licence cannot be obtained, not whether the licence is yet forthcoming. Thus if the licence is in the course of preparation or agreement at that date, or if the landlord is delaying in indicating whether he is willing to consent, the assignor will not be able to rely on the condition as presently drafted.

18–18   The assignment: implied covenants

Under the Law of Property (Miscellaneous Provisions) Act 1994, which came into force on July 1, 1995, the assignor may assign with full title guarantee or with limited title guarantee. It is important to be aware of the covenants implied by statute by the inclusion of those words, so that they can be expressly negatived or varied if necessary.[64] The

---

[59] National Condition 11(5).

[60] Referring to Condition 10. This does not mean however that the assignor has to follow the procedure laid down in Condition 10(1) in order to rescind: *Lipmans Wallpaper Ltd v. Mason & Hodghton Ltd* [1969] 1 Ch. 20.

[61] [1984] 1 All E.R. 657.

[62] *Balabel v. Mehmet* [1990] 26 E.G. 176. See para. 18–31, n. 83 below.

[63] *29 Equities Ltd v. Bank Leumi (U.K.) Ltd* [1986] 1 W.L.R. 1490, followed in *Ganton House Investments Ltd v Corbin* [1988] 43 E.G. 76. The Court of Appeal in *29 Equities Ltd* reserved their position as to whether the vendor could bring matters to a head by serving notice to complete: see *Shires v. Brock* (1977) 247 E.G. 127 at 129; *Jneid v. Mirza* [1981] C.A.T. 306.

[64] The implied covenants are not compulsory: exactly what is included is a matter of bargain between the parties. Section 8 of the 1994 Act permits the covenants to be modified, or they may be omitted entirely.

Full or limited title guarantee

statutory implied covenants, when leasehold property is sold with either full title guarantee or limited title guarantee, are as follows:

- the assignor has the right to dispose of the property as he purports to[65];
- he will at his own cost do all that he reasonably can to give the purchaser the title he purports to give[66];
- he is selling either the whole of the title of a registered lease, or the residue of the term granted by an unregistered lease[67];
- the lease is subsisting and the assignor has complied with its terms.[68] This covenant is normally modified, as is mentioned below;
- when the phrase "full title guarantee" is included, the property is free from all charges, incumbrances and all other rights exercisable by third parties,[69] and when the phrase "limited title guarantee" is used, that he has not charged or incumbered the property by means of any charge or incumbrance which subsists at the time of the disposition, and that he is not aware that anyone else has done so since the last disposition for value.[70]

In each case, with the exception of the covenant for further assurance, the assignor is not liable in respect of either any particular matter to which the disposition is expressly made subject, or anything which at the time of the disposition is within the actual knowledge of the purchaser.[71]

Sale subject to breaches of covenant

As just mentioned, inclusion of either a full title guarantee or a limited title guarantee imports a covenant by the assignor that the lease is subsisting at the time of the assignment and that there is no subsisting breach of a condition or a tenant's obligation and nothing that would render the lease subject to forfeiture.[72] As mentioned above,[73] this may well fail to reflect the true intention of the parties where the assignee is buying with knowledge of breaches of covenant, possibly paying a reduced price as a result. The most common situation where this can occur is in the case of failure to repair,[74] but other possible examples can readily be envisaged, such as

---

[65] Law of Property (Miscellaneous Provisions) Act 1994, s.2(1)(a).

[66] *ibid.*, s.2(1)(b); if title to the property is registered, this extends to the purchaser being registered at H.M. Land Registry with at least the same class of title as the assignor had; if title to the property is subject to first registration, this extends to giving all reasonable assistance to establish to the satisfaction of the Chief Land Registrar that the assignee is entitled to be registered as proprietor: *ibid.*, s.2(2).

[67] *ibid.*, s.2(3).

[68] *ibid.*, s.4(1).

[69] *ibid.*, s.3(1).

[70] *ibid.*, s.3(3).

[71] *ibid.*, s.6.

[72] *ibid.*, s.4(1); the covenant does not extend to anything to which the assignment is expressly made subject, or which at the time is within the actual knowledge of the assignee: *ibid.*, s.6.

[73] See para. 18–16 above.

[74] It is generally accepted that in practice repairing and decorating covenants are rarely complied with to the letter.

unauthorised alterations to the property. Where the deed of assignment clearly differs from the true bargain of the parties by importing the statutory covenant, rectification may be obtained,[75] but it is clearly preferable to limit the covenant expressly at the outset. Both sets of printed conditions provide for this by stating, in effect, that any statutory implied

Exclusion of condition of property   covenant on the part of the assignor shall not extend to breaches of covenants concerning the state and condition of the property.[76] If the lease is sold subject to other kinds of breach[77] then an appropriate special condition should be inserted. In the case of registered land, certain modifications of the implied covenant will need to be noted by entry on the register.[78]

Covenant by assignee   A final topic which must be mentioned is the statutory covenant on the part of the assignee, which is implied into all assignments for valuable consideration,[79] except in the case of assignments of new tenancies.[80] The assignee covenants that he and those deriving title under him will pay the rent due under the lease and perform the tenant's covenants, and will indemnify the assignor against failure to do so.[81] Where the

Continuing breaches   assignee agrees to take the property subject to continuing breaches of covenant, such as repair, the effect of the implied covenant may be to oblige the assignee to indemnify the assignor in respect of breaches existing prior to the date of assignment.[82]

18–19   Form of deed of assignment

Recitals   The deed of assignment should recite the possession of the assignor and where consent of the landlord to the assignment is required, should recite that such consent has been obtained.

Where title to the leasehold is registered, the transfer should be made in statutory form 32.[83] However, it appears

---

[75] See *Butler v. Mountview Estates Ltd* [1951] 2 K.B. 563 (a case under the previous system of implied covenants).

[76] National Condition 11(7); Standard Condition 3.2.2. As well as repairs this would appear to extend to covenants as to alterations and compliance with statutory requirements.

[77] *e.g.* user or an unauthorised sub-lease.

[78] Land Registration Rules 1925, rr. 76A and 77A: only modifications to the covenant implied by s.4 of the 1994 Act may be noted on the register.

[79] The requirement for valuable consideration is satisfied by the assumption by the assignee of the liabilities under the lease: see *Currie v. Misa* (1875) L.R. 10 Ex. 153; *Price v. Jenkins* (1877) 5 Ch. D. 619 (applied in *Johnsey Estates Ltd v. Lewis & Manley (Engineering) Ltd* (1987) 54 P. & C.R. 296).

[80] See para. 2–02 above for the definition of a new tenancy.

[81] Law of Property Act 1925, s.77(1)(C) and Sched. 2, Pt. IX; Land Registration Act 1925, s.24(1)(b). It appears that the covenant is by way of indemnity only and does not permit enforcement by the assignor in the absence of action by the landlord: see *Harris v. Boots Cash Chemists Southern Ltd* [1904] 2 Ch. 376; *Reckitt v. Cody* [1920] 2 Ch. 452; *cf.*, *Butler Estates Co. Ltd v. Bean* [1942] 1 K.B. 1 (in which the court decided that the relevant covenant then under consideration went beyond a mere indemnity).

[82] *Middlegate Properties Ltd v. Bilbao* (1972) 24 P. & C.R. 329, where Willis J. suggested that the usual watershed date of the assignment need not necessarily apply. See also *Gooch v. Clutterbuck* [1899] 2 Q.B. 148.

[83] Land Registration Rules, r. 115(1).

to be the practice of the Land Registry (contrary to the mandatory language used in the relevant rule) to accept transfers on the forms appropriate to transfer of the freehold.[84]

Deed   An assignment of a lease has to be by deed, even when the lease is merely an oral tenancy.[85]

18–20 Post-completion matters

Stamp duty   The deed of assignment will give rise to liability for stamp duty unless the appropriate certificate of value is contained within it, stating that the consideration does not exceed the relevant figure below which no stamp duty is payable.[86] An assignment or transfer of a lease with an unexpired term of seven years or more must be produced to the Inland Revenue by the assignee, who must provide the prescribed particulars of the transaction on the "Particulars Delivered" form.[87]

Registration   The transfer of a registered leasehold will need to be completed by registration of the transferee as proprietor.[88] An unregistered lease with more than 21 years left to run from the date of delivery of the assignment must also be delivered to the Land Registry, for the lease to be registered, whether or not the landlord's title is registered.[89]

Notice of assignment   The assignee will need to give notice of the assignment[90] to the landlord, and pay the necessary registration fee in accordance with the lease.

GRANT OF UNDERLEASE

18–21 Generally

The grant of an underlease raises many of the problems already noted in connection with the grant of a lease and with the assignment of an existing lease. It also raises some slightly different problems of its own.

Describe as underlease   The first point to note is that the underlessor should make it clear at the outset that what he is intending to grant is an underlease, and not a headlease. Failure to do so will result in the underlessee being able to escape from the contract.[91]

Length of term   It is essential that the landlord should retain a nominal reversion, as an underletting of the entire term granted by the

---

[84] Ruoff and Roper, *Registered Conveyancing* (1991 ed.) para. 21.20.
[85] *Crago v. Julian* [1992] 1 W.L.R. 372.
[86] Currently £60,000: Finance Act 1963, s.55, as amended by Finance Act 1993, s.201, for certificate pursuant to Finance Act 1958, s.34(4).
[87] Finance Act 1931, s.28(1) as amended.
[88] Land Registration Act 1925, s.22(1).
[89] *ibid.*, s. 123(1) as amended by the Land Registration Act 1986, s.2(1)(b).
[90] This is normally done using a pre-printed form from a law stationers.
[91] *Van v. Corpe* (1834) 3 My. & K. 269. This is especially so where the underlease is of part only of the land comprised in the headlease, since the underlessee will be exposed to forfeiture for acts carried out on land over which he has no control: *Darlington v. Hamilton* (1854) Kay 550; *Re Lloyd's Bank Ltd and Lillington's Contract* [1912] 1 Ch. 601.

headlease will be construed as an assignment of the headlease, rather than as an underlease.[92]

18–22   Investigation of title

Investigation of superior title

Under section 44 of the Law of Property Act, in the absence of any special condition in the contract an underlessee may not call for title to the freehold, nor may a sub-underlessee call for title to the lease out of which the underlease is created.[93] By inference therefore, they can call for the lease and underlease respectively.

Underlessee's intended use

Indeed, it is in the interests of the underlessor to make the lease available to the underlessee as soon as possible, since the latter will not be bound to accept an underlease if it transpires that the headlease contains unusual covenants of which he had neither notice nor opportunity to discover.[94] The underlessee's solicitor should be particularly on guard to detect covenants in the headlease which might prevent the underlessee's intended use of the property.[95]

Restrictive covenants

The risk of undetectable restrictive covenants affecting the freehold or other superior title should also be appreciated, though in many cases there is little which can be done to guard against it.[96]

Performance of covenants in headlease   The underlessee will require reassurance that the covenants in the headlease have been performed, since forfeiture of the headlease will result in the termination of the underlease also. As on assignment of a lease, the last receipt for rent due should be demanded as evidence of compliance with the covenants.[97] Where it is agreed that the underlease is to be granted subject to known breaches of the headlease, this should be covered by a special condition.[98]

Evidence of performance

Implied covenants

As has already been mentioned,[99] since July 1, 1995 it has been possible to incorporate implied covenants of title into the

---

[92] *Lewis v. Baker* [1905] 1 Ch. 46; *Milmo v. Carreras* [1946] K.B. 306; *Averbrian v. Willmalight* [1994] C.L.Y. 2799; exceptionally, where the mesne landlord has the benefit of the Landlord and Tenant Act 1954 and so the headlease is extended beyond its contractual termination date, this rule may be displaced: *William Skelton & Son Ltd v Harrison and Pinder Ltd* [1975] Q.B. 361.

[93] s.44(2), (4).

[94] *Flight v. Barton* (1832) 3 My. & K. 282; *Cosser v. Collinge* (1832) 3 My. & K. 283; *Melzak v. Lilienfield* [1926] 1 Ch. 480.

[95] Failure on the part of an undertenant's solicitor to investigate the provisions of the superior lease may constitute negligence: see *Hill v. Harris* [1965] 2 Q.B. 601. For leases which are "new tenancies" see Landlord and Tenant (Covenants) Act 1995, s.3(5), which codified the earlier law.

[96] See para. 18–08 above.

[97] See para. 18–16 above. Arguably, s.45(2) of the Law of Property Act 1925 applies to this situation, since "purchaser" includes a lessee or any person acquiring an interest in property for valuable consideration (s.205(1)(xxi)). But can the grant of an underlease count as land being "sold," sale being defined as "a sale properly so called" (s.205(1)(xxiv))?

[98] See para. 18–16 above.

[99] See para. 18–18 above.

grant of a lease, which includes the grant of an underlease.[1] The inclusion of the key words "with full title guarantee" and "with limited title guarantee"[2] imply, *inter alia*, a covenant that the superior lease is subsisting at the time of the grant of the underlease, and that there is no subsisting breach of a condition or tenant's obligation, and nothing which at that time would render the lease liable to forfeiture.[3]

Correspondence between covenants in headlease and underlease From the underlessor's point of view it is desirable that the covenants in the underlease should reflect, and certainly be no less stringent than, those in the headlease.[4] This can be achieved either by drafting the covenants to correspond to those in the headlease, or by inserting a separate covenant by the underlessee to comply with the covenants in the headlease. This does not mean that the parties should slavishly adopt the drafting of the headlease if it appears to be defective; but the substance of the obligations should correspond. The underlessee can hardly object to this, and indeed it is preferable from his point of view if the covenants in the underlease and headlease do correspond closely: it is irksome to have to remember to comply with two varying sets of covenants.

Ensuring correspondence of covenants

However it is not uncommon for different standards to apply to matters such as consents, where the concerns of the lessor in the headlease may differ from those of the underlease, particularly where the underlessor intends to resume occupation at the expiry of the underlease.

The draftsman must also take care to ensure that time limits and dates contained in the headlease are appropriately adjusted in the corresponding provisions in the underlease.

Future performance of covenants in headlease The underlessee should require a covenant by the underlessor and his successors in title to pay the rent due under the headlease and to comply with the covenants in the headlease to the extent that the underlessee is not covenanting in the underlease to comply with them.

Covenant by underlessor

18–23 Landlord's consent to underletting

This problem has already been discussed in the context of assignment of leases.[5] The same principles apply where

---

[1] In practice the incorporation of implied covenants for title into leases is not yet widespread.

[2] See para. 18–18 above

[3] Law of Property (Miscellaneous Provisions) Act 1994, s.4(2); the covenant does not extend to anything to which the underlease is made subject, or which at the time is within the actual knowledge of the underlessee, *ibid.*, s.6(2).

[4] Unless the underlessee is under an express obligation to perform, no right of indemnity will be implied: *Bonner v. Tottenham and Edmonton Permanent Investment Building Society* [1899] 1 Q.B. 161.

[5] See para. 18–17 above.

Need for special conditions as to refusal of consent

consent is necessary to the grant of an underlease.[6] Thus the grant of an underlease will often be preceded by a contract, subject to the landlord's consent being obtained. However, it should be remembered that the National Conditions as to consent do not extend to consent required for the grant of an underlease.[7] Thus an appropriate special condition covering the respective duties of the parties and the position if consent cannot be obtained should be inserted. By contrast, the Standard Conditions apply both to contracts to assign and to contracts to grant a new lease.[8]

ASSIGNMENT OF UNDERLEASE

Most of the relevant points here have already been canvassed in the preceding sections. Those outstanding are as follows.

18–24 Title

The property to be sold should be described as an underlease; false description as a lease may entitle the assignee to rescind.[9]

Investigation of superior title

Investigation of title   The generally accepted effect of section 44 of the Law of Property Act is that, in the absence of any special condition in the contract, the assignee of an underlease is entitled to sight of the underlease, but not of the headlease.[10] Nonetheless, the original underlessee will have had the right to see the headlease, and the assignee should always attempt to see a copy of it, both from the point of view of ascertaining any onerous restrictions and because he will probably be under a covenant in the underlease to comply with the terms of the headlease. This is particularly important where the assignee is paying a premium or is proposing to spend money on the property.[11] Difficulties in this respect can occur when the original underlessee failed to investigate the terms of the headlease, but even there an assignee who discovers by other means that it contains onerous covenants, or that the title to the underlease has been vitiated by breaches, will be able to rescind.[12] In practical terms it is most unusual nowadays for a landlord to refuse to provide a copy of a lease if his copying charges are reimbursed, in the unlikely event that the underlessee does not have a copy of the headlease available to show to his proposed assignee.

---

[6] See *White v. Hay* (1895) 72 L.T. 281.
[7] National Condition 11(5) only applies where the interest sold is leasehold for the residue of the existing term: Condition 11(1).
[8] Standard Condition 8.3.1.
[9] *Re Russ and Brown's Contract* [1934] 1 Ch. 34.
[10] See s.44(2), (3). Dicta in *Gosling v. Woolf* [1893] 1 Q.B. 39 at 40 suggest that the assignee is entitled to see the headlease; but *cf.* the report at (1893) 68 L.T. 89. See also *Drive Yourself Hire Co. (London) Ltd v. Strutt* [1954] 1 Q.B. 250 at 278; *Becker v. Partridge* [1966] 2 Q.B. 155; and, generally, J.T. Farrand, *Contract & Conveyance* (4th ed., 1983) p. 132.
[11] See *Imray v. Oakshette* [1897] 2 Q.B. 218 at 225, 229.
[12] *Becker v. Partridge* [1966] 2 Q.B. 155.

Precluding objection to covenants in headlease

Correspondence between covenants in headlease and underlease   National Condition 11(4) provides that no objection shall be taken on account of the covenants in the underlease not corresponding with the contents of any superior lease, as an attempt to deal with the problem of onerous covenants in the headlease. The Standard Conditions do not address the point.

Evidence of performance of covenants

Performance of covenants in underlease and headlease   As to performance of the covenants in the underlease, the National Conditions and Standard Conditions relating to production of the last receipt for rent will apply.[13] However, the purchaser will also require some assurance that the headlease is not subject to forfeiture. Section 45(3) of the Law of Property Act 1925 provides that on production of the last receipt for rent payable under the underlease the purchaser shall assume, unless the contrary appears, due performance of the covenants in the underlease, and payment of rent and performance of covenants under any superior lease.[14] It should be noted that the presumption is only prima facie, and if the assignor wishes to provide that the receipt shall be conclusive proof he will need to do so expressly. It may also be necessary to provide that no objection shall be taken to any breaches of covenant to which the assignee has agreed to take subject.[15]

The purchaser of the underlease should check that the underlease contains a covenant by the underlessor as to the payment of rent and performance of covenants in the headlease.[16]

Consent to assignment   The position as to any consent required from the underlessor for assignment is as stated above in relation to assignment of a lease.[17]

Consent of superior lessor

It is possible that the consent of the landlord under the headlease will also be required, and the assignee should seek confirmation of this and as to the superior landlord's entitlement to call for a direct covenant from the assignee. Even where the superior landlord's consent is not required, it is likely is that the headlease may require notice to be given of any dealings with an underlease, and possibly payment of a registration fee.

SURRENDER

18–25 Reasons for surrender

Surrender is the yielding up of a leasehold estate to the immediate landlord; it has the effect of causing the lease to merge in the reversion and thereby become extinguished. It may come about by agreement, by operation of law[18] or

---

[13] See para. 18–16 above.
[14] See para. 18–16 above for remarks on s.45(2) and similar provisions on the sale of a lease.
[15] See para. 18–16 above.
[16] See para. 18–22 above.
[17] See para. 18–17 above.
[18] See para. 18–26 below.

because one party has the right to surrender, or receive a surrender (*e.g.* if the premises are damaged by fire[19] or provisions requiring the tenant to offer to surrender before assignment).[20]

18–26   Form of surrender

By deed   An express surrender of a term of more than three years must be made by deed.[21] There is some doubt as to whether this requirement extends to terms of three years or less,[22] so for the avoidance of doubt a deed should be used here also.

Need for express surrender   However, consideration might be given as to whether an express surrender is necessary at all. It is possible to effect a valid surrender by operation of law without the need for a deed, by some act of the parties showing an intention to terminate the lease. Examples of such conduct are the grant of a new lease,[23] an extension of the term of the existing lease or the enlargement of the premises demised,[24] or the complete giving up of possession by the tenant and acceptance by the landlord.[25] But even where the parties propose acts which would amount to an implied surrender, they should consider whether a deed would be desirable to define their respective rights and obligations. It used to be possible to avoid paying stamp duty when a surrender was effected by operation of law instead of by deed, but this has now been made more difficult.[26]

Where the tenancy is one which is protected under the Landlord and Tenant Act 1954, Pt. II, an immediate surrender can effectively determine the tenancy,[27] but an agreement to surrender is void unless sanctioned by court order.[28]

18–27   Effect of surrender

Rent   The landlord is entitled to rent which has accrued due before the surrender.[29] He is also entitled to an apportioned payment in respect of rent payable in arrear which has not fully accrued due by the date of the surrender.[30] As regards

---

[19] See para. 13–16 above.
[20] See para. 12–15 above.
[21] Law of Property Act 1925, s.52.
[22] Woodfall, § 1–17.009, n. 49.
[23] *Rhyl U.D.C. v. Rhyl Amusements Ltd* [1959] 1 W.L.R. 465.
[24] *Baker v. Merckel* [1960] 1 Q.B. 657; *Friends' Provident Life Office v. British Railways Board* [1996] 1 All E.R. 336.
[25] *Hoggett v. Hoggett* (1979) 39 P. & C.R. 121; *Proudreed Ltd v. Microgen Holdings plc* [1996] 12 E.G. 127; *Filering Ltd v. Taylor Commercial Ltd* [1996] EGCS 95.
[26] Stamp duty is now payable on any document evidencing a surrender by operation of law: Finance Act 1994, s.243.
[27] Landlord and Tenant Act 1954, s.24(2) (so long as the tenant has been in occupation under the tenancy for a month).
[28] See paras. 12–15 and 16–24 above.
[29] Either under the personal covenant to pay or as use and occupation damages: see Woodfall, § 1–17.040.
[30] Apportionment Act 1870, ss.2–4.

rent payable in advance and paid before the surrender, the tenant is not entitled to any repayment in the absence of express agreement to that effect.[31]

Rent review and surrender The inter-relationship between surrender and rent review proceedings can be important. It has been held that surrender after a rent review date, but before the new rent has been determined, does not prevent the landlord proceeding to have the new rent determined, and requiring payment of the rent at the new rate for the period between the date at which the new rent becomes payable and surrender.[32]

Other covenants A surrender will not release the tenant from liability for breaches of covenant existing prior to the date of surrender; thus a clear distinction is drawn between past and future breaches.[33] Therefore if the tenant is to be released from liability from past breaches, an express release will be required. If the tenant surrenders with full title guarantee or limited title guarantee the surrender will include an implied covenant that the covenants of the lease have been performed.[34] Where no express release is being obtained from the landlord, this implied covenant must be expressly negatived in relation to any covenants with which the tenant has not complied;[35] even where an express release is being obtained, this would be wise, to avoid any argument as to whether the implied covenant or the release took precedence.

Express release from past breaches necessary

Obligations arising at expiry of term The landlord should be particularly wary of the effect of surrender on those obligations which are expressed to arise at or upon the expiry or sooner determination of the term, *e.g.* a covenant to leave in repair or to decorate. Such obligations will not survive surrender.[36] Thus the landlord who wishes to have them observed should require the tenant to enter into an express agreement to that effect, and make performance a condition precedent of the landlord accepting the surrender.

Removal of fixtures The rule that rights and obligations arising at the termination of the lease will not survive surrender is capable of working to the tenant's prejudice as well as the landlord's. In particular, the tenant will lose the right to remove tenant's fixtures at the date of surrender, and, if the surrender is preceded by a contract, from the date of the contract.[37] The tenant should be aware of this, and should

Trap for tenants

---

[31] *William Hill (Football) Ltd v. Willen Key & Hardware Ltd* (1964) 108 S.J. 482.

[32] *Torminster Properties Ltd v. Green* [1983] 1 W.L.R. 676.

[33] *Richmond v. Satin* [1926] 2 K.B. 530; *Dalton v. Pickard* [1926] 2 K.B. 545n.

[34] Law of Property (Miscellaneous Provisions) Act 1994, s.4: see para. 18–18 above.

[35] Typically covenants relating to repair and decoration: see para. 18–16 above.

[36] *Ex p. Hart Dyke* (1882) 22 Ch. D. 410 at 425; *Re A.B.C. Coupler & Engineering Co. Ltd (No. 3)* [1970] 1 W.L.R. 702.

[37] *Leschellas v. Woolf* [1908] 1 Ch. 641 at 650; *Ex p. Glegg* (1881) 19 Ch. D. 7 at 16. The analogy is with the vendor, who in the absence of express stipulation, cannot remove fixtures between contract and completion. But *cf. New Zealand Government Property Corp. v. H.M. & S. Ltd* [1982] Q.B. 1145, para. 11–13 above (right not lost by surrender by operation of law).

reserve the right to remove such fixtures before completion of the surrender or within a specified time thereafter.

Return of lease   The surrender should provide for the lease to be delivered up to the landlord.[38]

18–28   Surrender subject to underleases

Surrender of a lease will not affect the validity of a prior underlease, even where the granting of the underlease itself constituted a breach of covenant.[39] Indeed, acceptance of the **Landlord bound** surrender by the head landlord may preclude him from **by underleases** subsequently forfeiting the underlease as granted in breach of covenant, whether he knew of it or not.[40] Effectively the underlessor's obligations may be enforced against the head landlord following the surrender.[41] In view of this, the landlord should require disclosure of the terms of any underleases granted before accepting a surrender, and if necessary require them to be terminated before the surrender will be accepted.

In one case where the underlease provided that the rent review would operate in the same manner as the review in the headlease, the provisions in the underlease were held still to be operable even after the surrender of the headlease.[42]

From the surrendering tenant's point of view, underleases can also be a problem. A contract to surrender is prima facie **Surrender** an agreement to surrender in possession free from **subject to** underleases,[43] and so any underleases should be disclosed, **underleases** and the contract and conveyance made expressly subject to them.

Surrender followed by the grant of a new lease may be effected without the need to surrender and re-grant underleases and without prejudice to the respective rights and obligations of underlessor and underlessee.[44]

18–29   Surrender of registered lease

Surrender of a registered lease should take the form of a **Application to** transfer.[45] An application to close the title will need to be **close title** supported by the surrender, the lease and land certificate, evidence that the transfer was executed by the leasehold proprietor and every person appearing by the register to be interested in the lease,[46] and evidence as to reversionary title,

---

[38] *Knight v. Williams* [1901] 1 Ch. 256. This is particularly important in the case of a registered lease: see below.

[39] *Parker v. Jones* [1910] 2 K.B. 32; *Phipos v. Callegari* (1910) 54 S.J. 635.

[40] *Parker v. Jones* [1910] 2 K.B. 32 at 38, *per* Bucknill J.

[41] Law of Property Act 1925, s.139.

[42] *R&A Millett (Shops) Ltd v. Leon Allan International Fashions Ltd* [1989] 18 E.G. 107.

[43] *Leschellas v. Woolf* [1908] 1 Ch. 641 at 650.

[44] Law of Property Act 1925, s.150.

[45] *Spectrum Investment Co. v. Holmes* [1981] 1 W.L.R. 221 at 228.

[46] Land Registration Rules, r. 200.

where that title is not registered.[47] Where the surrender took place by operation of law, a statutory declaration evidencing the acts relied upon will be required in place of the transfer.[48]

Restrictive covenants subsisting
If it appears that restrictive covenants in the lease are intended to survive surrender (as for example a scheme of restrictive covenants in a shopping centre)[49] an entry should be made on the register in order to protect them.[50]

POSSESSION BEFORE COMPLETION

18–30 Generally

The last matter to be considered in this Chapter is one which in practice is common to many of the transactions already mentioned, namely the desire of one or both parties for effective completion faster than the legal formalities will allow. The pressure may come from a prospective tenant or assignee,

Need for early occupation
who urgently needs accommodation to avoid disruption of his business, or who wishes to derive some benefit from the premises immediately. A common example is the prospective shop tenant who wishes to fit out and be in a position to trade in the pre-Christmas period. On the other hand, a prospective assignor may wish to be rid of his obligation to pay rent as soon as possible. In either event, the solicitor may find that commercial reality conflicts with legal prudence, and for many clients commercial reality will prove the overriding factor.

It is perhaps all too easy for the solicitor to be cast in a negative role in such situations, placing legalistic obstacles in the way of the client's business goals. On the other hand, there is a duty on the solicitor to warn the client of real and substantial risks (which should not be confused with the solicitor's desire to keep to the usual well-worn paths of

Attitude of solicitor
conveyancing practice). What is needed from the solicitor is an awareness of the commercial importance of speed in the particular transaction and a sympathy to the client's practical problems, and at the same time a sound insight into the potential legal pitfalls. With forethought, some of the risks may be lightened, if not entirely obviated, and those which remain can be explained to the client without magnifying them beyond their proper importance seen against the commercial transaction as a whole.

18–31 Allowing the tenant into occupation prior to grant of lease

The first situation to consider is where a prospective tenant is allowed into occupation before completion of the lease. This

---

[47] Ruoff and Roper, *The Law and Practice of Registered Conveyancing* (1991 ed.), para. 21.31.
[48] *ibid.*
[49] See para. 10–11 above.
[50] Land Registration Rules, r. 205; Ruoff and Roper, *The Law and Practice of Registered Conveyancing* (1991 ed.) para. 21.38.

Agreement for lease or licence on undertakings can occur either under an agreement for a lease (possibly incorporating terms taken from the printed conditions of sale) or simply by the licence of the prospective landlord, the prospective tenant giving various undertakings as to the terms on which he occupies. Where the form of lease has been agreed, and the delay in completion arises merely from the logistics of engrossment and sealing, the tenant should always seek to be allowed to enter under an agreement for a lease, annexing the agreed draft to the contract. Where the form of lease has not been agreed, this will not be possible. Unless the arrangement can be construed as an agreement for a lease containing the usual covenants (which, as pointed out above, is unsatisfactorily vague)[51] no obligation to grant a lease can **Negotiation of terms** arise until the negotiation of terms is complete and the requirements of section 2 of the Law of Property (Miscellaneous Provisions) Act 1989 have been complied with.[52] This means that the prospective tenant who incurs the expense of moving into the property and possibly carrying out work to it will be at a grave disadvantage in negotiating the terms of the lease: until those terms are agreed his position will be precarious and he will therefore be under considerable pressure to accede to whatever terms the landlord puts forward. Therefore every attempt should be made to finalise terms before occupation is taken. In any event, the following matters will need very careful consideration by both parties.

Status of occupant   The practical importance of what might be thought a somewhat academic question lies in the ease or otherwise with which the prospective landlord will be able to recover possession of the premises should things go wrong.[53] A prospective tenant could be regarded as holding in a number of different capacities: as a licensee, as a tenant-at-will, as a periodic tenant, or as a tenant under an agreement for a lease.

If the agreement incorporates the National Conditions or **Conditions as to occupation as licensee** Standard Conditions, both contain provisions dealing with occupation before completion.[54] Both provide that occupation is as a licensee and not as a tenant.[55] However, unthinking reliance upon these printed conditions is not advisable. Both conditions contain in-built restrictions. The Standard Condition will not apply if the purchaser is already in lawful occupation of any part of the property and the National Condition will not apply if the purchaser is already in occupation as lessee or tenant: in each case this could be

---

[51] See para. 18–07 above.
[52] See para. 18–03 above.
[53] See the discussion of security of tenure in paras. 16–22 and 16–23 above. A classic example is *Javad v. Aqil* [1990] 41 E.G. 61, in which the intending tenant was permitted into occupation and paid rent on a quarterly basis on three occasions. Ultimately negotiations broke down and he claimed to have a periodic tenancy. The landlord had to litigate to the Court of Appeal, which held that the occupier was a tenant-at-will.
[54] National Condition 8; Standard Condition 5.2. In *Vangeen v. Benjamin* (1976) 239 E.G. 647 at 649 (a case on the grant of an underlease) Brightman J. held that this condition in the National Conditions applied to the grant of leases as well as to the sale of existing leases.
[55] National Condition 8(1)(i); Standard Condition 5.2.2.

relevant where the landlord is proposing to enlarge an existing holding by the grant of a new lease. Neither printed condition will apply if the purchaser is allowed access in order to carry out work, as will very often be the case. Thus specific incorporation of the relevant condition may be necessary. Furthermore, conditions providing for occupation under a licence, where in fact exclusive possession is given, must be

Street v. Mountford

treated with some caution after the decision in *Street v. Mountford*.[56] In that case occupation under a contract of purchase was instanced as one of the few cases where exclusive possession would not necessarily connote a lease.[57] However, the prospective landlord will need to ensure that the contract is binding and complete—otherwise occupation will not be referable to the contract and may lead to the inference of a tenancy.[58]

Payment for occupation

Another potential pitfall in the use of the usual printed conditions is inconsistency with any special condition, for example as to payment of rent. In *Joel v. Montgomery*,[59] Stamp J. held that the general condition providing that a prospective underlessee was in occupation as a licensee was overridden by a special condition providing that rent was payable in the period following occupation. This poses a dilemma for the landlord who wishes to receive some payment in respect of occupation prior to completion, but with care it should be possible to provide for such payment in a way consistent with occupation as a licensee rather than a tenant.[60]

Occupation after completion date

Another potential complication arises from the application of conditions primarily drafted with a sale of the freehold in mind to an agreement for the grant of a lease. In particular, occupation by the prospective tenant after any contractual date for completion could give rise to difficult problems. It could be argued by the prospective tenant that once the completion date is past he is entitled to occupation of right as tenant, and furthermore can obtain specific enforcement of the agreement and so should be equated with a legal tenant.[61] The printed conditions provide for the status to be that of licensee and not tenant until actual completion, but whereas it is uncommon for a purchaser of the freehold to remain in occupation under the contract long after the completion date, it is not uncommon for a prospective tenant to do so. Where this happens, and where the tenant is paying the rent and fulfilling the other obligations of the lease, it seems unlikely that the courts would permit the landlord to treat the tenant as a mere licensee occupying under the general conditions indefinitely. On the other hand, it would be a dangerous trap for the landlord if the prospective tenant's status changed from that of licensee to that of tenant in equity immediately

---

[56] [1985] A.C. 809; and see para. 16–22 above.
[57] *ibid.*, at 827. The same reasoning would seem applicable to occupation pending grant of a lease.
[58] *Bretherton v. Paton* [1986] 1 EGLR 172.
[59] [1967] Ch. 272.
[60] By requiring payment as mesne profits.
[61] *Walsh v. Lonsdale* (1882) 21 Ch. D. 9.

the completion date was past. It is therefore preferable to deal with the question by express stipulation.

Tenancy-at-will

An alternative to providing that occupation is as a licensee is occupation as a tenant-at-will.[62] Again, this will prevent the tenant acquiring protection under the 1954 Act but it may not be commercially acceptable given that a tenancy-at-will can be terminated without notice.[63]

Exclusion of 1954 Act

Where it is intended that a court order authorising the exclusion of Part II of the Landlord and Tenant Act 1954 shall be obtained, occupation and the contract should be made expressly subject to the order being obtained.[64] Ideally, the order should be obtained before occupation is permitted; it is likely that an undertaking by the tenant to join in a joint application for an order is unenforceable by reason of the anti-avoidance provisions in the Act.[65] If this cannot be achieved, the tenant may be permitted into occupation for a maximum limited period on licence (six months or less[66]), terminable if the order is not obtained by a stated date; so long as the order is obtained, the longer lease can then be granted.

Obligations pending completion   Further problems concern the obligations of the prospective tenant in occupation pending completion. Both sets of printed conditions contain relevant provisions broadly to the same effect: the purchaser is to pay and indemnify the vendor against all outgoings, to be responsible for repairs and insurance, to pay interest on any outstanding purchase money, and is entitled to any income from the property.[67] Such conditions may be entirely appropriate for the sale of freehold residential property, but they will not necessarily be suitable in the context of a proposed lease of commercial property. In particular, whereas on a sale of the freehold, the contract is all that there is to regulate the relationship between the parties, in the case of a contract for a lease, the prospective obligations of the parties will usually have already been spelled out in minute detail in the terms of the draft lease. It may therefore be appropriate to require the prospective tenant

Printed conditions

Obligations in draft lease

as licensee to undertake to comply with those obligations (but care is required to ensure that this does not conflict with the prospective tenant's status as licensee[68]); although one bold and creative interpretation of the National Conditions suggests that the obligation to pay "outgoings" extends to sums which would be payable under the lease after completion.[69]

[62] *Javad v. Aqil* [1990] 41 E.G. 61; see n. 53.
[63] See para. 16–22 above.
[64] *Cardiothoracic Institute v. Shrewdcrest Ltd* [1986] 1 W.L.R. 368: see para. 16–23 above.
[65] s.38(1).
[66] Occupation for a fixed period of six months or less confers no security on the tenant in the event that a lease is inadvertently granted: Landlord and Tenant Act 1954, s.43(3); and see para. 16–21 above.
[67] National Condition 8(1)(ii) and (iv); Standard Condition 5.2.2.
[68] *Joel v. Montgomery* [1967] Ch. 272.
[69] *Vangeen v. Benjamin* (1976) 239 E.G. 647. But "outgoings" would not necessarily cover all obligations under the draft lease, *e.g.* as to user.

Damage or alterations   Another worry is that the prospective tenant may during his period of occupation change or damage the property so as to diminish its value, and then for some reason refuse to complete.[70] This is only partially covered by the standard conditions.[71] In extreme cases, the vendor may obtain an injunction to restrain acts which would damage the property[72] but, since the draft lease will almost certainly contain detailed provisions as to the state of the premises and alterations[73], an obligation on the prospective tenant to comply with the terms of the draft lease will usually provide the best protection.

Occupation to carry out works   Indeed, frequently the purpose of allowing entry will be to carry out alterations or fitting-out works. If so, care should be taken to negative any general condition which might affect the tenant's right to do this.[74] The landlord should ensure that the agreement contains conditions as to the way in which the work is carried out, in the same way as a licence for alterations under an existing lease; and also for reinstatement in the event that the agreement for lease is rescinded.[75]

Expenditure by the prospective tenant   The expenditure of substantial amounts of money on the property prior to the grant of a lease places the prospective tenant in a vulnerable position; the main risk being that the lease may never be granted.[76,77]

Compensation for improvement   A different risk is that after the lease is completed, the tenant will not be able to obtain compensation for the improvement at the end of the lease. The provisions for compensation contained in Part I of the Landlord and Tenant Act 1927[78] do not appear to allow notice of intention to make an improvement (which is a prerequisite to an effective claim) to be served by a prospective tenant occupying as a licensee.[79] Thus if the tenant wishes to have any right to compensation, it should be expressly stipulated for.

Rent review   Finally, the relationship between the expenditure and the rent review provisions of the draft lease should not be overlooked. Any provision allowing improvements by the tenant to be disregarded in assessing the rent on review may not necessarily apply to improvements carried out by a licensee before the lease was granted.[80]

---

[70] See *Maskell v. Ivory* [1970] 1 Ch. 502.

[71] National Condition 8(iii); Standard Condition 5.2.2 (f)

[72] *Cutler v. Simons* (1816) 2 Mer. 104 at 105.

[73] See Chap. 11 above.

[74] See National Condition 8(1)(iii) and (v), though they may also be negatived by Condition 8(4); Standard Condition 5.2.2 (f).

[75] See para. 11–06 above.

[76,77] Whether any recovery can be made for benefits conferred by improving the premises is problematic: *cf. Lee-Parker v. Izzet (No. 2)* [1972] 1 W.L.R. 775 and *Lloyd v. Stanbury* [1971] 1 W.L.R. 535 at 546.

[78] See para. 11–07 above.

[79] Notice must be served by "a tenant of a holding": s.3(1). "Tenant" means any person entitled in possession to the holding under any contract of tenancy: s.25(1). In order to constitute a "holding" the premises must be held under a lease or agreement for a lease: ss.17(1) and 25(1). The point is not entirely free from doubt; *cf.*, para. 6–36 above.

[80] See para. 6–36 above.

Landlord's title Where it is impossible to make any investigation of the prospective landlord's title before occupation is taken, the right of the tenant to withdraw from the transaction should some serious defect in title be discovered should be preserved.[81]

Certainty

Obligation to grant and take lease As mentioned above, the long term position of the prospective tenant in occupation can only be safeguarded by a positive obligation as to the grant of a term. Thus it is vital that any agreement complies with section 2 of the Law of Property (Miscellaneous Provisions) Act 1989.[82]

Notice by landlord

Termination of occupation Under the printed conditions the position of a purchaser in occupation before completion is precarious. The purchaser is to give up occupation on termination of the contract or on notice from the tenant.[83] The prospective tenant should consider whether this provision should be modified, particularly where a substantial delay between occupation and completion is envisaged, and where he is undertaking the obligations of a tenant in the interim: an arbitrary notice requiring occupation to be given up could have disastrous effects upon the prospective tenant's business. The provision does, however, provide the landlord with considerable leverage to compel completion by a dilatory tenant. It should therefore be provided that notice to give up occupation may only be given on specified grounds, *e.g.* breach of the terms of the agreement or undertaking, or after some sufficiently distant long-stop date set for completion.

Specified termination grounds

18–32 Occupation pending assignment of lease

Risks relating to consent of landlord

There is often considerable pressure on the assignor to allow the prospective assignee into occupation pending receipt of the landlord's licence to assign, and formal completion. The requirement of the landlord's consent sharpens many of the risks mentioned above by introducing a factor which may cause the transaction to become abortive. Thus before the purchaser goes into occupation every attempt should be made to secure the landlord's consent in principle to the assignment.[84-85] It would be particularly foolish for the tenant to allow the purchaser into occupation where it is anticipated that difficulties may arise with the landlord, and for the

---

[81] As to possible defects in title, see para. 18–08 above. National Condition 8(3) or Standard Condition 5.2.7 could be used to negative the inference of acceptance of title.

[82] See para. 18–03 above.

[83] Seven days' notice under National Condition 8(2), five working days' notice under Standard Condition 5.2.5. In *Balabel v. Mehmet* [1990] 26 E.G. 176 the Court of Appeal considered the identical provision in the National Conditions (19th edition) and concluded that such notice had to be given even where the assignee was obliged to vacate if no licence to assign had been obtained within the period of three months specified in the special conditions.

[84-85] See para. 18–17 above. Any obligation on the assignor to obtain licences needs defining carefully: see *Creech v. Mayorcas* (1966) 198 E.G. 1091.

purchaser to expend money on the premises in such circumstances.[86]

Occupation as breach of covenant

The requirement of consent also raises problems of its own. In all probability the lease will forbid parting with possession of the premises as well as assignment, so that allowing the purchaser into occupation will constitute a breach of covenant, possibly entitling the landlord to forfeit the lease. This of course is a risk for both tenant and purchaser, but from the tenant's point of view it is particularly important that he is able to require the purchaser to give up occupation speedily should the landlord make any complaint, that the purchaser complies with the terms of the lease, and that the purchaser agrees to indemnify the tenant against any claim by the landlord.[87]

Unilateral offer of occupation by assignor

An interesting question which arises where the landlord's consent is delayed is whether the tenant can effectively throw the burden of the rent and other outgoings onto the purchaser by giving him the opportunity of going into occupation, whether or not the landlord's consent has by then been obtained. The wording of both the National Conditions and the Standard Conditions suggests that the purchaser is only liable where he actually takes occupation,[88] and indeed, it has been held by the Court of Appeal, in construing a somewhat similar special condition, that in order to make the purchaser liable, the occupation on offer must be lawful, that is, supported by some binding assurance from the landlord so as to confer some security.[89]

Premium for assignment

If a premium is payable for the assignment, the assignor may demand that the money be paid as a deposit on the assignee taking occupation pending completion. The agreement should make clear how the deposit is to be held, and under what circumstances it may be released.[90] Also, in connection with any premium payable, it may be necessary to negative the general conditions providing for payment of interest on the purchase money for the period of occupation.[91]

18–33   Occupation pending grant of underlease

The last case to be considered is occupation by a prospective underlessee pending the formal grant of an underlease. This

---

[86] See *Fischer v. Toumazos* [1991] 48 E.G. 123, in which exactly this occurred. The assignee was committed to paying the tenant's rent even though she could not trade from the premises.

[87] This does not appear to be covered by the standard condition as to indemnity against outgoings and expenses.

[88] "... is let into occupation": National Condition 8; "... lets [the buyer] into occupation ...": Standard Condition 5.2.1.

[89] *Cantor Art Services Ltd v. Kenneth Bieber Photography Ltd* [1969] 1 W.L.R. 1226.

[90] See *Tudor v. Hamid* (1987) 137 New L.J. 79: purchaser allowed into occupation of hotel upon payment of purchase price as deposit, held by Court of Appeal that in the absence of agreement to the contrary the sum was held as agent for the vendor, and that even if held as stakeholder it could be released to the vendor as soon as he performed his obligation to assign the property.

[91] National Condition 8(1)(ii); Standard Condition 5.2.2(d).

brings together the difficulties inherent in the grant of a lease, such as whether the prospective underlessee will obtain protected status against his prospective landlord, and those attendant on the assignment of a lease, namely whether the head landlord's consent is necessary, and the consequences of it being refused. In particular an intending underlessor should be wary of allowing occupation before the requisite licences **Danger where** are obtained where the proposed underlease is of part only of **underlease of** the property comprised in the headlease. He should be **part** reminded that by so doing he may run the risk of forfeiting the whole of the property, not only the part he is proposing to underlet; and that of course could be disastrous if he runs his own business from the remainder of the property.

19 VALUE ADDED TAX

19–01 Introduction

The first edition of this book contained no reference to Value Added Tax ("VAT") on property transactions, because virtually all such transactions were exempt supplies, a term which is explained shortly.[1] However, with effect from April 1, 1989 the regime changed and, overnight, property practitioners had to become familiar with the operation and scope of this tax.

This Chapter, which in parts will necessarily be more technical than much of the rest of the book, is set out as follows:

- General principles of VAT
- VAT considerations during the term of a lease
- VAT considerations arising on the grant of a lease and on the sale and purchase of a lease

GENERAL PRINCIPLES

19–02 Basis of charge

VAT is a tax administered for historic reasons not by the Inland Revenue but by H.M. Customs & Excise (abbreviated to "Customs" in this Chapter). It is charged on the value of a taxable supply[2] made in the U.K. in the course or furtherance of a business by a taxable person.[3] A taxable person is one who is registered or is required to be registered.[4] A person is required to be registered if he made taxable supplies during the previous 12 months the value of which exceeded the current registration limit.[5] A person who has made taxable supplies below the limit may register voluntarily.[6] The reason for wishing to register voluntarily is to enable input tax to be recovered.[7]

Co-owners Where property (including leasehold property) is jointly owned by two or more persons, and taxable supplies are made of that property,[8] the co-owners are treated as a single person for VAT purposes and are registered for VAT as such.[9]

---

[1] See para. 19–09 below.
[2] See paras. 19–06 and 19–09 below.
[3] Value Added Tax Act ("VATA") 1994, s.4(1).
[4] *ibid.*, s.3(1).
[5] £47,000 as at December 1995: *ibid.*, Sched 1, para. 1(1). In addition a person must apply to be registered if he has reasonable grounds for believing that the limit will be exceeded within the next 30 days.
[6] VATA 1994, Sched. 1, para. 9.
[7] See paras. 19–03 and 19–10 below.
[8] See para. 19–06 below.
[9] Finance Act 1995, s.26 if it comes into force. At present the authority is Mr G. W. and Mrs J. A. Green LON/91/2595Y, (9016) unreported.

Collection of VAT   VAT is assessed on the person who makes the supply[10] and it is that person's responsibility to account for VAT on a taxable supply.[11] Whether the customer has paid the VAT to the supplier is not relevant, and often the VAT element is concealed in the overall price, particularly in retail transactions. VAT is currently charged at the rate of $17\frac{1}{2}$ per cent.[12]

19–03   Input tax and output tax

The name value added tax explains how the amount of VAT payable is calculated. The seller is bound to account for VAT on the *net increase in value* of the item he is selling. It is necessary to understand the terms *input tax* and *output tax*. When a person is supplied with goods or services upon which VAT has been charged, he should receive an invoice detailing

Input tax   how much VAT has been charged.[13] This VAT is that person's "input tax".[14] Correspondingly, where a taxable person makes a taxable supply he must, at the end of the relevant accounting period[15] in which that supply was made, account for the VAT on that supply.[16] This is "output tax".[17]

Output tax   However, when accounting for his output tax, the taxable person is permitted to recover in full any input tax paid during that accounting period, so long as it is attributable to taxable supplies,[18] and this is achieved by his paying to Customs only the net amount by which his output tax exceeds his input tax. If recoverable input tax exceeds output tax, the input tax is recoverable in full.[19]

Limitations on recovery of input tax   In certain circumstances people who pay input tax are unable to recover it or to recover it in full. The most common examples are:

(1) People buying goods or services as consumers and not as traders. In this capacity such people cannot register as taxable persons,[20] and the input tax is part of the overall cost of the goods or services.

(2) People in their trade or business who make only exempt supplies, such as banking or insurance services. Where such people make partly taxable and partly exempt supplies they are known as "partially exempt" and are permitted to recover a proportion of their input tax.[21]

[10] VATA 1994, s.1(2).
[11] *ibid.*
[12] *ibid.*, s.2(1).
[13] See para. 19–04 below.
[14] VATA 1994, s.24(1).
[15] Normally a quarter, called a "prescribed accounting period", VATA 1994, s.25(1).
[16] *ibid.*
[17] *ibid.*, s.24(2).
[18] *ibid.*, s.25(2) and s.26 and Value Added Tax Regulations 1995 (S.I. 1995 No. 2518), reg. 101. For taxable supplies see below, para. 19–06.
[19] *ibid.*, s.25(3).
[20] See para. 19–02 above.
[21] This is beyond the scope of this work. See, for example, D. Goy and J. Walters, *VAT and Property* (2nd ed., 1993).

(3) Where the capital goods scheme applies.[22] This aligns VAT recovery of input tax on certain items, including land and buildings costing £250,000 (net of VAT) or more (but excluding rental payments), with the use of that land for the making of taxable or exempt supplies over a period of five or 10 years.[23] Where a lease which falls within the scheme is acquired then the amount of input VAT recovered is adjusted to reflect the extent of taxable and/or exempt use. This is achieved by reference to a formula applied annually by reference to the average input tax recovery position of the owner throughout the year.[24]

Where a person is unable to recover any of his input tax, then it follows that he is concerned to pay as little input tax as possible, and will wish to structure transactions with this aim prominently in mind. It must be said that, with the exception of persuading a supplier not to exercise the election to waive the exemption from VAT,[25] there is often little which can be done in terms of structuring the more usual commercial leasehold transactions so as to eliminate any VAT liability. With more complex transactions, ingenious tax mitigation becomes a possibility.

19–04 VAT invoices

When a taxable person makes a taxable supply he must issue a VAT invoice.[26] To be a VAT invoice the document must contain certain specified information.[27] Without a VAT invoice the recipient of the supply will not be able to recover VAT charged.[28]

19–05 Penalties and interest

VAT returns must be submitted within 30 days of the relevant prescribed accounting period.[29] Penalties exist for failing to

---

[22] Value Added Tax Regulations 1995 (S.I. 1995 No. 2518), Pt. XV. See also VAT Leaflet 706/2 "Capital Goods Scheme: Input tax on computers, land and buildings acquired for use in your business."

[23] The normal period for the scheme to run is 10 years, except where the lease has less than 10 years to run at the time it is acquired, when the period is five years: *ibid.*, reg. 114(2) and (3)(b) and (c).

[24] *ibid.*, reg. 115.

[25] See para. 19–10 below.

[26] Value Added Tax Regulations 1995 (S.I. 1995 No. 2518), reg. 13.

[27] *ibid.*, reg. 14.

[28] *ibid.*, reg. 29(2). See also J. F. Crossman LON/89/398 (5417) (unreported) where it was stated that it was within the discretion of the Commissioners whether or not to allow claims for input tax which were submitted after the end of the prescribed accounting periods and *ABB Power Ltd* [1992] VATTR 491 (9373) where stating that a tax point was a particular date was held to be insufficient to constitute a tax invoice. A further relevant case is *Austin Company of UK Ltd* LON/91/1990X (7981) (unreported) where the words "This is not a tax invoice" were sufficient to ensure that the document would not be treated as an invoice. See para. 19–03 above.

[29] Value Added Tax Regulations 1995 (S.I. 1995 No. 2518), reg. 13(5).

return or pay the tax on time and, even if returned on time, where the return is incorrect through innocent error.[30] If there is deliberate evasion of tax, criminal penalties will arise.[31] Where a person has overpaid VAT, Customs will repay such amount provided that to do so would not unjustly enrich the recipient.[32]

19–06   Supplies

The event which triggers a charge to VAT is a "supply". This, understandably, is a complex concept, and readers are advised to refer to a specialist textbook for further details.[33] The concept of a supply does not fit easily with property transactions, particularly the granting of a lease: it is nevertheless necessary, when analysing a transaction from the point of view of VAT, to envisage the landlord "supplying" the lease to the tenant; and similarly on the assignment of a lease of the assignor "supplying" the lease to the assignee.

Common property transactions

Here is an analysis of some common property transactions, in VAT terms.

Transaction	VAT treatment
Sale and purchase of freehold property	Supply of the property by the vendor to the purchaser
Assignment of a lease	Supply of the lease by the assignor to the assignee
Grant of a lease	Supply of the lease by the landlord to the tenant
Grant of an option for a lease	Supply of the option by the grantor to the grantee
Surrender of a lease	Supply of the lease by the tenant to the landlord
Expiration of a lease	No supply
Variation of a lease	Treated as a further supply of the lease[34]
Grant of a licence to the tenant (whether the landlord can or cannot unreasonably withhold consent)	Treated as a further supply of the lease

---

[30] VATA 1994, s.59. For misdeclaration of tax see ss.63 and 64.
[31] *ibid.*, s.60. See s.61 for liability of directors.
[32] *ibid.*, s.80.
[33] For example, D. Goy and J. Walters, *VAT and Property* (2nd ed., 1993).
[34] *Lubbock Fine & Co. v. C. & E. Commissioners* [1994] S.T.C. 101, E.C.J.

Sale of a business as a going concern (including sale of tenanted property)	No supply[35]
Dilapidations payments	No supply
Compensation payments under the Landlord and Tenant Act 1954, s.37	No supply

19–07 Time of supply

The time of the supply governs the date on which the person making the supply must account to Customs for VAT on that supply. A supply of property takes place when possession is given,[36] or if earlier when a payment is received or an invoice raised.[37] A lease is treated as supplied each time rent or a premium is received, or an invoice for such a payment is raised, whichever is the earlier.[38]

It follows that a landlord will wish to delay accounting for VAT on rental payments until the relevant rental payments have been received. It is therefore recommended that rent demands are not themselves VAT invoices,[39] but that a receipted VAT invoice is issued only when the rental payment is received. This will avoid not only the acceleration of the date of supply, but also either delay the landlord from having to account for VAT in the event that the rent is paid late, or ensure that no VAT is accounted for if the rent is not paid at all.

19–08 Value of supply

Where cash is received for a supply, then the value of the supply is the cash received less the VAT which is payable.[40] Where a consideration is shown as VAT inclusive, it is therefore possible to calculate the part which represents the consideration for the supply and the part which represents the VAT on that supply.[41] Where consideration is given otherwise than in cash (*e.g.* another interest in land), Customs are entitled to substitute market value in determining the value of

---

[35] Value Added Tax (Special Provisions) Order 1995 (S.I. 1995 No. 1268), art. 5.
[36] The time of supply in the case of a supply of services, *e.g.* a lease of less than 21 years, technically differs from that relating to supply of goods *e.g.* leases of 21 years or more or freehold interests, but in practice this makes no material difference.
[37] Value Added Tax Regulations 1995 (S.I. 1995 No. 2518), reg. 84(2).
[38] *ibid.*, reg. 85.
[39] See para. 19–04 above.
[40] VATA 1994, s.19(2).
[41] Currently the proportions are 40/47ths for the supply and 7/47ths for the VAT, based on VAT at $17\frac{1}{2}\%$.

the supply, even though there may not be a connection between the parties.[42]

19–09 Types of supply

As explained above,[43] a taxable person is permitted to recover input tax so long as it is attributable to taxable supplies. It is therefore important to understand the distinction between taxable and exempt supplies, and how the usual property transactions fit into this scheme.

Exempt supplies Where a transaction is an exempt supply, the taxable person is unable to recover his input tax relating to it. For taxable persons, therefore, exempt supplies are generally undesirable, as the input tax forms an irrecoverable overhead. For persons who are not taxable persons the distinction between exempt and taxable supplies is unimportant, as they cannot recover any input tax in any circumstances.

Generally, any grant, transfer or assignment of any interest in or right over land is an exempt supply.[44] This is subject to certain exceptions which are set out in the section below headed "Taxable supplies".

Surrenders of leases The surrender of a lease by a tenant to his landlord is an exempt supply, as is the surrender of any interest or right over land.[45] Where a *tenant* pays a premium to the *landlord* in these circumstances (generally called a reverse premium), the supply of the landlord agreeing to accept the surrender is an exempt supply.[46] In VAT parlance, a transaction in which the tenant pays the landlord a reverse premium to accept a surrender of the lease is termed a reverse surrender.[47]

Taxable supplies Taxable supplies fall into two categories: zero-rated supplies and standard rated supplies. The distinction is that in a zero-rated supply the taxable person has no obligation to account for any output VAT on the supply whereas in a standard rated supply he has to account for output VAT at the standard rate;[48] however in either case he is able to recover the full amount of input tax attributable to the supply. Currently the only supplies which are zero-rated and which relate to property transactions relate to buildings used as dwellings or for residential or charitable purposes[49] and as such are outside the scope of this work.

Zero-rated supplies

---

[42] VATA 1994, s.19(3).
[43] See para. 19–03 above.
[44] VATA 1994, Sched. 9, group 1.
[45] *ibid.*, Sched. 9, Group 1, Note 1, inserted by Value Added Tax (Land) Order 1995 (S.I. 1995 No. 282), art. 3.
[46] *ibid*, Note 1A.
[47] *ibid.*, art. 4.
[48] See para. 19–03 above.
[49] VATA 1994, Sched. 8, groups 5 and 6.

Standard rated supplies in property transactions

The following are the only relevant supplies which are standard rated in property transactions:[50]

(1) The sale of new freehold buildings. This is not relevant to the subject of this book, but is included for the sake of completeness.

(2) A supply which would be an exempt supply but in respect of which the supplier has elected that it should be a taxable supply. This topic is dealt with fully in the next section, headed "The election to waive the exemption".

(3) A supply of parking facilities, whether by lease or by licence.[51] However, where parking facilities are included in a letting of commercial premises, and relate to those premises, the rent need not be divided between the two supplies, and both will follow the type of supply of the main property.

(4) Where a landlord or an assignor pays a reverse premium to the tenant or the assignee (as the case may be) as an inducement to take the lease, or to accept an assignment of a lease, this is a standard rated supply and the tenant or the assignee must account for output VAT on the amount of the reverse premium.[52]

19–10 The election to waive the exemption (option to tax)

The election

The election procedure of the VAT Act 1994 permits a person to declare that any supply of any interest which he owns or creates in a building will be a taxable supply and not an exempt supply.[53] The election must be notified to Customs within 30 days of its being made.[54] A recommended form for the making of the election and its notification is set out in Appendix H of Customs Notice 742.

The person making the election need not own the property, or indeed have any interest in it whatsoever, at the time of the election. For example, a prospective purchaser of the property may make an election before he acquires it.

Revocation of election

The election can be revoked in only two circumstances:

(1) within three months of its date, so long as no tax is due to Customs, no input tax has been claimed and Customs give written consent; or

---

[50] VATA 1994, Sched. 9, group 1, item 1.

[51] VATA 1994, Sched. 9, group 1, item 1 para (h). See leaflet 701/24 on Parking Facilities.

[52] *ibid.*, s.4(2) and *Neville Russell* [1987] VATTR 194 (2484). Also see para. 19–15 below relating to rent-free periods.

[53] VATA 1994, Sched. 10, para. 2(1). An election cannot be backdated. See *Lawson Mardon Group Pension Scheme* LON/92/492 (10231) (unreported).

[54] *ibid.*, Sched. 10, para. 3(6) as amended by Value Added Tax (Buildings and Land) Order 1995 (S.I. 1995 No. 279). See also *Fencing Supplies Limited* [1993] VATTR 302 (10451) where charging VAT on rent was held to amount to an election.

(2) after 20 years, if Customs give written consent.[55]

The extent of the election It is not possible to make an election in respect of part only of a building.[56] "Building" has a wide meaning in this context and includes:

- all land within the curtilage of the building;
- any buildings to which it is linked internally or by a covered passage;
- complexes consisting of a number of units grouped around a fully enclosed concourse.[57]

The effect of the election on the right to recover input tax As an election converts exempt supplies into taxable supplies, any input tax incurred on expenses relating to the land, which would otherwise be irrecoverable (and therefore an overhead) become recoverable. These expenses may include professionals' fees, agents' fees, and the cost of building works.

Permission from Customs Permission from Customs to make the election must be obtained where there has been an exempt supply relating to that property prior to the election being made.[58]

VAT CONSIDERATIONS DURING THE TERM OF A LEASE

19–11 Service charges

Common parts. The VAT treatment of service charges for the common parts of a building[59] always follows the VAT treatment of the rent, whether or not separate management is employed for their administration. Thus if the landlord has elected to waive the exemption[60] on the rent, then he must also account for VAT on the service charges he levies and will therefore include it in the service charge demands.[61] As in the case of rent,[62] the service charge demand should not itself be a VAT invoice but a receipted VAT invoice should be issued on receipt of the service charge.

Separate services to tenants. Metered services supplied directly to tenants, such as heating and lighting, are standard rated supplies.[63]

---

[55] *ibid,* Sched. 10, para. 3(5) inserted by Value Added Tax (Buildings and Land) Order 1995 (S.I. 1995 No. 279) art.4(b).

[56] VATA 1994, Sched. 10, para. 3(3) as amended by Value Added Tax (Buildings and Land) Order 1995 (S.I. 1995 No. 279).

[57] *ibid.*

[58] *ibid.,* Sched. 10, para. 3(9) although under VAT (Buildings and Land) Order 1995 (S.I. 1995 No. 279), art. 4 in certain circumstances (described in VAT Notice 742, para. 8.6) prior permission to waive the exemption will not be required. Where permission is required, it will generally be given if Customs are satisfied that the proposed attribution of incurred input tax between the exempt use of the property and the intended taxable use of it is fair and reasonable. See VAT Notice 742, para. 8.8.

[59] See para. 8–02 above.

[60] See para. 19–10 above.

[61] VAT Notice 742, at para. 5.2.

[62] See para. 19–07 above.

[63] VAT Notice 742, at para. 5.7.

19–12 Insurance rents

The VAT treatment of payments made by tenants to landlords in respect of building insurance depends upon in whose name the policy is held.[64]

In whose name the policy is held

The policy may be in the names of the landlord, the tenant, or their joint names. This has different consequences for VAT purposes.

Landlord's name. The amount of the insurance contribution forms part of the consideration for the supply of the lease by the landlord.[65] Therefore if the landlord elects to waive the exemption in respect of the lease, VAT is also chargeable on any payment made by the tenant in respect of insurance.[66]

Tenant's name. Where the policy is in the tenant's name but payments are made via the landlord, then the payments are by way of reimbursement or indemnity and the payment is therefore not a supply.[67] Such payments are outside the scope of VAT.[68]

Joint names. For VAT purposes the landlord's interest is treated as nominal only and the same consequences ensue as where the policy is in the tenant's sole name.[69] There is therefore no supply.[70]

Cesser of rent

Where the landlord has insured against the risk of rent cesser,[71] he will receive insurance moneys instead of rent if the insurance is ever triggered. In such a case the landlord is not making a supply of the premises to the tenant, and is not obliged to account for VAT in respect of the proceeds of insurance, regardless of whether he has elected to charge VAT or not. It is therefore unnecessary, and indeed inappropriate, for the insured sum (*i.e.* the total of the landlord's rental income) to be increased to include VAT. Such an increase would serve only to increase the premium, most probably at the cost of the tenant,[72] and would not entitle the landlord to any greater proceeds of the policy than the total of his rental income.

19–13 Improvements carried out pursuant to section 3 of the Landlord and Tenant Act 1927

Under section 3 of the Landlord and Tenant Act 1927, where a tenant requests consent for the carrying out of

---

[64] See para. 13–04 above.
[65] There is only one supply by the landlord in these circumstances: VAT Leaflet 701/36/92, para. 43 and *Globe Equities Ltd* MAN/93/1449 (13105), (unreported).
[66] *ibid.*
[67] *ibid.*
[68] *ibid.*
[69] *ibid.*
[70] *ibid.*
[71] See para. 13–03 above.
[72] See para. 13–04 above.

improvements, the landlord may require the tenant to allow him to carry out the works and to rentalise the cost.[73] In such a case the tenant will be unable to recover the VAT on these costs, as he will not be paying directly for them. He will therefore wish the landlord to make the election to waive exemption in such circumstances,[74] which will therefore enable the landlord to recover the VAT on the cost of the works, and will thereby reduce the capital amount to be recovered through increased rental payments.

19–14 Tenants paying landlord's solicitors' and other professional costs

It is common for tenants to have to bear responsibility for payment of accounts rendered to their landlords by solicitors and other professionals.[75] The rules relating to the VAT treatment of such payments are complex. Different rules apply depending upon:

(1) the nature of the supply which the landlord is making to the tenant; and
(2) whether the landlord has elected to waive the exemption.[76]

Nature of the supply   **Licence granted under the terms of a subsisting lease, or variation of a subsisting lease**   Where the landlord has made an election, or is otherwise able to recover any VAT paid, the landlord's solicitor (or other professional adviser) renders a VAT invoice to the landlord. The landlord himself renders a VAT invoice to the tenant, in the same amount, which enables the tenant to recover the full amount of VAT paid. In practice, it is common for settlement of the professionals' accounts to be made directly by the tenant, and for the VAT invoices to be issued at a later date.

Where the landlord has not made an election, or is otherwise unable to recover the VAT on the professionals' accounts, the VAT invoice is still rendered to the landlord, but no VAT invoice is then issued to the tenant. The tenant is required to settle the professionals' invoices, but cannot recover the VAT element as the invoices are not addressed to him.

---

[73] Landlord and Tenant Act 1927, s.27. See para. 11–07 above. See also *Gleneagles Hotel plc* [1986] VATTR 196 (2152): an agreement by the tenant to carry out work on improving the premises was held to constitute a taxable supply and *Neville Russell* [1987] VATTR 194 (2484): money paid to enable firm to carry out refurbishments was held to be consideration for a taxable supply.

[74] See para. 19–10 above.

[75] *e.g.*, when a landlord is responding to a tenant's application for a licence to assign (see Chap. 12 above), or to carry out alterations (see Chap. 11 above), or in proceedings for the forfeiture of the lease (see Chap. 14 and para. 15–11 above).

[76] See para. 19–10 above.

Grant of lease or assignment of lease   The same rules will apply where the tenant is paying the landlord's professionals' costs on the grant of a lease, or the assignment of an existing lease.

Indemnity of landlord by tenant   The tenant may be required to settle the landlords' professional accounts in circumstances where no supply has been made by the landlord to the tenant. This may occur on abortive transactions, or when the landlord is enforcing the tenant's obligations in the lease.

Again the rules differ depending on whether the landlord has made the election. Where this has occurred, the professionals address their accounts to the landlord. The landlord pays the VAT portion and the tenant pays the VAT exclusive portion. The landlord is able to recover the VAT which it has paid.

Where the landlord cannot recover the VAT, the tenant is responsible for payment of the entire account, in the same manner as in the case where the landlord has made a supply, but has not waived the election.

19–15   Other miscellaneous circumstances

Notices of assignment, underletting and charge   Fees payable by a tenant to a landlord for the registration of an assignment or other transaction[77] will not attract VAT.[78] However if the fees are appropriated by the landlord's solicitor, then the landlord's solicitor must account for VAT at the current VAT fraction.[79]

Interest on overdue rent   This is outside the scope of VAT.[80]

Rent-free periods   The granting of a rent-free period is not a supply for VAT purposes, but it is merely an agreement of a price between two people at arm's length.[81] However, if the tenant undertakes to supply some form of consideration for this rent-free period, then this will constitute a supply for which VAT will have to be accounted.[82]

For example, where a tenant agrees to carry out improvements to a property in exchange for a rent-free period, the tenant is treated as making a supply to the

---

[77] See para. 19–14 above.
[78] Agreed statement between Customs and the Law Society, *Law Society Gazette* July 11, 1990 14.
[79] See para. 19–02 above.
[80] *British Property Federation VAT Newsletter*, Issue No. 3 October 1990, para. 1.
[81] s.5(2)(a) and *dicta* of Lord Grantchester in *Exeter Golf and Country Club* [1979] VATTR 70.
[82] *Ridgeon's Bulk Ltd* [1994] S.T.C. 47. Where the tenant undertook repairs to the premises there was held to be a supply from the tenant to the landlord, the consideration for which was the right to occupy the premises rent free.

landlord of an amount equal to the total of the rent forgone, and must account to Customs for VAT on this sum.

Payments by landlords to tenants for compensation for disturbance   Payments by landlords to tenants for compensation for disturbance pursuant to section 37 of the Landlord and Tenant Act 1954 are outside the scope of VAT.[83]

Payments by tenants in respect of dilapidations
Payments by tenants in respect of dilapidations[84] are outside the scope of VAT.[85]

VAT CONSIDERATIONS ARISING ON THE GRANT OF A LEASE, AND ON THE SALE AND PURCHASE OF A LEASE

19–16   Generally

In VAT terms, the grant of a lease and the assignment of a lease are very similar. Accordingly they are dealt with together in this section of the Chapter. For convenience the expressions "vendor" and "purchaser" are used, but these can equally be read as "landlord" and "tenant". The expression "purchase price" can equally be read as "premium", where the tenant is paying a premium on the grant of a lease, and the expression "contract" can be the lease itself, as well as an agreement for the assignment of a lease.

It is essential for both the vendor and purchaser to be clear (i) whether VAT is to be added to the purchase price as, if the vendor is obliged to charge VAT, he will be required to account for it to Customs whether he has charged it or not,[86] and (ii) if so, whether the vendor is entitled to charge VAT. This is because VAT charged when it is not properly due can never be recovered.[87]

19–17   Points to be ascertained by the purchaser

Matters to be raised by purchaser   It is customary for the purchaser to obtain information about the vendor's VAT position as part of the process of raising enquiries before contract.[88] These are the issues on which the purchaser will require information:

(1) Is the supply one on which it is possible to charge VAT? To the extent that the property is used as a dwelling or

---

[83] VAT Notice 742, at para. 4.9.
[84] See para. 9–24 above.
[85] VAT Notice 742, at para. 4.12.
[86] See para. 19–02 above.
[87] *Norwich Union Life Insurance Society* LON/90/1809X (7205) (unreported) and *P. Howard* LON/80/457 (1106) (unreported).
[88] See para. 18–05 above.

for a relevant residential[89] or relevant charitable
purpose,[90] VAT cannot be charged. If the property is of
mixed commercial and residential use (for example, a
public house) then an apportionment may be required.[91]

(2) Is the vendor intending to charge VAT? If the answer to
this question is yes, then the remaining questions will
also be relevant. If the answer is no, then it is advisable
for the purchaser to obtain a provision in the contract to
this effect. However this does not prevent the vendor
from subsequently making an effective election to waive
exemption, and therefore the purchaser should also
require a provision in the contract to cover the
eventuality that the vendor, in breach of contract, makes
such an election. This is explained in greater detail
below.[92]

(3) Is the vendor registered for VAT? The purchaser should
obtain a copy of the vendor's certificate of registration
together with confirmation that he does not intend to
de-register for VAT prior to completion.

(4) Has a valid election to waive exemption been made, and
not been revoked?[93] The purchaser should obtain copies
of any election in respect of the property, the
notification to Customs of the making of the election
and, where appropriate, the consent of Customs to the
making of the election.[94]

(5) Is the transaction to be a transfer of a going concern?
The purchaser will need to establish whether the
necessary criteria will be met.[95]

19–18   The purchaser's VAT position

If the purchaser intends to occupy the premises for the
purposes of his own business, then any VAT he pays will be
recoverable in accordance with his general VAT recovery
position[96] and the capital goods scheme.[97]

Purchaser may   However, if the purchaser is acquiring the property as an
need to make   investment (in other words, subject to one or more tenancies),
VAT election   then he must make an election to waive the exemption prior
to incurring any VAT.[98] The rules on the time of supply[99]
must therefore be borne in mind.

---

[89] VATA 1994, Sched. 8, group 5, n. 3. Relevant residential purposes broadly
comprise use as residential institutions but exclude prisons, hotels or
hospitals.

[90] VATA 1994, Sched. 10, para. 2(2).

[91] The apportionment will be made by reference to the extent of the premises
used for commercial purposes: VATA 1994, Sched. 8, group 5, n. 5.

[92] See para. 19–19 below.

[93] See para. 19–10 above.

[94] VAT Notice 742 at para. 8.8.

[95] This subject is beyond the scope of this book. See, for example, D. Goy
and J. Walters, *VAT and Property* (2nd. ed., 1993) for a detailed discussion.

[96] See para. 19–03 above.

[97] See para. 19–03 above.

[98] Value Added Tax (Special Provisions) Order 1995 (S.I. 1995 No. 1268)
art. 5(3).

[99] See para. 19–07 above.

19–19   The purchase price

Deposit   Where a deposit is paid to a vendor's solicitor as agent, the time of the supply is the time of payment.[1]
However, a deposit paid to a vendor's solicitor as stakeholder is not treated as having been supplied until it is released.[2]

The purchase price   It is essential for the contract to make clear whether the price to be paid is inclusive or exclusive of VAT. Two distinct rules must be borne in mind:

Price inclusive of VAT

(1) An election[3] made after the date of the contract entitles the person making the supply to add VAT to the price, *unless the price is expressly stated to be inclusive of VAT.*[4] As stated above,[5] a statement by the vendor that he will not make an election does not prevent a valid election subsequently being made. It is wise, therefore, for a purchaser in these circumstances to require not only a provision that the vendor will not make an election, but also a statement that if an election is made, the purchase price will be treated as inclusive of VAT.

(2) If an election has been made before the date of the contract, then the price is deemed to be inclusive of VAT, *unless the price is expressly stated to be exclusive of VAT.*[6] It is common for contracts expressly to state (where this is the case) that a purchase price is exclusive of VAT; in such a case it is usual for there to be a further provision stating that the purchaser will pay on completion any VAT which is or becomes due, and that such VAT forms part of the purchase price for the purposes of calculating interest due on late completion.

A provision in the contract that the price is inclusive or exclusive of VAT does not constitute an election to charge VAT.

Completion   If at completion VAT is charged, a VAT invoice should be produced.[7]

Rent apportionments   On the assignment of a lease, there is normally an apportionment between the vendor and the purchaser in respect of rents paid (in advance) or to be paid (in arrears). For VAT purposes any apportionments should be disregarded: VAT is charged only on the purchase price.[8]

Apportionments disregarded

[1] *Bethway & Moss Ltd* [1988] 3 CMLR 44 in which a deposit was held to constitute a payment in respect of a supply within what is now s.6(4). The decision was approved in *Moonraker's Guest House Ltd* [1992] S.T.C. 544.
[2] *Double Shield Window Co Ltd* MAN/84/227 (1771) (unreported).
[3] See para. 19–10 above.
[4] VATA 1994, s.89(2).
[5] See para. 19–17 above.
[6] VATA 1994, s.19(2).
[7] Value Added Tax Regulations 1995 (S.I. 1985 No. 2518), reg. 13.
[8] VAT Notice 742, at para. 4.11.

Late completion   If interest is charged following a late completion, then the amounts payable by way of interest are interest in nature and do not constitute an adjustment of the purchase price. Accordingly VAT is not chargeable on the interest element.[9]

19–20   Stamp duty on VAT

Here there is an important distinction between the rules on the assignment of an existing lease, and the rules on the grant of a new lease.

Assignment of a lease   Where the price includes VAT, then stamp duty is charged on the price plus the VAT.[10] Where VAT is not being charged then no account is taken of it.

Grant of a lease   Where the rent includes VAT, then stamp duty is charged on the rent including the VAT.[11] Where the landlord has the ability to charge VAT on the rent, then stamp duty is charged on the rent plus the VAT *whether or not the landlord has exercised the election to charge VAT.*[12] The only exception to this is where the rent under the lease is expressed to be inclusive of VAT so that even if the election to charge VAT is made, this would not increase the amount of rent payable by the tenant.

For the purposes of calculating the amount of stamp duty on the VAT part of the rent, it is important to know whether or not the VAT is reserved as rent.[13] Where VAT is reserved as rent, then it is treated as rent for stamp duty purposes.[14] However where VAT is not reserved as rent, it is treated as a series of annual payments for each year of the lease up to a maximum of 20 years, which attracts *ad valorem* duty at the rate of 1 per cent.[15]

VAT reserved as rent

19–21   Land Registry fees

Land Registry fees are calculated on the total price paid, inclusive of VAT.

[9] VATA 1994, Sched. 9, group 5.
[10] Statement of Practice SP 11/91 at para. 9.
[11] *ibid.*
[12] Statement of Practice SP 11/91 at paras. 6 and 7.
[13] Reserving VAT as rent has become common in practice and is accepted by both landlords and tenants as a means of mitigating the tenant's stamp duty liability.
[14] Statement of Practice SP 11/91 at para. 9.
[15] Stamp Act 1891, s.56 and Statement of Practice SP 11/91 at para. 9.

20 ENVIRONMENTAL CONSIDERATIONS

20–01 Introduction

Liability arising from the contamination of land, and from environmental protection legislation, is a risk to be addressed in commercial leases, as in other commercial contexts. It is becoming increasingly common, particularly in leases granted in 1990 and later, to find terms dealing expressly with environmental considerations, though this is by no means standard practice. Leases granted before 1990 are likely to be silent on the subject, save of course to the extent that environmental liabilities are covered by a general covenant on the part of the tenant to comply with statute.[1]

Considerations for landlords and tenants   Landlords and tenants need to keep in mind two considerations when agreeing the terms of a new lease, or interpreting an existing lease:

(1) the need for the owner and/or the occupier to comply with legislation in relation to the current use of the demised premises; and

(2) potential liabilities on the owner and/or the occupier stemming from the condition of the demised premises, for example where the property is contaminated by previous uses.

These two issues are dealt with in that order in this Chapter.

LIABILITY RELATING TO CURRENT USE

20–02 Applicable legislation

Authorisations   The tenant's use of the premises may require various consents or authorisations. Activities carried out without authorisation, or in breach of the conditions imposed on the authorisation, may constitute a criminal offence. Some of the main authorisations are listed in tabular form below.

---

[1] As to statutory compliance generally, see Chap. 7 above.

Presence of a hazardous substance on, over or under land	Hazardous substances consent: Planning (Hazardous Substances) Act 1990, s.4.
Operation of a prescribed process (*e.g.* metals manufacturing, the storage of certain chemicals in bulk, or the operation of a waste-oil burner)	Integrated pollution control or air pollution control authorisation: Environmental Protection Act 1990, s.6.
Disposal, keeping, treatment, deposit, etc. of waste (including office and other commercial waste)	Waste management licence: Environmental Protection Act 1990, s.33; or registration of exemption, if applicable: Waste Management Licensing Regulations 1994.
Keeping and use of radioactive substances and discharge of radioactive waste	Registration or authorisations for keeping or use of radioactive materials or for disposal or accumulation of radioactive waste: Radioactive Substances Act 1993, ss.6, 13 and 14.
Discharge of polluting substances or of trade or sewage effluent to controlled waters	Discharge consent: Water Resources Act 1991, s.88(1)(a) and Sched. 10.
Discharge of trade effluent to sewer	Trade effluent consent: Water Industry Act 1991, s.118.

20–03   Potential liability upon the landlord

Liability for operating without the necessary consent will generally fall upon the tenant as the person operating the process, discharging the effluent, etc. However, the possibility of the landlord also being liable cannot be discounted.

"Knowingly permitting" First, in certain cases liability may arise for "knowingly permitting" certain consequences, such as the discharge of polluting matter to controlled waters. "Permitting" in this context may mean giving leave or licence to do something.[2] Thus a landlord who grants a lease to the tenant for a purpose such as the deposit of waste, and who knows that the tenant does not have the requisite licence, may be said to be

---

[2] See *e.g. Shave v. Rosner* [1954] 2 Q.B. 113; *Lomas v. Peak* [1947] 2 All E.R. 574; *Kent County Council v. Beaney* [1993] Env. L.R. 225.

knowingly permitting the deposit. "Permitting", however, may also constitute failure to take steps to prevent something which it was within a person's power to prevent.[3] In this sense, a landlord who has contractual powers to prevent the unlawful deposit, release or other activity, and who knows the activity is taking place yet fails to exercise those powers, may be at risk.[4] Knowledge may be said to be a dangerous thing in this context: the more knowledge a landlord has of the tenant's activities, the more he may be said to be at risk of a charge of knowingly permitting. This does not necessarily mean, however, that a landlord should abstain from making any enquiry, since wilful blindness may in certain circumstances be equated to constructive knowledge and may equally incur liability.[5]

Joint causation   Secondly, it is conceivable that the landlord and tenant may be held to have jointly caused pollution. Case-law suggests that there can be concurrent causes of pollution where more than one person is involved in a chain of events resulting in contamination.[6] An example might be where the landlord has demised faulty plant or equipment which when operated by the tenant causes pollution. However, the mere fact that a landlord has constructed or provided a drainage system, through which polluting matter passes into controlled waters, will probably not be sufficient of itself to establish causation.[7]

Thirdly, problems can arise for a landlord who retains relevant consents in his name, where the conditions of those consents are then breached by the tenant. In *Taylor Woodrow Property Management Limited v. National Rivers Authority*[8] the defendant was the developer of an industrial estate, who obtained a discharge consent for a surface water drainage system. The consent remained in the name of the developer after completion of the development and the letting of units to various tenants. One of the conditions of the consent was that there should be no visible traces of oil or grease in the discharge. Due to the actions of one of the tenants, and in breach of a covenant in the lease against allowing deleterious materials to enter the drainage system, this condition was breached; subsequently the developer was convicted of knowingly permitting the discharge, and of breaching the condition under section 85(6) of the Water Resources Act 1991. The developer's appeal against conviction was unsuccessful: the court held that the developer could be guilty even though the act which breached the condition was some other person's. The court adopted the language of benefits

---

[3] *Berton v. Alliance Economic Investment Co.* [1922] 1 K.B. 759; *Bromsgrove District Council v. Carthy* (1975) 30 P. & C.R. 34; *Tophams Ltd v. Earl of Sefton* [1967] A.C. 50.

[4] See *London Borough of Tower Hamlets v. London Docklands Development Corporation*, Knightsbridge Crown Court, April 13, 1992 where the issue arose in relation to a construction contract.

[5] *Westminster City Council v. Croyalgrange Ltd* [1986] 1 W.L.R. 674; *Schulmans Incorporated Ltd v. NRA* [1993] *Water Law* 25.

[6] *Att.-Gen.'s Ref. (No. 1 of 1994) The Independent*, January 31, 1995.

[7] *National Rivers Authority v. Welsh Development Agency* [1993] Env. Liab. CS27; *Wychavon District Council v. NRA* [1993] 2 All E.R. 440.

[8] *The Times*, July 14, 1994.

Benefits and burdens
and burdens and pointed out that as the developer had taken the benefit of the consent, it must be subject to its burdens. The court also considered the relevance of the covenant in the lease against allowing deleterious materials to enter the drainage system. Whilst this was not relevant to the charge of breaching the condition, the court held it could be relevant to the charge of knowingly permitting, at least if the landlord could show that, knowing of the discharge, he had taken adequate steps to enforce the covenant, for example by obtaining an injunction against discharge in breach of the covenants.[9]

20–04 Compliance with notices

Notices
Another aspect of the current use of the demised premises relates to compliance with notices. Under environmental law, regulatory authorities have power to serve a range of notices requiring a response: these have various names, such as enforcement notices,[10] prohibition notices,[11] abatement notices[12] and remediation notices.[12a] In general, such notices are likely to be directed to the tenant as the party carrying on the relevant activity. However, in certain instances, a notice may be directed to the landlord as owner of the premises: *e.g.* in relation to statutory nuisance where the nuisance has not yet occurred but is anticipated, or where the nuisance relates to some structural defect in the premises.[13] The problem may arise where premises are inadequately soundproofed, so that the tenant's activities result in noise nuisance,[14] or where a piece of plant and machinery, such as a lift, creates excessive noise when in use.

As between the landlord and tenant, the issue here will turn on who is obliged to bear what may be the considerable costs of complying with the notice.[15] In particular, the issue is whether or not the tenant's liability is to be limited solely to those matters which are attributable to the tenant's use of the premises, as opposed to any historic use.

20–05 Common law nuisance

Where the use at the premises constitutes a nuisance at common law, it is the tenant who will in general be liable in damages or who will be subject to an injunction, as the person causing the nuisance. However, the landlord may potentially also be liable, depending on a number of factors.

---

[9] See n. 2 above.
[10] Environmental Protection Act 1990, s.13; see also s.42(5).
[11] *ibid.*, s.14.
[12] *ibid.*, s.80.
[12a] *ibid.*, s.78E.
[13] *ibid.*, s.80(2).
[14] *Network Housing Association v. Westminster City Council* [1994] 27 H.L.R. 189; see also Bettle [1988] J.P.L. 79.
[15] See para. 7–05 above.

Where the nuisance existed before the grant of the lease, then the landlord will remain liable if he knew, or ought to have known, of the nuisance.[16] Where the nuisance arises after the lease was granted, the landlord's responsibility may depend on the degree of continuing control exercised in law or in fact.[17] However, it should be noted that the leading cases in this area relate to structural defects in the premises and the landlord's responsibilities in relation to repairs, rather than in relation to the tenant's use of the premises.[18] The fact that the landlord may also have responsibilities in tort to a third party does not relieve the tenant of liability.[19]

Continuing control

20–06   Protecting the landlord

It will be appreciated from the preceding paragraphs that the landlord's position may in some circumstances be prejudiced by the way in which the tenant uses the demised premises. At a broad level, some degree of protection may be given by a general covenant by the tenant to comply with all applicable legislation in relation to the tenant's use of the premises.[20] More specifically, this may be framed to include compliance with the requirements of any competent authority (*e.g.* notices).

Covenant to comply with legislation

The landlord may also wish to ensure that any authorisations or licences which run with the premises are not prejudiced by the tenant's activities.[21] This may be facilitated by a covenant by the tenant to use all reasonable endeavours to maintain such licences or consents in force and not to do anything which would render them subject to revocation or suspension. A well-advised tenant would be unwilling to accept such a covenant unless the authorisations or licences in question were specifically identified in the lease.

In relation to potential common law liabilities, the landlord may seek an indemnity from the tenant for any claims asserted against the landlord in respect of loss caused by the tenant's use of the premises. Where those activities result in criminal liability on the landlord, *e.g.* for "knowingly permitting" pollution, such as an illegal discharge by the tenant to controlled waters, an indemnity will not as a matter of public policy be enforceable, and accordingly the landlord will have to rely on the general leasehold covenants as a deterrent.

Indemnity from tenant

---

[16] *Brew Bros Ltd v. Snax (Ross) Ltd* [1970] 1 Q.B. 612; *Sampson v. Hodson-Pressinger* [1981] 3 All E.R. 710.

[17] See *Brew Bros Ltd v. Snax (Ross) Ltd* [1970] 1 Q.B. 612 at 638; *Mint v. Good* [1951] 1 K.B. 517 at 528.

[18] See cases cited at nn.16 and 17 above.

[19] *Wilchick v. Marks and Silverstone* [1934] 2 K.B. 56; *St. Anne's Well Brewery Co. v. Roberts* [1929] 140 L.T. 1.

[20] See Chap. 7 above.

[21] See *Davy Ltd v. Guy Salmon (Service) Ltd, Chartered Surveyor Weekly*, July 23, 1992 (a case involving a petroleum spirit licence under the Petroleum (Consolidation) Act 1928).

20–07 Protecting the tenant

The tenant's concerns are likely to relate mainly to problems caused by the state of the premises taken in conjunction with the tenant's activities: *e.g.* inadequate soundproofing which results in noise nuisance, or some latent defect in the drainage system which results in the escape of polluting effluent.[22]

Fitness for purpose
Such issues go to the fitness for purpose of the premises, in relation to which there is no implied warranty; nor is the landlord likely to be willing to give any such express warranty.[23] For example in *Sutton v. Temple*[24] a lease of pasture was granted. The land was contaminated by poisonous flakes of paint which had been mixed into a manure heap. A number of the tenant's cattle died and the tenant refused to pay an instalment of rent which was due. It was held that nothing was agreed as to the fitness of the area for its purpose; the tenant was obliged to pay the rent "whether the land answer the purpose for which he took it or not".

The tenant's best protection is therefore likely to rest in a thorough survey prior to entering into the lease.

LIABILITY RELATING TO PAST USES

20–08 Nature of liability

Serious liabilities under environmental legislation may arise from past uses of the premises, or the adjoining premises, which have led to soil or groundwater contamination, or from problems in the structure and materials of the premises, such as asbestos fibres or lead paint. The remedial measures required may be long term, extensive and expensive. Such problems may be worsened by current activity: for example the use of inappropriate repairing or cleaning methods which release friable asbestos.

Under the currently applicable and proposed legislation, it is possible for liability for past contamination to extend to the current owner and occupier, albeit that they were not the originator of the problem. This is the result in part of the use

"Knowingly permitting"
of the expression "knowingly permitting" in some of the relevant legislative provisions,[25] and in part of the ability of relevant authorities to serve notices requiring remedial action on the current owner or occupier in certain circumstances. Under the Environmental Protection Act 1990, for instance, contamination could constitute a statutory nuisance in respect of which an abatement notice may in some circumstances be served on the current owner or occupier.[26] In such

---

[22] *R. v. C.P.C. (U.K.) Ltd* [1994] NPC 112.
[23] See para. 10–11 above.
[24] Lord Abinger, C.B., (1843) 12 M & W 52.
[25] See para. 20–03 above.
[26] Environmental Protection Act 1990, s.80(2). There are also powers of cost recovery for works by the enforcing authority under s.81(4). Following implementation of Part IIA of the Environmental Protection Act 1990 dealing with contaminated land (see below), statutory nuisance remedies will not be available to deal with contaminated land.

circumstances, it may be a difficult question as to whether the landlord or the tenant, or both, are ultimately responsible.[27]

"Person responsible" There is also doubt as to whether a tenant could be held to be the "person responsible" in relation to a nuisance which he did not cause: some authority suggests that such an interpretation might be tenable.[28]

Contaminated land The same problems may well arise under the provisions on contaminated land contained in Part IIA of the Environmental Protection Act 1990, as inserted by the Environment Act 1995.[29] Where land is contaminated in the terms defined by those provisions, so as to present a significant risk of harm to man or other living organisms, eco-systems or property or so as to pollute controlled waters, a remediation notice must be served by the enforcing authority (the district council or, in some cases, the Environment Agency) requiring either further assessment or remedial action.[30] Liability rests primarily with the person who caused or knowingly permitted the contaminants to be in, on, or under the relevant land. However, notice is to be served on the current owner or occupier, where the original polluter cannot after reasonable inquiry be found.

Original polluter To the extent that the contamination is referable to a known individual or company which is still in existence, the current owner and occupier will not be at risk save to the extent that they can be said to have knowingly permitted the contaminants to be present. However, it is quite probable that all or part of the contamination will not be so referable, where the identity of the original polluter is unknown, or where the polluter no longer exists, or the contaminants have migrated onto the demised premises from other property and cannot be attributed to a specific polluter. In such circumstances the **"Appropriate person"** "owner or occupier" for the time being will be an appropriate person to receive a remediation notice under section 78F(4) or (5). The "owner" is defined by section 78A(9) to mean a person (other than a mortgagee in possession) who, whether in his own right, or as trustee for any other person, is entitled to receive the rack rent of the land or who would be entitled to receive it if it were let at a rack rent. The person who is liable under section 78F may in many cases ultimately be determined by statutory guidance on exclusions from liability and apportionment of liability (the guidance not yet being officially available at the time of going to press). However, wherever liability rests under the Act, it may be the provisions

---

[27] As regards statutory nuisance, the court, on appeal, has wide power to apportion the expenses of compliance on appeal or in any action by the statutory authority to recover expenses; Environmental Protection Act 1990, s.81(4). See also s.161(3) Water Resources Act 1991 in relation to knowingly permitting water pollution.

[28] Section 79(7) defines the "person responsible" as the person "to whose act, default or sufferance the nuisance is attributable." See *Clayton v. Sale Urban District Council* [1926] 1 K.B. 415, and in Scotland (on different wording) *Clydebank District Council v. Monaville* 1982 S.L.T (Sh.Ct.) 46.

[29] Part IIA of the Environmental Protection Act 1990 is to be brought into force by commencement order. As at the date of going to press, no such order had been made.

[30] Environmental Protection Act 1990, s.78E as inserted by section 57 of the Environment Act 1995.

in the lease which ultimately decide which party bears the costs.

20–09 Allocation of risk between landlord and tenant

The key question relates to the allocation of risk between landlord and tenant. Such allocation may be by way of the more general lease covenants or by express provision.

20–10 General covenants

A number of general covenants may have a bearing on historic contamination; indeed, for leases drafted before such problems were fully appreciated the general covenants may provide the only allocation of liability.[31] Those which may be relevant are:

Repair

Repair It is conceivable, though not inevitable, that contamination may result in premises being out of repair, *e.g.* as a result of chemical corrosion of foundations or services. The repairing covenant will, however, be likely to address the symptom of the problem, as opposed to its cause. There is also the issue of whether contamination would constitute a latent defect which might fall outside the scope of the covenant.[32]

Statutory requirements

Compliance with statutory requirements and notices A covenant by the tenant to comply with notices served by statutory authorities might well have the effect of placing the risk of liability for historic contamination on the tenant, depending on how widely the covenant was worded.[33] This is probably the greatest threat to the tenant in pre–1990 leases. It is also questionable whether such a covenant would necessarily prevail over the power of any regulatory or appellate body to apportion liability under the terms of the legislation.[34]

Cleansing

Cleansing The standard covenant to cleanse demised premises or to leave them in a clean and tidy condition seems most unlikely to apply to the removal of sub-surface contamination, even though the sub-soil may as a matter of law comprise part of the demised premises.[35]

Service charge

Service Charge Expenditure on clean-up by the landlord may, depending on the relevant drafting, fall within the costs recoverable under the service charge.[36] In certain

---

[31] The passing of the Environmental Protection Act 1990 was probably the first general indication that this issue was to become of considerable significance.
[32] See para. 9–09 above.
[33] See Chap. 7 above.
[34] See para. 7–05 above
[35] See Chap. 4 above
[36] See Chap. 8 above.

circumstances, this could pose a serious difficulty for the tenant in terms of usual lease wording. Contamination may have little or no direct effect on the demised premises themselves (as, for example, where they comprise upper floors of a building) but may affect the common parts. For example, it is not unknown for the most highly contaminated soils to be covered over and used as car parking areas in the course of redevelopment on a "footprint specific" basis, *i.e.* where the layout of the building was designed to avoid disturbing those areas identified as most heavily contaminated.

20–11   Protecting the tenant

Caveat emptor

In relation to contamination, as with other possible defects in the demised premises, the tenant will be subject to the principle of *caveat emptor* in taking the lease. In the absence of misrepresentation or deliberate concealment by the landlord, the tenant will have no redress if contamination is later discovered.[37]

Enquiries by tenant

Desk top study

Searching for contamination   The most effective form of protection for the tenant is therefore to make appropriate enquiries before entering into the lease, so as to assess the likely extent of contamination and the risks it may present. The extent of such enquiries will vary depending upon the location of the premises, the proportion of the building being demised, the length of the term, the amount of the rent and the use to which the tenant is to put the premises. Clearly a tenant taking office premises in a multi-occupied building in an urban area will be more easily satisfied than one taking a lease of a retail warehouse on an estate on reclaimed land in a former industrial area. The former will probably be content with raising standard enquiries of the landlord; the latter will require professional advice from an experienced environmental consultant. The degree of stringency of the investigation will depend upon what is revealed by an initial "desk top study" into the past uses of the site and "targets" which may be affected by the contamination, *e.g.* residents of adjacent property, or groundwater resources. There is now a considerable amount of general and detailed guidance as to such investigation.[38]

The main problems relating to such investigations are their cost and ultimately their possibly inconclusive nature. With regard to the second aspect, it must be accepted that no investigation is ever going to be able to provide a totally conclusive picture of the presence or absence of contamination or its possible consequences. What it will do,

---

[37] See para. 18–05 above.
[38] See: Code of Practice for the Identification of Potentially Contaminated Land and its Investigation, The British Standards Institution Draft for Development DD175: 1988; Guidance Notes of the Interdepartmental Committee on the Redevelopment of Contaminated Land (ICRCL), for example ICRCL Guidance Note 59/83; Tackling Contamination: Guidelines for Business, the Confederation of British Industry (1994).

Risk assessment

however, is to provide the tenant with some information on which to take a reasoned decision on risk, and possibly material which will strengthen his negotiating position.

With regard to the cost of investigation, this must be viewed in relation to the value of the transaction, and as relative to the risks involved. Contamination of even modest premises may involve the tenant in high levels of cost and consequential loss. With the exception of established buildings in urban areas, it is likely to become much more common for "desk top" surveys to be carried out as part of the process of the grant, or assignment, of commercial leasehold premises.

Landlord's survey

It may be the case that the landlord has carried out his own investigations into contamination, particularly if the site has recently been subject to redevelopment. The tenant may be able to rely on a previous report, provided it was carried out thoroughly, and is available to the tenant with the benefit of a warranty from the consultant confirming that the tenant may rely on it.[39]

Where the property is found to have been contaminated   Where premises have been developed on contaminated land (*e.g.* retail development on a former landfill site), the tenant will wish to check that the appropriate precautionary measures, such as gas monitoring and venting equipment, have been properly specified, installed and maintained as part of the development.[40]

Precautionary measures

Not only should the tenant be safeguarded against being found liable for contamination arising outside his control, but he should also ensure that provision is made to cover the position where the initial precautionary measures taken in developing the contaminated site were inadequate, and subsequent contamination of the site occurred during the lease term. Such provisions should take account of the situation where use of the property becomes impossible due to contamination and the tenant wishes to break the lease, cease paying rent and/or avoid having to pay, or contribute to, remedial costs for action necessary for cleaning-up the site. It follows therefore, in terms of the lease itself, that the tenant may seek to have any costs and liabilities relating to pre-existing contamination expressly excluded or carved out from the standard clauses. Going further, an indemnity may be sought from the landlord in relation to any primary liability incurred by the tenant as the result of such contamination.

Tenant wishes to break lease

One possible solution which may be adopted where problems are known or suspected is for the perceived problem areas to be excluded from the definition of the demised premises. In some cases "pie-crust leases" have been granted which demise only the immediate sub-surface, excluding lower strata and groundwater. Extremely careful drafting will be needed for such matters as the extent of the demise and rights of support, and should be prepared in conjunction with the parties' technical advisers.

"Pie-crust lease"

[39] See para. 9–14 above.
[40] The tenant may also wish to instruct an expert to consider any subsequent monitoring data.

Consequential loss

One issue which is sometimes overlooked is the disruption and consequential loss which can result from the discovery of contamination. The tenant's business may be badly affected if intrusive site investigations or remediation have to be carried out during the term; indeed in extreme cases the premises may become unusable, for example where affected by significant levels of explosive gases.[41] This issue may be addressed by a provision for suspension of rent or, in extreme cases, a tenant's break clause,[42] and also by the inclusion of consequential loss within any indemnity provided by the landlord. Such provisions are likely to be acceptable to the landlord only in high risk cases, *e.g.* where retail development has been carried out on a former landfill site, following appropriate measures for gas control. Failure of those control measures would have sufficiently severe consequences to justify such an approach. Another area of potential exposure for the tenant is on rent review; where contamination affects fitness for purpose, the tenant will wish this to be taken into account. Similarly, the tenant will wish any clean-up operations carried out by the tenant, or at the tenant's expense, to be disregarded when ascertaining the reviewed rent.

Rent review implications

Ultimately, all of these issues are matters for negotiation, the outcome of which will depend on many complex factors, one of which will be the relative bargaining positions of the various parties to the transaction.

20–12   Protecting the landlord

Tenant's activities

The landlord's concerns are likely to relate to the possibility of the tenant's activities contaminating the demised premises or worsening existing contamination. The combination of present and future contamination raises very many questions in terms of joint and several liability, or apportionment of liability. The first step in managing this risk is for the landlord to gather as much information as possible on the likely activities of the tenant, any contaminative substances to be used and the precautions proposed to be taken against contamination. The following questions may be incorporated into a standard checklist:

- nature of proposed use;
- type of substances used, *e.g.* solvents, petroleum, chemicals;
- precautionary arrangements, *e.g.* bunding, impervious flooring;
- personnel, skills and training;
- past record—has the tenant any previous offences under environmental and safety legislation?

[41] Waste Management Paper No. 27.
[42] See para. 16–05 *et seq.*

The landlord may wish to exercise similar control in relation to assignment or underletting, and provision will need to be made for this.

Tenant's covenants

In terms of usual covenants, some protection may be provided to the landlord by the covenant against waste (express or implied),[43] the covenant to comply with general legislation, covenants against nuisance, the implied obligation as to tenant-like use[44] and the user covenant.[45] The landlord will also wish to exercise control over alterations to the premises to ensure that contaminative materials are not introduced, and that any existing contaminants (*e.g.* asbestos) are dealt with properly. These may usefully be supplemented by a general covenant to take appropriate precautions not to cause contamination (and possibly not to keep or use certain specified substances), to report significant spillages to the landlord, and to take appropriate measures in a timely fashion to rectify any contamination which does occur. How stringent these covenants should be will depend to a large extent on the nature of the premises and their expected use.

Rights of entry

Another potential problem relates to rights of entry. The landlord will need access to inspect the premises or to investigate possible contamination, and possibly to comply with statutory clean-up requirements. Drafting of the clause reserving rights to the landlord to enter the premises should be considered with this in mind.

Surveys

The landlord will also wish to ensure that the premises are in no worse a state in terms of contamination at the end of the lease than at the start. The problem here is frequently an evidential one. The safest solution is for a contamination survey to be carried out prior to commencement of the lease and the results agreed, and for a second survey to be carried out on termination of the lease or just prior thereto.[46] The tenant may then be required to make good any contamination caused during the term, or the landlord may have the right to do so in default, recovering the costs from the tenant. Whether this course is justified in any given case will again depend on the nature of the premises and the scale of risk of contamination by the tenant's use. The process may be equally desirable from the tenant's point of view to avoid mis-attribution of pre-existing contamination to the tenant: from that perspective it may be appropriate for the costs of the surveys to be shared between the parties.

20–13 Migration of contamination from other land

Both parties need to bear in mind that contamination may result from the migration of substances from neighbouring land, as well as from on-site sources. Under the new

---

[43] See para. 11–04 above.
[44] See para. 9–02 above
[45] See para. 10–08 above.
[46] In the case of long leases it may be appropriate for interim surveys to be carried out during the term.

Migration of contamination

provisions in Part IIA of the Environmental Protection Act 1990, an owner or occupier may be liable for the remediation of his own land to which contaminants have migrated from off-site: however, such an owner or occupier will not be liable in respect of further land into which the contaminants have passed.[47] It is also clear that an owner or occupier will not be liable for contaminants which migrated from the land before he became owner or occupier of it. This means that it is important for a tenant to assess the risks not only in relation to the demised premises before taking a lease, but also in relation to adjoining or neighbouring land which may be a source of migrating contaminants. Further, in relation to the negotiations for the lease, where a tenant accepts responsibility for contamination of the demised premises which was not present at the start of the lease, the wording of the relevant provisions should seek to avoid the tenant being made responsible for contamination caused by off-site sources over which the tenant has no control.

---

[47] The tenant should therefore be wary of contamination migrating to the demised premises from neighbouring contaminated property.

INDEX

ADDITIONS, 11–02
ALIENATION
  conditions for, 12–12
  consent to, 12–09 *et seq.*
    no fine payable for, 12–09
    reasonableness of
      criteria for judging, 12–13
      requirement for, 12–10
        burden of proof as to, 12–10
    refusal of
      common reasons for, 12–14
      timing of reasons for, 12–10,
        12–11
      unreasonable, effect of, 12–10
  construction of clauses and, 12–02
  covenants
    absolute, 12–08
    assignment, against, 12–03, 12–10
    parting with possession, against,
      12–05, 12–13
    qualified, 12–08, 12–10
    sharing possession, against, 12–06
    underletting, against, 12–04,
      12–10, 12–13
  Landlord and Tenant Act 1988,
    effect of the, 12–10
  part, of, 12–07, 12–10
  whole, of the, 12–07, 12–10
ALTERATIONS
  consent to, 11–05
  Disability Discrimination Act 1995,
    to comply with the, 11–05
  express covenants against, 11–02
  waste, relationship to tort of, 11–04
ANTI-AVOIDANCE PROVISIONS, 2–03,
  2–08, 16–23
APPEALS, 6–19
ARBITRATION
  advantages of, 6–13
  costs of, 6–18
  factors in choosing, 6–13
  independent expertise distinguished,
    6–13
  procedure, 6–15 *et seq.*
  proviso for, 15–09
  reference to, 6–10, 6–13, 6–14, 8–05
ARBITRATOR
  appointment of an, 6–13

ARBITRATOR—*cont.*
  award of an, 6–15
    appeal against an, 6–19
  costs, discretion to award, 6–18
  decision of an, challenge to the,
    6–19
  error of law by an, 6–19
  misconduct by an, 6–19
  removal of an, 6–19
  taxation of fees of an, 6–18
ASSIGNEE
  status of an, 12–14
  use proposed by an, 12–14
ASSIGNMENT
  benefit of a surety covenant, of the,
    3–15
  breach of a covenant against parting
    with possession, may constitute,
    12–05
  causes of action to a tenant, of, 9–12
  conditions to be included in the
    lease, 12–12
  consent to
    obtaining, 18–17, 18–24
    refusal of, 12–13, 18–17
  covenant against, 12–03
  covenants of indemnity on, 2–10,
    18–18
  deed of, 18–19
  excluded, 2–05, 3–08
    definition of, 2–05
  implied covenants on, 18–18
  ineffective, 9–12
  involuntary, 2–03
  lease, of a, 18–12 *et seq.*
  new tenancy, of a, 12–14
  offer back clause and, 2–15
  part, of, 2–11
  prohibitions against, 2–03, 12–03
  restrictions on, 12–08 *et seq.*
  underlease, of an, 18–24
  underletting and, 12–04
  value added tax as to notices of,
    19–15
  variation of tenancy following, 2–12
AUTHORISED GUARANTEE
  AGREEMENTS (AGAS), 2–01
  guarantor may enter, whether, 2–07
  limitations on obligations of, 2–06

A<small>UTHORISED</small> G<small>UARANTEE</small>
    A<small>GREEMENTS</small> (AGAs)—*cont.*
  new tenancies, as to, 2–06
  old tenancies, as to, 2–06
  safeguards for a former tenant
    under, 2–12

B<small>REAK</small> C<small>LAUSES</small>, 16–05 *et seq.*
  conditional, 16–08
  exercise of
    effect of, 16–07
    requirements for the, 16–06
  interaction with section 26 request,
    16–09, 16–28
  purpose of, 16–05
B<small>UILDING</small> S<small>TANDARDS</small>
  statutory obligations as to, 7–04

C<small>ALDERBANK</small> L<small>ETTER</small>, 6–18
C<small>APITAL</small> A<small>LLOWANCES</small>, 11–16
C<small>IVIL</small> E<small>VIDENCE</small> A<small>CT</small>, 1995, 6–17
C<small>ODE OF</small> P<small>RACTICE</small>, 1–02, 1–06,
  18–03
C<small>OLLATERAL</small> W<small>ARRANTIES</small>, 9–14,
  17–03
C<small>ONSENT</small>
  alterations and improvements, to,
    11–05
    conditions of, 11–06
    grounds for refusal of, 11–05
    unreasonable, 11–05
  dispositions, to, 12–08
    no fine payable for, 12–09
    refusal of
      common reasons for, 12–14
      criteria for judging, 12–13
      statutory proviso as to
        reasonableness of, 12–08
      timing of, 12–11
      unreasonable, effect of, 12–10
    statutory proviso as to
      reasonableness of prohibiting,
      12–08
C<small>ONSTRUCTION</small>
  suretyship provisions, of, 3–15
C<small>ONSTRUCTION OF</small> L<small>EASES</small>, 17–01 *et
  seq.*
C<small>ONVEYANCING</small>
  assignment of an underlease, 18–24
  assignment of a lease, 18–12 *et seq.*
    form of deed of, 18–19
    generally, 18–12
    implied covenants, 18–18
    landlord's consent required, 18–17
    National Conditions for, 18–13

C<small>ONVEYANCING</small>—*cont.*
  assignment of a lease—*cont.*
    notice of the, 18–20
    obtaining a landlord's consent,
      18–17
    post completion matters, 18–20
    registration of the, 18–20
    stamp duty payable on the, 18–20
    Standard Conditions for, 18–13
    terms of the lease, 18–15
      compliance with the, 18–16
      title of assignor, as to the,
        18–14
  grant of an underlease, 18–21 *et seq.*
    generally, 18–21
    obtaining a landlord's consent to
      the, 18–23
    performance of covenants in the
      headlease, 18–22, 18–23
    title of the property, investigation
      of the, 18–22
  grant of a new lease, 18–02 *et seq.*
    agreement on, 18–07
    allocation of costs, 18–04
    completion of the, 18–10
    draft form of, 18–05
    landlord
      disclosure of inherent defects by
        a, 18–05
      insolvency of a, 18–08
      title of a,
        investigating the, 18–08
      undertaking as to the costs of a,
        18–04
    Law of Property (Miscellaneous
      Provisions) Act, 1989, 18–03
    negotiation of terms, 18–03,
      18–06
    post-completion matters, 18–11
    pre-completion matters, 18–03 *et
      seq.*
    preliminary enquiries, 18–05
    references, 18–05
    registration of the, 18–07, 18–11
    searches
      local, 18–05
      pre-completion, 18–09
    stamp duty payable, 18–11
    survey, 18–05
    title of the property
      entry of notice on freehold,
        18–11
      investigation of the, 18–08
    Landlord and Tenant Act, 1954,
      exclusion of Part II, 18–03

CONVEYANCING—*cont.*
  possession before completion, where,
    18–30 *et seq.*
    generally, 18–30
    prior to assignment of lease,
      18–32
    prior to grant of lease, 18–31
    prior to grant of underlease,
      18–33
  surrender of a lease 18–25 *et seq.*
    effect of, 18–27
      covenants, on, 18–27
      removal of fixtures, as to, 18–27
      return of the lease, as to the,
        18–27
    form of, 18–26
    reasons for, 18–25
    registered, where, 18–29
    underleases, subject to, 18–28
COSTS
  grant of a new tenancy, of the,
    16–46, 16–48
  proviso in a lease for, 15–11
  rent review arbitration, of, 6–18
  services, of, 8–04
  statutory capital,
    expenditure of, 7–05
  undertaking as to, 18–04
  unsuccessful application for a
    licence, as to, 18–17
COVENANTS
  absolute, 11–02, 12–08
    prohibition on
      alterations, as to,
        consent, where, 11–05
  assignment, against, 12–03, 12–10
    qualified, 12–13
  breach of, 18–16
  cutting and maiming structure,
    against, 11–02
  death of a tenant, effect of the, on,
    3–08
  direct, 12–14
  easements, for the protection of,
    15–02
  express
    alterations, against, 11–02
    interest on rent, as to payment of,
      6–06
  external appearance, against altering
    the, 11–02
  headlease, in, 18–22, 18–24
  implied
    assignment, on, 18–18
    for title, 18–08
  insure, to, 13–02 *et seq.*

COVENANTS—*cont.*
  landlord, of a
    indemnity, as to, 15–08
    regulations, as to, 15–07
  onerous, 18–15
  parting with possession,
    against, 12–05
  performance of, 6–34
    evidence of, 18–16
    headlease, in, 18–22, 18–24
  planning compensation, as to, 15–05
  provision of services, as to, 8–02
  qualified, 11–02, 11–05, 12–08,
    12–10
  qualified, against assignment, 12–13
  quiet enjoyment, of, 16–02 *et seq.*
  rent, to pay, 6–01
  repair, to
    environmental considerations as
      to, 20–10
    landlord, of a, 9–19
    tenant, of a, 9–03 *et seq.*
  restrictive, affecting a freehold,
    18–08, 18–14
  sharing possession, against, 12–06
  statutory notices and planning
    applications, as to, 15–06
    environmental issues, 20–10
  underlease, in, 18–22, 18–24
  underletting, against, 12–04, 12–10
  waste, against, 11–02

DAMAGES
  breach of a repairing covenant, for
    landlord, by a, 9–27
    tenant, by a, 9–24
      measure of, 9–25, 9–27, 16–03
DEED OF ASSIGNMENT
  indemnity covenants incorporated
    into, 2–10
DEFECTS *see* REPAIRING
  COVENANTS, REPAIRS
DEMISED PREMISES
  appurtenant rights, 4–06 *et seq.*
    access, of
      adjoining property to, 4–12
      maintenance of, 4–07
    ancillary, 4–07
    communal facilities of, 4–10
    extent of, 4–07
    negating implied grants, 4–13
    parking, as to, 4–09
    sanitary facilities, as to the use of,
      4–10
    service media, as to, 4–08

DEMISED PREMISES—*cont.*
appurtenant rights—*cont.*
signs and advertisements, as to, 4–11
definition of, 4–01, 11–03
description of the, 4–02 *et seq.*
fixtures, as to, 4–05
floor areas, as to, 4–03
more than one parcel of land, as to, 4–04, 16–26
parts, in, 4–03
plan, as to the, 4–02
exceptions from the,
consideration of a tenant when making, 4–17
development, as to rights of, 4–18
entry, as to rights of, 4–17
express, must be, 4–14, 4–18
fire exits, as to, 4–15
service media, as to, 4–16
extent of the, 4–01 *et seq.*, 11–03
reservations from the, 4–14 *et seq.*, *see also* exceptions above
DEROGATION FROM GRANT, 10–11
DILAPIDATIONS, 9–24 *et seq.*
value added tax as to, 19–15
DISREGARDS, 6–36

EASEMENTS,
protection of, 15–02
ENVIRONMENTAL CONSIDERATIONS, 20–01 *et seq.*
common law nuisance, 20–05
contamination, as to, 20–08 *et seq.*
generally, 20–01
landlord
liability of a, 20–03
protection of a, 20–06, 20–12
legislation, 7–04, 20–02
liability
current use, as to, 20–02 *et seq.*
past uses, as to, 20–08 *et seq.*
allocation of risk, 20–09
general covenants, 20–10
nature of, 20–08
notices of, 20–04
tenant
liability of a, 20–03 *et seq.*
protection of a, 20–07, 20–11
EVIDENCE
discovery of documents, 6–15
extrinsic to construe leases, 17–03
parol evidence rule, 17–03
privileged documents, 6–12, 6–15
rent review hearing, at a, 6–17
varied rent, of, 6–21

EXPERT
appointment of an independent, 6–14
decision of an, challenge to the, 6–20
valuation by an independent, 6–16, 6–17

FACTORIES
statutory obligations as to, 7–04
FINE, meaning of a, 12–09
FIRE PRECAUTIONS, 7–04
FIXED CHARGE, definition of, 2–12
FIXTURES
chattels distinguished, 11–11
compensation for, 11–15
generally, 11–10
landlord's, 11–12, 11–14
removal of, 11–13
rent review and, 11–14
tenant's, 11–12
insurance of the, 13–03
removal of the, 11–13
rent review and, 11–14
trade, 11–12
capital allowances on, 11–16
FORFEITURE, 9–24, 12–02, 14–01 *et seq.*
breach of covenant, for, 14–03
clauses, 14–03
conditions, 14–02
exercise of right of, 14–04
generally, 14–01
insolvency, on, 14–03
irremediable breaches, for, 14–05
Law Commission recommendations as to, 14–08
mortgagees, as to, 14–04, 14–07
non-payment of rent, for, 14–06
possession proceedings on, 14–04
re-entry, proviso for, 14–03, 14–04
relief against, 14–06
rent arrears, for, 14–03
statutory requirements, 14–06
statutory termination scheme proposed, 14–08
underlessees, as to, 14–07
waiver of, 14–05

GUARANTOR, *see* SURETY

HABENDUM, meaning of, 5–01
HEALTH AND SAFETY AT WORK,
statutory obligations as to, 7–04
HOLDING OVER, *see* SECURITY OF TENURE

IMPROVEMENTS
  compensation for, 11–07
  consent to, 11–05
  covenants against, 11–02
  deemed premium, amounting to,
    11–09
  disregarded, 6–36
  generally, 11–01
  meaning of, 6–36
  proper, 11–07
  rates and insurance, as to, 11–09
  rent review and, 11–08
  valuation, on, 6–36
  value added considerations as to,
    11–09, 19–13
INDEXATION, 6–08, 6–38
INJUNCTIONS
  mandatory
    carry on business, to, 10–06
    enforce a landlord's obligations,
      to, 9–26, 9–27
INSURANCE
  bases of, 13–09
  disclosure of relevant matters and,
    13–10
  double, 13–04
  exclusions, limitations and excesses,
    13–08
  fault of landlord, effect of, on 13–10
  generally, 13–01 et seq.
  inherent defects, against, 9–15
  insurer, as to which, 13–05
  joint names, in, 13–07, 13–11
  lack of, 9–14
  landlord insuring, commission of a,
    13–05
  matters to be covered, 13–02
  misrepresentation, 13–10
  monies
    division of, where reinstatement
      impossible, 13–15
    shortfall in, 13–13
  non-invalidation clause, 13–10
  parties to, 13–04
  policy
    copy to be supplied to a tenant,
      13–10
    invalidation of the, 13–10
    voidable, 13–10
  proof of, 13–04
  reinstatement, as to, 13–11 et seq.
  risks, against what, 13–08
  shortfall in monies, 13–13
  sub-tenant, effect of activity of, on,
    13–10
  subrogation and, 13–06

INSURANCE—cont.
  sum of, 13–09
  third parties, as to, 13–06
  use of premises and, 13–10
  value added tax
    considerations as to, 19–12
  voidable policy and, 13–10
INTERLOCUTORY RELIEF, hardship to a
    tenant, where, 9–27
INTERPRETATION OF LEASES, see
    LEASES, interpretation of

JOINT TENANTS, 3–09

KEEP OPEN COVENANTS, 10–06

LAND REGISTRY FEES, 5–02, 19–21
LAND REGISTRY TRANSFER
  indemnity covenants incorporated
    into, 2–10
LANDLORD
  apportionment of costs of
    expenditure by a, 8–04
    certificate of the, 8–05
  company, where a, 3–06
  compensation for disturbance by a,
    19–15
  covenant to repair by a, 9–19
    breach of a, effect of a, 9–27
  covenants of a, performance of,
    6–34
  death of a, 3–04
  definition of, 3–03
  duties of a, third parties and tenants,
    to, 9–19
  expenditure of a
    apportionment of the, 8–02
    certification of the, 8–05
  generally, 3–02
  group of companies, where one of a,
    3–02
  insolvency of a, 18–09
  insuring, 13–05
  liability of a, 2–08
    implied, 9–02
    potential, 20–03 et seq.
  new tenancies, of, 3–03
  number of individuals, where a,
    3–05
  old tenancies, of, 3–03
  release of a, 2–08
    effect of, 2–09
  services, obligations to provide, of a,
    8–02
  single individual, where a, 3–04

LANDLORD—*cont.*
  suretyship provisions, effect of, on a, 3–15
  term of a lease, considerations to be taken into account by a, 5–02
  underlease by a, 5–02
  unoccupied property, implications for a, 7–02
LANDLORD AND TENANT (COVENANTS) ACT, 1995
  anti-avoidance provisions, 2–03
  assignment of part, as to, 2–11
  effect of the, 2–01 *et seq.*
  liability, as to, 2–04, 2–07, 2–08
  new tenancy, as to, 2–02
  old tenancy, as to, 2–01
  release, as to, 2–05, 2–09
  rights of indemnity, as to, 2–10
  safeguards for former tenants, as to, 2–12
LAW COMMISSION'S RECOMMENDATIONS
  forfeiture, as to, 14–08
  law of waste, as to the, 11–04
  repairs, as to, 9–01 *et seq.*
LEASES
  agreement for, 18–07
  arbitration clauses in, 15–09
  break clauses in, 6–08, 12–14, 16–05 *et seq.*
    interaction with section 26 request of, 16–28
    rent review timetable and, 6–10
  clear, 1–01, 8–01, 9–02
    subrogation and, 9–13
  construction of, 17–02 *et seq.*
  conveyancing of, 18–01 *et seq.*
  custody of, 18–11
  draft, mistakes in, 18–06
  drafting of, 1–02, 18–06
  execution of, 18–10
  grant of new, 18–02 *et seq.*
  head, 16–07
  hypothetical
    rent review provisions in, 6–27
    user clause in, 6–28
  interpretation of 17–01 *et seq.*
    contra preferentum rule, by the, 17–04
    ejusdem generis rule, by the, 17–04
    expressio unius rule, by the, 17–04
    extrinsic evidence, by, 17–03
    general principles of, 17–02
    parol evidence rule, by the, 17–03
    statutory rules, by, 17–04
  offer back clauses in, 12–15

LEASES—*cont.*
  options to renew, 16–10 *et seq.*
  pie-crust, 20–11
  prohibiting disposition without licence or consent, 12–09
  provisos in, 15–09 *et seq.*
  rectification of 17–05 *et seq.*
    discretionary remedy, a, 17–10
    requirements for, 17–06
      common intention, 17–07
        failure to record the, 17–08
      mistake, 17–09
  reversion of, restrictions on use affecting, 10–03
  surrender of, 18–25 *et seq.*
  term of, 5–01, *et seq.*
    length of the, 6–29
  termination of disclaimer, by, 3–08, 3–11, 3–15
    head, 16–07
    landlord's election not to reinstate, due to, 13–16
  user clauses in, 6–28, 10–01 *et seq.*, 18–03
  value added tax considerations, 19–16 *et seq.*
  variation of, 3–15
LETTING SCHEMES, 10–11
LICENCES, 6–22, 6–33

MODEL FORMS OF CLAUSES, 6–36, 6–37

NEW TENANCY, *see* TENANCY, new
NOISE, 10–02
NOTICES
  abatement, 20–04
  enforcement, 20–04
  prohibition, 20–04
  proviso for service of, 15–10
NUISANCE, 10–02
  common law, 20–05
  statutory, 20–04

OCCUPATION OF PREMISES, 16–16 *et seq.*
  completion, before, 18–30 *et seq.*
    breach of covenant, as, 18–32
    payment for, 18–31, 18–32
    pending assignment of lease, 18–32
    prior to grant of lease, 18–31
    unilateral offer of, 18–32
OFFENSIVE TRADE, 10–02

OFFICES SHOPS AND RAILWAY
PREMISES, statutory obligations as
to, 7–04
OPTIONS TO RENEW
breach of covenants and, 16–13
condition precedent, where a, 16–13
date of compliance, as to the, 16–13
drafting, 16–11
exclusion from new lease of, 16–11
exercising, 16–13
generally, 16–10 *et seq.*
overriding interests, as, 16–12
protecting, 16–12
registration of, 16–12
rent under new lease, as to, 16–11
OVERLOADING
floors, of, 15–04
wiring, of, 15–04
OVERRIDING LEASE
former tenant's right to an, 2–12
surety, for a, 3–16

PARTIES
generally, 3–01
landlord, 3–01 *et seq.*
surety, 3–11 *et seq.*
tenant, 3–07 *et seq.*
PARTNERSHIPS, 3–10
PERMITTED USES, 6–33, 10–08
PLANNING
applications, 15–06
compensation, 15–05
PLATE GLASS INSURANCE, 13–03
PREMISES, *see* DEMISED PREMISES
PRIVITY OF CONTRACT, 2–01 *et seq.*
PRIVITY OF ESTATE, new tenancies, no
place in, 2–04, 2–05
PUBLIC HEALTH, statutory obligations
as to, 7–04

QUIET ENJOYMENT
quiet enjoyment, covenant for,
16–02 *et seq.*
leasehold coveyancing, as to,
16–04
nature of a, 16–03
purpose of a, 16–02
qualified, 16–03

RATES
generally, 7–01
increased by improvements, 11–09
uniform business, 7–02

RATES—*cont.*
water charges, 7–03
REBUILDING, 6–34
RECEIVER
appointment of a, 9–27
functions of a, 9–27
RECTIFICATION OF LEASES, 17–05 *et
seq.*
REDECORATION
miscellaneous provisions, 9–23
repairs, after, 9–22
specification of, 9–20
timing of, 9–21
REFUSE AND EFFLUENT, disposal of,
15–03
REGISTERED TITLE, 18–08, 18–09
REINSTATEMENT
generally, 13–11
impossible, where, 13–15
landlord not wishing, 13–16
obligation of, 6–36
replacement or, 13–09
requirement of, 11–06
standard of, 13–14
time of, 13–12
value, 13–09
REMEDIES
breach of repairing obligations, for
landlord, by a, 9–27
tenant, by a, 9–24 *et seq.*
RENEWAL
costs of, 16–11
options for, 16–10 *et seq.*
breach of covenant and, 16–13
condition precedent, where a,
16–13
date of compliance, as to the,
16–13
drafting, 16–11
excluding from new lease, 16–11
exercising, 16–13
overriding interests, as, 16–12
protecting, 16–12
registration of, 16–12
rent under new lease, 16–11
RENT
arrears, forfeiture for, 14–03
assessment of, basis for, 6–23
best, 6–24
cesser of, no implied, 13–17
covenant to pay, 6–01
deduction from, 9–27
definition of, 6–01
deposits, 6–05
determination of new, 6–12 *et seq.*,
16–11

RENT—*cont.*
  free period, 6–02, 6–31, 19–15
  geared, 6–40
  headline, 6–23, 6–31, 6–37
  indexed, 6–38
  interest on unpaid, 6–06, 19–15
  loss of, insurance for, 13–03
  market, 6–24
  open market, 6–24
  payment of, 6–03
    reviewed, 6–22
  proviso for suspension of, 13–17
  rack market, 6–24
  reasonable, 6–24
  reservation of, 6–01, 8–06
    other payments, as, 6–04
    service charges, as, 8–06
  review, 6–07 *et seq.*
  statutory control of, 6–22
  suspension of
    express, 13–17
    implied, 13–17
    length of, 13–18
  turnover, meaning of, 6–08, 6–39
  use, effect of, on, 10–01
  valuation, basis of, 6–24 *et seq.*
  yearly, 6–24
RENT REVIEW
  activating, 6–09 *et seq.*
  arbitration
    procedure, 6–15
      costs of, 6–18
      decision challenged, 6–19
      evidence, 6–17
    reference to, 6–10, 6–13, 6–14
      advantages of, 6–13
      factors in choosing, 6–13
      independent expertise
        distinguished, 6–13
  award, 6–15
    appeal against an, 6–19
  break clauses and, 6–08, 6–10
  counter-notice by a tenant, 6–11
    time limits for a, 6–11
  default notice of, 6–11
  determination of the new rent
    third parties, by, 6–12 *et seq.*
    agreement, by, 6–09, 6–12 *et seq.*
  environmental considerations as to,
    20–11
  extension of time limits by the court,
    6–11
  frequency of, 6–08
  geared rents, of, 6–40
  hearing, 6–15
  hypothetical leases, in, 6–27

RENT REVIEW—*cont.*
  indexed rents, of, 6–38
  initiators of, 6–10
  inspection of property for, 6–15
  landlord, delay by a, 6–10
  long intervals of, 6–27
  memorandum of the, 6–21
  model forms of clause of, 6–37
  notice of, 6–10
    default, 6–11
    silence constituting acceptance of,
      6–11
    time of the essence, to make, 6–10
    trigger, 6–11
  payment of new rent, 6–22
  preliminary considerations, 6–08
  privileged documents, 6–15
  purpose of, 6–08
  sub-letting and, 6–32
  surety and, 3–16, 6–13
  time of, 6–10
  trigger notice of, 6–11
  turnover rents, of, 6–39
  undue hardship of a tenant and,
    6–11
  upwards only, 6–08
  user clause, where a, 6–28
  valuation
    basis of, 6–24 *et seq.*
    date, 6–24, 6–25
    development potential, where,
      6–33
    fitting out period assumed, where,
      6–30
    improvements to be disregarded,
      6–36
    matters to be assumed on, 6–34
    nature of interest for, 6–26
    original term, where an, 6–29
    planning permission, where, 6–33
    premises for, 6–26
    rent free period, where a, 6–31
    rent review provisions, 6–27
    tenant's occupation and goodwill
      disregarded, 6–35
    unexpired residue, where, 6–29
    user clause, where a, 6–28
    vacant possession, with, 6–30
    whole, as a, 6–30, 6–32
  valuation by an independent expert
    arbitration distinguished, 6–13
    procedure of, 6–16
    reference to, 6–13, 6–14
      advantages of, 6–13
      factors in choosing, 6–13

RENTAL VALUE
  alienation, effect of restrictions on
      the, 12–01
  diminution of the, 6–34
  improvements, effect of, on the,
      11–08
REPAIRING COVENANTS
  breach of
    landlord, by a, 9–27
    tenant, by a, 9–24 et seq.
  defects covered, 9–06 et seq.
    building and construction, as to,
        9–07
      specific provisions, 9–09
    damage distinguished, 9–07
    inherent, 9–09, 9–14, 9–19
    latent, 9–09
    work, whether repair, 9–08
  generally, 9–03
  insured risks excepted, 9–17, 13–08
  obligations of, 9–04
    limits on, 9–19
    mitigation of, 9–11 et seq.
  risks insured excepted, 9–17, 13–08
  spatial extent of, 9–05, 9–19
  standard of repair required by, 9–16
  survey desirable, 9–11
  timing of, 9–04
REPAIRS
  generally, 9–01
  implied liability for
    landlord, by a, 9–02
    tenant, by a, 9–02
  landlord's covenant as to, 9–19
    breach of, effect of, 9–27
    notice of disrepair required, 9–19,
        9–27
  Law Commission's
      recommendations as to, 9–01
  meaning of, 9–08
  renewal distinguished, 9–06, 9–17
  standard of, 9–16
  tenant's covenant as to, 9–03 et seq.
    breach of
      costs of proceedings, 9–24
      damages recoverable, 9–24
        measure of, 9–25
      effect of, 9–24 et seq.
      forfeiture, 9–24
    landlord's right of entry in default
        of, 9–18, 9–24
RESTRAINT OF TRADE, 10–12
R.I.C.S. GUIDANCE NOTES, 6–15,
  6–16

SECTION 146 NOTICE, 14–06

SECURITY OF TENURE
  exceptions, as to
    agreement, by, 16–23
    licences, 16–22
    statutory, 16–21
  generally, 16–01
  Landlord and Tenant Act 1954,
      under
    break clauses, as to, 16–28
    compensation, as to, 16–50
    effect of, 16–14
    grant of new tenancy
      costs, 16–46
      generally, 16–43
      length, 16–45
      opposing, 16–34
      order, 16–49
      property, 16–44
      rent, 16–47
      terms, 16–46
    operation of the
      concepts of the, 16–25
      continuation, 16–24
      determination, 16–24
      generally, 16–24
      interim rent, 16–32
      landlord, by a, 16–25
      month, as to, 16–25
      notices, 16–24
      period of, 16–25
      rules, 16–25
      time of, 16–25, 16–31
  opposing grant of new tenancy,
      16–34 et seq.
    generally, 16–34
    grounds for, 16–35 et seq.
      alternative accommodation,
          16–38
      breaches of covenant, 16–37
      delay in payment of rent, 16–36
      demolition of the property,
          16–40
      failure to repair, 16–35
      landlord's occupation, 16–41
      reconstruction, 16–40
      whole, to be let as a, 16–39
    successfully, 16–42
  premises
    meaning of, 16–16
    occupation of
      agent, by an, 16–17
      business purposes, for, 16–18,
          16–41
      excluded use, for, 16–21
      mixed use, for, 16–19
      tenant, by a, 16–17

SECURITY OF TENURE—*cont.*
premises—*cont.*
occupation of—*cont.*
unauthorised use, for, 16–20
rent renegotiation, 16–09
scope of Landlord and Tenant Act,
1954, 16–15 *et seq.*
sub-lessees, as to, 16–03, 16–16,
16–25
SERVICE CHARGES
environmental considerations as to,
20–10
expenditure covered by, 8–03
advance notice required of, 8–05
apportionment of, 8–04
certification of, 8–05
challenge to, 8–05
generally, 8–01
payment of, 8–06
reserve funds in respect of, 8–07
value added tax considerations as to,
19–11
SERVICES
apportionment of the cost of, 8–04
management expenses, 8–03
obligation to provide, 8–02
standard of, 8–02
variation of, 8–02
SPECIFIC PERFORMANCE,
landlord's obligation to repair, to
enforce a, 9–27
STAMP DUTY, 5–02, 18–11, 18–20,
19–20
STANDARD FORMS OF LEASE, 1–04
STATUTORY COMPENSATION, 16–40
STATUTORY NOTICES, 15–06
SUB-LESSEES, security of tenure of,
16–03, 16–16
SUBROGATION, 9–13, 13–06
SUNDAY TRADING, 8–04, 10–07
SURETY
advising a, 3–14
alternative to a, 3–15
breaches to be notified to a, 3–16
death of a, 3–15
duty of care to a, 3–15
former tenant, of a, 2–08, 2–12
generally, 3–12
guarantee of a, 3–13
indemnity of a, 3–13
insolvency of a, 3–15
liability of a, 2–07, 3–13
continuing, 3–16
disclaimer, following a, 3–15
provisions, 3–16
landlord, as to a, 3–15

SURETY—*cont.*
provisions—*cont.*
tenant, as to a, 3–17
purpose of a, 3–12
rent arrears to be notified to a, 3–16
variation in rent to be notified to a,
6–13
SURRENDER OF LEASES, 18–25 *et seq.*
effect of, 18–27
form of, 18–26
reasons for, 18–25
registered, 18–29
underleases, subject to, 18–28
SUSPENSION OF RENT, 13–17, 13–18

TENANCY
assignment of a, 2–11, 2–12
new
abbreviation for, 2–01
assignment of a, 12–12, 12–14
assignment of part of a, 2–11
identifying a, 2–02
indemnity of successive tenants of
a, 2–10
liability, as to
guarantor, of a, 2–07
landlord, of a, 2–08
tenant, of a, 2–04
meaning of, 2–02
privity of estate no place in a,
2–04, 2–05
release of a tenant of a, 2–05
effect of, 2–09
old
assignment of part of an, 2–11
indemnity rights of successive
tenants, 2–10
liability, as to
guarantor of a, 2–07
landlord of a, 2–08
tenant of a, 2–04
meaning of, 2–01
release of a tenant, effect of the,
2–09
release of a tenant of a, 2–05,
5–02
will, at, 16–22
TENANT
bankruptcy of a, 3–08, 3–09
collateral warranties of a, 9–14
company, where a, 3–11
covenants
performance of, by a, 6–34
repair to, 9–03 *et seq.*
death of a, 3–08, 3–09
definitions of a, 3–07

TENANT—*cont.*
  disposition by a
    freedom of, 12–01
    restrictions on the, 12–02 *et seq.*
  former
    guarantee of a, 2–08
    liability of a, 2–04
    safeguards for a, 2–04, 2–12
    surety of a, 3–15
  goodwill of a, 6–35
  improvements by a, 6–26, 6–36
  individual, where an, 3–08
  joint, 3–09
  liability of a, 2–04, 3–13, 7–02,
      9–02, 20–03 *et seq.*
  occupation of a, 6–35
  original, 2–04
    continuing liability of an, 2–04,
        5–02
    death of an, 3–08
  partnership, where a, 3–10
  release of a, 2–05, 5–02
  subrogation of a, 9–13
  successive, indemnity of a, 2–10
  survey by a, 9–11
  term of a lease, considerations to be
      taken into account by, 5–02
  third parties, rights of a, against,
      9–12
  unoccupied property, implications
      for a, 7–02
  use confined to a, 6–28
    protection of, 10–11
TERM
  commencement date, 5–03
  generally, 5–01
  length of the, 5–02
TERRORISM, damage caused by, 13–08
TITLE
  assignor, of an, 18–14
  conversion of, 18–14
  deduced, whether, 18–08, 18–14
  entry of notice on freehold, 18–11
  freehold, 18–14
  implied covenants for, 18–08
  investigation of, 18–08, 18–22,
      18–24
  paramount, 16–03
  predecessors in, 16–03
  registered, 18–08, 18–09
  unregistered, 18–08
  warranty of, no, 16–03

UNDERLEASES
  assignment of, 18–24
  contents of, 10–08

UNDERLEASES—*cont.*
  covenants against, 12–04
  forefeiture and, 14–07
  grant of, 18–21 *et seq.*
  length of, 5–02
  requirement of full value of, 12–14
UNDERLESSEE
  status of an, 12–14
  use proposed by an, 12–14
UNDERLETTING
  breach of a covenant parting with
      possession, may constitue,
      12–05
  consent to
    obtaining, 18–23
    refusal of, 12–13
  covenant against, 12–04
UNIFORM BUSINESS RATES, 7–02
UNOCCUPIED PROPERTY, liability for
    rates where, 7–02
UNREGISTERED TITLE, 18–08
USE
  adjoining premises, of, 10–11
  alienability, effect of, on, 10–10
  assignee, proposed by an, 12–14
  change of, 10–09
  classes, 10–08
    allied trades, 10–08
    high class, 10–08
    specified trades, 10–08
  modification by the Lands Tribunal
      of, 10–12
  planning, as to, 10–08
  proposed
    competing, 12–14
    not forbidden by the lease, 12–14
  protection of a tenant's 10–11
  rent, effect of, on, 10–01
  restricted to specified, 10–08
    attacks on, 10–12
  reversion, effect of, on, 10–03,
      10–04
  specific licence, requiring a, 10–05
  Sunday trading and, 10–07
  underlessee, proposed by an, 12–14
  vacant premises, to prevent, 10–06
  variation of, 10–08

VACANT POSSESSION
  fitting out period assumed, 6–30
  letting with, 6–30
VALUE ADDED TAX
  basis of, 19–02
  co-owners, as to, 19–02
  collection of, 19–02

VALUE ADDED TAX—*cont.*
common property transactions, as
to, 19–05
compensation for disturbance, as to,
19–15
dilapidations, as to, 19–15
grant of a lease, on the, 19–16 *et seq.*
improvements, as to, 11–09, 19–13
input, recovery of, 19–03
interest on overdue rent, as to,
19–15
interest payable for late payment,
19–05
invoices, 19–04
notices, as to, 19–15
output, 19–03
parking rights not included in the
demise, as to, 4–09
payments under the lease, as to,
6–04
penalties, 19–05
professional charges, as to, 19–14

VALUE ADDED TAX—*cont.*
purchase of a lease, on the, 19–16 *et
seq.*
rent-free periods, as to, 19–15
sale of a lease, on the, 19–16 *et seq.*
service charges, as to, 19–11
stamp duty on, 19–20
supplies, 19–05
supply
meaning of, 19–06
time of, 19–07
types of, 19–09
value of, 19–08
tenant's status for, 6–34

WAIVER, breach of covenant, of, 14–05
WASTE
constituents of, 11–13
disposal of, 15–03
Law Commission's
recommendations as to, 11–04
law of, 11–04
WATER CHARGES, 7–03